ORGANIZING AND MANAGING CLASSROOM LEARNING COMMUNITIES

Third Edition

Joyce Putnam

J. Bruce Burke

McGraw Hill **Custom Publishing**

Boston Burr Ridge, IL Dubuque, IA New York
San Francisco St. Louis Bangkok Bogotá Caracas Kuala Lumpur
Lisbon London Madrid Mexico City Milan Montreal New Delhi
Santiago Seoul Singapore Sydney Taipei Toronto

Organizing and Managing Classroom Learning Communities

1 2 3 4 5 6 7 8 9 0 MER   MER   0 9 8 7 6

ISBN-13: 978-0-07-339077-2
ISBN-10: 0-07-339077-1

Editor: Judith Wetherington
Production Editor: Carrie Braun
Cover Design: Maggie Lytle
Back Cover Art/Design: Melissa Dickson during TLC I (Fall 2005)
Photography: Grade school class and class close-up by Photos.com
                    Classroom with blackboard by Digital Vision
Printer/Binder: Mercury Print Productions

CONTENTS IN BRIEF

CONTENTS

v

ABOUT THE AUTHORS

Joyce Putnam is Professor of Teacher Education at Michigan State University. She received her Ph.D. degree from Michigan State University and has directed and coordinated teacher education programs there since 1973. Dr. Putnam was previously an elementary and secondary teacher. Her research interests include classroom organization and management and the process of how teachers learn to teach. She is the author of numerous journal articles and is the co-author with Jere Brophy of a chapter in the 78th NSSE Yearbook (Edited by D. L. Duke) dealing with classroom management. Dr. Putnam is engaged currently with the Professional Development School movement at Michigan State and with the redesign of their teacher education programs. She has a continuing commitment to school improvement through creating learning communities with collaborating teachers. In 2002, Dr. Putnam became Professor Emeritus at MSU.

J. Bruce Burke is Professor of Teacher Education and Senior Program Consultant for Graduate Studies on Education Overseas (GSEO) at Michigan State University. He received his Ph.D. from Syracuse University, where he was a Woodrow Wilson fellow. He is the author of *The Individual and the School,* a workbook for prospective teachers. He has written chapters, articles, and research reports in the areas of interpersonal communication skills, effective education, humanities education, and student perceptions of disruptive school behavior. He was one of the founders of the National Association for Humanities Education and a former director of the Humanities Institute at Michigan State University. Dr. Burke is a poet and is working currently on a volume that mixes poetry and reflection on teaching.

PREFACE

The authors have long been associated with alternative forms of teacher education. In particular, we have been associated with learning communities and cooperative learning. Over the years, as our experience with multiple-ability grouping has expanded, we have become increasingly convinced that cooperative learning benefits all students. Likewise, we have become convinced that understanding the classroom as a subculture provides realistic leverage for creating a cooperative learning environment. Since we could find no single text that integrated these two lines of thought, we decided to write our own.

This book views classroom management as integral to a larger conception of professional teaching. It treats classroom management, discipline, curriculum, and cooperative learning under the conceptual organization of learning communities. This learning-community perspective provides a coherent rationale for the how-to-do-it stuff of teaching. Without a theoretical foundation, teaching too often disintegrates into a patchwork of technical skills and decision making.

So here is a book that provides an introduction to classroom learning communities: what they are, how they function, and what they mean to the goals of democratic education. Section I presents the information and activities necessary for creating a learning community culture for the group using this text in their professional studies. It also presents the alignment of learning community concepts to National Standards for Teacher Preparation. Section II presents an update about the implementation of learning communities. Section III presents the more abstract material upon which the book's conceptual framework is based. Section IV presents two chapter-length examples (one elementary and one secondary) of learning community classrooms in action. Section V offers concrete guidance for each stage of developing a classroom learning community. Finally, Section VI takes a look at the future.

In order to make the discussions as vivid and compelling as possible, we have scattered a series of illustrative vignettes throughout the text. In all cases these vignettes are based on real life teachers and situations. Also, to help readers extend their understanding to the application stage, we have included an abundance of observation, interview, and reflection activities at the end of chapters.

ACKNOWLEDGMENTS

Scholarship should be a community activity. Certainly, this book was a cooperative activity, as we have benefited from the advice and counsel of many colleagues. We particularly want to thank the following people who provided invaluable feedback by field testing early versions of the manuscript: Carol Sharp, Glassboro State College; Frances Barger, Randi Nevins, and Janet Ronk, Michigan State University. Encouragement as well as wonderful suggestions were also provided by the following reviewers, who read the manuscript at various stages: Leo Anglin, Kent State University; Richard Arends, University of Maryland; Susan Florio-Ruane, Michigan State University; Thomas Good, University of Missouri; Nancy Winitzky, University of Utah; and Charles Wolfgang, Florida State University.

Without the support and encouragement of our chairperson, Henrietta Barnes, and our editor, Lane Akers, this book would never have been finished. The same might be said for Cindy Erickson, who typed and retyped the manuscript and somehow kept it all from getting lost on electronic disks. Finally, we want to thank the many classroom teachers with whom we work. Their sharing of their planning, instruction, and reflections helped us provide the many concrete examples and strategies that are found in our text.

Joyce Putnam, Professor MSU
J. Bruce Burke, Professor MSU

Joyce Putnam and Carol Sharp thank the MSU and Rowan Teacher Candidates and Professional Development School teachers who provided information as to the professional education needs of the candidates in early field and student teaching experiences. We also thank Lilly Levinowitz, Jane Graziano, and Louise Karwowski and the teachers in her Learning Communities course for providing specific feedback about course and field assignments. We also thank Rowan faculty and Toby Powell who suggested readings and references. Special thanks to Tanya Santangelo for her editing and content suggestions and to Kim Leverette for her help and suggestions. We thank Walter O. Quint, Tanya Santangelo, Laurel Byrne, and Patrick Westcott, members of the Rowan Teaching in Learning Communities I and II Committee for their recommendations and suggested additional assignment and rubric.

Joyce Putnam, Professor Emeritus Michigan State University
Carol Sharp, Dean College of Education, Rowan University

SECTION

I

Starting a Learning Community

OVERVIEW

Learning communities should exist in P–12 and college classrooms as well as in groups of educators as they work together to improve student achievement. One of the core principles in the teacher preparation program is the establishment of classroom learning communities.

The *study* of the conceptual framework for creating a Learning Community culture, as well as, *learning how* to create a learning community is an integral part of the preparation of tomorrow's teachers. It is intended that each professional education course work through the process to create a Learning Community culture.

The information and activities in Section I contribute to the process of your group's development in Stage 1—Beginnings and Stage 2—Establishing Expectations.

One of the norms of a Learning Community culture is that members help new members enter. During the professional education program experiences it is expected that candidates will actively contribute and participate in the formation of course and peer or professional learning communities each semester. Thus, university studies provide the opportunities to increase one's knowledge and skills through the practice of effective group membership and leadership in Learning Communities. One's ability to understand and apply the underlying conceptual framework and the actions and dispositions of learning community members and leaders will be observed and assessed over time, as they are a part of the teacher candidate performance standards. (INTASC 1-10)

Our recent fieldwork with *home schooling* led us to the conclusion that *Organizing and Managing Classroom Learning Communities* (2nd edition), provides the Parent-Teacher with information that will help in planning for and teaching home-schooled learners. The information in this book will help Parent-teachers and home-schooled learners with the knowledge and skills that they will use to gain a constructive social entry into PK-12 schools, community colleges and/or university class cultures.

The knowledge gained from this book will help home-schooled learners learn to observe and understand the development of the groups in their various classes. By being able to identify norms, roles, rules, and expectations, home-schooled children will understand the nature of the culture of the groups in which they are expected to function successfully. They will also understand the potential for effective group development and thus be able to contribute to the establishment of a successful learning environment.

The first stage of developing an effective Learning Community group is ***Beginnings.*** The stages for developing an effective Learning Community culture are described in Chapter 4, *A Pedagogy for Learning Community.* You will be reading about the stages of group development during this semester.

STAGE 1—BEGINNINGS
ACTIVITIES

Below are examples of activities that you can use in this class and in study-groups to help you start getting acquainted with other members in your section of this course. Strong academic outcomes are important for all people and the first stage in the development of a group culture puts you on the right path for further development of an effective Learning Community culture (group) when academic achievement is a goal.

The primary purpose of all of these activities is to provide an opportunity for you as a member of the course or group, including the teacher or leader, to share information that will help others become acquainted with you. At the very beginning of the course the nature of the information shared is more personal than related to the substance of the course. As time progresses the content of get acquainted activities changes so that the substance of what is being shared, is connected to what is being studied and practiced by an individual preparing for his/her career in education.

A second purpose of these initial activities is for you to practice keeping the focus on a speaker rather than changing the focus to yourself or others in the group. A third purpose is for you as a listener to consciously communicate nonverbally with the speakers indicating that you are paying attention and listening. Thus, later when you are listening to people whom you are interviewing or who are speaking to your class, you will be able to communicate nonverbally in ways that help the interviewees or speakers feel comfortable.

Individuals who know others in the group should be prepared to share new information about themselves so that their old acquaintances learn something new. Individuals who know the speaker should look for new information about the presenter.

All of the activities are created at a low risk level. However, you may still be uncomfortable with the task. It is important for the group and instructor to help and support you through the task. Likewise it is important that you help others who may be uncomfortable work their way through the task. It is necessary that individuals who are intending to or are currently working in the field of education be comfortable communicating in front of groups, in developing effective groups, and in participating in group work.

The procedures for activities 1–4 are the same. One member talks and the other members listen and communicate nonverbally that they are paying attention (posture, eye contact, facial expressions). The presenter then calls on two members of the group who will ask clarifying questions. The clarifying questions must extend the information presented. The group member will phrase his/her question so that a verbal link is made to something the presenter stated. The presenter may avoid answering the question by saying "I'm not ready to share that at this time." At the end of group sharing session, each member of the group will tell one thing that they learned about another member of the group. Once a person has been mentioned, no one else can tell something he/she learned about that member. Thus, all members of group will be mentioned in the closure session.

Activities 5–6 require the presenter to share his/her information. Then the other members of the group write a positive "first impression" adjective on a Post-it®. Then one at a time, the members of the group stick their Post-it® on the presenter's poster and explain in a sentence or two why they picked that adjective as their first impression of the speaker.

1. Memory Box

Each member of the class is to put a collection of personal objects in a box and bring them to class. The objects that you select should be reflective of memories you have of various parts of your life. The purpose of this activity is to provide the presenter with the opportunity to help other members of the class get to know him/her. For the listeners it is an opportunity to learn about your peers and to ask clarifying questions.

The format for the activity is for the group to sit in a circle so that everyone can see each other's faces. A volunteer shares the objects in his/her box and after they have finished the group may ask two or three clarifying questions. No other comments are permitted. The focus of the questions must be on the presenter and must not pull the focus from the presenter to someone else. Once the clarifying questions have been asked and answered, the speaker should select the next person to speak. This activity will take a class of 29 students and one instructor about 90 minutes. (E.g., 2 minutes to present per person, and 1 minute for clarifying questions per speaker.)

2. Sculpture from Junk Drawer

The instructor and group members empty their trash drawer into a paper bag and bring to the next class meeting. At the beginning of the activity, the contents of the bags are dumped onto a long table. Each group member then picks out items from the junk and constructs a sculpture that represents him/her. String, glue, and tape are used to hold the parts of the sculpture together. To finish the sculpture, the "artist" will create a sign that names his/her sculpture. The sculptures are displayed and each member of the group explains his/her sculpture and shares new information about him/her to the group. After a speaker finishes and the clarifying questions are asked and answered, the speaker selects the next speaker. This activity will take a class of 29 students and one instructor about 105 minutes. (E.g., 15 minutes to create sculpture, 2 minutes per person to present, 1 minute per presenter for clarifying questions.)

3. Name Tags

Members of the group are assigned the task of making a name tag for the next class. They are to create a name tag that represents something important about their experiences at the university, work, or vacations. The items that an individual selects for the nametag should reflect a particular value, feeling, disposition, type of character, or adjective, which furthers the information, shared with the group. After a speaker finishes and the clarifying questions are asked and answered, the speaker selects the next speaker. This activity will take a class of 29 students and one instructor about 90 minutes. (E.g., 2 minutes to present, 1 minute for clarifying questions.)

4. Picture Collage

Each member of the group is to create an 8½ × 11 collage using photos and documents that reflect where they are in their life at this time. For example: Who is important to them, what are they the most focused on currently, what are they struggling with, what goals do they have, and what goals have they just reached, etc.? After a speaker finishes his/her presentation and the clarifying questions are asked and answered, the speaker selects the next speaker. This activity will take a class of 29 students and one instructor about 75 minutes. (E.g., 1.5 minutes to present, 1 minute for clarifying questions.)

5. Successes

Each member of the group creates a success chart on desk pad size paper that shows the first part, middle part, and current time in his/her life. Each member then identifies academic, physical, and social/emotional successes in each period of his/her life.

Name: _____   Date: _____

Time in Life	SUCCESSES		
	Academic	Physical	Social/Emotional
Early (Years)			
Middle (Years)			
Current (Years)			

Individuals complete their charts so that they represent themselves and their successes over three life periods. To begin, the group selects a facilitator, timekeeper, recorder and reporter. Each member of the group then presents their information to *a small group of 10 to 15 peers*. After the presentation, each member in the small group writes a positive adjective, representing their first impression of the speaker, on a Post-it®. One at a time the members of the group walk to the presenters chart and post their note and looking the presenter in the eyes explain why they selected the particular adjective they posted. This part of the task takes about an hour. Next, the group decides on four insights into the group that they generated today. These will be reported to the whole group. After all have presented their charts, the charts are posted in the room. The small groups report to the whole group the insights they gained today. Each small group has 2 minutes for their report.

6. Shield

Individuals should make a shield (European, African, etc.) of their own design, on desk pad size paper. Each member should then draw three symbols on it to represent four contributions they have made to others during their life and three symbols that represent contributions others made to them. Each member of the group then presents their information to a small group of 10 to 15 peers. To begin, the group selects a facilitator, timekeeper, recorder and reporter. After each presentation, each member in the small group writes a positive adjective, representing their first impression of the speaker, on a Post-it®. One at a time the members of the group walk to the presenters chart and post their note and looking the presenter in the eyes explain why they selected the particular adjective they posted. This part of the task takes about an hour. Next, the group decides on four insights into the group that they generated today. These will be reported to the whole group. After all have presented their charts, the charts are posted in the room. The small groups report to the whole group the insights they gained today. Each small group has 2 minutes for their report.

7. Early Get Acquainted Activity

On the first day of class teacher candidates introduce themselves by doing the following: State their name, the name of the teacher candidate to their left, and then complete the following sentence: I, *Kathy Mill* am exploring education as a career because I (believe, need, want) ... and I see the field of education as a place where I can get that.

8. First Impressions

The whole group of students is divided into groups of 6 to 8 members. Each member has a stack of Post-its®, a large magic marker, and 1 sheet of poster paper. The individual writes on the poster the heading "First Impression of (teacher candidate's name). Each member of the group then writes one or two adjectives on the Post-it® that describe their first impression of each of the candidates. The first member of the group asks the others "What first impression have I made?" and the other members of the group individually post their adjective on the candidate's poster. This continues until all members have "first impression" feedback from all other members.

9. Small Group Discussion Roles

All of the members of the course need to carry out four roles in order to be an effective member of the course and study group. These four primary roles are that of *organizer, encourager, contributor, and synthesizer*. We are beginning this course with an explanation of the roles, as it is our expectation that you will develop the skills and effectively use them in course sections and in your study groups throughout your college program.

STAGE 2—ESTABLISHING EXPECTATIONS ACTIVITIES

Preparing to Practice the Roles in Groups

Using the primary role explanations (below), make yourself a set of 3 × 5 cards as follows: use four different colors (e.g., blue for contributor, yellow for encourager, green for organizer, and pink for synthesizer). Once you print a *Role* and its explanation on a card, sign your name to the card. During small group work in or out of class each group member will turn in to the center of the table an index card representing the particular role which was just carried out. Each member will do this when he/she feels he/she has demonstrated that particular role. *This procedure facilitates participants' practice and effective use of the various roles.*

Explanations of Primary Roles

1. *Organizer*—Asks questions and/or provides feedback when group gets off task, to help group refocus on task.
2. *Encourager*—Asks for opinions and information from members of the group who have not participated in the discussion on a regular basis.
3. *Contributor*—Provides information to further the group's discussion or quality of task completion.
4. *Synthesizer*—Pulls ideas, opinions, and information together and makes statements to show relationships among various contributions.

Four Additional Roles

Four additional roles are also necessary for effective small group work. A group *facilitator, a timekeeper, a recorder, and a reporter* must be identified each time a small group meets to work on a task.

The role of **the facilitator** is to direct the task by getting things started and being sure that everyone understands the tasks. When problems arise, the facilitator is responsible for getting questions answered and for obtaining information that is not available in the group. **The timekeeper** keeps the group informed about how much time they have to complete various parts of a task, and gives a warning toward the end of the time so that the group can review the recorder's notes. **The recorder** is responsible for the group's official notes, which are turned in at the end of a task or the end of several related tasks. **The reporter** helps to communicate the group's ideas, , questions, and problems to the whole group. However, when the small groups report to the whole group, it is the responsibility of all members to participate.

Procedure for First Small Group Discussions

The focus of this activity is four-fold: (1) to generate the ideas, opinions, and descriptions from all members of the group; (2) to provide an opportunity for all members of the group to practice the effective group member roles; (3) to provide an opportunity for individuals to practice the roles of facilitator, timekeeper, recorder and reporter; and (4) to practice keeping the focus of a study group's discussion on the topic so that the information generated can be used by individuals at later times. This activity for a large group of 30 members and instructor will take about 60 minutes.

First, course members are organized into groups of 6 to 8 people. Each group has 2 minutes to get organized and start the discussion. The discussion should last 20 minutes. At the end of the time for discussion each group should review the recorder's notes and the main points noted by the reporter.

During the discussion, the instructor's role is (1) to sit with each group and ask extending questions (model how to move discussion to more complex ideas), (2) to remind members when they demonstrate one of the effective group member roles, (3) to place their card on the table, and (4) to note examples of outstanding organizer, encourager, contributor, and synthesizer comments.

Once the whole group has reformed, each discussion group has 3 minutes to report the findings from their discussion. Each recorder provides the instructor with the group's notes at the end of class. The notes should include the names of the members of the small group. During the reporting phase, the instructor will monitor the content, organization of the presentations, and the number of group members who participate in the report.

After the reporting is finished, the instructor will then provide feedback to the class on their small group discussion skills. Each group will receive a copy of a feedback form filled out by the instructor. The purpose in providing feedback is that small group work is an integral part of the university learning experience and it is critical that each member of the group learn how to effectively carry out all of the roles. Providing feedback will reinforce the high standard for performance expected by all members in this type of activity.

Choose One of the Following Topics for Your Small Group Discussion

A. What educational experiences have you had that prepared you to be an effective and responsible member of a democratic society?

B. What evidence do you have that today's public schools, charter schools and home schooling are preparing today's P–12 learners to be responsible members of a democratic society?

C. What evidence do you have that today's preteens and teens demonstrate on a day to day basis that they have academic, personal, social, and social justice responsibility?

D. What evidence to you have that you demonstrate on a day-to-day basis that you have academic, personal, social, and social justice responsibility?

RUBRICS

A rubric for your use when working in small groups is provided on the following page. Each group should fill out one and turn it in to the instructor at the end of an in-class work session. Complete one form for each out of class study group meeting and turn in with study group report at end of project.

RUBRIC: SMALL GROUP WORK

Group Members: _____

Facilitator: _____   Timer: _____   Recorder: _____   Date: _____

	0 Dysfunctional	1 Moving Toward Effectiveness	1.5–3.0 Meets Standard Proficiency	3.5–4.0 Exemplary Practice
Problems identified	Complaints made to one or two members of group but behind dysfunctional group member's back	Member brings problem to whole group but group ignores or does not fully resolve	Problem brought to the group, members of the group act to help clarify and find solutions that work	Problem stated clearly and accurately at the time it first occurs
Problems articulated with all group members present	Complaints made behind dysfunctional group member's back	Tone and nonverbal communications (rolling eyes, sarcastic remarks) made in the group	One member of the group describes the problem using an "I" statement. There is agreement that the statement reflects the problem in the group	One member of the group accurately identifies the problem using an "I" statement and the person(s) contributing to the state that they will not do it again
Group members help to clarify problem	Individuals who are dissatisfied with the effectiveness of the group act grumpy and complain	Other members of the group nod in agreement	After initial I statement, other individuals use "I" statements to add their point of view; Person causing conflict/problem restates problem	After initial I statement, other individuals use "I" statements to add their point of view; Person causing conflict/problem restates problem using a clarifying statement
Group members help identify resolution, plan, or practice that is needed to end problem	Problems ignored	Problems brought to group but clarification of problems is not completed	Problem brought to group and most of the members participate in identifying resolution	Group has procedure established for resolving problems and uses it effectively without creating hostilities
Individuals contributing to problem able to articulate consequences to other members if problem continues	Individuals who contribute to the problem are silent or hostile thus stopping members of the group who want to resolve it	Individuals who contribute to the problem are silent or hostile when the problem is brought to the whole group. But, the problem is discussed even with hostility evident in group.	No one is hostile about problem behaviors. When something is recognized the contributors and other members make changes necessary so that things move forward	Problem behaviors do not occur in group as everyone acts in a responsible manner at all times

	0 Dysfunctional	1 Moving Toward Effectiveness	1.5–3.0 Meets Standard Proficiency	3.5–4.0 Exemplary Practice
When problem continues the group is able to work with the candidate and support him/her in changing actions	Group is unable to bring to the table the problem, or they bring it without identifying who is at the middle of the problems	Members of the group are able to use "I" statements to identify the individual(s) and problems but no changes occur	Members of the group are able to use "I" statements to identify the individual(s) and problems and the group expects the individuals to make the changes	Members of the group are able to use "I" statements to identify the individual(s) and problems and they identify clear changes in the group processes that will help resolve the problems
Individuals who contribute to problem say they will change	Individuals do not agree that they are part of a problem	Individuals who are part of a problem say they will change but do not change. The group spends much time trying to resolve problems rather than on work	Individuals who are part of the problem change after numerous reminders and discussions	When a problem is identified it is the last time that it occurs. Only limited time is spent on the problem
Individuals effectively use Small Group Roles: encourager, organizer, contributor, synthesizer; add evidence on back of this page	Members of the group do not take responsibility for encouraging, organizing, and synthesizing. Most members contribute to the discussion. Focus is on adding new information or restating what was already said	All members effectively encourage others to contribute; All members contribute to the group's organization and in clarifying the agenda and tasks at the very beginning of each meeting	All members demonstrate at some time ability to ask questions that expand learning. All members at some time accurately synthesize complex discussion	All members consistently demonstrate ability to ask questions and elicit information that is relevant to expanding his/her and others understanding about the topics being studied. All members synthesize and link aspect of discussion resulting in forward movement of the work
Assigned roles carried out: facilitator, recorder, reporter, time keeper; Add evidence on back of this page	Roles are dominant in the group, in that other members do not take responsibility for group's progress	Assigned roles	Members rotate roles and all members are effective in all roles	Depending on the work for a given session individual's volunteer for roles so that the most effective use of individuals is maintained
Members participate in small group reports	The group's reporter provides information to whole group	Recorder and Reporter report to whole group	All members of the group report to whole group	Outstanding audio visual representation of group's study

Learning Community Group member Disposition/Propensities are demonstrated. List on the back those that are observed giving examples	One or two members of the group consistently demonstrate 3 or 4 dispositions	Half of the group consistently demonstrate 5 or 6 of dispositions	All members of the group consistently demonstrate LC dispositions with only 1 or 2 reminders during a months work	Group is extremely effective and efficient. The quality and amount of work and learning is far above expectations. Group stands out from the performance norm
Teacher/leader dispositions demonstrated by small group leaders	Selection of leader takes time and uses up study group work time in getting organized	Rotation of role is established and members begin group work quickly. Not all dispositions demonstrated by all members	Leadership dispositions demonstrated by all members of the group when they are carrying out role	Leaders/facilitators are selected in advance and agendas set so that leader brings printed agenda to meeting
Individuals take responsibility for his/her tasks	At each group meeting at least one person does not have his/her task completed	At each group meeting no more than 1 person does not have all of his/her task completed	Completed on time, meet criteria for performance standard	All individuals complete their tasks, ask if they can help others, or support them
Total	NA or Total	NA or Total	NA or Total	NA or Total

RUBRIC FOR WRITTEN EDUCATION PAPERS

A. Clarity of Thinking and Writing

4–5	2.5–3.5	1.5–2	0–1
Report is free of jargon and surface language errors; it is consistent in tone and voice with documents prepared for professional peers and a critical public; the format, guiding questions, evidence, conclusions, and recommendations are obviously clear and reasonable; a strong coherent case is made in the study with assertions and claims consistently supported by strong evidence and reasoning	The reports are free of jargon and surface language errors; they are generally consistent in tone and voice with documents prepared for a peer professional audience and critical public; the format, guiding questions, data, conclusions, and recommendations are generally clear and accurate (either implicitly or explicitly); an apparent case is made for the learning that took place through the studies and the recommendations flowing from them—most assertions and claims are supported by evidence	The reports have a majority of the following attributes: there are some surface language errors and awkwardness in the handling of tone and voice; the style is occasionally too informal for a document prepared for a peer professional audience; the case and arguments are made for one or both of the studies is sometimes hard to follow, and has to be inferred (i.e., it is not explicit); the evidence and reasoning are loosely tied to assertions and claims	Report contains a combination of the following: a number of surface language errors and lack of consistency in tone and voice; inappropriate informality in style; lack of a clear position, case, or strategy to develop one; and the lack of explicit or implicit connections between claims and evidence

B. Sound Data Collection Procedures

3	2.5	1.5–2	0–1
Multiple sources are used, all of which are pertinent to the questions and hypotheses under study; the modes of inquiry are clear and could be replicated and/or checked out by other professionals	Multiple sources are used, and most seem pertinent to the questions and hypotheses under study; the modes of inquiry are generally clear, although some questions remain—not all could be replicated or reviewed for reliability	Several sources are used that seem relatively pertinent to the questions and hypotheses under study; the modes of inquiry are generally clear, although not all could be replicated or reviewed for reliability	The sources of data are limited, and not necessarily reliable; they would be difficult to replicate or substantiate; they are not clear, and obviously open to contention and/or question

C. Originality and Depth of Analysis and Thought

4.0–5.0	2.5–3.5	1/5–2.00	0–1
Selective and appropriate use of summary to establish the conceptual framework and foundation for in-depth analysis of the guiding questions, ideas and approaches; clear and logical connections between ideas and evidence are cited; a clear identification of the questions raised and/or problems cited; expected outcomes from the inquiry seem reasonable and needed, or suggest clear implications and show how an interviewee or youngster's life experience and learning opportunities might change because of them; future candidates, or futures teachers of a student who was studied would clearly value and likely use this report	Somewhat selective and generally appropriate use of summary as a foundation for analysis; generally sufficient data is used to substantiate claims; the analysis is generally reasonable and fairly well connected to some real, identified possibilities; some intended outcomes or implications are addressed as are some of the related requirements for future actions—future candidates, teachers or other educators would learn from this report	Predominantly an impressionistic summary with character generalizations; the behavioral evidence is weak, lacking sufficient or trustworthy data; the analysis seems scattered and without guiding theory; intended outcomes or implications are vague or must be largely inferred; little consideration of the needed experience and/or support needed for the subjects of the study	Primarily a list of character qualities with a set of data collected that is not well summarized or integrated; little or no evidence of analysis or of building a case or argument for selected needs; the intended outcomes or implications are not evident, nor are the strategies that are logically grounded in and connected to the information and ideas; little or no reliable evidence is presented

D. Grounding in Professional Expertise and/or the Research Literature

3.0	2.5	2	1–1.5	0
Draws appropriately from a wide variety of resources; demonstrates knowledge of some key resources, significant scholarly work and/or research pertinent to the questions/problems understudy; connects data, professional expertise and/or research within the framework of the study	Draws from a variety of sources; demonstrates general knowledge of some important resources, works and research related to the substantive areas of study; makes at least some connections among the data, professional opinion, and/or research and theory in the area	Draws from a limited range of resources; demonstrates limited knowledge of major works and research/theory for the areas under study; makes few connections among the sources of data, external expertise, research and the individuals studied	Draws primarily from one or two sources; demonstrates very limited knowledge of major works and research/theory for the particulars under study; makes few if any connections among the data, sources of expertise, research reports and individual cited	No literature review

E. Intervention Plan and Carrying out of Intervention for Action Research Study

4.0–3.5	2.0–3.0	1–1.5	0
Intervention includes goals that are tied to data about the learner, or person being studied, calendar of events, plan for documentation and evaluation, is clearly tied to findings, uses neighborhood and community resources, events are creative and illustrate non-traditional ways of working on area of the problem or concerns. Second semester includes summary of documentation and evaluation of the intervention and progress toward goals	Intervention includes goals that are tied to data about learner or who is the focus of the study, calendar of events, plan for documentation and evaluation, is clearly tied to finds, uses neighborhood and community resources. Outcomes and Evaluation is included in second paper after intervention	Intervention includes description of events to take place, may or may not include use of community and neighborhood resources. Outcomes and evaluation are mentioned but have weak links to person studies and intervention strategies	No intervention included in write up

CONTINUED DEVELOPMENT OF COURSE LEARNING COMMUNITY

Stage 1—Beginnings—As the semester progresses, candidates are encouraged to invest in higher level *Stage 1* getting to know you activities. For example, Activity 8: First Impressions, is an opportunity for candidates to share what they learned about each other. Thus, giving members data about how they are being experienced as a member of the group. Activity 5-Successes, actually provides deeper information than is warranted in the initial getting acquainted experiences and thus is a useful activity for later in the semester.

Stage 2—Establishing Expectations also continues to develop as course outlines, NCATC standards and instructor guidelines are reviewed. The expectation concerning the quality of candidate work are clarified as instructors provide specific feedback to early assignments.

Stage 3—Identifying and Resolving Conflicts—Continued development of the university course learning community will take the group to *Stage 3: Identification and Resolution of Conflicts*. It is an important stage in the development of a learning community that will last for only one semester. While unusual, it is important that the instructor process with the whole group, the course procedures for identifying and resolving conflicts that arise during the semester. In a university course that requires both individual and group accountability and responsibility. Below is a process that we found workable for instructors and candidates.

We recommend that instructors begin by dividing a sheet of paper into three columns or create three columns on a board or overhead if you choose to do this with your class. Then in the first column list the types of conflicts you observe and/or experience during a typical semester in your courses. In the second column, list the things that as an instructor you have or could have done to prevent the conflicts. Third, list the things that candidates have done to prevent the conflicts from occurring. Fourth, list what the instructor will do to prevent the conflict in the future. Finally, write out a procedure that you will use with the students should a conflict of the same nature occur again. For an example, see below.

Conflicts in which the Instructor has a role	Actions Instructor has taken to prevent or resolve conflicts	Actions Teacher Candidates have taken to prevent or resolve conflicts	Actions Instructor will take to prevent conflicts	Procedure to be used by Instructor and Candidates to identify and resolve similar conflicts
It is not clear what the instructor is grading in a given written assignment	Repeat directions; have student come to office for a one-on-one meeting; show an inappropriate example of the assignment (one that is not at the highest level).	Asking clarifying questions. Just do assignment guessing what the instructor wanted.	Rubrics will be provided for substance, writing, support for positions and related references.	The teacher candidate with the conflict will use the conflict identification and resolution process found in Chapter 10. If the conflict is about something that the instructor is responsible for then follow the first procedure. If it is with a peer then use the second procedure.

Conflicts between or among students where the instructor is not a part of it	Actions Instructor has taken to prevent or resolve conflicts	Actions Teacher Candidates have taken to prevent or resolve conflicts	Actions Instructor will take to prevent conflicts	Procedure to be used by Instructor and Candidates to identify and resolve similar conflicts
Member of small group does not complete his/her part of the task, is late, and/or creates stress for the group	Ignore problem as it is the candidates' problem; talk to the person who is acting irresponsible; or give the person who does not do his/her share of the work 2 grades lower than the other members of the group.	Tell instructor on candidate who is not responsible; Talk to others in the group about how terrible the candidate is; Talk directly to student and ask what can be done so that he/she does his/her share.	Teach group member roles and dispositions; Walk around class during small group work observing and recording specific student behavior; Provide feedback to individuals; In class have groups evaluate their group process and provide feedback to each other and instructor.	The teacher candidate with the conflict will use the conflict identification and resolution process found in Chapter 10. If the conflict is about something that the instructor is responsible for then follow the first procedure. If it is with a peer then use the second procedure.

During the semester it is a good idea, when the instructor is experiencing a conflict with the group, for the instructor to use the conflict resolution process with the entire class. Modeling for the candidates will help them see how they can transfer something they are learning about for use as a teacher as well as learning how to use the process personally. Providing practice in evaluating group processes and work also sets the stage for preventative actions. The instructor helps the candidates see that talking through something prior to it causing a crisis (when it is a question, or mildly bothersome) is one way to avoid continued irresponsibility and conflicts.

Stage 4: Maintaining and Expanding the Learning Community is the stage where if the group reaches this stage, the instructor can rely on individuals staying focused on contributing to academic, social, social justice, and personal development for themselves and others.

Stage 5: Closure and Disbanding is difficult in a university course due to the number of things that candidates have to complete at the end of each semester. It is easy for instructors to believe that eliminating work that lowers the standards of the course expectations will help them to be well liked. However, final reports verbal or written and final exams are all a part of the process that help students pull together and identify what they have learned and how much they have changed over the semester. It is also important to remember that it is unlikely that candidates will apply any knowledge or skills that they acquired at less than 85%. Thus, students who are not held to high expectations are unlikely to be able to apply the knowledge and skills taught in TLC 1 and TLC 2 in their field placements or in student teaching. Thus, instead of contributing to the candidates ability to achieve the program's performance outcome standards you would be contributing to their failure.

Stage 5 activities are helpful to candidates both in developing an appreciation for what you taught and what they have accomplished. For example, you can show photos (e.g., digital, slides) that you took at various stages of group development. As you go through the slides, ask the person in the picture what changes they had made since the beginning of semester until the time of the picture. Ask, when you look at the picture of you taken during the first week of the class, what changes have you made now that it is the end of the semester? Ask, what was the hardest thing for you to acquire? What was the funniest thing you did this semester as a part of this class? What reading had the biggest impact on you? In what way? Who in this class had the biggest impact on you? In what ways? What is caring?

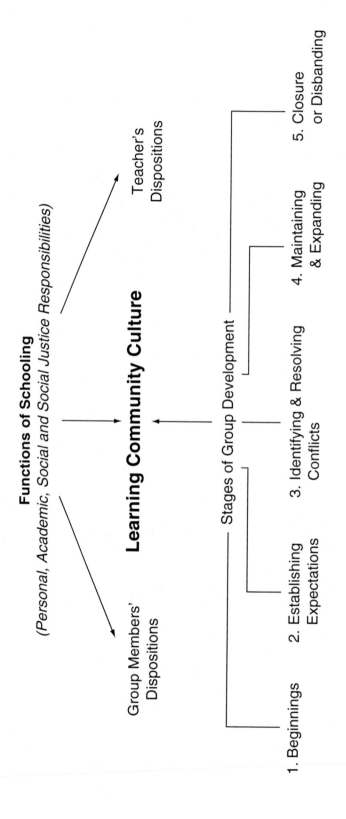

RELATIONSHIPS AMONG THE CONCEPTS INCLUDED IN THE LEARNING COMMUNITY CULTURE.

Functions of Schooling
(Personal, Academic, Social and Social Justice Responsibilities)

Teacher's Dispositions

Group Members' Dispositions

Learning Community Culture

Stages of Group Development

1. Beginnings

2. Establishing Expectations

3. Identifying & Resolving Conflicts

4. Maintaining & Expanding

5. Closure or Disbanding

ALIGNING LEARNING COMMUNITY CONCEPTS TO NATIONAL STANDARDS

By Carol Sharp, Ph.D.

INTASC Standard	Learning Community Concept(s)	NCATE Standards
1. Teachers understand the central concepts, tools of inquiry, and structures of the discipline(s) they teach and can create learning experiences that make these aspects of subject matter meaningful for students.	• Academic function of schooling • Instructional leadership disposition • Developmental perspective disposition • Stages of group development	• In-depth knowledge of subject matter. • Demonstrate knowledge through inquiry, critical analysis, and synthesis of the subject.
2. Teachers understand how children learn and develop, and can provide learning opportunities that support their intellectual, social and personal development.	• Developmental perspective disposition • Instructional leadership disposition • Supporting and expanding production—stage of group development • Levels of classroom culture	• Know how students learn and how to make ideas accessible to them. • In-depth understanding of multiple and instructional strategies (enabling) all students to learn.
3. Teachers understand how students differ in their approaches to learning and create instructional opportunities that are adapted to diverse learners.	• Social justice function of schooling • Instructional leadership disposition • Developmental perspective disposition • Supporting and expanding production—stage of group development	• In-depth understanding of multiple and instructional strategies (enabling) all students to learn. • Demonstrate knowledge, skills, and dispositions related to diversity. • Candidates interact and work with other students from diverse ethnic, racial, gender, language, socioeconomic, and religious groups.
4. Teachers understand and use a variety of instructional strategies to encourage students' development of critical thinking, problem solving, and performance skills.	• Instructional leadership disposition • Supporting and expanding production—stage of group development	• Thorough understanding of pedagogical content knowledge.
5. Teachers use an understanding of individual and group motivation and behavior to create a learning environment that encourages positive social interaction, active engagement in learning, and self-motivation.	• Personal responsibility function of schooling • Social responsibility function of schooling • Cooperative disposition • Stages of group development • Levels of classroom culture • Academic, Social, Social Justice, and Personal Functions of Learning	• Candidates establish educational environments that support student learning. • Candidates monitor student leaning and have a positive effect on learning for all students.

INTASC Standard	Learning Community Concept(s)	NCATE Standards
6. Teachers use knowledge of effective verbal, nonverbal, and media communication techniques to foster active inquiry, collaboration, and supportive interaction in the classroom.	• Social responsibility function of schooling • Social justice function of schooling • Instructional leadership disposition • Cooperative disposition • Levels of classroom culture	• Candidates integrate technology effectively. • Candidates use technology to support and improve student learning.
7. Teachers plan instruction based upon knowledge of subject matter, students, the community, and curriculum goals.	• Academic function of schooling • Instructional leadership disposition • Developmental perspective disposition • Beginnings—stages of group development	• Candidates develop meaningful learning experiences to facilitate learning for all students.
8. Teachers understand and use formal and informal assessment strategies to evaluate and ensure the continuous intellectual, social and physical development of the learner.	• Academic function of schooling • Social responsibility function of schooling • Personal responsibility function of schooling • Developmental perspective disposition • Supporting and expanding production—stage of group development	• Candidates accurately assess and analyze student leaning, and make appropriate adjustments to instruction.
9. Teachers are reflective practitioners who continually evaluate the effects of their choices and actions on others (students, parents, and other professionals in the learning community) and who actively seek out opportunities to grow professionally.	• Reflective orientation disposition • Self (and group) actualization disposition • Stages of group development	• Candidates reflect on their practice and make necessary adjustments to enhance student learning. • Candidates collect and analyze data related to their work.
10. Teachers foster relationships with school colleagues, parents, and agencies in the larger community to support students' learning and well-being.	• Dispositions of members of learning communities	• Candidates work with students, families, and communities as delineated in professional, state, and institutional standards.

SUGGESTED COURSE CALENDAR

(Note: Class times may be adjusted for candidates to work on Field Study Projects.**)**

First Semester

Week #	Class Topics/In-Class Activities	Assignments
1	Course Overview/Getting Acquainted	Read Chapter 1

2	Group Roles Practice
	Professional Writing (Reports)
	   Expectations/Rubrics
	Observation/Inference Statements
	   Activity (Ex. 1.1)
		Observations/Inferences—Ex. 1.2

3	Functions of Schooling Discussion of Ex. 1.2 Discussion of Purposes of Schooling—Ex. 1.3	Functions of Schooling Field Study Project—Ex. 1.6 (Due Week 6)
4	Functions of Schooling In-Class Panel—Ex. 1.4 Discussion of Purposes of Schooling—Ex. 1.5	Begin Neighborhood, etc., Ex. 1.4C Due Week 8. Read Chapter 2 Self Assessment Chart of Propensities and Summary Statement—Ex. 2.1 Begin Child Study Ex. 2.6
5	Propensities/Dispositions Discussion of Ex. 2.1 In Class small group work—Ex. 2.2	Actualization Study—Ex. 2.3 (Due Week 9)

6
Functions of Schooling
Field Study Project Due
	Propensities/Dispositions
	Discussion of traditional/learning
	   community classrooms—Ex. 2.4
	Discussion—Ex. 2.5
	Discussion of Functions of Schooling
	   Field Study Projects
		Read Chapter 3
		
		Self Assessment—Ex. 3.4

7 Individual Neighborhood, Community Study Parts 1 and 2 due	Culture Discussion of Classroom Culture—Ex. 3.1 Discussion of Self-Assessment—Ex. 3.4 Movie—Angela's Ashes	Measurement/Evaluation Field Study Project—(Due Week 11)
8	Culture Discussion of Ex. 3.3 Discussion of Ex. 3.5 Movie—Antoine Fisher	Group Field Project—Ex. 3.6 (Due for presentation Week 15) Read Chapter 4 Complete Ex. 4.2 (for Ex. 4.1 discussion)

9
Actualization Field
Study Project Due
	Stages of Group Development
	Discussion of stages of group
	   development—Ex. 4.1
	Discussion of Actualization
	   Field Study Projects
		Complete Ex. 4.2
		
		Complete Ex. 4.3
		
		Read Chapters 8 and 9

Week #	Class Topics/In-Class Activities	Assignments

10
Draft of Child Study Due
	Stages of Group Development:
	    Beginnings and Establishing
	    Expectations
	Discussion of Ex. 4.2
	Discussion of Ex. 4.3
		Final Report of Child Field Study Project
		    Ex. 4.4 (Due Week 13)
		Read Chapters 10 and 11

11
Measurement/
Evaluation Field Study
Project Due
	Stages of Group Development:
	    Identifying and Resolving Conflict and
	    Supporting and Expanding Learning
	    Community
	Discussion of Measurement/Evaluation
	    Field Study Projects
		Implement Child Study Action Plan
		    Ex. 2.6 after making revisions based
		    on feedback.
		Learning Community Plan—Ex. 4.5
		    (Due Week 14)
		Read Chapter 7

12	Stages of Group Development:
	    Disbanding—Transitions and Closure
	Making the Learning Community Vision
	    Explicit
	In Class Small Group Work—Ex. 7.1
		Read Chapters 5 and 6

13 Child Field Study Project Final Report Due	Forero and Henderson In Class Small Group Work—Ex. 5.1 In Class Small Group Work—Ex. 6.1 Discussions of Child Field Study Projects	
14 Learning Community Plan Due	Discussions of Learning Community Plans	End of semester self-assessment (Due Week 16)
15	Small Group Field Project Presentations	
16 (Individual) Final Community Assessment Part III Due	Discussions of End of Semester Self-Assessments and Final Exam	

Second Semester

Week #	Class Topics/In-Class Activities	Assignments
1	1. Getting Acquainted & Establishing Expectations for Course 2. Review of Chapters 1–7, Functions of Schooling, Learning Community, LC Teachers, Stages of Development (cooperative group presentations) 3 Starting Your Second Child Study and Action Research Project	A. Begin Second Child Study, Introduction to Chapters 9–12 B. Readings: Overview Chapters 8-12; and review Chapters 8 and 9 C. Activities 8.1 Observation D. Activity 8.2 Designing, Part A E. Activity 9.2 Designing , Part A.
2 (C. Due D. Due E. Due)	1. Small Group Discussions (Share Beginnings and Establishing Expectations-Plans; note feedback) 2. Presentation "Authoritative Teachers & Actions that Communicate You Care" 3. Observations, Inferences, Recommendation about "Beginnings" classroom observations.	F. 9.1 Observation G. Review Chapters 8 and 9 for Quiz H. Read Chapter 10 A. *Continue Second Child Study, Introduction to Chapters 9-12.*
3	1. Quiz Chapters 8 and 9 2. Instructor Introduction to Stage 3-Conflict Identification and Resolution 3. Activity 10.2-Bothersome Behavior Assessment 4. Review Child Study Progress in Small Groups: Members responsible for asking clarifying questions.	I. Revise 8.2 and 9.2 based on instructor feedback J. 8.2 B and C and D K. 9.2 B and C and D L. Small Group Create Activities for Course on the Topic of Bullying A. *Continue Second Child Study, Introduction to Chapters 9–12.*
4	Getting Acquainted and Learning Other's Expectations. Field Trip to Establish Process for Study of Community	A. *Continue Second Child Study, Introduction to Chapters 9–12.*
5 (1st Draft of Child Study Due)	1. Chapter 10-Bullying-Instructor Presentation, 2. Student led Whole Group, Small Group Bullying Activities. 3. Activity 10.4 Instructor Arranges Leader of Gang Prevention to Talk about Bullying	N. Add activities to your Stage I and II plans that support a bully free classroom O. 10.3 Observations, 1–9 P 10.5 Carry out interviews complete A & B.
6 (10.5 Write Up Due)	Chapter 10: Introduction to Steps in Conflict Identification and Resolution Activity 10.3 Activity 10.5: Identifying Building and District Discipline Policy Instructor Arranges Speakers	10.4 Small Groups work on study of materials and presentations to class Begin Implementation of Action part of Child Study
7	10.6 Communications Skills 10.7 Conflict Identification and Resolution Practice (Small Groups of 4)	Continue 10.4 Continue Implementation of Action Plan of Child
8	Chapter 10: Activity 10.7 Angry Parent (Pairs). Community Presentations	Continue Implementation of Action Plan of Child
9	Chapter 11: Maintaining and Expanding the LC. Activity 11.1 Concept Mapping	Continue Implementation of Action Plan of Child

Week #	Class Topics/In-Class Activities	Assignments
10	Chapter 11: Activity 11.2 & 11.3 Planning	Continue Implementation of Action Plan of Child 11.3 Work on Individual Plans started in Class
11	Chapter 11: Activity 11.4 Service Learning	Continue Implementation of Action Plan of Child Teach lessons 11.4 Add to Plans-Service Learning
12	Presentations: Community Studies	Continue Implementation of Action Plan of Child Study Teach Lessons
13	Chapter 12: Disbanding and Closure Chapter 13: The Future of LCCs	Continue Implementation of Action Plan of Child Study Teach Lessons
14 (Final Report of Child Study Due)	Individuals Report Expanded Community Studies	Continue Implementation of Action Plan of Child Teach lessons Complete End of Semester Self Assessment
15 (Final Draft of Plans Due)	Child Study Presentations	Study for Final Exam Complete End of Semester Assertiveness Assessment & Report on Changes to Date, Next Goals, and Strategies
16 (Self- Assessment Due) (Assertiveness Assessment & Plan Due)	Final Exam	

FIELD STUDY REPORTS & OTHER DOCUMENTS FOR INCLUSION IN ELECTRONIC PORTFOLIO

(Evidence of Meeting NJPTS/INTASC Standards)

Signature Assignments

Teaching in Learning Communities I (Include Assignment Product and Rubric)	Teaching in Learning Communities II	X when added to your portfolio	
Assertiveness Assessment Report and Professional Development Plan based on Assessment Data	End of Second Semester Assertiveness Assessment and Report on Progress, Plus Professional Development Plan based on new Assessment Data		
	Written Report Including Plan, Identification of School Policies, Practices, about, and strategies for Eliminating Discipline Problems (Primarily Bullying Behaviors)		
Functions of Schooling and Propensities Report (Based on application of Observation, Interview, Analysis, synthesis, and reporting skills)	Written Plan for Establishing a Classroom Learning Community and Stage 4 Subject Matter Plan that includes Concept Map, Performance Outcomes, Formative Assessments, Performance Evaluation Tasks, Instruction, Practice Activities, Service Learning Connections		
Written Report of Field Study on the Effects of Measurement/Evaluation on the Presence of Functions of Schooling			
Written Plan for Establishing Classroom Learning Community: Stages 1–3 (Stages of Group Development Plan)	Report about Experience in Establishing a Small Group LC and Subject Matter Instruction (Based on analysis, synthesis, of original plans, actual instruction, observations, learner artifacts and candidate's journal and reflections)		
Report Based on Data Collected from Observations, Analysis, Inferences and Reflections about a Variety of Classroom Learning Communities in Written or Video Form			
Community Exploration Report Including ties to Functions of Schooling and Network Map (Based on observations, interviews, analysis, synthesis reflections and reporting	Expanded Network Map and Report on Use/Applications of Resources and Contacts		
Child Study 1 (Initial Study, Action Research Plan, Report on Implementation and Evaluation of implementation and learner)	Child Study 2 (Initial Study, Action Research Plan, Report on Implementation and Evaluation of implementation and learner) Comparison and Contrasts between Studies 1 and 2		
End of Semester Self-Assessment	End of Semester Self-Assessment including description of changes in dispositions and related actions		
Study of One Disposition/Propensity: Actualization	Up-date on Candidate's talk and actions related to Actualization Disposition		

End of Chapter Activities

The activities related to each of the chapters are located at the end of each section. The activities in this book focus on *connecting* ideas presented in the chapter with your understandings of school and schooling, teachers and teaching and learning and learners all within the context of schools you attended and schools where you are now assigned. The primary study methods used in the activities are discussion, observing, interviewing, analyzing, synthesizing, inferring and formal report writing. The methods provide a structure for you to learn how to become a "***student of*** teaching and learning, schools and schooling, and learners and learning."

Teacher candidates will have an opportunity to select enrichment/extra credit activities related to some of the course activities. The instructor will provide information about this as part of his/her "Establishing Expectations" activities.

Several times during the next year you will have assignments that involve your interviewing people. One of the important aspects of the interview is your interpersonal interaction and a second are the clarifying questions you ask. Do not turn interviews into surveys by asking the individual "to write answers to your questions," and indicating that "they should email them to you or that you will pick up at a later time."

Professional Demeanor

A primary means for teacher candidates to acquire the "knowledge and skills of a teacher" is observing and working with PK-12 learners and teachers during school hours. A major portion of the teacher candidates' application of theory and research provided in this text requires them to carry out application tasks in schools.

PK-12 Principals, Teachers, and Parents have brought to the attention of the university faculty working with the teacher candidates in their schools, that it is important that university students dress professionally and bring a professional demeanor to the school site.

SECTION II

Current Ideas About Learning Communities

OVERVIEW

Since the publication of our text *Organizing and Managing Classroom Learning Communities*, in 1992, other authors have written about the worth of creating classroom Learning Community cultures (e.g., Solomon, Watson, Battistich, Schaps, and Delucchi, 1996, Rogoff, Turkanis, and Bartlett, 2001). Our initial work was based on Joseph Schwab's (1975, 1976) original ideas about the values in creating a classroom Learning Community culture coupled with the work of Stanford (1977), which focused on the *process* for effective group development or the *how* to create this particular type of classroom culture. Our text was based on Schwab's concept of a classroom learning community (1974, 1975, 1976) that P–12 learners are partners with teachers, parents, and others (the neighborhood and broader community) in their development and learning.

After the first edition of this text was published, Putnam and her university colleagues participated with teachers, whole schools and districts as they invested in creating classroom and school cultures that were reflective of the learning community principles. Putnam also worked with teachers in 18 international schools to create classroom learning communities. Across the US, many university professors and teachers have established and/or studied the classroom learning community culture. Thus, we now find that there is a larger literature and experience base about learning community classrooms, teams, and school cultures.

For example, in 1988 the Flint Community School District, an urban district located in Michigan, created a Professional Development School partnership with Michigan State University. As a part of this partnership, individual teachers with the support of MSU faculty began work on creating learning community cultures in their own classrooms. As the teachers got their learning community cultures established, they saw that there was a decrease in inappropriate student behaviors and an increase in attendance and achievement. For example, June Alexander, a third grade teacher, reported that she was shocked that attendance was nearly 100% on cold snowy/icy days. In the past her experience was that less than three or four students attended on these days. As Alexander's colleagues worked on establishing additional learning community cultures, Rowland Lillard, the principal, reported that there was a significant reduction in the number of students sent to the office for discipline (Putnam and Lillard, 1997).

Haberman (2004), identified characteristics of star teachers when they successfully created classroom learning communities. He begins with a description of what he means by a learning community. He states that "a group is a learning community when members share a common vision that learning is the primary purpose for their association and the ultimate value to preserve in their workplace and that learning outcomes are the primary criteria for evaluating the success of their work" (p. 52). Thus one of the characteristics of successful learning community star teachers was that they are turned on to learning and thus are able to model the value of life long learning to their students. "Students will model behavior of teachers they respect—teachers who have strong interests, who love to learn, and who are always reading something of interest" (Haberman, 2004, p. 52).

A second characteristic of the effective learning community teacher, reported by Haberman (2004) was that they focused on student effort. Third, these teachers saw effective instruction as a matter of life and death for students. Fourth, these teachers expected to have problems as part of their daily work and not as requiring extra efforts but as an integral part of their jobs. Fifth, the effective star learning community teachers accepted accountability for student achievement. Sixth, these teachers put the learning of all students above the convenience of the adults. Seventh, they did not blame students for not learning. Eighth, they defined their roles in terms of "whatever it takes" to solve the problems (Haberman, 1999).

Creating learning community cultures also necessitates that data about the individual students be used as the basis for individual work, the formation of student instructional groups and the various sizes of study, practice, and application groups. This means that new organizations and software are needed for student records, new ways of reporting, and new relationships with families and community are needed if data and experiences necessary for each child's academic, personal, social and social justice achievement are to be used. Using student data to form lessons and groups is essential to support students' equal opportunity to learn.

The nature of the learning community that was the focus of the Professional Development Schools in Flint, Michigan, and later the District's work, was based on learning community goals (i.e., development of academic, personal, social justice, and social responsibilities), beliefs about children (e.g., are good, want to learn, are capable), and theories of how children learn (e.g., constructive, authentic applications). Some teachers and administrators found that the goals, beliefs, and theories on which they had operated for years were being challenged. One of the greatest challenges for some teachers and administrators involved the beliefs and theories that held "when an urban learner fails, it is the fault of the home and community." Others were challenged by the idea that learner-self-concept was altered by their success or failure in learning at school and not merely by their home or community experience. Still others were challenged by the ideas of the social constructivist paradigm.

As administrators and teachers worked to understand the nature and goals of a learning community culture, as well as how to establish a genuine learning community culture, a conflict between those who worked to merely establish a kinder-gentler adult controlled environment and those who understood the principles of learning community was found. The latter group knew how to establish the relationship-building and listening mode (as described by Wolfgang, 2002) that is necessary if learners are to develop personal, social and social justice responsibilities. The teachers and administrators who were interested in a kinder-gentler adult controlled culture included those who did not have the beliefs, theories, knowledge, skills, and/or experiences necessary to create an authentic learning community culture. Frequently their own developmental level was at an intuitive-survival level (Wolfgang, 2000) or they had an authoritarian personality and they did not know how to allow students to learn to be responsible and accountable for their own behavior.

Wolfgang (2004) believes that some in-service teachers and many new teachers will not be successful in creating a learning community culture. We believe that these individuals will not create learning communities unless they find new values, beliefs, and skills and reach a new developmental level. For example, those teachers need to:

1. develop a sense-of-self as a teacher/leader that allows them to trust in the process of group development,

2. have as personal beliefs learning community norms,

3. have the knowledge and skills to be an effective leader of the process, and

4. believe in the good of K–12 learners.

These individuals may not have the personality, temperament or beliefs about children that are required for building caring nurturing relationships necessary for building authentic learning community cultures. For example, some teacher needs (e.g., to be liked, to maintain strong control, to not form warm emotional bonds) must be examined for their impact on learners and changed if these individuals are to become successful learning community teachers. For these individuals Wolfgang (1986) suggests a continuum for change. This continuum allows individuals to challenge their current beliefs and needs by trying out new actions and developing new views while not totally giving up their need for control, for being liked, or for being isolated. Creating a professional development plan with specific performance standards is one strategy that helps adults move through the development process. Conscious attention to the needed changes will help an individual's development move to new stages of moral development and progress at, for them, a "safe" pace until they have formed beliefs and actions that support their successful leadership of a learning community.

The professional development process and modeling by successful learning community teachers and administrator leaders were an important part of the Flint work. Professional Learning Communities provided the support for professional development.

Having a focus for adult learning provided the foundation for establishing the Professional Learning Communities. Having the opportunity to work as a member of a Professional Learning Community provided the members with the experiences and the benefits of being a member of a learning community as well as how to provide leadership for the development of other learning communities.

A group of the K–12 urban Professional Development School teachers who worked seriously at creating classroom learning communities were asked to share their ideas about "what the idea of the learning community meant to them," after establishing learning communities for at least two years. Some of their responses are provided below.

My classroom learning community is now a cooperative society in which a reflective teacher-manager-learner with a developmental perspective practices and promotes the academic, social, personal, and social justice outcomes of schooling.

The teacher and students all bring their individual cultures into the classroom and together they travel through the stages of developing the classroom learning community. High standards are held for all the students. Discipline problems no longer exist in our learning community and disappear as soon as all students become personally and socially responsible. I have observed how students from a learning community classroom can impact others and influence what goes on in other classroom cultures. I see the learning community students as very aware of what is going on around them and willing to help or support others when it is needed. **J. Howard**

I see a learning community as a process where a classroom becomes a community of learners in an effort to develop children who will grow into responsible adults ready or the larger community. The learning community culture teaches students how to live and work together in a responsible, cooperative, and collaborative way. It fosters personal and social responsibility with emphasis on the highest standards for academic learning. It is a culture which promotes positive pro-social behavior where respect and kindness prevail, all setting the stage for a future of life-time learners. **C. Ryan**

In a learning community everyone is responsible for learning and no one has all of the responsibility for learning. It is assumed (a norm) that everyone has valued information to share and that everyone is respected as a valuable member of the community. Discipline is reduced because more students are engaged in learning. **C. Wolgast**

Investing in the formation of a learning community classroom culture pays off for the entire year with each one of my classes. The time I spend on the first three stages provides me the time to teach the routines and procedures I need for laboratory classes, collect assessment data, and establish the norms for team work, using science equipment and working with a lab partner. My students are now ready to go when the bell rings, they know how to keep track of their grades, we have few if any discipline problems, and our equipment is no longer damaged as students respect it and each other. Grades have gone up and students study more of the subject matter now. **J. Ruddock**

The benefits I find in establishing a learning community classroom are that there are less discipline problems, student cooperate, collaborate, can work in teams, they care for each other, attendance has improved and they like school. The students like doing self-evaluations and participating in decision making. **J. Alexander**

My students now learn how to learn. **D. Shaffer**

Alarm clock, coffee, hair, make-up and school jumper. A bowl of cereal, check to-do list, pick up my blue desk-basket, and get into car. I am eager to get to school to begin the dance of the day. Like a dance, the day has beginning steps, pauses, and wild whirling, and ending steps. My learning community classroom has a calm feeling on everyone's part. We have time to chat, be friendly, learn new things, practice older things, and share with others. We are no longer operate at a harried pace because the norms, routines, procedures, rules created *time* for us. The new routines and procedures for me increased my record keeping, which increased the accuracy of the lessons I plan so I am teaching more and the students are learning more. **D. McFadden**

One of the Flint Professional Development School learning community teachers illustrated how she viewed her new classroom culture. On the following page is the picture that she drew that shows how a diverse set of students enters school with a set of community/neighborhood, and cultural values and then merge with the learning community values that are the foundation of her school and classroom. (See Figure 1)

The teacher preparation program working in the Professional Development schools was congruent with the beliefs, theories, and knowledge and skills necessary for creating effective learning communities. The teacher candidates reported that they were lucky when assigned to classrooms where the mentor teachers were learning to create classroom learning community cultures. Teachers who are learning, and expanding their own expertise by trying something different, and studying the effects on learners were the most effective mentors, according to the teacher candidates' evaluations of their mentors.

One example of an outstanding mentor teacher was a former music teacher who was placed in a fifth grade classroom. She used strong control methods (e.g., no one out of their seat ever, never say anything unless called on, sent to principal's office even if infraction was small). When asked why she managed her classroom in this method she said that as a music teacher she taught different classes and usually saw a group once or twice a month. She did not know the kids and they did not know her. The students' regular teachers simply dumped the students in her space and left. In order for her to get any of the music taught so they could put on the expected school productions, she developed the rigid management style as a survival strategy. The district eliminated music from the elementary school program and when she had to move to a classroom teaching, she simply took that management style with her. She wanted to create a learning community culture, which was on the opposite end of the management continuum.

She started the transition by folding a piece of paper in three columns. She wrote her current routines, procedures, rules, and norms in the first column. Then she wrote what she wanted to change to in the third column. In the middle column, she wrote out what the transition steps or alternative rules, procedures, and routines that she would use to move the students to accepting more accountability and responsibility for their behavior and learning. She also made a list of things that she would do that would communicate her genuine caring for her students. Her list included asking students about their lives outside of the school (inquiring about a sick parent; asking about a student's trip; asking about a problem with a sibling), providing specific (rather than general) feedback about students' understandings or misunderstandings and smiling, smiling, smiling. She also figured out a way she could meet with each of the students individually each day until she had established basic relationships. She started by having one student come to a "Presentation Corner" and show and/or describe to her something that they had learned since their previous one-on-one. She responded with encouragement, support, and at times challenged them in ways that helped them to increase the complexity of their thinking.

She took every opportunity she could find to talk with the students. For example, she was in the hall before school, greeting students, asking about their experiences out of school, checking up on how a sick parent or sibling was doing. She began before school "Special Sessions." This way she could talk or work with one or two students for a few minutes before the other students entered the classroom. The Special Sessions evolved into "Sign-Up Sessions" where students who wanted to talk, get help, or have something explained could simply sign up for a morning session and get an early entry pass from the teacher.

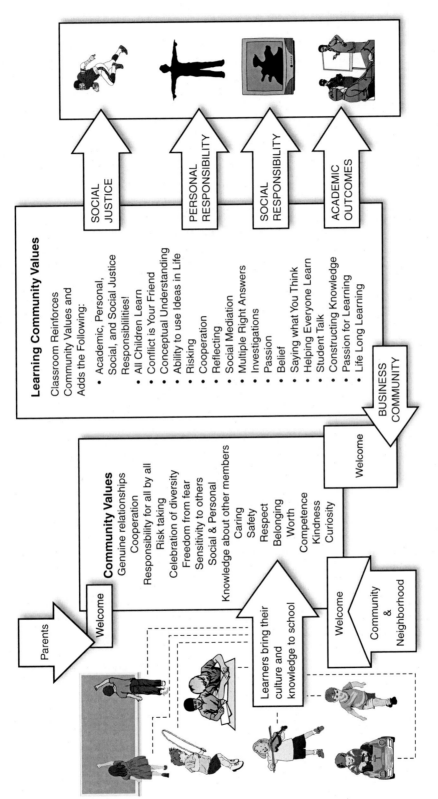

FIGURE 1

The transition took a while. She went backward when things did not go smoothly. Teaching the students to be responsible and accountable and eliminate their dependence on her external control was the hardest. However, within a day or two, she would talk with the students and together they would make a new effort. She learned that at the beginning reminders and asking students what was expected helped the students to get in charge of their actions. Each time they started up again, they made it a longer period without a problem. This former music teacher used her three-column paper to start the school year until the students she received each fall came to her from learning community classrooms. She relabeled the columns as "Column 1: What the students expect; Column 2: How to move to the learning community; and Column 3: Responsible and Accountable Individual Students in a Learning Community."

In the current literature, we found that multiple authors have added their ideas about the culture of *learning community classrooms* to the professional literature. This work is focused primarily on single classrooms or schools and does not include the complexity of cross-grade level learning communities.

Current research supports the idea that a classroom or school learning community culture contributes positively to K–12 learners from all SES levels in the areas of academic, social, personal and social justice responsibilities (e.g., Watkins, 2005). It is also clear those teachers who inappropriately feel sorry for or concentrate primarily on social support for students in poverty and excuse their lack of holding the students to high academic standards as "caring" are a part of the urban problem. As far back as 1960, Shouse warned us of this potential problem. He suggested that school or classroom learning community culture may only be helpful to disadvantaged students when there is a clear emphasis on academic performance.

In the current literature, we found articles that included the language "caring community." Given that Shouse (1960) and others (e.g., Thompson 2004) are concerned about students being harmed by teachers who "care" inappropriately by feeling sorry for them and not holding students accountable for achievement in academic, personal, social and social justice responsibilities, it is important that what is meant by *caring communities* be defined. We believe that it is important that learning community teachers are constructively caring individuals. In our text, a caring learning community classroom is one where the teacher communicates his/her caring through the constructive relationships built with students. The nature of these relationships is called relationship/listening and **holds all** students responsible for achieving academic outcomes, and personal, social and social justice responsibilities (thus, students are expected to care about, look out for, and support themselves and each other). It is possible for the learning community teacher to hold these high standards because she/he has a wide repertoire of knowledge and skills necessary to provide differentiated instruction so that success can be achieved by each learner.

The term Learning Community has an explicit definition of what is included as the outcomes of this type of classroom culture. Other types of classroom community cultures are not *learning communities* if they do not include accountability for academic, personal, social and social justice responsibilities.

One of the major improvements in the thinking about classroom learning community culture is about their connections to or inclusion of family and neighborhood/community partnerships. Epstein (1995) identifies six types of involvement for students, parents, and teachers in partnerships appropriate for classroom learning communities. These include parenting, communicating, volunteering, learning at home, decision making and collaborating with community (p. 706).

The MSU faculty and teacher candidates and the Flint Professional Development School teachers took Epstein's advice and created plans for making connections with the parents, neighborhood and community and their classroom learning communities. Once they started their efforts to make the connections they learned right away that sending a classroom newsletter home was merely one-way communication. The major thing that they did that was different than their past efforts, was to seek input from family, neighborhood and community members before they made decisions about things that would involve them. In other words, they sought their advice and ideas and actively included them in planning. In order to do this they had to establish a network not just among parents but also with members of the immediate school neighborhood and the larger community. Once the educators opened up their vision and decided to study/explore the neighborhood and community they learned a lot about the resources in the neighborhood and community as well as creating a network of contacts.

The initial relationships with neighborhood and community members were tentative and based on what teachers felt comfortable with and things that could be contributed to the students in a given learning community. Over time, the nature of the relationships changed so that family, neighborhood, and community members became regular members of the learning community classroom. As the system worked on district wide reforms the PDS buildings with classroom learning communities were open to the establishment of school advisory groups with parents and community members. Once the parents and community members saw that their input was heard and considered by the educators, and vice-versa, everyone became a legitimate part of the governance systems.

Through the school and neighborhood/community governance systems, the principals learned how parents and community members were thinking about things. It gave the principals a chance to explain why something the parents wanted was not possible or was illegal. The collaborative governance system also gave the teachers and/or principal a chance to explain and try out ideas for changes they wanted to initiate. The neighborhood, teachers, and community all supported the schools when decisions were made. The educators, parents and community members became authentic partners.

The classroom learning communities were also richer because of the new members. For example, parents, neighborhood and community members began to suggest things that they had to offer and the educators were willing to actively listen and no longer saw themselves as having all the answers or being threatened by outsiders. Because each classroom displayed a semester concept map illustrating what would be taught the parents and community members kept their eyes open for ideas as they went about their work in the community because they knew *what was going to be taught* in the future.

The parents and the community members also became important resources for the MSU university courses and field experiences. They actively participated in the design of neighborhood and community field experiences and they participated in course meetings providing a realistic point of view of what they expected of teachers in this urban district. For the teacher candidates, one of the greatest contributions was the parents and community members who provided opportunities for them to learn how to socialize effectively with adults in an urban community.

Planning and Instruction in a Learning Community

Current research supports the fact that effective planning makes a difference in student learning (e.g., Greenwood, 1991). Effective planning is the backbone of the Learning Community students' achievement and behavior. Greenwood, et.al., (1999), indicates that from their work and a review of studies concerned with academic engagement that it . . .

> was evident that plenty of room existed for increasing engagement and decreasing task management and inappropriate behavior levels. Even given the sophisticated instructional reform effort underway in these schools, students still spent on the order of 42% of their time looking at the teacher, raising their hand, waiting, etc., instead of reading, writing, talking about academics, or manipulating academic tasks. These data provided a provocative basis for reflection and of planning future changes in practices to increase engagement in academic responding (p. 16).

In the twenty-first century, instructional planning requires that teachers know subject matter and use district and state performance objectives (related to state and national testing), individual student data, their ability to differentiate instruction, and data about the social contexts of the community and individuals. Traditional planning strategies do not support the complex thinking, record keeping and achievement necessitated by the involvement of state and national government in outcomes and funding. Concept maps are a tool that helps teachers to gain an understanding of the conceptual linkages among the knowledge and skills they are responsible to teach (e.g., Novak, 1991). Concept maps also help learners understand the linkages among concepts they study (e.g., Novak, 1993). Concept maps are a tool that supports the teacher in linking knowledge and skills in ways that allow them to plan a single task or single instructional lesson that serves several performance outcomes. Concept maps also act as a tool that allows teachers to create conceptually linked long-range plans that illustrate the learning paths and destinations that teachers need to be able to see in order to create effective and efficient weekly and daily plans and evaluations.

For example, Ferry, Hedber, and Harper (1997), report that teacher candidates who used concept mapping as a tool in the construction of science related curriculum created curriculum content knowledge in the "form of more powerful integrated patterns" (p. 1). Additionally they report that "it was also found that the process of concept map construction enhanced candidate skills in planning instruction" (p. 1).

Novak (2004) helps us understand the idea of concept maps. He states:

> Concept maps are tools for organizing and representing knowledge. They include concepts, usually enclosed in circles or boxes of some type, and relationships between concepts or propositions, indicated by a connecting line between two concepts. Words on the line specify the relationship between the two concepts. We define concept as a perceived regularity in events or objects, or records of events or objects, designated by a label. The label for most concepts is a word, although sometimes we use symbols such as + or %. Propositions are statements about some object or event in the universe, either naturally occurring or constructed. Propositions contain two or more concepts connected with other words to form a meaningful statement. Sometimes these are called semantic units, or units of meaning. Figure 2 shows an example of a concept map that describes the structure of concept maps and illustrates the above characteristics. (1)

Novak (2004) created the diagram on the following page to help us understand the nature of concept maps. This helpful *concept map* illustrates what concept maps do.

Bartles (1995) states that "the real value in constructing a concept map is the visual representation of . . . connections . . ." (p. 548). She further states:

> With this tool, the connections are explicitly depicted and are visible to the person constructing the map as well as to anyone who observes the map. Without the concept map, connections are assumed; however, they may not actually exist or may be incorrect (p. 548).

Thus, a concept map is a hard-copy of the connections made by the person who constructed the map. The process of constructing concept maps also allows the person who is constructing it to evaluate the connections being made and alter them as he/she gains more information or clarity, thus the process allows for continued learning.

Currently there are a number of software programs on the market to assist professionals in the construction of concept maps. After reviewing a number of software programs and working with fifth year college teacher candidates who were using such software it is our opinion, that at this time, such software interferes with the development of the thinking required for curriculum and instructional plans. Typically, the software does not support the detailed work (thinking and illustrating connections) that is required of novice educators in the creation of instructional plans that meet State and District requirements as well as attending to the diverse needs of a group of K–12 learners. Novak, suggests that when creating concept maps, it takes three or more revisions to arrive at the necessary detail.

Later in Section II and in Chapter 11, we discuss the creation of concept maps as the first step in instructional planning. It is clear, based on the work of Novak and Gowin (1999) and others (e.g., Bartles, 1995) that concept maps are now being used to foster learning of K–12 students as well as evaluation tools. The difficult part of concept maps for many adults is that they simply have not had the experience of creating concept maps as a part of their elementary and secondary educational experiences.

Kim Leverette, an MSU-Team 3 graduate complained a lot during her first experience of having to create a concept map for a semester's instruction. She said that it was extremely hard work and took up her time. After completing her first map, she changed her view of the concept map from that of a "program required task" to "a tool for understanding what my students are suppose to learn and what I am responsible for teaching. The concept map allows me to focus on instruction that is meaningful."

Leverette mirrored her peers thinking. Almost all of them saw their first efforts at identifying what students would learn over a semester and making their subject matter connections visible as tough work. However, having worked through their initial resistance to push their thinking they used their concept maps as an instructional tool to illustrate academic linkages for their K-12 students. Recently Leverette

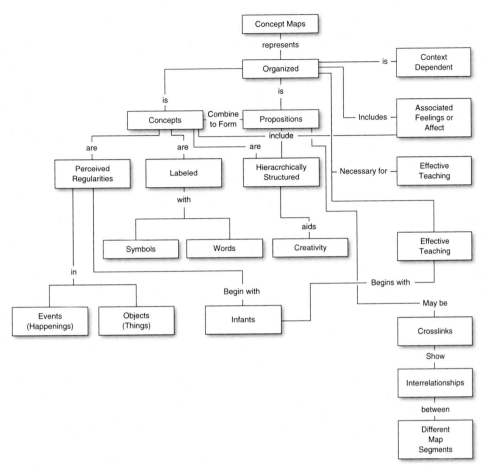

FIGURE 2   Novak's Concept Map Describing the Structure and Illustrating Characteristics of Concept Maps

told Putnam that "during a semester we modified and made changes as a learning community; therefore, everyone had a buy-in and could take personal responsibility for their learning. When a student would bring in something to share, we were usually able to add it to our concept map, helping the students to make additional linkages. Our concept maps became a driving force in the classroom." Leverette also mentioned that she thought that the planning required to produce a concept and its use in illustrating linkages for the students limited classroom behavior problems.

The use of *performance standards, rubrics, and portfolios* has increased over the last few years. Years ago, teachers identified behavioral objectives as a way to understand what it was they expected their students to learn from the lesson they taught. The new subject matter standards and performance outcomes are a result of the continued lack of student achievement. Many of the states, including Michigan and New Jersey, developed standards that are a central feature of the curriculum tested on state exams. The use of standards increased the work required by teachers in their planning. In some districts, the central office curriculum administrators and their committees have created new curriculum guides that illustrate at what grade levels performance of the specific standards is expected. The format and content of curriculum guides changed and the focus is now on the performance standards that all students are expected to achieve. Some Districts have included ideas for instructional strategies to aid teachers in standard based instruction. District curriculum guidelines no longer reflect the favorite textbooks, or subject matter promoted by favorite publishing companies.

The *standards* provide teachers with information about what remedial knowledge and skills a student who is struggling may need, as well as the direction for advanced learning for students who need academic challenges. The work on standards provided teachers with subject matter conceptual frameworks forcing textbooks to become resources rather than functioning as the curriculum.

The use of standards has increased the use of *rubrics* because it became necessary to be clear about what it was that was being assessed. It is critical that teachers communicate to their students what knowledge and skills would be evaluated. A part of the use of rubrics and standards is the expectations that students can do accurate self-assessments, carry out a performance/task analysis, and document their progress. These are not responsibilities that students learned in traditional classrooms.

We located at *www.mcrel.org/compendium/kSkillsIntro.asp.*, a brief history and a rationale as to why standards are important to teachers and learners.

The Case for Standards

Why are standards important? There appear to be three principle reasons advanced for the development of standards: standards serve both to clarify and to raise expectations, and standards provide a common set of expectations.

Former Assistant Secretary of Education Diane Ravitch is commonly recognized as one of the chief architects of the modern standards movement. In her book *National Standards in American Education: A Citizen's Guide* (1995), Ravitch provides a common-sense rationale for standards:

> Americans . . . expect strict standards to govern construction of buildings, bridges, highways, and tunnels; shoddy work would put lives at risk. They expect stringent standards to protect their drinking water, the food they eat, and the air they breathe. . . . Standards are created because they improve the activity of life. (pp. 8–9)

Ravitch (1995) asserts that just as standards improve the daily lives of Americans, so, too, will they improve the effectiveness of American education: "Standards can improve achievement by clearly defining what is to be taught and what kind of performance is expected" (p. 25).

Such a view is apparently shared by many. The polling firm Public Agenda conducted a number of surveys on the issue of standards over the last several years. They found that most Americans strongly support higher standards that are clear and specific (Farkas, Friedman, Boese & Shaw, 1994), believing that higher expectations produce better performance. Teachers, as well, support proposals to raise standards, which they expect to improve their students' academic performance (Johnson & Farkas, 1996). A recent finding indicates that students also see value in standards, saying that higher standards will make them work harder, and they expect to learn more as a result (Friedman & Duffet, 1997).

To learn more about the national standards and their history go to:

www.mcrel.org/compendium/kSkillsIntro.asp.

Finally, the use of standards is helpful to teachers as they plan their instruction, student activities, and performance evaluations. Some states have developed computer software to assist teachers in keeping records of the progress on specific standards for each of their students. This technology further supports the need for teachers to work toward individual plans of study for each learner due to differentiated learning styles and abilities. Individual learning plans and differentiated instruction (DI) provide all students with an "equal opportunity to learn."

Portfolios, while used for a number of years, came into full use as educators became clearer about the performance outcomes they expected from their students. Portfolios serve several purposes; among the most important are self-directed learning, learner reflections, and student goal setting.

The use of portfolios has expanded the use of *student directed* conferences. Based on the increase of the students' involvement in their learning, students are able to explain their progress, stumbles, and goals to teachers and parents.

Organization and Management in a Learning Community

The work between Flint Professional Development Schools and Michigan State University that focused on creating classroom learning communities resulted in changes in the roles of all participants including teachers, students, principals, parents, community members, teacher candidates and faculty. The new learning community culture required norms, rules and roles that were different from the ones found in the previously established traditional classroom cultures.

Thus, the first attempts at organizing and managing learning community classrooms, initially resulted in stress for all participants. The stress on the students was a result of the fact that the students were used to external controls and not used to being responsible for their own behavior. The stress experienced by the teachers was due to their being used to *controlling the behavior of their students* by the use of rules and consequences or an authoritarian stance. The university folks experienced stress because they were used to being guests in schools rather than participating members with on-going accountability and responsibilities to K–12 learners, the teachers, and principals, as well as, the university candidates. The principals' increase in stress came from the expectations for the development of a new institutional culture, which was supported by the central office but initially not by their immediate supervisors.

The teachers and their candidates worked to make clear the roles, rules, and norms that would allow for more responsibility and accountability on the part of the students. They identified the routines and procedures that would keep the classrooms running smoothly with the least amount of teacher time. As they created new ways to operate, they found that they could increase their instructional time and the time they had to work one-on-one with students. They came to realize that the rules, roles, norms, routines and procedures they worked out with the students made a difference in the efficient use of their time and increased the on-task time for students.

Discipline and Problem Student Behavior

Discipline and problem student behavior are major problems for teacher candidates, new teachers, and experienced teachers moving to new grade levels. According to Gordon (1999) in "Turning Frustration to Fulfillment: New Teachers Need More Help with Discipline" a new survey of 118 school districts across the country shows that nearly 10 percent of public schoolteachers quit during the first year and 20 percent leave within three years. The biggest barriers to new teachers' success, according to this survey—conducted by Recruiting New Teachers in Belmont, MA—are poor classroom-management skills (82 percent) and disruptive students (57 percent).

Wolfgang (1999) says that "*discipline* is the required action by a teacher or school official, toward a student (or group of students), after the student's behavior disrupts the ongoing educational activity or breaks a pre-established rule or law created by the teacher, the school administration, or the general society" (p. xi). He describes four categories from which the teacher's or administrator's discipline actions come:

- Relationship-Listening (a therapeutic process)
- Confronting-Contracting (an educational and counseling process)
- Rules and Consequences (a controlling process)
- Coercive-Legalistic (a restraining, exclusionary, and legal process) (p. xi).

Discipline problems that teachers confront come primarily from three places. The first is from the classroom environment or culture and are created by the teacher. Lack of organization and management of routines, procedures, or instruction contribute to these problems. The second is from a non-assertive personal stance and includes an immature perspective in that the student teacher wants to be liked by students rather than viewed as a responsible instructional leader. Thus, the teacher is the source of problems emanating from his/her own inappropriate behavior. The third is the student that brings his/her problem behavior to the classroom.

Before teacher candidates or novice teachers label classroom problems as the student's problem, they need to be sure that they are *assertive,* their *instruction is appropriate and interesting for each individual learner,* and that they have *systematically established the norms, rules, and roles for the classroom culture* they are creating. Effectively handling these allows the teacher to prevent most discipline problems.

Many teacher candidates have the task of creating their own two-way respect with the students as well as the potential problem of having to teach in a classroom culture established by the cooperating teacher. No matter what the nature of the cooperating teacher's classroom culture, the teacher candidate will have to establish themselves as an *authoritative and responsible* leader who respects the students and teaches students how to be respectful to others including themselves.

Cooperating teachers can effectively support the teacher candidate, in his/her approach to establishing the respect of the students, by how the cooperating teacher introduces the person into the classroom culture. Teacher candidates, who have a fall or year long teaching experience, start their student teaching experience by participating full time with the teachers starting with the preschool professional development and planning days. These teacher candidates have the opportunity to help establish the classroom culture right from the beginning of the year. Teacher candidates who begin their student teaching experience after the beginning of the school year need to plan clearly with the cooperating teacher about a strategy he/she can use to gain entry into the established classroom culture. Cooperating teachers are helpful when they introduce their teacher candidates as members of the teaching team and do not undermine them as they establish their sense-of-self as "being in charge as a teacher." Notes to parents co-signed by both teachers explaining the partnership is also helpful.

It is essential that teacher candidates and novice teachers become members of the instructional team and do not establish themselves as merely guests in someone else's classroom. For cooperating teachers who have established a learning community the norms will provide a means for the teacher and students to support the student teacher's entry into the community.

For teachers who have other types of classroom or community cultures, it will be important for the student teacher, cooperating teacher and the university supervisor to write a plan for gaining entry and earning respect. The plan should include specific actions the cooperating teacher will and will not take so that unintentionally she/he does not undermine the student teacher (new member).

After a teacher candidates gains entry and becomes part of the classroom culture it is important for them to have the opportunity to be on their own for increasing periods of time so that they develop their sense of self-in-charge. These times allow the student teacher the opportunity to refine his/her actions as an effective responsible, authoritative model. Since the times increase over several weeks, as the student teacher develops his/her confidence, the K–12 learners do not want to waste their time in out-of-control classrooms. At Gundry, Pierson, and Brownell Elementary Schools, these times were used for our Mentor Teacher/University Professional Learning Community Meetings.

Wolfgang (1996) analyzed 10 discipline models (e.g., The Judicious Discipline Model; The Positive Discipline Model; Assertive Discipline Model) and illustrated the range of teacher power that is involved in each. Wolfgang (1999) then analyzed the models and organized them into *"Three Faces of Discipline"* and based on the content he placed them on a *"Teacher Behavior Continuum" (p. xi).*

Teacher candidates and novice teachers may find some schools where the teachers have agreed to use a single discipline model. In other schools, individual teachers may have adopted a single discipline model. However, it is our intent that teacher candidates and teachers learn to function across the continuum so that they are able to establish a learning community culture (relationship-listening) and still effectively discipline a student who assaults a teacher or another student. Selecting those discipline actions that are appropriate for a specific student and his/her problem behavior and that successfully works for the candidate or teacher is a process for building **one's individual** discipline model.

No matter what mode of discipline a teacher candidate, novice or experienced teacher uses they must be able to handle problem behavior such as bullying, assaults, and sexual harassment. These behaviors require discipline actions on the part of the teacher. We provide vignettes with examples of candidates modeling these behaviors for practice in Chapter 10.

In a learning community culture, the effective teacher has a relationship-listening face as the primary mode of thinking about discipline. Due to the learning community teacher's effective establishment of rules, roles, and norms, establishment of the learning community culture and effective teaching, it is possible to act from a relationship-listening position most of the time. However, the effective learning community teacher is able to work across the continuum as the needs of individual students warrant. The learning community teacher's goal is to integrate every student into the culture as an effective learning community member so he/she is able to respond with discipline plans that *change* inappropriate student behavior.

Deiro, (1996) in *Teaching with Heart: Making Healthy Connections with Students,* suggests six strategies for creating healthy connections, one of which is creating a sense of community among students. Five strategies support the effective performances of learning community teachers. They include creating one-on-one time (Stages One and Four), using appropriate self-disclosure (Stages One, Three, and Four), high expectations of students while conveying a belief in their capabilities (Stages One, Two, and Four), networking with family and friends (Stages One and Four), and providing rituals and traditions (Stages Two and Five Learning Community development).

The model that we use for assessing, practicing, and evaluating progress in disciplining students effectively is as follows:

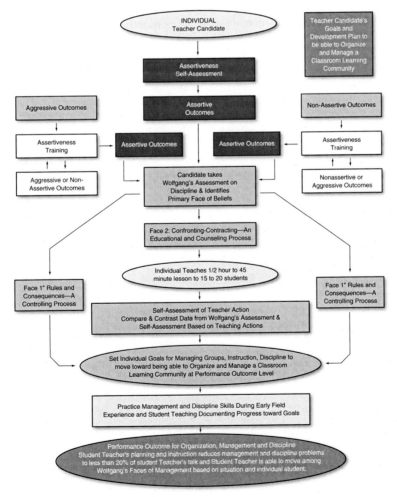

One of the types of problem student behavior that increased over the last few years is ***bullying*** in schools. From the 2001 American Association of University Women (AAUW) research report titled "Hostile Hallways: Bullying, Teasing, and Sexual Harassment in Schools," we learn that students are experiencing more problems in schools than they reported in 1993. Eckman (2001) reports that "they've come in a tidal wave—one news story after another announcing and denouncing the prevalence of bullying in U.S. Schools" (p. 1). Olweus (2003) states that "bullying and victimization are on the increase" (p. 12).

Pepler and Craig (Nov. 2004, *www.bullying.com*) of the Lamarsh Centre for Research on Violence and Conflict Resolution at York University report a list of nine research facts about bullying.

- Bullying will stop in less than 10 seconds nearly 60% of the time when peers intervene. (Pepler et al., 1997)

- Bulling occurs in school playgrounds every 7 minutes and once every 25 minutes in class. (Pepler et al., 1997)

- 85% of bullying episodes occur in the context of a peer group. (Atlas and Pepler, 1997, Craig and Pepler, 1997)

- Most bullying takes place in school and is reinforced by an audience. (Pepler et al., 1997)

- In 54 percent of cases, they reinforced the bully by watching, by not joining in. (Pepler et al., 1997)

- In only 25 percent of cases did peers support the victim. (Pepler et al., 1997)

- 83% of students indicate that watching bullying makes them feel uncomfortable. (Pepler et al., 1997)

- In playground observations, peers intervened in significantly more episodes than adults did (11% of episodes versus 4%). (Craig and Pepler, 1997)

It is suggested that the increase in bullying is due to the lack of response to bullying by adults in the schools. It is true that parents and the community are also blamed. Olweus (2003) found that "the attitudes and routines of relevant adults can exacerbate or curb students' aggression toward classmates" p. 12. Our focus is on the *adults* working in schools that have the responsibility and accountability to provide a safe environment for all students. Exactly, what is it that adults need to eliminate from school? Olweus (2003) states that a bully is

> The person who intentionally inflicts, or attempts to inflict, injury or discomfort on someone else in engaging in negative actions, a term similar to the definition of aggressive behavior in the social sciences. People carry out negative actions through physical contact, with words, or in more indirect ways, such as making mean faces or gestures, spreading rumors, or intentionally excluding someone from a group. p. 12

Today we also know that bullying takes place on the internet. Olweus (2003) further explains that bullying

> also entails an imbalance in strength (or asymmetrical power relationships), meaning that students exposed to negative actions have difficulty defending themselves. Much bullying is proactive aggression, that is, aggressive behavior that usually occurs without apparent provocation or threat on the part of the victim. p. 12

The stereotype of the bully is a male who is larger than his victim is. However, we now know that females are also bullies. Simmons (2002) dispelled the misconceptions that females are not bullies. She found that even though females are taught to be nice, "there is a hidden culture of girls' aggression in which bullying is epidemic, distinctive, and destructive" p. 3. While not openly aggressive in the same way that males are, females show their aggression non-physically, indirectly, and covertly. Unlike males, who frequently bully strangers or others who are just acquaintances, females bully those in their clique of friends. These types of covert bullying behaviors by females make it even harder for the adults in the school to identify and eliminate them.

Because student behavior may not always be what the adults in schools expect, it may be difficult for them to intervene appropriately. Canada (1995) and Simmons (2002) found that many girls of color were taught to defend themselves and not allow themselves to be victimized. Girls of color also were more likely to voice their anger and deal with their conflicts openly than were white females. Simmons (2002) reported that some African American females said that they were taught by their parents to defend themselves, even physically if necessary, rather than be taken advantage of. However, not all white girls avoid confrontation and not all girls of color confront everything. She found that some African American girls, in her study, that were raised by middle-class parents were socialized to speak indirectly and non-assertively in an attempt to appear nice and be accepted by whites. She also reported that, "girls from all walks of life have different experiences. Not all white middle-class girls avoid conflict, and not all other girls embrace it . . . Indeed, dominant middle-class notions of femininity are foreign to the experiences of many white girls" pp. 178–79.

Thompson, (2004) warns that the role of the media and teachers' and administrators' expectations must be considered as contributions to the problem behavior. She states, "when African American boys are presumed to be violent and aggressive merely because they are African American males, a self-fulfilling prophecy may occur. For example, Coloroso (2003), explains how expectations end up affecting how students behave. She uses a description of the actor, character actor, and type casting. She states:

Actor: Someone who behaves in a way intended to deceive or impress others.
Character Actor: Someone who specializes in playing the roles of unusual or distinctive characters.
Type Casting: To give an actor a series of parts of the same type, to the extent that the performer becomes associated with that kind of role and is overlooked for others.

When adults treat individuals by type casting they contribute to their behavior. The adults have created an environment where "the bully, the bullied, and the bystander are three characters in a tragic play performed daily in our homes, schools, playgrounds, and streets (2003, p. 3).

Khemsara (2003–04) brings to the discussion the importance of intervention. He states the "lack of intervention implies that bullying is acceptable and can be performed without fear of consequences." (p.1)

THE PROFESSIONAL LEARNING COMMUNITIES

One of the major changes related to learning communities is the development of Professional Learning Communities. Our work with Professional Learning Communities emerged from the MSU and Lansing and Flint Community Schools Professional Development Schools partnership and the Rowan PDSs.

In the 1990's research-universities began to work on authentic partnerships with schools and school districts. One of the purposes of this work was to create Professional Development Schools. The Holmes Group was created at a national level to bring these universities and their school partnership members together to exchange ideas and report progress as well as provide support and challenge.

One of the results of the Professional Development School movement was the creation of Professional Learning Communities among teachers and university faculty, among administrators and university faculty, then among teachers, administrators and university faculty, and finally among all stake holders including parents and community members within a school.

Holmes Middle School and Northwestern High School (also located in Flint, Michigan) created Professional Learning Communities as a part of their Professional Development School partnerships with the College of Education at Michigan State University. Both middle school and high school teachers reported that their learning community classes had a significant decrease in discipline problems (evident in school records) and an increase in the quality of individual and cooperative learning academic work (evident in course grades and test scores) (Bessie Straham, 1996, Art Wright, 1997).

However, the move to Professional Learning Communities provided a forum for solving problems that individual teachers had not resolved. For example, one of the urban eighth grade learning community teams reported that all but one of the students passed all of their classes (Pam Nagy, 2001). The teachers, MSU Teacher Candidates, parents, and students invested a lot of time and effort into tutoring and follow-up strategies, as well as new instruction strategies.

The teaching team had established a professional learning community, where the study of their students learning was the focus of their professional work. The question they asked as part of their research was "What do we need to do so that all of our students are successful in all of their classes?" One of the things they did during their prep-periods was to focus on individual students. For example, when one student was passing three out of eight classes, the teachers would identify instructional strategies and types of individual work that seemed to support this student's success in three classes. The other teacher adapted the ideas to their content areas and soon began to see that some students responded positively to these changes. Other students needed more effort on the part of the teachers before they turned around. Actions to improve student learning taken by these teachers in their Professional Learning Community is supported by work reported by Haberman (2004). Pam Nagy (2000) reported that after one semester her team learned that they needed to start their efforts at the very beginning of the year in order to increase the number of successful students from the beginning and thus have fewer individuals with whom they had to struggle to succeed as the year went along. For this Professional Learning Community a strategy that started as a remedial effort turned into a "starting the year correctly or getting students on the right track in September" plan.

Bessie Straham (Putnam and Straham, 1996) reported that there was an increase in attendance at Northwestern High School after the Professional Learning Communities were established. For the first time the percentage of attendance in the ninth grade Professional Learning Community team was higher than the attendance for eleventh and twelfth grade students. The Professional Learning Community ninth grade team also began to plan marking-period integrated curriculum. The teachers consciously helped the students see relationships among their courses. For example, the teachers used one assignment (when possible) in two or more classes and each instructor graded for specific course content. The ninth grade teachers' Professional Learning Community attributed the attendance increase to (1) improved planning and instruction, (2) increased constructive feedback to students, (3) better knowledge of their students, and (4) their new relationships with the eighth grade teachers and students at Holmes Middle School.

The Flint Community School District in 1998, as a part of a district reform effort, expanded the notion of learning communities and offered school buildings the opportunity to reorganize and create cross grade level learning community cultures. The district developed a long-range plan to give buildings a chance to develop their implementation plans and have the support of newly hired district consultants. The PDSs were among the first set of schools who chose to begin this effort.

It was difficult work for everyone and especially for teachers who had worked in isolation for their entire careers. These teachers found it difficult because now they needed to form Professional Learning Communities that kept the foci on the needs of all the team's learners, on needed changes in teaching, as well as on the development of new school governance systems. The teams created Professional Learning Communities where:

a. planning was a team effort (using concept maps and discussion),

b. content was influenced by state of Michigan Core Curriculum Objectives and the District's Performance Outcomes,

c. teaching was public (teachers no longer were isolated, agreed to carry out their part of the plans), and

d. parents and community members were part of the team's and the school's governance system.

Professional Learning Community teams were formed, by the elementary school teachers, in cross-grade level groupings (three grades). The teachers were also responsible for creating cross-grade-level classroom learning communities, providing students the opportunity to work with the same adults and peers over three years. The formation of the cross-grade level teams caused teachers to relocate in their buildings so that the teachers forming a learning community were located physically near each other. One school used their rejuvenation funds to change the entire make-up of their school in order to support the implementation of all of the learning communities in that school.

For some teachers physically moving to a new room was traumatic and difficult as the traditional school culture gave ownership of a given space to a teacher. The professional learning community culture asked teachers and administrators to make decisions about use of space (schools and schooling) based on students' needs and learning (learner and learning) and the team's needs for planning and effective instruction (teachers and teaching). Teachers who viewed themselves as stars wondered if they would lose their status when they became members of a team and others actually saw them in action. Still other teachers were not anxious to work with the *stars* as they thought that the star teachers were self-centered and would not make good team members.

Much has been written about Professional Learning Communities and several major reviews of literature have been completed in the last decade. Some of the most interesting and helpful includes the following: Hord, S. M., 1997; DuFour, R., Eaker, R., 1998; Shaughnessy, J., 1998; Wald, P. J., Ed., Castleberry, Michael S., Ed. 1999; DuFour, R., 2000; Moore, S., Shaw, P., 2000; Huffman, J. G., Hipp, K. A., 2000; Cowan, D., Capers, M., 2000; Huffman, J. G., Hipp, K. A., 2000; Huffman, J. G., 2001; DuFour, R., 2003; Mason, S. A., 2003; Schmoker, M., 2003; and Hipp, K. K., Huffman, J. B., 2003.

What we learned from our experience and the current literature is that the focus of a Professional Learning Community, like the classroom learning community, is on *learning*. For example, the Mentor Teachers' Professional Learning Community focused on the learning and performances of teacher candidates and on their new role. They studied the substance of the teacher preparation program, performance outcomes, how to observe, how to give positive and negative constructive feedback, how to and when to challenge and support the teacher candidates. They studied mentoring and coaching skills, and they learned how to interpret student data and use it in long range planning as well as in weekly plans. They learned how and carried out action research projects on their own. Through their practice they learned to think systematically, to be critical analyzers of studies, and how to be effective reporters so that they could model and provide instruction when needed, and evaluate action research carried out by the teacher candidates.

The Professional Learning Communities that were formed of cross-grade level teachers focused on the learning of "each and every" student in the learning community. For example, they studied student data and they learned how to interpret and use the data to benefit the students' achievement. They created new assessment tasks and new recording systems. Based on the needs of their students, they studied effective teaching strategies, carried out action research on new instructional programs and learned to eliminate those things that were wasting the learners' time.

PDS teachers reported that the cultures in their buildings changed so that there was support for each other's work, and an openness to each other's contributions and to the study of different ideas. Specific examples of school culture changes are provided on the following page.

University faculty reported that they observed changes in the school cultures in the PDS buildings and the experiences of the Mentor Teachers and Teacher Candidates. Eight of the changes that they observed are provided in the chart on the following page.

Before PDS	After PDS
If I tell others what I am doing they will think I am bragging.	When I share something I am doing my colleagues ask me questions to help my thinking.
If others see what I am doing they will criticize my efforts.	People know what I am doing and ask about my progress, they support my efforts and even make suggestions.
If I behave differently from other teachers, they say "I am making it harder for them."	We see that we all have strengths, something to contribute to the improvement of learner outcomes.
If the principal doesn't actively support what I am doing, I will be punished.	Teachers who have different roles, can enact these roles without fear of punishment by the administrators or teachers.
If I ask a teacher what they are doing, they do not share as they want to get "credit for it."	If I ask others what they are doing they are willing to share because we want to do the best for our learners.
Space belongs to the principal and "powerful" teacher, to be given as a reward to teachers who carry out "principal's vision."	All power and status is no longer located in a single person (the principal), it is shared among all the staff.
Cooperating teachers were to blame if a student teacher did not do well. (didn't give feedback, not good model)	Teacher candidate progress is a team effort. Mentors see their role as instructional, as making judgments about teacher candidate performances.
I am alone, isolated, doing my work.	We have a language that has shared concepts (teaching for conceptual and relationship understanding) we know what to look for, we know what to do.
I am the model for my Teacher Candidate.	Teachers see they all have different expertise. Send Teacher Candidate to others to see excellent models of asking higher order questions; implementing lab classes, long range planning.

Observed Changes in Practices

1. Teacher Candidates visit classrooms where teachers have been identified as "having expertise" in a given area (e.g., process writing, connected mathematics). Teacher candidates move between schools, too.

2. Teachers and Teacher Candidates invite other Teachers, Teacher Candidates and K–12 learners to learn how to do something in their classrooms.

3. Teacher Candidates seek out Teachers (other than their mentor) and Teacher Candidates to clarify their ideas, and get new ideas.

4. The focus for Teacher Candidates who have moved through the "survival" stage of their development is to access other Teacher Candidates and teachers to increase their expertise.

5. The long range semester plans that Teacher Candidates do provides an organization that permits Teacher Candidates to leave their teaching responsibilities and learn from the context and the Mentor Teachers are able to "allow" the change as they are comfortable with the Teacher Candidates' intent

for the K–12 learners and can carry on.

6. Teacher Candidates earn their place in the Professional Development School from their actions in the classroom, with members of the "professional learning community" and by not putting the Mentor in more of a risk situation than she/he can handle.

7. Mentor Teachers see themselves as contributing to the Teacher Candidates' learning. But, they no longer accept total blame when a Teacher Candidate is struggling to meet performance standards. Thus, Teacher Candidates have a chance to work out their problems.

8. Liaison Teacher can talk directly with Teacher Candidates, university faculty and Mentor Teachers creating a "Professional Learning Community" with the Teacher Candidate as its central focus.

The cross-grade level Professional Learning Communities also resulted in the teachers providing professional development sessions for the school district. They developed and offered a three day workshop focused on establishing classroom learning communities. After the workshop, the teachers were invited to offer independent study workshops with a focus on helping individual teachers actually create classroom learning communities. The PDSs teachers created a semester long staff development program for teachers from non-PDSs building. They included 7 steps in their plan: (1) they invited the independent study teachers to observe in their classrooms, (2) they shared readings that had helped them establish their learning community cultures and scheduled discussion about the other teachers' reactions, (3) they went and visited the non-PDS teachers classrooms, (4) together they wrote plans for establishing the learning community culture in the other teacher's classroom, (5) they helped the other teacher get started by observing and giving feedback, (6) they met with the teacher several times to provide support and answer questions, and (7) they used a learning community assessment form to provide the teacher feedback at the end of the year.

Teachers from the PDSs were among the first district teachers to take on responsibility for proposing and offering staff development workshops for district teachers.

Finally, as the Mentor Teachers and Teacher Liaison roles developed the university professors found that they used their time in the school doing things that they had not had time to do before. For example professors:

- worked with teachers on establishing different curriculum and instruction as a regular part of their classroom practice;
- worked with teachers and teacher candidates in the establishment of classroom learning communities;
- worked on integration of subject matter areas for instruction;
- observed and interacted to determine how the teacher candidate was doing in relationship to stated knowledge, propensities and performances;
- provided instruction to K–12 classes; and
- worked with Mentors to help them identify the levels of teacher candidate performances.

Learning to Teach

Teaching is an intellectual task, which means that much of what teachers do is hidden from those who come into classrooms and observe. Thus, teacher candidates must ask cooperating teachers questions in order to make the "invisible visible" and to get at the thinking that goes with the intentions and actions of the teacher. Equally important is the investment of candidates in communicating their thinking to their instructors, cooperating teachers and university supervisors. They have a responsibility to ask questions about candidates' performances and the underlying theories that candidates are implementing. They are also responsible for challenging candidates' ideas and performances so that candidates continue to develop and are able to meet the program's performance standards.

Journal writing is one way to keep others informed about candidates' thinking as well as helping each candidate identify the changes or development over time of his/her ideas, beliefs, dispositions, knowledge and skills. Likewise the journal is a way that candidates have to keep an account of their thinking and through reviews and reflections (meta-cognitions) complete self-assessments of their progress toward the program's standards. When the self-assessments are accurate, they provide the candidates with the data necessary for identifying their next set of professional goals and expected outcomes.

Stages of Teacher Development

Understanding the stages of development of the children one teaches is extremely important to understanding the complexity of the "whole learner." Equally important are the stages of development through which candidates and teachers progress. Knowing about the stages of teacher development is important to candidates who are responsible and accountable for their learning. Understanding how one can change over time helps him/her to understand where she/he is in their development at any given time. This knowledge also helps the individual recognize their progress when changes do occur.

Understanding one's thinking, how one learns, the perspectives one holds are ways that influence his/her own learning. One way to keep track of the changes experienced while in college is through journal writing and systematic record keeping. Periodic assessment of one's journal entries and course products allows the candidate to identify changes that are occurring, the opportunity to watch his/her own development, and the opportunity to influence the direction of his/her development. Below we have included summaries of two different development theories to give you a start in thinking about your own development.

Development Stage	Summary of Fuller Bown (1975) Pre-service Teacher Development
1. Pre-teaching	Pre-service teachers continue to identify with the pupils in observed classes rather than themselves as a teacher.
2. Early concerns about teaching.	Early concerns about survival, where they lost their idealistic fantasy of the teaching role and become concerned about their own survival as teachers.
3. Concerns about limitation of teaching context.	Pre-service teachers concerned about their own teaching performance, but not yet about whether the pupils were learning.
4. Concerns about student learning.	Concerns about pupil learning and began to see pupils as individuals with individual needs.

Candidates with whom we worked found that generally they went through the stages identified above. However, it is our experience that the length of time that one spends in any stage of development varies greatly. Putnam observed that in her experience at least ninety percent of the candidates reached stage four prior to the beginning of the second semester internship. She credits the candidates' concerns about student learning as an outcome of their program's stated performance outcomes and the nature of assignments that supported the focus on learners and learning.

Summary of Teacher Development Stages
by Katz (1992) in Stroot, S., etc., 1998

Stage of Development	Major Concerns and Focus	Things Person Says	Way things look in classroom
Survival	*Coping* on daily basis; question professional competence and desire to teach; *Focused* on themselves and own needs, have little understanding of their students & their needs. Don't acknowledge the truth of how things are. Blame everyone and anything but themselves. They blame the students, the principal, lack of materials, anything but themselves when they are not able to accomplish the task of teaching. Do not believe they have any control of their teaching context. React to situations rather than anticipate and prevent potential problems by using preventive management strategies.	Can I make it until the end of the week? Can I really do this work day after day? Can I get through the day in one piece? Things are going pretty well (even when they are not). I know what I am supposed to do, but it just doesn't work without the materials to do it the way it needs to be done. The principal will not support me when I need help with discipline. You might be able to do that in another classroom, but you don't know the baggage my kids bring to class. It won't work here! I can't follow the curriculum because I don't have enough materials to do it the way it needs to be done. Will agree with student center style, but will say it won't work with these kids.	Rules not clear. Routines not congruent with procedures for managing student behavior. Focused on act of teaching without considering whether or not the students are learning. Common to observe them as self-centered when teaching. They go through a planned lesson as though it was a script that could not be changed. Teacher-directed instruction with little or no input or interaction from students. Teacher is unsure of ability to maintain control of class so prefers to keep students in passive role. No recognition of students' reactions to lessons, no checks to see what extent students understand materials presented, no modifications of materials or lesson to address differing needs of individuals. If tries something new, makes quick decision about if new strategy works. If immediate success may try it again. If not, likely to revert to teacher-directed where teacher maintains power of control, even if not previously working.

Stage of Development	Major Concerns and Focus	Things Person Says	Way things look in classroom
Consolidation	Focus begun to shift to instruction and needs of individual students. Beginning to focus on individual children with unique problems and specialized needs. Interested in workshop and community as places to gather additional information.	Ask questions like How can I help a child who does not seem to be learning? How can I deal with a child with a specific discipline problem? How can I change my lessons to meet needs of low ability/high achieving?	Rules and routines are implemented. Majority of students well-managed, instruction activities meeting needs of the average student in class.
Renewal	Focus on professional development through local, state, or national organizations. Want to attend conferences, become members of their professional associations. Interested in enrolling in graduate work or examining own teaching through videotaping or action research projects. Want to visit other classrooms and have visitors in order to share and get new ideas.	What are some new materials, techniques, approaches, ideas, etc., that I can try? What is the teacher in my specialization doing in the next building? Have new ideas emerged since the last class I took?	Competent in teaching all children. Looking for new ideas because old ones are boring to them.
Maturity	Focus on insights, perspectives, and beliefs of teaching and children. Make excellent mentors because they have experienced all of the developmental stages and understand the needs of those moving through the stages.	Ask deeper and more abstract questions about their philosophy of teaching and the impact they may be making in and out of school. What are my philosophical perspectives? How will schools change society? What is my role to assist in change?	Will observe similar scenes as those of the Renewal teacher. It is through discussion with the teacher that the subtle differences emerge.

Candidates will observe that cooperating teachers can be found at all levels of teacher development. Some teachers may realize that they have functioned in a particular stage for a relatively long period of time. It appears that the culture of the school may support particular teacher thinking and actions thus making those teachers who are in different stages of development uncomfortable. This is one of the ways that members of a particular school culture "socialize" new teachers and teacher candidates to "fit in." Candidates who hear "We do it like this, at Holmes" or "That won't work with these kids" are hearing the type of talk whose purpose is to get the new members to "fit in."

Teachers from the Flint, Michigan, Professional Development Schools, reported that their involvement in Professional Learning Communities contributed to their getting "unstuck" and reaching the level of teacher maturity. Once engaged at this level of teacher development, they found that they became uncomfortable with their prior practice and thinking. Once at this level, they reported that their challenge was to continue this level of engagement and not withdraw when they were moved from a Professional Development School. Reassigned teachers recognized that the Professional Learning Communities, in which they had been engaged as part of their PDS work, had provided the support for the type of intellectual thinking and practice found in the maturity stage of teacher development.

As a candidate, you may wish to invest in better understanding your own stages of development. To expand on the ideas briefly presented above consider exploring Kohlberg's Moral Stages.

REFERENCES AND RECOMMENDED READINGS

Allen, R. (2003). *The Democratic Aims of Service of Learning.* Educational Leadership, Creating Caring Schools. March Vol. 60, No. 6, pp. 60–63.

Bartles, B. H. (1995). *Promoting Mathematics Connections with Concept Mapping.* Mathematics Teaching in the Middle School. Vol. 1, No. 7. November–December pp. 542–549.

Battistich, V., Solomon, D., Kim, D., Watson, M., and Schaps, E. (1995). *Schools as Communities, Poverty Levels of Student Populations, and Student Attitudes, Motives, and Performance: A Multilevel Analysis.* American Educational Research Journal, 32, pp. 627–658.

Baumeister, R., and Leary, M. (1995). The Need to belong: Desire for Interpersonal Attachments as a Fundamental Human Motivation. *Psychological Bulletin, 117,* pp. 497–529.

Beane, A. L. (1999). The bully free classroom: over 100 tips and strategies for teachers K–8, Free Spirit Publishing Inc., Minn., MN.

Belsey, B., Cyberbullying, Defined, www.Cyberbulling.com

Canada, G. (1995). Fist stick knife gun: A personal history of violence in America, Boston: Beacon Press.

Coloroso, B. (2004). The bully, the bullied, and the bystander: From preschool to high school—how Parents and teachers can help break the cycle of violence, Harper Resource of HarperCollins, NY, NY.

Cooper, D., and Snell, J. L. (2003). Bullying—Not Just a Kid Thing, *Educational Leadership, Creating Caring Schools, March* Vol. 60, No. 6., pp. 22–25.

Deiro, J. A. (2003). Do Your Students Know You Care? *Educational Leadership, Creating Caring Schools,* March Vol. 60, No. 6., pp. 60–63.

Eckman, A. (2001). Beyond Bullying: Knowing When to Step In—and When Not to, *Educational Update,* ASCD, Vol. 43, No. 6, September.

Epstein J. L., Salinas, K. C. (2004). Schools as Learning Communities, Partnering with Families and Communities, *Educational Leadership,* Vol. 61, Number 8, pp. 12–18.

Epstein, Joyce L. (1995). School/Family/Community Partnerships, Caring for the Children we share. *Phi Delta Kappan,* May pages 701–711.

Franklin, J. (2004). A Safer Place for Learning, *Education Update,* ASCD March, Vol. 46, No. 2.

Garbarino, J., and deLara, E. Words Can Hurt Forever, *Educational Leadership, Creating Caring Schools,* March Vol. 60, No. 6., pp. 18–21.

Haberman, M. (2004). Can star teachers create learning communities? *Educational Leadership,* Vol. 61, No. 8, May 2004, p. 52–56.

Haberman, Martin. (1999). Victory at Buffalo Creek: What makes a school serving Hispanic Children in poverty successful? Instructional Leader, 17 (2).

Lipson, J. (Ed.) (2001). Hostile hallways: bullying, teasing, and sexual harassment in school, AAUW Education Foundation, Washington D.C., Researched by Harris Interactive, NY, NY.

Marzano, R. J., and Marzano J. S. (2003). The Key to Classroom Management, *Educational Leadership, Building Classroom Relationships,* September, Vol. 61, No. 1, pp. 6–13.

McClure, J. S. (2003). Civilized assertiveness for women: Communication with backbone not bite. Albion Street Press, Denver, CO.

Olweus, D. (2003). A Profile of Bullying at School, *Educational Leadership, Creating Caring Schools,* March Vol. 60, No. 6., pp. 12–17.

Rowan, G. (2004). Teachers Matter: Evidence from Value Added Assessments, *Research Points,* Summer, Vol. 2, Issue 2, pp. 1–4.

Schaps, E. (2003). Creating a School Community, *Educational Leadership, Creating Caring Schools,* March Vol. 60, No. 6, pp. 31–33.

Schaps, E., Battistich, V., and Solomon, D. (1997). School as a caring community: A Key to Character Education. In A. Molnar (Ed.), *The construction of children's character, part II: 96th yearbook of the National Society for the Study of Education.* Chicago: University Press.

Scherer, M., Perspectives/Uncivil Liberties, *Educational Leadership, Creating Caring Schools,* March Vol. 60, No. 6, p. 5.

Simmons, R. (2002). Odd girl out: The hidden culture of aggression in girls. Orlando: Harcourt Brace.

Snider, M. and Borel, K. (2004). Stalked by a Cyberbully, *Maclean's Magazine,* May.

Stroot, S., Keil, V., Stedman, P., Lohr, L., Faust, R., Schincariol-Randall, L., Sullivan, A., Czerniak, G., Kuchcinski, J., Orel, N., and Richter, M. (1998). Peer assistance and review guidebook. Columbus, OH., Ohio Department of Education.

Thompson, G. (2004). Through Ebony Eyes: What teachers need to know but are afraid to ask about African American students. Jossey-Bass San Francisco, CA.

Weissbourd, R. *Moral Teachers, Moral Students.* Educational Leadership, Creating Caring Schools, March Vol. 60, No. 6, pp. 6–11.

Wong, H. and Wong, R. (1998). *The First Days of School.* Harry K. Wong Publications, Inc.

Woods, J. (2002). *Hostile Hallways.* Educational Leadership, Vol. 59, No. 4, December/January 2001–2002.

SECTION III

The Context of Schooling

OVERVIEW

Direct observation without any conceptual frame is impossible; some schema is bound to impose itself on the findings in the very process of seeking them, and the data reflect the expectation of the observer to who they are supposed to purely "given."
(Langer, 1967, p. 58)

Some people would tell us to judge schools by standards or analogies outside the domain of schooling. Some want schools to be judged successful by the degree to which they serve the needs of industry in competing with foreign business. Others want schools to function as community centers or social service agencies, and to meet the needs of the entire population from the cradle to the grave.

Suzanne Langer has pointed out that we cannot pretend to objectivity in our reflection on experiences in general. Her comment is especially germane in reference to schools and their functions in society. In a sense, the contents of our consciousness are "acts" of our dramatic schema for constructing meaning. The meanings we ascribe to schooling are deeply embedded in our own experiences and our own decisions.

The first three chapters of this book discuss schools, teachers, and classrooms from the perspective of learning communities, and discuss the organization of classrooms in terms of the purposes of schooling. The authors' believe that the legitimate functions of schooling are driven by four goals for all students: academic achievement, personal growth and responsibility, social responsibility, and social justice. We also believe that conceiving of the classroom as a learning community is a useful way of thinking about education designed to achieve these goals, without which teaching would be little more than training and indoctrination.

What Schools Are FOR?

Carolyn Barnes was worried. It was four o'clock in the morning, and she could not get back to sleep. The previous day she had received a letter from the school district superintendent's office reassigning her, to a fifth-grade class at Woodville School. The teachers' contract had worked against her this time! After teaching second grade at the Maple School for eight years, Barnes was being bumped by a teacher with more seniority in the tenure system. Because Barnes had started teaching 15 years ago as a fifth-grade teacher, according to the contract rules, the district administration could reassign her to a fifth-grade classroom in any building without consultation. Carolyn Barnes was lying awake angry and brooding. "It has been eight years since I've taught fifth grade!" she fumed. Then she began to recognize that behind her anger lay a fear that she might not be able to handle this new assignment.

Barnes pulled herself out of bed and went down quietly to the kitchen, trying not to wake up the whole family. She made some coffee and reminisced: She had started teaching fifth grade right out of the university and had married the same year. Marrying Jim Barnes was a good choice. His insurance business was beginning to provide a comfortable life for them and their two children. When they first married, she had taught so that they could save money to buy a house. She had quit teaching for three years when the children came along, but had returned to teaching as soon as she felt it was possible. The money was important, but she had also found that she missed the teaching. The district had welcomed her back and offered her a second-grade classroom at Maple School. She had loved teaching second grade. She had particularly enjoyed teaching reading

and had gone back to school to get a master's degree in reading instruction.

But now, Carolyn Barnes had to leave her colleagues, go to a different school, and return to teaching fifth grade. Maple School was located in an upper-middle-class, racially mixed neighborhood. Her students there came mostly from homes that valued education and participated in school functions. The new assignment was at Woodville School, an inner-city school, which also served a multiracial student population. General talk among teachers indicated that Woodville parents spent less time at school functions.

As Barnes sipped her coffee, her concerns multiplied. Her teaching career faced new complications. Her new students would be from lower-socioeconomic-class homes. The thousands of materials Barnes had carefully compiled, indexed, and referenced over the last eight years were second-grade-specific. Few would be directly usable in her new class. Further, she knew that most of her routines and procedures could not be adapted to the higher grade level. She would have to contact the principal for a set of teaching guides for the fifth grade at Woodville and then spend part of the summer reviewing the fifth-grade curriculum. She knew that much of the curriculum had changed in the last decade and felt sure that she would need extensive new knowledge to teach effectively.

The student population of her new class would be radically different from her previous classes, on four counts: (1) Half of her new class would be children for whom English was a second language. (2) On standardized tests, two-thirds of the class would score at least one year behind fifth-grade reading levels and a year and a half behind in math skills development. (3) Nearly a third of her class would be new to Woodville School this coming fall, and a third of the students who started school in her class in September would move before January. (4) Many of her new students would be from families whose low income levels would qualify the students for the breakfast and lunch programs at the school. However, her new students would be similar to the students at Woodville in that half the class would be noncaucasian. A third would be from single-parent homes. Half would be latchkey children, whose parent(s) worked full-time.

Carolyn Barnes had lots of questions about her new students—questions such as: "Why do they go to school?" "What is it that brings them back each day?" "Can I challenge them intellectually?" "How long will it be before they think school learning won't help them?" "What will their lives be like in the year 2010?" "What kinds of futures should I be preparing these youngsters to face?" Barnes finished her morning cup of coffee as the summer sun rose and decided to make a whole new pot of coffee. Even though her summer vacation had just begun, she knew that she would soon have to start preparing for her new class at Woodville School. "It's going to be a busy summer," she sighed.

Mark Hicks was sitting at his desk in his very first classroom, in the graying light of a late afternoon in August. He was enjoying the feeling of ownership: this was *his room!* He was also scared and frustrated. He had just a week until the Jefferson Davis High School opened its doors to students for a new academic year—a week to get ready for his first year of teaching. He had worked hard to get his degree and his secondary certification as a history and social studies teacher, and now he had his first job. They were going to pay him to do what he loved doing: teaching! He had accepted this job in a large southern state because they needed history and civics teachers, whereas social studies was overrepresented in the northeastern teacher population. Here he was; it seemed so sudden. He was in a room that was bare except for chalkboards, a few old-fashioned pull-down wall maps, and forty empty student desks.

Hicks had arrived at the school early, bringing with him not only everything he learned in his teacher education program but also his enthusiasm for teaching. The principal had seemed friendly enough and had given him a tour of the two-story school, along with some materials. "Here's your room—number 242, and this is your schedule of classes—U.S. history, world history, civics, and geography. Here's your schedule for chaperoning social and athletic events. Here are your attendance book and your copy of the school rules and regulations. And here's a copy of the master agreement." Hicks had also met the department chair, who had given him a set of teaching guides for his textbooks (the most recent text was five years old). From the chairman Hicks had found out that there was an honors program for 25 students, who were taught the required history courses by the chair.

Sarah Hatfield's room was next door to Hicks'. She had greeted him sincerely and said she had a "whole stack of dittos for student work sheets. You know: maps to label and pages for matching dates with places to keep these lazy students of ours busy and out of trouble." Hatfield advised Hicks, "Put up your set of classroom rules on the bulletin board, and hold them to it from day one!" She offered to help him get started, and her offer seemed to be genuine. For example, she offered to show him how to do the attendance report that was to be tacked up on the door within 5 minutes of the tardy bell.

As Hicks sat in the silence of his room, he felt the enthusiasm drain out of him. He was facing the enormity of his first teaching job. What an undertaking! He was going to teach two classes of civics, and one each of U.S. history, world history, and geography. He was also responsible for one study hall and a home room. His lunch period fell in the middle of his preparation time. When he asked about materials, he was told that there was no teachers' reference library. He had an educational supplies fund of $100 for two years. (The fund had been calculated by dividing the total allocation for social studies by the number of teachers.)

"What am I going to do?" thought Mark Hicks. "I must find the resources so I can do more than baby-sit these students! What is the purpose of schools, if so little is invested in teaching students what they need to know?" Such are the thoughts that occupied Hick's mind as he pondered his dilemma. The buzzing of a few stray flies seemed to accentuate his anxiety.

HISTORICAL PERSPECTIVES

Both Carolyn Barnes and Mark Hicks face situations which illustrate classic problems. Even though one is an experienced elementary schoolteacher and the other a new secondary schoolteacher, both have to struggle with the basic issue of the purposes of schooling. Teaching is a complicated business, compounded by many factors—perhaps too many variables for any single human being to master. Each school building and each school district is unique in some sense, as is each school year and each school day.

Some school boards are not supportive of good teaching because they do not recognize it when they see it. What they do see does not look like the classrooms they experienced as students. Place some twenty-five to forty children in a classroom, and the variability multiplies. Each child brings to school a world of perceptions and expectations built out of intersecting quadrants of meaning: family, church, and neighborhood. To this heterogeneity each teacher brings a microcosm of histories, norms, and understandings. Seen in the light of such complexity, the problem of schooling in our time is how any meaningful activity can be carried out in the seeming chaos of particularity. Even taking a stab at bringing order, organization, and discipline to such diversity, which is what Carolyn Barnes and Mark Hicks are contemplating, calls for incredible courage and imagination.

We know lots of teachers like Barnes and Hicks. They are hard-working and committed to kids, and they do care about what they teach and how it is received. However, no matter how dramatic the personal investment of such teachers, their efforts will *not* be ultimately effective unless they and the schools and communities in which they work have a clear vision of the functions of schooling. Teachers cannot make responsible and consistent decisions about teaching practice if they do not have a clear notion of the purpose of schools. Without a clear vision of the mission of the school, no one can make a decision on specific issues such as what should be taught, how the teacher should teach it, and what management and organization procedures are most appropriate in classrooms. Barnes and Hicks find themselves in their situations through no personal fault and not because of professional deficit. In the United States there is a historical tension between competing visions of the purposes of schooling—between idealized promises that schools will provide the glue to hold together a multicultural society and practical definitions of schools as the educators of the work force in each new generation.

Visions of schooling in America traditionally have held out a promise we made to ourselves to build a better society—that is, a more open, fair, and democratic society. This promise, however, has not been delivered to certain segments of our population. From the beginning of the republic, the schoolhouse has been linked essentially to the society. Thomas Jefferson (1743–1826) argued for free public education in order to provide the republic with a literate and informed electorate. He thought that the great evil against which a democracy must fight was the "tyranny over the mind of man." Jefferson saw education as weapons in the fight against ignorance, superstition, and the power of the few over the many (Greene, 1978). Though Jefferson's educational system was meritocratic, it was based on the spreading of knowledge as the guarantee of public liberties.

Horace Mann (1796–1859) provided the rationale for the "common school," whose curriculum would make of an immigrant society a common nation, a melting pot which would merge many traditions into one strong new national identity. Alexis de Tocqueville (1805–1859) worried about the effects of the industrial revolution on the common man. The factories made individuals dependent upon managers who acted for the owners. The owners themselves often lived at a distance from the industrial site. Schools were seen as training grounds for the industrial work force.

In the twentieth century, many schools even looked like factories, with dull, long, dark corridors, and they were dominated by clocks and bells. Some social critics (e.g., Linda McNeil, 1987) carry the "schools as factories" analogy further. Schools had the function of sorting students as if they were raw material to be processed. The "highgrade ore" made the next generation's leaders, while the "low-grade ore" were destined to be workers on the production lines. Universal education was necessary, so this view of schools goes, to provide workers with minimal literacy so that they could read directions and keep records. Further, emphasis on the socialization role of schools in preparing students for the drudgery of the factory's repetitive work required schools to habituate future workers to dullness and routine. Instead of promoting creative and autonomous thinking, schools tended to emphasize respect for authority. They turned out compliant workers who took orders without questioning the manager's reasons.

If the function of schools in an industrial society was to prepare compliant workers for factory roles, does the postindustrial era present a challenge to educators with its demand for independent and creative thinkers? More on this later.

Preparing workers for industry was not the only function of schools in America. Jefferson's idea of an educated electorate making democracy strong fostered a concern that schools ought to produce something more than skilled factory workers. For example, John Dewey (1859–1952), an American philosopher who wrote extensively on schools, schooling, and public policy, had a vision of schools in which students were active participants in their own learning, rather than passive recipients of filtered information. Dewey's vision of education as primarily a discovery process has had a huge impact on educational theory but little effect on the day-to-day curriculum of classrooms. Teachers and administrators through most of the twentieth century have not been persuaded that children can learn "on their own," and so the inquiry approach has been viewed with suspicion. Dewey argued that not only do people learn better what they learn on their own but also the experimental inquiry model is the paradigm of scientific knowledge itself. If schools built their curricula on a discovery approach to learning, Dewey predicted, students would both learn more and develop their own access to knowledge.

However, local communities in America have not been willing generally to support school curricula that emphasize development of students' higher-order thinking and creativity. Traditional teacher education programs did little to educate preservice teachers to use materials other than those their own K–12 teachers used. Jerome Bruner tried to create curricula that were built on a discovery approach; these were successful in design but failed to achieve public acceptance (Bruner, 1983). Bruner's Man: A Course of Study (MACOS), for example, was a terrific integrated social studies K–12 curriculum which was built around a discovery or inquiry approach to constructing social studies concepts and principles. One reason it failed was the political furor it created. Instead of treating students as passive recipients of givens (facts and figures) to be learned in order to pass tests, MACOS engaged the minds of students and challenged them to experiment in creating explanations for various social and cultural phenomenon. If educators and society had valued cognitive independence and originality as desirable academic outcomes of schooling, MACOS might have been accepted as a desirable curriculum.

What people think of as the functions of schools controls how they think about teaching—that is, our ideas of appropriate subject matter, methods of instruction, classroom organization, discipline, and control methodology are derived from our beliefs about the purposes of schools. When Carolyn Barnes and Mark Hicks review their personal beliefs about the goals of schooling, reflect on society's expectations of schools, and examine the circumstances of their particular schools, they get in touch with the reality of their particular contexts. It is on the basis of such complex realities that responsible plans for instruction and classroom organization can be made. Teachers cannot simply accept whatever "society" might tell them schools are for, because there are so many competing visions of schooling.

Over the two centuries of American schooling, a variety of functions have been ascribed to schools. Some economists, for example, argue that schools serve to keep adolescents off the job market for several years, thereby reducing competition for the available jobs. Indeed, there is some evidence to support this argument. As the average age for entering the job market has risen during this century, so too has the average number of years in formal schooling increased. Social workers, on the other hand, might argue that schools function to keep children off the street and out of trouble long enough so that maturation will occur. Social workers may believe that keeping children in school tends to hold down the crime rate by providing custodial services, when both parents work full-time.

The position one takes about the legitimate functions of schools affects the design and content of instruction in classrooms. Historically, schools began as agents of religious communities. Social, religious, and moral education were of the same cloth, blurring distinction between academic and religious goals. In America, the public school was supposed to be separate from the church and was thought to have primarily academic goals: the teaching of reading, writing, arithmetic, and basic logic and speech skills. In the twentieth century, however, the school has taken on more and more societal roles. The weakening of first the church and then the family social structure in our society has placed greater and greater responsibility on the school to fulfill a variety of socially valuable functions (D. K. Cohen, 1988).

Early in the twentieth century, school subjects were seen as exercises for preparing minds for real-world tasks. Such subjects as Latin, mathematics, and physics were seen as valuable not necessarily because of their intrinsic value as subjects of study but because they trained students in mental discipline. [See *Report of the Committee of Ten on Secondary School Studies* by the National Education Association (NEA), 1894.] If the mind was a muscle, so the argument went, then the school functioned as a gymnasium in which to exercise it. In the Depression era of the 1930s, the NEA organized a commission on educational policies. Its report, *The Purposes of Education in American Democracy,* identified school aims as: "(1) self-realization, (2) human relations, (3) economic efficiency, and (4) civic responsibility" (as cited by Ornstein and Levine, 1985, p. 457). In the 1950s and 1960s, schools were seen as agents for further national agenda, namely defense and expanded opportunity for the disadvantaged. The Sputnik and Vietnam eras put great pressure on schools to defend America from threats without (the spread of communism) and from threats within (the ravages of poverty and "racial discrimination). By the 1970s, schools were seen as expanding their functions to reach multicultural, bilingual, and handicapped students.

In the 1980s John Goodlad and his associates surveyed what people (parents, students, and teachers) wanted from their schools. What he found (Goodlad, 1984) was that Americans want everything from their schools (see Goodlad's chapter entitled "We Want It All," pp. 33–60.). The four sets of goals Goodlad identified were: academic goals; vocational goals; social, civic, and cultural goals; and personal goals (pp. 53–56). We not only "want it all" for our children, we want it for all our children. We are not satisfied with success for only a few. However, some *unified vision* of what constitutes the educated person is needed to achieve all these goals. Once, the literate person was someone who could read and write his or her own language. Now, we talk of math literacy, science literacy, computer literacy, and social literacy as expectations for schools. Who will our children be when they grow up and have full responsibility for our society? Can we envision their needs?

The confusion about where we as a society are going and about the purposes of schools came home to the authors in a conversation we had with teachers in an urban school. The teachers talked about their despair of preparing students for jobs that no longer exist. When pushed to explain what they meant, they said that the factories are all automated now, which means that there are fewer and fewer jobs for which their school's graduates can qualify. The teachers' expectations for their students are linked to previous conceptions of the functions of schooling—namely, that schooling exists only to prepare workers for factories. The loss of factory jobs in this particular urban area has convinced these teachers that their students have bleak futures. Educators who possess no clear directions are right to think that their students will not participate in the American dream of employment, self-sufficiency, and full citizenship. Because educators have a dismal outlook and no clear vision of the functions of schools in postindustrial America, students find that what they are asked to do in schools is meaningless and intellectually unchallenging. The problem here is the link between these teachers' expectations of dismal futures for their students and the students' perception of schoolwork as boring and meaningless.

Because these teachers do not have a clear vision of their students' futures, they find it very difficult to evaluate either the appropriateness of changes they may want to bring about or the efficacy of the official school curriculum. In other words, they are confused about the present functions of schooling in their city. This leads to their having little sense of control over their own professional lives. If they cannot see what roles their students will have in society, they cannot create appropriate instruction for their students. This may explain why these teachers (and others elsewhere) are so focused on "self-esteem issues" in discussing instructional activities. They communicate that if they could improve their students' self-esteem, the students might achieve more academically. They argue that schools can, at least, help students feel better about themselves, and that this result would be beneficial for society. These same teachers see no reason to motivate students to learn academic subjects, because they do not see any benefit for the students. "What would the students do with an academic education?" they ask. None of these teachers can imagine one of their students becoming the governor of the state or the President of the Union. They do not make the connections between academic achievement, on the one hand, and increased self-esteem and an improved quality of life, on the other.

The implicit theory of the function of schooling in these teachers' perspective is the *social reproduction theory*. This view of schools argues that it is the function of schools to recreate the past in the lives of students. One difficulty of the social reproduction theory is that it assumes that the future will be like the past. A more fundamental difficulty has been the tendency to focus the school on practical and instrumental goals: that is, on preparing students for specific types of employment and social roles. For example, future farmers took agricultural technology courses, future mechanics and factory workers enrolled in the vocational technology courses, and future homemakers studied home economics. Only students who planned to go to college would take the academic sequence of courses. The social reproduction theory does not ask teachers to reflect about what qualities are possessed by the "educated person," or about the social justice embedded in the current pattern of courses, as the basis for formulating curriculum and instruction. Thus, when there is rapid change in the social and economic order, schools which conceptualize their functions as reproducing the status quo suffer a loss of direction and confusion as to purposes.

The last decade of the twentieth century is a time of intensive social and economic change. It is no wonder that educators are confused about school functions. Our society is involved in multiple transitions of huge proportions. There is a new awareness of the "global village quality" to our lives. We are linked by satellite communications, driven by digital computers, and extended by other electronic devices. What happens in one part of the world happens to all of us. Events in Beijing or Kuwait are viewed and reacted to by the entire world, not just by a few million isolated people in a province of China or in the Middle East. We are interconnected not merely by electronics but by other powerful forces. For example, one of the consequences of terrorism is the internationalization of social consciousness. East-West Cold War differences dissolve in the face of terrorism, because all states share equally in the disruptions of social order, no matter what the kind of social order.

FUNCTIONS OF SCHOOLS

In our own struggle to identify and to state explicitly what we believe to be the purposes of schools, the authors have come to agree with Schwab's four functions of schooling: academic, social, personal, and social justice (1974). Each function is a legitimate educational goal individually, but collectively they support, supplement, and substantiate each other. Whether we call these functions "purposes," "goals," or "outcomes," they remain the irreducible essentials for education. They form the four building blocks of classroom learning communities.

Few would argue with us, for example, about the academic function of schools. Students need to learn the content of academic subjects: reading, writing, mathematics, history, sciences, and many others. When people urge teachers to return to the "basics," they usually mean the traditional academic subjects. However, we cannot imagine any genuine mastery of, say, basic math skills that does not have an impact on the social responsibility, personal maturation, or equity issues connected with it. A person who does not learn basic math is denied opportunity to exercise social responsibility. Deficient math skills inhibit personal maturation, and a person who fails to achieve self-sufficiency in basic math is denied access to opportunity. This is an affront to social justice, especially when a pattern of failures can be traced across minority groups. It is easy to see the interconnectedness of the academic subjects with social functions, and the consequences of neglecting to teach any such subject to students.

Because we believe that the social functions of schools (academic, social responsibility, personal maturation, and equity) are central to the educational process in a democratic society, it follows that we see teachers as responsible for teaching across all these functions. In a classroom learning community, instruction is structured to elicit both knowledge and a commitment to using the knowledge responsibly. The classroom learning community teacher teaches academic subject matter, for example, not only for understanding but also for ownership of what is understood. By "ownership," we mean a commitment to make positive use of what is learned for the benefit of oneself and others. When students' "play dumb," they do not own their knowledge. It is irresponsible not to use what one learns. Alfred North Whitehead (1861–1947), the British mathematician and philosopher, said that unused knowledge is positively harmful to the individual and society. The teacher should not teach merely for the sake of the test, nor should the students learn simply in order to pass the test. The learning-community teacher teaches toward out-of-school applications of subject matter through in-school practice of problem-solving paradigms.

The classroom learning community itself, as we shall see, is an involving learning environment that provides opportunities for practice and polish of the social, personal, and justice outcomes of academic development. The classroom becomes the laboratory for exploring not only content knowledge but also the personal understandings and appropriations that make such knowledge powerful.

These functions form the foundations for our recommendations about managing and organizing a classroom learning community. They serve as the criteria against which we can evaluate what we think we should do and give us guidance on how it's going once it's under way. The authors' recommendations for effective professional practice are rooted in this interpretation of the functions of schools. This is where we begin, but it is also a commitment to help fashion the kind of world we believe will be needed to enable human beings to thrive in the twenty-first century.

Given the complexity of the modern world, we believe that schools that foster learning communities must provide all students with equal access to knowledge. Academic knowledge cannot thrive unless schools support the development of personal and social responsibility in their students. Finally, unless social justice and the democratic values that go with it are promoted, both individuals and society suffer.

Academic Outcomes

People who are not "plugged in" to the data bank in this information age are figuratively in the dark. The information explosion has made it impossible for any single individual to know all that is needed to function effectively in contemporary society. Individuals must learn how to use multiple sources of information, relying on a network of resources. Therefore, individuals can no longer afford to see others as competitors for a few rare and valuable rewards. Rather, they must come to see others as valued sources of information about the world. Likewise, they must also see themselves as a resource to others. Rather than arguing for a mere tolerance of differences, we intend to present the case for the positive valuing of differences to broaden the knowledge base which we use in judging and deciding courses of action.

The idea that the function of education is to make one literate includes the notion that knowledge is liberating. The child who learns the mysteries of fractions or division is changed fundamentally. More than just "skill acquisition" (how antiseptic that sounds!) is involved. Knowing how to do fractions frees a person to exercise power in this world-power that the person could not exercise before knowing fractions. People who acquire knowledge learn to see with their own eyes, to judge for themselves. Children who learn to read also learn how to take charge of their lives in productive and inventive ways. No wonder children get excited when they discover that they can read! They are excited about what is happening to them, or more accurately, they are excited by what they are becoming capable of doing.

Personal Responsibility

Teachers often think that the problems of classrooms are how to get students to quit behaving badly. "How do I get him to stop stealing?" "How do I persuade her to stop lying or cheating?" "What can I do about drugs?" We do not argue that these behaviors are not problems to students and to teachers, but we do argue that specific remedies for these problems are conditional at best. That is, prescriptions to cure classroom disruptions are contextual, depending upon the situation and the characters interacting. While this book contains many suggestions for positive actions appropriate to a variety of situations, it focuses on helping teachers change classrooms from passive, custodial units to active learning communities. (Chapters 2 and 3 describe what we think learning communities are.) The changes invite students to become active participants in a community of learning and, thereby, to take responsibility for their own learning.

In order to achieve such changes, we have to recognize that the schools are not working for many students, just as the economics of the society do not work for the urban poor. For many an urban teenager, the human need for affiliation is met by a gang. The school is foreign territory to such youths. Their gangs provide the protection and identity they need, but at a high price. Likewise, the drugs that these teenagers take and trade provide an immediate satisfaction that cannot be matched by the delayed gratification preached in schools. The magnitude of such problems cannot be addressed by simply urging teachers to care more about their teaching and about their students' lives. No amount of caring is enough to solve problems which are basically societal in nature.

Social Responsibility

Teaching for social responsibility is revolutionary stuff. It was revolutionary in the golden age of Pericles' Athens when the democrats sought to build a free and open society. They failed, but twentieth-century educators have continued the effort in this country. The conditions of schooling that are necessary for universal education to take place require certain basics: Schools need to be *safe* places. Schools need to be *open and active* environments. Schools need to be *fair* in requiring all members to be treated by the same standards of conduct and achievement. Finally, schools need to be *collaborative and cooperative* societies, rather than competitive collectives. These conditions turn out to be characteristic of learning communities.

Schools need to be safe places for students, because without safety, students and teachers are drawn into a web of protective postures and a focus on survival that prevent students from learning new things. Schools need to be open and active environments because the kind of knowledge and skills we seek to have our students acquire is characterized by a personal vitality and dynamic participation in the cultural and natural environment. Fairness is called for because of the Jeffersonian vision of a just and equitable social order that makes democratic government possible. Schools need to be cooperative societies because the students need to learn how to rely on others, giving and receiving help in a common effort to achieve group goals. Such activities will be necessary social survival skills in the increasingly interdependent world the future seems to be preparing for us.

Social Justice

Our promises of a just, fair, and equal education for a democratic society have yet to be achieved. In emulation of a phrase used by President Franklin Delano Roosevelt (1882–1945) fifty years ago—"a third of a nation ill-fed, ill-clothed, and ill-housed"—we can now say, "a third of a nation ill-educated." How a nation treats the lower third of the population is a better measure of the quality of life in that society than any other. Our vision of schools in America has embraced this promise to build a better society, a more open society for all its members. If this is what schools are for [and Goodlad's report (1984) seems to confirm this interpretation of the goals of schools], then educators carry a tremendous burden and a moral imperative to get on with the business of teaching for all.

Often, conditions in schools are the opposite of those considered positive for a learning community. Schools are *unsafe* in many cities, necessitating the use of guards to patrol the hallways and conduct body searches at the entrances. They often are *closed* rather than open societies, encouraging passivity as a model of acceptable student behavior. In spite of 200 years and more of democratic aspiration in America, *unfair and unequal* treatment of some students prevails. The last and saddest of all realities of our schools is that they remain bastions of unremitting *competition*. See Kohn's book on the destructive effects of competition in America, *No Contest* (1986). The teacher's words slip out so easily:

"Let's see who can finish first."
"Who is the fastest?"
"How many words did you spell correctly?"
"Do you have all the problems completed?"

THE REFORM OF SCHOOLS AS LEARNING COMMUNITIES

Because the problems we face in schools and society are so large and so numerous, we are tempted to look for excuses not to work for improvement. The current conditions of schools and classrooms can be used as a rationale not to change; for example, "With the students I have this year, I'll be surprised if we get anything done!" Indeed, learning does suffer if students misbehave (Baker, 1985). If a substantial part of teachers' time is focused on keeping control and dealing with discipline problems, little attention will be paid to learning. Another way to put this is:

> When crime and violence create an atmosphere of fear and hostility at school, the efficiency of the education of all students is impaired. Teachers who function as baby sitters or police officers are not teaching. Students whose teachers do not teach cannot learn. (Baker, 1985, p. 487).

Lack of discipline in classrooms inhibits learning, but that does not mean that authoritarian attention to discipline will create a learning community. The evidence seems to run in another direction. One study of "disruptive students" in a Texas junior high school turned out to be a study of "disruptive teachers" (Burke, 1982a). This finding is supported by what Baker reports of a study of inner-city schools in London. Children seem to be more affected by school characteristics than has been otherwise supposed. "Students who transferred from behaviorally 'bad' elementary schools to 'good' secondary schools became good students and vice versa" (Baker, 1985, p. 483).

We believe that there is a clear link between societal problems and problems of teaching practice. The degree to which students see lying, cheating, stealing, drug use, and sexual abuse as norms in our society is precisely the same degree to which teachers will have to cope with these behaviors in classrooms. The notions of a rapacious competitive society which seem to characterize the language of the streets and the mythology of Madison Avenue (e.g., "life in the fast lane") are not only inaccurate descriptors of adult norms of cultural and economic life but also perpetuators of pseudoidentities, such as that of the "rugged individual." In fact, most adult roles in our society hinge on possession of cooperation skills. Relating well to others is a basic survival skill in an era in which the relationships between races and nations are of paramount concern. Slavin (1985) points out that success came to humans as a species not because they were bigger, faster, or stronger than tigers or elephants, nor because they were smarter than other animals. Intelligence alone was not enough to make for human survival. "What has really made us such successful animals is our ability to apply our intelligence to cooperating with others to accomplish group goals," Slavin writes (1985, p. 5). Indeed, it is hard to imagine any activity valued by humans that does not require cooperation with others for success.

The image of extreme individualism, privatism, and isolated self-reliance among Americans is frankly a myth. Our love of heroes acting privately against great odds is romantic rather than factual. Stories abound in western literature of rugged individuals (nearly always white men) who through cunning, strength, and purity of motive overcome huge odds, or evil powers, or mindless bureaucracies. Such stories are great fun and great escapes from reality—but that is just what they are, escapes. In fact, we rely on each other to profound degrees. Educators must be concerned with promoting cooperation. Schmuck and Runkel put it this way:

> *The increasing complexity of social conditions locally and worldwide has brought to the forefront the importance of learning to cooperate. . . . The future will hold an even more compelling need to deal with interpersonal, intergroup, and intersocietal tensions and conflicts. (Schmuck and Runkel, 1985, p. I)*

Some would say that schools try to deal with too much and that is why they are failing with academic basics. William Bennett, the former Secretary of Education, wanted schools to return to the basics. Others, like Cremin (1977), would have schools share the socializing and teaching functions with other groups in society. Still other critics, such as Illich (1973), would have schools abolished, since they perceive them as obsolete agents of class oppression.

All who would tell us what perfection is forget that educators have to work in a real world that is sloppy, complex, and richly interwoven. We cannot wait until things get better before we try to do our best work. We cannot blame the system for our failures to act on what we know. Schools, like all social institutions, change slowly. However, they are not likely to change at all, if educators do not work for change. The risk for educators is that we cannot wait to act until we know enough, if "knowing enough" means having all the answers. In fact, acting is a way of finding answers, as well as new questions to ponder.

Acting on the basis of partial information is necessary, if we are to do more than simply follow the advice of Voltaire's Dr. Pangloss (in *Candide*), to till our gardens. The knowledge generated through the actions we take is often more useful than abstract knowledge presented in scientific paradigms. The "action science" of the professional marketplace provides a knowledge base for changing school norms. Nevertheless, until we decide what schools are for, we cannot act except out of habit or hidden agenda. Another way of putting this idea is that without public discussion and communication about the functions of schooling, we remain stuck in a closed and protective culture. Teachers need to have a personal sense of what schools are for; without a personal interpretation of the meaning of schools, they cannot provide a rationale for their work. If they do not have consistent, professional reasons for their practice of teaching, teachers are left with such vacuous rationales as: "That's the way things are done here." When teacher roles are taken on without linkage to the functions of schools, they end up as straitjackets. We believe that just as students can learn to be helpless, so teachers can learn to be authoritarian and privatistic. Then they become stuck in patterns of protective behavior and need to find a way to get unstuck.

The first step toward getting unstuck is to acknowledge being stuck. At the beginning of this chapter, both Carolyn Barnes and Mark Hicks acknowledged that they were stuck in difficult if not impossible situations. What makes the difference for teachers in such situations is taking the time to identify what they believe to be the purposes of schools. They are able to get on with the business of professionally planning their teaching when they know what they believe to be essential in schooling. Barnes began to feel at home with the higher-level class, although she freely admits that she has much yet to learn before she will become "as good a fifth-grade teacher as I was a second-grade teacher." Mark Hicks taught at Jefferson Davis High School for two years, but then left to find another school with values that more closely fitted his own. He eventually found a teaching job in a school which he acknowledges is not perfect but which does more closely share his vision of what schools are for.

Performance Outcomes and Activities (NJPTS 1, 2, 3, 6, 7, 8)

CHAPTER 1
What Are Schools FOR?

PERFORMANCE OUTCOMES

Teacher Candidates will

1. Define and describe functions of schooling.
2. Link contributions of specific talk and actions observed in schools, to functions of schooling.
3. Apply discussion group roles effectively.
4. Use observation skills accurately, use interview skills effectively.
5. Create useful data collection tools, use effective note taking skills, and analyze and synthesize data accurately and effectively.
6. Use systematic study and reporting skills effectively.

OVERVIEW OF CHAPTER 1 ACTIVITIES

The end-of-chapter work for Chapter 1 links the acquisition and/or practice and application of scholarly skills to the expansion of your knowledge about the functions of schools, through a focus on the following tasks:

1. activities for accurately discriminating between observations and inferences;
2. activities to practice observation and note taking skills, and to identify actions and talk that support the functions of schooling through classroom and school observations;
3. an activity for creating interview questions and letters to introduce you and your task to the administrator and interviewee, to practice gaining entry for interviews, and to practice seeking permission for interviewing;
4. activities to practice interviewing skills and interview note taking skills, and collecting data about the functions of schooling from interviews;
5. activity to create a letter to introduce the idea of study in a school site, as a means to enhance understanding of the concept of a classroom learning community; and
6. activities focused on the substance of Chapter 1 that support the linkages to the study of learning-community concepts.

A secondary purpose of Chapter 1 study activities is to set the framework and expectations for scholarly study throughout the candidates professional education teacher preparation program.

BACKGROUND INFORMATION FOR OBSERVATIONS AND INFERENCES ACTIVITIES

Effective teachers base their instructional decisions on a solid foundation of reliable information about students, standards, and the learning environment. Thus, observation and data collection are crucial skills for effective teacher practice and reflection. Because nonprofessionals, teacher candidates and novice teachers often confuse their observations with their inferences about what they observed, we start with a brief review of the distinction between observations and inferences. This exercise is also helpful to experienced teachers as review of their inference-making skills so that they are able to work and talk with early field experience and student teachers in increasing their skills.

As previously noted, it is sometimes very difficult to separate what we experience from the meanings we give to experiences. In the extreme cases, some teachers see what they want to see. Research on teacher expectations has confirmed this blurring between observations and inferences (Brophy, 1979). We know, for example, that teachers who expect to see their students succeed act as though students' success were already a reality. The impact of their actions is that students experience success-oriented expectations and work to meet those expectations. These teachers hold high expectations for the students and thus provide different instruction and materials for those students. At times, teachers also actually "see" success, even when the student's work is not successful student work. Thus, they do not provide quality corrective feedback and end up interfering with the student's progress. The self-fulfilling prophecy is involved in such attitudes toward learning.

Holding high expectations for all students and securing confidence in the reliability of our information base is thus a very important step in the assessment process.

Observations and Inferences

Observations are those aspects of experiences that we can relate directly to some physical or quantitative feature of an event. We see, hear, touch, or smell a physical object or event. If two or more people experience the same sensations, they will report similar if not exactly the same perceptions. *Inferences* are the meanings we make of our perceptions. We say that we draw an inference from observations. A positivist definition would be that observations are facts, whereas inferences are interpretations of facts. We know, for example, that the same event can be interpreted differently by different people. A teacher who calls on 3 boys who are the first students to raise a hand after a question is asked, can be viewed by one person as rewarding the student for eager participation in the class and by another person as expressing a sexist preference for male students. Thus, two people can see the same event very differently.

Also, two people can view different events and see the same underlying meaning. There are no methods, however, for predicting in advance whether what we see or experience will be the result of preconceptions about what we will see or the consequences of the interpretations we instantly make of sensory experiences.

The learning community culture is based on the constructionist view that there are no innate meanings to events but only constructed meanings from our sensory perceptions. The issue is whether the meanings we make of the events we observe are adequate explanations of what happened. An inadequate explanation might be made by someone who is inexperienced or might be the result of either a deliberate or an unconscious prediction that was made to avoid "seeing" certain data. Another possibility is that there was not enough data available to make a fair explanation.

Imagine the following situation:

In a fifth-grade classroom, some twenty-five children are sitting in rows of desks, quietly working on their math problems in a mathematics workbook. The teacher sits at the desk behind the students, watching them as they work.

1. The principal enters the room, sees the students working quietly in their workbooks, and concludes: "What a hard-working class! So quiet! This is a good teacher!"
2. A student returns from a visit to the school nurse, enters the room, and sees her fellow students working in the workbooks. She nods to the teacher, goes to her desk, gets out her workbooks, and thinks, "What a rotten bore! This teacher is a loser!"
3. A parent enters the room, looks around, and leaves quickly, thinking, "Teaching is certainly an easy job. Just sit and watch children; nothing more than babysitting."
4. A student teacher enters the room, observes the students working for a while, and thinks, "How does this teacher do it? How does she get these children to sit quietly for such a long period of time? I wonder if I will ever be this good?"

5. A school psychologist enters the room and watches the faces of the teacher and the students. She says to herself, "These children look tense, and the teacher looks determined. At this rate, the teacher will develop an ulcer and the students will develop a dislike for mathematics."

6. A teacher educator visits the room and sees the same things as the above observers. She says to herself, "Here is a teacher who needs help. She treats the class as if it were a single person and she does not want a single deviation or change in pace. We had better not put a student teacher in this room."

The point of these examples is that people's particular perspectives, knowledge, and experiences help to focus their interpretations of events. Understanding the multiple views helps teachers to question their first impressions and to consider potential alternative views.

Recently the authors made the following observations in a classroom we visited:

Observation 1: There were thirty-two students present.
Observation 2: There were thirty-six desks in the room.
Observation 3: One student said, "That story we read for homework was 'bad.'"
Observation 4: Another student said, "I don't like this class when we have that kind of homework."
Observation 5: All the walls, including the bulletin boards, were covered with student work, and student projects were hanging from the ceiling.
Observation 6: The work on the walls and hanging from the ceiling was all done within the last month and a half.

In addition, to the classroom observations, the history of the school site and any available facts about it are treated as observation data. For example,

Interview question 1: Ask the principal or teacher. How many students were enrolled in the class we observed? This would have given us additional observational data (e.g., the principal might have said that there were thirty-two students enrolled in the class).
Interview question 2: Ask student 1—What was it you liked about the book?
Interview question 3: Ask student 2—What is it that you don't like about having a story to read for homework?

Other people's inferences also become part of the observers' observations. For example, consider the statement: "The teacher said that he believed that the basketball team would be state champions." It is an observation in that the statement is "the teacher's inference about the basketball team."

For the purposes of this text, when we use the term "infer," we mean a report of an individual's reasoning about a particular situation. That is, when people make inferences, they add meaning to their observations. Following are some inferences based on the above observation data that we could have made about the classroom we visited:

Inference 1: The room was cluttered.
Inference 2: Four students, or 11 percent of the class, were absent.
Inference 3: Students liked the homework.
Inference 4: Students did not like the homework.

In doing classroom observations and in making inferences, we find that it is important to check out what we think we see and what we think it means. Therefore, it is not sufficient to say things like "There were thirty-six desks and thirty-two students; thus there were four students absent." The classroom we visited had four extra desks and when we asked we learned that they were placed one in each of four circles and used during small-group discussions. With the 4 extra chairs, the teacher could place them in small groups (she divided her class into four groups for small group work), then the teacher was thus able to move freely around the room and sit in on each small-group discussions without disturbing anyone.

Following are two practice exercises for discriminating between observations and inferences.

Exercise 1.1
Identifying Observation and Inference Statement

A. In-Class Instruction—Whole Group of Small Group

1. Instructor Leads Group in a Review of Observations and Inferences and the connections of these skills to Reflection.
2. Instructor Leads Group in identification of observations and inferences through viewing of a movie or video about classrooms or schools.
3. Class is organized into small groups and the Instructor provides an activity for practicing identifying and creating observation and inference statements.

B. In-Class Activity—Individual Task

To be sure that you understand the difference between observations and inferences, read each of the following statements and indicate whether it is a statement of observation or an inference that could be made about a classroom.

CIRCLE ONE

STATEMENTS

1. Observation
   Inference

   1. The homework that the students handed in was too difficult for them.

2. Observation
   Inference

   2. Thirty of the thirty-two students received a grade of C or above on the homework.

3. Observation
   Inference

   3. I think that this classroom represents an example of a learning community.

4. Observation
   Inference

   4. The teacher said that he was not concerned about the grades students received but was concerned about the concepts they developed, about changing their misconceptions, and about everyone in the room succeeding.

5. Observation
   Inference

   5. Parents of the children in this class value education.

6. Inference
   Observation

   6. We felt that we would like to be students in this classroom.

Now go back and circle the part of each statement that supports your judgment.

Exercise 1.2
Practice Observing and Inferring

Part A.—HOMEWORK.

Record observations about an interaction you observe in the next couple of days. With a partner, go over your statements about the situation and determine whether they are observation statements or inferences. Next, list several logical inferences that could be made based on the observation statements you recorded. Bring your observations and related inferences to the next class.

The following format will be used for this task. You will need to add additional rows to this table.

DATA COLLECTION
DISTINGUISHING BETWEEN OBSERVATIONS AND INFERENCES

NAME: DATE:

Dates	Type of Inter-actions	Notes	Ob. Inf	Inferences that could be made based on observation statements

Part B.—IN-CLASS ACTIVITY.

In groups of three go over the observation and inferences for each member of the group. To the best of your ability be sure that all observations and inferences are technically accurate. Then individually, for each of your inference statements write a statement describing the additional information you would need to observe in order to determine that your inference was accurate. Review these statements as a group. After the discussion each member of the group should adjust his/her statements so that they are as accurate as they can be technically. Have the group leader turn in the copies to the instructor.

The Functions and Purposes of Schooling Academic, Personal Responsibility, Social, and Social Justice Responsibilities, Values and Actions

THE FUNCTIONS OF SCHOOLING

The following activities focus on connecting ideas about the functions of schooling with real school situations. Exercises 1.3 and 1.4 use small-group discussion to explore your ideas about the functions of schooling. Exercise 1.4 is a panel discussion with community members. Exercise 1.6 is a study project in which you will use school-based observations and interviews to provide an opportunity to connect the idea of functions of schooling with school as experienced by learners. You will use observation, inference, and reflection to further study the four functions of schooling presented in Chapter 1. You will also use interviewing as a means to study the structures of schools and their impact on the purposes of schooling. Finally, you examine one or more of the original sources referred to in Chapter 1, as a means to further expand your understandings.

Exercise 1.3
Exploring Personal Ideas about the Functions of Schooling

In-Class Activity—Small Group Discussion
Teachers, teacher educators, administrators, school board members, parents, preservice teachers, and others answer the question "What are schools for?" in many different ways. In Chapter 1, the authors described the purposes of schooling as we see them. In this exercise, you have an opportunity to analyze your personal beliefs, and to compare and contrast them with others' beliefs about the purposes of schooling.

A. The purpose of the first part of this exercise is to enable you to explore your ideas about the functions of schooling today. Working with a study group of from four to six other people, brainstorm two lists: (1) the functions/purposes of schooling that individuals in the group believe schools now promote and (2) the functions/purposes that the group members believe schools should promote. Assign a group facilitator, to help move the discussion along and to promote the brainstorming process. Assign a timekeeper to remind the group about the time frame given for this task so that the group can accomplish as much as possible. Assign a recorder to keep notes that can be turned in at the end of the group's discussion. Finally identify a reporter who will facilitate the group's report to the class.

B. What do you personally believe are the purposes of schooling? After the group discussion, and taking into account any new ideas that you received during the discussion, summarize your response to the above question in writing.

C. Turn in your personal summarized response to the question prior to leaving class.

Exercise 1.4
Parent, Business, Community Members' Expectations for Schools, their Children and the Teachers

In-Class Activity—Panel Discussion

The purposes of this activity are to provide teacher candidates with the opportunity (1) to practice social responsibility skills, (2) gain experience in asking important and sometimes difficult questions of people you do not know; and (3) give you the opportunity to being a community network.

The instructor will invite parents, business people, minister, mom at home, mom working, grandparents and guardians raising kids, dad at home, dad working, and community members to discuss what they think the functions of schooling are. The members selected will represent the schools and neighborhoods where you are assigned. When they are invited, the instructor will ask them to prepare to tell you what it is that they want from their schools, from their teachers, from their administrators, and from their children and youth. They will also be asked to describe how they would like their child treated in school.

Part A: Panel Presentations and Question and Answer Period

On the day of the panel discussion, as the panel members arrive, teacher candidates get up and greet individuals as they arrive, introduce yourself and introduce the guest to one or two other candidates. It is your responsibility to contribute to the comfort level of any guest who may be somewhat shy as a speaker for your course. Also, while the panel is speaking, you must maintain appropriate eye contact with the speakers and communicate nonverbally that you are listening.

Prior to the Panel Discussion, candidates will write one question that you would like to ask a member of the community. After the panels' presentations, the instructor will act as a facilitator so that as many individuals as possible have a chance to ask their questions.

At the end of the Panel Discussion and question/answer period, the class will take a break; it is the social responsibility of each member of the group to thank individuals as they prepare to leave. Be sure to include in your thank you one thing that you learned from the guest's comments.

After the members of the community leave, the class will divide up the Panel members and write thank you notes to them. The instructor will see that they are mailed. Thank you notes will include concrete examples of contributions the speaker made to the panel discussion.

Part B. Debriefing—In Class

Teacher candidates will identify new information they heard, information that reinforced their prior thinking, information that was new or a surprise to them, times when they were uncomfortable, and how they will make use of the experience to practice establish a network with community members.

Part C. Investigating the Neighborhood and Community and Creating a Network where your Field Placement Is Located

An important part of a teacher's responsibility is to connect with the parents, guardians, and members of the neighborhood and community in which they teach. The networking that teachers can create pays off in parent and community support and respect, additional resources, and students feeling respected.

Many new teachers are so busy surviving in the classroom that they do not invest in learning about their school's neighborhood and community. Unfortunately, they create their role in isolation of the neighborhood and community and when they look back years later, they find that they unconsciously built a wall between them. University faculty find that this is the area that in-service teachers provide the least support and challenge for their student teachers.

One of the ways for you to avoid the isolation is to create a process for studying and gaining entry into a neighborhood and community now. Thus, it will become an automatic part of your role as a learning community teacher. You have a school field placement this semester and you will have one each semester as a part of your teacher preparation program. By beginning the study and process of gaining entry to a new neighborhood at this time, you will have a process to practice for the next three years.

The activity has three parts: *the first* is a self-assessment about what you know already about the school, neighborhood and community; *the second* is an exploration of the community; and *the third* is an end of the semester self-assessment about what you learned over the semester and how you used the information you gained to improve your students educational experiences. Complete the writing for this task on your computer using the formats suggested.

Early Field Experience and Student Teaching Format

PART 1: SELF ASSESSMENT ABOUT STUDENTS, SCHOOL, NEIGHBORHOOD, AND COMMUNITY

Name: _____ School Assignment:_____ Level: _____

Community Name:_____ Date:_____

I. Neighborhood
A. List what you know about the neighborhood in which your school is located.
B. Explain how each of the items you listed will help you provide higher quality educational experiences for your students.

II. Community at Large
A. List what you know about the community at large.
B. Explain how each of the items you listed will help you provide higher quality educational experiences for your students.

III. Students
A. List what you know about your students. P–6 select six students to write about and 7–12 select one student from each of six classes.
B. For each student explain how what you know about him/her helps you provide higher quality educational experiences for him/her individually.

IV. Schools
A. List what you know about the school to which you are assigned.
B. How will you use this information to improve the quality of educational experiences you provide for your students?
C. List what you know about two other schools (at different levels than where you are assigned).
D. How will you use this information to improve the quality of educational experiences you provide for your students?

V. School System
A. List what you know about the school district.
B. How will you use this information to provide high-quality educational experiences for your students?

VI. Professional Knowledge
A. List the professional knowledge, about schools and communities that you gained from your university course work that you will be able to use in order to provide high quality educational experiences for your students.
B. How will you use this knowledge to improve the educational experiences you provide your learners?

VII. Knowledge Gain from Personal Experiences
A. List the knowledge you have gained from your experiences about the linkages between school and community.
B. How will you use this knowledge to provide high quality educational experiences for your students?

PART II: INVESTIGATING AND GAINING ENTRY NEIGHBORHOOD AND COMMUNITY

Your role in this activity is to be a student of the neighborhood and community. You are acting as an investigator or an anthropologist who makes the "invisible visible."

The product of this part of the neighborhood and community study is a network map. To create the map, you will (1) identify questions, (2) interview people, (3) ask for referrals to other members of the community who will help you expand your understandings of the neighborhood's norms and values. Below is the beginning of a network map. The names of the people, and the concept(s) they talked with you about are recorded in the circles and the lines show who referred you to whom.

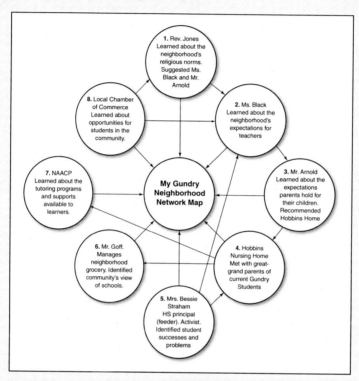

After you have interviewed enough individuals to get a sense of the neighborhood it is time to write up your investigation. Organize your data so that you tell a story about the norms, values, and unique features of the neighborhood.

Turn your network map and your story in to the instructor at the 7th week class session. Plan to use your neighborhood and community networks in a small group exploration task related to exercise 3.6 in Chapter 3.

It is your choice to follow your neighborhood study with a study of the broader community. If you choose to do this, follow the directions for the neighborhood study. Turn this in with Part III during week 16 of the course and it will provide extra credit.

PART III: END OF SEMESTER SELF-ASSESSMENT

Students, Neighborhood, Community, School, and School System/District
Due Week 16 of Semester. Do Assignment on Your Computer

Name: _____ School Assignment:_____ Level: _____ Date:_____

(Use this format and write the Self-Assessment on your computer)
Review what you wrote in the initial assessment, review your neighborhood network map and story, and if you did them review the community map and story.

A. After reviewing your data answer the questions below explaining how you used the information you learned. If you did not use the information simply write, "Did not use information in this category to improve instruction," then write why you believe that you did not make use of it.

   1. Knowledge about the neighborhood.
   How did you use information about the neighborhood to improve the educational experiences of your students?

   2. Knowledge about the community.
   How did you use information about the community to improve the educational experiences of your students?

   3. Knowledge about the students (6 you identified).
   How did you use information about the students you gained to improve the educational experiences of your students?

   4. The school to which you are assigned.
   How did you use information about the school to improve the educational experiences of your students?

   5. The two other schools about which you provided information.
   How did you use information about other schools in your feeder system to improve the educational experiences of your students?

   6. The school district/system.
   A. How did you use information about the district to improve the educational experiences of your students?
   B. Explain what you know now, about linking school and community, student and family, curriculum and neighborhood/community, and the system and community, in order to improve educational experiences.
   C. If you did the community network map and story, compare and contrast the neighborhood and community stories. Write a story using what you learned about similarities and differences between the neighborhood and broader community.

Exercise 1.5
Purposes of Schooling

The purposes of this activity are to provide the candidate with the opportunity to identify his/her current personal views of the functions of schooling and link them with the functions identified with a classroom learning community and to continue to practice the application of effective group member skills.

In-Class Activity—Small Group Discussion
The large group is divided into small groups of six to eight members. Each group should choose a facilitator, timekeeper, recorder, and reporter. The facilitator should remind everyone in his/her group members that they are to demonstrate all of the roles of effective group members during the discussion. You should place the card on the table when you believe you carried out one of the roles. At the end of the discussion, you and the other members of the group should review the cards in the center. You and each of the other individuals will describe what you said that made you think you were demonstrating a particular role. The group should provide constructive feedback after you speak. Upon reflection, you can provide constructive feedback to yourself noting your ideas in your journal. Remember that you are working toward you and every other individual being an effective group member so that everyone learns as much as possible during the year.

After reviewing the application of small group discussion skills the facilitator of the group will lead the group's review of the content of their discussion. The recorder records the additional points made. At the end of the review, the group will reach consensus on three to five synthesizing statements. The statements should reflect the different points of view identified during the discussion. The reporter will report these statements to the whole group and the recorder will turn them in to the instructor.

Questions to Focus Small Group Discussions

1. What do you see as the futures for your students?
2. What do you see as the futures for students in the schools you attended?
3. What do you see as the futures for students in the Camden Schools?
4. What do you see as the futures for students in the Cherry Hill Schools?
5. What do you see as the common threads among these students' futures?
6. What do you see as the differences among these students' futures?
7. What difference does it make to the students you teach what vision of their future you hold?
8. What are the functions of schooling from your point of view?
9. Think about the most effective teacher you have had and then describe the functions of schooling that he/she reflected in his/her practice.
10. How does the social reproduction theory of schooling interfere with the following four functions of schooling: academic, personal, social and social justice responsibilities?
11. What is an educated person?
12. What are the reasons that some educators support the social reproduction theory?
13. What contributions are made to learners and our country by teachers and schools, which support academic, personal, social and social justice purposes of schooling?
14. What functions of schooling have you experienced during your formal education experiences?
15. As a teacher candidate or teacher, what do you need to know and be able to do in order to become a leader who consistently supports the four functions of schooling (academic, personal, social and social justice responsibilities)?
16. What will you look like to your students if you support the four functions of schooling? What would it mean if a student said that you walk your talk?

(Note: Items may be used as Essay Questions on Future on Exams)

Exercise 1.6
Functions of Schooling—Academic, Personal Responsibility, Social Responsibility, and Social Justice Values/Actions

The purpose of this exercise is to provide the first of three different databases for identifying school experiences that contribute to each of the four functions of schooling as presented in Chapter 1. The final report from this project should be placed in your Portfolio as Evidence of Meeting INTASC/State Standards. You will add to the report at a later date and you will add the updated report to your Portfolio which will also illustrate your growth since your first report.

The first database is constructed from your observations in a school.

The second database will be generated from responses of the pupils and teachers, who were observed, to questions constructed by the reader after their observations and from interviews of neighborhood and school personnel.

The third database will be generated from interviews with neighborhood members and school personnel.

Part A Observations

What are you looking for? The format presented below will serve as a model to help you to organize and write up your findings. Four functions of schooling were presented in Chapter 1 (i.e., academic, social, personal, and social justice responsibilities). You are looking for examples of situations that students experience as part of their school curriculum that contribute to their acquisition of one or more of these functions of schooling. The products of your small-group discussion (Exercise 1) may include other functions of schooling. When you begin your observations be sure to also look for support or lack of support in the school environment for these functions of schooling.

Time The time that you should spend on the observations is a minimum of two half-days (one morning and one afternoon) in an elementary, middle, or high school. This includes the time during which students are entering the school grounds, classes, lunch hours, time between classes, time spent in clubs or other after-school activities, and the time during which students are leaving the building at the end of the day.

EXAMPLE   The Function of School: Social Justice Responsibility
Observation Field Notes, Reflection Notes, and Inferences

Name: Date: Grade Level Observed: School:
Subject Matter taught during observations: Times From   to

Observation Notes	Reflection Notes (Notes not made during observation or clarifications)	Inferences	Questions
Teacher said students would use cooperative learning study groups. Students moved to groups of 4 and 5. Students asked each other questions to clarify understandings.	Not all students participated. Noise level did not appear to bother any students. It was too loud for me. Student volunteers to facilitate.	Students do not understand their responsibility to the group.	What are the specific behaviors taught to students that qualify as cooperative learning?

Use the following data collection format for your school and classroom observations. (Add Rows to Your Forms). The first form is to be used for recording your observations, etc., of academic outcomes opportunities that you observe.

The Purpose of Schooling: *Academic Outcomes*
Observation Field Notes, Reflection Notes and Inferences
Observation Data Collected in a Minimum of
5 School/Classroom Situations (Same Building)

Name: Date: Grade Level Observed: School:
Subject Matter taught during observations: Times From   to

Observation Field Notes	Reflection Notes	Inferences	Potential Interview Questions

Use a form similar to the one below and record the personal responsibility occasions you observe.

The Purpose of Schooling: *Personal Responsibility*
Observation Field Notes, Reflection Notes and Inferences
Observation Data Collected in a Minimum of
5 School/Classroom Situations (Same Building)

Name: Date: Grade Level Observed: School:
Subject Matter taught during observations: Times From   to

Observation Field Notes	Reflection Notes	Inferences	Potential Interview Questions

The following form is to be used for recording your observations of the social justice responsibility occasions you observe.

The Purpose of Schooling: *Social Justice Responsibility*
Observation Field Notes, Reflection Notes and Inferences
Observation Data Collected in a Minimum of
5 School/Classroom Situations (Same Building)

Name: Date: Grade Level Observed: School:
Subject Matter taught during observations: Times From   to

Observation Field Notes	Reflection Notes	Inferences	Potential Interview Questions

Part B Reflection on School Observations
Review all of your observation notes, inferences, and your list of potential interview questions. Synthesize the information by looking for links and patterns that show up in your work. What are the main questions that seem to reoccur? What patterns are there that further investigation will help you understand the source or direction of the patterns? What actions, verbal and nonverbal communication did you see that you believe were linked to positive supports for the functions of schooling? What actions, verbal and nonverbal communications did you observe that you believe were linked to nonproductive or non-democratic functions of schooling? What things did you start to wonder about and wish that you had better or more information? What are you learning about schools and schooling, learning and learners, teachers and teaching and the functions of schooling?

Part C Identification of Research Questions
Write two or three research questions that you will study as you go forward with your interviews. The questions need to come from your observations, inferences, and reflections. Once you have written your questions, write a paragraph that explains the linkages to your initial data, inferences, and reflections. (e.g., How does the way the teacher addresses the functions of schooling impact the culture of the Learning Community? What functions of schooling are evident in teacher talk? What functions of schooling are evident in teacher actions? What functions of schooling are evident in student action?)

Part D Interviewing School Personnel, Community Members and Students Rationale for Interviews

You have now completed the collection of observation data in and around a single school and its classrooms. The next part of this study is to collect data from the adults and children who are members of this school's community.

The *purpose of this part of the study* is to provide an opportunity to learn how adults and learners, in a particular school, think about the functions of schooling and their relationship to what students, teachers and administrators do and say as they go about their work in a given school. While this type of thinking may not be at a conscious level people are acting on their beliefs. Thus, it is important for you to design questions that will give individuals a chance to reflect and tie their actions to the beliefs they hold about the functions of schooling.

For this part of the experience you will:

Step (1) Select People to Interview,

Step (2) Create interview questions and try them out on peers,

Step (3) Contact Interviewees and explain purpose of interviews, set up interview appointments, and carry out interviews.

The people you will interview must all be connected to the same school. The variety will provide you with a general sense of how adults and students see their school environment and what they believe are the functions of schooling.

1. Selecting People to Interview

Select a set of people to interview who are teachers, parents, students, principals, assistant principals, volunteers, custodians, security personnel, cooks, lunch supervisors, secretaries, bus drivers, resource personnel, university faculty working in the school, and community members.

2. Generation of Interview Questions Based on School Observations and Reflections

Write questions that you will use to interview each person. The same content is appropriate for the different role groups, however the *structure* of the question will need to change depending on the person/role group. For example, a question asked of the principal *(As principal what do you believe are the functions of schooling that your students should acquire when attending your school? When your students leave here what should they take away with them?)* needs to be altered for a parent *(As a parent, what do you believe are the functions of schooling that your child will get out of going to Gundry school? What should she/he learn while at this school? What should she/he get out of his/her experiences at Gundry school?).*

Other types of questions that you will consider include the following: How does this school carry out this function? What goes on in the halls, classrooms and playground that contribute to the students developing this outcome? What do you say and do that contributes to the students acquiring this function?

Using some of the suggestions offered earlier, construct an interview data collection sheet for each of your interviews.

After creating the lists of questions and data collection sheets you will use with each role group, try out your interview questions on someone that is not in your class. During this interview, focus on the questions that the interviewee asks you, and his/her responses. If you are getting responses that seem unrelated to schooling, then rework your questions and pilot them again with a new person.

3. Contacting Interviewees, Setting Up Appointment, Interviews, and Data Collection

Contact the individuals you will interview, explain the purpose of the interview and what you are learning, and set up a time and place to meet with them. Be sure to tell them how long the interview will take. Also, explain that you will be analyzing data and reporting to your class. Inform them that you will not be using their names, but rather the role group which they are representing. To set up appointments with the principal, contact him/her directly. Contact teachers directly and work with them to identify and talk with the students.

Be early for your interview so that you have your data sheets, questions and other materials all ready so that you can begin the interview on time. Begin by reintroducing yourself, the purpose of your interview/what you are studying and thanking them in advance for meeting with you.

Be sure to take notes while you are interviewing. If you need to go back and check out exactly what the interviewee said or meant, ask an objective clarifying question.

Interview two people for each of four role groups.

Part E Analyzing and Synthesizing Data, Reporting and Reflecting

1. Analyzing and Synthesizing your Data

Once your have collected all of your data, review your notes and figure out what patterns are embedded in the data, what anomalies are apparent, and what comparisons and contrasts are evident. Be sure to compare your interview data with your observation data. Review your data analysis and identify the types *of biases that may be built into* your data. For example, did all of the parents you interviewed come from the same socio-economic level?

2. Reporting Your Findings

After completing your data analysis and reflection write a report using the following format:

1. Title and author page
2. Introduction
3. Describe the question(s) you were studying and what you were trying to learn about that question.
4. Explain the process you used for your study. Include both observation and interviews.
5. Present your data as collected. Include both observation and interview data.
6. Describe your findings using the analysis of both observation and interview databases you completed.
7. State your current conclusions.
8. Describe your new questions and indicate why these came to mind after your study.
9. List of references used in presentation of report.
10. Appendix A: Observation Field Notes
11. Appendix B: Interview Field Notes

You will find a rubric for use in the evaluation of the research report. This is a project in process and you will be adding to it at a later date. Use the rubric as a standard as you complete your report. Turn in your report along with a copy of the rubric on which you have noted your self-assessment.

Once you have received your report back with feedback, put the report in your Portfolio. This is a great project that will help you demonstrate your professional ability to study an environment as well as show your growth over a period of time.

Expanding Your Understandings

At the end of the exercises in each chapter, you find a list of references that are part of the bibliography for the chapter. They present additional information about the substance of that chapter. For some chapters you will also find web pages that may be helpful to you in your work. Teachers and teacher candidates who piloted these materials indicated to us that these were particularly interesting and helpful to them.

On the following page is a list of some of the original resources that we used in the text of Chapter 1 as well as recently published references. We provide these as a recommended readings list, to support those people who wish to pursue one or more of the ideas studied in this chapter in order to personally gain a better understanding of a particular concept. Your instructor will provide you with additional suggestions.

RUBRIC FOR EVALUATION OF CHAPTER 1 STUDY PROJECT

	0 Must be Revised in order to receive any credit	1 Below minimal performance level	2 Close to Standard	3 Meets Standard at the Sophomore Level	4 Exemplary Includes skills expected later in Program
Introduction to Report & Description of Study Question	Includes a paragraph that simply restates the functions as presented in the text	Includes expanded statements of functions and presents basic question for study	Includes clear easy to understand explanations of functions of schooling	Introduction tied to study question, clear description	Graduate school level writing, includes abstract that has clear data organization and findings
Classroom Observation Notes and Inferences	Notes are skimpy; may focus on one element; inferences may be restatements of notes	Notes include 2 or 3 elements; inferences are weak but included	Includes clear notes on teacher, students, environment, & content; inferences are clearly linked to data, includes talk and actions that contribute to functions	Accurate and clear ties of teacher and student talk and actions to all 4 functions of schooling; Where a function is absent shows data that supports that finding	Graduate School Level writing, original observations notes are reorganized for data analysis and synthesis
Interview Questions	3 to 4 questions, are short and do not suit role group	Many questions, some are redundant; Follow up questions might get only restatements of first response at times	Questions are clear and to the point; are different to meet role group needs; No yes or no questions.	Same as 2 plus Questions appear to elicit complex data; follow up & clarifying questions result in interviewee answering questions at deeper level	Same as 3 plus the nature of questions would be appropriate for MA Thesis.
Interview Notes and Inferences	Notes skimpy or seem unrelated to real talk, inferences restatements of notes	Notes lack depth of interview contributions; confusing organization and not clear linkages to inferences	First response data, follow up questions look good but don't raise level of interviewee responses	Notes clear, inferences tied clearly to data; follow up questions resulted in deeper or more complex responses from interviewee	All of 3 plus data and inferences could result in action research study
Data Analysis	Does not appear	Includes a few ideas that may be embedded in data	Identified patterns, anomalies, compares and contrasts	All of 2 plus some of the patterns or anomalies do not fit stereotypes of those interviewed	Analysis of data includes use of "significant" correct formulas and enough interviewees to use them correctly

	0 Must be Revised in order to receive any credit	1 Below minimal performance level	2 Close to Standard	3 Meets Standard at the Sophomore Level	4 Exemplary Includes skills expected later in Program	
Data Biases	Unable to identify any	Mentions surface level biases; all white people interviewed	Identifies two or three probable biases and explains clearly why and potential problem with the data	All of 2 plus biases are accurate	All of 2 and 3 plus identifies potential biases and indicates potential effects on findings.	
Reflections and New Questions	Repeat of data analysis. No new questions	Does not take thinking further than data, questions do not stretch thinking	Reflections are simple ideas that take study further in the current direction, new questions	Reflections are extrapolations of data; questions clearly take work in new direction	New questions are presented as future study.	
Writing	More than 4 spelling, format and grammar errors	Internal consistency is weak; spelling structure is simple; paragraphs not linked	Spelling OK except for words computer does not catch, only 1 or 2 grammar errors, some organizational errors	Grammar, spelling and clear links within paragraphs, clear transitions from paragraph to paragraph, no errors	All of 3 plus complex data is supported, clarified by tables and charts.	
Totals						

Total Score for this project: _____

RECOMMENDED READINGS

Apple, M. W. (1993). Official Knowledge: Democratic Education in a Conservative Age. New York: Routledge.

Aronowitz, S. & Giroux H. (1993). Education Still Under Siege. Second Edition. Critical Studies in Education Series. Connecticut: Bergin & Garvey, Greenwood Publishing Group.

Banks, C. A. M. & Banks, J. A. (1997). Reforming Schools in a Democratic Pluralistic Society. *Educational Policy.* 11(2), 183–93.

Beane, J. A., & Apple, M. W. (1995). The case for democratic schools. In M. W. Apple, & J. A. Beane (Eds.), *Democratic Schools,* (pp. 1–25). Alexandria, VA: ASCD.

Bruner, J. S. (1983). In search of mind: Essay in autobiography. New York: Harper Colophon Books.

——— (1966). Toward a theory instruction. New York: W. W. Norton.

Dewey J. (1933). How we think (rev. ed.). Boston, Mass.: D. C. Heath.

——— (1944). Democracy and education. New York: The Free Press. (Originally published in 1916.)

Everhart, R. (1984). Reading, writing, and resistance. London: Routledge & Kegan Paul.

Goodlad, J. I. (1984). A place called school: Prospects/or the future. New York: McGraw Hill.

Schwab, J. J. (1978). The practical: A language for curriculum. In I. Westbury and N. J. Wilkof (eds.). *Science, curriculum, and liberal education.* Chicago: University of Chicago Press.

Slavin, R. E. (1983). *Cooperative learning.* New York: Longman, Inc.

The Learning–Community Teacher

When students are asked what kind of teachers they want in their classrooms, they describe, in effect, learning-community teachers. Lewis and Lovegrove (1984) studied student perceptions of desirable teacher characteristics for maintaining classroom organization and control. The highest characteristic on the students' list was "calmness." Students argued that teachers should avoid getting angry, yelling, or in general acting like the misbehaving kids. Further, the students wanted clear rules, reasonable authority, appropriate punishment, and fairness. But, above all, Lewis and Lovegrove tell us: "the best teachers are more likely to be seen as taking responsibility for maintaining a learning atmosphere in their classrooms and not rejecting their disciplinary role or attempting to place the responsibility elsewhere" (1984, p. 100).

The classroom learning community that we envision is led by a teacher who accepts the discipline-related functions of teaching as part of the work of teaching. The instructional responsibility for classroom learning requires the teacher to be involved with the quality of life in the classroom—a situation which is best described as "community." A learning-community classroom does not prevent disruptions from occurring, but it does provide the norms for dealing with disruptions and getting on with instructional activities. The following two vignettes provide contrasting examples of classroom teachers.

Alice Tompkins is a middle-school English teacher. She teaches seventh- and eighth-grade English classes and serves as the faculty adviser for the school newsletter. She says that she is a frustrated writer and will someday quit teaching and devote her life to writing critical essays for the little journals. Her friends consider this to be only her private fantasy. In fact, she loves teaching poetry and literature to young people who are still in their formative years. She is known as a strict disciplinarian: "I take no back talk from anyone, much less my students," she says. She has a set of thirteen rules for classroom decorum on her bulletin board; the list is put up before the school year begins and stays up all year. If a student breaks one of Tompkins' rules, she records it in her record book and deals out punishment (ranging from extra homework or detention to talks with the vice-principal) according to the severity of the infraction.

Tompkins says that she is strict because she cannot waste precious class time on distractions and disruptions when there is so much information for the students to learn and so much literature for them to read and appreciate. She is big on "appreciating literature." She loves teaching literature, she says, "because it is dealing with the most cherished memories of our society, shared with us by the best writers of the past." She sees her role as giving information, selecting the best examples of good literature, and introducing students to the classics. "They do not know it now," she says, "but they will thank me later for being a tough teacher with good taste." She thinks that there is a basic body of knowledge which all citizens should know. She is proud that her classes contribute to the increase of cultural literacy. Her students know who are the ten most important American writers; they can name the most important poets and dramatists. They say that Tompkins is fair and not too hard, if you pay attention to what she says is important. What she says is important is always on the quizzes, just like she says it will be. If she gives you a date for a poem, the students say, make sure you remember it, because it will be on a test.

John Dyer is a fifth-grade teacher in a professional development school (PDS), a school affiliated with a nearby university and a base for a lot of student teaching and internships, as well as teaching research. Dyer considers his classroom a community within a larger village. If the school is a village and the principal a mayor, then Dyer thinks it is all right to call his class "Dyer's Neighborhood," even if it sounds corny. He talks a lot about his "neighborhood" and what makes it work. There is much to do because there is much to learn. Everybody has a role. John Dyer says he likes to use social metaphors when he is talking with the students and their parents about the class, because it emphasizes the active role that every student must play if the neighborhood is to be a successful and satisfying place to live and learn.

All the subjects are taught in Dyer's class. However, he prefers to call the teaching "investigations." He sees teaching mathematics, for example, as a matter of inviting students to conduct investigations about numbers and other mathematical phenomena. Instead of lecturing, he most often poses problems or dilemmas for class discourse. He sees his role as engaging students in meaningful "math talk." In order to achieve high student participation in class discourse, Dyer spends a lot of time early in the year developing a common vocabulary with his students. They learn to talk about their "theories," to "infer from their observations," to "challenge someone's assumptions," to "test an idea by finding an example," and most of all, to "respect others and their ideas."

Though Dyer's students see him as a resource who knows a lot of stuff, he portrays himself as a learner. "Life is a journey, not a destination," he likes to say to his students. He spends a great deal of time each day "thinking with his students." "What's happening?" is a question he asks a lot.

Because his classroom is part of the larger community of a school and that the school is a PDS, many adults visit Dyer's classroom, including interns and student teachers. He insists, however, that everyone who comes into his room become a participant in the ongoing discourse. He puts it this way: "You cannot be in Mr. Dyer's Neighborhood without being a good citizen." Even visitors who come to watch Dyer teach are often drawn into the community conversation by students who ask them what they think about this or that. Some first-time visitors to this class get frustrated by being asked by an enthusiastic fifth grader, "What's your theory about what is happening here?" He is focused on how students in his class make sense out of their experiences, in and out of school. John Dyer acknowledges that his class is somewhat chaotic, but he says he likes that because life is also chaotic. "The most important thing," he says, "is to try and figure out whether any real learning is going on. Are we pushing back our collective ignorance and actually gaining in the race against indifference?"

The contrast between these two teachers may, at first glance, appear to be not that significant. Many would account for the major differences between them on the basis of their environments, that is, one teaches at middle school and the other is a primary teacher. We do not think so. We believe the contrast between Alice Tompkins and John Dyer to be extreme, on the basis of an examination of their underlying assumptions about teaching and learning. The clash between their assumptions is deeply cultural. Tompkins believes teaching to be the distribution of knowledge and the shaping of the right attitudes and social behaviors. She thinks of knowledge as a closed set of standardized information. Therefore, learning is a matter of acquiring something that the teacher disperses to pupils.

Dyer, on the other hand, sees teaching as something like coaching. Knowledge is something that the students put together in their heads; it is essential to encourage student participation in the classroom activities. Participation in the discourse of the class makes what is being learned a public event, not a private individual affair. This is the aspect of the learning community that makes it a cultural process. Bruner (1990) puts this idea well when he writes that, "by virtue of participation in culture, meaning is rendered *public* and *shared*" (pp. 12–13). Dyer thinks that this kind of classroom is a reflective community, because students spend a lot of time thinking about what they have done and planning for new events.

Argyris and his associates (1985) illustrate the contrast between reflective cultures and protective cultures. We think that this distinction applies to these two teachers and their classrooms. Classroom learning communities can be characterized as reflective cultures led by teachers like John Dyer, who see themselves as reflective professionals. Protective school cultures are ones in which teachers like Alice Tompkins see themselves as managers of discipline and dispensers of knowledge. Reflective teachers like John Dyer, as life-long learners, model the collaborative and learning process. Reflective teachers talk about themselves, their efforts, and their rewards in current learnings.

The contrast between reflective and protective cultures is even more profound in their respective treatments of the nature of knowledge itself. Protective cultures tend to see knowledge as a complete "body"—something received from the past. Reflective cultures tend to treat knowledge as a constructed reality embedded in particular contexts. Likewise, students of reflective teachers perceive their teachers not as finished products but as growing and struggling adult learners. The key feature in these students' perception is their acknowledgment of their teachers as members of their own learning communities.

We use *community* much as it was used originally (in about the fourteenth century), to signify a group of people who are associated by common status, pursuits, or relationships (Onions, 1966, p. 196). *Community* can also refer to the quality of relationships, in the sense that a community exemplifies humans sharing resources and experiences. The word "community" also contrasts with other words for social organization which are more formal, such as "society," "state," and "nation." It is interesting to note that the word "community" is invariably used in a positive sense (Williams, 1983)—a rare phenomenon, as most words have both a positive and negative connotation. We pose the word "community" as the opposite of the condition of isolation; that is, a community is not an enemy of the individual as are some collective social organizations. One can be isolated in a crowd or a collective, but not in a community. In a community we are members—linked, connected, in communication with other members. Because humans are connected to many groups, are members of families, it is appropriate to talk of *communities,* as a plural phenomenon. "Community" can also mean commitment or concern for some common cause, as in the term "community action." Thus, the word "community" always carries with it a sense of identity and all the complexity that is embedded in the idea of belonging.

A classroom learning community cannot be simply created by teacher fiat. One does not command community to occur! Schwab (1976) gives us some idea of the complexities involved in setting up a learning-community environment when he suggests that community comes from "rewarding collaboration, communication, helping and being helped, toward goals we have set ourselves" (p. 235). A community is not so much a collection of like-minded believers as a commitment to shared differences. The range and variety of developmental and environmental differences in one classroom are significant. A learning community gathers up differences and celebrates them, because differences are rich resources which improve the quality of group interaction.

A heterogeneous community not only increases the richness of individual experience within it but is critical for the learning process itself. We do not learn from sameness but from the differences around us. The contrasts, differences, and even oppositions found in typical classrooms can be understood as a positive resource. A learning community begins to form when all class members are accepted as they are, for what they are. Instead of being blamed for their differences, the students are credited for them. As we discuss in Chapter 3, students learn from the social context of a classroom. They make sense out of what they experience in their classroom out of who they are in relation to others. We wish to reinforce the principle that the learning-community culture is appropriate for students with learning disabilities, for science labs, for art classes and other classroom organizations.

We have suggested that a classroom learning community does not arise simply out of the accidents of time and place, nor because of casual historical associations (as in, "I go to Mason High"). Schwab (1976) characterizes a community as a group of people who share "a set of internalized propensities, of tendencies to feel and act in certain ways" (p. 241). If we define "community" in this way, then a community is not constructed out of external signs, such as flags, mottos, and pledges of allegiance, no matter how important such signs are for symbolizing commonalities. Rather, community is the product of how people relate to each other. Bellah (1985) writes of the tendency among contemporary Americans to replace the word "community" with the popular term "lifestyle." He contrasts the meanings of the two terms this way: "Whereas a community attempts to be an inclusive whole, celebrating the interdependence of public and private life and of the different callings of all, lifestyle is fundamentally segmented and celebrates the narcissism of similarity" (p. 72). In other words, community includes, while lifestyle excludes.

We are drawn toward Schwab's idea of community as a state of internal dispositions of its members; what Schwab calls "propensities." *Propensus,* the Latin root of "propensities," means inclination or leaning. Describing the members of a community as having particular "inclinations" avoids an implication that the cultural manifestations of community (its physical and social environment) control the quality of community. Further, Schwab's idea is consistent with our own notion that a classroom group cannot understand the social dynamics within the group unless it is self-consciously aware of its own operational theories or cultural norms. (See Chapter 3.) Therefore, creating a learning community is a process of encouraging and promoting the development of certain propensities as the classroom's cultural norms. The propensities that we discuss first below are representative dispositions possessed by all members of a classroom learning community, teacher and students alike. Later on, we will describe four additional propensities that are especially fit to the teacher as community leader.

PROPENSITIES OF LEARNING-COMMUNITY MEMBERS

We have adapted Schwab's seven propensities for a learning community (1976, p. 246) to make it clear that the goal of schooling—and, therefore, all that goes on in classrooms—is the internal growth of the students toward adult membership in the larger society.

1. **Identifying Common Needs and Purposes**   Unless internalization takes place, we teach for naught. No collection of human beings becomes a community without a sense of common goals, or a common vision of the future. Students need to discover their commonalities and differences within a classroom. They need to know themselves better, as well as to gain an understanding of others. An inclination to see a connection between one's own needs and the group's goals characterizes communities. Students discover that they are not alone in their confusion, puzzlement, or frustration with themselves and with schools. The relief in this discovery encourages group bonding: they find identity, even if at the beginning it is only an identity of a mutual predicament. Eventually, identity formation leads to generation of individual and group purposes. It makes sense that if a group can identify a given set of common problems, the next step is for them to search for potential common solutions.

2. **Seeing Peers as Colleagues**   The classroom learning community encourages students to perceive others as possessing rich resources of experience, skill, and knowledge which complement their own. Fellow students are colleagues or collaborators, increasing one another's potency. Rather than seeing others as competitors for a few meager rewards, students in the classroom learning community see their peers as partners on the joint enterprise of learning. The talents of another person do not detract from one's own stature, but can supplement and strengthen the pool of skills from which individual community members can draw. Teachers sometimes have trouble in grasping this radical notion, because the tradition of making students compete with each other for the teacher's attention, course grades, and school awards is a long one.

3. **Seeking Self-Actualization and Group Actualization**   In a classroom learning community, teachers encourage students to welcome problems which are challenging and will expand their capacities. Students come to delight in the joint exercise of the class's resources. Instead of seeing

problems as obstacles to be avoided, students in a classroom learning community find satisfaction in solving problems and sharing knowledge. Aristotle defined happiness as the "full exercise of one's talents." In this sense, a community is happy to struggle with its problems. Actualization also implies that there is developmental work yet to be done. To actualize means to bring potential into vivid operation. There is a sense of adventure in a classroom learning community, a taste for the trouble of growth, that is often called the "satisfaction of achievement." The imagery is one of active pursuit, rather than passive receipt of something. The teacher in a classroom learning community, as a life-long student, also communicates an enthusiasm for the struggle of learning.

4. Recognizing Other Groups as Similar   One amazing result when a class develops into a learning community is the development of a perception of other groups as having similar internal relationships. Contrast this with the more common notion that foreign groups could not possibly be as humane, or friendly, or whatever, as our group. Hostility toward the strange or foreign derives from a failure of self-knowledge. As competition decreases and collaboration becomes the norm, it becomes easier to see that other classes or groups are as satisfying for their members as one's own class or group is for its members.

5. Reflecting on Past Actions   A classroom learning community is characterized by public reflection on what has happened. This propensity to reflect involves observing, thinking, and talking about the past, including the immediate past. Self-confrontation occurs in shared reflection, so that the gap between intention and effect can be shared publicly. The mismatch between what we thought would happen and what actually happened is identified and acknowledged in a community. In an atmosphere in which sharing reflections publicly is the norm, the members of the class are not afraid of failure, because events can be talked about. Risks can be taken in a reflective culture because of the social norm supporting experimentation and the trying out of new ideas. Negative results receive as much attention as positive results, when the class thinks out loud about what has happened. In fact, negatives often prove to be especially important to the class because they give clues to what led to mistakes or errors. Building on the correcting of past errors, new events can be planned and tested publicly. Young children especially need to learn how to reflect on their actions, so that they can learn to see the things that happen as circumstantial rather than as character flaws. Very young children do not separate their own being from their doing and so think they are "bad" if they make a mistake. Group reflection on events influences students powerfully to view events as external circumstances to be examined for understanding, and not as internal character flaws to be evaluated and blamed. We will return to this theme later on.

6. Helping and Being Helped   A classroom learning community invites its members to value helping one another, while placing no stigma on being helped. From a community perspective, needing help is seen not as weakness but as human. We all need help at something, sometime, from someone. The community does not view helping as the "superior" position. Being helped is getting on with the business at hand, not a lesser state of being. When the person being helped is not considered to be of lower status, it is easier to ask for help. Not only students but also teachers aides have access to help. "Help me out," when said in a classroom learning community, is not a form of helplessness, but an expression of a temporary need in a given situation. Later in this chapter, we discuss the developmental perspective as a key to operating in a learning community. Here we assert that everyone in a classroom learning community is learning something, somewhere along the developmental continuum. Because everyone is a learner, community members are not tempted to play "power games" with what they know (as in: "I know something you don't know.").

7. Celebrating Accomplishments   A community remembers significant events from the past, and its members enjoy talking about their individual and collective successes and failures. "Great goofs we have made" is a favorite memory in the classroom learning community. In fact, enjoying remembering failures is so basic that it can be used as a test for genuine community. Social organizations that cover up past mistakes, hide the failures, and deny that anything ever goes wrong are certainly not communities. Schwab (1976, p. 246) lists celebration as the last and maybe most important propensity of learning communities. Celebration is the propensity to collect symbols of past successes and to memorialize past griefs. In other words, a community develops a historical memory. Recitation of past events celebrates and empowers group identity. This may be what is missing from many contemporary urban classrooms: a sense of identity with class and school. What is meant here is not just that students "should" feel some loyalty or school spirit, but a deeper sense of identity, in which students feel that their destiny, what they are becoming, is tied up with their schooling. As long as schools and classrooms are adjuncts to the main business of students' lives, their educational impact will remain superficial, even trivial.

Focusing on the characteristics of classroom learning communities as developing a set of propensities is a different approach to creating classroom organizational structure. When teachers plan to create classroom learning communities, they engage in work that is very different from preparing a collection of strategies for dealing with potential student discipline problems. Valuing the seven propensities discussed above leads to seeking a quality of relationships in classrooms that enriches both the internal and the external lives of its members.

PROPENSITIES OF LEARNING-COMMUNITY TEACHERS

While the above seven propensities describe the inclinations of any learning-community member, there are additional dispositions or propensities that are characteristic of learning-community teachers. Developing a classroom learning community requires a teacher to possess these four additional propensities:

1. Instructional leadership
2. A developmental perspective
3. A cooperative disposition
4. A reflective orientation

We think of these propensities as operational heuristics, because they are frames for organizing action. A "heuristic" is a way of finding out something, a way of proceeding. An "operational heuristic" is, therefore, a way of discovering how to proceed. Guiding principles are built into each of these propensities, and thus a teacher who possesses these propensities knows how to proceed.

1. Instructional Leadership   Classroom learning-community teachers think of themselves more as instructional leaders than as classroom managers. Focus on the teacher as a classroom *manager* tends to imply uncritical acceptance of the influence of the twentieth-century business world on school organization. Historically, powerful forces invited us to think of schools according to the heuristics of the industrial revolution, which created the factory as the central organizational unit. The tremendous success of manufacturing and industry influenced the way we think about all social institutions. The evolution of the one-room schoolhouse and academy into large-scale "school systems" was an understandable development as concerns borrowed from the business world crept into educational policy. "Productivity," "division of labor," and "quality control" are all concepts derived from business. As universal education became the norm in the twentieth century, schooling became "big business." Leadership in schools shifted from an instructional base to a preoccupation with issues of management, whether of the school or the classroom.

The power of this conceptual shift was compelling. School administrators started to talk like businesspeople, and teachers started to act like workers rather than professionals. The sentiment of many Americans by the end of the nineteenth century was, "The business of America is business." This sentiment is expressed when educators speak of education as a "people business." Schools were conceived of as factories, taking the "raw materials" (youth), "processing" (teaching) them, and "producing" (graduating) the labor supply for the next generation of workers. The schools we built even looked like factories, and it seemed that what was needed for schools, like factories, were managers.

When institutional management becomes a substitute for instructional leadership, a different set of assumptions about teaching holds sway. It is common to find classroom management courses which are organized around strategies for controlling students. One reason for the divisiveness of management conceptualizations of education is that management is sometimes seen as an adversarial position, as in the relationship between management and labor in the business world. Management can be seen as an abstract, even a neutral term, describing a particular ideological interpretation of human relationships (R. Williams, 1983). The employment of a class of people who are paid to administer ever-larger bureaucratic enterprises creates an artificial distinction between employers and employees. The artificiality is illustrated when management is characterized as pursuing the generalized good for the organization, but employees (students) are seen as selfish individuals attempting to satisfy their own needs.

The kind of classroom management which sees teachers as responsible for "handling things" distances teachers from the "objects" they manipulate and inspires a tendency to treat students as objects. A result of this kind of management is that open sharing of goals and plans tends to be undervalued. When teachers feel that they cannot share with students the purpose of lessons and assignments nor the decision-making process, they are really denying their students access to knowledge. The idea of managing, of handling things, tends to elicit visions of impersonal relationships. The more that procedures are routinized and educational content is packaged, the less human beings have to interact about.

In contrast, the classroom learning community is built on the premise that teacher and students are members of the same society—a society in which all individuals share human status and play a variety of roles. In large part, the teacher's role consists of instructional leadership. The key to leadership is motivating others to collaborate in shared activities. The teacher can still "manage the class" in the sense of bringing together the resources and organization to empower student learning. In a learning community, individuals thrive because of the high value placed on individual differences. Instructional leadership overcomes the isolation of individuals—who are locked into performance expectations and invites the risk taking that underlies all learning the moving from the familiar into the unknown. The culture of the classroom learning community is understood as one in which teacher and students can interact with safety and satisfaction. Community within a classroom cannot be commanded. Community is built by all the members who share a common history, common values, and common goals. The teacher's role as instructional leader in the community, far from being an isolating one, is a fully involving social enterprise.

2. Developmental Perspective   A developmental perspective assumes that individuals, as well as institutions, pass through stages of growth as they mature. These stages are conceived of as dynamic and not merely as "phases" one goes through on the way to becoming an adult. Each stage that we experience includes and transcends the previous stages in a way the earlier stages cannot do with the later. The movement is developmental when the knowledge, skills, and values gained transform who we are. Thus, development is not a mere collection of experiences but a process of transition, a movement to new cognitive and moral territory.

To say that classroom learning-community teachers take a developmental perspective means they take a particular position about how humans learn and grow. They reject the idea that education is basically something for children to do on the way to becoming adults. Consider Dewey's comment that "acquisition of skill, possession of knowledge, attainment of culture are not ends: they are marks of growth and a means to its continuing" (Dewey, 1939, p. 628). In this sense, life is a journey, not a destination. Again, Dewey said it well:

We exaggerate the intellectual dependence of childhood so that children are too much kept in leading strings, and then we exaggerate the independence of adult life from intimacy of contacts and communication with others. (1939, p. 629)

If teachers are seen as learners—still developing, evolving, and growing—then it is necessary to see what they do as having a developmental history which they can share with their students in the classroom learning community. This means that everyone in a community is somewhere on a continuum of personal development, and no one is a finished product (that happens when we die). If people develop throughout their lives, as we believe they do, then individuals can hardly be blamed for being at the developmental stage they happen to occupy on the continuum of growth. This concept, which applies to students as well as to teachers, is a freeing concept. Individuals are responsible for their actions, but they may not be responsible for the developmental space they currently occupy, which represents one facet of the range of possible spaces a person is capable of occupying. In other words, it makes little sense to blame someone for not being someone else at a given time. For example, the classroom learning community teacher does not blame a student for having reversal problems in learning to read. Evaluation of progress in development is an aid to learning, because humans need corrective evidence of their progress or lack of progress. However, much of what passes for evaluation in schools has been status analysis, rather than progress reports. Status analysis is the comparison of one person with others. A developmental perspective assumes that incremental progress, step-by-step improvement, and change can and do occur.

Although the research on development continues and there is a lot that we do not know, we know enough to begin to take seriously the scientific basis of developmental theory. Sprinthall and Thies-Sprinthall (1980) suggest that the series of studies on adult functioning now in the literature have reached similar conclusions. What these studies have found is that predictions of successful adult functioning based on assessment of individuals' stage development are more accurate than those based on the traditional measures of academic aptitude or even previous grades in scholastic settings. McClelland (1973) pointed out that there is a curious circularity to scholastic aptitude and school success. Scholastic aptitude tests predict grades in school, yet neither the tests nor the grades predict success in life. What does predict performance in complex human tasks is psychological stage development (Sprinthall and Thies-Sprinthall, 1980). In the classroom learning community, individuals are invited and encouraged to learn at their own rate and within their own stage of development.

3. Cooperative Disposition   As a nation, Americans are beginning to question the value of competition as the prime motivator for all successes (Kohn, 1986). Notions of competition and aggression as natural human instincts necessary for survival are being challenged by our increasing awareness of cooperation and conciliation as effective and satisfying modes of operation. People like to cooperate; they gain satisfaction from mutuality and collaboration. At present, there is a strong educational movement to mitigate the effects of competition in schools by using cooperative learning strategies (Slavin, 1980) and multiability groups (E. Cohen, 1986) in classrooms. Traditionally, cooperation and competition have been understood as mutually exclusive, but they may interact within individuals according to each one's need for confirming personal identity or testing skills publicly (Owens, 1987). Cooperation may be understood in a variety of ways. D. W. Johnson and R. T. Johnson (1985) tend to see cooperation as structure; that is, they interpret cooperation as a better way of organizing instruction by structuring relationships. Others see cooperation as a trait; for example, studies have shown that girls are more cooperative than boys, and that Mexican-American children are more cooperative than others (Kagan and Madsen, 1972). Slavin (1983) sees cooperation as a powerful strategy to improve learning for the low achievers, while not slowing the progress of the high achiever. Sharan (1980) treats cooperation as collaboration, doing work together. He found that cooperation causes race relations to improve while expanding high-level cognitive functioning for students who started at both low and high levels. Kohn (1986) reports that studies of performance differences between competitive and cooperative working conditions provide overwhelming evidence in favor of cooperation. "Superior performance not only does not *require* competition; it usually seems to require its absence" (p. 47).

Cohen (1982) studied the use of cooperative tasks in structuring multiability groups in integrated classrooms. That is, Cohen studied what happens when students of different ability levels are mixed in groups and given cooperative tasks. She found significant positive interaction between multiability activities and academic tasks. Using small groups and rich, multiability activities increased the participation rates of poor readers in academic tasks. The traditionally low-status poor readers increased their involvement in classroom activities and improved their reading ability, while the more successful readers did not suffer any loss in academic progress.

Creating cooperative learning groups is not an easy task in a culture that so highly values competition. Children in America begin school believing that doing well means beating someone else (Aronson, 1978). Therefore, teachers have to teach the skills and values of cooperation; cooperation is a task structure which must be learned. New roles and procedures for interaction within the group need to be practiced by students. When this occurs, cooperation directly affects the redistribution of rewards in the classroom and as a result eases the basic inequities of classroom status.

We have learned (J. L. Green, 1983) that tasks and activities do not themselves structure learning. Rather, teachers and students interacting within the classroom, modifying and reacting to each other's messages and behaviors, construct the learning environment. It is for this reason that we emphasize a cooperative *disposition* as a goal and a means in a learning community classroom. Teachers and students need to internalize the cooperative norms in order for positive effects to occur. The curriculum evolves through exchanges between teacher and students, and through the interaction of students with subject material. The learning community is an environment of shared meanings, so that instructional decisions can be made in contexts understood by all the members of the class.

Some teachers are suspicious of cooperative learning and multiability task structuring. They tend to think that cooperation in learning is cheating in some way, as though only individualistic learning gained in competitive battle is genuine. The authors' beliefs are contrary to this traditional view; we believe that individualistic interpretations of learning are based on a faulty theory of knowledge. Knowledge by its very nature is a collaborative affair. Scholars cooperate within research teams and across generations, testing and refining what is called "knowledge." If we had to depend on what we could know individually, our knowledge would be very meager indeed. A disposition to share what one knows and to test it publicly is characteristic of the members of learning communities. Schwab describes it this way:

> Collaborations have a clear contribution to make to effective division of labor in a society. In such a pattern of school life, tasks can be discriminated which require the dovetailing of diverse talents. . . . Each person discovers, then, in the course of completing the task . . . that different clusters of talents exist in different persons. (1975, pp. 34–35)

What the class members discover is that success, far from being a matter of competitive combat, is the product of the conjoining of talents to achieve goals.

A cooperative disposition is often hard to maintain in a litigious society. In an atmosphere in which people sue at any trivial slight, teachers are tempted to be protective and private about their professional work. Cooperation, therefore, will probably not succeed if it is seen as merely a strategy for attaining certain instructional goals. The propensity to cooperate and encourage cooperation among others feeds on open and public discourse about the effect of events upon us. Cooperation is not something done in private, but a public activity that involves others and empowers by the very fact of pooling talents.

4. Reflective Orientation   Our belief in the value of a reflective orientation on the part of teachers is linked to our assumptions about the developmental nature of the learning process. We oppose the view that education is a quantitative process of "filling up" empty youth—who are deemed to be ignorant, inexperienced, naive, and uncivilized—with enough facts, skills, and wisdom to make them into socially responsible adults. Such a view is not only a mechanistic view of teaching, but also condemns people to stable unchanging characteristics that may be evaluated as "good" or "bad."

Human beings are incredibly complex and adaptive creatures. Thus, any mechanical explanation of teaching and learning will fail to account for the complexity of what goes on in classrooms. If we examine all that happens in a classroom—the actions, the work, the thoughts and feelings we have about ourselves and others, the impact we have on others and they on us—we begin to develop a sense of the complexity of classroom reality. However confused we may become about the complex world of the classroom, it does not mean that knowledge about classrooms is relativistic. That is, an explanation of teaching and learning in classrooms must fit or match the experiences of teachers and students in classrooms in order to be considered a useful theory.

Karl Popper (1974) argues against relativism and for the reality of knowledge and ideas about ourselves and the world. That is, what we know has power to prompt more learning. What we think we know becomes knowledge only when private, personal ideas and meanings are tested in public. Knowledge is basically a social phenomenon. The public testing of the inferences we make about our perception of the world can change ignorance to new knowledge. Popper puts it this way:

> It is through the attempt to see objectively the work we have done—that is, to see it critically—and do it better, through the interaction between our actions and their objective results, that we can transcend our talents and ourselves. (1974, p. 196)

A learning-community teacher approaches a classroom with a reflective orientation. Traditional teachers tend to assume that knowledge is given—a received set of truths, standards, or rules for social conduct. When people do not measure up to the standards, traditional orientations tend to blame individual students or colleagues for faults or defects in their character or personality. On the other hand, teachers with a reflective orientation tend to think about human conduct and the social context in which it occurs. Moral seriousness is inherent in the process of reflecting about human affairs as problematic. The thoughtful person, as Dewey wrote, "makes a problem out of consequences of conduct, looking for the cause from which they probably resulted" (1939, p. 856).

We like Dewey's rule of making a problem out of the consequences of conduct, because teacher reflection is recursive, looking back for patterns of behavior, seeking to find linkages between intention and effect. Teachers get stuck in nonproductive or unhelpful behavior when they are unaware of conflicts between intention and action. Instructional error results from getting stuck in unexamined assumptions which drive teaching actions. In Chapter 3 we examine how the culture of the classroom and the school can trap teachers and students into unexamined assumptions about the "way things are." Here we argue for considering a reflective orientation as an approach to the learning community classroom.

A reflective orientation keeps teachers open to the multifaceted nature of human cognition. Reflective teachers also see the disruptions and distractions of some forms of student behavior as problems to be understood and solved, rather than as traits to be crushed or trials to be endured. Reflection is a process of making sense of complex classroom events and not a single set of guidelines for problem solving. Teachers engage in reflection, we believe, when they publicly test their theories (beliefs) against their instruction (actions). We say, "publicly," because human beings are capable of self-deception and need the feedback of an audience, whether that audience is the teacher's students or a colleague.

Reflection is a process that includes *both* thinking *and* talking about human activity. Reflective teachers think in advance of action, during instructional activities, and afterward. However, such thinking in itself is not sufficient to create reflection. To be reflective, teachers' thoughts must be shared and compared with others' perceptions of the same events.

In this sense, we would reserve the term "reflection" to mean thinking and public discourse, in order to distinguish it from private mental exercises, such as meditation. No matter how refreshing or focusing meditation and other private mental exercises may be (and we are certainly not against them!), they are not a substitute for the active process of considering the links between intentions, actions, and consequences. The problem with private mental exercises is that they do not include a feedback loop and that they therefore limit the range and array of decisions based upon them. Teachers intend to assist student learning. That is their professional role. Reflection focuses on evaluating the degree to which what we intend actually occurred because of our instructional actions.

We assume that what we do as teachers is helpful, because we certainly intend to be helpful. However, this is a testable assumption. The teacher can ask his/her students whether a particular strategy is working as intended; for example: "Is it helpful if I repeat the question before I answer it?" Notice that, in order to ask such a question, the teacher must *be aware* of the choice made to link a particular strategic action (repeating the question before answering) with the intention to be helpful to the students. Awareness requires an examined theory of teaching, a self-conscious plan of action, and a set of educational goals.

A reflective orientation requires the teacher to state publicly the plan and goals of instruction. Teachers and students cannot talk together about what went right and what went wrong in an instructional episode unless they share publicly an awareness of what they were trying to achieve together. This may seem self- evident, but we have found that teachers often cannot identify what their goals were, nor say why they were using one strategy rather than another, nor explain the educational theory upon which their instructional actions were based. Clearly, if teachers do not know what they were trying to do in a lesson, they cannot very well reflect on the quality or effectiveness of their instruction.

Thus, reflection requires a public statement of instructional plans prior to the instructional action. In a learning-community classroom, the teacher discusses publicly with the students the instructional plans, the choice of activities, and the evaluation criteria for measuring outcomes. Such discussion includes student interests, values, and reactions to instructional goals. Without student input and feedback, the teacher can only guess at the results of instructional activities.

A learning-community teacher may invite a colleague or supervisor to observe the classroom and to share feedback on instructional performance. When that happens, the teacher will have to be specific about what is intended to happen and the strategies to be used to achieve instructional goals. Otherwise, the teachers cannot talk with each other about the common ground of professional activities observed. Without such advance organizers for professional observation, teachers are left with random observations that cannot be molded into any coherent or useful feedback.

A reflective orientation includes a taste for criticism. Learning communities are built on criticism in the best sense of that term. Members of a community are critical not as a means to cut one another down but as a way of expressing support. People who do not care, or who are bored by or indifferent to what is going on, cannot be critical. Only people who share a common set of experiences can make critical judgments and give effective feedback. Teachers and students in learning communities are reflective about what is happening, not so much to be evaluative ("How am I doing?") as to the descriptive ("What is going on here?"). Therefore, critical reflection seeks a description of events and the impact made on participants. A shared understanding of what happened and what it means is the goal of reflection and the basis for new instructional decision making.

All social interactions produce meanings that cry out for interpretation. Since the meanings are constructed by the participants of events, the teacher must ask the students what sense they make of what is happening. Reflecting on human events has a moral seriousness, because we do not experiment with human activities; all are real. Dewey's concern for practical commitment in teaching is well-advised. Teachers cannot treat their students as guinea pigs by constructing experiments as a means for satisfying intellectual curiosity. Instead, they must be concerned about the social and personal consequences of every deliberate action. In this sense, the consequences of all social actions are problematic and require reflective treatment. What happens in a learning community is meaningful to the members of that community and therefore demands responsible action. Problem solving within a community is bound to the community in the sense that the concerns of the members of a community define what is problematic to them. Often the perspectives within a classroom are unconscious and not discussed publicly; this means that the problematic orientation of a group can be inaccessible even to insiders. This phenomenon is discussed in Chapter 3, where we turn to the cultural nature of classrooms and schools.

Performance Outcomes and Activities (NJPTS 2, 3, 5, 6, 7, 8, 9, 10)

CHAPTER 2
The Learning-Community Members and Teachers

PERFORMANCE OUTCOMES

Teacher Candidates will—

1. Define roles, responsibilities and propensities of learning community teachers and students (members).
2. Describe the difference between an effective Learning Community teacher with an authoritative style and teachers with a laissez-faire or authoritarian style in traditional classrooms.
3. Describe the difference between an effective Learning Community teacher and an authoritative teacher in a traditional classroom culture.
4. Link specific beliefs to relationships, actions and specific learning-community dispositions.
5. Complete a self-evaluation and report at any given time his/her progress in developing talk and actions for all propensities or dispositions.
6. Demonstrate ability to use small group discussion skills in class.
7. Design a Child Study/Action Research Project (Due at end of Semester).
8. Assess assertiveness, create, implement, and evaluate plan to support or move closer to an assertiveness disposition and actions.

OVERVIEW OF CHAPTER 2 ACTIVITIES

The activities for this chapter are designed to provide opportunities to make connections between beliefs, actions, and the learning-community propensities. To provide these opportunities, the activities focus on self-assessment, on assessments based on observations of teaching and learning, and finally on the propensities themselves.

The activities begin with a self-assessment opportunity (2.1). It provides a structure for identifying the congruence between one's current belief-related actions and the learning-community propensities. A second exercise (2.2) provides you the opportunity to identify actions/behaviors that you would use for each of the functions of schooling, learning community dispositions and the roles for effective group members. A third set of exercises (2.3–2.5) focus on classroom observation, interviews with educators, and reflection focused on the actualization propensity. It is recommended that the other propensities, which were described in this chapter, be explored in a similar manner. Activity (2.6) begins with a semester long child study. Finally, Activity 2.6 provides you with the process for identifying your level of assertiveness.

Please note that the terms *propensities* and *dispositions* are used interchangeably in the program.

Exercise 2.1
Learning-Community Teachers and Propensities

Learning-community teachers hold beliefs and act in ways that are congruent with the classroom learning-community propensities. They work in ways that support their continuous questioning of *what is intended, what is happening, and why they and other members of the community are doing some particular thing.* The purpose of this exercise is to provide you the opportunity to assess your current beliefs and actions to determine their congruence with learning-community propensities.

The propensities identified in the chapter are listed on the following worksheet, which also provides a structure for self-assessment and reflection. For each propensity, identify the beliefs/values that you hold, at this time, that are relative to the propensity. You will identify those that are congruent with the learning community and those that are incongruent.

Part A—Observations

You will do this chart twice, once for yourself as a group member and once as a teacher or leader. First, think of yourself as a member of a group and identify your dispositions that are congruent (that support the propensity) and those that are incongruent (that do not support the propensity). Second, identify your related actions that are congruent and incongruent with that propensity. Third, follow steps one and two again, this time thinking of yourself as a teacher. Fourth, identify the consequences of the identified beliefs and actions for yourself and for others. Fifth, review your self-assessment with a peer, and record additional insights about your actions and their consequences.

Use the following chart on page 95 to provide a structure for tying your prior knowledge and ideas to the concept of learning community. Complete the first section, thinking of yourself as a member of a learning-community. Then complete the second section thinking of yourself as a teacher.

Special Note: *Instructional Leadership* requires that a teacher be authoritative and that they are responsible for student learning and have students actively engaged in learning at all times. It is irresponsible for teachers to permit learners to behave inappropriately or be out of control. Effective planning and assertiveness are two of the indicators of *Instructional Leadership.*

Dispositions	Congruent Values & Actions as a Member	Incongruent Values & Actions as a Member	Congruent Values and Actions as a Teacher	Incongruent Values and Actions as a Teacher	Consequence to you and others of your values & actions as a member or teacher
AS a GROUP MEMBER	AS a GROUP MEMBER	AS a GROUP MEMBER	AS a TEACHER LEADER	AS a TEACHER LEADER	AS a TEACHER LEADER
Identifying common needs and purposes					
Seeing Peers as Colleagues					
Seeking self- and group actualization					
Recognizing other groups as similar					
Reflecting on past actions					
Helping and being helped					
Celebrating accomplishments					
AS a TEACHER LEADER	No responses in this area for member		AS a TEACHER LEADER	AS a TEACHER LEADER	AS a TEACHER LEADER
Instructional Leadership					
A Developmental Perspective					
A Cooperative Disposition					
A Reflective Orientation					

Reflective Insights from discussion with a peer:

Part B. Summary Statement

Not all people have all the propensities listed or have them all to the same degree. However, the absence or severe weakness of a propensity makes a difference because the values and actions connected to the propensities define the learning community culture.

To pull together what you learned from the self-assessment and reflection, first write what you think would be your strengths as a learning-community teacher. Then, taking into account your incongruent actions and values, write about the effect these have on the students you teach. The following chart may help you think through your self assessment.

What Fits You Now	What Doesn't Fit You Now	Questions
Which of the Learning Community ideas do you currently use?	What ideas do you disagree with at this time?	What questions do you have about the content and its applications?
Which ideas do you currently apply that are not congruent with the Learning Community culture?	What ideas do you have trouble applying?	What actions do you need to take in order to develop the Learning Community Teacher dispositions?

Exercise 2.2
Identifying Behaviors that are Necessary for Effective Implementation of Learning Community Roles and Dispositions (Knowledge)

All members (members, teachers or leaders) of Learning Communities, whether classroom or professional Learning Communities, are responsible for engaging in roles and dispositions that support the Learning Community culture. These include 7 dispositions and four group roles for members and an additional four dispositions for teachers and leaders.

Whether P–16 students or adults we all need to identify behaviors that are indicators of the dispositions and roles. On the following page are listed the dispositions and group roles. For each one, identify actions or behaviors that you would need to teach to group members in order for a Learning Community Culture to be established and maintained.

Dispositions for Group Members	Behavior or Actions for Group Members		Behavior or Actions for Teachers or Leaders	
	Looks like; Sounds like	Does not look like; Does not sound like	Looks like; Sounds like	Does not look like; Does not sound like
Identifying Common Needs & Purposes				
Seeing Peers as Colleagues				
Seeing Self & Group Actualization				
Recognizing Other Groups as Similar				
Reflecting on Past Actions				
Helping and Being Helped				
Celebrating Accomplishments				

Dispositions for Teachers	Behavior or Actions for Teachers		Behavior or Actions for Leaders	
	Looks like; Sounds like	Does not look like; Does not sound like	Looks like; Sounds like	Does not look like; Does not sound like
Instructional Leadership				
A Developmental Perspective				
A Cooperative Disposition				
A Reflective Orientation				
Other				

Effective Group Member Roles	Behavior or Actions of All Members of Effective Groups		Behavior or Actions of Teachers or Leaders of Effective Groups	
	Looks like; Sounds like	Does not look like; Does not sound like	Looks like; Sounds like	Does not look like; Does not sound like
Encourager. Asks for opinions and information from members				
Synthesizer. Pulls ideas, opinions and information together and makes statements to show relationships among various contributions.				
Organizer. Asks questions and/or provides feedback when group gets off task, to help group refocus on task.				
Contributor. Provides information to further the group's discussion or quality of task completion.				
Other				

ROLES TO BE TAUGHT TO MEMBERS OF GROUPS

Assigned or Negotiated Roles in Effective Groups	Behavior and Actions Demonstrated in Small Groups
Facilitator	
Time Keeper	
Recorder	
Reporter	
Other	

Exercise 2.3
In-Depth Study of One Disposition—Actualization: Openness, Problems and Problem Solving

Purposes and Instructions

One of the learning community propensities is seeking actualization; problem solving is a characteristic of this process. What you are trying to understand is, first, what problems and their responses look like in the classroom setting. Second, you are trying to understand whether what was observed supports or does not support the learning-community propensity. The purposes of the observation are to identify typical problems that arise during a school day in classrooms and the responses to these problems. Schedule opportunities to observe a classroom during the school day, or observe your own classroom if possible. Using the guide below, collect relevant data. Once you have collected this data, look for patterns from which you can infer patterns for dealing with problems. Finally, reflect on the nature of the observed problems and the way they are handled. Determine how the patterns are or are not illustrative of a learning community.

Typical problems that cooperating teachers indicate that teacher candidates face include student defiance, talking over the teacher candidate when he/she is teaching, not following directions among other things. Cooperating teachers indicate that teacher candidates' lack of assertiveness is the major reason they have management problems. Poor planning and weak instruction is another reason. Use this opportunity to observe the problems that experienced teachers face and how both the students and teachers respond to the problem.

Observations

1. It is important that you work with the principal so that he/she will help you identify and explain to the teacher that you will be observing and what type of examples you are looking for in order to increase your understanding of effective teaching and learning.
2. Set up an appointment to observe in a classroom for two half days at different times or on different days of the week.
3. Create an observation form using the format on the following page.

DISPOSITION—ACTUALIZATION

I. DATA COLLECTION FROM CLASSROOM OBSERVATIONS

Describe the Problem Observed. Was it related to Personal, Social, Social Justice, or Academic responsibilities or a combination?	Describe the student's(s') Responses to the Problem you Identified	Describe the Teacher's Response to the Problem you Identified	After Observation Notes Go over your notes and things that you observed but did not have time to record

II. Analysis of Observation Data

Using the notes from your observations, identify the following:

1. Describe the patterns in types of problems you observed.
2. Describe the patterns in individual student's responses to problems.
3. Describe the patterns in the group's responses to problems.
4. Describe the patterns in the teacher's responses to problems.
5. Describe the differences in the teacher's responses to problems and on what the differences appeared to be based.
6. What specific problem solving characteristics did you observe that contribute to actualization of individuals and the group?
7. What additional things would need to occur in the classroom, for actualization to actually result in individuals and or the group?

III. Inferences Based on Observation Data

Using your observations notes and the analysis of data notes, list the inferences you can draw from the problem-solving patterns which you documented in the classroom.

IV. Reflection

Describe how the patterns are congruent or not congruent with learning community dispositions.

V. Checking Out Your Inferences and Reflection Statements

Set up an appointment with the teacher whose classroom you observed. Ask the teacher to tell you about his/her ideas about the role of teachers and students in problem solving. Ask clarifying questions so that you are clear about his/her ideas about what she/he should do to prevent as many problems as is possible and to solve them when they do occur. (Example of a clarifying question: what roles have the students been taught to use when they work in small group?)

VI. Identifying Supportive and Helping Behaviors in the Classroom

Using a structure similar to the one above, identify classroom examples of the other propensities. We suggest having different people look for propensities and sharing the findings in small-group discussions. Interviewing the teachers of the classes you observe will help you to understand the teachers' values and their own interpretations of their own and their students' actions. For example, for the propensity "Helping and being helped," the following will help focus your observations:

A. Observations

1. Observed occasions on which help was asked for

2. Observed occasions on which help was provided

3. Observed consequences to learners and teachers

B. Analysis of observation data: Identify patterns.

C. Inferences: What inferences can you draw?

D. Reflection: How are patterns congruent or not congruent with learning-community propensities?

E. Meeting with the teacher: What are the teacher's values and interpretations about what you observed? Since teachers' actions are based on their knowledge, skills, and what has been reinforced over the years, it is important for you to give the teacher time to reflect on why they are doing or not doing something. Most teachers, upon reflection are very articulate about their actions. However, it is infrequent that they have an opportunity to talk at an in-depth level about their thinking and thus, need a moment to process or follow their actions back to the source. Adults frequently have two types of answers to questions; one is the immediate response and the other is the response after reflection. Our society frequently appears interested in only the quick response rather than the in-depth thoughtful responses.

Exercise 2.4
Speculations about Traditional and Learning-Community Classroom Cultures

Small-Group Discussion

This small-group discussion will provide an opportunity to speculate about the benefits and costs of traditional and learning-community classroom cultures to children, society, teachers, administrators, parents, and teacher educators. The intention is to enable individuals to tie their prior knowledge to the ideas presented in Chapters 1 and 2, and: (1) to raise questions for further exploration, (2) to provide insights into the functions of schooling and their relationships to the learning community propensities, and (3) to clarify the benefits and costs of the two types of classroom cultures. Ideas generated by these deliberations will be challenged, supported, or replaced by ideas formed later.

Here is a plan that provides one means for initiating the small-group discussion. First, select a facilitator, a recorder, reporter, and a timekeeper for the discussion. Then begin by reviewing the functions of school and the learning-community propensities. Next, list examples of the areas of experience and knowledge (e.g., liberal arts courses, experience as a student, discipline knowledge) that should be drawn upon for the discussion. List enough examples to enable individuals to explore from diverse perspectives. The format below is provided as a suggestion for how to record information gathered from the speculative discussion. Example notes are provided.

RECORDING FORMAT FOR DISCUSSION GROUP

Traditional Classrooms

Characteristics of Traditional Type of Classroom Culture	Benefits: What type? To Whom?	Costs: What type? To Whom?	What questions do you want to answer when you next observe?
For example, learning outcomes defined by textbook or state exam	*. . . fits current administrative management models, may be required by state*	*. . . not all children learn, instructional methods usually leave out teaching children to think and focus on memory or steps*	*Who does this benefit?*

RECORDING FORMAT FOR DISCUSSION GROUP

Learning Community Classrooms

Characteristics of Traditional Type of Classroom Culture	Benefits: What type? To Whom?	Costs: What type? To Whom?	What questions do you want to answer when you next observe?
For example, outcomes related to agreed-to functions of school, district performance outcomes and state mandates	. . . gives all children a chance to learn as methods fit nature of subject matter to be learned	. . . traditional teachers need to learn new values and performances; . . . teacher educators need to create LCs and new methods for people learning to teach	Where do teacher candidates and university faculty experience building a learning community?

Exercise 2.5
Discussion Questions Chapter 2

Small Group Discussion

Follow the procedures established in earlier class sessions for small group discussions. Be sure that your recorder turns in the group notes to the instructor at the end of the session. For this discussion, the reporter should keep a tally of who demonstrates which roles during the discussion. All individuals should be using these in multiple situations and they should have started to become internalized.

1. What are the primary differences between a classroom learning community and a traditional teacher? What effects do these differences have on learners?
2. Which of the dispositions are most needed in your current classroom right now? What would the addition of these dispositions add to the culture? What effects would these have on the learners? How would things change?

3. Describe three activities you could use in the next couple of months that would help to foster the dispositions. What actions would you or the teacher need to take on a daily basis in order to reinforce and establish these dispositions?

4. How do your beliefs and current performances as related to teaching and learning support the teacher dispositions? What beliefs and actions do you have that interfere with your demonstrating the teacher propensities/dispositions?

Exercise 2.6
Child Study

Child Study: Guidelines

The purpose of this child study is to provide you the opportunity to begin to learn to focus on individuals in addition to the classroom group and small groups of learners. Since effective planning is based on the academic and other needs of individual students, it is important for you to begin to develop the knowledge and skills for assessing individual learners. (INTASC STANDARDS 2, 3, 5, 7, 8, 9)

Phase I: TLC 1—Process and Reports

A. Planning and Implementation
1. Identify the 3 students with whom you will work with over the semester or year.
2. For each of the students list all of the information you know about them at this time.
3. Look over your notes on the 3 students and select one about which you are most curious. Describe what you observed that you find interesting. Explain what inferences you are making based on the limited data you have to date.
4. Describe what makes you curious about this child. What is it that makes you think that it is important to choose this student as the first about whom you will learn more?
5. What will you do to learn more about the learner you selected?
   a. Data Gathering:
      (1) What do you say in order to get support from family and student for you to expand your knowledge about this student? Write it out.
      (2) Who would you talk to (family, student, previous teacher, principal, social worker, speech therapist, Title I teacher, special education teachers, principal, others)? Make a list. Are there voices missing?
      (3) What will you ask? Write interview questions for each role group.
      (4) How will you record information from interviews?
      (5) What system will you use to record observations you make during the regular day to day school times?
      (6) Begin a collection of artifacts created by your learner.
   b. Data Analysis
      (1) After organizing your data—
         (a) How did you organize your data? (What organizers did you use?)
         (b) What patterns emerged?
         (c) What hypothesis do you now have?
         (d) What new questions, concerns, ideas, or issues emerged after you learned more about the learner?

(2) Forming generalizations—

    (a) After analyzing your data what do you think is the primary purpose in further study and support of this student?

6. Based on what you learned about this student to this point during the semester what do you recommend as an action that would result in support for the learner and increased achievement? (Create an Action Plan)

    a. Write a summary of the items above and then write a plan of action that you would recommend for this student.

    b. What strategies do you intend to implement? Describe the activities including who from the neighborhood, community and family are involved. Include a calendar of events.

    c. What do you predict will be the impact/result/outcomes if you effectively implement your strategies?

    d. What recording system will you use to systematically collect data that will be useable at a later time?

    e. How will you evaluate the activities, your plan and the outcomes?

    f. What documents will you collect?

B. End of TLC 1 Reports Include:

1. Formal Report to Instructor of Action Research Project

    a. Section I: Introduction including background information and reasons you selected this student to expand your knowledge about;

    b. Section II: Original and later questions and hypotheses; Describe what data you used to change your questions;

    c. Section III: Describe data you wanted to collect;

    d. Section IV: Describe the process you used for data collection and any problems you found and how you solved them;

    e. Section V: Describe how you analyzed your data, what organizers you selected or created, and what you learned;

    f. Section VI: Describe how you carried out your action plan and student responses. Summary of Plan as Implemented.

    g. Section VII: Describe data you collected during implementation of action plan. Describe how you analyzed your data and your findings.

    h. Section VIII: Based on your findings (data) make clear conclusive statements.

    i. Section IX: Based on data make recommendations for next steps that would support this student's progress.

2. Part Two Report to Instructor:

This part of Your Report to the Instructor is *Written* as a letter of information with the Principal as the audience. This part of your report should not be shared with anyone prior to it being signed by your instructor.

    a. Letter to Principal Introduction

        (1) Where did you start—with what you wanted to learn and to do and wanted the student to learn and do?

        (2) Where did you end?

        (3) How did your thinking change?

        (4) In what areas were you trying to help the child develop and grow?

        (5) What was it that made you think that your plan would contribute to the child?

        (6) What seemed to help? What did not appear to help? How do you think the child has benefited from your support?

        (7) What is your assessment of the learner's academic progress?

    (8) When you review your collection of artifacts including those from the student's work what patterns emerge? What insights did you gain from this review?

    (9) What recommendations do you have for supporting this learner in the future?

  b. Letter to Student and Family (Not to be shared with anyone.)

    (1) Write letter in language and sentence structure readable by family.

    (2) Do not include professional jargon.

    (3) Focus letter on learner and not on your actions.

    (4) Describe progress you observed student make during the semester.

    (5) Include suggestions of things that parent and child could do that would support the student's continued progress. Suggestions must be appropriate for the home structure of the student.

3. Attachments

In a folder include your papers, data, notes, initial reports, initial action plan, revised plan, notes to or from those with whom you worked, and documentation of what you and student did and accomplished. This is merely an organized collection of materials relevant to this work.

RUBRIC FOR CHILD STUDY*

Child Study (Potential 56 points) Rubric	
Final Reports	
I. Report to Instructor	
A. Clarity of Thinking and Writing	
5 = the reports are free of jargon and surface language errors; they are consistent in tone and voice with documents prepared for professional peers and a critical public; the format, guiding questions, evidence, conclusions, and recommendations are obviously clear and reasonable; and a coherent case is made in *both* studies with assertions and claims *consistently* supported by *strong* evidence and reasoning.	
3–4 = the reports are free of jargon and surface language errors; they are *generally* consistent in tone and voice with documents prepared for a peer professional audience and critical public; the format, guiding questions, data, conclusions, and recommendations are *generally* clear and accurate (either implicitly or explicitly); an apparent case is made for the learning that took place through the studies and the recommendations flowing from them—most assertions and claims are supported by evidence.	
2 = the reports have a majority of the following attributes: there are some surface language errors and awkwardness in the handling of tone and voice; the style is occasionally too informal for a document prepared for a peer professional audience; the case and arguments made for one or both of the studies is sometimes hard to follow, and has to be inferred (i.e., it is not explicit); the evidence and reasoning are loosely tied to assertions and claims.	
1 = the reports contain a combination of the following: a number of surface language errors and lack of consistency in tone and voice; inappropriate informality in style; the lack of a clear position, case, or strategy to develop one; and the lack of explicit or implicit connections between claims and evidence.	

B. Sound data collection procedures	
3 = multiple sources are used, all of which are pertinent to the questions and hypotheses under study; the modes of inquiry are clear and could be replicated and/or checked out by other professionals;	
2.5 = multiple sources are used, and most seem pertinent to the questions and hypotheses under study; the modes of inquiry are generally clear, although some questions remain—not all could be replicated or reviewed for reliability;	
2 = several sources are used that seem relatively pertinent to the questions and hypotheses under study; the modes of inquiry are generally clear, although not all could be replicated or reviewed for reliability;	
0–1 = the sources of data are limited, and not necessarily reliable; they would be difficult to replicate or substantiate; they are not clear, and obviously opened to contention and/or question.	
C. Originality and Depth of Analysis and Thought	
5 = selective and appropriate use of summary to establish the conceptual framework and foundation for in-depth analysis of the guiding questions, ideas and approaches; clear and logical connections between ideas and evidence are cited; a clear identification of the questions raised and/or problems cited; expected outcomes from the inquiry seem reasonable and needed, or suggest clear implications and show how a youngster's life experience and learning opportunities might change because of them; a youngster's future teachers and parents would clearly value and likely use this report.	
3–4 = somewhat selective and generally appropriate use of summary as a foundation for analysis; generally sufficient data is used to substantiate claims; the analysis is generally reasonable and fairly well connected to some real, identified possibilities; some intended outcomes or implications are addressed as are some of the related requirements for future actions—a youngster's future teachers and parents would learn something new from this report, and would value it.	
2 = predominantly an impressionistic summary with character generalizations; the behavioral evidence is weak, lacking either sufficient or trustworthy data; the analysis seems scattered and without guiding theory; intended outcomes or implications are vague or must be largely inferred; little consideration of the needed experience and/or support needed for the youngster and how its success might be further monitored.	
1 = primarily a list of character qualities with a set of data collected that is not well summarized or integrated; little or no evidence of analysis or of building a case or argument for selected needs; the intended outcomes or implications are not evident, nor are there strategies that are logically grounded in and connected to the information and ideas; little or no reliable evidence is presented.	

Intervention Plan and Carrying out of Intervention

4–3.5 = Intervention includes goals that are tied to data about learner, calendar of events, plan for documentation and evaluation, is clearly tied to findings, uses neighborhood and community resources, events are creative and illustrate non-traditional ways of working on area of the problem or concern. (Second semester includes summary of documentation and evaluation of the intervention and progress toward goals for learner)	
3–2 = Intervention includes goals that are tied to data about learner, calendar of events, plan for documentation and evaluation, is clearly tied to findings, uses neighborhood and community resources. (Evaluation data included in second semester paper)	
1 = Intervention includes description of events to take place, may or may not include use of community and neighborhood resources.	
0 = No intervention included	
E. Grounding in Professional Expertise and/or the Research Literature	
3 = draws appropriately from a wide variety of resources; demonstrates knowledge of key resources, significant scholarly work and/or research pertinent to the questions/problems under study; connects data, professional expertise, and/or research within the framework of the study.	
2.5 = draws from a variety of sources; demonstrates general knowledge of some important resources, works and research related to the substantive areas of study; makes at least some connections among the data, professional opinion, and/or research and theory in the area.	
2 = draws from a limited range of resources; demonstrates limited knowledge of major works and research/theory for the areas under study; makes few connections among the sources of data, external expertise, research and the individuals studied.	
1 = draws primarily from one or two sources; demonstrates very limited knowledge of major works and research/theory for the particulars under study; makes few if any connections among the data, sources of expertise, research reports and individuals cited.	
0 = No literature review.	

II. Initial Letter and Final Letter written to student and member of the family (10 Points)	First	Second
A. Clarity of Thinking and Writing (3 points)		
1. Letter is written using language understood by family.		
2. No jargon is used.		
3. Letter includes examples of the support being elicited (e.g., talk with you) or received from the family.		
4. Letter does not contain anything that might be offensive to learner or family.		

5. Observational data is included.		
6. Generalizations are not included.		
B. <u>Message is positive and supportive of the learner. (4 points)</u>		
1. Specific examples of learner's progress after you worked with learner during the year or at the beginning of the year (since you met learner at beginning of the year) are included.		
2. Specific examples of learner's strengths are included. Ones you observed since you met learner or ones further developed during the year.		
3. Specific examples of something you want to work on with learner (or you suggest next year's teacher begins to work on with the student).		
C. <u>Recommendations for further support of learner (3 points)</u>		
1. Recommendations fit with the analysis and findings reported to principal.		
2. Recommendations are doable.		
III. Initial Letter and Final Letter Written to Principal/Teacher (6 Points)		
A. Clarity of Thinking and Writing (4 pts)		
1. Introduction includes summary of process and project. (2 pts)		
2. Describes what was learned from data. (1 pt)		
3. Describes recommendations for further support of the student. (2 pts)		
B. Message is positive and sportive of the learner. (1 pt)		

*The original child study rubric was created by Judith Lanuer, Ph.D. and Joyce Putnam and used in the Michigan State University Teams 3's-Teacher Preparation Program.

Exercise 2.7
Assertiveness Assessment

During the time you are studying Chapter 2 take the Assertiveness Assessment. Analyze your score and based on your findings, write a set of performance outcomes that will support your continued disposition and actions as assertive or that will move you toward an assertive disposition and actions. The plan will include: performance outcomes, activities, and evaluation methods. At the end of the semester retake the assessment, write a report about your progress and create a data based plan (performance outcomes, activities, and evaluation tools) for you to implement next semester.

CREATING A PLAN TO DEVELOP YOUR ASSERTIVENESS

Getting Prepared to Create a Plan: Given that you are interested in being a successful teacher, the focus of your assertiveness plan must include goals, strategies and situations where you can practice being assertive with P-12 students and educators. Begin your planning with the review of several books whose topic is assertiveness. Find a strategy that, if you create a specific plan and follow through with it, will work for you in increasing your assertiveness.

Assessment: 1. Begin by reviewing your rights. (See table.) 2. Review your assertiveness questionnaire and answer the questions at the bottom of the questionnaire. Then analyze your findings and become clear about when and with whom you have assertiveness problems. 3. Next, specifically describe a minimum of three of your problem scenes. For example: My friend Karl (who), when we carpool to our field placement (when), often goes on and on about his problems with his lesson plans (what). After listening to him for several weeks I now just try to look interested and think about something else (how). He is my only way to school and I think if I interrupt him he will get angry and think I just don't care (fear). I would like to offer suggestions to him, ask him about my problems, and discuss how to solve our lesson plan problems (goal).

    Davis, Eshelman, and McKay (1988) suggest that your problem scenes "…include who the person involved is, when it takes place (time and setting), what bothers you, how you deal with it, your fear of what will take place if you are assertive, and your goal. Always be specific!" (pp. 140–141). The problem scenes help you understand what is going on now and helps you clarify what it is you want or need.

Write Three Goals: One goal should focus on your personal life. Two goals must focus on people and situations you will encounter in school settings as you prepare to become a teacher. (When I am with other teacher candidates, I will initiate give and take discussion about our work, ask and answer questions about how to improve, share my insights and actively listen to others' and support others and myself in our successes.)

Write an Assertiveness Plan: In "The Relaxation & Stress Reduction Workbook," Davis, Eshelman, and McKay (1988), suggest the "LADDER" as a strategy for creating a plan to increase one's assertiveness. You may choose to take an Assertiveness Training class as a major part of your strategy.

Describe how you will evaluate your progress toward your goals: In order to be clear about the progress you are making (formative evaluations) and when you have really achieved your goal (summative evaluations) you will need two ways to evaluate your progress. How will you document your progress as you go along? What would have to occur for you and others to say that you achieved your goal?

ASSERTIVENESS QUESTIONNAIRE FOR TEACHER CANDIDATES

(This questionnaire is adapted from Sharon and Gordon Bower's *Asserting Yourself*.)

In the "A" column check those items that apply to you. In the "B" column rate all of the items from 1-5 for discomfort.

1.	Comfortable
2.	Mildly uncomfortable
3.	Moderately uncomfortable
4.	Very uncomfortable
5.	Unbearably threatening

Who are the people with whom you are non-assertive? When do you behave non-assertively?
What do you want that you have been unable to achieve with non-assertive styles?

A. B.
— — parents
— — classmates
— — strangers
— — old friends
— — person of other gender
— — employer
— — 1-5 year olds
— — spouse or mate
— — salesclerks, waiters
— — more than two or three people in a group
— — asking P-12 students to do something
— — taking charge of elementary students
— — taking charge of middle school students
— — asking peers for help
— — asking authority figures for help (professors, cooperating teachers, principals)
— — taking charge of secondary students
— — people of different ethnicity
— — people of different race
— — parents/guardians of students

A. B.
— — asking for help
— — asking questions
— — taking charge
— — explaining an idea
— — dealing with attempts to make you feel guilty
— — getting constructive negative feedback
— — getting general positive feedback
— — asking authority figures for help
— — giving specific negative feedback
— — giving specific positive feedback
— — asking for a date or appointment
— — asking for service
— — taking or sending back things that are not right
— — saying no
— — asking to be included
— — going to a new environment

A. B.
— — approval for things you have done well
— — to get help with certain tasks
— — to get others to do the thinking for you on a project
— — more attention or time with significant others
— — more time with cooperating teachers
— — more time with professors
— — confidence in speaking up when
— — something is important to you
— — confidence in speaking up when
— — something is important to your students
— — to have a feeling of helplessness and the sense that nothing ever really changes
— — to change majors
— — greater comfort in new situations
— — greater comfort in situations where you are a minority
— — comfort with people who supervise you
— — to be listened to and understood

Who are the people who threaten you?

What situations threaten you?

How does non-assertive behavior contribute to the achievement of the things you want?

The items in the table below are presented by Davis, et al., (1988, pp. 133-134).

MISTAKEN TRADITIONAL ASSUMPTIONS	YOUR LEGITIMATE RIGHTS
1. It is selfish to put your needs before others' needs.	You have a right to put yourself first sometimes.
2. It is shameful to make mistakes. You should have an appropriate response for every occasion.	You have a right to make mistakes.
3. If you can't convince others that your feelings are reasonable, then you must be wrong, or maybe you are going crazy.	You have a right to be the final judge of your feelings and accept them as legitimate.
4. You should respect the views of others, especially if they are in a position of authority. Keep your differences of opinion to yourself. Listen and learn.	You have a right to have your own opinions and convictions.
5. You should always try to be logical and consistent.	You have a right to change your mind or decide on a different course of action.
6. You should be flexible and adjust. Others have good reasons for their actions and it's not polite to question them.	You have a right to protest unfair treatment or criticism.
7. You should never interrupt people. Asking questions reveals your stupidity to others.	You have a right to interrupt in order to ask for clarification.
8. Things could get even worse, don't rock the boat.	You have a right to negotiate for change.
9. You shouldn't take up others' valuable time with your problems.	You have a right to ask for help or emotional support.
10. People don't want to hear that you feel bad, so keep it to yourself.	You have a right to feel and express pain.
11. When someone takes the time to give you advice, you should take it very seriously. They are often right.	You have a right to ignore the advice of others.
12. Knowing that you did something well is its own reward. People don't like show-offs. Successful people are secretly disliked and envied. Be modest when complimented.	You have a right to receive formal recognition for your work and achievements.
13. You should always try to accommodate others. If you don't, they won't be there when you need them.	You have a right to say no.
14. Don't be anti-social. People are going to think you don't like them if you say you'd rather be alone instead of with them.	You have a right to be alone even if others would prefer your company.
15. You should always have a good reason for what you feel and do.	You have a right not to have to justify yourself to others.
16. When someone is in trouble, you should help them.	You have a right not to take responsibility for someone else's problem.
17. You should be sensitive to the needs and wishes of others, even when they are unable to tell you what they want.	You have a right not to have to anticipate others' needs and wishes.
18. It is always a good policy to stay on people's good side.	You have a right not to always worry about the goodwill of others.
19. It's not nice to put people off. If questioned, give an answer.	You have a right to choose not to respond to a situation.

RECOMMENDED READINGS

Bellah, R. N. (1985). *Habits of the heart: Individualism and commitment in American life.* Berkeley: University of California Press.

Cohen, E. G. (1986). *Designing group work: Strategies for the heterogeneous classroom.* New York: Teachers College Press.

Dewey, J. (1939). *Intelligence in the modern world.* Ratner, J. (ed.). New York: The Modem Library.

Huffman, J., Hipp, K. A. (2000). *Creating Communities of Learners: The interaction of shared leadership, shared vision, and supportive conditions.* Paper presented at Annual AERA meeting, New Orleans, LA, April.

Norlander-Case, K. A., Reagan, T. G., and Case, C. W. (1999). *The professional teacher: The preparation and nurturance of the reflective practitioner.* Jossey-Bass Inc., San Francisco, California.

Popper, K. (1974). *Unended quest: An intellectual autobiography.* LaSalle, 111. The Open Court Press.

Putnam, J. (1982). *Planning for a Classroom Learning Community.* AERA Annual Conference, NY, NY. March.

Putnam, J. (1983). *Classroom Management and Organization: Teacher Decisions For Establishing a Learning Community Classroom.* Annual AERA Conference, March.

Schaps, E. (2003). *Creating a school community.* Educational Leadership, ASCD. March, Volume 60, Number 6, pp. 31–33.

Schwab, J. J. (1976). Education and the state: Learning community. *The great ideas today.* Chicago: Encyclopedia Britannica, Inc.

Shaughnessy, J. (1998). *Initial guidelines on becoming a learning community.* OERI Event No. 36, November 16. Northwest Regional Educational Laboratory, Portland, Oregon.

The Culture of the Classroom Learning Community

When teachers begin to establish a classroom learning community, students invariably feel strange at first. The mental routines of ingrained habits are hard to break, and most students have been acculturated to traditional kinds of classrooms and schools. Such acculturation takes place without students being aware of it, and thus they see the traditional classroom as normal and the learning community as strange, even abnormal. In order to make progress toward accepting the classroom learning community as the norm, they must first experience a new acculturation. Typically, when people experience transitions from one culture to another, they experience feelings of loss and failure. Leaving behind familiar, traditional classrooms therefore feels bad to students, even though the classrooms they have experienced may have been hostile or oppressive.

Any transition from one culture to another is painful, no matter how beneficial the new one will ultimately be. William Perry (1978) writes about the grief involved in having to give up a part of oneself in order to move on to a new stage in life: "It comes to me as a sort of theorem, that when you have taken one step in development, you cannot take another until you have grieved the losses of the first" (p. 271). Perry's comment rings true to teachers who see how wrenching change can be for children. The depth of the changes we propose in classroom organization and instruction becomes clearer when we understand the changes in cultural terms. This chapter describes the classroom as a culture, and also describes and gives examples of classroom action research which provides teachers with a systematic way to obtain feedback and engage in professional reflection.

The use of the word "culture" for what goes on in classrooms makes it possible to understand the complexity of classroom organization and the assumptions which operate in them. Any social unit can be defined as a *culture*. Schein (1985) describes cultures as agencies that teach their members "the correct way to perceive, think, and feel in relation to [their] problems" (p. 9).

A culture may also prescribe *what* the group members are to think—that is, the content of acceptable thought. This content is often perceived as "common sense" and thus is taken for granted. What is taken for granted is powerful stuff within a community, because it drops out of awareness; it becomes "the way things are." A culture's basic assumptions shape the meanings the members make of the world: their working theories about reality. It is necessary to distinguish between cultural theories and the overt behavior of the members of the culture. If all our behavior were driven by theory, we would be automatons, determined by cultural norms. However, our behavior is a curious combination of individual responses to contextual situations and responses which are theory-driven. The result is that we can never be sure, when observing an instance of human behavior, whether what we see is a cultural artifact or a response to a given situation.

For example, students may leave the classroom promptly at the end of the last school period, rarely staying around afterward to socialize or to ask questions. Interpreting this pattern of behavior as a symptom of a theory about the classroom culture might be a mistake, because school bus schedules may require students to leave quickly. Only through an examination of the layers of cultural meanings embedded in the class and the school could it be determined whether the rush for the door was a function of culture or a pragmatic necessity.

Seeing the classroom learning community as a culture helps us to understand why outsiders (such as principals) frequently misinterpret what is happening inside a class. Hall (1977) labels this cross-cultural incongruity "situational irrationality." That is, behavior that seems sane in one context can appear crazy in another context. The school principal's office operates under the rules of its own culture. For example, when a principal interrupts instructional activities with frequent announcements on the public address (PA) system, teachers and students may well perceive the principal's behavior as strange, even crazy. Likewise, the classroom learning community's use of public argument about classroom rules may seem strange to the principal. A principal might say, "You don't ask students what to do, you tell them!" To him, classroom forums may seem ridiculous. The clash of two culturally different frameworks produces irrational interpretations.

If we are to understand what seems irrational in another culture, we must try to get inside that culture. The difficulty should not be minimized. Hall tells us that we experience

obstacles in the path to understanding because culture equips each of us with built-in blinders, hidden and unstated assumptions that control our thoughts and block the unraveling of cultural processes. (1977, p. 220)

We cannot expect to understand the hidden and unstated assumptions of a culture from the outside. Because cultures are wholes in which all the parts interact with each other, it is necessary to know how the whole system is put together.

LEVELS OF SCHOOL CULTURE

The process of coming to understand a particular classroom culture is like peeling an apple. Three layers, or "levels," as Schein (1985) calls them, can be distinguished. The surface layer, like the apple skin, is the obvious, visible appearance of the classroom. The next layer represents the expressed values and goals of the class. Like the pulp of the apple, this is the meat of the classroom learning community's business, what it professes to be about. At the core of the apple is the basic program for reproduction. The seeds contain genetic codes which can create an entire apple tree. Just so, at the core of a classroom's culture are the basic assumptions of the learning community.

The class members' level of conscious awareness diminishes at each layer. That is, the material which belongs to the first level is easily identifiable and comes from the features of the physical and social environment—for example, the physical look of the classroom. The next level is less obvious and often requires interpretation or verification—for example, the classroom motto or list of rules posted on the board. The deepest level of the culture is often hidden—namely the operational theories or basic assumptions of the teacher and students. Table 3–1 shows the hierarchy of these levels.

Level 1: Physical and Social Environment

As soon as one walks into a classroom, the first level of culture is apparent. Look around. Are the walls decorated or drab? Are the windows clean? Are the materials on the wall student productions or commercial photographs? Are the classroom doors open? Are you met by someone as you enter? Do students speak to you? Is the noise level high? Or is the room quiet? If it is quiet, what kind of quiet prevails—a serious, get-on-with-the-business-at-hand quiet, or a quiet-as-a-funeral-parlor aura? Are the students smiling, or are their faces dead-pan? All these features and more are indicators of the classroom culture.

An experienced educator can easily interpret the signs of classroom culture at this level. For example, describing an effective bilingual school, T. P. Carter and M. L. Chatfield (1986) wrote: "A walk

TABLE 3–1   Levels of Classroom Culture

Levels	Awareness
Level 1: Physical and social environment	
Artifacts, decorations, and creations (e.g., student art on walls; trophies)	Visible but often not decipherable
Use of space, environmental conditions (e.g., clean or dirty walls; open or closed doors)	
Overt behavior of students (e.g., high or low noise, cheerful or depressing talk)	
Level 2: Values and goals	
Statements testable in physical environment (e.g., "We're proud of our room"; "This is an open community"; "We're a risk-taking class."	Some degree of awareness
Statements testable by social validation (e.g., instructional goals; philosophy; motto; morale)	
Level 3: Operational theories	
Theory of reality, time, and space (e.g., seeing time and space as common or scarce commodities)	Tends to be: Invisible
Theory of human nature (e.g., believing people to be basically trustworthy)	Taken for granted Often unconscious
Theory of ethics and morals (e.g., believing that substance is more important than appearance)	
Theory of knowledge (e.g., believing that knowledge is contextual and right answers are situational)	

Source: Adapted from Schein, 1985, p. 14.

through the grounds and classrooms of Lauderbach community school can provide a keyhole peek at a community school process" (p. 201). They go on to describe features of that environment which make it distinctive: senior citizens going in and out of the classrooms, a volunteer center where a busy group is assembling materials for instruction, the sounds of people chatting in several languages (English, Spanish, and Chinese), and a brightly painted yellow chair used in the center of a story reading area as the chair of honor. Anyone who visits this learning community long enough will be able to interpret the meaning of these visible signs of its culture.

Level 2: Values and Goals

At the second level of a classroom culture, meanings are less clear and need further investigation. Every organization has an avowed mission, a set of goals and expressed values about its function. A classroom learning community may have a list of curriculum goals or a display representing its beliefs about learning hanging on the walls. The meanings of such a list or display, however, may not be immediately clear. If a class member says, "We're proud of our classroom," an observer needs to check on whether pride is made evident by such signs as care and upkeep of the physical environment. If there is a sign over the chalkboard that reads, *Mens sana in corpore sano* ("A sound mind in a sound body"), the observer needs to ask how the sign relates to the classroom instructional philosophy. Are all the students encouraged to participate in sports? Do the physical activities include both group and individual development activities? Are the most prestigious students the athletes who play on the varsity teams? Are academic achievements valued equally with sports? A variety of evidence should be collected to clarify the meaning of the motto within a particular classroom culture. Without such deeper probing, we cannot tell whether the motto is a living reality in the culture or simply an empty Latin phrase.

This level of classroom culture deals with the values embedded in the activities which fill the time of the class members. Does the teacher emphasize "academics"? You can interview the students to discover how that emphasis is actualized. How much time do they spend in core subjects? What is the percentage of time going to math/science? Are they required to do research papers and essay examinations? On the other hand, if the teacher asserts a belief in joint decision making with the students, you can inquire about how much time is set aside for cooperative planning and discussion of materials. If the teacher's role is seen as a catalyst for student learning, how time is used as a resource can be interpreted as a function of the teacher's commitment to collaboration. An example of evidence that value is placed upon teacher/student collaboration is regularly scheduled brainstorming sessions between teachers and students, in which students get as much "air time" as the teacher does.

The values expressed by the members of a classroom culture may or may not be verified by examining the evidence for their public effects. A teacher may value the idea that intrinsic rewards are the best motivators for learning, but a researcher who studies the classroom instruction may find heavy emphasis on controlling rewards and negative feedback. When students are continually exposed to negative feedback about their competence and when teachers repeatedly use extrinsic rewards, students' sense of well-being and intrinsic motivation are undermined (Deci, 1975). If there is incongruity between expressed values and observed behavior, an observer will have to look more deeply into the classroom culture in order to understand its basic assumptions.

Level 3: Operational Theories

The operational theories of any organization are the basic assumptions its members hold about the meaning of what they do in their group. Operational theories are often not part of the group members' immediate awareness. Often they are not even written down and can only be inferred from the overt behavior of the group members. In school classrooms, there may be rules governing how the world of a particular classroom works. For example, Florio-Ruane (1983) reported on the effects of a collaborative effort between university researchers and school teachers to study writing instruction. The goal of the study, Florio-Ruane wrote, was "to bring together members of different speech communities to deliberate on the problem of teaching writing and, perhaps, to create a new speech community marginal to the others" (1983, p. 5). However, the speech community of the teachers and the speech community of the researchers had different histories, cultures, and professional objectives. Florio found that the two groups had very different views of both the data collected and the very forum for discussion itself. She wrote, "Another surprise concerned how the institutional structures within which we worked supported those differences" (1983, p. 6).

At this deepest level of cultural meaning, the relational structures are *designed* to support the particular perspectives of the group members. The theories about the nature of the world that lie at the core of a social organization, whether large or small, act like rules for conduct. For teachers, the rules of practice give meaning to the activities of the practice. Cherryholmes describes the process this way:

> These rules vary from those that are legally constituted, such as state laws concerning educational assessment; to those that are explicitly stated but not legal, such as school district policies concerning grading systems and final exams; to those that are not stated at all, such as beliefs that teachers use to guide their testing procedures within a classroom. (1985, p. 65)

It is particularly these rules—the beliefs of a teacher—that constitute the compelling force for practice within a particular classroom culture. Operational theories may touch on any of the basic areas of human relationships and knowledge. They may be theories about what is real and may find expression in how a teacher uses space within the classroom or time within a schedule. In some classrooms, for example, everyone is in a great hurry. The teacher and students may tell you things like, "There is so much to do and so little time to do it." They may be unaware that they are acting out a deep operational theory about the scarcity of time. Nevertheless, they feel uncomfortable unless they are talking fast, running to and fro, and generally expressing that they feel pressed for time. Likewise, seeing how some teachers use the space in their classrooms will reveal their underlying operational theories. In one classroom, for example, the teacher's desk may be barricaded like a fortress against incursions from students and the rest of the world. The teacher does not have to be aware of such an operational theory to be driven by it.

Operational theories may touch on human nature, such as the belief that people are basically trustworthy or untrustworthy. Theories of ethics can also be found at this level, communicating what is "right behavior." Even matters of knowledge itself may be governed by unwritten rules, or operational theories. The current emphasis on rote learning and recitation in teaching the "basics" may be governed by a belief that knowledge is a fixed set of facts to be mastered.

The operational theories of a culture are hard to pin down, precisely because those who are driven by them are often almost unconscious of them. A teacher must deal with this level of culture as the primary content for assessment if major cultural changes are to occur. Many failed attempts to develop learning-community classes can be traced to teachers' failure to understand the culture children bring to the classroom at the start of the year. When people cross cultural contexts they frequently fail to see the basic assumptions and beliefs of those who live and work in the different culture.

From our perspective, Schein's (1985) view that culture is the outcome of group learning is critical. He tells us that when people encounter a common problematic situation and figure out how to solve it, this is the stuff of culture formation (p. 183). It follows that if a culture is to change, a new set of circumstances must be created in which people can share experiences. "New shared experience begins the formation of a new culture" (1985, p. 184). We will argue that this is precisely what successful learning-community teachers do—namely, create conditions under which students can share a problem-solving enterprise, come to consensus about norms of interaction, and support each other's achievements.

If the cultural assumptions of a classroom are to evolve into learning-community assumptions, the process must be consistent with the kind of propensities discussed in Chapter 2. That is, learning communities are constantly in the process of learning about community. Learning-community teachers create situations in which students struggle with their old ideas, recognize those that are ineffective, and seek new ideas which may be tested in public discourse. This kind of change happens inside the heads of students. Students who are members of classroom learning communities are, in effect, engaged in the process of modifying their culture.

THE INDIVIDUAL AND THE GROUP

The process of creating a learning-community culture demands that the teacher be sensitive to the dialectical relation between the one and the many, the individual and the group. Relating to a group is a double-edged sword. The group both protects and threatens personal autonomy. The group is a source of both safety and stress for the individual. People bargain about the roles they play within the group in order to reduce stress and maintain protection. Visible in the early stages of group development are dissensions, nonconformity, and conflicts about the norms of the group and the roles individuals are expected to play. Conflict is the *normal* state of affairs in healthy groups, because individuals cannot fully satisfy all the group's expectations. R. Schmuck (1980) explains the interaction between the individual and an institution, such as a school, as a many-faceted phenomenon.

> The school is a social institution composed of a multitude of parts. It is an integral aspect of the community, a complex organization, and a loosely knit collection of small groups. It is also an arena in which faculty members work together or apart, in which committees are formed or dissolved, and in which crucial problems are solved or ignored. The school is a complex organization composed of both formal and informal relationships among faculty members and between faculty and students. (1980, p. 169)

The organization of group culture can be experienced by the individual as frustrating and confusing. This is particularly true of social organizations such as classrooms. Individuals can be caught in "double binds" (see Bateson, 1972), in which social rules cause personal problems but are not open for discussion. Social stress results when individuals encounter choices in which whatever they decide will be considered wrong. Many social organizations are "limited-learning systems" (Argyris, 1982) because they limit individual choice and choice-testing. In fact, the function of some groups in relation to the individual is to reduce the number of options from which the individual can choose. "They require that members assume the double layers of vulnerability inherent in camouflage and games of deception. Discussion of these conditions is taboo, as is discussion of the process by which one is caught in them" (Argyris, 1982, p. 94).

A culture which is run by a limited-learning system forces individuals to take the blame for design failures. Cut off from specific feedback, individuals cannot sort out the sources of their reputed errors. For example, Coleman (1966) found that black children tended to believe success was a matter of luck, which is beyond a person's control, whereas white children more often attributed success to effort. Likewise, low-status children are often described by teachers in terms of personal characteristics, such as personality traits. When teachers do this, they are likely to be pessimistic about the prospects of change or improvement for such students. It makes a funny kind of sense; if teachers think that one trait or another causes students to succeed or fail, then a given student either "has it" or "doesn't have it." If a teacher holds such a perception of reality, it is easy to sort individuals out as "good" or "bad." When students internalize such thoughts about themselves, a dangerous inertia sets in.

Explaining students' progress in terms of an abstract construct, such as a personality trait, denies them access to concrete feedback about what they do and its effects. If they do not have access to community feedback about the effects of their actions on others, they cannot change their actions to match the effects they intend. Thus, traditional classroom cultures are seen as limited-learning systems which *both* protect individuals from awareness of error *and* condemn them to feelings of not being in control. The traditional classroom creates conditions which protect and threaten individuals at the same time. This double binding makes it inevitable that little genuine learning or self-correction can happen in such classrooms.

What tends to block change from traditional classes to learning communities can be summarized by the following model for limited-learning systems, based on Argyris.

1. *Teachers and students hold operational theories which drive their actions.*

2. *Faced with difficult issues that are threatening, teachers and students avoid expressing negative feedback and thereby feel like they are losing control. Such reaction increases the likelihood that errors will continue.*

3. *In order to maintain a sense of control, classroom members will tend to focus on the faults of others. Teachers, for example, can play endlessly with the diagnosis of student problems and "what we can do with them."*

4. *Teachers will tend to focus on higher level abstractions when dealing with threatening issues. This avoids relating issues to observable data and concrete explanations. For example, some teachers blame school disruptions on the abstract notion of the "Social and Economic Status" of their students.*

5. *Teachers and students alike have an aversion to testing theories and inferences. Perhaps such aversion is prompted by the suspicion that such testing might produce information that is hard to explain or put attributions in doubt. (1982, pp. 98–99)*

When a classroom is a closed collective, the individuals in the class have highly ambivalent feelings toward the class. They feel simultaneously attracted to the group for protection and repelled by the group's behavior. As a result, teachers and students tend to feel isolated and neglected. Classrooms, however, need not be isolating and self-sealing. In the next section, we describe a better option for organizing the classroom and interactions of the individual and the group: the learning community.

LEARNING COMMUNITIES AND COOPERATIVE GROUPS

We believe cooperation to be a powerful mechanism for changing classrooms into learning communities. However, cooperation is difficult to learn in a competitive society. Even though there is convincing evidence (see Kohn, 1986) that competition is detrimental to our well-being, its hold on social organizational structures and our private value systems continues to be strong. In fact, competitive values in the traditional classroom are so common that no single change will dislodge them. The quality of class-rooms cannot be improved simply by reorganizing their social structures, nor by changing the beliefs of individual teachers. Our consumeristic society reinforces competition so pervasively that it seems natural to many educators to focus on winning, finding the best speller, the fastest mathematics calculator, etc., as though all learning were analogous to athletic contests.

Much current research has focused on the benefits of cooperative learning for students (e.g., Slavin, 1983; D. W. Johnson and R. T. Johnson, 1985; Slavin et al., 1985). There is also research which recognizes that much of what has been learned about cooperative learning with students also applies to teacher cooperation (e.g., Arnn and Manigeri, 1984; Rorschach & Whitney, 1986). We have learned that cooperation is more effective when groups are relatively small, problems complex, and tasks interdependent (D. Johnson et al., 1981). Further, we have learned that it is necessary to teach participants in cooperative groups the roles they will play in making the group effective (E. G. Cohen, 1976; Glachan and Light, 1982). As a result, we know a great deal about what it takes to create a cooperative teamwork environment.

Cooperation requires teambuilding activities. Arnn and Manigeri (1984, p. 34) described the features they found that made teamwork effective. First, teamwork is functional, drawing upon the collective strengths of team members and producing more than individuals can produce by working separately. Second, teamwork is attractive to the team members, who derive satisfaction from the collaboration and the resulting productivity. Their sense of pride is linked with feelings of competence and worth. Third, teamwork is intentional, not a random event. Team members recognized that they are developing teamwork skills, which takes time and energy on their part. Fourth, teamwork increases the perception that all members make specific contributions to achievement of results. A team is more than simply a collection of individuals who happen to work in a group; the members of a team blend the knowledge and skills of many into a new reality in which individual strengths are enhanced and individual weaknesses are compensated for.

The reason we focus on developing teamwork in cooperative groups is our conviction that successful inquiry requires the shared perceptions of others, what is often called "feedback." If students are to gain an understanding of the impact they have on the world, they must have access to the observations and judgments of others. Only through inquiry can students become aware of what can be done to improve their learning in any of the four domains of school learning: academic subjects, personal growth and responsibility, social responsibility, and equity. If this is to happen in classroom learning communities, the level of leadership offered by the teachers must be of a very high order. Teachers need to be sensitive to the human needs of security and safety, while at the same time challenging their students with new visions of what they may become. Students need both structure and challenge. K. Green (1985) shows how dangerous mere technical skill is when educators see themselves as managers without roots or professional conscience. The qualities that Green believes educators need are *rootedness* and *vision.* Students need a strong association with the past to protect them from capricious change while they explore the frontiers of their own learning and understandings. Without such a balance, they have too many possibilities and can become lost. Thus, the teacher's leadership in a classroom learning community is essential, to maintain the tension between historical roots and visions of what students may become.

Cooperative groups are seen as the means for inquiry into possibilities. In cooperation, students learn to develop a propensity to seek reliable (tested) data to inform their choices of what they can do and what they are becoming. Elizabeth Cohen (1972) suggests that multiability group work is also a "strategy for solving two common classroom problems: keeping students involved with their work, and managing students with a wide range of academic skills" (p. 6).

Sharan (1987) provides a definition: "Cooperative learning stresses that knowledge is given meaning not only by the content of study but also by the social milieu, including peers and teachers, and the process by which it is pursued" (p. 6). Sharan, along with others, believes that when students study by giving each other mutual assistance and also getting help from the teacher (not merely by working exclusively with the teacher or alone), they find their studies more motivating, more informative, and more instructive. However, he points out that groups must be managed in ways that will "enhance and promote the contributions of individual students, and do not impose upon them conformity to the wishes of some people within the group" (1987, p. 6). R. Schmuck (1985) links cooperative learning to Dewey's philosophy about learning through social discovery. He states that "a key to unlocking Dewey's philosophy about cooperation and learning is in the development of group dynamics as a discipline" (1985, p. 2).

D. W. Johnson and R. T. Johnson (1985) reviewed their findings concerning research conducted over several years. They identified implications for using cooperative group strategies. These implications may be treated as guidelines for developing cooperative learning activities:

1. *Cooperative procedures may be used successfully with any type of academic task, although the greater the conceptual learning required, the greater will tend to be the efficacy of cooperation.*

2. *Whenever possible, cooperative groups should be structured so that controversy among group members is possible and is managed constructively.*

3. *Students should be encouraged to keep each other on task and to discuss the assigned material in ways that ensure elaborative rehearsal and the use of higher level learning strategies.*

4. *Students should be encouraged to support each other's efforts to achieve, to regulate each other's task-related efforts, to provide each other with feedback, and to ensure that all group members will be verbally involved in the learning process.*

5. *As a rule, cooperative groups should contain low-, medium-, and high-ability students.*

6. *Positive relationships and feelings of acceptance and support should be encouraged.*

7. *The more positive attitudes toward subject areas should be capitalized on by encouraging students to take further math, science, foreign language, and other classes of interest.*

8. *The fairness of joint outcomes should be discussed and pointed out to students. (D. W. Johnson and R. T. Johnson, 1985, pp. 120–121)*

We find that teachers who use a technical approach to the teaching of cooperative learning or multiability tasks tend to drop the strategy from their repertoire of teaching activities after some time passes. By "technical approach" we mean employing the schema of cooperative tasks in instruction without possessing background information on the principles of cooperative learning. Teachers from two different schools in which we work provide examples of responses to opportunities to learn more about cooperative learning/multiability tasks in their classrooms, after they had tried a technical approach. These teachers indicated that they had used cooperative grouping strategies before and were not impressed with the results. They were frustrated by the downtime they observed in their groups. They saw no positive consequences that compensated for the increase in noise levels. The group products were frequently achieved by one or two members and thus did not represent true cooperation. In these schools, we observed faculty who had established a routine for student work in small groups. The routine included telling students, "Move to your cooperative learning group and. . . ." In the groups, the work was done by one or two members, and teachers did not check to see that all students had acquired the expected learnings or contributed to products.

Effective teaching is more than applying principles of management or instruction to create popular learning activities. Effective teaching is more than teacher performance. Students need to be motivated to learn. Instructional materials should be at the appropriate level, neither too easy nor too hard for the students. Sufficient time should be allowed for the activity. Furthermore, correct subject matter information is required to facilitate student learning. Slavin (1987d) suggests that quality, appropriateness, incentive, and time are four important elements for effective instruction in cooperative groups (p. 92).

Cooperative learning groups with multiability tasks designed into the learning activities seem to provide many positive results for student achievement. Slavin (1987) compared projects in which cooperative learning methods were used in elementary or secondary classrooms. He found that a pattern of research "supports the usefulness of cooperative learning for improving self-esteem and for improving the social outcomes of schooling, such as intergroup relations, (and) attitudes toward mainstreamed students" (1987d, p. 242).

Slavin also points out that the primary debate about grouping over the past half-century has "revolved around the questions of whether instruction must be adapted to students' individual needs" (1987d, p. 89). He suggests that accepting the idea that students need to have materials taught at their level does not force us to use any particular form of instructional grouping. He observes that "there are many means of accommodating student differences" (p. 89). Teachers have been grouping students for efficiency for years. However, most grouping patterns have involved ability; that is, students were sorted by level of school tasks achieved. Slavin has shown that ability-grouped lessons are ineffective for increasing student achievement. He suggests several alternative means of grouping that offer considerably better evidence of effectiveness, do little or no psychological damage, and have less segregative potential than ability grouping. Heterogeneous grouping distributes students in groups with mixed ability levels and is the most common learning-community pattern of organizing classrooms. Slavin points out that cooperative learning in particular has a strong integrative effect on students of different ethnic backgrounds who work together cooperatively on a routine basis.

Once students have been organized into cooperative groups, some regrouping for reading and/or mathematics is possible. The research indicates that such regrouping can be effective instructionally, if two conditions are fulfilled:

> *Instructional level and pace must be completely adapted to student performance level, and the regrouping must be done for only one or two subjects so that students stay in heterogeneous placements most of the day . . . [for] mathematics . . . and reading and mathematics taken together. (Slavin, 1987e, p. 113)*

Slavin concluded that when grouping had been done without adapting the pace or level of instruction or in more than two different subjects, regrouping had no benefits.

What happens to high- and low-ability students when they are grouped was studied by Lucker and associates. They found that there is "no support for the notion that high ability students might suffer in interdependent classes while low ability students improve" (Lucker et al., 1976, p. 121). The results of this study show that students in "the upper 25% on reading ability benefited just as much from the interdependent method as did students in the bottom 25%" (p. 121). When first-graders were studied by stratifying gender and academic ability, the results showed that cooperative interaction, as compared with competitive and individualistic learning, promoted higher achievement and the discovery of superior cognitive reasoning strategies (D. Johnson et al., 1981).

Warring et al. (1985) suggested that positive relationships between male and female elementary-aged students may be built by participation in cooperative learning activities (p. 58). In two studies of sixth- and fourth-graders, these researchers found that relationships formed within cooperative learning situations did generalize into unstructured class, school, and home activities (p. 53). Slavin and Madden (1979) reported that programs involving cooperative interaction between students of different races are most likely to improve race relations in desegregated schools (p. 169). Likewise, Sharan and his colleagues (1984) reported that "cooperative-learning methods promoted distinctly more positive social integration of the two ethnic groups than the Whole-Class method, whereas the latter produced some negative social-psychological consequences for the students in these desegregated classrooms" (p. 137). They concluded that "ethnic contact alone in classes conducted with traditional forms of instruction that lack cooperative, egalitarian patterns of social interaction is not adequate to the task of promoting interethnic integration in multi-ethnic classrooms" (p. 137). R. T. Johnson and D. W. Johnson (1980) support the idea that, when handicapped students are liked, accepted, and chosen as friends, mainstreaming becomes a positive influence on the lives of both handicapped and normal-progress students.

Effective cooperative learning schemes could take advantage of current theories and empirical findings associated with cognitive approaches to learning. Certain findings are particularly relevant to cooperative learning activities: oral summarization (Ross and DiVesta, 1976) and elaboration (Reder, 1980). Research on metacognition (e.g., J. H. Flavell, 1979; Markman, 1979; Schallert, 1982; A. L. Brown, 1978) shows the difficulty students have in monitoring their learning. Cooperative learning groups help to structure situations to promote student metacognitive behavior. This is equally true for students with learning disabilities.

There is a temptation to make grouping—any sort of grouping—the focus of classroom organization, rather than using it as a means for teaching personal/social responsibility, academic subject matter, and social justice values. It is easy to get caught up in the "management of the grouping activities" to such an extent that the "real purposes" for their use are lost. Keeping in mind both long-range and immediate goals helps students to succeed. Carter (1986) studied teachers' ideas about classroom management and tried to map out how teachers' thinking about management is organized. She described teachers who "solve the problem of order" from two perspectives. One type "guided students through work paths that made progress, movements, and smoothness comparatively more probable" (p. 51). A second type focused on those students "who were most likely to block the flow of the activity and reduce the probability of its success" (p. 51). The first type of teacher focused on the central goal and worked to achieve that end. The second type of teacher was "distracted from the key role of the activity" (p. 50). This sort of teacher used mental resources to persuade a few visible students to become involved in the class and to afford them opportunities for participation. It seemed as though the "real goal" was order rather than student achievement.

Implementing classroom learning community can lead to many beneficial consequences for both teachers and students. Still, like all genuine change in social organizations, a move toward learning-community structures for the classroom can create stress. We believe that the real danger, however, comes from trying to keep change from happening. Research into the problems of teacher stress has found that the kinds of stress that are the most debilitating are those associated with boredom and unexciting routine. Blase (1986) reports that when teachers lose enthusiasm for their work, "maladaptive behavior develop[s], behavior that teachers believe result[s] from work stress and its unrelenting interference in their ability to provide quality education experiences for students" (p. 31). In other words, while developing a classroom learning community is difficult, even demanding, it is not associated with the kind of stress Blase discovered among teachers who felt that they had to concentrate on rote and recitation instructional strategies. The "back-to-basics" curriculum movement has created more demands for teachers to "cover" subject matter, thereby linking teachers to a kind of "production quota" in student scores on standardized tests.

Goodlad's massive study (1984) produced ample evidence that rote learning, memorization, fill-in-the-blanks exercises, and multiple-choice testing dominate the contemporary classroom. Blase's (1986) research shows the link between teacher stress and an overemphasis on rote learning and mediocre instructional objectives. Teachers find it difficult to remain positive about their teaching when they feel locked into the routine of lower-order cognitive operations. When teachers lose a sense of control over their own destinies, they become like their students, many of whom likewise feel that the school is alien territory and the subject matter is not relevant to their future.

The cultural nature of learning communities provides arenas of trust and a sense of personal empowerment. Fallows (1989) writes about American culture in comparison with the Japanese culture and observes that whether or not Americans are able to draw upon their roots in releasing their creative capacity "depends on two things: whether the radius of trust is large enough and whether people feel they can control their destiny" (p. 25). The classroom learning community supports individuals acting decently toward one another, while at the same time it promotes their creative capacity to own their actions. The educational goal of American democracy—educating all U.S. citizens so that they will become a literate and responsible electorate—may have its best chance for fulfillment in classroom learning communities.

Performance Outcomes and Activities (NJPTS 2, 3, 5, 6, 9)

Chapter 3
The Culture of the Classroom Learning Community

PERFORMANCE OUTCOMES

Teacher candidates will

1. Define and describe levels of classroom culture.
2. Identify the cultural characteristics of three different classrooms and one school.
3. Identify the things that at this time are blocking the change from a traditional to Learning Community culture in one classroom or this class and accurately list those things. List those things that you could do that would bring you closer to becoming a Learning Community teacher/leader.
4. Practice in planning for an investigation, identifying questions, carrying out data collection, analysis, synthesis, reporting, and identification of next questions.
5. Practice working effectively as a small group member, identifying problems and strengths for group work, practice giving constructive feedback to small group members, practice receiving and acting on constructive feedback from members of small group.

OVERVIEW OF CHAPTER 3 ACTIVITIES

The activities below focus on the classroom as a culture. Exercise 1 provides an opportunity to identify levels of classroom culture. Exercises 2 and 3 provide an additional opportunity to assess levels of culture related directly to measurement and evaluation practices and the broader contexts of the classroom (e.g., families). Finally, exercise 4 provides an opportunity to assess one's goals as a professional and to explore the congruence between such personal goals and the goals of a learning community culture.

Exercise 3.1
Classroom Cultures

In this chapter, we suggested that thinking about the classroom, as a culture is helpful to the learning community teacher. The purpose in this exercise is to provide the opportunity for you to identify levels of classroom cultures, and to reflect on the classroom in which you are currently assigned for your field work.

A. Work with two or three of your colleagues to make a list of all the specific examples of hidden agendas (e.g., use of busywork to avoid providing instruction, ignoring classroom behavior in order not to have to be assertive) that you can identify. Make the list in such a way as to illustrate the three levels of classroom culture and their meanings.
B. Go through your list and specify aspects of classroom culture that reflect your professional values and perspectives. Discuss these aspects with your peers or colleagues. Write about your findings.
C. Compare your group's conclusions with those of other colleagues (preferable in small groups). Based on this discussion with your colleagues, what further questions and issues about the classroom culture and hidden agendas (e.g., use of busywork to avoid providing instruction) remain for you to consider?

Exercise 3.2
Potential Effects of Measurement/Evaluation on Learning Communities

As you know, our talk may reflect the values on which our actions are based. We say *may reflect,* because some people do not "walk their talk." That is, their talk and actions are incongruent.

Measurement and Evaluation are an important part of the Learning Community classroom and the lives of the Learning Community members. It is critical for Learning Community teachers and their students to know the level and quality of the learners' accomplishments so that group, individual and whole class work fits the needs of the learners. Thus, in a Learning Community school, classroom assessments and evaluations are built into the culture as desirable and helpful. In many of today's schools and classrooms measurement and evaluation have gotten a bad name due to the values, talk and actions of educators.

Purposes of Exercise

The purposes of this exercise are as follows:

1. to identify the impact of school measurement and evaluation practices on the four functions of schooling discussed in Chapter 1,
2. to make connections between school practices and the levels of culture,
3. to assess the current role of measurement, assessment, and evaluation in the culture of the school and classroom, and
4. to provide on-going application and improvement of your skills in identifying questions for you to study, in writing clear interview questions, in carrying out interviews, in analyzing interview data, and reporting what you learn.

A. Interview Questions and Data Collection

Write questions that you will use to interview one principal or assistant principal and one teacher in the same school. The same content is appropriate for the 2 role groups; however, the *structure* of the question will need to change depending on the role group. For example, a question asked of the principal *(As principal what do you believe are the most important evaluations carried out in your school? How are the data from these evaluations used by you, the teachers, and the students? When your students leave here, how will they feel/think about being evaluated? What do your teachers think about their evaluations? How do you and the teachers use these data?)* needs to be altered for a teacher *(As a teacher, what do you believe are most important assessments and evaluations that you carry out with your students? If I interviewed your students, how would they say you and they use the data from your assessments and evaluations? How do you use these data?).*

Other types of questions that you will consider include the following: How does this school carry out the measurement or evaluation responsibilities? What goes on in the halls, classrooms and playground that contribute to the students developing a sense of the constructive contributions of evaluation to their learning? What do you say and do, that contributes to the students seeing the importance of using evaluation data?

Using some of the suggestions offered in Chapter 1, construct an interview data collection sheet for each of your interviews.

After creating the lists of questions and the data collection sheets you will use with both role groups, try out your interview questions on someone that is not in your class. During this interview, focus on the clarifying questions that the interviewee asks you, and his/her responses. If you are getting responses that seem unrelated to what you want to learn, then rework your questions and pilot them again with a new person. Be sure to time the practice interviews so that you can accurately inform those you will interview.

B. Interviewing

Contact the non-educators you will interview, explain the purpose of the interview and what you are learning, and set up a time and place to meet with them. Be sure to tell them how long the interview will take. Also, explain that you will be analyzing data and reporting to your class. Inform them that you will not be using their names, but rather the role group they are representing. To set up appointments with the principal and teacher contact them directly and work with them to identify the time they can meet you.

Be early for your interview so that you have your data sheets, questions and other materials all ready to begin the interview on time. Begin by reintroducing yourself, communicating the purposes of your interview, the question(s) that you are studying and thanking them in advance for meeting with you.

After each interview take a few minutes and review your notes. Add any information that you observed, but did not have time to write down. Clarify any ideas that you wrote but which were confusing as you reread your notes.

C. Analyzing, Reporting and Reflecting

Once you have collected all of your data, review your notes and figure out what patterns are embedded in the data, what anomalies are apparent, and what comparisons and contrasts are evident. Be sure to compare your interview data with observations you made in this school during previous assignments. Review your data analysis and identify the types *of biases that may be built into* your data. For example, did you interview only a teacher whose classes always score in the top percentiles or grade levels?

D. Review the levels of culture. Then answer the following questions:

1. What did you learn about the culture related to measurement, assessment and evaluations?
2. What data supports your judgments?
3. What did you learn about the functions of schooling and culture of the school and classroom?
4. What impact might measurement and evaluation have on the functions of schooling as outcomes? What is your rationale for this answer?
5. What levels of culture are apparent in the interview responses? What supports your judgments?

E. Reporting Data

After completing your data analysis and reflection write a report using the following format:

1. Title and author page
2. Introduction
3. Describe what question you were studying and what you were trying to learn about that question that are related to the purposes of this Exercise.
4. Explain the process you used for your study. Include preparation and both interviews.
5. Present your data as collected. Include both observation and interview data.
6. Describe your findings using the analysis of both observation and interview databases you completed.
7. State your current conclusions.
8. Describe your new questions and indicate why these came to mind after your study.
9. List of references used in presentation of report
10. Appendix A: Observation Field Notes
11. Appendix B: Interview Field Notes
12. Appendix C: Letters sent with the approval of instructor and letters to be sent after instructor approves them.

REPORT RUBRIC: CONTRIBUTIONS OF MEASUREMENT AND EVALUATION TO SCHOOL AND CLASSROOM CULTURE AND FUNCTIONS OF SCHOOLING

	0 Must be Revised in order for teacher candidate to receive any credit	1 Below minimal performance level	2 Close to Standard	3 Meets Standard at the Sophomore Level	4 Exemplary Includes skills expected later in Program
Introduction	Includes a paragraph that simply restates the functions as presented in the text	Includes expanded statements of functions and presents basic question for study	Includes clear, easy to understand explanations of functions of schooling, measurement and evaluation	Includes all of 2 and links text information to observation data to clarify and illustrate ability to make linkages	Introduction includes background, related studies, questions and an abstract
Question	Question restates one or more of purposes; Questions short, don't all fit topic or role group or long list redundant questions not organized	Questions are in authors own words but only restate the purposes of the Exercise. Question organized for smooth flow in interview	Includes purposes of assignment; Questions are clear & linked to the task purposes, organized for flow in interview; May tie to former interviews or observations	All of 1 & 2 plus Questions are clear and tied to functions, culture and Learning Community	Questions are at level of MA thesis requirements
Study Process	Disorganized did not know what he/she was doing.	Somewhat systematic but got off track at times	Systematic	Wrote clear plan and implemented it with minor errors; Level of questions kept getting more complex	Organized and carried out a systematic study before as planning & implementation had no errors
Data	Does not appear	Includes a few ideas that may be embedded in data	Identifies patterns, anomalies, compares and contrasts	Same as 2, plus ties anomalies, comparisons and contrasts to research questions	Data presented in graphs and charts and tied to primary and secondary research questions
Findings	Appear to be made up; not clearly linked to data	Appear to have some links to data but are questionable	Findings might or might not be replicable, make sense	Findings clearly tied to data; could be replicated	Same as 3, plus linked to new questions to be investigated
Conclusions	Not clear or tied to data	Some tied to findings, some not	Clearly tied to findings	Clearly tied to questions, findings	Same as 3, plus tied to new questions

	0 Must be Revised in order for teacher candidate to receive any credit	1 Below minimal performance level	2 Close to Standard	3 Meets Standard at the Sophomore Level	4 Exemplary Includes skills expected later in Program
New Questions	Superficial if included	Clearly stated question, but does not have a clear tie to the study	Clearly stated 2 or 3 questions, clear ties to data, analysis and conclusions	Same as 2 plus questions take the study further or in new direction while based in these data	Level of new questions at MA level.
References	From text	From text and 1 other	From text and 3 others	From text and 5 others	List of references reflect question
Biases	Does not include ideas	Superficial ideas included	1 or 2 biases reported and based on instructor's analysis; they are potentially correct ones	Identifies two or three probable biases and explains clearly why there are potential problem with the data. Uses information from notes to support judgments	Same as 3, plus cover all possible ideas that come up in the data.
Interview Notes	Notes are skimpy; may focus on one element; inferences may be restatements of notes	Notes include 2 or 3 elements; inferences are weak but included	Includes clear notes on teacher, students, environment, & content; inferences are clearly linked to data, includes talk and actions that contribute to functions	Accurate and clear ties of teacher and student talk and actions to all 4 functions of schooling	Used participant observation research analysis of data.

Totals

Project Score: Comments:

Exercise 3.3
Linking Learning Community Classroom to Community

Relationships of Classroom to School, Family, Neighborhood, and Community

The purpose of this exercise is to assist you in thinking about the relationship between the culture of the learning-community classroom and its relationship to the family, neighborhood, and general school community culture outside the classroom. The chart below will help you with your assessment. After you complete the assessment you will then participate in the small group discussions. Questions for the discussion group follow the Chart.

DATA SHEET: Tying Prior Knowledge about Family, Neighborhood, School, Special Needs Students & Classroom Culture to Classroom Learning Community Ideas.

Name_____   Date _____

What do you see in the classroom that is linked to professional knowledge you have been studying, relative to family, parents, and community?	List of Observations		What did you study?
What do you infer is the impact of these things (actions, talk, environment) on the teachers and students?	List Impact on Teacher's Actions/Talk	Impact on Student Talk/Actions	Impact on Environment
What would be the impact on the teacher and students of ignoring the students' families, the neighborhood and the community at large?	List Impact on Teacher	List Impact on Students	List Impact on Parents
What levels of culture are evident in your data?	List Level I Evidence	List Level II Evidence	List Level III Evidence
What did you observe about how special needs students are incorporated into the class?	List types of differentiated learning styles and abilities plus special needs students may have	List the impact of special needs students on the other students and the teacher.	

Small Group Discussion

The purposes of this small group discussion include giving each teacher candidate

1. the opportunity to share his/her observations and inferences with peers and to receive feedback about their ideas;
2. the opportunity to hear other's observations and inferences and provide them with specific feedback about their ideas;
3. the practice in stating his/her ideas and backing them up with data; and
4. the opportunity to consciously link the ideas of family, neighborhood, community, special needs candidates, functions of schooling, classroom culture to the ideas of a classroom Learning Community.

Select a facilitator, recorder, reporter, and timer. Then review the purposes of the small group discussion. Organize an agenda so that each person shares the information on their data sheet. Each person in the group must give specific feedback about the presenter's observations and or inferences. Members of the group should carry out the small group roles in ways that assist the group in making worthwhile progress.

At the end of the session, the group will create a summary of the data provided and a statement about what they learned from information shared and feedback provided.

The group leader will turn in the data sheet created by each person in his/her group, the summary statement, and the statement of what was learned to the instructor prior to their leaving class.

Exercise 3.4
Accurate Self-Assessments and Setting Professional Development Goals

---

ASSESSMENT INSTRUMENT
MY GOALS AS A TEACHER

Purpose of the exercise to help you to assess your goals and priorities as a teacher candidate or in-service teacher and thereby to become more reflective.

INSTRUCTIONS:

Step 1   Suppose for a moment that you are a veteran teacher about to be recognized for your outstanding service to the profession. The statements in each category below (A to I) represent ways in which you might be especially remembered by your students. Think about what you might like them (or others who know you as a teacher) to say about you.

Step 2   Rank-order the items in each category below as: 5—most important to me; 4—important to me; 3—neither important nor unimportant to me; 2—not very important to me; 1—least important to me."

RANK ORDER CATEGORY

A. _____   It was a meaningful class.

_____   Students learned a lot and cared about getting a good education.

_____   I helped them to feel good about themselves.

_____   I was fair.

_____   They thought that the teacher knew what was good for them and administered it for them.

A Example Ranking
4
5
3
1
-

B. _____ The school or class was interesting and enjoyable; students liked it.

_____ I taught them a lot and made them learn; learning something and accomplishing a task was the important thing.

_____ I cared about their ability to deal with reality, take responsibility, and be interdependent.

_____ I was a good teacher.

_____ I was "stronger" than they were. I had the attitude "This is something we have to do."

B Example Ranking
4
5
3
1
2

C. _____ It was a good year. They had a good feeling about the year, and it was a good part of their lives.

_____ I gave them a boost in reading or math.

_____ I helped them to be good citizens—to accept that there are rules we have to follow.

_____ I dealt with them on the level.

_____ I stuck to what I said and made them do what was required.

D. _____ They remember the good times, the special things we did in class.

_____ They got some new knowledge.

_____ I taught them to respect the rights of others.

_____ I had a sense of humor.

_____ I provided strictness and clear discipline.

E. _____ They remember people they met in the classroom.

_____ Academically, things stuck in their minds; they remember the subject matter. I was interested in them; I was a caring individual, big on love.

_____ I helped them to feel good about themselves.

_____ They thought that the teacher knew what was good for them and administered it for them.

F. _____ They felt comfortable in my class.

_____ I made them want to learn the material.

_____ I cared about their ability to deal with reality and take responsibility.

_____ I was a humanist.

_____ I was "stronger" than they were. I had the attitude "This is something we have to do."

G. _____ They remember the good times, the special things we did in class.

_____ They learned a lot and got a good education.

_____ I helped them to become good citizens.

_____ They came to me with problems and could talk to me.

_____ They stuck to what I said; I made them do what was required.

H. _____ They remember people they met in the classroom.

_____ I really made them work and learn the material.

_____ I taught them to respect the rights of others.

_____ I was a person who affected their lives in a positive way and helped them to get started on the right track.

_____ I was strict.

I. _____ I was helpful.

_____ They learned a lot about school subjects.

_____ I was well-liked and am remembered with a smile.

_____ I was soft-spoken with my students.

_____ I made them behave.

Step 3   To score the instrument, circle your "5" responses in each category. These responses represent one way to categorize your goals. Each category (A to I) includes five rather broad goal orientations that teachers might hold to be central in classroom organization and management. The goals are listed below in the order in which they appear in each category. Count the number of 5's you circled for each goal, and enter the total in the space in front of each goal.

ORDER OF APPEARANCE of GOAL ORIENTATION IN EACH CATEGORY	Number of "5s" in items A-I	Comments
First: Building a robust learning environment		
Second: Assuring academic/ task-oriented learning		
Third: Socializing personal and social growth		
Fourth: Focusing on student-centered learning		
Fifth: Controlling student behavior		

Example of Data from 2 Ranking Examples ORDER OF APPEARANCE of GOAL ORIENTATION IN EACH CATEGORY	Number of "5s" in Example items A-I	This shows the way the example rankings would be scored
First: Building a robust learning environment		
Second: Assuring academic/task-oriented learning	11 (2 tallies)	Individuals must be knowledgeable if they are to be successful in their career choice and as leaders
Third: Socializing personal and social growth		Social and Personal responsibility critical dispositions for students who will be leaders
Fourth: Focusing on student-centered learning		
Fifth: Controlling student behavior		

Step 4   Now it is time to draw inferences. Some research reports suggest that operating from clusters of these goals enhances how students report on the effectiveness of their teachers. We believe this to be consistent with what we have been saying about the purposes of schooling in the learning community. Which goals represented in this assessment instrument do you believe are congruent with the purposes of schooling for the learning community outlined in this chapter? What rationale can you provide for your answer?

Exercise 3.5
Elements of and Resources from Families, Neighborhood and Community for a Learning Community

DISCUSSION QUESTIONS

Knowing the neighborhood, community, schools, and district in which you learn to teach and when you become a professional is critical to your being an effective educator. It is important because of the relationships you will build with families, the knowledge you will gain about the resources available for your use in order to provide the most effective learning experiences possible for your students. Taking advantage of talking with and learning about the members of the neighborhood, community and district provides you with opportunities to become skillful and comfortable in talking with and learning about others who are different from you.

The purpose of the following items is to provide you with suggestions of areas to consider as you begin the group project. These categories provide a foundation for thinking about your preconceptions, about your first impressions, about ideas you hold that are being challenged or reinforced, about areas that need a focus and about things you may not have yet considered.

1. What do you know about the organization of your school? And what do you need to do (learn) in order to become a more effective teacher candidate at that school this semester?
2. What do you know about the zone or feeder system that your school is a part of and how is it organized? And what do you need to do (learn) in order to become a more effective teacher candidate this year?
3. What do you know about the goals and dreams of your students? And what do you need to do (learn) in order to become a more effective teacher candidate this year?
4. What do you know about the goals and dreams that the families have for their children? And what do you need to do (learn) in order to become a more effective teacher candidate this year?
5. What do you know about the school system or district, how it is organized, it's goals/missions/vision? And what do you need to do (learn) in order to become a more effective teacher candidate this year?
6. What is the school system's position about the use of NJ Core Curriculum standards?
7. What do you know about the school and community and the support-systems they have for their families and your students? And what do you need to do (learn) in order to become a more effective teacher candidate this year?
8. What do you know about the community and what your students experience outside of school? And what do you need to do (learn) in order to become a more effective teacher candidate this year?
9. What do you know about the homes of your students and what they experience outside of school? And what do you need to do (learn) in order to become a more effective teacher candidate this year?
10. Who supports each of your students? If a given student was having a problem, who in their family would you contact "feeling confident" that the student would get the needed support?
11. What are "student support groups"? What is your role in these groups?
12. What is the vision of the "learning communities" as being developed in your school? What is your role in the "learning community" to which you are assigned?
13. How does the work of a learning community and the curriculum and teaching differ from traditional classrooms?
14. What resources are available in the community that you could use to increase the effectiveness of your teaching and the achievement of your students? And what do you need to do (learn) about community resources in order to become a more effective teacher candidate this year?
15. What role do the churches in the neighborhoods around your school play in the children's lives?

16. What roles do the churches play in the schools? (e.g., One Church-One School)
17. What community groups are neighborhood "grass-root" organizations? How do these differ from other community organizations?

Exercise 3.6
Investigation, Analysis of Data and Reporting

Tying your knowledge through a small group study to the neighborhood community in which the school you are assigned for fieldwork is located.

Step One: Preparing for the Group Project.
Start this work by creating a study group that you will work with the entire semester. Each study group is made up of individuals who are assigned to the same school system. Each group can have up to eight members. However, if there are nine members in the class from one district, then two project groups should be established.

Step Two: Self-Assessment.
In order to carry out the group study project of the community it is important that each member of the group complete a self-assessment of his/her current knowledge of the neighborhood and community. The members of the study group should each complete the following self-assessment individually. On your computer write out your assessment using the format below. Once each of you has completed the self-assessment share your findings with the other group members. Once all the members of the group have shared their current information about the community you are ready to move to step three.

SELF-ASSESSMENT

What do you know about Students, School, Neighborhood, and Community Where You are Assigned for Field Experience?

Name: _____ School Assignment:_____ Level: _____ Date:_____

I. Neighborhood
  A. List what you know about the neighborhood in which your school is located.
  B. Explain how each of the items you listed will help you provide higher quality educational experiences for your students.

II. Community at Large
  A. List what you know about the community at large.
  B. Explain how each of the items you listed will help you provide higher quality educational experiences for your students.

III. Students
  A. List what you know about your students. P–6 select six students to write about and 7–12 select one student from each of six classes.
  B. For each student explain how what you know about him/her helps you provide higher quality educational experiences for him/her individually.

IV. Schools
  A. List what you know about the school to which you are assigned.
  B. How will you use this information to improve the quality of educational experiences you provide for your students?

    C. List what you know about two other schools (at different levels that you are assigned).

    D. How will you use this information to improve the quality of educational experiences you provide for your students?

V. School System
    A. List what you know about the school district.

    B. How will you use this information to provide high quality educational experiences for your students?

VI. Professional Knowledge
    A. List the professional knowledge about schools and communities that you gained from your university course work that you will be able to use in order to provide high quality educational experiences for your students.

    B. How will you use this knowledge to improve the educational experiences you provide your learners?

VII. Knowledge Gain from Personal Experiences
    A. List the knowledge you have gained from your experiences about the linkages between school and community.

    B. How will you use this knowledge to provide high quality educational experiences for your students?

Step Three: Organizing for the Group Project.

Your study group will work together during the semester and will create a report (using technology) that will be presented to all the members in the course during exam week. Establish your project groups.

Now that you have completed your self-assessment and shared the information with the group, the next task is to design, implement and report a research study that increases your knowledge about the impact of neighborhood and community on schools, schooling, learners, learning and teachers and teaching. The purpose of this task is to provide experiences that will support your development, skills, and comfort level in exploring the neighborhoods and communities in which you are assigned or in which you accept teaching positions. Below we provide a list of items that form the foundation for your study. Without this ability, you are not and will not be able to make the linkages between school and community that are necessary for effective teaching and high student achievement.

The first step in this study is for you to use the data from your individual self-assessments and the following topics to create your research questions. Be sure to include the study of areas that you found you lacked in depth knowledge when you did the self-assessment, then include questions from each of the categories listed below.

Topics for your Research
    A. Race, Diversity, Gender, Ethnicity, Racism

    B. Education

    C. Sports

    D. Religions

    E. Business

    F. Social Structures in Community

    G. Fine and Performing Arts

Second, based on your network within the neighborhood and community create an investigation plan and calendar. Using your current contacts will help you get started in your investigations. Keep your eyes open to finding individuals who would be effective community resources for learners in the school system. Be sure to indicate what contribution they can make and how a teacher would make contact with them. If your school assignment is in a neighborhood and community in which you do not have any contact, we then suggest that the historical society in the community is a good place to begin your investigations. Your investigations will result in data and a network map of your contacts.

Third, view the videos Angela's Ashes, and Denzel Washington's film, Antwone Fisher, (2002). You should look at each of these stories and identify the effects of poverty on learners and learning. Then list the stereotype comments that middle and upper class individuals usually make about individuals who are at the poverty level. Analyze your list and for each comment describe one thing that you will do as an educator to not let the values underlying stereotype comments impact your expectations for learners, what you will teach, the standards you will hold and the methods of instruction you will use in your teaching practice.

Fourth, write up your research report using the following format.

a. Title and author page.
b. Introduction and rationale for why you selected your research questions.
c. Describe what questions you studied and what you were trying to learn.
d. Explain the process you used for your study.
e. Present your networking map.
f. Present your data as collected. Include both observation and interview data.
g. Describe your findings using the analysis of both observation and interview databases you completed.
h. State your current conclusions.
i. Describe your new questions and indicate why these came to mind after your study.
j. List of references used in presentation of report.
k. Appendix A: Observation Field Notes.
l. Appendix B: Interview Field Notes.
m. Appendix C: Photos of your work and contacts in the community.
n. Appendix D. Information about Community Resources that could be used by teachers in the community.
o. Appendix E. Small Group Rubrics for Each Group meeting.

Fifth, using your research report as the foundation, create an audio-visual presentation that presents your experience in carrying out the study and your findings. Be sure to include all members of the group in the presentation.

COMMUNITY STUDY REPORT WRITTEN AND AUDIO VISUAL

Criteria	0	1	2–3	4
Rubrics for Small Group Work	One or two turned in; unable to distinguish problems resolved	One or two rubrics showed resolutions of small group problems	Uninformative rubrics turned in for all group meetings	Rubrics tell story of the group's development over the semester.
Goals of Study	Goals not stated	Goals are stated clearly but there is not any to the self-assessment data.	Goals linked clearly to self-assessments of all members of the group	Same as 2–3 plus clear presentation of individual's needs after looking over topics
What was learned (new information) about neighborhood and community	New information is the type that can be gathered from historical writings, no investigations into the communities are apparent	New information from written documents and field trips into community; At least 3 of the research topics are included	Same as 1 plus observation and interview data support by pictures, tapes, and documents that are evidence that all members of the group investigated deeply the nature of the research topics; All topics are included	Same as 2–3 plus organization of new information is linked through illustrations to self-assessment and research topics.
Resources for Report	Few Resources used; Used only references suggested in course materials or class.	About one field trip and one interview per member of the group is basis for report; wide use of written resources	Group field trips into the community and interviews were above 16; wide use of written resources including original documents for important aspects of the history	Rich data base is result of field trips into diverse parts of the community and from interviews with diverse members of the neighborhood and community
Use of Data	No concrete examples of how data will be used by educators to increase the effectiveness of teaching and learning	One or two examples of how new information will be used by educators to increase the effectiveness of teaching and learning	Multiple accurate examples of how the teacher candidate will make use of these data or similar data to increase teaching and learning effectiveness.	Same as 2–3 and Resource pamphlet created for distribution to others and to the schools in which the teacher candidates are assigned

COMMUNITY STUDY REPORT WRITTEN AND AUDIO VISUAL

Criteria	0	1	2–3	4
Interviews	Not all members carried out interviews with individuals different from themselves	At least half of the group interviewed diverse people	All members of the group interviewed diverse people and collected important reported information	Same as 2–3 plus follow up interviews were carried out when groups found new questions based on first interview data
Writing	See Report Writing Rubric			
Audio Visual	No Audio Visual Report Provided	Overheads or Poster reports presented	Group used computer or video technology to tell the story of their study and findings	Quality of audio visual presentation is such that it can be used by the school district to introduce new teachers to their community

REFLECTION GUIDE

Now look over your responses to the self-assessment instrument once again. Now that you have completed your work in this chapter and had time to think about it how were your responses congruent with the learning community purposes of schooling? What changes if any would you make in the self-assessment at this time? In what ways do your choices about goal orientations interfere with learning-community goals? What is your rationale or explanation for your responses to either or both of these questions?

RECOMMENDED READINGS

For reading some of the original sources used in this chapter, we recommend the following texts. Additional references are also provided for your perusal.

Brophy, J. E. (1982). Classroom organization and management. (Occasional Paper 54). East Lansing: Michigan State University, Institute for Research on Teaching.

Brophy, J. E. and Putnam, J. G. (1979). Classroom management in the elementary school. In D. L. Duke (ed.). Classroom management: The seventy-eighth yearbook of the National Society/or the study of education. Chicago: The University of Chicago Press.

Good, T. L. and Brophy, J. E. (1987). Looking in classrooms (4th ed.). New York: Harper & Row.

Goodwin, D. L. and Coates, T. J. (1976). Helping students help themselves: How you can put behavior analysis into action in your classroom. New Jersey: Prentice-Hall.

Johnson, J. (1977). Use of groups in school: A practical manual for everyone who works in elementary or secondary schools. New York: University Press of America.

Stanford, G. (1977). Developing effective classroom groups: A practical guide for teachers. New York: A & W Visual Library.

SECTION IV

The Classroom Learning Community

OVERVIEW

Praxis involves critical reflection—and action—upon a situation to some degree shared by persons with common interests and common needs. Of equal moment is the fact that praxis involves a transformation of that situation to the end of overcoming oppressiveness and domination. There must be collective self-reflection; there must be interpretation of present and emergent needs; there must be a realization. (Greene, 1978, p. 100)

Because the classroom learning community is both an idea and an action, it is a form of *praxis*. This means that discussing the implications of cooperative organization of learning environments is not enough; there must also be what Maxine Greene calls "transformation" and "realization." This section presents a pedagogy for the classroom learning community (Chapter 4) and two examples of learning communities, one at the elementary level (Chapter 5) and the other at the secondary level (Chapter 6). We believe that it is important not only to write about learning community in a theoretical context, but that actual implementations of learning community in real classrooms also need to be described. The two classroom implementations presented in Chapters 5 and 6 are very different from one another, but we would expect them to be different, and not simply because of the difference between elementary and secondary school curricula. Every learning-community classroom is different from all others, because people do act on their common interests and needs in their unique situations.

These examples offer very different interpretations of learning community, but each can be described as a version of learning community. Both chapters provide samples of what learning-community teachers may think about, how they may interact with students, and the kinds of activities typical of their classroom organization. We selected these cases because they represent contrasting goals for the students in each classroom. The primary teacher described in Chapter 5 focuses on developing personal and social responsibility and academic learning as major goals for her class. The secondary teacher described in Chapter 6 (who is a composite of several secondary teachers we studied) focuses typically on academic learning goals for her students.

In Chapter 4 we present a pedagogy for learning community in terms of stages of group development. The stages are discussed and arranged sequentially for purposes of analysis and explanation. However, in real classrooms, as in life generally, events are not as orderly nor as neat as they may appear in the pedagogy. Often, things happen simultaneously. In the two case studies presented in Chapters 5 and 6, the boundary lines between stages are fuzzy. For example, Forero in Chapter 5 starts thinking about norms and expectations from the start of her school year planning, and so stage I and stage II activities overlap in her classroom. Likewise, Henderson in Chapter 6 starts working on resolving student conflict about norms for participating in math exercises on the first day of class.

Therefore, the examples provided in these chapters are to be understood as representative. They were selected to illustrate particular visions of the learning-community teacher. They are not to be considered exhaustive; nor is either of them intended to represent a single "right way" of "doing learning community." Instead, they provide food for thought, ideas, and practices to compare, and they suggest professional visions of what classroom learning communities could be.

A Pedagogy For Learning Community

Thinking about the classroom as a **learning community** may profoundly change the way one thinks about teaching, the relationship between teaching and learning, and the profession of teaching as work. This chapter explains why this is so by offering a pedagogy for learning community. The Greek word *paidagōgos* referred to a slave who escorted a child to school. Over time, the word came to designate a teacher, one who guides or leads students through lessons. "Pedagogue" literally means leader of youth and—like the word "pedant," which originally meant "schoolmaster"—has acquired a pejorative connotation, namely, as one who overly values book learning. Those who enter the teaching profession have to come to terms with the U.S. public distrust of teachers, which is confusing to new teachers because the public, at the same time, values schooling.

The negative associations connected to the words "pedagogy," "pedant," and "teacher" can be explained historically. The role of the teacher in previous societies was performed by someone of lower class (in ancient Roman, often a Greek slave). Further, the content of the lessons often was not seen as essential or practical. In the Middle Ages, teachers were clerics, churchmen, who supposedly had their eyes on other-worldly rewards. Also, teaching has focused traditionally on language instruction. Professor Higgins, Shaw's chauvinistic linguist in *Pygmalion,* insists that "class" and "culture" are matters of "right speaking." Dealing with words seems to the public somehow less vigorous or less authentic than dealing with deeds. In early days in the United States, a schoolteacher was apt to be a schoolmarm. The young woman who practiced at teaching until she got married was so common an image that teaching soon came to be considered "women's work."

Some modern writers (such as Thelen, 1981) suggest that the original linkage between teaching and slavery continues in current usage when teachers are characterized as public "servants." This interpretation of public service is open to dispute. On the one side, the linguistic history of the word "service" links it to "servitude." On the other side, service is associated with broader democratic concepts which emphasize citizen responsibility for the affairs of the community and state. Perhaps the way one chooses to "read" the word "service" may well be related to how the concept of "work" is understood. Negative interpretations of service may derive from European notions about work itself as suspect. Laborious or mechanical work has been considered "servile" and to be preformed by "servants." A laborer may be accepting this negative interpretation of work when he refers to himself as "just a working man." The Jeffersonian democratic tradition, however, breathed a fresh breath of air into the term "service." The idea of public service became a higher ideal, as all work became respectable. Ironically, in the United States, where work with one's hands became identified with real work, those who work with their minds have come to be seen as somehow less vital.

The authors, however, choose to see public service as a positive value in a democratic society. Teaching as public service is quite properly called "pedagogy." We use the word **Pedagogy** to mean the theory of teaching that informs and shapes the practice of teaching. The pedagogy we present in this chapter provides a framework for thinking about developing a classroom learning community. Chapters 7 to 12 present recommendations for procedures and activities for organizing and managing a classroom learning community. This chapter may be considered a pedagogy for learning community because it describes a theory of classroom organization and management which attends to the developmental and educational needs of children as *full human beings,* rather than dealing with the control and management of students. What is managed in this pedagogy are instructional designs, materials, schedules, roles, rules, and routines—*not students.* Students are conceived of as partners with teachers in the joint enterprise of teaching and learning.

Many of the sources for our thinking about the classroom learning community have been identified in preceding chapters. However, before we continue with specific guidelines for thinking about the classroom as a learning community, it may be useful to review the research, practice, and perspectives which provide evidential and conceptual support for constructing learning-community classrooms.

Cooperative Learning

Both research and theory about the instructional value of cooperative learning support the concept of multiability grouping in some kind of collaborative social structure. The research of such leaders as David Johnson and Richard Johnson in Minnesota, Robert Slavin at John Hopkins, and Elizabeth Cohen at Stanford, among many others, offers convincing evidence that individuals fare better in cooperative groups than in competitive settings. Collaboration is more satisfying than competition. Again and again, researchers have demonstrated that students at the lower end of the learning pace or rate make more gains and achieve higher test scores in heterogeneous cooperative groupings than in homogeneous competitive groupings. Those at the advanced end of the developmental continuum maintain their achievement levels while advancing in their social development. Everybody wins; who can criticize instructional strategies with such an outcome?

Conceptual Learning Theory

Since the work of Jean Piaget (1896–1980) and Lev Semyonovich Vygotsky (1896–1934), psychological research on the development of reasoning and language in children has emphasized the contextual nature of learning. Advances in understanding of how children acquire and process information have been associated with an appreciation for the complex interplay between the child and the social environment. Two principles that seem to be agreed upon, whatever the particular learning theory, are: (1) learning is an active process which is deeply contextual, and (2) learning is developmental. Learning happens when students are actively constructing meaning for their experiences, and learning is contextual in the sense that what we learn is linked to where and with whom we learned it. The ability to recall, restructure, and apply information that has been learned seems to be tied to the conditions under which it was learned (Minsky, 1986). When students can shape their experiences into a meaningful pattern, the retrieving of the information is greatly improved. Learning is developmental in the sense that there appear to be stages of growth that are sequential in nature. Change in cognition proves to be something like change in the social order, that is, it is not a continuous, smooth process, but a jump from step to step. A student stays at one stage until she/he acquires enough experience, mastery, or whatever is needed to prepare for the next stage. Then one day, the cocoon splits open and the butterfly emerges. All of a sudden, a child who has been studying mathematical concepts sees new relationships.

Dewey and the Social Nature of Knowledge

John Dewey (1859–1952) was an eloquent spokesperson for the democratic tradition in education (1939, 1933). He was committed to the idea that all knowledge was social in nature. Facts were not facts until they were communicated to others and tested publicly. Dewey defended progressive education because it linked knowledge and action. He believed that the scientific method applied as much to social and political issues as to matters of nature. We see the current interest in action science as an extension of the Deweyian concern to include practical and moral issues in the scientific domain. Schwab's elaboration of learning-community propensities (1976) evolved from Dewey's ideas about the communal nature of knowledge, both its production and its dissemination. Schwab's learning community is democracy in action at the classroom and school level.

Effects of Teaching Research

Since the major paradigm for educational research shifted from studying the characteristics of effective teachers to studying the effects of teaching, significant gains have been made in the knowledge base about teaching. Research on teaching promises to "transform the practice of teaching in the way that the practice of medicine has been and continues to be transformed by medical research" (Medley, 1977). This means that we are better able to begin to separate the valuable from the worthless in the lore of the teaching profession. In learning to ask the right questions about the effects of teaching, we have begun to learn some of the answers. The classroom learning-community conception of teaching as a collaborative act within a social context is supported by this evolving knowledge base on teacher effects. Teaching is both a complex cognitive skill and an improvisational performance (Borko and Livingston, 1989). Teachers must have what Shulman (1987) calls "pedagogical content knowledge," the combining of knowledge about subjects with knowledge about what works to enhance learning, under what conditions. Also, teachers need to have many, varied, and detailed strategies in their heads so that they can respond creatively to students (Yinger, 1987). This view of teaching challenges the traditional notion of teaching as technological mastery of some predefined set of "methods of teaching."

GROUP DEVELOPMENT

The pedagogy for learning community described in this chapter has also evolved from the authors' thinking about the work of Stanford and Roark (1974) and Stanford (1977) and their emphasis on the stages of group development. They originally identified seven stages: beginnings, norm development, conflict, transition, production, affection and actualization. Stanford (1977) later reduced the number of stages to five: orientation, establishing norms, coping with conflict, productivity, and termination. We believe these stages to be genuine developmental stages in the sense that they are structurally essential in building groups and sequentially interdependent. To put it another way, without anyone of these five stages, groups—especially learning communities—cannot be effective. Likewise, the sequential nature of the stages means that the quality of later stages depends upon the quality of the earlier stages. For example, without adequate attention to matters related to "beginnings," such as orientation activities, it would be very difficult for "norm development" to be an efficient and effective experience.

To suggest that the classroom is a learning community which needs to be created anew each year is to suggest a different view of the classroom—to suggest that the classroom is not just a place where teachers "do things to students" so that they may learn. Rather, we take an interactive view of the classroom, as suggested by Copeland (1980). In a learning community, teachers and students alternatively influence and are influenced by each other (Copeland, 1980, p. 164). In a community, members may be of equal status, but they play many different roles with each other, not only throughout the school year, but also during each school day. This chapter describes many roles the teacher and students have to play in order to create and maintain a classroom learning community. Each section deals with a different stage in the learning community.

Throughout the chapter, we emphasize the quality of communication among the members of a learning community. We suggest that attention to the communication content and patterns among students (in student-to-student interaction) is as important as the communication between teacher and student. The current pressures on schools to emphasize academic outcomes (e.g., state assessment tests, basic skills testing, and even minimum teacher competency testing) tend to divert educators' attention away from student growth in personal and social responsibility and the development of democratic social values. Stressing academic outcomes to the exclusion of social and emotional outcomes is neither desirable nor, in the last analysis, possible (see Joyce and Weil, 1986). Goodwin and Coates remind us that we must prepare students to live in a complicated world, which means that:

Schools must take an active role in preparing them (students) to design and fashion the kinds of lives they want to live. To function effectively in our society they must develop emotionally and socially; this requires learning to communicate, make decisions and relate well to other people. (1976, p. 161)

Students who cannot communicate effectively are not likely to be successful academically, and thus the presumed dichotomy between academic and social development is a distortion of reality. Likewise, to separate teachers' beliefs about teaching and learning and their expectations for students from their professional communication skills produces a serious distortion of the holistic nature of classroom management. Take, for example, the problems associated with establishing classroom order and discipline. Often the usual social expectations for male and female role behavior are communicated unintentionally by teachers, because the cultural conditioning of these expectations go so deep. Maher and Rathbone (1986) point out that the expectation that boys will be active while girls will be passive creates pressure on teachers to discipline active boys and ignore quiet, obedient girls.

Young women and men who seek to become teachers in our society have the special burden of overcoming a cultural bias which associates ideas of control and discipline with traditional conceptions of male dominance. Maher and Rathbone suggest that helping females to become teachers means helping them to confront and overcome doubts about personal autonomy:

Establishing one's authority and finding one's voice—as a leader, organizer, and teacher—constitute formidable tasks for any inexperienced teacher, especially in a culture that does not tend to take its young women (or its classroom teachers) very seriously. (1986, p. 227)

We especially notice the close connection between classroom discipline and communication skills that is made in the use of the phrase "establishing one's authority and finding one's voice." The issue is *not* learning to project vocally in order to command respect! The feelings we have about ourselves (our self-esteem) do interact with the skills we have available to affect our social environment. Thus, it should not be surprising to find that sexism is expressed in social expectations, classroom management, communication skills, and personal attitudes and values, and that all these qualities are mixed together. In order to develop more democratic forms of classroom management, we will have to untangle and examine the various realities which press upon the classroom as a learning environment. Whatever piece of the puzzle we pick to examine and understand, it will lead us to the interlocking network of factors which make up the social system of the classroom as a living entity. Many social institutions establish and maintain a sense of community and commonality which survive over time. A school develops a particular culture that can remain remarkably stable from year to year. Every classroom, however, changes radically each year. A classroom learning community must be created each year and then maintained throughout the year. At the middle-school and high school levels (and in departmentalized elementary schools), the mix of teachers and students may change every hour through the day and then be reshuffled at each marking period. Secondary teachers in such schools are faced with the task of establishing a learning-community environment with each class—a task which is formidable but not impossible.

This chapter addresses the **_Propositional Knowledge_** which underlines the developmental stages of learning community. Examples of how propositional knowledge has been handled by teachers at both the elementary and the secondary levels will be offered in subsequent chapters. Here we look at a five-stage development of the rationale and theoretical basis for the classroom learning community (adapted from Stanford, 1977):

1. *Beginnings.* The process of orientation
2. *Establishing expectations.* Teaching norms, roles, procedures, and rules
3. *Identifying and resolving conflicts.* Building personally and socially responsible behavior
4. *Supporting and expanding production.* Getting on with the business of learning
5. *Disbanding the community.* Transitions and closure from endings to new beginnings

The pedagogy we offer concentrates on the basis for action, and therefore assumes that educators are available for taking actions, making choices, and reflecting on both their actions and their choices. This is not an easy assumption, nor one to take lightly, because many theories, when examined, assume that people are not free to choose from among various courses of action but are driven by one or another compelling force. Putting aside the human capacity for self-deception, the authors believe people to be essentially free to choose among competing actions, values, and goals. We believe that this human quality makes us responsible for what we do, even if there are hundreds of mitigating factors. It is ultimately the individual teacher who will choose the kind of classroom environment to create for learners. In any given situation, the teacher will find more or less support for his/her choices. If that assumption makes sense, then the following rationales for the stages of a learning community will also make sense.

STAGE I. BEGINNINGS

An Asian schoolteacher who took a course with one of the authors reminded us of the Chinese saying, "A good start is halfway to success." This old saying reminds us that we must invest thought and preparation at the start of an enterprise if we are to hope for success in reaching our goals. This truism is relevant not only to human affairs in general but especially to the creation of a classroom learning community.

How teachers structure their classrooms (either intentionally or unintentionally) not only sends messages about the teachers' expectations but also their students' expectations of success or failure (E. Cohen, 1986). There is evidence that how students feel about their chances for success or failure is related to the teacher's expectations of the students (Frieze, 1980; Ames, 1982). What teachers expect of their students is communicated in a variety of ways at the beginning of the school year: how the room looks (the arrangement of furniture, and what is or is not hanging on the walls); the teacher's facial expression, dress, and demeanor; the first words the teacher speaks; the attention she/he pays to some students and not to others; and what substance the teacher chooses to focus on (whether what matters to the teacher, what matters to students, or what matters to both receives the most attention). All these and more affect the start-up of a new class.

Beginnings are also affected by the expectations that students bring to the classroom. Lisa Saunders, a teacher, tells about the time a new student entered her history class in February. She introduced him to the group, assigned him to a partner, and proceeded to get the class engaged in the lesson. In a few minutes the new student raised his hand and asked: "Is this eighth-grade history?" When he was assured that it was, he replied that he had never seen a history class where the students talked instead of the teacher. He said, "In history, I am used to taking notes while the teacher talks."

Even though teachers cannot control the expectations students bring to class at the beginning of the school year, or even to a new start in the middle of the school year (as with the student above), they do influence the expectations the students continue to carry. The teacher's decisions and actions will support or challenge the students' preconceived ideas. Thus, the teacher must clarify his/her own thinking about expectations and what is communicated during the first days of school.

The "getting-started" period of the new school year offers special opportunities to set the stage for successful learning. As a play is offered in a setting, suggesting mode, time, and place for the words and action to unfold, so the classroom is a setting for the students' expectations, both positive and negative. By every gesture, tone, and word, the teacher defines such critical issues as:

- "How we'll treat each other in this classroom"
- "How we will learn and study together"
- "How I feel about being a teacher and having you as my students"
- "The behavior standards which teacher and students are expected to meet"

It is not surprising that when researchers studied teachers they found that the better-organized teachers "had clear expectations about what they would accept in the students' behavior and what they would encourage" long before they met their students on the first morning (L. M. Anderson and C. M. Evertson, 1978, p. 9). A good start begins with advance preparation and planning, done before the school year begins (Brophy and Putnam, 1979; Brophy, 1982). This means that the teacher should be clear about the purposes of schooling and about his/her expectations, besides making procedural preparations. Advance planning gives teachers a sense of purpose which is communicated to students both directly in meaningful statements and assignments and indirectly in positive attitudes and directional teacher behaviors. Students are able to sense when a teacher is rudderless and floundering in a sea of "busyness."

Preparation and planning permit teachers to clarify in their own minds standards for student behavior in the classroom that are congruent with desired outcomes. Once teachers are clear about their own expectations, they can communicate them to students. Students tend to accept the teacher's standards, if they know what they are. Anderson and her colleagues (1980) describe their observations of student behavior and assert that "a high level of cooperative, on-task behavior (on the part of students) reflects student acceptance and knowledge of the teacher's behavior standards" (p. 345). Students will figure out hidden agendas and standards eventually, but it makes sense that: (1) publicly stated agendas are more likely to be accepted early in the school year, and (2) agendas that are explained in terms of their utility to the class will be viewed favorably.

Being well organized clearly helps to get the school year off to a good start. Anderson and Evertson's study (1978) of better-organized teachers revealed that better-organized teachers had the following characteristics:

- They had clear expectations.
- They communicated their expectations from the beginning.
- They were sensitive to students' concerns and need for information.
- They monitored their students closely during the first few weeks.
- They analyzed tasks of the first few weeks for purposes of reflecting and planning.

While these characteristics are not the exclusive features of learning-community teachers, they are necessary to preparing for a learning-community environment.

What does it mean to the learning-community teacher to be well-organized? Being well-organized means that learning-community teachers have developed, for the given year, a conscious plan that links their understandings to their instructional actions. Their understandings about the purposes of schooling, the specific desired outcomes for their students, and their actions (from preparing their classroom environments, to greeting students on the first day, to selection of instructional activities) function both as criteria and as rationales for what the teacher and students do. Being well-organized, to learning-community teachers, means much more than creating a technical checklist of teacher actions (e.g., check off students' names in an attendance book or put up colorful bulletin boards) to be sure that they won't forget important items.

There is much to think about while planning and implementing the beginning stage of a classroom learning community. The heuristic we use to think about beginnings includes the following ten concepts, which must be reflected on during the orientation process.

1. Purposes of schooling

2. Readiness

3. New beginnings

4. Inventory and planning

5. Initial actions

6. Framing

7. Assessing

8. Celebrations

9. New students

10. Changes in culture

The first eight of these concepts provide structure for thinking about starting the school year, while the last two relate to beginnings that occur throughout the year. Our purpose in using this heuristic is to facilitate thinking about beginnings while helping to avoid the problems of focusing only on technical survival.

Purposes of Schooling

Learning-community teachers support all four of Schwab's functions of schooling: academic achievement, personal responsibility, social responsibility, and social justice (equity) values and behaviors as outcomes (1975, 1976). However, each new year is an occasion for teachers to review: (1) what these words have come to mean during the last year; and (2) what these words mean in terms of what will be expected of the students, what will be taught, and how it will be taught.

Teachers may explore both congruence and incongruity in their thinking by asking themselves such questions as "What do I mean when I say that all my students will reach the academic goals this year?" and "How do I think about this differently?" Teachers can also ask themselves "What would the ideal graduate of my class do in various situations?" or "What student outcomes (exactly) am I willing to be responsible and accountable for this year?"

Readiness

Being ready for the new year includes being sensitive to the impact of changing times on oneself (the teacher) and on students. Teachers and students bring to school their excitement and anxiety, their happiness and fear, and their elation and depression. Everyone has questions about what is going to happen at the start of a school year: "Who will be in my class?" "How will I be treated?" "How will I feel?" "Will I be liked?" "What can I expect?" (Stanford, 1977) These questions are asked by teachers and students alike. Teachers wonder about their relationships with students, with new administrators, and with new teachers in the building. Students wonder about their relationships with teachers and with other students.

By the end of the summer, students and teachers are generally ready for the start of the new school year, but are they ready to get started in a particular classroom? Teachers can capitalize on their own and students' readiness for "getting on with" and making new friends, colleagues, and associates. Wise administrators and teachers provide an orientation time at the start of the school year. It is important for teachers to create information and getting-acquainted times when students can overcome their vulnerability. Both teachers and students can begin to feel safe when they know what is happening, what is going to happen, and what degree of control they will be able to exercise over themselves and their environment.

New Beginnings

Ideally, students begin the new year with a sense of hope for achievement and satisfaction. For a student, beginning of school heralds resolves to turn over a new leaf, get a fresh start, and be the person he/she wants to be. Likewise, teachers feel they can get on with a new chapter in their career. The new year is a propitious time for starting new projects and holding on to the enthusiasm for as long as possible. One way to assure that enthusiasm will last a while is to resist the temptation to signal to students that past patterns will be honored in the learning-community classroom. Teachers can help students to break with patterns of failure and frustration by not expecting their new students to be like last year's students; or like their brothers or sisters; or like others of their sex, race, or religion.

Inventory and Planning

Prior to the start of a new school year, teachers can benefit from review of their past experiences. As they make plans for the new year, they can draw upon what seemed to work well in the past, and upon the conditions under which it seemed to work well. This is also the time to incorporate new ideas into curriculum plans. In taking stock of past successes and failures, the teacher can profit from asking, "What have I been putting off doing or trying out in my teaching?" The new year presents an opportunity to try out a high-risk strategy that has a good chance for success. With careful planning, and when hope and energy levels are high, risky schemes can succeed.

The learning-community teacher should make explicit plans for beginning a new classroom learning community. The plans should include organizing the classroom environment, the subject matter, and the instructional strategies—and communicating the plans publicly will contribute to clarity about what is expected and how it will be accomplished.

Initial Actions

While students do bring to class their preconceived ideas (based on the teacher's reputation—what friends and siblings have told them), the actual first impression is hard to resist and lasts a long time. For some students, the teacher's smile and first comments set the tone of a whole school year. After school, students talk to their friends and the adults in their homes about what they like or dislike about their teachers, on the basis of the most minute data. Did the teacher mispronounce a student's name? Did the teacher smile and call on students to do a task they could do? Did the teacher seem to like the students, and to like what was being taught? Did the teacher wear a nerdy shirt? Did the teacher laugh or admit liking a popular music group? Did the teacher admit to making a mistake? Did the teacher ask for help? Was the classroom bright and cheerful? It can take months to undo an initial bad impression, and likewise a teacher can be forgiven lots of gaffs if students' initial impressions are favorable.

Framing

A picture frame defines the limits of the expanse framed; it also provides support for the glass and other material within the frame. A teacher "frames" the school year by defining the limits of role responsibility in the classroom. Student responsibility is a key element of the learning-community frame. L. Anderson and R. Prawat (1983) suggest that teachers who "give away" responsibility to students must also provide instruction on how to exercise control. The teacher provides the cognitive strategies for internal control by modeling. "In short, teachers must first accept responsibility before they can ask students to accept it" (1983, p. 65).

How the teacher behaves toward students is a cue (model) for how students will think the teacher wants them to treat each other. The teacher must demonstrate respect for students, their feelings, their ideas, and their needs, so that the students will learn to be respectful. This is a part of what we mean when we say that the teacher frames the central concerns of the classroom learning community.

Assessing

When we say that teachers "assess," we mean that they watch and weigh the effects of their actions on students. All actions produce reactions. The teacher's responsibility extends to monitoring student reactions and seeking, through reflection, to understand them. In fact, some of the initial actions of the orientation stage of group development are designed to help the teacher to gather information about where the students are in relation to specific learning goals. Assessing students' developmental stage is critical, since it affects the choice of appropriate content and strategies not only for the first few days but also for the full year.

Since we argue that classroom discipline falls within the domain of organization and instructional design, we assume that most of the discipline problems of a classroom can be avoided, prevented, or at least reduced by careful attention to the planning and execution of instructional and management decisions. Early assessment of student reactions aids in appropriate decision making. Brophy (1987) argued that management decisions should be driven by concern for the quality of instruction rather than by concerns for controlling students. Likewise, Brophy wrote:

> *Socialization decisions should be driven primarily by concerns about self-sustaining positive qualities in students rather than concerns about compelling conformity to demands through threats and sanctions. (1987, p. 3)*

Assessing students early in the school year can provide information about their self-concepts as well as their cognitive development. A focus on students' developmental needs helps to orient the teacher away from thoughts about "controlling kids" and toward thoughts about appropriate instruction. The very process of collecting, storing, analyzing, and making decisions on the basis of data leads the teacher to an accepting position vis-à-vis students. That is, teachers are more likely to accept students and value their uniqueness when they possess information about students' learning and social context. Thus, assessing students leads not only to better-informed instructional decisions but also to greater valuing of students for their own sake.

Celebrations

Celebrations are signs of group memory. By cultivating the capacity to celebrate individual and group achievements, the teacher invites the students to remember key events valuable to the group. In so doing, the teacher creates group consciousness: the community acquires a history. Just as every family has an individual history and unique celebrations, so every classroom learning community has a collective memory. Celebrations are both a product of group history and a reinforcer of group consciousness.

At the beginning of the school year, the classroom contains a collection of individuals who have little or no common history. One way of looking at the teacher's orientation tasks is to see them as exercises in creating the beginnings of group history. A group history will grow no matter what the teacher does; the issue is whether the teacher will self-consciously use this phenomenon to create a positive classroom community. By selecting what to celebrate early in the first week, the teacher communicates to the students what is valuable to the group. Will everyone simply say, "TGIF" at the end of the first week? Or will the teacher choose to invite celebration about meeting an initial group goal? (An example might be to have everyone know everyone else's name by Thursday.)

A celebration can be a small recognition of a small step achieved (e.g., it can note the effort and achievement of an individual) or a larger time-out to enjoy some occasion (e.g., a holiday or birthday), but every celebration should involve the whole group. The teacher who excludes some students from the group celebrations will face powerful negative consequences. Schwab (1976) reminds us of the energy for community building that celebrations provide. Celebrations can bring back memories of "crises surmounted, defeats survived, triumphs, all shared within a kinship conferred by common roots" (p. 240). The learning-community teacher provides illustrations of how things change over time. For example:

- "Remember when last month you didn't know, and look at what you can do now."
- "Remember last month when this problem started, and now see how things have changed."
- "We all have tried to solve this and now it is past."

The learning-community teacher plans for celebrations of the class's shared experiences and thereby helps students to focus on what they have in common.

The concerns about beginnings discussed above can apply at various times during the school year, whenever reorientation is appropriate. Beginnings can occur at any time throughout the school year—for example, (1) whenever a new student joins or leaves the class and (2) whenever any change occurs in the classroom community culture.

New Students

When a new student is assigned to a class, orientation procedures must be repeated. Both the student and the class need to adjust: the student needs to gain entry to the class, and the class needs to make room for the student. The transition from alien to class member can be rocky. Disruptive behaviors may occur, simply because students need to test the environment. The teacher and the class need to help the "new kid on the block" to learn the culture of the class—its norms, rules, roles, and procedures. The new student will have to have time to adjust to insider information about accepted signals that operate within the class culture. He/she can be helped to learn how to survive in the class by being given an explicit review of the cultural norms—for example, information about how assignments are handled. Such details as when homework is due and where it is turned in, procedures for asking questions, when it is OK to laugh, and when everyone has to work are manifestations of class culture that need to be learned by the new student. Direct attention to orientation matters by the teacher will assist the new student, provide a model of helping for the class, and provide a review of negotiated norms for the rest of the class. When the student succeeds in negotiating membership in the class, the event may well become an occasion for celebration.

Changes in Culture

Various events during the school year signal changes in classroom culture for which the teacher needs to plan. Vacation breaks produce disruption in the continuity of the classroom culture. Reorientation is required to rebuild the sense of commonality of purpose. A new beginning during the school year does not mean throwing out old agreements; it is a reaffirmation of the class's identity and norms for interaction.

A variety of things, including scheduled vacation breaks, can cause changes. An extended period of snow days, for example, can disrupt the class. A winning season for the school football or basketball team can become a disruptive force, if not dealt with as a reality for students. One school we know went through the winter with an undefeated basketball team and ended up the season in the state championship game. It was interesting to observe how differently teachers treated the growing disruption of academics by the school spirit and general excitement. Some teachers tried to control it by ignoring it.

Some tried to ban the topic of basketball from the class lessons and discussions. By and large, the most successful approach seemed to be acknowledging the powerful influence basketball success was having on the school as a whole and the players in particular, and then proceeding with the lesson at hand.

Reorientation can also be seen as a making room for newness within the community. Whether that newness comes in the form of a new student joining the class or an event that rocks the class, accepting newness and adjusting to it may expand the cultural norms of the class, but it also is a good model for coping with reality.

Summary

In the first stage of development of a classroom learning community, the beginnings of activities are framed. The activities are related to the purposes of schools, and the energy invested in readiness for fresh starts is drawn on. Orientation is planned and reactions are assessed. Finally, accomplishments are celebrated. The teacher also recognizes that a new start is necessary with every change in the community population (whenever a new student joins the class) or in the school culture. Issues connected with beginnings keep cropping up during the school year, but when such issues have been initially dealt with effectively in the fall, the severity of disruptions is limited and an easier maintenance of learning-community norms is assured.

STAGE II. ESTABLISHING EXPECTATIONS

The second developmental stage in creating a classroom learning community is establishing expectations. In this stage, teacher and students negotiate; practice; and apply specific norms, rules, roles, and procedures which will support the functioning of the community. This is the stage most often neglected by beginning teachers. Many teachers begin the school year by posting class rules prominently and telling students that breaking the rules will result in this or that consequence. Lists of rules are often experienced by students as demands which limit them and which define the classroom as the teacher's domain.

The stage in which expectations are established focuses on issues of student socialization. Expectations must be explicitly communicated by both teacher and students, so that a community can be forged out of a collection of individuals. Brophy (1987) defines student socialization as "actions taken with the intention of influencing students' attitudes, beliefs, expectations, or behavior concerning personal or social (including oral and political) issues" (p. 2). When a teacher acts to influence students, he/she is influenced in return. Reinforcing particular student behaviors will have an impact on the teacher as well. Communication always goes two ways—even when it is meant to go one way! If a teacher yells at a student, the yelling affects both student and teacher. If a teacher speaks softly and smiles, again both are affected.

All communication is a modification of behavior. It would be fanciful to assume that one could direct someone else's behavior without being affected oneself. In the stage in which expectations are established, the teacher's responsibility is to communicate clearly with the students about the mutual interdependence created by the classroom learning community. Behaviors appropriate to the mutuality are negotiated. The organized teacher has already analyzed the academic tasks usually accomplished at this grade or instructional level (L. M. Anderson and C. M. Evertson, 1978). Some would argue that the teacher should also take responsibility for structuring the social negotiations for the classroom norms (L. M. Anderson and R. Prawat, 1983). However, we believe that these actions on the part of the teacher should be considered part of the role expectations of the professional teacher rather than a separate domain of power the teacher wields over students. The teacher takes initiative as a means of sharing information with the students. Shared information leads to shared responsibility.

In contrast to many traditional teachers, the learning-community teacher is open about the conditions of the classroom and school environment. How the school board or school principal may limit teachers' freedom to choose their own class rules is a subject for discussion. The teacher may also be frank about his/her own tolerances for certain behaviors. For example, if a teacher has a low tolerance for noise above a certain decibel, this becomes a factor in the discussion. How the teacher is affected by high noise is treated as a consideration in rational rule formulation, rather than a non-negotiable demand by an authoritarian teacher.

A teacher who treats the students as capable people who need information to act responsibly is inviting them to respond accordingly. However, such an invitation is, in itself, often not enough to engender student responsibility. Students who are deeply distrustful of any information shared by teachers will not likely be transformed by initial teacher actions. Even so, the demonstration of shared information and responsibility by the teacher signals a willingness to deal with whatever realities students may bring to the classroom. The open teacher is not held captive by a need to hide information from students as a power ploy. When students in the primary grades receive explicit information and signals early in the school year, they soon learn about the classroom environment, and they settle in more quickly and more safely (Shultz and Florio, 1979).

Our heuristic for thinking about the stage of establishing expectations includes four concepts. The first concept is *norms,* and it provides a means for thinking about the necessary characteristics of the classroom learning community. The other three, *roles, rules,* and *routines,* help us to think about the organization of the classroom learning community.

Norms

Norms are contrasted with the rules of a classroom in that norms are at once larger and more intimate than rules. Rules govern specifics. Norms describe cultural expectations. Though norms are often unacknowledged in a group, we believe that both the teacher and the class benefit when norms are expressed as openly as possible. The term "norm" refers to a standard by which a group, culture, or community judges itself. A norm is the "right-and-proper" behavior within the group. Because groups will inevitably develop norms, whether or not they are acknowledged, we believe that it is better for them to be developed openly so that they can be examined and, if found wanting, changed. The argument here is for open examination, discussion, and negotiation of classroom norms.

In Latin, *norma* means "carpenter's square." By extension, a "norm" is any standard or pattern by which judgment is made. In comparatively recent times, the term "normal school" has been used to mean a standard or common school. In anthropology, the "norms" of a group are the standards by which the individual's behavior is evaluated, and this is how we use the word.

The primary focus of classroom norms has to do with the discourse of the group—that is, how the members of the group interact with and engage each other. An example of a norm might be the expectation that everyone in a class deserves respect, whereas an example of a rule might be "No put-downs allowed." The concept that everyone deserves respect is larger and may have many concrete manifestations that could not be covered by a discrete list of rules.

The norms of a classroom learning community have much to do with the style of interaction among the members. A typical list of learning-community norms might include:

- Seeing oneself and others as mutual resources, rather than as competitors
- Reflecting on personal and group actions
- Having respect for other communities
- Being responsible for one's own learning
- Supporting the idea that everyone is learning
- Celebrating accomplishments and the failures of the group

Schwab (1976) sees learning-community norms as propensities or internal dispositions toward acting in a certain way.

One of the critical propensities of a classroom learning community is cooperation (G. Stanford, 1977). Members of the class listen to what each other say and become interdependent (M. Cohen, 1987). Interdependence among class members is demonstrated by peer collaboration. When students see each other as valuable resources for success at the assigned tasks, rather than as competitors for a few rewards and privileges, learning is more fun. The plain truth is that it is more pleasant to cooperate than to compete.

Rules

Ideally, in the classroom learning community, one rule would be sufficient (e.g., "We will treat people and things with respect"). The ideal conditions under which this would be true would be that all members of the community would understand what was meant by "learning community." Teachers, however, are faced with a dual responsibility: teaching the concept of "learning community" while at the same time living in some approximation of a learning community. That is, students are learning about the community while they are experiencing it. Thus, both teachers and students may find that more rules are helpful. The saying "The government which governs least governs best" seems to apply to rules. Good and Brophy (1987) suggest that the best course is to have the fewest possible rules in a classroom, along with broad guidelines for behavior. The elementary classroom may require several explicit rules, as students are still being socialized into schooling. (For example, it may be necessary to have the explicit rule "No hitting" at the elementary level.) By secondary school, students have usually been sufficiently socialized to know what is appropriate and to have developed internal controls. However, at any age level it is appropriate for a class to talk about the kinds of rules that may be needed to promote the greatest good for the greatest number. Given the constraints of classroom space, limited time and materials, and the problems of human interaction, some minimal rules for getting along are probably necessary no matter what the grade level. The teacher's responsibility is to identify and establish the rules that are necessary for teaching appropriate behaviors in the community.

Good and Brophy (1987) also suggest that teachers analyze their rules to determine the cost/benefit ratio. For example, rules that do not result in intended outcomes or are incongruent with the classroom learning-community norms should be eliminated. A set of rules that requires teachers to focus excessively on management has too high a cost and should be revised.

Roles

The idea of "role taking," as opposed to status giving or power exchanging, is critical to the classroom learning community. People in a learning community are equal in status but have different roles in play. The difficulty is that many of the roles needed to maintain a classroom learning community have to be learned, because they are not familiar to the class members. Success in creating a classroom learning community will depend to a great extent upon students' learning a variety of interactive group roles. G. Stanford (1977) suggests the roles of organizer, linker, and contributor, and encourager. E. G. Cohen (1986) suggests that the roles of facilitator, recorder/reporter, clean-up, and timer be assigned to students working in small groups.

Stanford's roles are ones which all members of the community need to acquire. They contribute to the ideas of what it means to be personally responsible and responsible to the community (a form of social responsibility). Cohen's roles are represented as a means to alter inequities in power and status among students. For these roles, Cohen suggests that the teacher must maintain the responsibility for role assignments. It is through making decisions about who will carry out which role that the teacher can support low-status students' move to equitable positions within the learning community.

No matter what roles a teacher chooses to emphasize and no matter what names are used for the roles, one thing is clear about assigning roles to students: roles have to be taught. It is not enough to describe the roles the teacher expects students to play. Students must practice the roles, get feedback on their performance from teacher and peers, and then practice some more. Furthermore, it is necessary that all students learn all the roles. Roles should be rotated, and all students need to be effective in each role. (Besides, no one wants to be the permanent recorder in a study group.) Direct instruction in roles may be necessary in some cases, because students may have never experienced the roles either in previous classrooms or outside the school.

Focusing on roles played by members of the classroom learning community is also a way of emphasizing equality of status among members. Differences can be accounted for by the variety of tasks that are completed to accomplish group work. Evaluation, then, can focus on role performance as it contributes to the intended outcomes, and not on character analysis.

Routines

Like roles, routines must be taught to students. Routines facilitate more engaged time for students (Emmer, Evertson, and Anderson, 1980). The more quickly a class masters the routines of the community, the more time the teacher will have to communicate about substantive issues with the students. The routines of a learning community will support the cooperative culture, namely the norms, rules, and roles of the class. Routines for students to help each other, for working in groups on multiability tasks, for maintaining the classroom physical environment, for taking responsibility, and for celebrating the accomplishments of individuals and of the group need to be designed.

Student teachers often have problems with the routines of managing the class. One of the reasons is that pupils perceive the student teacher's changes or modifications as *disintegration* of the master teacher's routines (Leinhardt et al., 1987). For this reason, the student teacher is well advised to make shifts in routines explicit. This communicates purposefulness rather than inattention. It is also good practice for any teacher who is seeking to modify routines.

A startling fact is that many teachers pay little attention to developing transition routines. Students find it confusing when the teacher charges on to a new topic or project without any routine for transition. Effecting smooth transition to a new activity requires teacher and students to have routines for stopping and starting activities. The old advice that speech teachers gave to students is an example of a transition routine: "Tell them what you are going to tell them, then tell them, and then tell them what you told them." At minimum, a transition should alert students that activities are shifting from one subject to another. Effective teachers practice transitions all the time—for example, "Yesterday, we . . . ; today, we will . . . ; and tomorrow, we will. . . ." Another example is, "Now that we have finished this section, we will review all the main ideas before we go on." There is some evidence that overly long transitions may indicate that the teacher is off-task rather than the students (Gump, 1985). Expert teachers tend to use more routines during transition times (Leinhardt, Weidman, and Hammond, 1987). Since the transition time is often when attention wavers and purposeful teacher and student activities tend to slide, the practice of using routines helps to avoid undue downtime.

Summary

Establishing expectations is a clearly defined stage in the development of an effective group. It is a time when teachers and students create standards for how they will work together during the academic year. We believe it is the teacher's responsibility to exercise leadership in the agenda-setting, problem-posing interactions of this stage. However, that responsibility does not extend to publishing a prepackaged list of prohibitions and requirements like the ones that are often found in authoritarian classrooms. Attention to norms, rules, roles, and routines becomes a community project when the values and beliefs of students are taken as seriously as those of the teacher. Inviting students to take themselves seriously as socially responsible members of the community is more powerful than any punitive system and causes them to internalize fair play and justice—concepts that cannot be taught by indoctrination. Indoctrination always carries with it the connotation of force: "Do it or else." Establishing expectations in a classroom learning community is an exercise in building trust which lays the groundwork that allows students to take the risk of learning.

STAGE III. IDENTIFYING AND RESOLVING CONFLICTS

All teachers, at some time, will have to deal with classroom disruptions, whether they occur among students or between students and teacher. No matter what type of culture teachers set up in their classrooms, they will face the necessity of responding to certain types of common disciplinary problems. When classroom learning communities are established systematically, many of the problems which normally arise because of a lack of information or because expectations are not clear will not appear. Classroom learning-community teachers, like any other group of effective teachers, will lay out their expectations very explicitly, so that students will not create problems because of lacking or inaccurate information. However, in the classroom learning community, conflicts are seen as normal; that is, conflicts are the cues that we normally use to discover where either misunderstandings or differences in values exist.

We find that classroom learning-community teachers have two basic types of conflicts to identify and resolve: (1) conflicts that arise within the dynamics of the classroom group and (2) conflicts that are brought into the classroom from the outside. The first sort of conflicts arise around issues related to establishing and maintaining a classroom learning community. The second sort arise from the problems individual students bring into the learning community classroom from their personal and social environments—for example, children abused at home will need attention in school. The teacher's role is to identify conflicts and problems, and to seek ways to resolve conflicts and solve problems, so that the full range of personal and social responsibility and equity growth can occur in the classroom learning community.

Conflicts Related to Establishment of Community

Conflicts occur during the early stages of community building as students learn new norms, rules, roles, and routines. Any change in social systems will produce some conflict among its members. As students develop their awareness of the responsibilities they are expected to carry, they may challenge these norms. Some conflicts arise as a natural outcome of the creation of an environment that fosters the exchange of ideas rather than traditional teacher-centered teaching (e.g., involving messages such as "Don't talk unless I call on you," "Everyone's eyes up here," "I'm waiting"). There is a kind of safety, after all, in letting teachers take all the responsibility for what happens in classrooms.

Learning-community teachers understand conflict to be a normal part of life. J. Johnson (1977) points out that conflicts will arise whether or not the collection of individuals develops into a cohesive group. He predicts that both process and content conflicts will occur. Problems that arise as students learn how to become members of the community and how to take responsibility for the community are part of the normal learning cycle that prompts resistance to anything new. Johnson (1977) suggests that one can expect to find "collision of roles, norms and values as a group attempts to resolve differences" (p. 21).

In the early stages of learning-community development, it is possible that conflicts arise simply because students are testing the social environment. Conflicts occur while the community is creating a safe area for social interacting and before trust among members has been established. In the effort to establish trusting relationships, a teacher creates risk for students. It could even be said that the rule is: Trust comes from taking risks. A student of the authors was disappointed in us; her expectations were that we would "do more" for her, and she said: "I should be able to trust you!" We said, "No, what we have been doing is risking. Trust comes later on, and as a result of our risking together."

As students become invested in the environment, they also change and these changes may bring about their own conflicts. For example, Elizabeth Hermann, an English teacher we know, began to have new conflicts in her class during the month of February. Young women in the class had begun to express their opinions about the material they were reading. Previously nonassertive females were expressing their positions strongly, responding to other members of the community in new and assertive ways, insisting that others listen to them, and insisting that their ideas be considered. Hermann realized that these young women had developed more confidence in themselves as they better understood the principles of equity embedded in the classroom learning community. Therefore, they were asserting themselves in new ways. They were creating new conflicts because they were challenging established interaction patterns. Hermann understood that identifying this conflict for what it was during class time would bring new learning, because it would bring to the surface assumptions about role expectations that affect the quality of student achievement. She saw that the individuals were growing and that the community needed to change to accommodate their productive changes. After establishing classroom learning communities in her high school for 10 years, Hermann has come to understand that her students grow in spurts and starts. She has learned to use conflicts created by student growth as support for more student development. She challenges the comfortable statuses and roles that students had assumed were stable. This leads to the clarification of new norms or new understandings of the old norms, rules, and roles that are a part of the classroom learning community. These conflicts are natural expansions of individual development toward valuing social and personal responsibility, social justice, and academic outcomes. We believe that these conflicts signal that students are buying into the community and that they have begun to see that they have a stake in their community.

Other conflicts arise as individuals learn specific subject matter. Once community members have begun to see themselves as members of a community who trust one another, a kind of polarization on content issues occurs. People begin to disagree openly about what they know and what they value. Johnson (1977, p. 21) believes that content issues are most obvious and easy to deal with. This may be because when these occur there already is a "community." When members of the community find that they have genuine differences about content issues, they know that they can trust each other enough to discuss and resolve them. For example, conflict arises when students develop new understandings about various subject matters. This type of conflict may arise when the teacher intentionally plans for students to debate their views and publicly share their opinions as a part of the process for understanding ideas, issues, or actions. The use of cooperative learning, multiability, and experiential instructional strategies within a learning community enhances the opportunities for "learning" conflicts. Again, without conflicts of this type, there would be little improvement in the quality of achievement.

These types of conflicts and their resolutions can contribute to students' understandings of various perspectives, values, and behaviors. Helping students to learn to live with ambiguity, not to become dysfunctional in the face of equal options, and to use conflict as a means of strengthening relationships and coming to deeper understandings are parts of how a classroom learning community functions.

Conflicts Related to Problems Students Bring to Class

When students bring their problems into the classroom learning community, the teacher is responsible for helping, within the limitations and commitments of the community as a whole. Students need help "to utilize their abilities, energies, and talents in ways that promote their development and learning" (H. Perkins, 1969). This category of conflict may be thought of by many as "discipline." The traditional view of discipline emphasizes teacher control of student behavior in order for learning to occur (Neill, 1962). We believe that the teacher has the authority and responsibility to promote problem solving and responsible behavior by students. However, the teacher cannot permit the problem behavior of one or a few students to interfere with others' learning.

Complementary to our view is the work of Lewis and Lovegrove (1984), who point out that students have certain expectations of teachers when it comes to the topic of discipline. They identify five factors that students value in teacher behavior in discipline situations (see Figure 4-1). Teacher calmness minimizes student embarrassment in tension-filled situations. Minimizing student embarrassment has been recognized (Good and Brophy, 1987) as part of the long-term socialization of the student. Lewis and Lovegrove also state that students support rules based on "authority integral to the teacher's role of coordinator of the learning environment" (1984, p. 100). That is, students support teachers' actions to protect them from disruption of their learning, rather than teachers' capricious exercise of personal authority or preferences. By "fairness," Lewis and Lovegrove mean that students feel that teachers should give a fair warning to students and should clearly identify the appropriate miscreant.

Misbehavior can be defined in a multitude of ways but is best defined situationally. For example, the norms for accepted behavior in two middle schools in which the authors work are very different. In one school, students can either eat lunch in the school cafeteria or leave the school grounds to eat lunch at local restaurants, while in the other school, students cannot leave the building during lunch period. In the first case, a student walking across the street is viewed as "on lunch period and appropriate," while in the other context, the same behavior is considered "misbehavior." Another example is that, in one school, students receive demerits that are recorded in the office when they do not bring books or pencils to class. In the other school, students simply borrow a pencil or look on with someone else if they do not bring their book. In addition to school norms, there are differences among the behaviors that bother individual teachers. Our work with both preservice and in-service teachers over the last two decades has convinced us that some student behaviors will bother some teachers and not others. The teachers' ideas about the purposes of schooling, their cultural backgrounds, their experiences as teachers, their values, and the knowledge and skill they have for responding to particular problems may all contribute to these variations. Many scholars believe that disruptive behavior is defined by its context. People also disagree about what constitutes disruption.

We are convinced with Gnagey (1981) that it is impossible to list generically what is misbehavior. Gnagey suggests that the only realistic position is that "any behavior is deviant if the teacher (principal, school board) deems it so" (p. 50). In the classroom learning community, behavior that has a long-term harmful or destructive effect on the individual or the group is defined as misbehavior. At the same time, different but neutral or constructive behavior can be supported by the teacher and school norms. From the learning-community perspective, criteria for determining what is an effective classroom must include student results in all areas (personal and social responsibility, academic concerns, and social justice). Disruptions to learning, when handled in congruence with these norms and goals, can contribute to student learning.

Based on observations of student and teacher behavior in an urban junior high classroom and a suburban junior high classroom, Lasley concludes that "teachers are instrumental in both causing and preventing discipline problems" (1981, p. 149). He suggests that teachers contribute to problems when they ignore students' cultural backgrounds and learning needs, and that acknowledging the presence and importance of such factors can reduce or eliminate certain kinds of problems. For example, Lasley

Factor	Descriptions
1	Teacher calmness
2	Rule clarity and reasonableness
3	Appropriate punishment
4	Fairness
5	Acceptance of responsibility

(*Source:* Lewis and Lovegrove, 1984, p. 100.)

FIGURE 4-1   Student Expectations of Teachers

reports that students in both the urban and the suburban classrooms displayed coping behaviors. These behaviors in the suburban school were more often tacit and subtle, and thus were acceptable to teachers with largely middle-class value systems. Urban students' coping behavior includes verbal jousting and posturing, which are antithetical to middle-class value systems. In both the urban setting and the suburban setting, students saw their coping behaviors as acceptable. However, teachers in both settings, who held similar middle-class value systems, saw one set of coping behaviors as acceptable and the other as unacceptable.

Students bring many personal problems from their out-of-school lives to the classroom learning community. Many urban learning communities are in neighborhoods where physical sickness, poverty, child abuse, drugs, crime, hostile-aggressive behavior, and social pathology are common elements of the students' out-of-school experiences. Chapter 10 will deal with five specific problems which most teachers confront, and which cannot be ignored. These five problems are (1) drugs, (2) dishonest behavior, (3) child abuse, (4) suicide, and (5) hostile-aggressive students' destructive behavior. Each of these problems is destructive to the individual who has the problem and, at times, to others. We have selected these problems for three reasons: (1) their serious consequences for the student, (2) their disruption of the learning environment, and (3) their effect on some teachers, who find them frightening and overwhelming.

The problems we have selected to explore in Chapter 10 are not the same as those that teachers usually faced in the 1960s. Problems like students "used to have" still do exist in the schools of America, but the typical problems in classrooms today are representative of more serious social ills. Problems such as throwing paper wads and talking back are not our concern in Chapter 10, nor are problems such as those that Carter (1985) describes, which were created by a teacher's inappropriate management behavior. The teacher intervened so frequently, to defend order, that her actions blocked the flow of activity and reduced the probability of success (p. 93).

The serious problems which arise in classrooms today are caused by the influences of the outside world on the class and not by the ineffectiveness of the teacher. These problems cannot be prevented by an effective teacher nor by well-organized instruction. These problems are brought into the classroom and emanate from the personal lives of students. Whenever these kinds of student problems disrupt learning, the teacher must take action to restore a supportive learning environment. We address these major issues and how to resolve the conflicts they create in Chapter 10.

Summary

The authors consider conflict to be a normal part of the development of a classroom learning community. The identification and resolution of conflict is a sign that the class is making progress toward an effective learning-community culture. Conflicts about norms and the clash of ideas are to be expected in the classroom learning community, and yet there are still other conflict-creating problems that come from outside the classroom (see Chapter 10).

STAGE IV. SUPPORTING AND EXPANDING PRODUCTION

By the time a class reaches the developmental stage of productivity, the community is starting to function smoothly. Teacher and student attention shifts from establishing the community (becoming acquainted and learning roles and procedures) to fine-tuning and making changes to improve the quality of community life. Both teachers and students have a vision of what the new community looks like (e.g., the norms of the community have been established). Members of the classroom learning community have begun to believe that when problems arise they will be resolved. The agenda is filled with activities relating to all four of the functions of schooling.

Both teachers and students monitor activities for productivity, to make sure that they are moving toward mutually agreed-upon goals and purposes. Thus, our heuristic for this stage is monitoring. The form of monitoring we support is reflection. We suggest that the teacher and the students monitor the progress of the community by asking questions about the meaning of daily activities. As events occur, they can ask about the connections between what was planned and what actually happened. Was there congruence between actions and beliefs and their consequences? Reflection on congruence or its lack results in powerful monitoring of classroom learning-community productivity. The productivity stage is full of learning activity. The monitoring questions we ask concern the progress made toward achieving community goals.

STAGE V. DISBANDING THE COMMUNITY

Nothing in the world lasts forever. The lifetime of a given classroom learning community is short, usually lasting only one year, though it may last two years in some cases. During a given year, both individuals and the community go through transitions, as a result of change. The community members move from one stage to another, from one state to another. They change from "not knowing" to "knowing," and in that sense, they become different people. The authors choose to use the term "transitions" to describe this stage because we value individual and group changes, getting on with the business at hand, achieving new levels of reality, and being sensitive to feelings about leaving something behind. G. Stanford (1977) suggests that it is the teacher's role to acknowledge the end of the year or other events that create transitions and to facilitate the movement of the group through this stage.

Being explicit about the temporary nature of a given classroom learning community underscores the risk of making an investment in the community. We assert that any school day is a part of the here and now, and that students and teachers are engaged in a normal phase of life as they progress through the school year. We believe that a classroom learning community maintains a healthy tension between membership in a community and the sense that time is passing.

Two ideas are involved in this stage: transition and closure. Attention to closure means planning for things to end. Speaking about change and endings as normal parts of events helps to facilitate our transitions to the new. There is a sense in which we must say "goodbye" to the old in order to really possess the new. Those who cling to the past are not ready for the new. This applies in learning, as well as in life. For example, counting on one's fingers may be a genuine help during the early stages of learning numbers, but, at some early stage, literal finger counting has to be given up, in order to advance in mathematics.

We seek to understand what is happening in this stage. We ask: "What is happening? When will it end?" The teacher and students need to be aware that some transitions are structural or formal—examples are the end of the marking period, the end of the school year, and when a student leaves the community to move to another school. Other transitions are caused by classroom learning-community actions—for example, solving a problem, undertaking a new responsibility, or revising norms because of new understandings. Three sets of questions help us to monitor and facilitate the passage of individuals and the community through transitions and closure. These monitoring questions are:

1. What changes are occurring? Are these changes contributing to increased quality of life? How can we remember? How will things be different in the future?

2. What will we miss? What have we gained? How will we be different? How are we different already?

3. What occurred in this community? What has happened to me and to the group? What have I/we given to others?

Performance Outcomes and Activities (NJPTS 4, 5, 6, 7)

Chapter 4
The Pedagogy for Learning Community

PERFORMANCE OUTCOMES

Teacher Candidates will

1. Describe each of the stages of group development in a Learning Community.
2. Use small group roles effectively on a regular basis.
3. Generate ideas about talk and actions that contribute to the establishment of a learning community culture in a classroom.
4. State examples of talk and actions in traditional classrooms that act as roadblocks to the establishment of a learning community classroom.
5. State examples of talk and actions in traditional classrooms that can act as supports for establishing a learning-community classroom culture.
6. Create initial plan for Stages 1–3 for establishing a classroom learning community.

Exercise 4.1
Stages of Group Development

Small Group Discussion

The pedagogy of the learning community, as presented in this chapter, may make you feel comfortable in some ways but not in others. The purpose of this exercise is to enable you to (1) identify issues and questions regarding your assessment of the pedagogical process of the learning community and (2) identify your personal knowledge, performances, and dispositions that may or may not contribute to your success as a learning community teacher.

Overview small group task. First, identify for each individual in the group, the questions she/he has about establishing a learning community classroom. Second, identify the knowledge, skills, performances, and dispositions that each member holds that will contribute to his/her success in establishing a classroom learning-community culture. Third, identify the talk, actions, and dispositions that each member holds that will interfere with his/her success in establishing a learning-community classroom culture. Assess your personal information as it relates to each stage of the development of a learning community culture.

Begin your small group discussion by establishing the facilitator, timer, recorder and discussion questions or expected outcomes of your work. The group reporter will turn in a synthesis of the data collected for each of the three parts of this task.

At the next class, each member of the group will turn in his/her individual Questions and Self-assessment Report. In addition to the items you identified during the small group discussion, add the following information. First, add a description of how you will attend to the issues and answer the questions you identified. Second, add a description of how you will turn your incongruencies into congruencies or eliminate them.

Exercise 4.2
Classroom Observation Notes and Inferences

You have been reading about classroom learning communities. The purpose of this observation is to provide an opportunity for you to identify concrete examples of things that happen in classrooms that are and are not indicators of a classroom learning community culture.

Establishing a classroom learning community culture is a process. It takes a teacher who is both knowledgeable about the specific culture of a learning community and skillful in moving a group of students through the effective group development process in a timely fashion. Many teachers establish elements that one would find in a classroom learning community but do not create the culture of a learning community. This activity is not designed to be judgmental of a given classroom culture. It is designed to assist candidates in their growth toward identifying concrete examples of the learning community culture, as well as examples of culture that would not be a part of the learning community culture. Once examples and non-examples of a learning community are identified, teacher candidate skills in establishing learning community culture are strengthened.

During observations over a week's time, note those things that appear to support the idea of a learning community culture and those things that would not be found in a classroom learning community. For each of the supportive factors you identify write your reason as to why you think the factor contributes to a learning community culture. For each of the nonsupportive factors write your reason as to why you believe the factor does not contribute to a learning community culture. Once you identify a factor, do not continue to record it. Record a factor only once.

OBSERVATIONS OF SUPPORTIVE AND NONSUPPORTIVE FACTORS OF A LEARNING COMMUNITY

Date and Times	Supportive Factors		Nonsupportive Factors	
	Observations	Inference and Rationale	Observation	Inference and Rationale
Score				

Total Score:

Name:

OBSERVATIONS OF SUPPORTIVE AND NONSUPPORTIVE FACTORS OF A LEARNING COMMUNITY

Date and Times	Supportive Factors		Nonsupportive Factors	
	Observations	Inference and Rationale	Observation	Inference and Rationale
Score				

Total Score:

Name:

Exercise 4.3
Identifying and Analyzing Norms; Identifying Related Behaviors and How to Teach Them to Group Members

Statement of Norms	Relationship to Functions of Schooling	Dispositions/ Propensities Link *Group Member* Dispositions to the Norms and Functions of Schooling	Describe the Distinctions that must be taught to Group Members	What would you teach your students in order to establish these norms? How would you go about teaching them? How will you reinforce the behaviors? How will you evaluate?
Respect for others and their property	Personal and Social Responsibility		Distinguish between respectful, disrespectful and kidding-around behavior:	
Cooperation	Social Responsibility		Distinguish between cooperation and passive behavior:	
Interdependence	Social Responsibility, Social Justice		Identify outcomes that result from these relationships:	
Completion of Tasks, Self-evaluations	Academic		Identify outcomes that result from establishment of these norms:	
Other:				
Other:				

Small Group Discussions

Use the procedures established in previous sessions of this university course for the organization and effective implementation of small group discussions. Turn in your group's notes to the instructor at the end of class. Following are questions to help you start your group discussion.

1. What are the Stages of Group Development used to establish a learning community.
2. What does the teacher and students do in each stage to move the group toward a learning community culture?
3. What are the things that a teacher should plan prior to the first day of school if she/he intends to establish a learning community culture?

| | | SELF-REPORT | NAME | | DATE |

Stages of Learning Community Group Development	Questions and Issues	List what you will do to answer the questions and resolve the issues	Personal Knowledge Skills, talk, actions & Dispositions that are Congruent with a Learning Community	Personal Knowledge, Skills, Talk, Actions and Dispositions that are *Incongruent* with a Learning Community	List what you would do to change each of the *Incongruent* items so that they became congruent or no longer existed
1					
2					
3					
4					
5					

Exercise 4.5
Learning How to Plan for Establishing a Learning Community Culture

Creating a Plan Establishing a Classroom Learning-Community Culture

The purpose of this activity is to provide you with the opportunity to think through and create a written plan for beginning to establish a classroom learning community. This exercise leads you through concrete activities that you will implement to get started once you begin teaching a small group or a classroom of learners. Use the following questions as guidelines for the development of a concrete plan for establishing a classroom learning community culture.

I. Assessment

    A. What is the nature of the classroom culture your students currently experience? List and describe the things you see that serve as evidence of their experience.

    B. What is the average number of other students' names that a student knows?

    C. If possible create and use a socio-gram to assess the nature of the relationships among the students.

    D. List differentiated learning styles and abilities, and special needs present in classroom group

II. Performance Outcomes

List the outcomes in behavioral terms, that you expect from each student if you plan and implement an effective Stage One-Beginnings, Stage Two-Establishing Expectations, and Stage Three-Identifying and Resolving Conflicts.

III. Preparing for Stage One: Beginnings Activities

    A. Design three Beginnings Activities that meet the criteria for establishing a Learning Community Culture.

        1. Create one activity that would be suitable for the beginning of the year or the beginning of your teaching responsibilities.

        2. Create the second activity appropriate for students who have been together for about three weeks.

        3. Create the third activity so that it is appropriate for students who have worked effectively together for about three months and is based on subject matter.

    B. Preparing for Stage Two: Establishing Expectations

        1. List all of the routines, procedures, norms, and rules you expect to establish in your classroom or group.

        2. For each one describe its contribution to the Learning Community Culture.

        3. Describe how you will teach the routines, procedures, norms and rules to your students.

            a. For those items that need an activity, design that activity.

            b. For those items that need role plays to illustrate the behavior, write out the role play you'd use.

            c. For those that need consequences, write out the consequence you would establish.

            d. For each routine, procedure, norm, and rule describe how you will reinforce them as part of your daily teacher talk and actions.

C. Preparing to Move Through Stage III: Identifying and Resolving Conflict.
1. Read Chapter 1, in Charles Wolfgang's *Solving Discipline Problems*.
2. Describe your place on the Discipline Continuum.
3. Write out how you will handle the following problem.
   Three students in your group or class do not follow your directions or requests. If you ask them to get their materials out, they simply do not do it. If you ask them a question, they just ignore you. What actions will you take to get these students to be effective members of your learning community?

Keep a copy of your plans, you will use them later.

RECOMMENDED READINGS

Bartles, B. H. (1995). "Promoting Mathematics Connections with Concept Mapping," Mathematics Teaching in the Middle Schools, Mathematics Teaching in the Middle School, Vol. I. No. 7, November–December.

Brophy, J. E. (1982). Classroom organization and management (Occasional Paper 54). East Lansing: Michigan State University, Institute for Research on Teaching.

Brophy, J. E., and Putnam, J. G. (1979). Classroom management in the elementary school, in D. L. Duke (ed.). Classroom management: The seventy-eighth yearbook of the National Society for the Study of Education. Chicago: The University of Chicago Press.

Good, T. L., and Brophy, J. E. (1987). Looking in classrooms, 4th ed. New York: Harper and Row.

Goodwin, D. L., and Coates, T. J. (1976). Helping students help themselves: How you can put behavior analysis into action in your classroom. Englewood Cliffs, N.J.: Prentice-Hall, Inc.

Johnson, J. (1977). Use of groups in school: A practical manual for everyone who works in elementary or secondary schools. New York: University Press of America.

Novak, Joseph D., Gowin, D. Bob. (1999). Learning How to Learn, Cambridge University Press.

Stanford, G. (1977). *Developing effective classroom groups: A practical guide for teachers.* New York: A & W Visual Library.

Stage I: Beginnings

Putnam, J., and Burke, B. (1992). Organizing and Managing Classroom Learning Communities. McGraw-Hill. Chapter 8, Stage I Beginnings. (See this chapter for concrete examples of activities and how to plan for the beginnings stage of your group development.)

Stage II: Establishing Expectations

Putnam, J., and Burke, B. (1992). Organizing and Managing Classroom Learning Communities. McGraw-Hill. Chapter 9, Stage II Establishing expectations. (See this chapter for concrete examples of activities and how to plan for establishing the expectations you have for your group's culture.)

Wolfgang, C., Solving discipline and classroom management problems, Methods and models for today's teachers. NJ John Wiley and Sons, Inc., Chapter 13, pages 233–246. (Note: This chapter provides a clear example of the multiple expectations and procedures teachers must think through.)

Stage III: Identifying and Resolving Conflicts

Putnam, J., and Burke, B. (1992). Organizing and managing classroom learning communities. McGraw-Hill. Chapter 10, Stage III Identifying and resolving conflicts. (See this chapter for concrete examples of procedures to use in identifying and solving conflicts.)

Wolfgang, C. (2001). Solving discipline and classroom management problems, Methods and models for today's teachers. NJ John Wiley and Sons, Inc. (This book reviews in depth the major discipline models.)

5

CHAPTER

A Primary-Level Classroom

This chapter describes a first-grade teacher and her students as they establish a classroom learning community. We have given the teacher the name "Janet Forero," and the description is based on a real case study reported by Putnam (1984a). In order to develop a classroom learning community, this teacher (1) fostered group responsibility for learning, (2) fostered individual responsibility for learning, (3) used heterogeneous groups, and (4) employed task and objective monitoring systems. In addition, she used three strategies which also contributed to creating a vision of learning community: (1) identifying what students were to know and/or be able to do by the end of the school year; (2) collaborative planning between the teacher and students; and (3) explicit organizing focused on development of personal responsibility, responsibility to the classroom group, and academic responsibility.

Forero thought about her teaching role as that of a goal-directed decision maker. For example, she frequently asked herself, "What are you trying to get done?" (Putnam, 1984a; p. 3). She viewed instruction as a complex series of preactive, interactive, and postactive decisions. Thus, teaching for Forero was a process of finding answers to a set of questions that she continuously asked herself:

1. *Preactive*   What do I know? What is expected? Who are the learners?
2. *Interactive*   What does she/he understand? What do I need to change?
3. *Postactive*   What happened? What comes next?

This description is based on the report of a year-long study of this teacher and her primary-age students (Putnam, 1984a).

When interviewed about her thinking as a teacher, Forero revealed several distinctive features. One feature of her thinking was her tendency, at the beginning of the planning process, to assess the quality and adequacy of the information she possessed. She would then determine what additional data needed to be collected for her decision making. A second feature was her propensity to make decisions based on her students' achieving long-term goals. Very early in the year, she identified the academic, personal responsibility, and social responsibility goals for which she would hold the students accountable by the end of the year. A third feature of her thinking was how she integrated preactive and interactive teaching decisions. Rather than thinking about planning as a teacher behavior separate from instruction, she saw planning as integrated with instruction in the form of decision making. Forero's decision-making strategies supported her effort to guide her class through the five stages of development of an effective classroom learning community: beginnings, establishing expectations, conflict resolution and problem solving, productivity, and transitions and closure. Table 5–1 illustrates how Forero used group development for the stages of creating a classroom learning community. Forero cycled through the five developmental stages each time she started a new integrated unit of instruction. She organized and taught between five and seven units each year. Forero followed an action-research model for her roles in the classroom. She used a five-function heuristic in monitoring her classroom learning community: data collection, data synthesis, data-based decision making, data-based instruction, and evaluation and verification (Putnam, 1984a; p. 8). Data collection included taking in new information and recalling data previously collected. Data synthesis was the process in which Forero integrated new and old data, then narrowed down the data to a usable size and/or form. Data-based decision making followed from the synthesis and was based on it. Forero next taught the units and lessons she and the students had planned, paying close attention to the students' responses and performances and adjusting the instruction to fit her updated ideas about what specific students needed in order to succeed. Finally, she verified her decisions by observing her students and evaluating her teaching against the standard of her students' learning.

Key to Forero's success in planning for and establishing a classroom learning community was the content of the information that she processed and the relationships she valued. She believed that her students' relationships with each other would be related to the kinds of rules, routines, procedures, and instructional activities that were selected. She wanted students to be problem solvers as learners. Establishing a learning community in which students had the opportunity to solve problems and make decisions meant that she had to promote rules, routines, procedures, and instructional activities that would provide opportunity for students to be responsible and accountable.

The remainder of this chapter is in five sections, corresponding to the stages listed in Table 5-1. The section on stage I describes Forero's planning and decisions as she prepares for starting school and her yearly task of establishing a classroom learning community. The section on stage II describes how she initially worked with her students to establish a classroom learning community. The sections on stages III, IV, and V briefly describe how Forero and her students cycled through these stages during the rest of the year.

TABLE 5-1   MODEL FOR CREATING AND MAINTAINING A CLASSROOM LEARNING COMMUNITY

Stage I: *Beginnings*   Establishing the classroom learning community (3 weeks at beginning of school year)
            Components include:
            A. Planning for new school year
                Data collection
                Data synthesis
                Preactive decision making (identifying goals, activities for learning names,
                getting acquainted, and assessment)
            B. Implementing plan
                Interactive data collection
                Interactive decision making
Stage II: *Establishing expectations*   Occurs simultaneously with stage III
            Components include: Socializing students on how to live together in the classroom learning community
Stage III: *Conflict identification and resolution*
            Components include:
            A. Preactive decisions
            B. Simulations for learning how to solve conflicts
            C. Reflective thinking, synthesis, and postactive decisions
Stage IV: *Supporting and expanding production*   (eight months of school year)
            Cycle for each of five units of instruction:
            A. Preparation
            B. Implementation
            C. Reflection
Stage V: *Closure and transition*   (last two weeks of year)
            Components include:
            A. Reviewing the year
            B. Reflecting on what was achieved (the first step in planning for the next year)

STAGE I. BEGINNINGS

Preparation

Forero started each school year by thinking about what she knew about the curriculum and the students. She reviewed the information in the texts and thought about specific goals she wanted her primary students to achieve in reading. She gathered new data by reading the cumulative recording forms, talking with teachers who had taught her students the previous year, and looking at schedules of school events. She took notes and made lists during this phase. She eventually organized the information that she gained into six categories. This information represents assessment data collected prior to her actually working with a new group of students. (See Table 5-2.)

Forero's first category, "self," was a list of things that she identified as her current interests, strengths, philosophy, and weakness. "Teaching and learning" was a list of her assumptions, which she identified as being based on her knowledge and experiences about learning, concept of teaching, and transfer of knowledge/skills by students to situations other than the initial instructional context. She included on this list the things that she had learned since the previous fall. Some of these things had come from courses she took, in-service experiences, and inferences based on her systematic collection of data about her students during the previous academic year. "Students" was a list of things that she had learned about this year's students' previous experiences and performances by studying their cumulative files, by talking with teachers, and from her casual observations of the students during the previous year. "Environment" was a list of things that she brainstormed as ways to enhance learning through the use of the classroom and the nearby community. This list included ideas for setting up the classroom, for making field trips, for utilizing community resources, and for working with parents. "Curriculum" included a list of academic, personal responsibility, and social responsibility outcomes, along with topics that could be considered as the basis for curriculum development for the year. Finally, "community" was a list of the desires, expectations, and hopes of her students' parents.

Forero's lists show that her preactive planning required time to think, collect new data, talk, and organize information. It also shows that she was a teacher who consistently made decisions based on tested information.

Planning Decision Making—Establishing Expectations

Using the data that she had collected and synthesized, Forero then made a series of preactive decisions concerning:

1. The nature of the classroom community she wished to establish
2. Specific student outcomes
3. A related classroom organization and management model
4. Evaluation recording systems
5. Specific content and processes that would make up the framework of the curriculum

TABLE 5-2   ORGANIZING WHAT IS KNOWN

1. Self
2. Teaching and learning
3. Students
4. Environment
5. Curriculum
6. Community

Source: Putnam, 1984a; p. 10.

The Nature of the Classroom Community

Forero's decision about the **Nature of Her Classroom Community** was made several years prior to our study. Her concept of a learning-community classroom had been developed over several years. It had emerged from her initial concept that the classroom group should function as an effective family. At the beginning of each year, Forero reviewed her beliefs about the classroom learning community. She recommitted herself to the concept and made her assumptions and related classroom activities more explicit as her understanding developed. Her reflection helped her to see that a new year required new commitments to her kind of teaching and to her ideas of the classroom community.

During the year that the authors studied Forero, she verbalized her decision to establish a classroom learning community which featured an interactive instructional style. She described this community as one in which students orally, nonverbally, and in writing interact with each other and the teacher, while the teacher modifies her thinking, speech, and actions based on what she observes and infers. This decision prompted her to organize her class in a way which would maximize student responsibility and accountability and minimize her role in managing student behavior so that she could attend to the instructional interactions.

Three major decisions and related planning were the focus of the rest of Forero's thinking in this period. She made decisions about student outcomes (goals), classroom coordination, and instruction and curriculum.

Academic and Social Outcomes

Each year Forero selected the **Academic, Personal, and Social Outcomes** for her students. She saw these decisions as very important, and she made a commitment to hold herself accountable for her students' achieving the selected goals. During the year of this study, she was teaching students from two grade levels, and so she constructed two sets of outcomes. Based on her notes on standard expectations for students at each grade level that she taught, the academic work presented in textbooks, curriculum guidelines, and the explicit expectations of other teachers at both the same and the next grade level, Forero identified specific goals for her students. She individualized her expectations in the form of objectives. When she did not initially have enough data on a student, she waited until school started to interact and collect additional assessment data. She listed her objectives and noted whether each objective applied to all students or to an individual or a subset of students.

Classroom Organization

Forero's basic **Classroom Organization** decisions were guided by the idea that rules and routines for student behavior must be congruent with and must support the learning community concept. Thus, her criteria for evaluating her decisions were based on what the community would need to develop: (1) group work, (2) cooperation, (3) maximum teacher instructional time and student engagement, (4) community members who would take positions of leadership in the classroom, and (5) use of the out-of-school community.

Rules

Next Forero identified her **Rules** about behavior in helping and individual work, in small-group work, and in working with members of the classroom learning community and the larger community outside of class. She checked to see that these rules were congruent with her concept of the learning community. For example, her classes had the rule, "Help others when you are asked and know how to help and have time to help. Say no when you are asked to help and you do not know how to help or do not have time." She saw this rule as supporting the ideas of both personal and social responsibility.

Student Attitudes

Forero also identified four **Attitudes** students needed to acquire: (1) Be positive. (2) Enjoy learning. (3) Realize that teachers are responsible for teaching and students are responsible for learning. (4) Realize that helping and asking for help are your responsibilities. During her planning time, Forero identified specific student behaviors to suit these attitudes. (The attitudes and behaviors were then explicitly taught during stage II, establishing expectations.) Table 5-3 is a list of eight behaviors that she wanted her students to learn because she felt that these behaviors would help the students to achieve more academically.

Procedures and Routines

Forero also identified **Procedures and Routines** that would be congruent with her concept of community. She evaluated these to be sure that they contributed to (1) student participation in the learning community, (2) engaged time, (3) teacher instructional time, and (4) students' accountability for their own learning and behavior. She defined "routines" as sequences of behavior that did not involve problem solving. In her room, routines included: (1) turning in homework; (2) folding hands and looking in the eyes of a leader at the beginning of a whole-class presentation; (3) taking home every night a book at independent reading level and reading from it to someone who was older than the student, having a slip signed by the listener, returning the slip, answering questions about the book, and marking a chart; and (4) storing certain things in assigned places. She taught her students that "procedures" were events or sequences of steps that required decision making and interactions with other students in the class. She identified five procedures to use in teaching responsibility to the students. (See Table 5-4.)

Task Completion and Achievement of Objectives

Given all that Forero wanted to accomplish with her students, she had to keep track of students' **Task Completion and Achievement of Objectives.** Good record keeping was necessary in order to monitor her students' progress. She kept records on students' acquisition of specified academic outcomes, on their demonstrations of responsibility and accountability, and on examples of interactive teaching and

TABLE 5-3   Student Behavior for Getting and Giving Help

1. How to offer help to someone
2. How to know when you need help
3. How to ask for help
4. How to listen to the helper
5. How to help (tutor)
6. How to say that you cannot help
7. When to say that you cannot help
8. How to say that you do not want help

Source: Putnam, 1984b, p. 9.

TABLE 5-4   Procedures Which Enhance Student Responsibility and Accountability

1. Voting to decide something
2. Problem identification
3. Evaluation of oneself and others (receiving and providing feedback)
4. Before-school studying
5. Initiating requests to be evaluated or helped

Source: Putnam, 1984b, p. 13.

learning. Her record-keeping systems, which were mostly public, aided her in using up-to-date information about the students as she worked with them individually and in groups. For example, over each student's desk she decided to hang a string and a clamp-type clothespin. As students completed tasks related to a unit of study, she would give them pieces of a figure to glue to a basic shape which was then clipped to the string. This system allowed Forero, whether she was working individually with students at their seats or they came to her in another part of the room, to glance at the forms above their desks to determine what tasks they should be doing or where in the series of activities they were working. She could also assess the group's progress by systematically looking around the room. As she planned for the next day's work, she was able to make decisions about an individual's tasks based on this recording system. Forero also developed a recording system for keeping track of the objectives that the students had achieved. She decided on a system that would allow her to record (in her grade book) when students first achieved an objective and when they "learned" or transferred that particular knowledge or skill to a new situation. These two systems were supported by many checkoff-charts for recording acquisition of individual skills and building of vocabulary, as well as completion of homework and at-home reading.

Content and Processes

Finally, Forero made decisions about the **Content and Processes** that would be included in class during the year. Her first decisions about topics were always tentative, and she viewed them as a list of potential alternatives. After she and the students completed the study of the initial topic she had picked, they decided together what to study next.

Her decision about the first topic of instruction for the year was based on the following criteria. First, the topic should involve creating a problem-solving activity which would allow her to observe students' behavior and achievement. She wanted to relate observable student behavior to the objectives she had identified for the first period of six or seven weeks. The topic also had to be one about which Forero knew the content and, preferably, one with which she had had personal experience. Further, the topic had to be one that the students already knew something about, one with which they had had some prior experience, and one which offered many opportunities to explore various contents with hands-on experiences. Finally, the topic had to provide for cooperative working experiences. Forero believed that topics that met these criteria allowed her to assess students and, at the same time, to model the learning activity. During instruction, she would absorb and store information about her students rather than spending a lot of public, interactive teaching time processing content or procedural information. Likewise, the first topic would be treated as a guide for the students, a model of how the classroom would run throughout the school year.

After Forero selected the first topic (e.g., apples), she planned an assessment activity related to the topic (e.g., making applesauce and writing an experience story) that allowed her to collect specific data about the students' social skills and academic knowledge and skills. The assessment activity also allowed her and the students to collaboratively plan the rest of the unit of study. She planned the assessment activity to include whole-class discussion, decision making, lecture, smallgroup work, and individual work.

Unlike many teachers, Forero spent little or no time on "decorating her classroom" before the students arrived. Instead, during the beginning and establishing-expectations stages, she and the students set up the environment together as a way of getting to know each other and what each expected of the school year. Thus, a secondary criterion that Forero used in deciding what to do during the first days of school was that the activities should result in products (group and individual) which could be put up in the room to decorate, inform, and teach.

By the time she reached this point, Forero had made preactive decisions about identifying:

1. An organization and management system

2. The first area of study and a tentative list of topics for the curriculum

3. A list of goals for the year

4. Objectives for the first unit which were related to year-long goals

5. Potential instructional strategies (e.g., cooperative learning and working with senior citizens at the center four blocks from school)

6. Systems for keeping track of individuals' task completion and achievement of objectives

At the beginning of the year, all these decisions were in formulation; that is, Forero kept all these decisions tentative until after the orientation sessions and the completion of her first assessment activity.

Implementation

During the first school days, Forero and her students worked together to "decorate" the room and to establish how they would "be together" as a learning community. During a period of fifteen days, the collaborative decision making of this teacher and her students evolved into a routine that allowed the students to discuss, plan, problem-solve, and make decisions together. The structures for the learning community were established in this time frame. On the fifteenth day, the researcher was able to say, "Oh, this is how this community will function. This is how the teacher and the students will be together" (Putnam, 1984b, p. 12).

Forero introduced eight procedures and/or values during the first fifteen days of school which may be taken as characteristics of the learning community she sought to establish. Early introduction of valued practices formed the foundation of her classroom learning community and acted as an advance organizer for what life in the learning community would be like. (See Table 5-5.) Forero provided her students with answers to the orientation questions usually raised by students when they enter a new group (Putnam, 1984b): "Who is in the group?" "What is expected?" "How will I be treated?" "How should I behave?"

The descriptions below give a clue to the activities that occurred while Forero was establishing a learning community. The time was spent on developing the concept of community (or family), as well as on providing instruction and feedback relative to behavior that would be expected in the classroom learning community.

Physical Environment

When the students entered the room, they saw it as divided into three parts. The front part of the room contained a desk for each student, the "teacher's desk" (which was to be frequently used by students during the year), a two-story loft, a seven-foot bench, a chalkboard, a bulletin board, and a cubby box or shelf for each student's personal things. The other two parts of the room were set up with round tables and chairs for small-group-work. Seven posters were taped to the front board.

The room had not been decorated before the students arrived, because of Forero's belief that the community was a shared responsibility and that the students needed to participate in the creation of their physical environment as well as their social environment.

TABLE 5–5   Key Characteristics of a Learning-Community Classroom

1. Emphasis on student and teacher participation in decision making
2. Acceptance of a range of feelings and the stress of transition. An emphasis on communication
3. Talk about the class as a family
4. Linking to students' families via writing, homework, and expectations for support
5. Self-disclosure by adults and students
6. Integration of social and academic skills, building on themes discussed the first days of school (e.g., family and linking)
7. Use of first names by everyone
8. Student and teacher statements about quality of behavior with specific examples provided

Source: Putnam, 1984b, p. 8.

Learning Names and Getting Acquainted

On the first day of school, the teacher stayed near the door. As the students entered the room, the teacher greeted each one individually. She called them by name or asked their names, and she looked each one directly in the eyes as she greeted him/her. She asked each student about a family member, a pet, or some personal matter. She introduced students to each other, saying, "Tim, do you know Javier? Javier, this is Tim. Please go over to the desks and see if you can find the one with your name taped to it. If you see someone having a hard time finding the right desk, you can help. Then sit in your seat. We have a lot to do today." She kept an eye on the students as they looked for the desks with their names on them. If a student was having difficulty, she said, for example, "Tim, William is having a hard time finding his desk. Can you find his name?" After all the students were in the room, she walked over toward the desks and continued talking: "I wonder where Chris' desk is; has anyone seen her name on a desk?"

When everyone was in his/her seat, Forero started a whole-class session by asking the students to fold their hands and look directly in her eyes. Then she said, "We've got to get to know each other. You can call me Janet. I think that Forero is a hard name to say." She introduced the other adults in the room (a researcher and an aide) by their first names. Then she walked around the group and mentioned each student's name and something the student had said to her upon entering the room. "Michael said he was sorry summer was over. Michael, what was the reason?" Michael responded,"I want to go to the lake to swim some more." Then she put her hand on one student's shoulder and asked the group in general who knew that student's name. She listened to callouts; after several people had said the student's name, she asked a student who had not volunteered. When possible, she made connections between what was of interest to one student (e.g., "cooking") and what was of interest to another student (e.g., "reading"), mentioning both students' names.

STAGE II. ESTABLISHING EXPECTATIONS

Establishing expectations is the stage of development which includes implementing and framing the culture of the community. Examples that contribute to the learning community are establishing permissions and prohibitions, community participation, room procedures, recess procedures, homework procedures, norms, and ways to give and get attention. These are described in detail below.

Identifying Permissions and Prohibitions

Forero started by saying, "If we are going to work together, we've got to figure out how to be together. We spend so much of our life here at school. We'd better learn to be like a family when we're together. That means some things will be all right for us to do and some are not all right." Forero and the students took turns mentioning things to do and not do: Listen, so that you will know what another person says. Don't laugh when someone doesn't know something or makes a mistake. Raise your hand to take turns talking when meeting in the whole group. Do something else if you can't get help and you have to wait behind more than three people. Go to the bathroom or get a drink when you need to. Ask to borrow something. Put things back where they came from. If you have a serious problem and you can't solve it by getting someone's help, signal for everyone's attention by flicking the light. Keep track of your papers and your work. Help others to learn. Ask for help when you need it. Try to do things on your own before you ask for help.

Forero then said, "It sounds like we understand that in this classroom we will treat each other and things with respect." She wrote the words "We will treat each other and things with respect" on a piece of chart paper. The paper was on the wall the next day.

Starting the Concept of Participation in Community—Deciding Things by Voting

Forero said, "In this room sometimes we vote on things, and sometimes we will try to get everyone to agree." She described what voting meant, giving examples. A student asked if the class could vote about what to do if someone "is not good." Forero asked everyone who wanted to be good to raise his/her hand. Forero looked around the room, told the students to look around the room and then she said, "It looks to me like everyone wants to be good, so I don't think that we will have a problem." She explained that today they would select a picture to write about.

Taped to the chalkboard in front of the class were eight pictures. The pictures included: (1) children baking something; (2) an adult and a child hugging; (3) a child hitting a baseball; (4) a child in an autumn woods; (5) children with an animal; (6) two children doing artwork in school; (7) a man and a boy sitting on a porch step, apparently talking; and (8) a child sitting alone, perhaps thinking. Forero asked the students to describe each picture or something the picture reminded them of. She made sure that each student responded at least once. She reminded students who spoke out of turn or interrupted another student to wait and to listen to the person who was speaking so that they could know what that person had said. She asked them to raise their hands when they wanted to speak to the group, because they were meeting as a whole class. She also asked students to look at the other students in the group when they were talking, rather than just looking at her. During the discussion, Forero used students' comments, added her own comments, and made explicit links with the behavior in the pictures and "family actions" (e.g., talking to adults, being alone, working alone, working together, working with a brother or sister, or with an adult or someone older, and making things).

Finally, she said that they were going to vote on the eight pictures, to pick the topic that they would write about, on this first day of school. She explained that each child could vote only once, and then, as the children voted, she recorded the votes under each picture. There were twenty-five students, and after the first voting there were twenty-nine votes. Forero said, "Please close your eyes and think about whether you voted one time or two times." She then reminded the students, "Raise your hand to vote for the picture that you want to write about today." The vote was held again, and this time there were twenty-five votes. The picture that won was the one of the man and boy talking on a step.

Forero placed the picture on one side of a bulletin board. She and the students then worked together to compose a story about the picture. Forero wrote the story on chart paper and when it had been completed, it was placed on the bulletin board next to the picture. She asked what she should write for "author." The group agreed on "The Class." She told the students that they would be putting up other pieces of their work.

Bathroom Procedure

On the first day of school, Forero taught the students the procedures for using the bathroom. She said that procedures for going to recess and using the bathroom were one way when they were all working together in one group; permission was needed to leave the group. However, when they weren't working in one group, the students could use the bathroom when they decided to leave their work, needed to go to the bathroom, and no one else was in there. She then asked the students when they were to ask permission and when they would decide on their own to use the bathroom, and listened to their responses.

Next, she talked about how the bathroom near the classroom was like the bathrooms the students had at home; that is, since everyone uses the same bathroom, they needed a way to signal to other people when the bathroom was being used. Students suggested that they knock, have a sign, leave the door open when the room was not in use, or sign up. She said she agreed with the sign because that would take the least time and would keep the bathroom private. She picked up a piece of tagboard to which she had tied a string, and asked what the sign should say. She called on students who raised their hands, told those who called out to raise their hands, and then called on them after one or two others had turns, so that they could contribute their ideas. She asked a student to repeat what she had said earlier about how to get a turn to share an idea when they were meeting in the whole class. Students suggested words, which Forero wrote on the board.

She encouraged the students to think of as many words as possible to represent "occupied and vacant." She then pointed to three or four of the words in turn, asking students to raise their hands if they thought that word would work. She reported to the class that more people thought "busy" and "open" were the best words. With a large felt pen, she then wrote the words on opposite sides of the sign and asked one of the students to put the sign on the hook on the bathroom door.

Going to and from Recess

Forero saw recess as a break from academic work rather than as a physical education class. On a normal day, either she noticed or one of the students told her that it was time for the break. (Forero and the students went over an agenda and noted the times for various activities at the beginning of each day.) When the class members were not working together as a whole class, students left for breaks individually, in pairs, or in small groups. Forero would dismiss students to go outside as she worked with them individually, or she would walk by the desks of students she had worked with earlier and quietly asked them if they were ready to take a break. Sometimes she said, "You need to take a break; you are having so much trouble with this; just leave it for a few minutes, go outside, and maybe when you come back you can get it." Sometimes, she said, "You and Mareal wanted to organize a game for today. Why don't you get her and the equipment, and go outside and set things up. Then when the others come, you will be ready."

When the students were working in a whole group and it was time to take a break, she dismissed the students by rows, telling them to get their outerwear and go outside. If they wanted to go first to the bathroom, they would stay in their seats, take their turns, and then go outside.

Whether she dismissed students individually or as a group, she always reminded them of what the activity after break would be. (For example, "When you come in from break, I'm going to read you a story about helping," or "Leave things as you have them so that you can get right back to your work when you come in.") She wanted the students, toward the end of the break, to begin to think about what was going to happen in the classroom when they came back (mentally preparing themselves to get quickly on task). Thus, during the first days of school, when it was time for the students to come back from break, Forero would walk around and gather three or four students together and say, "It is time to go back to the room. Please go to the room and put your sweaters on the coat rack and begin your work. If you want to, you can get a drink or go to the bathroom, but if the water fountain or the bathroom is full, go to your seat and wait. What is the next thing that we are going to do?" As soon as a student replied with "Tell us a story" or whatever was next, she said, "I can see that you are thinking about what we will do next." By the time two such groups of students had entered the room, she was back at the door and others were lining up. Again she spoke to small groups, repeating her message.

During the year, students learned to monitor their own behavior. They came into the room, went out for breaks, and left at the end of the day individually or in small groups. Lines were not used as a means for moving students from work to break or to lunch. Instead, students moved to the next activity as they completed their transactions with the teacher about the current activity. Students moved together in clusters, walking on the sidewalks to places off the school grounds or to the school-wide activities (e.g., assemblies). "People walk and talk without disturbing other people," Forero taught her students. Thus, when Forero moved her students from the room to an assembly, she would ask, "What will the other teachers and students and the principal be expecting from us? If all of us are to enjoy this activity, what will we each have to do?" She would look at the student who was responding to her question and would listen intently. Then she would ask another student what the previous student had said. (This would serve as the reminder of expectations for behavior in specific situations.) When a previous experience had not been what was expected as standard behavior, Forero would use her observations of that time to ask what had gone wrong or what was the problem and how they could overcome the problem this time.

Teaching Routines: The Home Envelope

Forero followed a pattern in teaching routines. She taught a routine by providing examples, having two or three students model while she provided specific feedback. During the next couple of days after introducing a new routine, Forero provided positive and negative feedback until the students had internalized the new routine.

Forero introduced the home envelopes to students by showing one to the class. Then she showed them the pile of envelopes. Each student had an envelope, and she had written their names on their envelopes so that they could keep track of them. She told them that the envelopes were part of an important routine because they helped the students to communicate with the people who lived in their houses about what they were doing in school. She said that this routine provided them with a systematic way to handle their homework and communication between the classroom community and the "home family." The students were to put in their envelopes their home reading books, the slips to be signed by their listeners, notes from the school to home, and homework. They were to take the envelopes home every afternoon and bring them back each morning. She said that the envelope was the student's responsibility, and not the responsibility of their father, grandmother, brother, aunt, or mother.

Next she created a role-play on the spot. She asked one student to take an envelope and go out the door and another student to leave the envelope on the desk and go out the door. They were to pretend that it was the next day, and they were to come into the room. Forero positioned herself near the chart on which she would keep a record of home reading (where she stood each morning for the next several days when the students were entering the room). When the student with the envelope came into the room, she said, "I see that you have your envelope. Did you read to someone last night? Who? Put your coat on the rack and bring me your signed slip." After the student walked to the rack and over to Forero, she looked at the slip and pretended to make a check on the chart next to the student's name. When the next student entered the room without the envelope, Forero, asked, "Where is your envelope?" The student said, "I didn't take it; I left in on my desk." Forero said, "What is your responsibility concerning the envelope?"

During the next couple of days, Forero positioned herself near the chart when it was time for the students to come into the room. She watched the students as they entered and directed those entering with envelopes and signed slips to the chart, those without envelopes to their seats, and those with envelopes but no signed slips to their seats. Students who had their envelopes but hadn't read to someone at home the night before was one problem Forero worked to solve. A second problem was students who did not have their envelopes.

Forero asked the students who did not have their envelopes to think about where they had left them. She closed her eyes and put her index fingers by them to model thinking. Some students went to their lockers and returned with their envelopes. Some said such things as "My mother wanted to keep it," "My brother burned it up," or "My grandmother said she gave it to you before school." Forero talked to each about the consequences of not being able to do something in school because the envelope was not there (e.g., being unable to write in a journal or practice a poem that was in the envelope). She said to the student who had said her grandmother had given it to Forero that at break she would call the grandmother. Before break, the girl came to Forero and said that her grandmother didn't have it but she couldn't remember where it was. She asked one boy to call home and have someone bring him his envelope.

During the first days the students who had not read to anyone met individually with Forero (during break, or right before lunch), and together they figured out whom the students could read to. For students who had no one available at home, Forero found students in higher grades who could meet them at noon, at break, or before school and serve as the listener and sign their slips. By the third day of school, all students had taken and returned their envelopes once. By day four, all but two students had done it twice. On the fourth day, Forero had the class think about where they would put their envelopes when they went in the door at home. She then told them to always put their envelopes in the same spot. Only one student continued to have problems with materials after the first 15 days of school.

Establishing Norms

One example of how Forero established expectations for behavior in the classroom community is how she introduced the norm of helping and being helped by others.

When the students came back from their break on the first day of school, Forero told them that it was important to help other people. She gave examples of how she, her child, husband, mother, father, sisters, and brothers helped one another. Then she asked the students to give examples of how they helped others outside school. Next, Forero told how she helped students in the classroom and asked the students to give examples of how they helped each other in school.

She then read a story, the point of which was helping, and showed posters of children and adults helping each other and their peers. After the story, the students were asked who, what, where, when, and why questions, with a focus on who was helping and who was not. Forero then asked the students to say how they thought the children and adults were helping in the poster pictures. The discussion switched to helping in the classroom. She asked questions such as: "How does the teacher help students?" "How do students help themselves?" "How do students help each other?" "How do students help adults and visitors who come to the classroom?" "How do students help the teacher?" "How do students help their families to know what they are learning in school?" "Who at home can help students by listening to them read and answering their questions?" Forero wrote the students' suggestions on the board, along with expectations that she would be making explicit and teaching during the first three weeks of school.

Feelings, Attitudes, and Motivation to Learn

Forero also led conversations about feelings. The purpose of these discussions was to communicate to the students that not all things that people have to do are things they actually "love." She talked about how important it was to do things (learn your sight words) so that you would be an outstanding reader. She communicated that things are sometimes hard to do, but that it is important to keep working at them.

Forero told the students about several personal examples to differentiate between "like," "love," and "dislike." She asked students to give examples of things that they liked to do, loved to do, and disliked doing. She also related the concepts of helping to the students' interpersonal relationships and things that happen at home. She then related the concepts to things in school, making the point about having to do things that we don't like to do. She mentioned things the students had said. Then she read the story "Things I Like."

After Forero finished the story, she asked, "What is an illustrator? Does anyone know what an author is?" Several students raised their hands and before Forero could systematically call on anyone, someone had defined author and someone had defined illustrator. In each case, Forero asked other children to paraphrase the correct answer.

She then said that soon the students would be authors and illustrators. This comment elicited some grumbles. Forero responded by saying, "I don't think that is the right attitude." She asked why particular students did not like writing. She then elaborated on the task and said that in about two weeks the students would each have made a book that they could take home.

Teaching How to Pay Attention and How to Communicate with the Group

Before school started one morning, Forero planned with three students presentations that they would give to the class. Each presentation was done first "poorly" and then in an appropriate fashion. One student first read to the class with the book in front of her face and mumbling, and then she held the book down, looked up at the audience periodically, and used a clear, projected voice. Another student flicked the lights to get the group's attention and started to tell his problem before the group stopped talking and started looking at him. Then he flicked the lights, waited until he had everyone's attention, looked at the class, and spoke in a clear, projected voice. The third student gave an unclear set of directions and then asked people to do the task. Students said they didn't know what to do. Then she gave the directions again, demonstrating how to do the task and pointing to a chart she and Forero had made to illustrate the directions.

After each simulation, Forero asked her students what was difficult or helpful about the presentation. Next, she asked the speakers what was helpful or unhelpful about the class's behavior.

STAGE III. CONFLICT RESOLUTION AND PROBLEM SOLVING

Forero expected that her students would have problems, but she also expected them to learn how to figure things out as the classroom learning community developed. She taught them a strategy for problem solving. To help teach problem solving and how helping was associated with solving problems, Forero and two students planned a little roleplay about someone's pencil being taken.

During the opening activities, as planned, Steve yelled, "Marty took my pencil."

Forero looked at Steve and said, "Steve, did you see Marty take your pencil?"

"No," said Steve.

"But your pencil is gone?"

"Yes."

"What can you say that you know is true?"

"My pencil is gone."

Forero said, "Steve, I have your pencil. I forgot to put it back when I was at your desk before school this morning."

Forero then told her three conclusions about the pencil event. First, "When something happens, report observations only and don't blame people for things you don't observe." Second, "If you have a problem and can't solve it yourself or with another student and/or the teacher, flick the lights to get everyone's attention, and we'll solve it as a group." Third, "If you need something, ask. Someone will help. If you are asked to help, do what you can."

Interspersed with her communication about problem solving, Forero taught the concepts of *observation* and *inference,* as well as when to say "Yes, I can help" and when to say "No, I can't help." For example, the students were to say yes if they had the time and understood the content the person was trying to learn. They were to say no if they didn't have time or didn't know the content. Forero's strategy for teaching students how to make good decisions was to give an example and label what she was doing.

Knowing how to tutor (help) someone was a related problem-solving skill she also taught. Before school in the morning, she taught pairs of students to role-play "tutoring helpfully" (learning occurs) and "tutoring destructively" (no one learns but blanks are filled in or answers written down). After the demonstrations and class discussion, for approximately two days Forero provided the students with numerous opportunities to give and receive help. When problems arose, she stopped the class, stated the problem, and asked what they had said before about this type of problem. When a specific problem arose, she would have students roleplay the situation. Feedback between the person being helped and the helper was incorporated into the tutoring process. Finally, to reinforce the constructive helping idea, Forero had pairs of students who had worked together meet with her so that she could talk with them about what they had said to each other and check out whether the tutee knew the material. If the tutee did know it, she would say, "This worked for you." If not, she role-played them through the process, pointing out that the tutee was to "learn, understand, and be able to do what was expected." Other types of feedback Forero gave to support the establishment of the helping process were as follows:

1. "You had to ask three people to find someone to help you with this. I'm glad you stuck to it, now you have this done."

2. "Your work is not done, and I saw you helping Frank most of the morning. You like to help. You'll have to figure out how much time you can spend on helping and how much time you need to do your own work."

Peer helping was an integrated part of the community norms. Daily, Forero cued students about the helping process by such comments as "Marcus can help you with this if you have trouble; he has already mastered it" and "You've got this right now; you can help others who are working on this, when they ask you."

STAGE IV. SUPPORTING AND EXPANDING PRODUCTION

Forero divided the production stage of development into three phases: preparation, implementation, and reflection. She saw these phases as organizers for the productive activities in her classroom learning community. During the school year in which we observed Forero, she and the students planned and implemented five integrated curriculum units during the production stage. This section provides examples of how she and her students worked together for most of the year.

Preparation

Forero organized her curriculum into five integrated units over the year. She held collaborative planning sessions with her students at the beginning of each unit. She and her students planned together what she would teach, what they would learn, and how they would learn it. Remember that Forero had already, during her preactive planning, actually identified the specific objectives for which she planned to hold all students accountable. During the early stages of the group's development, as she collected and analyzed assessment data about each student, she refined these objectives. Thus, she began with some clear ideas about what knowledge and skills each student needed to acquire during the year.

Forero used collaborative planning because she saw this strategy as providing a foundation that would help students to learn how to become personally and socially responsible for their learning. The planning sessions included making decisions about the substance of the curriculum and the activities that would be included. Forero followed eight steps in the planning process (see Table 5–6). Below is a brief description of each of the steps Forero used initially to teach her students how to plan, as well as the steps she used later in the production stage in her learning community.

Step 1

Forero told the students that they were going to make applesauce. She explained her interest in the activity and the topic it represented. She told the students that she was very interested in apples because she grew up on a truck farm where her family had raised vegetables and fruits. She talked about helping her mom and dad pick vegetables and apples. She told about (1) getting punished by her parents when she climbed an apple tree that was too little and she broke it, (2) being praised by her parents when she helped, (3) what types of family events she liked, and (4) what she knew about apples (on the basis of growing them, making things from them, and eating them). Then she asked the students what they knew about apples. When a student would tell about something that was similar to someone else's contribution, Forero would ask, "Who else said something like that?"

Step 2

Forero and her students then participated in the concrete activity, which Forero calls "the initiating common experience." For the first unit of the year, it was making applesauce. While the students were making and eating applesauce, Forero interacted with them and made first observations of their language development, social and cooperative skills, writing and reading skills, and memory patterns. Later she made notes on 3 × 5 cards about what she had learned. She then used the information she had collected to determine individual instructional needs. (See step 8.)

TABLE 5–6   STEPS IN COLLABORATIVE TEACHER-STUDENT PLANNING

1. Forero described a concrete activity in which everyone would participate, as well as her rationale for suggesting the activity.
2. The class did the concrete activity (e.g., a treasure hunt or making applesauce).
3. Students answered who, what, where, when, and why questions for a group experience story.
4. Students answered who, what, where, when, and why questions for an individual experience story and wrote stories about their previous experiences related to the concrete activity topic.
5. Forero and students answered two questions that led to the identification of the potential subject matter to be learned and some ways in which it could be learned.
6. Forero met with students to identify specific tasks for which they would be held accountable.
7. Forero and individual students identified specific objectives for which they would be held accountable. (These specific objectives were related to the original set of outcomes for which Forero was holding herself and the students accountable.)
8. Forero monitored students' progress as they tried out tasks; she adjusted the tasks to individual students' needs.

Source: Putnam, 1984b, pp. 13–14.

Step 3

Next, Forero and the students discussed the event. The students answered who, what, when, where, and why questions and produced both a collaborative group experience story and a written or verbal individual experience story. Forero began the discussion by saying, "Can we appreciate diversity, welcome individual learning, and still develop one applesauce story? Some of you can read, and some are learning to make a circle correctly. How can we all use this experience?" Forero and her students then talked about the meaning of the terms "appreciate," "diversity," "cooperation," and "learning." Forero then focused the discussion on the applesauce activity.

In writing the collaborative experience story, Forero and the students discussed each word and sentence until they agreed on it. For example, Forero asked, "What did we do to the apples?" The students responded with a variety of suggestions, including "squashed," "squooshed" and "squished." Forero wrote the words on the board, and the students said each word, talked about what it meant and whether it was fun to say or hear, and identified what sounds would be studied in each word. Forero then indicated which students would study which specific vowel combinations. The students later voted on which word to use in the story, based on its usefulness.

After the sentences had been agreed on and written, the group then selected a title and decided who to list as the authors of the story. After the experience story was completed and written on the board, Forero had the students use it in reading and writing activities during the study of the first unit. Nine activities were generated for which the students used this one story. Activities were assigned, based on the teacher's assessment of students' needs. See Table 5-7 for a list of the nine activities.

Step 4

While the class members worked, either individually or with a partner, on the objectives associated with the nine activities (using the experience story), Forero met with individual students to write down their personal experiences related to the initiating common experience. All the personal experiences in this unit of study dealt with apples. Students wrote their personal stories or dictated them to Forero, who typed them directly on a ditto. In each instance, the student was identified as the author. Forero analyzed the finished personal stories for their potential use as instructional materials.

Step 5

Together, Forero and her students identified the subject matter to be learned. Forero set the stage for a discussion and brainstorming session by asking, "What can we learn?"

TABLE 5-7   NINE ACTIVITIES USING THE SAME EXPERIENCE STORY

1. Handwriting
2. Oral reading
3. Sequencing of cut-apart sentences
4. Recognizing sight words
5. Substituting synonyms for story words
6. Creating a new story with cut-up words from the apple story
7. Changing descriptive words and explaining the changes in meaning
8. Developing word-recognition skills
9. Creating new sentence structures to communicate better or the same messages

Source: Putnam, 1984b, pp. 15–16.

Forero wrote the titles of all the subject-matter areas on the board (e.g., math and social studies). The collaborative curriculum development began when she asked questions such as:

"Besides what we learned during the initiating common experience, what else do we know about apples? When do you find apples in the store? Why do adults say you can have an apple instead of a candy bar? If you brought an apple to eat at recess and your best friend wanted part of it, how would you solve this problem?"

Forero provided direct guidance as the students responded to the questions, so that science ideas were classified on the board as science, math ideas as math, and so forth. She also asked students to read their personal stories to the class to generate additional ideas. For example, Christa read the following:

Apple Bark
Author: Christa

My mother and I like to make apple bark.
We use red delicious apples, a pan, a hot
    plate, a spoon and a cookie sheet.
We make the apple bark in our kitchen.
We make it in the fall. Usually we make it
    around Halloween time.
We make it because we all like it. We take
    it with us on walks and when we go
    in the car. It is a good snack.

After the story was read, the students asked the author questions. This discussion resulted in two study topics. Because several questions concerned cooking, hot plates, temperature, and burning, one study topic was electricity and energy—an interest that emanated from the children's focus on the hot plate and how it worked. Another group of questions was about things you can make with apples, resulting in designation of healthful snacks (without preservatives) as a study topic.

Once the study topics had been selected, Forero asked, "What can we do?" and followed up with specific questions designed to identify activities. The students made some good suggestions (e.g., taking a trip to an orchard and making an apple pie), but not all were appropriate (e.g., making a hot plate). Forero responded to the suggestions in a supportive manner, giving examples of what could be learned from the suggested activities. She then asked the students to classify their ideas under the appropriate topic. She added ideas and discussed the classifications with the students.

Reflective Thinking, Synthesis, and Decision Making

Between step 5 and step 6, Forero thought about the lists and considered the probability of student success if the plan of study were implemented. The questions she asked herself were: Is this plan related closely enough to the year-long outcomes? Is the plan flexible enough to allow me to adjust tasks and activities to meet individual learning needs? How interested are the students? Should they work on a number of activities at one time, or should everyone participate at the same time in a given activity? If Forero decided not to move ahead, she redid step 5, and if she decided to move ahead, she implemented step 6 (Putnam, 1984a, p. 14).

Step 6

Forero met individually with each student to select from the list of activities the things that the student would do and the specified objectives that the student would be learning. The individual discussions were continued in small groups and in whole-class deliberations. The final result was a list of things that each student would work on during the unit.

Step 7

Whenever there was a major shift in activity, Forero gave detailed directions. For example, when the whole class would work on one activity, she listed the steps and tasks on the board. When individual work was to be done, she met with the appropriate people. Again, she listed tasks, and listened and talked through the steps that students would be expected to follow. She illustrated how the monitoring system would work.

Step 8

While the class worked in small groups, in pairs, or individually, Forero and each student met regularly to talk about (1) content and responsibility and (2) the level of students' accountability. Through these conferences, a list of refined objectives was developed. Forero did the following in each student conference: (1) She told the student what observations she had made about his/her independent work during the common initiating experiences. (2) She showed the student the written or taped work. (3) She told the student specifically what she/he currently could and couldn't do. (4) She gave examples of what the student would be able to do by the end of the unit.

After the student had worked a while on the topic, Forero determined the level of student accountability. During the next conference, she would tell the student which level of knowledge she/he would need to demonstrate (e.g., practice, application, or transfer) to receive academic credit. Students who were being introduced to new content usually were held accountable for practice-level demonstration. Students who had already reached the practice stage were moved to application. Only when a student was able to actually use the new knowledge or skill in a new situation did Forero record credit for new knowledge or skill gained. For example, a student might be asked to distinguish between an exclamation point and a period by reading paragraphs and indicating the difference through voice and nonverbal expression. During the year, students became adept at defining their tasks as instructional, practice, application, or transfer.

Finally, Forero and each student worked out a way to keep track of their progress. Both task completion and acquisition of new skills or knowledge were recorded.

During the first part of the year, collaborative planning took about ten days. (See Table 5-8 for an outline of the ten-day planning sequence.) Seven to ten days was the range of time that Forero and her students took for the organization of their new units of study during the rest of the year.

When collaborative planning was completed, the learning community was ready to embark on an extended study. The students were ready to learn the things they had identified and to do the things they had selected. The period of extensive study was labeled the "study episode."

Implementation

All the planning and talking resulted in teacher, students, and materials being ready for an extensive study period, or study episode.

During the study episode, students completed activities and worked toward the planned academic objectives. Both task and academic objectives were adjusted during the study episode. If Forero and a student determined that the objectives were inappropriate (i.e., when she had misassessed and later found that the work was based on prerequisites the student didn't have, or when the student already knew how to do what had been planned), they immediately identified alternative tasks and objectives. The study periods lasted from two to five weeks, averaging about four weeks, depending on the work pace and motivation of the teacher and students.

During the study episode, Forero focused on the following four topics for interactive decision making:

1. *Instruction.*   What do I say or do to provide instruction about a particular concept/skill/fact with a particular child?

2. *Outcomes.*   If necessary, what changes in the objectives for which a given student is being held accountable will I suggest and/or agree to?

3. *Activities.*   So that students will be successful, how must I reorganize an activity or change an activity?

4. *Student behavior.*   What must I do to make sure that this individual will get in control of his/her behavior and become responsible for his/her learning?

Each day's study period was organized into three parts: (1) determining tasks, (2) working, and (3) closing. In the first part of the study period, the group shared news from the classroom and decided what tasks needed to be done next and by whom. In the second, a variety of work activities were engaged in: Forero instructed individuals, small groups, or the whole class, while students worked individually or in dyads or small groups. In the third part, Forero focused on closing activities, reviewed group behavior and individual progress, reminded students about home tasks, and planned for the next day. Frequently, Forero created the next day's agenda with the students and wrote it on the board.

TABLE 5-8   A TIME LINE FOR TEACHER/STUDENT PLANNING

Monday	Tuesday	Wednesday	Thursday	Friday
Week 1:				
1. Teacher shares personal experience.	Students make personal monitoring system for experience steps.	Class determines story, by answering the who, what, when, where, and why questions. Discusses all possible sentences and comes to consensus or vote.	Teacher meets with students to identify specific skills to practice, apply, or transfer.	Teacher assigns lesson, based on students' skills and understandings.
2. Teacher shares her planned experience for class.	Do experience.	Teacher writes story on board as it progresses. Reads it as a model, then has class join in choral reading.	Students choose monitor for skills record keeping (usually use teacher's checklist).	Cut story into sentence strips.
3. Identify steps to complete "doing" experience.	Share orally how students and teacher can tell about experience— what outline questions to use for guidance.	Students copy story.	Work on reading story and developing skills.	Students identify sentences for sequencing of events.

Monday	Tuesday	Wednesday	Thursday	Friday
4. Model a monitor for keeping records of progress.	Write outline on board.	Students practice story in pairs.		Sequence and put together story.
				Explain why order is accurate.
Week 2:				
1. Cut individual words apart.	Students choose step needing completion or catch-up.	Students who have completed class experience (and steps) choose new, related experiences.	Meet with teacher and identify what is to be learned.	Create closure for the group initiating the experience, and for all students.
2. Reconstruct sentences.	Class brainstorms about other, somewhat related experiences.	Develop materials and process for doing new experiences.	Meet with teacher and identify level of understanding one is accountable for (e.g., practice, transfer, transformation).	All students select new tasks, systems for monitoring, objectives, and/or new skills.
3. Identify and code (by underlining) words to know in isolation by sight memory.	Teacher writes content headings on board and lists words to represent ideas student generate.	Choose a monitor for experience steps.	Select a monitor system.	
4. Choose words you would like to make substitutions for (beautiful/pretty, good/delicious, etc.).	All discuss possible activities.	Begin experience.	Work on experience and objectives.	

Forero came into individual instructional contact with each student every day. Individual contact was anywhere from eight seconds to several minutes long. Students helped each other and were helped by others at various times. All students functioned as helpers and got help from someone at some time.

The break (recess) came in the middle of the work session, and the number of students who left the room averaged ten out of twenty-five. The students who stayed to work and those who left varied from day to day. As one student said, "I stay in when I want to learn, and I go out when I want to play."

Students rarely got off-task during study periods. When they did, it was usually because of something like a student saying he/she didn't feel well and being left along to sit in his/her seat. Sometimes a student who had entered the group later in the year attended to her/his work during only part of the study time and then walked around. When this happened, the teacher and other students took action to help the new student gain entry into the group and to socialize her/him to the community's expectations. Sometimes brief social conversations occurred between students who passed each other on their way to do something task-related. Children would leave their tasks when they wanted to go to the bathroom or the drinking fountain.

When disruptive off-task behavior did occur, a class meeting was called. Either a student or Forero flicked the lights to get everyone's attention and then stated the problem. For example, once a student said, "There is so much talking in here I can't work at my desk," and once Forero said, "Seven people have interrupted Susan and me, and I can't help her." The problem statement was followed by a question asking people to recall whether the problem had been discussed previously and, if so, what had been said. When the problem appeared to be new, whoever was causing the disruption was asked to say what was happening and to explain why. Finally, Forero would ask, "What are we going to do about this?" If the problem was that the interruptions were occurring because directions were unclear, Forero stopped everything, redirected the students, answered their questions, and then went on. Generally, students would give her suggestions on how the problem behind the disruption could be handled.

Reflecting

As the study unit closed, Forero met with each student. These conferences helped to create a sense of closure for the students in relation to the tasks that they had been working on, and to initiate the transition to the next unit of study.

As students completed their activities and reached their objectives, Forero would discuss with the class a closing date for the unit of study. By the closing date, she would have evaluated all the students' progress. Daily class discussions were held during the last two or three days of study. Students then shared with each other the new knowledge and skills they had acquired (e.g., reading with voice inflection, reading stories they had written, telling how many sight words they had learned, telling how a problem had been solved, and describing new information or understandings they had acquired). Students who had not completed their tasks or reached their objectives held conferences with Forero to see whether they could determine the cause (e.g., they might not have paid attention in class, there might have been too many or the wrong objectives, or the pacing might not have been right for an individual student). These conferences always ended with an agreement between the teacher and the student to try to make better decisions next time.

During each student conference, Forero evaluated the student's progress by examining what he/she was able to do as measured against the assigned objectives. She recorded her evaluation and reviewed previous evaluation data. On occasion, to document individual student performance, she had the student complete a written test. The written tests required different students to do different things (recall, transfer, transform, or recognize) based on the criterion level of their objectives.

The data from this phase helped Forero to verify her previous evaluation of students and her records. She looked for data that conflicted with the decisions she had already made, because she understood that disconfirmation was as important as confirmation when testing a hypothesis. She used the data to begin planning for a new unit of instruction.

Forero designed her instruction so that her class completed a full cycle of the five stages of group development about four times throughout the year. The material of stage V, transition information, became new data for use in starting another cycle.

For example, after Forero and her students had cycled through a unit for the first time, she started a second unit of instruction. Once again, she started by thinking about what she had learned about her students, what she had committed herself to help them achieve, and the tentative decisions she had made about curriculum the first time around. She was now able to make decisions about specific student needs and to adjust her specifications for individual outcomes. The focus during the second cycle was on refining the students' social behavior and attitudes toward the helping goal and on supporting more student responsibility. She worked to get students to initiate contact with her ideally once a day and at least once in two days. While she assumed responsibility for working with students, she saw their initiating contact as critical to their future success as active and participating learners.

During the year, after each new cycle began, Forero's attention shifted from teaching students how to function in the learning community to what they were accomplishing. She looked for opportunities for the students to read stories they or others had written (e.g., stories about when residents of a senior citizen's home four blocks from school were invited to visit the class). She worked with students to help each one plan a lesson and teach it to the whole class. The lesson was usually a craft or project of some type that fit into the unit of study. Forero's goal was to provide students with procedures for preparing and giving directions. The criteria for how "good" a lesson was included how the products turned out and how many questions people had to ask.

Summary

Students in Forero's class were aware of the expectations and outcomes they were being held accountable for. They were able to describe what they were doing and what they were learning from any particular assignment. Students showed their assertiveness by voluntarily telling visitors about their academic and/or personal and social progress. For example, one day Tonly reported that he could recognize a set of sight words on which he had been working. On another occasion, Margaret announced that she was now able to raise her hand in class. In addition, students did their work, asked for help, and helped others when they could, without cues from Forero. They said "no" when they didn't think they could be helpful or when they had several tasks of their own to complete, but when they could, they contributed time to help others who were having a difficult time learning something.

Behaviors related to helping were observed regularly. Students made decisions about when they would ask for help, offer help, decline help offered to them, and decline to help others. The result was that they developed a sense of community, of working together so that everyone would learn. It is this sense of community and being responsible for and having pride in one's own and others' learning achievements that seem so vital to learning community. An example may help illustrate this point.

> One of the students had had trouble both in becoming socialized to the learning community classroom and in learning to read. The first time he actually read to the class (not saying words he had memorized), everyone broke into spontaneous applause. At the end of the year, the boy asked the researcher if she remembered when he didn't do his work. When the researcher said yes, he said, "Well, I always do it now." The researcher said she remembered when he would yell or cry when the teacher didn't let him make cookies or dunk for apples because he had not worked on his tasks. She asked, "Should the teacher have let you do those things?" He replied, "Oh, she always wanted me to. I couldn't (because) I didn't do my work. But I always do my work now. I can do lots more than just read." (Putnam, 1984b, p. 29)

Brophy (1983) defined classroom motivation as having three components: (1) Students value learning for its own sake. (2) Students value learning rather than merely performing. (3) Students value actual processes of learning, as distinct from outcomes. Forero's students talked about their experiences in ways that showed their motivation in Brophy's terms. They made clear distinctions between outcome and task. Unlike Anderson's (1984) findings, in which students were concerned primarily with getting seat-work done, students in Forero's classroom explained what they were learning to do as well as how they were doing a specific task. In addition to having learned new things, they frequently initiated conversations with the researcher, in which they said that they had acquired some new set of understandings or behaviors and could now do something they couldn't do previously.

STAGE V. TRANSITIONS AND CLOSURE

Bringing closure to the school year included two specific steps. First, Forero brought closure to the current classroom learning-community activities, and second, she planned with the students things that they could do during the summer and gave them an idea of what to expect the next year.

Closure involved reflecting on the year's experiences. Students listened to tapes of their reading and writing from earlier in the year, looked at pictures they had drawn, talked about experiences they had had, and took things home. The room began to regain the appearance it had had at the beginning of the year.

Performance Outcomes and Activities (NJPTS 6)

Chapter 5
A Primary-Level Classroom

PERFORMANCE OUTCOMES

Teacher candidates will

1. Analyze written and video learning community classroom case studies and accurately identify the learning community cultural elements, dispositions, roles, and functions of schooling illustrated in the case studies.
2. Compare and contrast written learning community classroom case studies.
3. Compare and contrast the elements of learning community case studies with observation and interview data collected in schools.

The activities for this chapter provides the opportunity to analyze learning-community classroom cultures and to compare and contrast them with the ideas presented in the preceding chapters. The tasks also provide an opportunity for you to reflect once again on your professional beliefs and actions and to compare them with the essential learning-community elements.

Exercise 5.1
The Study of Classroom Learning Communities

Application and Reflection on the Text

There is no single vision of "the perfect" classroom learning-community. Instead, there are multiple versions. There are teachers who call their classrooms learning communities however, upon systematic study it is apparent that they are not CLCs. This is because all the functions of schooling or the group and/or teacher propensities are not present and/or the group is locked into one of the stages of group development. The case presented in Chapter 5 is one classroom teacher's version of a classroom learning community, as she and the students during one school year established the LC culture. The information for this case was collected as part of an ethnography over a ten-month period.

The purposes of this activity are for you: (1) to practice analyzing classroom situations to determine their congruence or incongruity with the learning-community vision explicated in the preceding chapters, and (2) to use another teacher's actions as a basis for better understanding your own beliefs and practices.

1. We suggest that you and several of your peers or colleagues compare the teacher's actions with the vision of the learning community presented in the previous chapters. What congruencies and incongruities did you find? Make a list in the space below. For example: What functions of schooling are evident? What is the evidence? How were the stages of community development handled?
2. Now, by way of reflection, once again examine your own beliefs and practices. How do they compare with the vision of the learning community presented in this chapter and with the teacher's beliefs and practices? What might you do to make your beliefs and practices more congruent with the vision presented here? Would it be beneficial to you or your students? Why? Why not?
3. If this were your learning community, what would you do to strengthen the learning-community ethos?

Exercise 5.2

View the Documentary Film: To Be and To Have (French multilevel classroom) and identify the observable elements of a classroom learning community. List your observations on one half of a sheet of paper and on the other half identify the function of school or disposition, that your observation reflects.

RECOMMENDED READINGS

Anderson, L. (1984). The environment of instruction: The function of seat work in a commercially developed curriculum, in G. Duffy, L. Roehler, and J. Mason (eds.). *Comprehension instruction: Perspectives and suggestions.* New York: Longman, pp. 93–103.

Brophy, J. E. (1983). Classroom organization and management. *The Elementary School Journal,* XXX–286.

Putnam, J. (1984a). *Developing an elementary school learning-community classroom.* (145, November). East Lansing: Michigan State University, Institute for Teaching.

_____. (1984b). One exceptional teacher's systematic decision-making model (Research Series 136, January). East Lansing: Michigan State University, Institute for Teaching.

CHAPTER

6

A Secondary-Level Classroom

Harriet Henderson entered teaching with a thorough grounding in her discipline areas: mathematics, which was her major, and social science, in which she had a minor. She believed that her teaching must aim at four long-range goals for her students: (1) academic outcomes, (2) development of personal responsibility, (3) development of social responsibility, and (4) development of social justice values and attitudes. When Henderson graduated with her undergraduate degree and teacher certification, she believed that her preparation had provided her with the necessary professional knowledge and skills to *begin* a successful teaching career as a general mathematics teacher.

When Henderson told her friends that she had accepted a job teaching general mathematics to middle-school students, many of them predicted that she would never be happy because general math was not really "her subject." They also told her that she was much too altruistic to be a successful teacher in the 1990s. Her friends suggested that she was asking for trouble and wondered why she didn't know what everyone else knew, that general mathematics students were unmanageable and not interested in learning. Henderson was aware of these stereotypes of general mathematics students. She also was aware that general mathematics classes were considered to be the testing ground for the "new math teacher." She knew that when math teachers achieved seniority, most would choose to leave general mathematics and take algebra or trigonometry classes. In addition, she knew that teachers and administrators talked about the discipline problems that occurred in general math classrooms.

In contrast to the stereotypical responses of her colleagues, however, Henderson was much more positive about her assignment. She believed that all students can and will learn if the environment is stimulating, interesting, challenging, and supportive. She based this optimism partially on her study of Brophy's ideas (1985) about creating student motivation to learn. Further, she valued the work done by some of her professors in mathematics and mathematics education related to the professional possibilities of teaching general mathematics. She was also familiar with the sociology of the classroom, as described in G. Stanford and A. E. Roarks' works (1974) on identifying stages in the development of effective classroom groups. She knew how to plan a curriculum that provided for the integration of the four functions of schooling and how to design classroom organization congruent with these goals. She could assess her students and use the resulting data in deciding what and how to teach. She felt confident about bringing her skills and understandings to the teaching of general mathematics.

During her student teaching experience, Henderson had engaged in an action-research project that focused on her teaching practice. She had collected pre- and post-test data for four general mathematics classes. In two of the courses, she had used traditional methods of teaching. In the other two classes, she had used group development stages which employed cooperative learning. Henderson had chosen to use a teaching strategy designed by Fitzgerald and Shroyer (1986) called "independent exploration material." The academic tests, questionnaires, and data from observations completed by the cooperating teacher and university field instructors had provided Henderson with descriptive information that helped her to evaluate the contrasting outcomes. She was able to see that the principles of instruction and theories of motivation she had studied could be applied successfully in general mathematics classes. As a result of her action research, she began to talk about teaching as involving a continuing series of studies that would facilitate her professional growth and help her to understand how her students were thinking.

Today Henderson is a successful general mathematics and social studies teacher. She is now even more confident that middle-school general mathematics students can get excited about understanding mathematics. She attributes much of her success to information she learned as a preservice teacher and to her ability to transform this information into effective teaching practice. She also continues to study her own practice and has begun graduate study in the field of education.

The beginning of each year excites Henderson anew and confirms her choice of teaching as a professional career. As she plans each year's work, she tries to be clear about her longrange goals and her plans for establishing a learning community in each of her five classes—four general mathematics classes and one social studies class. In this chapter we describe how Henderson plans for and develops middle-school learning communities in general mathematics.

PLANNING

Henderson, like other learning community teachers, plans thoroughly for her learning-community classes. She organizes her planning into nine steps, and it begins two weeks before the start of school. Following is a description of the nine steps in her planning process.

Step 1

The first step in Henderson's planning process includes collecting materials such as the school calendar for the upcoming year, curriculum materials and supplemental resources, the district's curriculum guides for middle-school mathematics, and the textbooks.

Step 2:

She thinks about things to consider while planning, and she makes extensive lists. Items on Henderson's lists include new instructional materials, new ideas for activities, agreements among mathematics teachers in the district, improvements she wants to make based on last year's experiences and on her students' achievements, and the particular instructional strategies that she wishes to employ during the year (e.g., jigsaw, Student Teams-Achievement Divisions, Teams-Games-Tournaments, lecture, multiability, role-plays, videotapes, and computers).

Step 3

Henderson continues her planning by writing her goals for the year. This includes selecting topics to be taught in each class over the year. These topics function as organizers for the units of instruction. By writing the goals and objectives for each topic, she develops a clear understanding of the year's work for each of her classes. Later she will schedule the topics on her calendar.

Step 4

Henderson then asks school counselors to pull files for all her students. She scans through each file, looking for four things: (1) the student's latest reading comprehension test score; (2) health problems that might need attention (e.g., diabetes); (3) scores on mathematics tests, including subtest or skill-specific scores, mathematics comprehension and problem solving scores, and reading comprehension scores; and (4) general information about the student's interests and strengths. This task generally takes several hours because Henderson teaches approximately 156 students. (She has a friend who teaches at a school where one can simply make a request for information from the counselor and in a few days receive a computer printout by class.) Henderson records the data in four columns on a copy of her class list. Her notes are usually brief and pointed, including only information she knows she can use in making her decisions.

Step 5

Next, Henderson finds out which rooms she will be using for her classes, whether during certain hours she will be a floating teacher, and the particular constraints of the physical environment.

Step 6

The next step in Henderson's planning is noting on a desk-size year-long calendar the events of the school year. She records vacations, assemblies, planning and conference days, marking periods, semester exams, special community events that are of interest to mathematics students and teachers, birthdays of important mathematicians, and anniversaries of events that will have an impact on the life of a classroom community. She also notes the beginning and endings of units she wishes to teach to each class. This step allows her to adjust her long-range plans so that she will not have to begin three new and different units on the same day or to give exams for three different courses on the same day. Thus, she can construct a schedule which avoids problems of timing, such as scheduling a major new activity right before exams for a marking period or scheduling highly interdependent multiability and cooperative learning tasks on the first day after students return from a break. She has learned that vacations or changes in routine attendance patterns affect the way the students interact and participate in the classroom (G. Stanford, 1977). This type of long-range scheduling gives her the opportunity to pace her own work.

Step 7

By now, Henderson is ready to plan her classroom organization. This planning includes identifying and listing the procedures, routines, rules, norms, expectations, and roles that are necessary for each class in order to enable students to have effective and efficient learning experiences. Here Henderson reflects back on student behavior that has proved supportive of the teaching strategies she plans to use, as well as on the problems that occurred in her classes the previous year. Henderson uses her classroom organization as a guide for being explicit about the roles, rules, norms, and procedures that she wishes to establish in learning communities.

Henderson thinks about each class as a separate classroom culture and is aware that every classroom culture must be constructed each year. She bases her organization plans upon: (1) proposed yearlong outcomes, (2) multiple types of instructional strategies, and (3) principles of motivation and learning.

Henderson lists the rules, roles, norms, and procedures she wants to establish during the first weeks of school. She has one major rule: *Help each other to understand, but take tests on your own.* She lists four roles—environmentalists, small-group facilitator, record/reporter, and timer—and later she puts these roles on charts. She identifies procedures that will help students to achieve all the goals she is setting for them. For example, she works out (1) procedures for moving seats from a whole-group arrangement to small-group arrangements with as little downtime as possible, (2) procedures to help students interact with her or peers about their mathematics misconceptions, and (3) procedures enabling her students to work in pairs with the classroom computers.

Henderson does not organize her class primarily to keep students "quiet." If that were her intent, she would list procedures and rules to support a teacher-centered classroom [e.g., how to enter the room, take a seat, do the "sponge" (á la Madelene Hunter) activity, correct homework, turn in homework, hand out graded papers, listen to the teacher lecture, do guided practice, and do homework assignments]. Such routines alone would not reflect Henderson's concern about promoting personal and social responsibility, the development of students' understandings, and the use of multiple teaching strategies to achieve multiple outcomes.

Step 8

Henderson is now ready to plan for each class as a separate course. The product of this step will be a course outline for each class. She begins by reviewing her notes on the students in her classes. This provides her with information about the students' interests, experience in content areas, and related achievement, as well as indicators of low and high status and power students (see E. G. Cohen, 1987). Next she selects areas to be assessed (e.g., problem-solving thinking, computational skills, computer skills, and specific knowledge and skills related to the year's unit topics and her stated goals and objectives). Then she reviews the lists of rules, norms, roles, and procedures she wants in each class. On the basis of this information about her students, her management style, and her assessment plan, she proceeds to select initial instructional activities. These initial activities are designed to provide more assessment data and also to serve as opportunities to teach various multiability study-group skills and values, including roles; norms and procedures such as cooperation, listening, and responding to others; interdependence; giving feedback; task completion and turning in completed work on time; grading individuals and groups; getting feedback; movement to small-group work from whole-class activity; getting and returning materials; and daily activities such as attendance.

Henderson thinks about the introductory unit from many perspectives. She asks questions such as, "How will the instructional activities help to produce new information about these students?" She wants to know about their grasp of mathematical facts, skills, and procedures. She wants to assess how they react to group organization, whether any students have special needs, and what their social interaction skills are like. She wonders whether some of the students already have high expectations of leadership and achievement. Henderson shapes her initial instruction with care. She wants to have a good chance of getting answers to her questions. She will spend much of her time monitoring her students and giving them corrective feedback as the new classroom cultures begin to develop.

Once school begins, Henderson will lead her classes through the first three stages of group development and into the productivity stage in about twenty days. She starts the year by teaching short units selected to elicit high student interest; to provide opportunities for students to practice roles, procedures, and norms; to utilize multiple teaching strategies; to provide opportunities that offer all students the potential to succeed; and to have an opportunity to assess the students' reactions and conceptual sophistication.

Henderson knows that aspects of her organization plan will need to be adjusted during the year. She is aware that changes in school routines (events such as assembly, a week of fire drills, and vacations) will contribute to the deterioration of some aspects of the community. Thus, she will take actions during the year to maintain the quality of the learning-community interactions.

To conclude step 8, Henderson writes a course outline to give to her students. The course outline includes the classroom rules, mathematics topics and questions to be studied, expectations about class participation, and a letter to parents or guardians with a form that they are to sign to indicate that they have read the course outline and the letter.

Step 9

Finally, Henderson prepares for the first day of school. She begins by making several posters to hang up in her room. Each poster communicates part of the information that the students will need to carry out the various roles necessary for the learning community to function well. The posters will function as visual representations of the information Henderson will give the students during the first days of school, and later as reminders of the roles. (See Figure 6-1.) In addition, some posters provide examples of **Sentence Starters** for the students to refer to during their initial cooperative learning small-group experiences; for example, ways to ask questions for any student to use while playing the "encourager" role (e.g., "What do you think . . . ?"). The charts in the room illustrate the roles (e.g., organizer, encourager) that all students are to play as a way of accepting responsibility for the effectiveness of their group. Other roles (e.g., facilitator) are assigned by Henderson in order to equalize power and status among the students (E. G. Cohen, 1988, 1982). Henderson makes explicit the roles students are expected to play and clarifies how they are to begin interactions with others by giving examples of student discourse.

Henderson knows that there will be particular times when students will need additional support so that the classroom learning community, once created, can be maintained. These times will come after the first report card period, at the end of fall athletics, after Thanksgiving, after the winter break and the spring break, when the wrestling and cheerleading teams are chosen, and before and after the spring concert and play. Thus, she has already starred such places on her yearly calendar as signals reminding herself to pay particular attention to maintaining classroom learning-community activities.

ROLES FOR EVERYONE	ASSIGNED ROLES	ENCOURAGER
Encourager Asks others what they think, or to give more information.	**Facilitator** Directs group, can contact teacher.	"What do you think . . . ?" "Tell us more about. . . ." "We haven't heard from you about. . . ." "Did you have an idea about . . . ?" "Did you mean . . . ?"
Organizer Reminds members of the group to stay on-task; suggests ways to function efficiently and effectively given the task and purposes.	**Recorder/reporter** Takes notes and reports to class. Checks to see that report reflects the perspective of the group.	
Linker Links ideas presented by different people; synthesizes information; Information provided by multiple people.	**Timer** Watches time to be sure that task is completed and report is ready to give.	ORGANIZER "Is that related to . . . ?" "I think we are off track. . . ." "One way we could work would be to. . . ."
Informer Gives information; suggests places or ways to get information.	**Environmentalist** Works with members of the group to be sure that materials are available, that the classroom environment is setup so that the activity can be accomplished, and that materials are returned at the end of the hour.	"It seems that we are not getting anything done, I think we should do. . . . What do you think?"
INFORMER "I think we could do. . . ." "The readings said that we could. . . ." "My notes indicate that it is. . . ." "No one seems to know but we could get . . . to find out."	LINKER "Javier and Alice said . . . , and Bob indicated that . . . , so we have two different ideas about this." "Your idea is similar to the one we used in class yesterday. . . ."	

FIGURE 6-1

IMPLEMENTATION

By the beginning of the school year, Henderson is ready for her students. She knows something about them, has a plan for the first weeks of school, is clear about what she wants to accomplish during the year, and has an idea of what the school year will bring. When she attends the opening school staff meetings, she looks for information that may influence her schedules or affect the expectations that she now holds. She is excited about having the chance to talk with other teachers and to share professional and personal information.

Day One

On the first day of school, Henderson follows her plans for the individual classes. For example, in the third-hour general math class, she meets the students at the door and asks them to hand her their bar-coded identification cards so that she can scan them with the computer wand, then to select a seat and fill out the information sheet that is on each desk. (These tasks are also written on the board.) By the time all the students are in the room, seated, and filling out the information sheets, Henderson has already entered the attendance data from the computer wand into her computer, and pressed the printer code for her attendance record.

Henderson wants to establish herself as the instructional leader on the very first day. To her, this means providing students with explicit information about what will occur in the classroom and providing answers to questions often asked by students in her previous courses. She begins the class by announcing the course title (seventh-grade general mathematics) and says that general mathematics classes generally have a bad reputation but that she disagrees. She thinks that these classes have had a "bad rap." She tells the students that she is excited about this class and about the mathematics that they will study during the semester. She knows that the content is very important for success in today's world, and she thinks that the students will find the class challenging and interesting.

Next, she provides information about her expectations and her view that she is the responsible instructional leader. For example, she tells the students that they will be able to sit in the seats they chose today until next Monday, when she will bring in a new seating plan. She states that the new plan will be based on information that she collects during the first days of school and probably will change several times during the semester, as needed. She also tells the class that they will work individually, in pairs, and in small groups during the year and that she will determine the membership of pairs and workgroups based on (1) the task assigned, (2) information about individual students, and (3) her professional knowledge about ways of organizing that contribute most to student learning. She then hands out a course outline and reviews its content.

Next, Henderson carries out activities designed to help students answer their questions about who is in the group, how they will be treated, and norms and role expectations. She begins with an orientation activity that has two purposes: first, for the students to introduce themselves, and second, for each student to practice listening and paraphrasing what another student has said. She tells the students to introduce themselves to the group by telling their names (using the names they wish to be called) and then telling about a mathematical problem they encountered and solved during the summer months. Several students call out, "I don't use math!" She says, "That could be so; listen to the examples, and if you still need some help, I'll work with you." She tells them that they are to describe their problem and the solution they figured out. To illustrate the assignment, she gives two examples. Then she calls on two students to restate her directions and asks if there are others who want to clarify the task. After everyone has had an opportunity to make a contribution, she asks what was helpful to understanding the assignment and how it was helpful.

She then gives the students time to think about a problem, make some notes, and prepare to introduce themselves to the group. She walks around the class and answers individual questions. She uses directed questions to help students who still seem to have trouble identifying a problem to tell. She mentions things in her questions that may cue students (e.g., "Did you need money to go someplace?" "Did you need to know how long, how much, how many, what part of?"). Once she sees that all students have something started, she asks them to talk quietly to themselves to rehearse what they will say when she calls on them. She then provides directions, saying:

> Listen very carefully to each speaker. After a speaker has finished, we will ask clarifying questions. Negative comments are not permissible. Once a person has finished their introduction and answered clarifying questions, she/he will draw the name of a person out of an envelope, and that person will be the next speaker.

Previously, she has written all their names on pieces of paper. Now, she tells the students that the second person will start by stating one thing about the person who has just finished. She mentions that it is sometimes interesting when the next speaker links his/her comments to the previous speaker's ideas or experiences. She says, however, that linking to the previous speaker's contributions is not a requirement for this exercise. While the students introduce themselves, Henderson takes notes on her observations about individual student thinking.

After all students have introduced themselves (which takes about one minute per person), she asks whether anyone has noticed anything about the group. She calls on students, who contribute the following ideas: "Some people had a hard time figuring out how they used math," "Everyone has used math outside school during the last year at least once," and "Some people just seem to go on and on when they talk." Henderson comments that these students summarized their ideas for the class.

Henderson places a poster on the board. She says that there are three rules for her classes (she has modified her single rule). These are her rules on the first day of school:

1. Help each other to understand (except when taking tests).
2. No putdowns.
3. Do tests by yourself.

Henderson also tells her students that she has some particular expectations for the class. She explains that she expects all students to help in keeping the room orderly so that class time will not be wasted on putting away things from other classes. She shows the students that they have access to particular drawers, shelves, etc., and not to others (explaining why not) and that each student has a particular space assigned as his/hers when in this class. She tells students that she expects them to participate in class activities and to complete their assignments, both in class and at home. She asks students to paraphrase or state in their own words what she has communicated about the rules and expectations. One student asks, "What ya going to do if we don't do these things?" Henderson replies, "I don't expect that to happen. Perhaps someone will forget and I'll remind them." She paraphrases and responds to other questions and concerns which students raise about class rules.

Henderson announces several procedures and routines that she and the class will follow (see Table 6-1). She describes the purposes of these as being to help the class run smoothly and to eliminate as much nonconstructive confusion as possible.

At the end of this presentation, Henderson reviews with students what they are to do when they come into the room tomorrow: "(1) Have your ID cards out for me to scan. (2) Go directly to your seats. (3) Read the agenda on the board for your class, and prepare to do the first thing on the agenda."

Henderson hands a packet of bright orange cards to the students seated at the front of each row (see Figure 6-2). She says that each student should take a card and then pass the packet back. She asks the students to answer the questions printed on the cards and to hand her the completed cards as they leave the room. She says that she will read the cards and then put them in an envelope and store them until the end of the school year. Then, in June, she will give the cards back to them, and they will be able to see what they were thinking about at the beginning of the school year.

TABLE 6–1   HENDERSON'S CLASS PROCEDURES

1. Have your ID card out when you enter the room (so that it can be read by the computer wand).
2. Read the *agenda* for the day, and get ready to do the first thing on the agenda.
3. Make an *appointment* with me: *if* you have questions that were not answered in class, *if* you need clarification about comments on your papers, or *if* your papers include a note indicating that I want to talk with you.
4. A *resource* person in each study group will be assigned to get materials for group work and to return them to their storage space.
5. A *facilitator* for studygroup work will be assigned.
6. A *recorder/reporter* for study-group work will be assigned.
7. A study-group *timer* will be assigned.
8. After homework papers are discussed in class, *papers* will be passed to the front of each row and then to the left. The person in that seat will place them in the third-hour file.
9. Homework (from third hour) will be *returned* with written comments every Friday.

Name you wish to be called: _____

Something you would like me to understand about you:

A comment you would like to make about something you would like to review next June:

Turn the card over and on the back write a prediction about what you think this class will be like.

FIGURE 6–2

When the bell ending the class rings, Henderson chats with students as they hand her the cards and leave the room. She goes to the board and erases the agenda for the past hour, placing a check by the agenda for the next class. She then goes to the door and greets her next class as they enter her room.

Day Two

The bell for the end of second hour rings. As the second-hour students leave the class, Henderson erases the second-hour agenda, puts a colored chalk check by the third-hour agenda, and picks up the computer attendance wand. She then walks to the door, so that she can welcome the students and also monitor their activity as they enter the room. She calls the students whom she knows by name and asks the ones whose names she does not yet know to say them to her. She also suggests that they try to think of some way to help her learn quickly to remember their names. Henderson frequently reminds students, "Don't forget to read the agenda."

All the time that she is talking to the students as they enter the room, she holds out the computer wand to record the bar-code identification numbers from the students' ID cards. She then follows the same pattern as on day one for recording attendance, and about ten seconds after the final bell rings, she is standing in front of the class.

As the students enter the room, they can readily see both the class procedures that are posted by the door near the ceiling and the class rules that are posted above the door. The agenda reads:

Agenda—Third Hour

Homework: None due

Assessment: Discussion of *roles* and *behavior* in an effective mathematics class

1. Facilitator, recorder/reporter, timer, synthesizer, researcher, and organizer (The posters with definitions of these roles are on the side walls of the room.)
2. Cooperative behavior in a study group

Activities for learning small-group roles:

1. Puzzles
2. Tangrams

Homework: Write a story problem for fifth-graders.

Henderson praises her students for quickly taking their seats and being ready to start when the class begins. She turns to the agenda and tells the class that today's class purposes are to work on a mathematics problem and to practice working cooperatively in small study groups.

Henderson says that today they will engage in several mathematics activities, all with the same rules. She tapes a piece of newsprint to the wall (see Figure 6-3) and describes the rules. She says:

> For the first activity, each of you is assigned to a small group. Each person in the group will receive an envelope with four pieces to a puzzle. The pieces have numbers on them. Take the pieces out of the envelope and put them on your desk, number side up. Do not try to do anything else until I give you the rest of the directions.

She then points to students, telling them to move their desks slightly to form several groups of four students each. One student says that he wishes to work with a certain other student. Henderson tells him that she will keep that in mind for another time but that today she has decided that the group will be formed this way. Once the groups are formed, she hands out the packets of envelopes to one member of each group, who is called the resource person. She says, "Here is your set. Give one envelope to each member of your group. At the end of the activity, it is your responsibility to return the items to the envelopes and return the set of envelopes to me." Henderson goes to the front of the room and states, "I am ready to give the rest of the directions." She waits until she gets their attention, her body posture and eye movements communicating the message that she expects them to get ready quickly. As soon as she has everyone's attention, she says:

> Each group now has the pieces of a computation puzzle. Your goal is for each person in your group to have a set of pieces that adds up to 60. The rules, however, state that you may only give someone a piece that you think they need. You may not take a piece from another person or group. You may not speak to anyone or make a gesture that shows that you want a particular piece. The purpose of this activity is to provide experience with a mathematics task and practice in paying attention to what other people need while solving your own problem. You may use your calculators. Tell me what you must do if you are going to complete this task.

No group is allowed to start until Henderson judges that everyone understands the task. Then they begin. She walks around observing the students and enforcing the rules.

After the group completes the first task, Henderson asks each group to tell about their experiences in solving the task. What was hard? What did they observe? What would they do the next time to

---

1. Don't talk.
2. Observe what others need.
3. Give other people your pieces.
4. Don't take pieces away from others, and don't show nonverbally what you want.

FIGURE 6-3   Rules for activities

increase cooperation in finishing the task? The students say that keeping track of everyone's set of puzzle pieces was hard. One student says that when he had pieces that added to 60 but no one else did, he had a hard time giving away his pieces so that others could complete their parts of the task. Another student says that it was frustrating to see what someone else needed when the others in the group didn't see it.

After the general class discussion, Henderson hands out another set of envelopes. The groups follow the same rules and observe that the task is getting easier. Finally, Henderson distributes tangrams to the groups and tells them to work together to arrange the pieces in a square. (A tangram is a Chinese puzzle made by cutting a square of paper or cardboard into five triangles, a square and a rhomboid. The pieces can be arranged in many different configurations.) Once the squares are assembled, Henderson puts another piece of newsprint on the wall, which asks seven questions, as follows:

1. How did you feel when you needed a piece someone else had?
2. Did you see anyone give someone a piece they didn't need?
3. Did you find it hard to wait for pieces?
4. Did anyone try to solve someone else's puzzle?
5. What do you have to do to be an effective participant in this task?
6. What do you think is the purpose of this activity?
7. When is the task completed?

She assigns a group facilitator and a recorder/reporter, pointing to the role definitions on the wall chart. The students discuss the questions in their groups, and the recorder jots down their responses. After the groups have talked about the purpose of the tasks they have done (learning to cooperate in completing a task), Henderson asks them to report on their discussions. Each group is asked to add new information to what has already been presented. Then Henderson tells the resource person to put the packets into the third-hour basket and asks all the students to turn their desks back to the front so that she can introduce and explain the homework assignment. She tells them that they will be doing more small-group work the next day.

To introduce the homework, she tells the students that they will be working with some fifth-grade students in a nearby elementary school during the semester. She explains that for today's homework assignment, each student is to write a math story problem that fifth-graders will find interesting. She says that the story can involve any type of mathematics. Henderson reads two examples of the type of problems she wants the students to write, and gives examples of topics, such as shapes, measurement, money, and probability. The homework assignment is to write out a first draft of a problem and bring it to class tomorrow. She asks several students to repeat the directions for the homework assignment and gives an example of a potential problem. When one student gives inaccurate information, she gently corrects the information. As the students leave after the bell, she answers several questions about the homework assignment. She asks one of the students if he can come to the room during the lunch period, telling him that she wants him to practice the steps in peer editing so that he can model the process in class the next day. He agrees to come and asks for a hall pass.

Alone briefly, Henderson goes to the board and erases the agenda, checks the next agenda, puts the overhead on the table in front of the screen for her next class, picks up her computer wand, and goes to the door.

Day Three

Henderson meets the third-hour students at the door, calls them by name, and records their ID card numbers with the computer wand. Beginning with the first student to enter the room, she asks each one, "Do you have your draft of the story problem?" When one student admits that she does not have a completed story problem, she says, "You have about a minute to get something on paper." As before, she asks the class members to read the agenda for the class session.

Following the pattern of the first days of school, Henderson is starting the class by reading the agenda within forty-five seconds of the last bell. The agenda is as follows:

Agenda—Third Hour

Homework:

1. Story problem
2. Discussion of topics interesting to fifth-graders

Assignment   Discussion of *roles* and *behavior* in an effective mathematics class:

1. Facilitator, recorder/reporter, timer, synthesizer, researcher, and organizer
2. Cooperative behavior in a study group

Activities for learning small-group roles:

1. Reviewing story problems
2. Peer editing

Homework: Rewrite story problem for fifth-graders.

Henderson starts today's class by asking about the purposes of the previous day's tasks. Once the students have described the purpose as promoting group cooperation to complete a task, Henderson says that they will be doing similar group work today, but working in pairs. Today's purpose is to improve the quality of the story problems. The students, working in pairs, will contribute to one another's work. (She knows that the students have already done peer editing in their English classes.)

Henderson asks the students to describe their story problems to the whole class. She says that it is not necessary for them to read a completed draft now, and asks that they just tell the topic (e.g., clothes) and the question (e.g., "How much more money is needed?"). Students who do not have a draft are told to exchange seats with those in the last row and to write out their problems while the others talk. After each student speaks, the teacher asks why the problem she/he presented would be interesting to fifth-graders.

Next Henderson says, "Now we will edit the story problems in pairs." She puts up a poster that has the steps for peer editing written on it. The students ask questions about how to do peer editing in math, and Henderson takes out a story problem that she has prepared, saying that she and a student will demonstrate how to do the task. She tells the students in the back of the room to stop writing for a few minutes so that they can watch the demonstration. After Henderson and the student complete the role-play demonstration, she asks the students to move their seats quickly and quietly and proceed with the peer editing. She comments that when students have a question while they are working, they are to raise their hands and she will respond as soon as possible. She stands in front of the room for thirty seconds to see whether all the pairs have started to work, and then walks directly to two students who have not yet started.

She asks, "What is the first thing you are to do?" The students tell her that they don't know. She tells them to read step 1 on the chart.

One of the students reads the chart. Then Henderson asks again what is the first thing to be done. The student says, "I don't want to do this!"

The other student says, "Yeah."

She says, "You don't want to do this. There will be other things we do that you won't particularly like, but when you are in this room, your job is to learn mathematics and do the work. If you want help to write a different problem or think of a more interesting problem, I'll help with that. Otherwise, the two of you can get started."

The student who had said he didn't want to do the task, now says, "My problem is dumb."

Henderson asks the pair whether she should work with them to develop a better problem. The student says he'll work with his partner first and if he can't get a good problem, he'll get her to help.

Henderson circulates during the work period. She notes the types of problems students had in writing. She asks questions about the tasks the problems require. She asks them to tell her how they would think through a solution to the problems they have created. Students who have written overly simple problems are challenged to think harder and to write a new draft. As students finish the editing process, she tells them that they can begin their homework, which is to rewrite their problem based on the feedback they received.

Three minutes before the bell will ring to dismiss class, Henderson calls for the students' attention and asks them to discuss the purpose of working in pairs today and the results of their efforts on the mathematics problems. After the students have paraphrased the opening-purpose statement and reported on their progress, she gives them their new homework assignment. She asks whether there are questions, requests that the students put the chairs back where they belong, and checks each row for straightness as they leave the room.

Day Four

Henderson again meets the students near the door and asks them about their homework. Some students say they finished it before they left class yesterday. One student says she can't find hers. One student forgot and left it in her locker. To these comments, Henderson replies, "The expectation is that homework will be completed before you enter the room. You have a minute before the last bell rings." The girl who left her homework in her locker asks whether she can go to get it. Henderson says, "You must have it for class." The student says, "Will you count me late?" Henderson says, "If you hurry, I will not mark you late this time. However, if it happens again and you can't get back before the bell rings, I will mark you late."

Agenda—Third Hour

Homework: Edited story problems
Assessment: Discussion of *roles* in an effective mathematics class

1. Facilitator, recorder/reporter, and timer—roles assigned by the teacher
2. Synthesizer, researcher, organizer, and encourager—roles that are the individual's responsibility

Using smallgroup roles:

1. Work in group to study and evaluate story problems.
2. Work in group to practice giving directions to fifth-graders.

Henderson starts the class by reminding everyone that the class expectation is that homework will be completed and brought to class each day. Everyone has this responsibility. She comments that most of the class members have met this expectation with the two homework assignments.

"Ms. Henderson!"

"Yes, LeTresha."

"Alex, my brother, is in fifth grade. He said he thought my problem was dumb. I don't want to have my name on it if you are going to give it to the fifth-graders at Grudry Elementary School."

"I can understand that, LeTresha. You think it would be embarrassing if the fifth-graders thought your problem was dumb. The activity that we are going to do today should give you an opportunity to improve it, if you and your work group decide that it needs to be changed. That is true for any of the problems."

Henderson says that she wants to talk about the two types of roles that she has put on charts. She explains that there are roles that all students must take when they are in her class. She points to a chart that reads:

Roles for Individual Class Responsibility:

1. *Organizing:*   Keeping the group on task
                    Keeping the group on topic
                    Reminding the group of the goal
                    Asking for a vote, or agreement

2. *Contributing:*   Sharing information
                     Sharing ideas
                     Suggesting other resources

3. *Encouraging:*   Calling on other members to contribute their ideas
                     Listening in such ways as to draw out other members

4. *Making connections:*   Linking contributions together
                           Pointing out the relationship among ideas
                           Summarizing

As Henderson reads each role description, she gives one example and then asks someone in the class to give another example. Her explanation demonstrates how to encourage someone who has not shared ideas with the group. "One way to encourage," she says, "is to ask someone directly what he/she is thinking." She then asked the group to give an example. Theodora raises her hand and says, "I said to Stanley yesterday, 'You don't like my problem.' I could tell; he was rolling his eyes when I read my problem." Henderson asks Theodora what reasons made her think that this is an example of an encouragement. Theodora says, "Well, I knew he didn't like my problem, but he wasn't saying so. I was encouraging him to be honest.' Henderson suggests that Theodora could be more encouraging by being more positive. Theodora could have said, "Stanley, what would make my problem a more interesting problem?"

When no one can contribute a second idea, Henderson then gives an example that she observed while the students were working together the first three days of class. Henderson then says, "When you all accept responsibility for each of these roles, the group will start to be more productive and more satisfying."

Next, Henderson points to the chart that reads:

Workgroup Roles Assigned by Teacher

Facilitator	Starts the group.
	Makes sure that everyone knows what the task is.
	Gets materials and hands them out when needed.
	Puts all materials away at the end of the small-group session.
Timer	Reminds the group of how much time they have for the task.
	Notifies the group when two minutes are left.
Recorder	Writes down what people say.
	Completes forms to be turned in at the end of the group work.
	Organizes information to give to the group reporter.
Reporter	Reports to the whole class and/or the teacher the results of the group's efforts.
Environmentalist	Organizes the movement of furniture for group work purposes.
	Sees to it that the room is rearranged at the end of the class.

Henderson points to show the students how she wants them to move their desks for today's small-group work. She then hands out teacher-assigned role cards to members of the groups and asks the environmentalist to take charge of getting the groups formed as quickly as possible. Next, she gives the directions for the small-group task.

October

Several weeks after the beginning of the school year, the researchers find that Henderson's class is running smoothly and that students are helping each other to understand the subject matter. They initiate asking questions of the teacher and each other when they need help, and they carry out individual and small-group tasks efficiently, with a focus on understanding.

At the begining of the hour, we find one of the students reading the ID cards and sending the attendance information to the office via the computer. The teacher is interacting with the students about the activities they did during their last unit of study and is listening intently as one of the students tells her about how he challenged his older sister with the problems they had been working on.

The agenda for the third-hour class is on the board when the group comes into the room. It reads:

Agenda—Third Hour
Objectives:
    Practice using stretcher to draw similar figures.
    Discover and communicate similarities between the original figure and a new figure.

Small-group work:
    Assigned resource people—Pick up materials on group trays after introduction of activity.

The students enter the room, read the board, and talk with each other until the bell rings. Then they attend to what Henderson has to say.

We find that Henderson's general mathematics students are involved in the study of similarity and equivalent fractions. Henderson has selected materials published by Addison-Wesley (Lappan et al., 1986). Henderson introduces the unit with a demonstration; at the conclusion of the demonstration, members of the class label the product she has constructed. She then gives directions to the class about how to do the small-group activity. She reminds the students of the objectives for the lesson, indicating that "drawing practice" is one of the objectives. She then tells students to move their desks for small-group work and asks the resource people to pick up trays that contain rubber bands, blank sheets of paper, tape, and two work sheets.

Henderson has developed a procedure for organizing work-group membership for a unit of study. Students work in different groups each time a new unit of study begins. She assigns the roles of the facilitator, recorder/reporter, resource person, and timer for three days of group work, and then reassigns them. This helps to keep the status and power of the members of the group equitable, but does not cause confusion by making students change roles daily for the fifty-minute period.

On this day we find that the facilitator and the other three or four students in each group all begin the task. They help each other with the materials and drawing skills. Then they work as a group to complete the first work sheet. By this time in the school year, the students are accustomed to Henderson's way of running the class. While the students are working, the teacher stops at each group and asks questions about the problems they are having with drawing and about their observations. She suggests (as the text directs: Lappan et al., 1986, p. 9) that students who complete both worksheets use more paper or the chalk board and a three-band stretcher to draw another figure. Ten minutes before the end of class, Henderson tells each group to meet and record their observations about the figures. Five minutes before the end of class, she asks each group to report their observations. She reminds students that she is looking for someone who will be able to synthesize the group reports.

When the bell rings, resource people pick up the trays and put them back on the shelf, with all the materials (except for the work sheets) organized. The work sheets are turned in by the recorder to the teacher. The other members of the groups put their desks back in the original places before they leave the room.

November

Returning to visit Henderson's room after Thanksgiving break, we find students off-task, not following established routines for beginning class, and resisting getting started. Henderson knows that this is a predictable problem, and she takes action to stop what is happening. It takes work to recreate the smoothly functioning learning-community environment after breaks. She knows that if she does not attend to the cues, the learning community will deteriorate over time and she will end up wasting valuable instruction time in just "managing the students."

The first thing that Henderson does is acknowledge the variety of feeling messages that the students are communicating (e.g., "It is hard to get back to work after a vacation," "I want to talk to my friends," and "These people are wasting my time"). We hear the following conversation.

Henderson: "LaTrica, it sounds like you want to visit with your friends today. Did you have a chance to spend a lot of time together over the long weekend?"

LaTrica: "Yes, and now we have to be quiet all day again."

Henderson: "You feel it is more interesting to be able to talk to your friends than to learn mathematics. You are unhappy about being back in school."

LaTricia: "Ya, this school is. . . ."

Henderson: "Javier, I heard your brother was hurt in a car accident. What is happening with him?"

Javier: "He's OK. He is back in school today."

Henderson: "It sounds like several of you are having trouble getting back in the routine of things. Remember, on the last day of class before break we planned what we would do in class today. What was our agenda?"

Angel: "I don't really remember, but it was something about. . . ."

From this point Henderson and the students get back on the mathematics tasks at hand. At the end of the class, Henderson tells the students what they will be doing the next day and reminds them that they should have their ID cards ready when they enter the room and should read the agenda for specific information about what groups to get into at the beginning of class the next day.

January

After winter break, we visit Henderson again and find that students entering the third-hour class are telling each other to hurry up so that they can get going. Before vacation Henderson and the group planned an activity for this first day back that would provide the students with an opportunity to select mathematics topics of interest and discuss them in small groups. On the last day of class before break, students listed several topics that they thought would be interesting to discuss two weeks later in their first class after vacation. Before school today, several students came to the room and added new topics to the list. The list is posted on the wall where it can be read by everyone.

On the last day before break, they also identified criteria for selecting group members, the size of groups, the product to be generated through discussion, and the topics that were eligible for consideration. They decided that a group of no more than five and no fewer than three students would self-select and would appoint roles of facilitator, recorder, and timer. The criterion for topics was, "The discussion must contribute to all members learning something new about other members of the group." The product was to be an algorithm, a shape, or a statement (probability or hypothesis) that would reflect the discussion.

At the end of class, Henderson says, "Your groups seemed busy today. I learned a lot of interesting things. Remember that your product is due for display by first hour in two days. Also remember to look at the agenda when you come in tomorrow. I'll be ready to introduce the new unit, and I hope we'll have time for one activity."

May

Henderson knows that at the end of the school year students may become anxious about going on vacation; bored with routines, procedures, and content that they have worked with over the whole academic year; and worried about losing the group relationship that they have developed. Sometime during May, Henderson observes that the students have begun the process of closure. She hears comments such as "Get out of my face! You're always the one who has to. . . ." "Remember when we discovered that. . . ?" "We should do another *big* project like we did in February!" and "Everyone in *this class* who tried out for next year's football cheerleaders got picked." She initiates a conversation with the students in which she acknowledges that the process for ending this group's experience has begun. Her purpose is to set up with the students an explicit plan for bringing closure to the class. This plan will be in the form of a calendar of academic work and socialization experiences to end the year and promote the students' movement forward.

The plan that Henderson and the students develop includes a schedule to complete the final unit of study and to intersperse study with closure activities, primarily during the last two weeks of school. The closure activities are to include showing a video that students will make outside of regular school hours (a humorous sketch entitled "General Math Class"); showing slides of various activities that the students completed during the year and reading the prediction cards that they put away at the beginning of the year ("Remember when . . ."); presenting to the department chair a framed work entitled "Mathematics Collage," signed by all the members of the group, to be hung in the hallway (immortalizing their experience); giving make-believe (oral) gifts to classmates. The students and Henderson identify a facilitator for each of the closure projects and work out a way for students to sign up for the activities they wish to work on outside school. The purposes of these activities are to review the year, to tie up loose ends, to help the students to acknowledge their feelings about the experiences they have had together and about the group's breaking up, and to help the students to celebrate their experience in the class.

June

A visit to Henderson's third-hour class in June finds the group participating in one of the year-end socialization activities. The students have created a piñata and filled it with make-believe gifts. Giving make-believe gifts is one way to celebrate the class's experience. In May, when Henderson and the students developed the calendar for ending the year, the students drew names. They then each thought up a present that was both related to mathematics and appropriate for the person whose name they had drawn. Next, they wrote a description of the gift on a 3 × 5 index card, rolled the card and tied a bow around it, wrote the person's name on the outside, and put it into the piñata. The student facilitator for this activity checked off each student's name on a chart when he/ she placed the "gift" in the piñata, to keep track and make sure that everyone had completed the task.

As students enter the classroom, they move their seats into a circle. Then the facilitator opens the piñata, and members of the class help distribute the "gifts."

One at a time, the students open their "gifts" and read them to the rest of the class. For example, the card Mark opens reads, "Mark, you've had a hard time with estimating all year. Your gift will make it possible for you never to have this problem again. I give you an invisible set of rulers to use in estimating distances. This packet includes invisible rulers for 1 mile, 100 yards, 10 miles, 5 feet, a minute, a light year, a probability of 75 percent, and 'just a second'." Mario, who had wanted to draw designs all year, received a trip to every art gallery in the world that shows contemporary artwork.

We also visit school on the last day, a day that is usually hectic and one many teachers and students feel is a waste of time. At Henderson's school on the last day, students report to each class for a brief time, pick up their cards, and move to the next class. In May, Henderson and the students had decided that they would each think about "the best thing that happened" (in this class) and would be prepared to tell it during the last get-together. For this final activity, the students sit in a circle and tell their "best things," starting with the teacher or a volunteer. After the last student in the circle tells her "best thing," the students applaud and leave the room to go to the next class.

Henderson has found that engaging students in closure plans gives them a direction to move toward. They are able to participate in a variety of things and to keep their attention on academic work right to the end of the year, because their socialization needs are also being attended to. Carefully executed closure plans also function as a transition to the coming year, because they help students to fix their achievements in memory and to carry a feeling of confidence forward to their next experience.

Performance Outcomes and Activities (NJPTS 6)

Chapter 6
A Secondary-Level Classroom

PERFORMANCE OUTCOMES

Teacher Candidates will

1. Analyze written and video-learning community classroom case studies and accurately identify the learning community cultural elements, dispositions, roles, and functions of schooling illustrated in the case studies.
2. Compare and contrast written learning community classroom case studies.
3. Compare and contrast the elements of learning community case studies with observation and interview data collected in schools.

Exercise 6.1

The purpose of this activity is to reinforce the idea that learning community cultures can look very different even though they are based on a common set of principles.

A. Begin by following the process you used to study the elementary learning community culture. Once you have identified the learning community cultural elements in this case study get together with a group of six to eight peers and compare your findings. How are they similar and/or different from your colleagues ideas?
B. Second identify the important ideas or elements of a classroom learning community culture that both Henderson and Forero established in their classes.
C. Third identify the apparent differences in their learning community cultures.
D. Finally, once again think about your own ideas and compare them to Henderson and Forero. How are your ideas similar and/or different from Henderson and Forero's ideas? (Use your self-assessments and related charts that you completed in earlier work.)

RECOMMENDED READINGS

Brophy, J. E. (1985). Classroom management as instruction: socializing self-guidance in students. *Theory into Practice, 24* (4), 233–240.

Documentary Film: To Be and To Have (French multi-level classroom)

End of Semester Self-Assessment
Students, Neighborhood, Community, School, and
School System/District

Name: _____ School Assignment:_____ Level: _____ Date:_____

REVIEW WHAT YOU WROTE IN THE INITIAL ASSESSMENT.

A. After reviewing your initial assessment data write how you used the information you provided in the first assessment (and new information you gathered) to improve the experiences you provided your students. If you did not use the information simply write, "Did not use information in this category to improve instruction," then write why you believe that you did not make use of it.

1.   Knowledge about the neighborhood.
2.   Knowledge about the community.
3.   Knowledge about the students (6 you identified).
4.   The school to which you are assigned.
5.   The two other schools about which you provided information.
6.   The school district/system.

B. After reviewing your initial ideas about how you would use the information, you had to improve the educational experiences for your learners explain how you in fact used the information. If you didn't make use of the information simply write, "Did not use information in this category to improve instruction," then write why you believe that you did not make use of it.

1.   Neighborhood
2.   Community
3.   Students
4.   Schools
5.   School Systems
6.   Professional Knowledge
7.   Personal Knowledge

C. Explain what you know now, about linking school and community, student and family, curriculum and neighborhood/community, and the system and community, in order to improve educational experiences.

SMALL GROUP DISCUSSIONS—COURSE CULTURE

The purpose of this activity is for you to have the experience of identifying the three levels of culture in a group that is familiar to you. Use the procedures developed early in this university course for organizing and facilitating an effective small group discussion. Turn in the notes from your discussion group to the instructor at the end of the session.

1.   What are the Level 1 indicators of the type of culture in this university course?
2.   What are the Level 2 indicators of the type of culture in this university course?
3.   What are the Level 3 indicators of the type of culture in this university course?
4.   What Level 1, 2 and 3 additional indicators would you expect to develop over the semester as you work toward establishing a learning community culture?
5.   What Level 1, 2, and 3 indicators would you expect to eliminate over the semester as you work toward establishing a learning community?

OVERVIEW

In the first section of this book, the authors presented a theoretical description of learning communities by discussing the functions of schools (Chapter 1), the propensities of learning-community teachers (Chapter 2), and the classroom considered as a culture (Chapter 3). In Section II, Chapter 4, we presented a pedagogy for a learning community. We also offered the reader two concrete descriptions of learning communities in operation, at the elementary level (Chapter 5) and the secondary level (Chapter 6). This section presents the developmental stages of classroom learning communities with specific recommendations for what should be done to implement each stage.

The developmental stages of learning communities are sequential; in the descriptions which follow, they are cast in the framework of a typical school year. In each stage there are three phases of activities which are also sequential and cyclical: preparing, implementing, and reflecting. The time frame does not matter in this context, because each activity is repeated at many levels—daily, weekly, by term, or even by school year. The cycle of preparing, implementing, and reflecting characterizes both the teacher's organization of work and the learning which is going on in the community. Students and teacher are constantly preparing, implementing, and reflecting. We use this cycle as an organizer because it is a simple guide through which a frame of reference for any work going on at any time can be suggested immediately. Teachers do not just jump in and start doing; they have to plan, and they have to check on what they learned the last time they did a similar activity.

Likewise, the authors are aware that we cannot ask you, the reader, to jump into the chapters which follow without first being prepared. Chapter 7 is different from the rest of the chapters in this book, in that it is a midpoint workbook. It offers you an opportunity to consider in some depth what your own views are with respect to the functions of schools, the nature of learning, the cultural norms for a classroom, teacher roles, and subject-matter goals. In other words, Chapter 7 allows you to create your own "advance organizer" for developing learning communities. Therefore, the writing style addresses you directly, as in the activities sections which accompany this chapter and other chapters. In Chapter 7, the authors give you direct advice on thinking about, writing down, and reflecting on essential matters of professional practice.

Of course, you are free to jump past the exercises described in Chapter 7 and get on with reading about the stages of developing classroom learning communities. We strongly recommend, however, that you take advantage of this opportunity to create your own vision of teaching in general and learning community in particular. "Where there is no vision, the people perish," according to Proverbs. We agree, and we add that, in particular, having a vision of an entity as complex as a learning community is necessary in order to negotiate the demands of each developmental stage. In a sense, therefore, we are asking you to think about what lies ahead. Pause here and consider before proceeding; otherwise, what is offered in Chapters 8 through 12 may seem overly prescriptive. The development of a learning community calls for interaction among its members. We challenge you to consider now what vision you bring to the process of developing a learning community.

Assertiveness and Earning Respect of the Students in Your Classroom

Since we initially published our book for establishing and maintaining classroom learning communities more and more reports from K–12 students as well as teachers indicate that they do not see their schools as safe places to learn or work. Increases in drugs and violence are common in schools located across the spectrum of school locations. Problem student behavior is no longer considered an urban problem or a middle school and high school problem. Most teachers entering the field of teaching in the early part of the twenty-first century will encounter problem behavior no matter where the school district, in which they accept a job, is located.

Student teachers and even new teachers do not have a two or three year "honeymoon period," during which they can learn how to effectively teach and manage students. No longer is there a strong "position-respect" that comes with being labeled a teacher. Changes in our culture mean that student teachers, new teachers and even experienced teachers who switch grade-levels must be prepared to take charge, establish an effective learning community culture and demonstrate their ability to engage all students in effective tasks, which result in expected achievement of specified outcomes and excellence. Teachers who are not prepared to begin at an effective level will create unmanageable problems and probably leave the profession within three years.

The two problems we selected for further exploration are faced by all new teachers. They are: (1) respecting and earning the respect of their students and (2) identifying and eliminating bullying in their classes. We chose the problem of respecting and gaining students' respect because teachers who communicate that they do not respect students on principle and do not know how to earn the respect of their students will create management and discipline problems that they will not be able to handle. We placed an emphasis on the problem of bullying because of an increase of its occurrence in schools, the increase in the public's interest and response (e.g., talk shows, newspapers, journals) and an increase in the findings from studies about bullying that would help teachers.

Being non-assertive, whether due to communication weaknesses, upbringing or the perception one holds of him/herself, is one of the ways that people create relationship and management problems for themselves. For non-assertive teachers, the result is that twenty-five to thirty students suffer from the teacher's actions. Being non-assertive in the classroom communicates a lack of respect to the students. It also contributes to an environment that appears to "sanction" disruptive or bullying behavior.

McClure (2003) suggests that there is a lot of confusion about the concept of assertiveness. She reviews the definitions of aggressive, passive and assertive:

> Aggressive adj. 1. inclined to move or act in a hostile fashion. 2. assertive; bold; enterprising; Aggress v.i., to start an attack or quarrel;

> Passive adj. 1. Receiving or subjected to an action without responding or initiating an action in return. 2. Not participating or acting; submissive; inert; Pass v.t. To relinquish a right; and

> Assertive adj. Inclined to bold assertion; positive; and Assert v.t. 1. To state or express positively, affirm. 2. To defend or maintain, for example one's rights. To express oneself forcefully or boldly. (p. 40).

Given the two definitions for aggressive (adj.) she states that it is easy to see why people may be confused about what it means to be assertive.

A second point that McClure (2003) makes is a misunderstanding that the terms passive, aggressive and assertive fall on a continuum. She asserts that they are not on a continuum and the passive, aggressive and passive/aggressive characteristics are dysfunctional while the assertive characteristics "form a healthy and functional realm of their own" (p. 40). She provides the following two charts (p. 41) to illustrate this point.

PASSIVE

- Goes off in a huff to manipulate
- Sighs a lot
- Says he or she is angry while smiling
- Tries to sit on both sides of the fence to avoid conflict
- Is afraid to take risks
- Shows stage fright when speaking in front of a group
- Clams up when he or she feels treated unfairly
- Asks permission when it isn't necessary
- Complains instead of taking action
- Buys approval by appearing selfless, a good sport

AGGRESSIVE

- Puts others down
- May respond too vigorously, making a negative impression
- Expresses ideas and opinions strongly
- Is often first and very competitive
- Doesn't ever think he or she is wrong
- Takes over a group
- Exhibits bossy, pushy behavior
- Takes charge, task-oriented, gets important things done
- Moves into people's space, overpowers
- Jumps on others, pushes people around

ASSERTIVE

- Operates from choice
- Knows what is needed and develops a plan to get it
- Is action-oriented
- Demonstrates firmness
- Is initially trusting
- Assumes responsibility for self
- Has realistic expectations
- Emphasizes the positive nature of self and of others
- Deals with others fairly and justly
- Behaves with consistency
- Takes proactive positions
- Takes appropriate action toward filling needs and wants without denying right of others

Byrmu (1988, pp. 149) created a summary that shows how the characteristics of passive, aggressive, passive/aggressive and assertive behavior appear when applied by an individual.

FACTOR	STYLES			
	PASSIVE	AGGRESSIVE	PASSIVE-AGGRESSIVE	ASSERTIVE
TREATMENT OF RIGHTS	Gives up own	Usurps Others	Sneakily usurps others	Maintains own
METAPHOR	Doormat	Steamroller	Doormat with Spikes	Pillar
VERBAL BEHAVIOR	Qualifies, Apologizes	Blames, Accuses	Uses sarcasm indirectly	Speaks mind openly
NONVERBAL BEHAVIOR	Averted gaze, Soft voice, Cowers	Stares, Loud voice, Invades others' space	Sideways glance, Sarcastic tone, Shifts limbs	Direct gaze, Varied voice, Balanced
RESPONSE	Flight	Fight	Hit and Run	Engagement

It is important to understand the linkage between being assertive and your rights as a human being. McClure (2003), states "basic rights are simply universal human standards for how to treat each other ethically" (p. 35). Davis, Eshelman, and McKay state that: "You are assertive when you stand up for your rights in such a way that the rights of others are not violated" p. 132. Years ago it was believed that people were either assertive or they were not. Years later researchers (e.g., Wolf, 1958; Lazarus, 1966) learned that almost everyone was assertive in some situations, but passive or aggressive in other situations. They defined assertiveness as "expressing personal rights and feelings" (p. 212). Based on this definition assertiveness training became popular in the 1970's. During the 1970's, researchers (e.g., Jakubowski-Spector, 1973), further studied individuals and they learned that individuals who demonstrate assertive behavior infrequently, do not believe that they have a right to their feelings, ideas, opinions, or beliefs. These people probably learned as children that their ideas and feelings were not as valuable or correct as others. This negative belief about oneself hinders a teacher from becoming an effective classroom teacher. Davis, et al., (1988, 2003) state that ". . . when you are an assertive person, you can be more relaxed in interpersonal situations. Working with 25 to 150 students a day clearly demands mature healthy adult-student relationships.

To determine where you are in your development McClure (2003), created an assessment "Taking Stock of Your Rights" (pp. 32–35). She included in this assessment everyday examples of how you exercise your rights while you respect the rights of others. She concludes:

> . . . exercising human rights is as much a duty as a right. This duty is to the larger human community. Our assertiveness actively affirms basic standards of behavior necessary for civilized relationships. The equality that we are establishing is not an equality of status, aptitude, or ability, but an equality of fundamental rights as human beings. It is the one universal and abiding bulwark against bigotry, intolerance, and discrimination of all kinds. (p. 36)

It is very important that student teachers, new teachers and those changing grade levels are effectively assertive, as this supports them in communicating caring, respect, and expectations that all students will achieve. Effective assertiveness also supports the teacher in not letting disruptive behavior get out of hand. This prevents many of the discipline problems that teachers create for themselves. It also means that when a student brings problem behavior (e.g., bullying, hitting) to the classroom, that the teacher is able to stop it before it harms the rest of the students. It also allows them to communicate that students will treat others with respect and caring and contribute to an environment that promotes learning for all students.

To be sure that you are developing the assertive norms and skills you will need to be an effective teacher take McClue's "Taking Stock of Your Rights" and identify some behaviors that you want to change. Write three goals that you will reach when you have changed the behaviors. Write one goal that will have an effect on your personal life. Write two goals, related to behavior changes that will have an effect on your success as a candidate and new teacher.

Respecting and Earning Student Respect

One of the problems that early field experience students, student teachers and new teachers bring to the classroom is that they "need" to be "liked" by their students. Further, they are unclear about what an appropriate caring relationship is when the relationship is between a teacher and student. This is a problem because frequently new teachers do not understand that "being liked" is an outcome of students feeling that they are respected, held to high standards, provided quality instruction and given complex worthwhile tasks. Deiro (2003) tells the following story:

> When you enter Ms. Bennett's 3rd grade classroom, you hear classical music playing softly. Students sitting in small groups . . . couches are arranged casually . . . , purposefully giving the space the ambience of a cozy home rather than a traditional learning environment. On Ms. Bennett's desk sits a jar of lemon drops from which she rewards students from time to time . . . Meg is a student . . . does not perceive Ms. Bennett as a caring teacher. Meg explains, "she thinks about us having fun, but she doesn't think about our feelings. A caring teacher is

a teacher that is responsible and reliable and doesn't need to give candy or lemon drops or anything else. A caring teacher acts like we are older and more sensible and not just 8- or 9-year-olds. We are somebody." Meg views her 2nd grade teachers as caring. "She says my 2nd grade teachers were different. They taught us like we were older than 2nd grade." (p. 60)

Bennis, Schein, Steele, and Berlew (1973, 3rd edition), make it clear that the caring relationship between a teacher and student is an influential relationship. They believe that relationships between teachers and students are formed to *promote learning* and academic growth. The relationships between teachers and students are not formed for mutual satisfaction as we expect in emotional-expressive relationships.

Bennis, et al. (1973) identify three characteristics of the influential relationship as follows: (1) The central concern of the influential relationship is planned change/growth (for teachers it is student learning); (2) The successful conclusion of the influential relationship is termination (for teachers, the student should move on/graduate to the next level); and (3) The power in the influential relationship is asymmetrical (for teachers they know and give more to their students). Deiro, (2003), states that with "this asymmetrical balance of power comes a responsibility for the change agent to handle the power ethically and respectfully. The way in which teachers handle their asymmetrical power shapes and determines what students perceive as caring behavior" (p. 2). Glenn and Nelsen (1988) point out that in influential relationships, (as in teaching and parenting), using an *authoritative* approach increases children's perceptions of caring and trust. Deiro (2003) concluded that

> A teacher's respect and an ethical use of power are key to students' perceptions of caring. With respect, teachers can communicate caring to students when disciplining them, correcting their assignments, lecturing, or playing with them . . . respectful treatment can go a long way toward creating a caring learning environment, promoting the academic growth of students, and enhancing a teacher's ability to make a difference in student's lives. (p. 4)

The first two stages of creating a learning community culture provide the information about

what occurs in each stage, as well as how to begin the creation of a caring learning community culture. Equally important as is the process of group development in the establishment of a learning community are the quality of the teacher's instruction, learner tasks, and his/her classroom management skills.

The process for Stage I-Beginning is a first step in communicating the teacher's respect for and interest in each student. It also offers the students the chance to see that the teacher's actions demonstrate his/her value for each student. It also supports the teacher in demonstrating how important it is for each student in the classroom to get to know all of the other students. This begins the sense of community for the students rather than the sense of isolation or clicks. When invited by a teacher to work with them to create a learning community we continue to be astonished to find how many students did not know the names of the other students in their classes.

Stage II-Establishing Expectations is the second stage in the development of a learning community classroom. The stage is focused on the establishment of a classroom management system. Wong & Wong (1998) define classroom management as ". . . all of the things that a teacher does to organize students, space, time and materials so that instruction in content and student learning can take place" (p. 84). The process of this stage of group development supports the development and implementation of a *quality* classroom management plan that is essential if students are to achieve. Thinking through the roles, rules, routines, procedures, and norms that will be established in the classroom culture can be done by the teacher alone, in professional learning communities, or in teacher and student discussions. New teachers must create a written plan that spells out the actions for the development of a learning community. Experienced teachers who know the management system can include the students in discussion as a part of establishing the plan.

Emmer, Evertson, and Worsham (2003) found in their research that effective classroom managers included beginning the school year with a positive emphasis on management by arranging the room in a way that supports effective and efficient management, as well as systematically identifying and implementing rules and operating procedures. In a learning community classroom the rules, roles, routines, and procedures would be congruent with the norms of a learning community (e.g., contributing to the achievement of personal, social, social justice, and academic performance outcomes).

Once a teacher is experienced in working with large groups of students in problem solving and reaching consensus then they may choose to involve the students in the identification of the rules, roles, routines, and procedures that will support the development of learning community norms. While including students in the identification of rules helps them buy into them it is possible for new teachers to gain the buy in of their students through discussions and role plays of the predetermined rules. To further the individual buy in, new teachers can have each student sign in on a "Support the Rules" chart once he/she can explain why a rule is important in the classroom.

In Chapters 8 through 12, we provide guidelines for establishing, maintaining, and disbanding the classroom learning community.

RECOMMENDED READINGS

Bower, S. A., and Bower, G. H. *Asserting yourself*, Reading, Mass., Addison-Wesley.

Davis, M., Eshelman, E. G., McKay, M. (1988, 2003). *The relaxation & stress reduction workbook,* New Harbinger Publ, Inc., Oakland, CA.

Heath, S. B., and McLaughlin, M. W. (Editors, 1993). *Identity and inner-city youth, beyond ethnicity and gender.* Teachers College, Columbia University, NY, NY.

Hurmence, B. (Editor, 1984). *My folks don't want me to talk about slavery: Twenty-one oral histories of former North Carolina slaves.* John F. Blair, Publisher, Winston-Salem, North Carolina.

Jakubowski-Spector, P. (1973). "Facilitating the Growth of Women Through Assertive Training." *The Counseling Psychologist,* 4, 75–86.

Lazarus, A. (1966). *Behavior Rehearsal vs. Non-directive therapy vs. advice in effecting behavior change.* Behavioral Research and Therapy, 4, 209–12.

McClure, J. (2003). *Civilized Assertiveness for women: Communication with backbone . . . not bite.* Albion Street Press, Denver, Colorado.

CHAPTER

Making the Learning–Community Vision Explicit

This chapter describes how you can create an advance organizer for use in planning for and establishing a learning community. Your advance organizer will detail characteristics of the learning community you will be establishing. In other words, you can be a participant throughout this chapter rather than a passive reader.

Teachers prepare for the beginning of the school year in many different ways. For example, Forero (Chapter 5) identified specific outcomes toward which she would work before she thought much about specific units, activities, or the classroom's physical environment. Some teachers with whom we work reverse this sequence, while others seem to keep both goals and activities simultaneously in mind. In this chapter, you will be able to design an advance organizer in which you can make explicit the connections between the functions of schooling for expected student outcome (what will be learned in relation to the four functions of schooling) and the classroom learning-community culture (how its members will live together day by day).

The first step in creating an advance organizer is to answer a series of questions designed to keep the focus on identifying characteristics of the culture that is to be established. The questions include:

- What functions of schooling will guide your decisions?
- What are your year-end curriculum goals for learners?
- How will the physical environment of your classroom be created and maintained?
- What norms, roles, rules, and procedures are necessary for your learning-community culture?
- What will your classroom learning community look, sound, and feel like? That is, what overall impression would someone who visited your learning community receive?

We begin by identifying the functions of schooling in a learning community. These functions provide the foundation for the design of the rest of the advance organizer.

FUNCTIONS OF SCHOOLING

One way in which you could identify the functions of schooling would be simply to borrow ours—the four described in Chapter I as a way to begin examining your own thinking. Figure out exactly what these functions mean to you by writing the label for each function (e.g., social justice) as the title at the top of a page; then set a timer for three minutes, and start writing. Write everything that comes into mind about the particular function until the timer rings. Repeat the process for each function. This should help to capture what you think each of these functions is about. Writing out your thoughts will push you to specify what meanings you think are implied by these purposes of schooling.

Once your "fast-write" pages are completed, organize what you have written by rewriting the statements. As you rewrite, analyze the statements to see whether they fairly represent your commitments about what schools are for. It may be helpful to set your statements aside for several days; taking a fresh look at them after such a pause may enable you to adjust their substance so that they will express your point of view more adequately.

Another good way to identify the functions or purposes of schools is to follow the example of Forero (Chapter 5). She figured out what functions of schooling she would support by reflecting on what she knew about teaching and learning, society, math, social studies, literacy, science, and her own beliefs and values. Her strategy was to create a concept map.

A concept map can be created in six steps, as follows:

1. Brainstorm to make a list of terms pertaining to outcomes—for example, "State theories," "Help others," and "Provide illustrations."

2. Organize related words into categories.

3. Label the functions of schooling reflected by each category (e.g., "State theories" should be labeled as an academic function).

4. Cross out any specific items that will not really receive systematic attention. The deleted items may be areas that would be nice to include if time were really available or areas that are traditionally mentioned as "important" but seldom taught.

5. Draw lines to connect items in a given category to items that are related in other categories.

6. Analyze the representation of the functions, and write a statement defining each function. This statement should reflect your ideas about the mission of the classroom learning community.

GOALS

What are your goals for the year? After you define your own concepts of schooling's functions, your next decision is about what you intend to hold yourself and your students accountable for during the school year. Holding students accountable also means that you accept responsibility for helping all students in your class to reach the goals. Thus, learning-community teachers state explicitly what they accept responsibility for accomplishing during a specific period of time. Your goals will also provide criteria for evaluating progress through the year and for deciding specifically what you will teach and how you will teach it.

Your goal statements for the year may be as global as "All students will act in school in ways that demonstrate personal and social responsibility and social justice values," or they may be stated in terms of specific outcomes, such as "Demonstrate problem solving in mathematics as described by the National Council of Teachers of Mathematics (NCTM) standards." Still other goals may be stated in out-of-school terms; that is, they may communicate what you want students to take away from the school setting and apply in their out-of-school lives. For example, "When confronted with a situation in which inequity for any person is evident, the learner will take actions to change the situation."

We suggest that you follow five steps, listed below, to decide what is worthy of being included in your goal statements.

1. Think about students, our society, and what you have identified as the functions of schools. If you are early in the process of learning to teach, reviewing curriculum guides may be a necessary part of your first step in identifying your goals. However, experienced teachers should not lean too heavily on curriculum guidelines.

2. Write out goals without reviewing material from curriculum or teacher guides. Goal statements may represent different segments of time. Some may be written for a marking period or semester or year.

3. Analyze your written goal statements to determine what will have to be learned/taught/evaluated if the students are to achieve each stated goal. You can use these statements as cues for writing specific objectives at a later time. (See Chapter 11.) List the learnings.

4. Review your curriculum guides, school missions, and teacher guides to that you can add worthwhile things that you may have left out in the first draft. Revise and edit your goal statements to reflect your more comprehensive thinking after reviewing the curriculum.

5. Reflect on your goal statements for several days until you feel ready to make the commitment to take on the responsibility for helping all your students to reach the goals. If, after due consideration, some of your statements appear to represent unattainable goals, delete or rewrite them. Keep repeating this last step until you have a set of goals that are: (a) worthwhile, (b) supportive of the learning-community philosophy, and (c) reflective of what you are willing to be held accountable for.

PHYSICAL ENVIRONMENT

How will your classroom environment be created and maintained? In planning a physical environment for a classroom learning community, a teacher needs first to identify elements that promote shared responsibility and the type of instruction that promotes equity and intended learner outcomes. These elements should support individual responsibility and access to materials and equipment by establishing open traffic flow. Elements should also assist in the selection of materials used to create the classroom context.

Both teacher and learners share responsibility for the environment. In fact, it is essential that students participate in creating the physical environment of their classroom, so that they will develop a sense of ownership of the physical space they occupy. For this reason, learning-community teachers identify opportunities for students to contribute. Listing such opportunities (e.g., develop and maintain a terrarium, select and maintain a pet, design bulletin boards, create and select artwork for display, and clean storage areas once a semester) is the first step in clarifying visions about the environment.

The second part of your advance planning for the classroom environment should contain your plans for using space and storing materials. Such planning helps you to focus on ways to prevent disruption and promote maintenance of an orderly environment in an activity-filled classroom space. A key to the arrangement of furniture is a seating plan that allows for whole-group direct instruction, individual work, easy movement from whole-group to small-group work, and class discussions. Many teachers create the environmental design in their heads, based on their experiences. We recommend a computer or paper-and-pencil sketch for the purpose of systematic analysis.

Once you have created a design, consider whether or not the arrangement of furniture permits easy flow of traffic and easy access to materials, both when getting them out and when putting them away. For example, bottlenecks can occur in areas where students are getting out and putting away materials. Traffic patterns that emphasize one-way flow help to minimize "traffic accidents" among students at bottlenecks. For younger children, going to and from small-group instruction areas can present another possibility of bottlenecks.

The third part of your environment vision should be the "decoration" of the classroom. In a learning community, visual and audio representations can promote: (1) shared responsibility among students and teacher for the environment, (2) equity, (3) appreciation of diversity, and (4) recognition of both group and individual achievements. Visual representations (e.g., posters) of the community's focus on academic, personal, and social responsibility and social justice outcomes contribute to orienting students. Having a tape recorder to play selected music also helps create a comfortable environment.

TABLE 7-1   IDENTIFICATION AND ANALYSIS FORM FOR NORMS

Statement of Norms	Relationship to Functions of Schooling	What Must Be Taught
Respect for others and their property	Personal and social responsibility	Distinguish between respectful, disrespectful, and kidding-around behavior.
Cooperation	Social responsibility	Distinguish between cooperation and passive behavior.
Interdependence	Social responsibility	Identify outcomes that result from these relationships.

TABLE 7-2   IDENTIFICATION AND ANALYSIS FORM FOR ROLES

Roles	When Assigned by Teacher	When Decided by Group	Contribution

Everyone:
  Encourager
  Informer
  Organizer
  Synthesizer
	Each person takes all roles, as part of group responsibility.	When group is not functioning well.	Social responsibility

Individually assigned: Facilitator	At beginning of unit.	When someone is absent.	Social justice

We suggest that you sketch a couple of floor plans as a means for assessing your image of a preferred classroom arrangement. Experienced teachers can challenge their own thinking by asking, "What would be gained and lost by a new physical arrangement?" Preservice teachers can begin by reflecting on the classroom environments in which they have been students.

NORMS, ROLES, RULES, AND PROCEDURES

An advance organizer specifies norms, roles, rules, and procedures that are related to the specific purposes of schooling to which a teacher has made a commitment. The identification process includes thinking about intended outcomes and stating specifically what is needed. Once you have stated your norms, roles, rules, and procedures, you can analyze them for their congruence with the intended goals and for potential unintended effects. Unintended effects are things that might happen but can be prevented by thorough, thoughtful planning (e.g., avoiding conditions in which a student uses a procedure for getting help as a means to get others to do his/her work.) Finally, your analysis should seek out any inconsistencies or incongruities among the norms, roles, rules, and procedures or with the overall learning-community philosophy. For example, rules that keep students from making decisions or becoming personally responsible for their actions are incongruent with the purposes of schooling. Such rules need to be changed.

We find that identifying norms, roles, rules and procedures is facilitated by using analysis forms, because these forms provide a visual representation of the elements that need to be identified and analyzed by the teacher. For example, communicating vague impressions about norms to students gives them conflicting messages and thus leads them to behave inconsistently. When you are identifying norms, you should list concepts that reflect "the way we will live together." For example, respect, cooperation, and interdependence are norms that are consistently identified in learning-community classrooms.

TABLE 7-3   IDENTIFICATION AND ANALYSIS FORM FOR RULES

Rule Statement	Intended Outcome	Unintended Outcome	What Must Be Taught	Connections
No put-downs.	Respectful environment.	Problems don't get settled.	Problem-solving strategy	Academic Personal Social responsibility
Help when you can.	Everyone learns.	A student does someone else's work.	Tutoring	Social responsibility Academic
Ask for help when you need it.	Everyone learns for understanding.	Some students get others to do their work.	How to ask clarifying questions	Personal responsibility Academic

TABLE 7-4   EXAMPLES OF PROCEDURES

A. General assessment
   1. Procedures to promote teacher instructional time and student on-task time
   2. Procedures to support a variety of instructional strategies
   3. Procedures to promote shared responsibility for teacher and students
   4. Procedures to promote communication with parents
B. Instruction
   1. *Instructional time and student engaged time*   Develop procedures for:
      a. Efficient transitions
      b. Getting and putting away materials
      c. Taking attendance and other school procedures
      d. Occasions which happen on an irregular basis (e.g., visitors, parent aides, requests from office), so that they will occur with the least possible disruption to the learning process
   2. *To support successful implementation of instructional strategies*   Develop procedures for:
      a. Student access to teacher's written and verbal feedback
      b. Getting and putting away materials
      c. Managing individual and small-group instructional formats; includes
         (1) Seat work that promotes students' continuation of engagement as they move from activity to activity on their own
         (2) Selection of seat/independent work criteria (e.g., relevance, challenge, internal cues to continue)
         (3) Gaining teacher's help while student is engaged in independent work and teacher is working with others
         (4) Calling on students in ways that promote equity in speaking time, feedback, and interactions with teacher
      d. Whole-group interaction; includes
         (1) Getting started
         (2) Bringing closure
         (3) Getting and returning paperwork
   3. *Procedures which promote shared responsibility*   Develop procedures for:
      a. Solving problems, so as to prevent crises from arising in the future
      b. Housekeeping, so as to promote student accountability and responsibility, and shared teacher and student ownership of classroom
C. Communication with parents and community

Once you have listed all such norms, the next step is to identify the school functions which they support. Finally, based on your prior knowledge, you should identify what you will need to teach explicitly to students, so that the norms can be established successfully. For example, you might predict that students who have been in traditional classrooms may have trouble distinguishing between comments that show respect, disrespect, and "just kidding around."

TABLE 7-5   IDENTIFICATION AND ANALYSIS FORM FOR PROCEDURES

Name and Purposes of Procedure	Steps in Procedure	Intended Outcome	Unintended Outcome	Connection to Functions Schooling

Set up small work groups.	1. Environmentalist identified for each group for 1/2 marking period.
	2. Work day— designated person:
	  a. Signals others to move chairs and tables for group work
	  b. Gets materials from counter
	  c. Distributes materials per directions on board
	  d. Collects and puts materials away at end of period
	  e. Signals members to put chairs and tables back into regular classroom positions at end of session
		Students on-task immediately on small-group work days.	Others in group take no responsibility for helping environmentalist.	On-task behavior necessary for academic outcomes, cooperation, and interdependence.

In some classrooms, what teachers and students believe to be respectful actions may conflict. In these settings, creating shared understandings would be a first step toward establishing a norm about respect in the learning community. See the norms form in Table 7-1 on page 219 for an example.

Identifying roles for members in the learning community is another aspect of the advance organizer. Two sets of roles function as organizers for community membership. The first set includes the roles of encourager, informer, organizer, and synthesizer, which all members must play responsibly at all times. The second set includes roles assigned to facilitate equity in power and status among students (E. Cohen, 1986) in the community. Being clear about how often small-group assigned roles will be changed and about how to handle absences is part of the teacher's advance planning. Being clear about how roles relate to the functions of schooling is necessary to avoid conflicts between daily living and long-term outcomes. See the roles form in Table 7-2 on page 219.

Identifying rules involves formulating clear statements, identifying intended and unintended outcomes, and identifying what will need to be taught so that the rules can be expected to contribute to the community. Once again, the connection between the rules and the functions of schooling needs to be made. Table 7-3 on page 220 illustrates how one teacher thought about her rules.

Finally, the identification of procedures occurs. Here the first step is to identify procedures that will be needed to help the community function properly and smoothly. Table 7-4 on page 220 contains examples of procedures for consideration. These examples are organized in three categories: general assessment, instruction, and communication with parents and community. We have found these categories helpful in managing a classroom learning community.

Finally, the procedures chart in Table 7-5 on page 221 is useful in analyzing procedures. The process includes identification of a procedure, steps in the procedure, intended and unintended outcomes, and connections to the functions of schooling.

VISION OF CLASSROOM LEARNING COMMUNITY

After you have specified the functions of schooling; the goals; the room environment; and the norms, roles, rules, and procedures, you can draft your vision of the learning community in operation. Start by thinking about an ideal learning-community day—a day when the community is in place and things are functioning as you believe they should on a regular basis.

The statements that you have already created will provide the basis for your vision description. Your draft can be in any one of several forms. For example, you might describe a day and how it moved along, you might present several vignettes or short stories illustrating typical learning-community occurrences, or you might write as if from a student's perspective. Whatever the form of your draft, its substance should communicate how the action in a learning community differs from that in a traditional classroom. Thus, selecting critical characteristics to use as illustrative occurrences of learning community contributes to the presentation of the distinctions.

Once you have drafted your vision statement, you can begin the final step of your advance organizer. Read through all your statements, starting with the functions of schooling. As you read, locate instances of congruity and incongruity between rules, procedures, functions, goals, and norms. Incongruity is most likely to be found between norms/functions/goals and rules/procedures, and is caused by tension between ideal outcomes and the past experiences of teachers and students.

Performance Outcomes and Activities (NJPTS 6)

Chapter 7
Making the Learning Community Vision Explicit

PERFORMANCE OUTCOMES

Teacher Candidates will

1. Using the information in this chapter, reanalyze the written learning community classroom case studies (Chapters 5 and 6) to determine which of the learning-community cultural elements, dispositions, roles, and functions of schooling the teachers planned to establish.
2. Compare and contrast written learning community classroom case studies to your Stage 1, 2, and 3 plans for establishing a learning community.
3. Use the ideas in Chapter 7, to increase the authenticity of previously written plans for establishing Stages 1, 2, and 3.

Exercise 7.1

Assess your written Stages 1, 2, and 3 plans for each of the following:

A. Functions of Schooling

Read through your plans for establishing a Classroom Learning Community and assess which of the functions of schooling are a clear part of your plans. Organize your data to show where in your plans you are introducing, reinforcing and practicing things that support the functions.

You may find that you introduce a function of schooling in one stage and practice it in another stage. Then create a chart such as the following chart to help you organize and communicate your findings. Turn in the chart to the instructor when you have made all final edits.

FUNCTIONS OF SCHOOLING

	Social Justice	Academic	Social	Personal
Stage 1	**Introduced in activity:** **Reinforced in activity:** **Practiced in activity:**	Introduced: Reinforced: Practiced:	Introduced: Reinforced: Practiced:	Introduced: Reinforced: Practiced:
Stage 2	Introduced: Reinforced: Practiced:	Introduced: Reinforced: Practiced:	Introduced: Reinforced: Practiced:	Introduced: Reinforced: Practiced:
Stage 3	Introduced: Reinforced: Practiced:	Introduced: Reinforced: Practiced:	Introduced: Reinforced: Practiced:	Introduced: Reinforced: Practiced:

If you find that there are holes in your plans, go back and edit your plan so that you have a plan that covers the systematic establishment of the functions of schooling in your class.

B. Identifying What You Expect Students to Learn about Each of the Functions of Schooling

Read through your written plans. Now write out in your own words what you think the students will learn about each Function of Schooling. If you have a hard time doing this because your plans do not make it clear, write out the goals you would like to have the students reach and then go back and edit your plans to assure that the students would achieve your goals. After you have updated your plans then do this task.

C. Identifying the Norms, Roles, Rules and Procedures You Will Establish

Read through your written plans. Now make a list of the norms, a list of the roles, a list of the rules, and a list of the procedures/routines that you planned to establish. Analyze each of the lists and determine if there were areas you have left out that would cause you to have problems when you begin teaching. For each of things you need to add go back and edit your plan so that you have covered those areas. (The additional references for reading will help you think this through.)

D. Identifying the Procedures for Identifying and Resolving Conflicts.

Read through your written plans. List the procedures you are planning to put in place to identify and resolve conflicts. Next, think about students that have problem behaviors, such as not doing what you ask them, not paying attention to you when you are providing instruction and explaining content, or interrupting you all the time. What have you planned to do to show the students how these situations will be handled? To further improve your plans, write out role plays you would use with students to show them how your conflict resolution procedures support you being the in-charge teacher.

Keep a copy of your written plans, as you will use them next semester.

REFERENCES AND RECOMMENDED READINGS

Stage I: Beginnings

Putnam, J., and Burke, B. (1992) Organizing and Managing Classroom Learning Communities. McGraw-Hill. Chapter 8, Stage I Beginnings. (See this chapter for concrete examples of activities and how to plan for the beginnings stage of your group development.)

Stage II: Establishing Expectations

Putnam, J., and Burke, B. (1992). Organizing and Managing Classroom Learning Communities. McGraw-Hill. Chapter 9, Stage II Establishing expectations. (See this chapter for concrete examples of activities and how to plan for establishing the expectations you have for your group's culture.)

Wolfgang, C., Solving discipline and classroom management problems, Methods and models for today's teachers. NJ John Wiley and Sons, Inc., Chapter 13, pages 233–246. (Note: This chapter provides a clear example of the multiple expectations and procedures teachers must think through.)

Stage III: Identifying and Resolving Conflicts

Putnam, J., and Burke, B. (1992). Organizing and managing classroom learning communities. McGraw-Hill. Chapter 10, Stage III Identifying and resolving conflicts. (See this chapter for concrete examples of procedures to use in identifying and solving conflicts.)

Wolfgang, C. (2001). Solving discipline and classroom management problems, Methods and models for today's teachers. NJ John Wiley and Sons, Inc. (This book reviews in depth the major discipline models.)

Stage I. Beginnings

The start of the new school year is an exciting time for both teachers and students. As the instructional leader and responsible adult, the teacher carries a major responsibility for planning and facilitating the group's interactions, and for moving through the stages for establishing the learning community.

During the first days of school, the time when the plan for stage I is implemented, the teacher's role consists of facilitating, monitoring, and processing. Facilitation leadership promotes orientation of students to each other and the classroom culture. The teacher also monitors students' reactions to learning activities, and their impact. Once the activities are finished, the teacher leads the group in discussion about: (1) the processes they engaged in, (2) the expected socialization outcomes, and (3) the expected subject-matter outcomes. Teachers should model for students the use of reflection to develop a better understanding. Reflective experiences help everyone to adjust future activity.

Once the learning-community advance organizer has been completed, it serves as the framework for planning, implementing, and reflecting for the rest of the year. The advance organizer is used to guide teacher planning and evaluation of the learning community. Planning involves the specification of learning, monitoring, and reflection strategies.

For a teacher the beginning of the school year signals that the time has come to begin anew the process of building one or more new learning communities. For some students, learning to be a member of a classroom learning-community culture will be a new experience. Likewise, for teachers who have not previously worked to systematically establish a classroom learning community, this process will be a new experience. In these classrooms, past experiences may even get in the way of the smooth creation of the new culture. Internalized norms for teacher and student behavior and practices that are incongruent with a learning-community culture act as roadblocks to the establishment of learning communities. While this is not a reason to abort efforts to create a learning community, the teacher should be aware of it, and should monitor and adjust practices as needed to ensure that they will support and contribute to the establishment of the learning community.

This chapter will describe ways to prepare for, implement, and reflect on the first of the three stages involved in establishing a classroom learning community. The first three stages are: stage I—beginnings; stage II—establishing expectations; and stage III—identifying and resolving conflicts. Stages II and III are described in Chapters 9 and 10, respectively.

PREPARATION

Having a clear plan based on the advance organizer facilitates the learning-community teacher's work and the group's progress. Here are some questions teachers need to ask themselves at this initial stage: "How will we begin the school year?" "How will we get acquainted?" "What sequence of activities will help to establish a learning community and my specified instructional goals?" "How will new students gain entry into the classroom group?" "How will major changes be handled?"

Planning for the First Days

Five guidelines are useful for designing activities for beginning the school year. These beginning activities are merely first steps in developing a classroom learning community. The guidelines are:

1. Design activities that inform students about life in the learning community.
2. Design activities that help teachers and students to learn each other's names, to become acquainted, and to begin to build trust.
3. Design activities to foster appreciation of other students' multiabilities.
4. Design activities that promote students' development of a voice in their schooling, gaining more and more confidence in asking clarifying questions and getting information, providing supportive/constructive feedback, giving help, encouraging others to participate, and seeing themselves as active participants in the learning community.
5. Design activities that assess what students know and can do.

Informing Students about Life in the Learning Community

Students without previous experience in classroom learning communities need to know what life in a learning community is like. Students who have been in other learning communities need to know the specific characteristics of this year's version. Explicit and specific examples will help. Teachers can describe things that occurred in previous community groups, exhibit pictures, display products, and in general provide information. Introducing all activities by making explicit connections between the activity and the expected outcomes is one means to start giving students a picture of "life in our learning community." After each activity, teacher and students can process their experiences and clarify their impressions of learning-community culture. Orienting activities followed by discussion provide a common experience that enables students and teacher to work together to build their group into a genuine community.

When learning-community teachers design activities, they make sure that they include students in a variety of roles for creating and maintaining the classroom physical environment. They include activities that describe ways for students to help each other learn. Teacher and students need to talk extensively about those elements of community life that are new experiences for them. They should think together about how they can learn to be more like a democratic community, rather than merely a collection of individuals.

Learning Everyone's Names, Getting Acquainted, and Initial Building of Trust

Relationships within a learning community are based on expectations that all students will know and respect each other. Traditional classrooms have been shown to be highly organized in established social cliques. Homogeneous groups tend to reinforce cliques. In a learning community, students work across ability levels. Thus, some beginning school activities are designed to sanction cross-group talk and respect for diversity. Low-risk activities that have clear and specific steps contribute to building communication and respect across established social groups.

Especially during the first week or two of the school year, activities should provide enough time for students from diverse social groups to complete assigned tasks satisfactorily and for students to gain some sense of personal accomplishment. Otherwise, activities could seem meaningless to students. Clear directions provide structure and support to students during initial interactions. Some students may feel tense because their interpersonal skills are at a low level; well-designed activities and clear directions ease such tensions.

Fostering Appreciation of Multiabilities

A classroom learning community calls upon a wide variety of talents. Individuals in a learning community come to appreciate both their own abilities and the multiabilities of others in the group. Teachers at the Averill School, for example, promote the idea that everyone knows something and is able to do something and that no one knows or is able to do everything. They encourage students to believe in their own capacity to contribute not only to their own individual learning but also to the good of the whole.

E. G. Cohen (1986) describes multiple activities that she recommends to help in creating multiability tasks. To foster the appreciation of diversity, Cohen suggests that teachers design multiability tasks that involve general answers or several ways to solve problems; that are challenging, interesting, and rewarding to the learners; that provide opportunities for different students to make different types of contributions; that incorporate the use of multimedia; that require learners to use a variety of skills and to call on a wide variety of knowledge; and that incorporate reading, writing, constructing, and designing skills. Activities of this sort contribute to equity in status and promote the purposes of schooling.

Establishing Each Student's Voice

To be a member of a learning community, students need to find and express their own voices. Students do not develop their own voices unless they are treated as real people. The classroom learning-community culture demands that students relate to each other as members who have equal status and who deserve respect. Thus, initial activities are needed to provide opportunities for students to gain more and more confidence in their ability to participate fully in the class by asking clarifying questions, synthesizing information, providing supportive and constructive feedback, giving information, and encouraging others to participate actively in the learning community.

One way to empower student voices is to arrange seating so that all students can see one another's faces, especially when they are speaking during get-acquainted activities. In rooms where there are too many students to use an oval or a discussion circle, the fishbowl strategy helps. In this strategy, a large outer circle is formed around a central circle made up of six chairs. Five students are selected (or volunteer) to participate. Each student presents personal information, or talks about a selected discussion topic. Participants share with each other, ask questions and generally clarify or paraphrase what other members of the group say. The sixth chair is available for other community members (including the teacher) to sit in when they wish to ask a question or paraphrase the comments of one of the five participants. After all five have given their short presentations, a new set of participants takes over, and so on, until all have had a turn.

Planning to empower student voices involves identifying and avoiding potential situations that may tempt students to act in traditional ways. Instead, the teacher should prepare students to behave in the alternative ways that are appropriate for a learning community (e.g., the students should look at a person who is speaking and should learn how to ask for help). Additionally, teachers need to prepare explanations about the importance of gaining one's voice within a learning community (e.g., that it is essential to their learning) and how students can acquire their voices (e.g., by questioning, supporting, and challenging).

When students use traditional classroom behavior during the early weeks of the school year, the teacher can promote development of their voices by stopping the action and discussing what is happening, why it should change, and how to change it. For example, if students continue to look only at the teacher while a peer is talking, the teacher should interrupt and remind them to turn and look at the speaker.

Assessing Students and Having Students Assess Themselves

Finally, learning-community teachers need to plan how they will get to know the students. Teachers should assess students' prior knowledge and skill, their prior experiences and interests, and their current joys and fears.

One strategy that works well is to have students talk and write about things to accomplish, things to change, and things they would like others to support them in doing. Such sharing provides a way for members to get more information about each other as well as a means for setting some group goals. Finding out about common needs enables development of a support system for students who think they are "the only one who . . ." and also provides a basis for mutual support between the teacher and the students.

One self-assessment activity that we often see used as a get-acquainted strategy has the potential for helping individuals to inventory and plan the new year. After a discussion about multiple abilities (e.g., everyone knows something and can do something, and no one knows or can do everything), students are given worksheets to focus their reflection. The worksheet in Table 8-1 was created to structure students' self-assessment. It encourages them to look at their current situation, to acknowledge what they want to do differently, and to identify the kinds of support they need.

Teachers with whom the authors work use the completed worksheets in different ways. One teacher uses them to get students to begin keeping a journal of their development. Each week this teacher and her students take time to reflect on what they have accomplished, what may be getting lost, and what they may need to ask others to provide as support. Another teacher uses the self-assessments as a means for determining what his students perceive as their primary strengths and weaknesses and what their ideas are about the purposes of schooling. After reviewing the students' assessments, he discusses the purposes of schooling as they relate to his course. He then asks students to expand what they have written by adding information about functions of schooling that they may have left out. Such activities help to develop shared understandings and expectations.

In addition to student self-assessment activities, other kinds of assessments related to the purposes of schooling and specific goals for the year or semester can also be used. Assessments related to understanding subject matter, once conducted, should be shared in personal conferences and in written feedback. Students should come to understand that assessments provide valuable information at the

TABLE 8-1   EXAMPLE OF SELF-ASSESSMENT TASK

Personal		Environment	
Already Working for Me	**Need to Develop**	**Already Supportive**	**Working Against Me**
I. Assessing the current situation I'm a good problem solver. I want to try. I write good short reports. II. What I want to do differently Finish my work. Get better grades. III. What I need to accomplish my goals Support from teacher. Better reading skills.	Ability to keep my attention on a task. Knowing what I read.	Teacher won't embarrass me. Friend will remind me (nag).	I don't want people to know. This subject is boring. Friends may laugh.

beginning of school. Once a baseline has been established, recording progress during the semester or year will give students and the teacher a way to judge progress. Teachers who already use formal pretests need to add the communication with students and some form of student recordkeeping to their current practice.

One indication that assessment and evaluation are not functioning in the spirit of learning community is students' confusion. When students cannot tell what they are learning, or why, or when they receive surprising grades for a given marking period, what is indicated may be a lack of teacher clarity about expectations, a breakdown in communication, inappropriate self-assessments, or inappropriate recordkeeping, or perhaps all four.

Using the guidelines suggested above will help assure the occurrence of activities designed to provide assessment while getting acquainted and learning about life in a learning-community classroom. After designing these activities, the next step is reviewing them to verify their congruence with learning-community norms (acting in personally and socially responsible ways, promoting equity, and emphasizing values for learning subject matter). Assessment activities are reviewed by analyzing the congruence of both the process and the content of each activity with learning-community norms.

For example, teachers will want to think about activities in terms of their potential first impressions. How teachers start the year—that is, the kinds of first impressions they make upon students—tends to frame the whole year. To make these first impressions congruent with learning-community concepts, teachers need to plan in detail how they will set the context for their students. Teachers can ask themselves the following questions about first impressions: "What will I say about classroom learning community?" "What values will I emphasize?" "What do I want students to think about during the first few days/hours of the school year?" "What attitudes will be elicited by these activities?" "How will students see me? Helpful? Friendly? Accessible?" "If parents ask students about what happened in school, how will they answer, based on these first activities?"

Planning for New Students

When new students enter the class after the school year has begun, they have questions like those the rest of the class asked at the beginning of the year. Thus, when new students join the class, teachers and students need to help the new student gain entry into the learning-community culture. Though teachers need not repeat the activities used at the beginning of the year, they should give special attention to the new student so that the whole class will develop shared understandings.

Two perspectives shape the activities designed to assist the entry of a new student into a class. The first is the new student's point of view as he or she seeks to gain entry into a group. Since few people have "gaining-entry skills," the classroom learning-community members must accept responsibility for helping the new student to gain entry into the group. The second perspective relates to the collective point of view of the community members: How can they enlarge their community and make a place for a new member? Once a group moves beyond the orientation stage, individuals undoubtedly will have suggestions for activities to help a new student go through his/her "beginnings" and eventually become a full member of the community.

Major Changes During the Year

"Beginnings"—at the start of the day, at the start of an activity, at the start of school after a holiday or an unplanned "day off" (because of snow, fog, or wind, for example)—need special attention from the teacher. Attention needs to be directed to explicit directions concerning what is expected. How is today's expectation connected to prior expectations? What is different about what is wanted? Students need information in order to be successful with each new beginning and also to eliminate or minimize the temptation to "guess" what the teacher is thinking about and wants. New beginnings are also situations in which traditional classroom behavior may reemerge. Attention to learning-community norms helps to minimize or prevent deterioration of the learning-community culture.

Many students value revisiting the social activities they enjoyed during the first weeks of the school year. They may feel that they learn more about each other at different times. Deepening of relationships comes about through structured activities provided by the classroom community and provides a comfortable way for students to practice their socialization skills and to develop more genuine relationships with their peers.

IMPLEMENTATION

A thorough plan for establishing a learning community guides teachers in getting started. Such a plan includes specified activities and schedules that increase the likelihood that learning-community attitudes and behaviors will develop systematically, early in the school year. A scheme for implementing the plan is presented in this section.

Even though teachers work hard for weeks ahead to prepare their plans and materials, the first day the students arrive is traditionally thought of as "the first day of school." As the first minutes tick by, excited teachers and students ask, "What is going to happen here?" The question is answered during the initial days of school. In the learning-community classroom, students may wonder, "Is this different?" if they have previously been members of classroom learning communities.

Now is the time to systematically implement the planned activities. New classroom learning-community teachers may feel pressure to abort their thoughtful plans and to revert to traditional teacher actions (e.g., to merely pass out textbooks and recite what the course outline says). Remember, however, that students' first impressions should include indicators of the culture to be established. Students who only listen to the teacher lecture about lists of things students should not do will not become informed about a learning community.

For individual students who participate in purposefully planned stage I activities, many questions are answered, including the following:

How will I be treated?

Who are these other people in the group?

Where do I fit in?

Will others like/accept me?

What does the teacher expect of me?

Where is *my* space?

Teacher-tested, successful stage I activities focus on the environment, on sharing names and personal information (getting acquainted), and on building trust. How teachers integrate this process affects schooling outcomes for students.

Physical Environment

Teachers can reduce the tension of "first impressions" by creating an inviting room environment that is subsequently altered through student participation in co-creating the learning environment. Selected activities lend themselves to the spirit of the co-construction of the community, using the guidelines noted earlier. We have observed on numerous occasions that classroom learning-community teachers prepare their rooms for the beginning of the school year differently than do their colleagues who are not learning-community-oriented. Learning-community teachers see the room environment as something that should be co-constructed. The effect is that they do limited amounts of decorating or putting up instructional bulletin boards before the students arrive on the scene. For example, Elizabeth Hermann creates large charts with definitions of the roles she will teach during stage II. Other than that, the materials in the room during the first week come from the activities in which the students participate as they get acquainted and progress through stages I and II.

Another teacher, before the first day of school, puts two name tags for each student on a bulletin board. As the students enter the room she snaps a Polaroid picture and thumbtacks it to the board above one name tag. She gives the other name tag to the student. When students introduce themselves later, she records information about them on 4 × 6 cards and tacks them next to the students' pictures. As students become better acquainted, they add their observations about their peers to the cards.

Lisa Saunders puts the hour and subject matter up as titles for bulletin boards (e.g., "Seventh-Hour History") and wall space before the first day of school. During the first days of school, she has the students place samples of their writing in the space representing this section. The writing products vary depending on the particular getting-acquainted activities used. For example, once she had students draw visual representations of their view of the "subject-matter area" and then describe it in prose. Another time, her students completed a subject-matter writing task.

In another teacher's classes, students create the boards and displays all year long. Therefore, at the beginning of the year the teacher creates interactive instructional bulletin boards, and students work with the boards to accomplish their beginning tasks. Her initial boards serve as models of the quality of boards that she expects students to create during the year. By communicating her expectations verbally, visually, and in writing, she easily gets across her message: that creating a quality visual representation helps learning. She effectively communicates to students that merely laminating a few pictures will not meet the standards of this particular classroom learning community's environment.

Primary Grades

Getting Acquainted

Primary-grade teachers have two major responsibilities. The first is to teach primary-grade children "how to go to school" (Brophy and Evertson, 1978) as well as basic skills (such as learning to read, and mathematical understandings and computation). Socialization for school includes learning each other's names, getting acquainted, and learning the norms for listening and responding to each other.

Activities traditionally used by teachers in primary grades to help students to learn each others' names (e.g., having students sit in a circle and toss around a bean bag, roll a ball, or pass along a rope while calling out one another's names) can be used as activities in this stage of group development. The teacher needs to make explicit connections between the activities and the knowledge, skills, and propensities necessary for community development (e.g., learning names, cooperating, listening and responding to each other). Linking these expectations as outcomes of the activities supports community building. For example, a teacher who is working to create a learning community will not say to his/her students, "Be quiet so others can talk." Instead, such a teacher will say, "Listen to what others say so that you can learn their names and what they like to do. This way, you will know them." Note the differences in the explicit reasons stated by the teacher. Once an activity has started, the teacher takes actions to facilitate the stated outcomes. For example, during the activity the teacher will ask children who are listening to repeat or paraphrase what prior speakers have said. The teacher will support listening by asking, "What have people said about X so far? Did anyone notice whether someone else has similar/different ideas?" or "Who said something that no one else mentioned?" Sharing times, when children tell about something they are proud to have done or like to do, can be structured so that listening children have a chance to respond with what they are learning. The teacher may ask, "What is it that Javier likes to do?" or "What is Arthur's last name?" To be consistent with the learning-community concept, teachers need to ***Promote The Idea That Listening Is What One Does In Order To Learn,*** rather than in order to be quiet.

Activities which incorporate the use of children's photographs and the knowledge they have accumulated about each other during the first days of school support the development of genuine relationships and academic outcomes. For example, one primary teacher takes pictures of each child during the first day of school. She shows the pictures to the children at the beginning of the second week, asking them to link names with the pictures. Later she has a group of students draw from an envelope a set of five of the pictures. The group then work together to write a story that incorporates what they have learned about the people in the five pictures (e.g., facts, feelings, likes, dislikes, what they are good at, where they live).

Some teachers transfer the procedure they use to help children learn people's names and getting acquainted in the classroom to learning about others in the building. This procedure explicitly addresses becoming acquainted with people in the multiple settings in which primary-grade children find themselves (e.g., the principal, community helpers, visiting parents, and children from other rooms who read to them or tutor them).

Developing Ownership of the School Environment

Activities that teachers do with primary-grade children (such as taking a tour of the classroom, taking a tour of the building, or walking through the lunch line) help the children to gain information about their environment. As the year progresses, experienced teachers find ways to send primary-grade children on errands so that they will become confident about their ability to find their way around and to relate to the larger school environment.

Kindergarten children in one teacher's room took turns in making photographs of the school building as they toured it. Later they arranged the photos on a board in the order of the tour. The teacher then recorded all the information that the children could recall about the specific places. The photos and the experience stories were placed on the walls as an illustrative outcome of a group project. When the teacher began to send students on errands, she pointed to the photos of where they were to go, thereby helping them to connect their destinations with prior experiences.

Middle Grades

Though middle-grade students have learned how to go to school (Brophy and Evertson, 1976), each year they find themselves in a new group of students. They may know some of the other members of the class, and their best friends may even be in the class, but this is not enough. A characteristic of the learning community is that all members get to know each other. Teachers in learning communities promote and facilitate both cross-social group relationship building and the entry of students who are new to the school.

Getting Acquainted

Loralee Sealey, a fourth-grade teacher, designed a plan for starting the school year that was consistent with her beliefs that early days of school should "establish expectations and procedures to maximize learning time." In her plan, Sealey makes a "deliberate attempt to build group skills systematically."

One of the initial products of her first-day activities is a class directory. Assessment of students' ability to apply "process writing skills" that they have learned in prior years is one of her interests, and getting acquainted is another. Students write information about themselves in the form of character descriptions, which they then share with a partner. The partners introduce each other to the class. Later the information from the descriptions is incorporated into the room directory. The directory also includes students' addresses and telephone numbers.

Another teacher, using a variation of this idea, includes photos of the students, birthdays and special celebrations, and names and telephone numbers of the students' parents/grandparents/friends. An idea for the cover of a class directory may be developed by the group, and a single member may be asked to do the actual drawing. We suggest avoiding competition for this privilege by using the process for selection as an opportunity for practice in group decision making. Another possibility would be to have each student design and create his/her own cover, creating a personalized directory.

Sealey also uses creation and sharing of personal collages as a getting-acquainted activity. Students receive directions for making a collage that reflects their personal likes, interests, strengths, and dreams. Sitting in groups, students look at the collages created by their group members, and identify similarities and differences. The group members then work together to write a paragraph about the collages created by their group. Later all the groups' collages are posted, along with the paragraphs reflecting the group's analysis of their pictures.

Creating a poster representing oneself or a classmate is another way for students to get acquainted and to talk with one another about things that interest them. The directions for this activity could include an interview, a draft, feedback from the subject of the poster, and final drawing. When it is time for posters to come down, they can be stored so that they can be looked at again at the end of the year.

Middle schoolers like to "bury" things. A time capsule is often a popular project. At the beginning of the year, students place objects that are important to them in a "capsule" and "bury" it. The capsule is "dug up" at the end of the school year for review. One junior high class placed artifacts in the shell of a car and buried it when they were sixth-graders; then they dug it up as eighth-graders. Again, the primary purposes of this activity are to enable students to talk about themselves and what is important to them, to be listened to by their peers and the teacher, and to make links to school subject matter.

Developing Ownership of the Environment

For the most part, middle graders know how to go to school. If they attended the school the previous year, they know where the materials are kept, where different teacher's rooms are, how to access information from the office, and how to get around. However, some students may not have figured out how to get the context to work for them. These students and the students who are new to a particular school will need information and "local strategies" for making the environment work for them. Therefore, teachers and experienced students can work out together, during stage I, a strategy for providing new students with information about their school and its inhabitants.

For example, two teachers may work together and with their experienced students to create "treasure hunts" for their classes. Of course the treasures are people, resources, and places in the school/community. Once each class has designed a treasure hunt, they swap. Teacher A and her students use teacher B's treasure hunt, and vice versa. The students work in pairs or small groups to find the treasures. Once the hunt starts, each morning's opening activities focus on sharing what the class has learned so far. The spirit of the hunt is to work to learn things so that they can be contributed to the whole group. Daily, class members write about their "findings" and post their records.

Physical arrangements within the classroom for middle students can be as varied as the furniture and space allow. For example, Sealey has her students sit in small groups with their desks facing each other all the time. She works on the premise that most of the time students will work in cooperative groups or will need to be able to ask peers for assistance on individual work. She wants the "regular" arrangement to be one that causes the least possible disruption to the available engaged learning time. For individual work (e.g., individual testing/evaluation), she manipulates the environment. She finds that there is less downtime with this plan. Sealey also believes that students learn to manage themselves in this environment from the beginning of the school year. She focuses on appropriate behavior as related to different classroom activities and the group seating plan. For example, since students may be more tempted to talk with peers when they are facing each other, Sealey tells her students when it is OK to confer and when it is not appropriate. Thus, during the first days of school, she reinforces the habit of listening either to her or to other students who are speaking to the class as a whole. She also purposefully observes the nature of the interactions in the various groups and provides explicit feedback. This approach may initially take more teacher monitoring, but for a teacher who holds similar beliefs, it is the most convenient approach in the long run.

High School

Getting Acquainted: English Courses

Virginia McKniff, during the first two days of school, uses letter writing both as a means to get acquainted with her students and as a means to help the students in her eleventh- and twelfth-grade International Baccalaureate English class to get acquainted with each other. Next she uses the development and writing of a character sketch as an orientation activity. To do this activity, the students, during the third day of class, read "First Confession" by Frank O'Connor, a short story in which a character is described in depth. McKniff and the class list on the board direct and indirect means of characterization that they find in the short story. For their homework, students write a list of ten questions, for use in an interview, that they think would give them the information necessary for writing a character sketch. On the fourth day of school, students present their questions in a round-robin fashion. All the questions are written on the board, and then they are discussed, modified, and weeded out until a list of fifteen to twenty questions remains. Students then select the questions that they will use in their interviews.

Criteria for evaluation of the sketches are discussed ahead of time and can include the physical and personal characteristics of the person, along with class members' perceptions of his/her character, a favorite speech pattern, a habit, and so on, plus the general criteria that are used for all written assignments. On the fifth day, students work in pairs to carry out the interviews. Each student is responsible for providing a character sketch on the following Monday. The sketches are then read aloud in class without names, and students explain why they think the character sketch is a particular person.

Developing Ownership of the Environment

Several high school teachers with whom the authors have worked initially questioned whether secondary students would develop a sense of shared ownership of the classroom environment. These teachers found, however, that their students, given the opportunity, were eager to share responsibility for the environment.

Two different schools of thought about the classroom environment were represented in this group of teachers. One group treated the classroom as a temporary space for activity. These teachers took out the materials themselves, returned them to the storage areas, and were careful not to let the rooms get cluttered. Bulletin boards for the most part either remained empty or contained permanent displays (e.g., announcements from the principal's office, a copy of the Constitution, or a newspaper article related to the discipline area). The other group used bulletin boards for displays related to each topic they taught. Students rarely looked at the materials, but the teachers nevertheless believed that they had done "their part."

A teacher candidate studied the problem of getting her high school students to develop shared responsibility for the class environment. She began by asking class members to record what they believed was being studied in other classes. Next she provided a class period during which students could create a bulletin board or display representing a concept they were studying. She subdivided the class into small groups and listed each group's contribution to the display. Every two weeks, one subgroup from two of her six classes was assigned the task of creating a new display; again, names accompanied the products. She found that students first began to talk to each other about the displays for their own classes and later began to notice the displays from other classes. At the end of the first marking period, students were able to say what concepts had been presented in their classes' displays and in other classes' displays. Using a consensus model at the end of the first marking period, each class created a list of "display guidelines" to provide a quality standard.

Other teachers who engage high school students in shared environmental responsibility operate on the same heuristic as the teacher candidate: (1) Treat the assignment as serious and worthwhile. (2) Provide class time for starting new activities that create new norms for activity. (3) Bring the display content into class discussions. (4) Give credit to group participants.

Cross-Grade Activities

Helping New Members to Gain Entry to the Community

One stage I activity that we have seen used from first grade through high school can be adapted to meet the needs of any group of students and any teacher. The product of this activity is a slide-tape or video presentation. The authors know teachers who have used this as their primary organizer for moving through the beginnings and establishing expectations stages. Each teacher and her/his students write a presentation that will inform students who enter their class at a later time about the school, the students, the teachers, and the class expectations. Writing the script requires developing a shared understanding of the ideas (e.g., who is in the class, and what the rules are) to be included. The students plan the sequence of pictures and write the script for the product. Depending on the grade level and prior experiences of the students, they receive more or less help in the technical development of the final product. The teachers who have used this strategy employ it as a means to create readiness to understand the teacher's expectations for the classroom and a means to tell others what has been learned during the first few weeks of school. Once the product is finished, the teachers and students create a process for selecting members of the classroom to show the film and tell new students "inside information" so that they can become successful members of the classroom/school community. A video can serve the same purposes.

Another aid for students entering mid-year was the use of a video made by the previous year's students at the end of the year. In this instance, the creation of the video was a stage 5 endeavor. The video presented the norms, expectations, and experiences that the particular group of students thought captured the essence of their learning-community year together. Students provided their addresses, and each agreed to write to a member of the next year's class. After viewing the video, the next year's teacher and students sent letters asking questions, and they also invited some of the previous year's students to come and talk to them about what else they could expect.

Making the Purposes of Schooling Explicit

Illustrating for students the importance of the different purposes of schooling associated with a classroom learning community is an ongoing process. At the beginning of the year, providing information about social justice behavior outcomes or about what constitutes personal or social responsibility is as difficult as communicating about academic outcomes. That is, students who have been socialized in traditional classrooms think about completing tasks and learning in traditional ways. Because the learning community focuses on learning for understanding and teaching for conceptual change, the teacher needs to introduce and, as time goes on, to repeatedly point out these differences. This will help students to see that their current perceptions of schooling and learning may be different from the conception espoused in the learning community.

Helping Students to Benefit from Starting a New School Year

As mentioned in Chapter 4, starting a new year can be difficult and exciting for individuals. Teachers and college professors who have been teaching for a long time talk about how they still get the "beginning-school" thrill each year and/or each semester, as they begin new classes or long-term workshops. For students who need a second chance, the beginning of a new school year is a time when teachers can deliberately make a difference and a lasting impression. A fresh start can diminish or even break the stereotype that teachers treat younger brothers and sisters according to the reputation of the family and older siblings. Consciously providing opportunities for students to discuss their perceptions of how they are treated and identifying the similarities and differences among students (those who are oldest, youngest, single children) is one means of confronting this problem. After students describe their experiences, follow-up questions can provide a new direction for teachers and students.

Included in the discussion are questions such as: "How might this year be different from last year?" and "What is a unique feature?" Providing opportunities for individuals to communicate values helps in finding something unique in each individual and gives another means of trying explicitly to initiate support for individuals.

Teaching the Value of Working Together

One old tradition that students seem to learn in school is that working together is "cheating." Since this perspective is the standard students bring to learning-community classrooms, they lack the knowledge and skills to participate in the group effectively. Remember that one classroom learning-community norm is cooperation and interdependence; that is, students should work together. This norm provides support for the individual who is trying to learn something but is having difficulty; the class has a responsibility for helping the individual to learn, and he/she can get help when needed. Classroom learning-community norms also support the idea that helping others to learn is responsible rather than irresponsible behavior. Again, the literature makes it clear that working together supports development of the habit of "collaboration." When people work together, the product is better than what results when people work in isolation. Confronting the problems involved in developing individual responsibility in group work and in changing students' preconceived ideas about working with others provide the basis for teaching the value of working together.

The activities in this area occur in two phases. First, students need an opportunity to participate in a consensus decision-making activity. Activities such as "Stranded on the Moon" and "Lost in the Mountains" work well in presenting the idea that working together enables everyone to learn more. Use of the class subject matter in creating an activity is very useful and may help the students to connect the activity with subject-matter outcomes. Once the activity is completed, the second phase involves processing what students observed and problems they encountered. Processing includes identifying problems that may occur in other activities (e.g., when students do not bring to class materials that they are responsible for and that are needed for task completion) and exploring what students would say to each other and how they would handle the problems.

Using Celebrations as Benchmarks for Progress

One classroom teacher had a difficult time learning 180 student names in a short amount of time. She set three goals for the "beginnings" stage. Each goal was related to a different time period. First, within a week she needed to be able to name all 180 students when they were in their seats in the classrooms. Second, she needed to be able to recognize the students when they were in the classroom but in different places. Third, she needed to be able to recognize the students and their names when she saw them around the building and in after-school activities. She made these goals public and enlisted the students' help. The first class celebration was to take place when she had achieved all three goals and when all the students in each of her classes also knew the names of everyone else in their section. She worked publicly on her goals. When she would see students at lunch and not know their names, she would tell them, and then she would say, "You have to help me or we'll never make it to the first celebration." She and the students always planned a first celebration that was worthwhile and would set the tone for other celebrations during the year.

Another teacher works with her students during the first part of the year to identify "things we will celebrate." The list is updated periodically. As students become more comfortable in the culture, they begin to suggest celebrating personal successes.

REFLECTING

As the initial days of school pass, the teacher asks herself/himself, "What is the impact of the initial activities and interactions on the members of the community?" In stage I, teachers guide their students to begin to ask such questions as, "What can I do?" "What do I know?" "What needs to be changed?" "Who is in this group?" "How will I be treated?" and "What is expected?" They also foster the ability of their students to ask planning questions such as, "What can I do better?" and "What can I learn?" These questions provide the basis for teacher monitoring of student progress toward the establishment of the learning community.

Thus, in this stage, ongoing monitoring and reflection is based on questions about short-term getting-acquainted outcomes and about setting the context for long-range goals. Daily, learning-community teachers ask themselves, "What does all this have to do with and contribute to the identified long-term outcomes?" and "Are we making progress toward a learning-community culture?"

One sign of progress is that students begin to predict the appropriate expectations of them and responses from others. We recommend that teachers use daily notes as the basis for a record of their observations and ideas about how things are getting started. Reviewing these notes later will help them to capture the essence of a particular class experience, rather than relying only on their own memory and experience. Both Carole Shank and Jane Boyd use journals to capture their observations. They report that the journals provide them with data about patterns of behavior changes in climate and with ideas for teacher/pupil or teacher/parent conferences. Shank writes her journal notes at the end of each day before she leaves school. Boyd prefers to do hers at home at night. Kathy Beasley and Judy Thompson talk together after school about their observations and inferences concerning individual students. One teacher shares her observations about the student's place and voice in the community, and the other asks questions. She reports her own observations, and she both supports and challenges the other teacher's ideas. Each teacher then decides whether any particular action needs to be taken in order to better integrate particular students into her own class culture.

We find that the heuristic presented in Chapter 4 (see related items listed below), provides a useful learning-community framework for assessing the effects of the activities during the first days of school and their probable contributions or impact. As the planned activities occur, the teacher looks for evidence that members of the community are finding answers to the following questions:

1. Who are the members of the classroom community?

2. What are the goals for the community and individuals?

3. What is expected of each member of the community?

4. What can we accomplish this year?

5. How will this year be different from prior years for students?

6. What are the teacher's and students' first impressions? Are they congruent with the learning community ideas?

7. What will it mean to be responsible learners in this culture?

8. What are the differences between observations and inferences about classroom culture, learners, teachers, and curriculum?

9. What can we learn about ourselves and others?

10. What will we be able to demonstrate as our accomplishments this year?

11. Do we have anything to celebrate? Are we celebrating?

Performance Outcomes and Activities (NJPTS 2, 4, 6)

Chapter 8
Stage 1. Beginnings

PERFORMANCE OUTCOMES

Teacher Candidates will:

1. Gain the knowledge and skills for professionally preparing for, carrying out, and reporting data from classroom observations that furthers their knowledge about teachers and teaching and learners and learning and schools and schooling.
2. Gain the knowledge and skills to identify Stage 1. Beginnings teacher and student behavior.
3. Gain the knowledge and skills to create an effective plan that when implemented will likely move students through Stage 1. Beginnings with activities that are congruent with the functions of schooling for learning communities.
4. Refine interview skills, data analysis and use of data.
5. Continue practice in carrying out child studies.

Exercise 8.1
Observing to Assess Establishment of Stage I Outcomes

A. Preparation for and Classroom Observations

The first activities in chapters 8–12 are classroom observation tasks. The four steps that you will use for these activities are: (1) preparing for the classroom observation; (2) carrying out the observation; (3) interviewing the teachers; and (4) analyzing and making sense of the observation and interview data.

You will be observing in schools where there are few learning communities established. However, some teachers, use Stage 1. Beginnings activities as a way to start the school year or semester. Begin your preparation for the observation by listing actions you might see if the students had progress through or were part way through Stage 1 group development. One of the questions you are answering in this activity is: What is the nature of the relationships among students in the situations listed below?

Make arrangements with the teacher for you to do 3 twenty minute observations. Arrange a time that you will meet and interview the teacher. Use the following observation form to collect your classroom observation data. After the observations complete column three.

A. CLASSROOM OBSERVATION FORM TO ASSESS ESTABLISHMENT OF STAGE I OUTCOMES

Focus of Observation	Observation Notes (What did you see and hear?)	Summary/Inferences & questions you will ask the teacher when you interview him/her
How many names of other members in the class does each student know?		
What is the nature of diversity valued in others by group members?		
What is the nature of trust that exists or is being built between students and between teacher and students?		

B. Take the questions you identified in Column three and list them in a format that will support your note taking.

C. Interview the teacher.

D. Identify the Nature of Relationships Among the Students and Between Students and Teacher(s) by analyzing and summarizing your observation and interview data.

E. Write up your report using the data to support your assertions.

Exercise 8.2
Designing and Implementing a Stage I Activity

Over time in the fall semester and since the beginning of this semester you have had opportunities to organize a plan for establishing a classroom learning community. The original work that you did in planning was to help you establish a process for linking concrete teaching behavior with the learning community ideas by thinking about long-range plans. The purposes of *this* activity and the first activity for chapters 9–12 are for you to

(1) expand your previous plans of one of the *Stage 1. Beginnings* activities for a group of 18 students (or a whole class),
(2) teach the activity,
(3) evaluate student outcomes, and
(4) reflect on your teaching, outcomes, and specify what you think should be taught next in order to move this stage of group development forward.

Remember that *in reality, the highest quality group development activities (for all stages of group development) have links to school subject matter whenever possible.*

A. Create a Detailed Plan for One Stage 1. Beginnings Activity

1. Explain in writing what subject matter you expect to teach in this lesson.
2. Write subject matter performance outcomes for (choose one content area) math, reading, music, art, physical education.
3. Write performance outcomes for Stage 1 outcomes.
4. Write a detailed description in chronological order of the activity you will teach. Be sure to indicate both what you and the students will be saying/doing.
5. List the materials that you will need for this lesson.
6. Write out what you will say to introduce this lesson. Be sure to include communication of purposes and subject matter and community building outcomes.
7. At the end of the lesson you will process the experience with the students. Write out what you will say, questions you will ask, how you will summarize information at the end of the lesson with/for the students.

B. Teach the Lesson to a group of at least 18 P–12 students or a classroom of students.

C. Reflection on the Instruction of Your Planned Lesson

Answer the following questions as a guideline for a written reflection.
1. What did you observe while you were teaching? (list)
2. While you were teaching, what were you thinking? *Do not describe what you did or said,* list the things you thought (the things that went through your mind).
3. List the decisions you made while you were teaching. Indicate which of the decisions you had not planned to do and explain why you made this decision.
4. For each of the outcomes you listed in your plan, list who accomplished that outcome. Describe the data you have for each student that met an outcome that indicates he or she achieved the outcomes. What data did you have that shows that the student did not know or was not able to do the behavior in your performance outcomes?
5. What did you observe about student learning that you believe was unusual or different?

D. Recommendations

1. What do you recommend as a follow-up and expanding activity?
2. Why do you believe that this is the best thing to do next?
   a) During informal periods in the classroom
   b) During small-group work
   c) During class discussions
   d) During independent work
       Who asks? Who helps? And who talks to whom about what?

To do this activity construct a diagram of the room. Then Tally interactions of teachers and students and students to students. You will need to collect data in the same class 3 times for at least 20 minutes each time.

3. After you summarize your data, what inferences would you make about relationships in this classroom? Use data to explain your inferences.

E. Based on your analysis of the limited data you collected in this activity, what would you recommend doing to further support the group's progress in Stage 1? It may help you to think about what you would do if you were called in as a long-term substitute in this class and knew you would be there the rest of the year.

STAGE ONE: BEGINNINGS

Characteristics of a Classroom Learning Community	Describe the activities you would use to introduce and reinforce the ideas embedded in the listed characteristics of a Learning Community	List the comments and questions you would use after each activity that will give the learners practice in assessing their knowledge and performances, in listening to feedback, and in establishing their ability to reflect.
1. All members get to know each others' names and important things about each other		
2. All members develop ownership of the classroom environment and school environment		
3. All members know they have personal strengths and areas for growth		
4. All members know they have to listen to the teacher and each other to learn		
5. All members begin to learn to work together and value working together		
6. All members begin to learn how to help each other when needed (do not give answers)		
7. All members know how to respond to each other showing cooperation and support		
8. All members begin to develop personal responsibility for helping to achieve classroom goals and tasks		
9. All members begin to develop their understanding of the purposes of schooling in a Learning Community Classroom (academic, personal responsibility, Social Responsibility, and Social Justice)		
10. During the school year new members have opportunities to become members of the group		

RECOMMENDED READINGS

Deiro, J. (1996). *Teaching with heart: Making healthy connections with students.* Corwin Press, Inc. Thousand Oaks, California.

Deiro, J. (2003). *Do your students know you care? Caring is not just a way of acting; it's a way of thinking.* Educational Leadership, Creating Caring Schools. Volume 60, Number 6, March, pp. 60–63.

TLC 2 CHILD STUDY

Now is the time to begin your second Child Study. This semester the focus of your study is on a child and his/her connections to the subject matter of the major you are taking in college (e.g., history, mathematics, art, music, social studies, physical education, etc.,) and reading/writing. Begin immediately by identifying potential students for your action research study. Take into consideration recommendations of cooperating teachers as your work can contribute to their support of the student.

Child Study: Guidelines

The purpose of this child study is to provide you the opportunity to practice focusing on individuals for the purposes of individualizing support and instruction, whether in whole, small groups or one-on-one. Since effective planning is based on the academic and other needs of individual students, it is important to develop the knowledge and skills for assessing individual learners and creating plans of action that increase their success and achievement. (INTASC STANDARDS 2, 3, 5, 7, 8, 9)

Phase I: Second Semester Child Study Action Research Project, Process and Reports

A. Planning and Implementation

1. Identify the 3 students with whom you will work with over the semester or year.

2. For each of the students list all of the information you know about them at this time.

3. Look over your notes on the 3 students and select one about which you are most curious. Describe what you observed that you find interesting. Explain what inferences you are making based on the limited data you have to date.

4. Describe what makes you curious about this child. What is it that makes you think that it is important to choose this student as the first about whom you will learn more?

5. What will you do to learn more about the learner you selected?

   a. Data Gathering:

   • What do you say in order to get support from family and student for you to expand your knowledge about this student? Write it out.

   • Who would you talk to (family, student, previous teacher, principal, social worker, speech therapist, Title I teacher, special education teachers, principal, others)? Make a list. Are there voices missing?

   • What will you ask? Write interview questions for each role group.

   • How will you record information from interviews?

- What system will you use to record observations you make during the regular day to day school times?

- Begin a collection of artifacts created by your learner.

b. Data Analysis

After organizing your data—

How did you organize your data? (What organizers did you use?)

What patterns emerged?

What hypothesis do you now have?

What new questions, concerns, ideas, or issues emerged after you learned more about the learner?

c. Forming generalizations—

After analyzing your data what do you think is the primary purpose in further study and support of this student?

6. Based on what you learned about this student to this point during the semester what do you recommend as an action that would result in support for the learner and increased achievement? (Create an Action Plan)

a. Write a summary of the items above and then write a plan of action that you would recommend for this student.

b. What strategies do you intend to implement? Describe the activities including who from the neighborhood, community and family are involved. Include a calendar of events.

c. What do you predict will be the impact/result/outcomes if you effectively implement your strategies?

d. What recording system will you use to systematically collect data that will be useable at a later time?

e. How will you evaluate the activities, your plan and the outcomes?

f. What documents will you collect?

C. End of Fall Semester Reports Includes:

1. Formal Report to Instructor of Action Research Project

a. Section I: Introduction including background information and reasons you selected this student to expand your knowledge about;

b. Section II: Original and later questions and hypotheses; Describe what data you used to change your questions;

c. Section III: Describe data you wanted to collect;

d. Section IV: Describe the process you used for data collection and any problems you found and how you solved them;

e. Section V: Describe how you analyzed your data, what organizers you selected or created, and what you learned;

f. Section VI: Describe how you carried out your action plan and student responses; Summary of Plan as Implemented;

g. Section VII: Described data you collected during implementation of action plan; Describe how you analyzed your data and your findings;

h. Section VIII: Based on your findings (data) make clear conclusive statements;

i. Section IX: Based on data make recommendations for next steps that would support this student's progress.

2. **Part Two Report to Instructor:**

This part of Your Report to the Instructor is _Written_ as a letter of information with the Principal as the audience. This part of your report should not be shared with anyone prior to it being signed by your instructor.

A. Letter to Principal Introduction

1. Where did you start—with what you wanted to learn and do and wanted the student to learn and do?

2. Where did you end?

3. How did your thinking change?

4. In what areas were you trying to help the child develop and grow?

5. What was it that made you think that your plan would contribute to the child?

6. What seemed to help? What did not appear to help? How do you think the child has benefited from your support?

7. What is your assessment of the learner's academic progress?

8. When you review your collection of artifacts including those from the student's work what patterns emerge? What insights did you gain from this review?

9. What recommendations do you have for supporting this learner in the future?

B. Letter to Student and Family (Not to be shared with anyone.)

1. Write letter in language and sentence structure readable by family.

2. Do not include professional jargon.

3. Focus letter on learner and not on your actions.

4. Describe progress you observed student make during the semester.

5. Include suggestions of things that parent and child could do that would support the student's continued progress. Suggestions must be appropriate for the home structure of the student.

3. **Attachments**

In a folder include your papers, data, notes, initial reports, initial action plan, revised plan, notes to or from those with whom you worked and documentation of what you and student did and accomplished. This is merely an organized collection of materials relevant to this work.

CHILD STUDY (POTENTIAL 36 POINTS) RUBRIC

Final Reports	
I. Report to Instructor	
A. <u>Clarity of Thinking and Writing</u>	
5 = the reports are free of jargon and surface language errors; they are consistent in tone and voice with documents prepared for professional peers and a critical public; the format, guiding questions, evidence, conclusions, and recommendations are obviously clear and reasonable; and a coherent case is made in *both* studies with assertions and claims *consistently* supported by *strong* evidence and reasoning.	
3–4 = the reports are free of jargon and surface language errors; they are *generally* consistent in tone and voice with documents prepared for a peer professional audience and critical public; the format, guiding questions, data, conclusions, and recommendations are *generally* clear and accurate (either implicitly or explicitly); an apparent case is made for the learning that took place through the studies and the recommendations flowing from them—most assertions and claims are supported by evidence.	
2 = the reports have a majority of the following attributes: there are some surface language errors and awkwardness in the handling of tone and voice; the style is occasionally too informal for a document prepared for a peer professional audience; the case and arguments made for one or both of the studies is sometimes hard to follow, and has to be inferred (i.e., it is not explicit); the evidence and reasoning are loosely tied to assertions and claims.	
1 = the reports contain a combination of the following: a number of surface language errors and lack of consistency in tone and voice; inappropriate informality in style; the lack of a clear position, case, or strategy to develop one; and the lack of explicit or implicit connections between claims and evidence.	
B. <u>Sound data collection procedures</u>	
3 = multiple sources are used, all of which are pertinent to the questions and hypotheses under study; the modes of inquiry are clear and could be replicated and/or checked out by other professionals;	
2.5 = multiple sources are used, and most seem pertinent to the questions and hypotheses under study; the modes of inquiry are generally clear, although some questions remain—not all could be replicated or reviewed for reliability;	
2 = several sources are used that seem relatively pertinent to the questions and hypotheses under study; the modes of inquiry are generally clear, although not all could be replicated or reviewed for reliability;	
0–1 = the sources of data are limited, and not necessarily reliable; they would be difficult to replicate or substantiate; they are not clear, and obviously open to contention and/or question.	

C. Originality and Depth of Analysis and Thought	
5 = selective and appropriate use of summary to establish the conceptual framework and foundation for in-depth analysis of the guiding questions, ideas and approaches; clear and logical connections between ideas and evidence are cited; a clear identification of the questions raised and/or problems cited; expected outcomes from the inquiry seem reasonable and needed, or suggest clear implications and show how a youngster's life experience and learning opportunities might change because of them; a youngster's future teachers and parents would clearly value and likely use this report.	
3–4 = somewhat selective and generally appropriate use of summary as a foundation for analysis; generally sufficient data is used to substantiate claims; the analysis is generally reasonable and fairly well connected to some real, identified possibilities; some intended outcomes or implications are addressed as are some of the related requirements for future actions—a youngster's future teachers and parents would learn something new from this report, and would value it.	
2 = predominantly an impressionistic summary with character generalizations; the behavioral evidence is weak, lacking either sufficient or trustworthy data; the analysis seems scattered and without guiding theory; intended outcomes or implications are vague or must be largely inferred; little consideration of the needed experience and/or support needed for the youngster and how its success might be further monitored.	
1 = primarily a list of character qualities with a set of data collected that is not well summarized or integrated; little or no evidence of analysis or of building a case or argument for selected needs; the intended outcomes or implications are not evident, nor are there strategies that are logically grounded in and connected to the information and ideas; little or no reliable evidence is presented.	
Intervention Plan and Carrying out of Intervention	
4–3.5 = Intervention includes goals that are tied to data about learner, calendar of events, plan for documentation and evaluation, is clearly tied to findings, uses neighborhood and community resources, events are creative and illustrate non-traditional ways of working on area of the problem or concern. (second semester includes summary of documentation and evaluation of the intervention and progress toward goals for learner)	
3–2 = Intervention includes goals that are tied to data about learner, calendar of events, plan for documentation and evaluation, is clearly tied to findings, uses neighborhood and community resources. (Evaluation data included in second semester paper)	
1 = Intervention includes description of events to take place, may or may not include use of community and neighborhood resources.	
0 = No intervention included	

D. <u>Grounding in Professional Expertise and/or the Research Literature</u>	
3 = draws appropriately from a wide variety of resources; demonstrates knowledge of key resources, significant scholarly work and/or research pertinent to the questions/problems under study; connects data, professional expertise, and/or research within the framework of the study.	
2.5 = draws from a variety of sources; demonstrates general knowledge of some important resources, works and research related to the substantive areas of study; makes at least some connections among the data, professional opinion, and/or research and theory in the area.	
2 = draws from a limited range of resources; demonstrates limited knowledge of major works and research/theory for the areas under study; makes few connections among the sources of data, external expertise, research and the individuals studied.	
1 = draws primarily from one or two sources; demonstrates very limited knowledge of major works and research/theory for the particulars under study; makes few if any connections among the data, sources of expertise, research reports and individuals cited.	
0 = No literature review.	
II. Initial Letter and Final Letter written to student and member of the family (10 Points)	
A. <u>Clarity of Thinking and Writing (3 points)</u>	
7. Letter is written using language understood by family.	
8. No jargon is used.	
9. Letter includes examples of the support being elicited (e.g., talk with you) or received from the family.	
10. Letter does not contain anything that might be offensive to learner or family.	
11. Observational data is included.	
12. Generalizations are not included.	
B. <u>Message is positive and supportive of the learner. (4 points)</u>	
1. Specific examples of learner's progress after you worked with learner during the year or at the beginning of the year (since you met learner at beginning of the year) are included.	
2. Specific examples of learner's strengths are included. Strengths you observed since you met learner or strengths further developed during the year.	
3. Specific examples of something you want to work on with learner (or you suggest next year's teacher begins to work on with the student).	

C. <u>Recommendations for further support of learner</u> (3 points)	
1. Recommendations fit with the analysis and findings reported to principal.	
2. Recommendations are doable.	
III. Initial Letter and Final Letter Written to Principal/Teacher (6 Points)	
A. Clarity of Thinking and Writing (4 pts)	
1. Introduction includes summary of process and project. (2 pts)	
2. Describes what was learned from data. (1 pt)	
3. Describes recommendations for further support of the student. (2 pts)	
B. Message is positive and supportive of the learner. (1 pt)	

Stage II. Establishing Expectations

The second stage of creating a classroom learning community involves establishing expectations. As indicated in Chapter 4, Stage II is the stage in which the teacher and students make explicit, practice, and establish the specific norms, roles, rules and procedures that will form the foundation of the functioning classroom learning community culture.

This chapter provides suggestions for planning activities for establishing expectations, implementing the plan, and reflecting on its impact. Monitoring and reflecting strategies are also suggested. The implementing section includes examples of activities that learning-community teachers find useful in teaching norms, roles, rules, and procedures. The reflecting section includes strategies for use in monitoring and adjusting the impact of activities and for determining progress in the establishment of the community.

PREPARATION

Learning-community teachers use the advance organizer as the basis for their plans in stage II. Since norms, roles, rules, and procedures have already been defined in the advance organizer, the primary task of the learning-community teacher in stage II is to plan how to introduce them to students, by providing: (1) descriptions of the norms, roles, rules, and procedures; (2) reasons for their existence; (3) illustrations of what they look like in the learning community; (4) practice opportunities; (5) feedback to individuals and the group; and (6) consequences for the individual and the community when they are not used.

One way to do the necessary planning is to outline explanations for the proposed existence of the learning-community norms, roles, rules, and procedures. In effect, teachers need to figure out ways to communicate to students their thinking about each norm, role, rule, and procedure in the advance organizer. The content of such an outline would be explanations of what every statement in the advance organizer means (e.g., how a norm called "cooperation" is manifested in the classroom).

To identify reasons for the existence of each item in this part of the advance organizer (e.g., why cooperation is important to the learning community), it would be helpful to list below each explanation its contribution to life in the learning-community culture. This step also helps to clarify any final incongruities that may exist among the norms, roles, rules, and procedures. For example, teachers can do a final check on congruence between expectations embedded in the norms (e.g., cooperation and interdependence), the rules (e.g., "Treat each other with respect"), the roles (e.g., encourager and linker) and the procedures (e.g., student participation in maintenance of the classroom community). Learning-community teachers also eliminate any rules that do not support student responsibility and accountability (e.g., "Do not talk unless you are given permission by the teacher"). Teaching rules that are incongruent with learning accountability and responsibility communicates a mixed message to students and works to defeat the teacher's intention of creating a learning community. Likewise, procedures that interfere with a cooperative culture could defeat the idea of shared responsibility and thus must be eliminated.

The learning-community teacher also gives illustrations or examples of what the statements in the outline translate into when they become actions in the learning-community classroom. These illustrations, which can be expansions of the steps or actions listed on the worksheets in the development of the advanced organizer, provide students with concrete examples of abstract ideas.

Initial practice opportunities can range from having one or two students walking through an example to staging elaborate role-plays that include all students in the class, depending upon the grade level and past experiences of students. We recommend that roles and procedures be taught in conjunction with subject-matter activities that occur normally in the classroom. For example, the teaching of students to act as encouragers should occur in small-group discussions about content that is being taught in the course, so that the students will have an opportunity to link their actions with learning outcomes. Eventually, practice opportunities need to be provided for all students. Connected to the practice opportunities is a plan for feedback.

The next consideration is planning specific statements to use in giving students feedback about the appropriateness of their actions as they initially try to act in congruence with expected norms, roles, rules, and procedures. Positive and negative feedback helps students to understand which of their actions are actually appropriate and which are inappropriate. For teachers who tend to provide general feedback (e.g., "That is good" and "I like how you are sitting still"), written statements can help them to provide students with the specific feedback they need. For example, "When you asked Milly the question about her ideas, you were acting as an encourager," and "This week we provided time to help each other to understand the lessons each day, and for the first time everyone answered all the questions on the quiz correctly." Because changing a communication pattern is difficult, preplanned statements to be used as written or adapted can be helpful.

Finally, learning-community teachers also plan how they will communicate accountability. Students should be held accountable for consistent performance, once the teacher knows that the students understand the learning-community expectations. As shown in Chapter 5, Forero provided support while students were acquiring the expected behavior. Her consequences were related to their intended outcomes. For example, when students left work at home, Forero required them to have someone bring it in, because the work was connected to the day's instruction and its absence meant that the student could not participate fully. The norm that everyone was to learn was connected to the rule that students must bring their materials to class.

The reason for such specificity is that effective instruction of norms, rules, procedures, and roles includes providing clear explanations, demonstrations, activities for practice, and feedback. That is, direct instruction aids the establishment of expectations.

Planning also includes figuring out a sequence in which the activities will be taught. Certain activities may require a logical or special sequence. Sequencing decisions are based on the effects of predicted or past experience. The desired overall effect is part of the community culture. For this effect to happen, students will need to know the connections among norms, roles, rules, and procedures, as well as their connections to the purposes of schooling.

Without a specific plan, a teacher might teach rules but not relate them to norms. Students would thus perceive rules as isolated "do" or "do not do" behaviors, and would not connect them to "the ways we will live together in this learning-community classroom culture." Procedures present a special case, in that some are needed from the first day students arrive, others not until later. Introducing procedures that support community life as needed seems to be a way to connect procedures and the overall culture without creating confusion.

IMPLEMENTATION

The learning-community teacher's primary roles in establishing expectations are to communicate clear and explicit instructions and to monitor and assess the impact of the activities.

Two questions which the authors use as a basis for assessing the impact of the implementation of plans to establish expectations are: "Who is doing what?" and "What do students understand?" Answers to these questions can be found through discussions about: (1) what students see as the similarities and differences between the learning community and their past experiences of school, (2) what they believe the teacher is trying to do, and (3) what they believe the teacher is trying to get them to do. Conversations, as well as direct observations of student talk and actions, provide a basis for figuring out what students think, linkages they are making, and the initial value they attach to the notion of a classroom learning community. Another way to determine the impact of activities is to analyze students' perceptions. Keeping track of students' perceptions helps the teacher to determine how the group is progressing toward a learning community.

While teaching students roles, norms, routines, and rules, learning-community teachers watch for opportunities to provide practice, feedback, and correction. At times, they stop the flow of activity and illustrate the accuracy of students' actions relative to norms, rules, procedures, and roles. These events provide students with positive and concrete references which they can practice at other times. Teachers with whom we work have indicated that prior to cooperative group training they would give negative feedback but did not stop and provide feedback when the class was running smoothly. The effect of providing negative feedback only is that students have to guess what is appropriate. Providing positive examples helps students to see the limits and range of the teacher's expectations.

Asking themselves the following questions may help teachers to find important concrete examples: "Are there approximations of learning community during specific parts of the day/class that I can point out? How are they accounted for?"

In general, during stage II, teachers help students to learn the classroom learning-community culture. Specifically, students learn the range of acceptable actions. Teachers monitor the establishment, support movement in appropriate directions, and eliminate inappropriate actions.

Given below are some activities that can facilitate the socialization of students to learning-community expectations. We have grouped our suggestions by norm development, rules, roles, and procedures.

Activities for Teaching Norms

Norms describe the classroom learning community cultural expectations. The norms are the standard by which the learning-community classroom group will judge itself. Thus, the norm is the standard for right and proper behavior, or the convention for living together, in the classroom learning community. The norms are discourse, cooperation, and respect for other communities.

Discourse

The nature of the discourse among learning-community members reflects their respect for each other as people, their respect for their own and others, ability to learn, honesty in assessing their own ability to get help or help others, and concern for the individual as well as the group. Specific skills related to learning-community discourse include listening, explaining, synthesizing, asking, encouraging others to participate, empathizing, and questioning. These skills can be taught and practiced in isolation or in an integrated manner.

For primary graders in a classroom learning community, discourse can be viewed as a way to develop skills for helping oneself and others. It also includes deciding whether one needs help, deciding whether one can help, deciding whether one should help, and knowing how to get and give help constructively, on the basis of the primary set of decisions and skills that primary graders need for functioning in a learning community. Also included is listening to learn, asking for help and information, explaining what or how or why, and identifying when something doesn't make sense. These skills, coupled with taking turns, actually form the basis of the norms that prevail in most traditional primary classrooms. The focus in the learning-community classroom upon helping others and taking responsibility for one's own learning changes the socialization norms for going to school.

One primary-grade teacher used a story entitled "Helper-Helpful and Harmer-Harmful" (Putnam, 1976) to introduce these concepts to her students. She transformed the two story characters into objects. Harmer-Harmful was made from a prickly seed pod, onto which she glued frowning eyes and mouth. Helper-Helpful was made from a "furry" piece of material onto which she glued pleasant features. After she read the story about the two characters, she and the students talked about how children in school "help" and what they might do that is "harmful." Before the discussion, she asked the students how they could get her attention if they wanted to talk. She said that she could call on each person in the order they were sitting, or she could call on people who raised their hands, or she could call on some who raised their hands and some who didn't. "But," she said, "what is important is that everyone has a turn to talk." She told them that she could not hear what they were saying if they were all talking to her at once. She asked that they pay attention to what people were saying so they could say things that added to the topic. During the discussion the teacher reminded students to wait their turn, indicated when they had waited, indicated who would be next, told a particular student that three others would talk before him, and told all the students that they were listening and learning. Sometimes she would call on someone and ask what the last person had said. After the discussion, she and the students wrote about times when the children had helped others and times when others had helped them.

We find that it is difficult to teach children to decide when they need help, how to initiate asking for help, and how to get help that they may need. It is equally difficult to teach students how to decide whether they are capable and knowledgeable enough to help others. Also, students need to know practical criteria that they can use in deciding whether they should be helping others or continuing with their own work.

Discourse related to asking for or giving help can be taught through role-play and reinforced during times when students are working independently. Using role-plays provides teachers with opportunities (1) to model thinking out loud as they take on the task of deciding whether they need help and asking for it and (2) to assess the students' ability to decide and communicate the type of help they need.

Teachers can model (1) thinking related to deciding they need help, (2) deciding that they can figure something out themselves, (3) asking for help effectively and ineffectively, and (4) helping someone effectively and ineffectively. After the concepts have been introduced, the students role-play their versions. For younger students, teachers work with a dyad. First they talk through a situation, and then they have the students practice the role-play, reinforcing the critical elements. Older students, once the teacher gives them the context, can work in small groups to create role-plays to present to the class.

Middle and high schoolers have had opportunities to make traditional discourse skills habitual. For students at this age, working together toward individual and group goals is the new idea.

"Practicing Pairs" is a strategy that, at the beginning of the year, provides students with the opportunity to work together as partners and to learn actions that promote a learning community. One student of a pair listens to the other explain something, and then the listener paraphrases the speaker's message. If the paraphrase is correct, then the speaker verifies both the cognitive and the feeling messages that were communicated. The listener focuses on remembering what the speaker communicates, without asking clarifying questions. After the speaker is finished, the listener restates or paraphrases the speaker's message. The speaker indicates whether or not the listener has received the message. Then the listener identifies the main ideas of the message and adds the supporting evidence. The original speaker listens to determine whether the messages heard were those intended. After the first practice is finished, the students swap roles and repeat the process. Once the pair have each acted as speaker and listener, they work together to list ways to improve their explanations and their paraphrases. They also identify and list the things that the speaker said that helped the listener to understand and remember and the things that the listener did that helped him/her to get and remember the message.

After all the pairs of students have made their lists, the teacher asks them to share their findings. Now the teacher turns the focus to the process the students experienced in order to raise their awareness. Once the findings have been reported, the teacher asks for more information about the process: "What helped?" "What needs to be improved?" and "What content was learned?" The teacher or one of the students lists new contributions on chart paper, the chalkboard, or an overhead projector. The contributions are then organized into lists reflecting the assignment (e.g., things that contributed to explanations, things that were helpful or not helpful, things that would improve explanations, effective and ineffective listening strategies, things that would improve the listener's understanding of the message, subject-matter concepts, and skills learned).

We suggest that a summary of subject-matter and process findings be copied and placed on a bulletin board, so that teachers and students can then monitor: (1) the changes from a primary focus on process with subject matter second to the reverse and (2) increase in process skill levels. Remember, when the teacher gives directions for an activity, both subject matter and process outcomes should be explicitly identified. After the activity, the teacher should explicitly focus the processing of the activity on both substance learned and process.

Teachers and students can select the topics for the "Practicing Pairs" explanations from two sources: personal experiences and school subject matter. "Practicing Pairs" can be repeated with different topics, so that, whereas at first the activity was focused on two skills—(1) explaining and (2) listening and paraphrasing what the speaker communicated—later other skills can be added, such as synthesizing, questioning, encouraging, and asking. The goal is to move students from working skillfully in pairs to working skillfully in small groups. The pace will depend on the grade level, students , experiences, and the explicitness of the assignments and processing outcomes. After the "Practicing Pairs" assignments become complex enough to encompass a full set of discussion/interaction skills, and the students have learned to label, demonstrate, and identify others' effective use of discussion-group skills, the process can be repeated, with students working in small groups (five to six people).

Cooperation

Members of a learning community founded on interdependence and cooperation act in particular ways. Basically, teachers and individual students take action to promote learning about school subject matter, personal responsibility, social responsibility, and social justice. Students take responsibility for their learning, for helping others learn, for accomplishing group goals, and for seeing themselves and other students and adults as resources. Thus, when a teacher is setting up a classroom learning community, students need to be taught actions that are congruent with the ideas of interdependence and cooperation. One aid to such teaching is to post a list of actions that will remind students about interdependence and cooperation (see Figure 9-1).

Activities that facilitate learning how to cooperate contain processes that require groups of students to work together to come up with a solution to a problem or a product. Such activities include directions that focus on cooperation as the necessary element.

One such activity is creating complete sentences from individual words. For this activity, write five complete sentences using a capital letter for the first word in each sentence and a period after the last word, and then cut up the sentences into individual words or phrases. (The sentences should come from the course content. For example, knowing what to accept as scientific evidence is something to learn, and adaptation is a concept related to humans, dinosaurs, and explorers. Mathematics equations or scientific formulas could be used instead of prose. Tangrams and puzzles also work.) Then the teacher puts a set of five complete sentences into an envelope for each group.

When the class meets, the teacher has the students form groups of five, and distributes words to everybody in each group. Directions for the first experience with this activity include: (1) The goal is for each person to have one complete sentence in front of him/her. (2) Each person does his/her own work.

(3) Students or the teacher may give words to others when they see that they need the words. (4) Help others only by talking. (5) The task is finished when each student has a complete sentence. When the groups are finished, the teacher tells them to list the things they saw, thought, and said that helped or hindered the group's work.

Then the teacher distributes a second set of sentences to each group. Directions this time differ only in that no one may talk. Again, when a group's task is done, the group members should identify what they saw and thought, and should discuss their actions.

After both experiences are finished, the teacher should help the class to discuss what they paid attention to in order to help complete the task. Generally, students report: having had to pay attention to what others were doing; not wanting to break up their personal sentences to provide necessary parts for someone else; and having felt frustrated when it was clear what someone else should do and that person didn't see it.

Verbal group puzzles, also called "mystery games" (Stanford, 1977), also can help a group to understand cooperation and interdependence. These puzzles are designed to fit any school subject matter. Individual students are given clue cards which they share with their group. By synthesizing facts on the clue cards, the group can answer a question. The teacher reads a question and the background information. Then she/he asks students to share their clues and questions, discuss the information, and agree (reach consensus) on a response to the question.

A seventh-grader used a newspaper article to construct the following mystery game. The clues were cut up and distributed. A group facilitator was selected. The student author read the following to start the action.

> You are going to identify three events. These particular events happened in our lifetime and each has historical importance. You need to identify three events correctly. Clues provided.

Any of these events described here will give a small group practice in encouraging others to speak, synthesizing information, organizing and staying on task, and providing information in a timely fashion.

Respect for Other Communities

Other classrooms, other schools, other neighborhoods, and other cultures are all examples of different communities. As the classroom learning community is created, students and teachers develop a sense of pride in, respect for, and ownership of their own community. The principle "Respect other communities" ascribes the same feelings to members of other communities.

Activities for Teaching Rules

Rules for a classroom learning community should be congruent with the explicit norms. For example, a rule that is congruent with a respecting-others norm is "No put-downs allowed." Rules that interfered with students' talking to each other, getting help, or receiving help would not be congruent with learning-community norms.

---

1. Be a resource for others.
2. Support everyone's learning.
3. Take responsibility for your own learning and understanding.
4. Initiate seeking help to understand.
5. Reflect on your actions and their effects.
6. Celebrate individual and community achievements.

FIGURE 9-1

Actions for Interdependence and Cooperation

A rule can be a general statement (e.g., "We treat people and things with respect") that is then taught by examples. For example, students can brainstorm all the ways that they can show respect (e.g., "When others are having a problem learning, don't distract them by asking them to help you" and "When you find something, put it in the place designated for lost items, so that the owner will be able to find it").

We suggest that to teach rules, teachers must communicate the rules and their purposes, illustrate or model examples, and nonexamples, provide practice/support/feedback, and monitor. Learning-community teachers monitor closely to establish rules quickly.

Primary-grade students need opportunities to connect their behavior to the expectations the teacher has communicated about rules. Teaching the students how to make decisions about their behavior, so that they will be complying with the rules, means providing them with opportunities to see a variety of positive examples for a given rule, as well as examples of inappropriate behavior. One of the most successful strategies we have observed for teaching rules to primary children involves role playing in which students demonstrate the behaviors that comply or do not comply with the rules. The teacher asks students to role-play a variety of situations (e.g., making supportive comments, finding lost/dropped items, using instructional materials, sharing). For several days after the role-play, the teacher asks, "How is what you are doing right now an example of following the rules?" or "How is what you are doing right now an example of breaking a rule?" Note that the focus is on the student's explanation of congruence or incongruity. After the student explains, the teacher follows up by asking, "Do you need to change what you decided to do?" For students who have a difficult time becoming socialized to the classroom expectations, a picture or symbol can be used as a reminder. Reminders are helpful to students who are learning how to internalize classroom learning-community social control. Note that the emphasis is on students' talking and reflecting on their explanations of behaviors and verbalizations about what to continue or eliminate.

Activities for Teaching Roles

Teaching interactive group roles is a key to helping individuals to become successful learning-community members. Teaching students how to interact in whole-class and small-group learning situations contributes to the smooth running of the classroom and the success of each individual. Students need to learn two sets of roles. The first set consists of roles that each individual group member should be able to assume in any interaction—the roles of organizer, linker, contributor, and encourager (Stanford, 1977). The second set, suggested by M. Cohen (1987), include: timer, recorder, facilitator, and equipment person. Role-plays and other activities provide students with practice in roles while also allowing them to observe others carrying out roles and receiving and giving feedback.

Use of Stanford's roles (1977) has proved very helpful in establishing responsibility for the group. All students should be taught to take on the four roles of organizer, linker, contributor, and encourager whenever they are members of groups. When students are working in groups, they need to pay attention to the task, to keep on topic, and in general to move the agenda along.

The role of **Organizer** provides a means for people to act responsibly when they are not the group facilitator. Helping the group to make progress is the responsibility of all group members. The **Linker** or **Synthesizer** role involves tying what is being said together to help others or oneself make sense of or clarify what is happening. Illustrating similarities and differences in positions, ideas, or propositions contributes to quality outcomes. Providing information or sources for information is the function of the **Contributor** role. Finally, the role of the **Encourager** involves helping others to make their points, clarifying the meanings of others' statements, and including individuals who are not participating. The teacher can hand out 3 × 5 index cards in four colors (e.g., blue for the organizer, yellow for the synthesizer, pink for the encourager, and green for the contributor) to help students to acquire specific effective roles. When a student becomes aware that she/he is carrying out one of the roles, she/he places the appropriate card on the corner of the desk. The goal is for each student to "try on" each role. Students should be asked to state what they said that they identified as an example of each role.

Facilitator, timer, recorder, and equipment person are examples of roles that contribute to the status and power of members of a class. Assigning the role of facilitator to students who have less power at the beginning of the year helps those students to gain status in the class, because the facilitator has contact with the teacher. The teacher responds to the facilitator when the group has questions, and the teacher also addresses questions or comments for the group to the facilitator.

To teach the assigned roles, teachers need to let students know what actions are expected for each role. There are several ways to accomplish this. First, bulletin boards or charts hung on the walls provide support for students as they learn the expected role actions. Second, a videotape of a group carrying out the roles as they do a task or a role-play can provide concrete examples. Third, any small-group activity will provide the basis for practicing the roles of facilitator, timer, recorder, and equipment person. Once the roles have been assigned and the groups are working, the teacher monitors individuals' actions. When actions are congruent or incongruent, the teacher interrupts to indicate why. One teacher hands out chips when she sees actions congruent with role expectations. Thus she is able to avoid interrupting, except when the actions need to be changed.

Activities for Teaching Procedures

Procedures needed to facilitate smooth functioning are like rules and roles in that they facilitate the creation and maintenance of the classroom learning community. Routines are needed, through which students can help each other, get feedback, get into and out of group work, evaluate the efforts of the group and individuals, take responsibility, and celebrate. Also, as in other classroom cultures, routines for maintaining the physical environment need to be established.

Six steps are effective for teaching procedures to students. We recommend that they be taught only when actually needed. First, provide an explanation of a given routine. Include the reason for the routine, as well as the steps students should follow to accomplish it. Second, illustrate the steps in the routine. Third, depending on the grade level, either have the students go through the routine or ask them to verbally reflect back the rationale and the steps. Fourth, provide the opportunity for students to practice the routine. Fifth, give feedback. Sixth, monitor students throughout the period during which the routine is being established. Provide positive and negative feedback, and hold students accountable for consistent use of the routine.

REFLECTING

Giving time to establishing expectations and also providing consistent follow-up and support contribute to the establishment of the community. Two types of reflection are warranted. First, reflect on the initial establishment of expectations. Second, reflect periodically to be sure that the expectations are maintained and refined.

Teachers should walk a fine line between allowing time for things to work but not persevering when things clearly are not working. Assessment questions that provide directions for the initial reflections include: What is going well? What are students learning? What stands out? What happened? What makes these norms, rules, routines, and roles either work or not work so far? These questions provide a basis for assessing reflectively what progress is being made toward the establishment of a learning community. Analyze once again the nature of the procedures and expectations as a means of clarifying what has been happening. After the initial implementation of plans for establishing expectations, look for possible incongruities that may not have been evident on paper. When students are having trouble capturing the idea of a learning community, or when they develop misconceptions about norms, rules, roles, or procedures, the concept and the related actions need to be clarified. Reteaching and reinforcement may be needed.

Once the roles, norms, rules, and procedures have been established, the next reflection task concerns maintenance of learning-community expectations. The first step in maintenance is to identify cues that indicate the desirability of an intervention to prevent disruption (e.g., intervention is needed when no students start tasks after the teacher gives directions). Distinguishing between cues that do and do not need a response (e.g., when a student goes to get materials at an appropriate time, no intervention is needed) is necessary, so that teachers can act responsibly and not nag students. When a response is necessary, the type of response will depend upon the need. For example, different responses are needed to physical problems, to curriculum problems (such as when the work is too hard or too easy), and to individual behavior problems.

When procedures have been lost or when unplanned procedures have emerged, teachers need to evaluate the existing procedures and reestablish any lost procedures that are critical to the community. To do this, they should call the problem to students' attention, review the rationale and steps for essential procedures, add new signals as reminders, and then monitor the situation until the desired procedures have been established.

Learning-community teachers often ask themselves questions such as: "What is the meaning of what is happening in the classroom?" "How could it be better?" "What has been learned? By whom?" "What remains a problem?" and "What problems have been overcome?" Reflecting on questions of this type provides a means for figuring out how to adjust plans for upcoming days. The task is to identify specific activities, to develop support for one's own behavior, or to construct feedback that will contribute to the learning-community establishment—or to try all three of these approaches.

Tables 9-1 and 9-2 offer examples of how some teachers assess the impact of instruction relative to procedures and rules, and how they determine what else is needed. Using notes that they took during classroom observations (monitoring), they answer the questions: "What is the impact of the procedures?" and "What do the rules promote?" Tables 9-1 and 9-2 show these teachers' thoughts. By considering outcomes, they became able to identify what else needed to be done. Their notes, thus, provided the plan for making adjustments that would further the establishment of the learning community.

Reflection on the classroom community yields information about whether or not adjustments need to be made—for example, adjustments in tasks, rules, procedures, or roles. Further teacher/pupil discussions may be needed. Evidence of progress toward intended outcomes as they relate to establishment of expectations should also be monitored. Specific possibilities to consider include adjusting activities, clarifying misperceptions, and adjusting pacing.

TABLE 9-1   ASSESSING PROCEDURES: WHAT IS THE IMPACT OF PROCEDURES?

Procedure	Outcome	Benefit	Needs Work
Feedback on homework.	Students get feedback.	None yet.	Teach use of feedback in increasing learning.

TABLE 9-2   ASSESSING RULES: ARE THE EFFECTIVE CLASSROOM RULES EFFECTIVE?

Rules	Evidence of Outcomes
A. Do rules promote individual responsibility and accountability? Students respect each other and property.	Decrease in verbal put-downs since first week in school.
B. Are rules flexible? Do they promote the intended outcomes? Late homework for a serious reason is OK.	Students hand in homework in a timely fashion.

Performance Outcomes and Activities (NJPTS 2,4,6)

Chapter 9
Stage II. Establishing Expectations

PERFORMANCE OUTCOMES

Teacher Candidates will:

1. Gain the knowledge and skills for professionally preparing for, carrying out, and reporting data from classroom observations that furthers their knowledge about teachers and teaching and learners and learning and schools and schooling.
2. Gain the knowledge and skills to identify Stage 2. Establishing Expectations teacher and student behavior.
3. Gain the knowledge and skills to create an effective plan that when implemented will likely move students through Stage 2. Establishing Expectations with activities that are congruent with the functions of schooling for learning communities.
4. Refine interview skills, data analysis and use of data.
5. Continue practice in carrying out child studies.

Exercise 9.1
Observing to Assess Establishment of Stage II Outcomes

(Reminder: The first activity in chapters 8–12 are classroom observation tasks. The four steps that you will use for these activities are: (1) preparing for the classroom observation; (2) carrying out the observation; (3) interviewing the teachers; and (4) analyzing and making sense of the observation and interview data.)

You will be observing in schools where there are few learning communities established. However, teachers, do establish norms and roles, rules and procedures even though they are not congruent with a learning community culture. Begin your preparation for the observation by listing actions you might see if the students had progress through or were part way through Stage 2 group development in a learning community. Make arrangements with the teacher for you to do 3 twenty minute observations. Arrange a time that you will meet and interview the teacher. Use the following observation form to collect your classroom observation data.

ASSESSING THE ESTABLISHMENT OF NORMS/ROLES, RULES, AND PROCEDURES

List those observed.	Describe data that support the establishment or not established (If a teacher reminds students about norm/role, rules or procedures and students do not initiate the action on their own . . . it is not established and absent from the culture)	Inferences & Questions you will ask when interviewing the teacher
I. Norms		
II. Rules		
III. Roles/jobs		

A. List Your Questions in a Format That Will Support Your Note Taking.

For example, certain rules are usually established in a classroom that provide for safety and courtesy. What rules did you observe that might be for safety and courtesy? Who makes the rules? How are rules communicated to the students?

B. Interview the Teacher.

C. Identifying the Nature of Relationships Among the Students and Between Students and Teacher(s)

1. The question you are answering in this activity is—"What is the nature of the relationships among students in the situations you observed?"
2. What do the rules and who made them communicate to the students about how the class will function?
3. What do the roles and jobs you observed students carrying out tell students about the students' place in the classroom culture? In some classes, students have jobs that contribute to keeping the environment clean and orderly. In some classes teachers lead discussions while other students take part in leadership roles.
4. How do the norms you observed affect the way the classroom functions and how students participate in having control over their learning?

Exercise 9.2
Designing and Implementing Stage II Activity

Use the data you collected in 9.1 above as a baseline for your planning.

A. Create a Detailed Plan for Stage 2. Establishing Expectations

For Stage 2 plans, create a lesson activity for each of the following: Norms and roles, rules, and procedures. For each lesson:

1. Explain in writing what subject matter (if any) you expect to teach in this lesson.
2. Write subject matter performance outcomes for (choose one content area) math, reading, music, art, physical education.
3. Write out what norm or role you will teach.
4. State the purpose of the norm or role and its contribution to the community.

5. List what the students need to know and be able to do in order to understand and demonstrate the norm or role.
6. Write performance outcomes for Stage 2 norms/roles outcomes.
7. Write a detailed description in chronological order of the activity you will teach. Be sure to indicate both what you and the students will be saying/doing.
8. What pupil activity will you support explicitly after this lesson as a means for reinforcing or establishing the norm?
9. List the materials that you will need for this lesson.
10. Write out what you will say to introduce this lesson. Be sure to include communication of purposes and subject matter and community building outcomes.
11. At the end of the lesson, you will process the experience with the students. Write out what you will say, questions you will ask, how you will summarize information at the end of the lesson with/for the students.

B. Based on your knowledge of the students in the class teach the Lesson to a group of at least 18 P–12 students or a classroom of students.

C. Reflection on the Instruction of Your Planned Lesson
Answer the following questions as a guideline for a written reflection.

1. What did you observe while you were teaching? (list)
2. While you were teaching, what were you thinking? *Do not describe what you did or said,* list the things you thought (the things that went through your head).
3. List the decisions you made while you were teaching. Indicate which of the decisions you had not planned to do and explain why you made this decision.
4. For each of the outcomes you listed in your plan, list who accomplished that outcome. Describe the data you have for each student that met an outcome that indicates he or she achieved the outcomes. What data did you have that shows that the student did not know or was not able to do the behavior prior to your teaching?
5. What did you observe about student learning that you believe was unusual or different?

D. Recommendations

1. What do you recommend as a follow-up and expanding activity?
2. What instructional activities might be needed to see that the role or norm is connected in the students' minds with life in the classroom learning community?
3. Why do you believe that this is the best thing to do next?
4. What did you learn from your observations while you were teaching?

Exercise 9.2
Identifying Classroom Norms

Use the following formats for classroom observations. Make you own observation forms on your computer, then after your observations enter your data, copy and use for analysis, synthesis and reporting.

OBSERVATION AND INTERVIEW FORM FOR IDENTIFYING CLASSROOM NORMS

Norms promote listening, learning, encouraging other to participate, linking, synthesizing, cooperation, assertiveness, and self-monitoring of progress toward explicit outcomes.

Norm Describe the Norm	Evidence Norm is Established & Frequency of Occurrence	Evidence Norm is Not Established	Questions You will ask when interviewing the teacher

ACTIONS THAT PROVIDE FOR ADJUSTMENTS AS YOU ESTABLISH A CLASSROOM LEARNING COMMUNITY CULTURE

1. Task Adjustments	2. Rules, Procedures, & Role Adjustments	3. Interactive Adjustments	4. Monitor Progress toward intended outcomes
A. Reduce student frustration or potential for it through:	A. Clarify rules, procedures and roles that have lost their sharpness	A. Adjust pacing	A. Acting in personally responsible ways
1. Adjusting types of activities	B. Remove rules, procedures or roles that no longer have a purpose	B. Adjust teacher talk	B. Acting in socially responsible ways
2. Adjusting level of difficulty	C. Identify new rules, procedures, norms or roles that have emerged over time and are implicitly held by members of the learning community	C. Add or delete repetition of examples given in instruction	C. Achieving subject-matter outcomes
3. Adjusting relevance		D. Differentiate required student tasks	D. Acting in ways that promote social justice
4. Adjusting relationship between tasks & students' interests		E. Evaluate student participation structures	
5. Providing instruction in prerequisite skills/knowledge		F. Monitor general student behavior:	
B. Plan breaks before students disrupt the learning environment		1. Scan, walk around, ask unobtrusive on-task questions, provide specific feedback, challenge, and support	
		2. Identify behavior which requires teacher intervention, decide on action, take action in the most unobtrusive fashion possible, and monitor the effects of the action.	

STAGE TWO: ESTABLISHING EXPECTATIONS

Statements of or Descriptions of:	Reasons for their existence	Descriptive Examples of what they look like in the LC; How these are similar to and different from those in traditional classrooms	Practice Opportunities (What activities will you provide so that all students have an opportunity to learn?)	Examples of Feedback to Individuals and Group	Consequences to individuals when they are not followed; Consequences to the group when they are not followed
1. Descriptions of Norms					
2. Descriptions of Roles					
3. Descriptions of Rules					
4. Descriptions of Procedures					

Exercise 9.3
The Study of the Stages of Human Development and Their Application to Planning

The purpose of this assignment is to provide the opportunity to tie knowledge about human growth and development to planning activities at appropriate levels so that they meet the needs of the students and support the establishment of an effective learning community.

This assignment has three parts. The first is data collection and organization to increase your knowledge about growth and development, the second is using the data to answer questions relevant to teacher candidates and their thinking about organization, management, and instruction, and third is a task that puts into practical activities the knowledge you gained about the stages of human development.

Part I: Data Collection and Organization

Select two age levels from the following: 4–7, 8–11, 12–15, or 15–18 years old. Think of this task as a comparison of two students at different stages in the areas of intellectual, physical, and social/emotional growth and development. Using books, websites, and/or visual materials create an illustrated, written, and referenced comparison of two students who are in two different growth and developmental stages you selected.

The following web site will help with your initial data collection *http://childdevelopmentinfo.com/index.htm*. The following website will give you an overview of pamphlets that you can find in your Education Building Resource Center *www.responsiveclassroom.org/bookstore/pamphletcc.html*. These pamphlets will also provide data about what you can observe at the different stages of development.

Part II: Using Knowledge about Human Development to Answer Questions Relevant to Teacher Thinking

When you finish your written and illustrated comparison of students at two different developmental levels, answer the following questions:

1. What is intellectual development?
2. What do effective teachers do in establishing their classroom learning community environment to support intellectual development?
3. What is social-emotional development?
4. What do effective learning community teachers do in their classrooms that supports the social-emotional development of their students?
5. What is temperament?
6. How do teachers make effective use of the diverse temperaments that exists in a learning community classroom?
7. How do the stages of group development support intellectual and social/emotional development?

Part III: Application of Knowledge to Teacher Planning

1. Select a concept from school subject matter in which you are interested.
2. Write two subject matter performance outcomes (intellectual). Write one for each of the two developmental stages you studied.
3. Write two social performance outcomes that reflect Stage I, II, or III Learning Community norms. Write one for each stage of human development you selected.
4. Create two activities, one for each set of outcomes (intellectual and social). Be sure that the activities reflect the differences in developmental stages.

RECOMMENDED READINGS

Cohen, E. G. (1986). *Designing groupwork: Strategies for the heterogeneous classroom.* New York. Teacher College Press.

Galvin, K., Book, C. (1975). *Person to Person, an introduction to speech communication.* National Textbook Company, Skokie, Illinois.

Oakes, J. (1999). *Limiting students' success and life chances: The impact of tracking.* In A. C. Ornstein and L. S. Behar-Horenstein (eds.), Contemporary Issues in Curriculum (2nd ed). Needham Heights, Mass., Allyn and Bacon.

Schmuck, R., and Schmuck, P. (1975). *Group processes in the classroom* (2nd. Ed.). Dubuque, Iowa. W. C. Brown.

Stanford, G. (1977). *Developing effective classroom groups: A practical guide for teachers.* New York. A & W Visual Library.

Stage III. Identifying and Resolving Conflicts

Whenever learning-community norms are being shaped, conflicts will arise. One type of conflict is related to life in a learning community, and a second type is related to problem behavior brought into the community by its members.

The learning-community classroom we advocate has norms of conduct and relational expectations quite different from those of the traditional classroom. In traditional classrooms, the hierarchical and authoritarian concentration of power resides in the teacher. In the learning-community classroom, power is redistributed among the members of the class, so that students as well as the teacher are empowered to enact their roles within a society of learners. As teachers and students learn new roles and begin to establish new relationships, the internalization of learning-community norms will bring conflict. This conflict is normal.

Learning communities are distinctly different from traditional classrooms. That difference is that *conflict* is understood as a sign of the group's development. The group's developmental health is increased when the conflicts are resolved rather than suppressed. The conflicts that arise within a learning community arise because of the diversity of interests, backgrounds, and stages of human development among the members. Suppressing conflict in the name of uniformity and control requires exaggerated efforts to deny human diversity. Sameness, uniformity, and conforming are the weapons of control that are characteristic of the traditional classroom (and of a masculine culture). Resolving conflicts within the classroom learning community empowers individuals to grow while bonding the group together.

Conflict related to a student's problem behavior is not the fault of the learning community. A given student's problem behavior may have been developing over years or months. The conflict it creates for the learning community is that the purpose (learning) of the entire community is disrupted or blocked by the disruptive behavior of that one individual.

The teacher has three responsibilities when this type of conflict occurs. First, the teacher as a responsible adult must stop disruptions, so that the learning environment will be restored. Thus, the teacher supports the students' right to learn and his/her own right and responsibility to teach. As the community comes to be established, students will learn to assert their own rights and responsibility to learn. Second, the teacher is responsible for systematically working with the individuals who have the problem behavior to facilitate their socialization into the community. Third, the teacher is responsible for helping the student to get appropriate help to solve the problems that underlie the disruptive behavior.

To provide the leadership necessary to identify and resolve conflict in the learning-community classroom, a learning-community teacher acts as an assertive adult. Assertive behavior is required in order to stand up for one's own rights and duties as the instructional leader, while not violating the rights of others. Nonassertive behavior is interpreted as violating one's own rights by failing to express honest feelings, thoughts, and beliefs, or by expressing them in ways such that others easily disregard them (Kubowski and Lange, 1976). Effective learning-community teachers act assertively to establish and maintain the community. At times, teachers must assert both learners' rights and their own rights in order to deal with destructive/disruptive student behavior.

Asserting one's responsibility and rights leads teachers, at times, to take disciplinary action. Brophy (1987) defines disciplinary interventions as "actions taken to elicit or compel changes in the behavior of students who fail to conform to expectations, especially behavior that is salient or sustained enough to disrupt the classroom management system" (p. 3). Brophy and Rohrkemper (1980) studied the hostile-aggressive student problem and concluded that teachers should work with students who have problematic behavior, rather than merely punishing or expelling them from their classes. They concluded that it is necessary, "at least to the extent that it is possible for them (teachers), to divert time and energy from their primary instructional goals to work on students socialization goals" (p. 77). Brophy and Rohrkemper believe that teachers who possess effective student socialization strategies should use them and that other teachers who do not possess effective strategies should develop them. We agree with Brophy and Rohrkemper and others who support the idea of working with students to help them to become constructive contributors and learners (both in the learning community and in society at large). All teachers will be faced at times with situations that call for responses to misbehavior that occurs repeatedly and continues to disrupt learning. It is possible for teachers in these situations to feel a need to punish a student. The effect of punishment, however, is to suppress the behavior, or to attempt to do so. Punishment does not solve any problems or eliminate disruptive behavior. Punishment is used as a last resort and can be either effective or ineffective.

Good and Brophy (1987) suggest several principles that teachers should consider if they need to punish their students. According to Good and Brophy, the first thing to consider and an important choice to weigh is the "way the teacher presents it to the students" (p. 270). Their suggestion is congruent with our idea that the learning-community teacher should avoid starting "power struggles" with students. While learning-community teachers work to get students to control themselves, they can and will control misbehavior when necessary.

Good and Brophy (1987) also suggest that effective punishment is contingent upon teacher tone and manner. Specifically, in relationship to misbehavior, the teacher makes a clear distinction between a student's misbehavior and the teacher's acceptance of the student as a person. The teacher warns the student when it appears that punishment must be administered after the next disruption. The teacher makes it clear that the student's decisions and actions to disrupt the learning environment will cause the punishment to be administered. Once the time comes to administer punishment, the teacher remains flexible and clear about how the student can redeem herself/himself, and also makes it clear again why the student is being punished (Good and Brophy, 1987, pp. 270–271). Actions that do not result in suppression of the misbehavior are ineffective punishments and should be stopped. Additionally, Good and Brophy suggest that there are three inappropriate punishments that should not be used, for a variety of reasons: abusive verbal attacks, physical punishment, and extra work (pp. 269–270).

Walker and Shea (1984) suggest three principles that should guide teachers' decisions about discipline. These principles are: "(1) the principle of normalization, (2) the principle of fairness, and (3) the principle of respect for the dignity and worth of the individual" (p. 211). These principles mean that teachers should seek courses of action which will return the class to normal conditions as quickly as possible, be fair to students, and express valuing of the student as a person. Carl Rogers (1962) reminds us that effective relationships with students depend on genuineness, empathy, and unconditional positive regard. The following three sections present ideas for preparing for and implementing strategies, and reflecting on the impact of stage III efforts.

PREPARATION

Preparing for the third stage in establishing a learning community involves assessing one's own policies, the potential conflicts that may need to be handled, and school policies and practices. In addition, preparation includes identifying a way to solve conflicts and figuring out how the process will be taught to students.

Self-Assessment

Figuring out one's own policies relative to the identification and resolution of conflict starts with answering assessment questions about oneself. These questions include:

- "What are the roles of the teacher and pupils in the learning community?"
- "What do I believe and know about socializing students to be contributing members of the community?"
- "How do I respond to classroom disruptions and problem behavior?"
- "How do I feel about particular behavior?"
- "What strategies do I have for helping learning-community members resolve conflicts?"
- "What strategies do I have for working with problem behavior that students bring to the community?"
- "What problem behavior is most troublesome?"

Initial responses to these questions provide the basis for exploring and clarifying, and bring one's values, probable actions, and thinking into congruence.

For example, some beginning teachers have conflicts between wanting the students to like them and their responsibility, as instructional leaders, to promote student learning. Discussing what it means to be liked, how one comes to be liked, and the primary role of the learning-community teacher will help to clarify a teacher's ideas. At one level, it is easy to agree that permitting the community's learning function to be disrupted is unacceptable. In a discussion it is even easy to agree that teacher behavior that permits disruption in goal attainment is nonassertive, irresponsible, and unacceptable in a learning community.

Even so, learning-community teachers who assert the rights of learners and themselves may, for the short term, feel "That student doesn't like me." This will occur, at times, even when the teacher (or a student) provides an articulate rationale for his/her assertive stance. However, not only is permitting irresponsible behavior to continue incongruent with the learning-community foundation but also it is not what students really want. Remember that Nash (1976) found that students want teachers to be fair and to keep the culture functional.

Clarifying what it means to be liked helps teachers who have this concern to explore related values and actions. Thus, we suggest that teachers who are primarily concerned about being liked by students and peers further explore their own beliefs and values, and the congruence of those beliefs and values with the concept of learning community. Concern about being liked will interfere with a teacher's role as a learning-community leader. Focusing on a student's short-term discomfort (because of not getting his/her own way), or on one's own short-term discomfort (because the student says unkind things) will block responsible action.

Another possible internal incongruity for teachers is confusion between the ideas of earned and unearned respect. We see unearned respect as the unconditional regard of one human being for another. It may be given because of a person's role as teacher, principal, or student. Unearned respect, in such an instance, has nothing to do with whether the person is effective in the role. For teachers and learning-community students, in contrast, earned respect is connected to the community process as it is experienced by each member and the understandings acquired.

The process of assessing one's own values and actions and their congruence with the learning-community culture provides a means for identifying potential conflicts between the community's stated purposes and the teacher's values and behavior. The resulting awareness provides valuable information about the congruence between one's values and actions and a learning-community culture.

Potential Problems and Responses

Identifying potential conflicts provides a basis for planning responses. Possible responses to predicted problems can be assessed for their congruence with the learning community. A teacher might anticipate that some students will not carry out their responsibilities in a small-group task. Since work for small groups is constructed upon principles that include contributions from all members, students who do not do their part cause conflicts. The consequences of this lack of personal and social responsibility may include the following: (1) group members are not allowed to learn from this individual, (2) the product is not complete, and/or (3) the individual has not learned what was intended.

Potential responses to students' problem behavior are generated by teachers from many resources. For example, the work of Wolfgang and Glickman (1986) provides review and analysis of models for responding to problem behavior. While Wolfgang and Glickman recommend eclectic and developmental approaches to problems, most frequently models of the type reviewed (e.g., assertive discipline, according to Glasser 1969) are implemented without thought of the classroom culture or context, and without regard to the individual learner and teacher. Since the learning community is based on particular norms, not all discipline responses are appropriate. For example, discipline responses that promote student dependency on the adult for self-control are incongruent with learning-community expectations. An assertive discipline model, requiring blind obedience to authority, is also incongruent with learning-community life or outcomes.

Likewise, some models are inappropriate for some teachers. For example, one teacher, who was afraid of her students, was not able to effectively implement coercive models. This teacher reported that she used an assertive discipline model. Classroom observation showed that she listed misbehaving students' names on the board. However, after putting a number of checks after their names for each additional disruption, she stopped responding to their disruptive behavior. She stopped when the next check mark would mean that she would tell the student to leave the room. When first asked about the observation that no students were sent out of class, she indicated that the model was working and that as soon as the students "knew they would be out the next time" they stopped being disruptive.

Later, when she reviewed observation data and saw no decrease in disruptive behavior or time off-task, she questioned the accuracy of the observation data. Still later, viewing a videotape prompted her to protest, "The principal wants me to use this. I knew the model didn't work. It is just these kids!" Further exploration led the teacher to question how she would ever be able to "kick students out of her class." She did not believe she could actually get them to leave if they resisted her command. Therefore, she felt that she must not actually confront the disruptions to learning directly because she would "lose." For this traditional classroom teacher, the incongruence between her belief that she was powerless and a power model contributed to her classroom problems.

A more helpful response to problems is to teach students how to respond constructively to problems. Learning-community teachers teach students strategies for solving problems for use when conflicts arise. Planning such a strategy and its instruction enables teachers (1) to promote their own self-confidence (just knowing that they have a plan will help); (2) to communicate to students that both students and the teacher are responsible for solving problems, because they are all members of the community; and (3) to demonstrate leadership in establishing the learning-community expectations.

Teachers have several options in planning for general conflict solving. For example, they can select a model created by someone else, or they can create their own model based on reflection of their past experiences and/or observations of others who are effective problem solvers. Most traditional classroom cultures do not teach students how to effectively solve conflicts. This means that many students in a new learning community will initially need to develop a sense of responsibility about conflict resolution, along with the knowledge and skill to be effective in solving conflicts. Thus, teaching and modeling effective resolution are necessary in the process of establishing the learning community.

Another option is use of the author's conflict-resolution guide, which we developed by working with teachers. (See the checklist in activity 10-4 at the end of the chapter.) It has roots in Gordon's no-lose conflict-resolution model (1974). It identifies: (1) problem-solving steps; (2) the teacher's role in conflict resolution, both when the teacher is involved in the conflict and when the teacher is not involved; and (3) the problems teachers have in teaching or using responsible resolution strategies.

In the checklist, the problems, which are labeled "Monkey Wrenches," are used to illustrate the nature of the problems encountered by teachers with whom we have worked. Problems similar to these arise with any resolution strategy other than an authoritarian teacher model in which the teacher makes the decisions and the students respond blindly to authority. Since using a conflict-resolution model takes time, it is worthwhile, feasible, and necessary to teach students the process so that they will be able to responsibly identify and respond to problems on their own. This model is worthwhile in a learning-community context, in which teachers work with students to facilitate their becoming responsible and accountable for their decisions and behaviors (see Figure 10-1).

Step 1. Reach Agreement

The first step in our recommended conflict-resolution process is to reach agreement that there is a conflict and that those involved will work on resolving it. We find that, in traditional classrooms, when an individual identifies and tries to resolve a conflict alone, the frequent result is either a power struggle, conflict escalation, or no change. For example, if the teacher perceives a conflict and the students do not, the teacher does not have the cooperation of the other participants in working toward resolution. Problems arise at this step when teachers begin to perceive everything as conflicts and/or tells students what will be done about the conflicts.

Step 2. State the Conflict

The teacher next makes a conflict statement, in order to help in clarifying what the conflict is about. Frequently we find that students and teachers identify responses to conflicts as the conflict. In this case, conflict resolution starts with the wrong premise. That is, individuals are trying to resolve disagreement on a response to a conflict that is not clear to anyone, rather than identifying and understanding the problem/conflict/issue and then working together to find responses. Problems at this step arise when (1) the statement is about solutions rather than about the conflict; (2) any one participant does not feel his/her perspective was heard; or (3) the teacher is going through a process but has already determined the outcome and the students know about it.

Step 3. Identify and Select Responses

Brainstorming and recording solutions to the conflict is the third step. Each solution is then analyzed for its short-range and long-range consequences for the immediate conflict, the individual, and the ethos of the learning community. Problems arise at this stage if the teacher does not accept suggestions from the student. This creates a feeling that the teacher is controlling the student's input.

I.   *Reach agreement.* Make sure that all involved agree that:
    A.   There is conflict.
    B.   All members of the learning community will work together to resolve the conflict.
II. *State the conflict.* Make a conflict statement, and separate:
    A.   Conflict of solutions.
    B.   Conflict of needs.
III. *Identify and select responses.*
    A.   Brainstorm alternatives.
    B.   Assess long-term and short-term consequences. Discard solutions that have negative consequences.
IV. *Create a solution.* The solution should satisfy the needs of all parties involved in the conflict.
V.   *Design and implement a plan.* What? Who? When? How?
VI. *Assess the success of the plan.* Identify checkpoints at which you will follow up on the implementation of the plan. When the conflict has been resolved, evaluate the process and the outcome.

FIGURE 10-1
Guide for Conflict Resolution.

Step 4. Create a Solution

Next, the teacher designs a suitable response that takes into consideration consequences for individuals and the group. A combination of several solutions identified during brainstorming helps to create a comprehensive response. Problems arise at this step if students see the teacher as manipulating the discussion to get his/her own preferred response.

Step 5. Design and Implement a Plan

A plan must then be designed and the proposed solution must be implemented. Since most solutions have several components (e.g., different individuals do different things), the implementation plan includes specifics about what will happen when, who will act, and under what conditions. Students who do not feel that their perspectives have been heard will not invest in carrying out the plan.

Step 6. Assess Success

The sixth step involves monitoring, adjusting, and assessing. Once the plan has been implemented, students and teachers monitor the immediate results as well as individual's follow-through. When adjustments in the plan are warranted, they are made. The final action is to review and assess the success of the implemented plan. This allows members of the community to tie their plan and actions to the resolution of the conflict. Problems arise at this step if, when the plan is not effective, the teacher punishes or takes actions that are not a part of the plan.

    The above conflict-resolution steps can be used also in connection with conflicts that arise when students bring their problem behavior to the classroom. While many types of behavior are problematic, socialization into a learning community prevents some of them from occurring (e.g., failure to complete tasks and general disruptive behavior due to boredom). The problems of students who are not particularly affected by a learning community are our next concern. We call these "crisis problems," because of their serious effects on the individual and potentially on the learning community.

Crisis Problems

Teachers indicate that five specific problems cause stress for them and their students in learning-community classrooms: (1) drugs, (2) dishonest behavior, (3) child abuse, (4) suicide, and (5) hostile-aggressive students.

Drugs

Who is responsible for helping students who are on drugs get referrals to individuals or agencies with the expertise and resources to help them? Our answer is, any person who knows that the student is in trouble. This includes his/her teacher. We believe a primary responsibility of our society is to nurture and protect its children. In America today, the serious threat to the health and well-being of our children is drug use. According to the Children's Defense Fund (1990), 17,674 children are arrested for drunken driving every year and 76,986 children are arrested for drug offenses (p. 3). Statistics related to children and drug abuse are clouded by the impact of parental substance abuse, and as a result, children may be "counted" under abuse/neglect data. A study of the 4,164 delinquent children who are under the direct supervision of the Department of Social Services in Michigan revealed the following: 41 percent use drugs regularly, 18 percent are drug-addicted or seriously abusive, 42 percent use alcohol regularly, and 17 percent either abuse alcohol or are alcohol-addicted.

Commonly abused drugs include alcohol, tobacco, cannabis, stimulants, inhalants, cocaine, psychedelics, depressants, and narcotics. The drug of choice in late childhood and early adolescence is alcohol. However, they indicate that while cigarettes and alcohol are the primary drugs abused in many elementary and middle schools, substance abuse in high schools requires sophisticated knowledge about a range of abuse substances and their effects.

Teachers should watch for symptoms such as those listed in Figure 10-2. These symptoms are clues to the teacher that the student may be in trouble. It is not always possible to determine whether children are using drugs, but the presence of any of these symptoms should at least alert the teacher to a potential problem.

Osborn and Osborn (1981) suggest that changes in behavior that teachers observe over time may also be indicators of a student problem (e.g., a student may become more compliant, may seem fatigued and do things at a slow speed, may become more moody, and/or may pay less attention to his/her appearance). In other words, such indicators may include changes in a student's relationships with others, feelings about himself/herself, emotional stability, work habits, and sense of time.

In addition, Osborn and Osborn (1981) have suggested five environmental factors, listed in Figure 10-3, that teachers should be aware of. These factors may be signs that students are interested or involved in drugs.

Oetting and Beauvais (1988) indicate that "drug use by young people is rooted in personal attitudes and values and in the youth's relationships with the family and peers" (p. 15). They believe that youths'

Red, watery eyes	Red, raw nostrils
Profuse perspiration and body odor	Constant licking of lips to keep them
Runny nose	moist
Sunglasses worn at inappropriate times,	Tremor of hands
to hide dilated pupils	Staggering and disorientation

(*Source:* Waiters, 1971, p. 156.)

FIGURE 10-2

Symptoms which should alert teachers to possible drug use. Note, however, that these symptoms can also be caused by other ailments.

primary problem is not addiction to the drug, but rather, that the students are experiencing emotional and developmental problems that have made them susceptible to becoming involved in lifestyles that include drug abuse. Newcomb and Bentler (1989) emphasize "that even though child or teenage drug use is an individual behavior, it is embedded in a sociocultural context that strongly determines its character and manifestations" (p. 242). School counselors need to assess all the psychosocial elements of a case; see Oetting and Beauvais (1988). From the perspective of these experts, drug use may be treated as part of the problem but not the entire problem. Teachers can be helpful in sharing this perspective with their students.

Many teachers find that they must deal with both prevention and intervention; each approach has different implications for different students. Prevention programs may be appropriate during preadolescence "because of the closer association between use and abuse during this developmental period" (Newcomb and Bentler, 1989, p. 246). However, some prevention programs may be inappropriate for adolescents, because this is a period of experimentation, exploration, and curiosity.

Although it is important to delay the onset of regular drug use as long as possible, to allow time for the development of adaptive and effective personal and interpersonal skills, it may be less important to prevent the use of drugs than the abuse, misuse, and problem use of drugs. . . . "Prevention and intervention should focus on the misuse, abuse, problem use, and heavy use of drugs to meet internal needs, cope with distress and avoid responsibility and important life decisions and difficulties." (Newcomb and Bentler, 1989, p. 246)

The problems brought to the classroom by students who abuse drugs require teachers to be informed about substance abuse and to be knowledgeable about the strengths and weaknesses of various programs. Unfortunately, we still have little reliable information available on these subjects. However, by keeping up to date, working with school counselors, and being aware of students' needs, teachers can respond realistically to the problems of students who use drugs.

In a review of programs related to alcohol and drug education in the elementary schools, Bradley (1988) indicates that in successful programs for preventing substance abuse, the two areas most frequently addressed are the development of appropriate social skills and the nurturance of self-esteem. We recommend Bradley's article on alcohol and drug education (see the Bibliography) as a resource for information about programs for elementary and middle schoolers. Those who have studied the nature and extent of alcohol and drug abuse among middle-school youths conclude that prevention programs are needed at both the elementary and the middle school levels to reverse current trends toward escalating the drug problem.

Dishonest Behavior

Most in-class dishonest behavior falls into either the category of stealing, as when students take things that belong to others, or the category of cheating, as when students use other peoples' work (answers, papers, projects) as their response to a given assignment, whether homework, classroom work, or tests. Many teachers find dishonest behavior to be one of the most difficult issues that they have to handle.

---

1. Use of drug terminology in conversation.
2. Drug phrases written on book covers, notebooks, desk, or walls.
3. Cigarette papers found on floors or in trash.
4. Plastic baggies or other drug paraphernalia in desks, cubbies, or lockers.
5. Magazines which are pro-drugs.

FIGURE 10-3
Environmental signs of drug use.

This may be because the covert nature of this kind of disruptive behavior means that teachers have to determine, usually based on information other than their own direct observation at the time the misbehavior occurred, who did what, if anything.

Cheating is a kind of dishonest behavior that frustrates teachers. First, cheating is a behavior that is, for the most part, incongruent with the classroom learning community, because the philosophy of community and the actions of the participants are primarily focused on helping, cooperation, and interdependence. Cheating can be reduced by the effect and nature of attitudes related to the classroom learning community. For example, working together in structured ways on projects and papers is acceptable behavior when cooperation and the goal of having everyone learn are key to the culture. Achieving understanding is a more important norm than just finishing papers and completing tests. However, teachers must work with students to help them to understand, appreciate, and accept the differences between learning practice conditions and individual evaluation.

Assertive behavior by the teacher supports the norm of honesty. Teachers who exhibit passive-aggressive behavior (giving pop quizzes or using tests that are inappropriate for what has been taught in the class) contribute to the cheating problem. Teachers can take action to reduce the probability of students' cheating. For example, they can be clear about the differences between group and individual work. Individual work is usually completed in class under supervision. When teachers wish to evaluate individual student achievement for various reasons, at various times, students may copy responses from their classmates. Houston (1986) found that college-age students copied less when they were assigned to particular seats than when they were allowed to select their own seats. He also found that students copied more when they knew and studied with the students they sat next to during tests. In testing situations, a concerned teacher monitors the class by walking around the room so that she/he can view the students from all angles.

Why do students steal? Psychologists have suggested that stealing may be connected to a problem of poor self-image. Stealing may be a way of asking for love, or seeking attention, or getting even with someone. Today, students' reasons for stealing may be related to doing drugs and the support of an expensive habit. Their immediate concern may not be love or attention but physical survival. Whatever the reason, theft is a major problem.

Stradley and Aspinall (1975) state, "theft should be treated as a major problem with special penalties attached" (p. 125). They believe that offenders should be counseled "in a positive way and treated in a fair manner" (p. 145). They also believe that parents should work closely with the school, to help their child. If, however, parents are unwilling to work with the school, they suggest, "there is little that the school can do except to take a strict disciplinary approach with the student" (p. 125). Today's classroom teacher also has a responsibility to report incidents of stealing as indicated in the particular school's building policy.

Stealing is a problem that a teacher must handle, whether something is taken within the classroom or whether a student reports that something was stolen from him/her outside the classroom. Stealing within the classroom community can be prevented by reducing the temptation to steal, through procedures which support efficient handling of personal goods and handing out and return of materials. Orderliness in the classroom environment helps both the teacher and the students to keep track of equipment and materials. Routines for borrowing school property or other people's belongings should be established. For example, a student who borrows an item for use in the classroom to accomplish an assigned task (such as an extra textbook or a pencil) can temporarily trade his/her ID card or shoe for the item to be borrowed.

When students report that articles have been taken from them outside the classroom, the teacher should see that the school's policy and related procedures for handling such incidents are followed. Each school has particular strategies for responding to these problems.

Miller and Klungness (1986) point out that, "among professionals there is a general consensus that treatment success is critically dependent on consistent labeling of all suspected or known stealing episodes by all of the significant adults in a child's life" (p. 33). Dodson and Evans (1985) suggest that school theft "has complex psychological and social underpinnings" (p. 522). They found that students perceive school theft as a serious problem. To develop a better understanding of school theft, they suggest, studies need to be carried out in the early grades, as they may help us understand how it starts and how perceptions are formed.

Williams (1985) suggests that, for young children, theft may be simply normal experimental stealing or may even be caused by an undeveloped understanding of property rights—not knowing that objects belong to a person or a group. However, even developmental stealing is a problem for others, and socialization of students to personal property norms is necessary. She suggests that parents and teachers act as socialization agents when they:

1. *Give young children verbal or visual cues as needed to help them understand the concept of personal property.*
2. *Recognize and label the child's possessing of items that he does not own as stealing.*
3. *Clearly state rules regarding property ownership and [ask] for permission to use items belonging to others.*
4. *Consistently apply appropriate consequences after every instance of parent-defined stealing.*
5. *At a later time, discuss the theft, its consequences, and its effect on others. . . .*
6. *Refrain from reinforcing the child for periods of "not stealing," but reinforce the child for specific prosocial behaviors. (Williams, 1985, p. 21)*

Williams also recommends that, in addition to the above suggestions, four guidelines can help when a teacher is required to deal with theft detections, as follows:

1. *Clearly state rules and authority to search a child's possessions based upon the establishment of probable cause, particularly for older children and youth.*
2. *Carefully observe and monitor the behavior of all children and record instances of unusual behavior.*
3. *Refrain from being a "detective" and indiscriminately searching a child's possessions.*
4. *Ask children about unusual behavior or the possession of questionable objects. (Williams, 1985, p. 22)*

Child Abuse

Child abuse, according to the Position Statement of the American School Counselors Association (ASCA), is (1) any infliction by other than accidental means of physical harm upon the body of a child and/or (2) any unrelenting psychological damage to children and/or denial of the child's emotional needs (ASCA, 1988, p. 262). According to the ASCA, child neglect is defined as the failure to provide necessary food, care, clothing, shelter, supervision, or medical attention (p. 262). The ASCA also recognizes that corporal punishment by school authorities might well be considered child abuse. Corporal punishment has recently become illegal in Michigan.

In *Children 1990,* published by the Children's Defense Fund (1990), each day 1,849 children (about 675,000 a year) are abused or neglected (p. 3). In the first nine months of 1990, the Michigan Department of Social Services investigated approximately 50,000 cases; 15,881 families were documented as having actual abuse and neglect cases. It is possible that these 15,881 families include approximately 25,000 children. Physical neglect prevailed as the most common problem, which includes issues of food, clothing, and shelter. More specifically, approximately 10,000 cases of physical neglect were documented as well as 5,000 cases of physical injury and 2,000 cases of sexual abuse. Most children impacted by abuse were young, about age three. During any given year, the Michigan Department of Social Services assumes direct responsibility for approximately 16,000 children who are victims of child abuse and neglect.

Many states have child abuse reporting laws. Spiegel (1988) points out that "second only to parents, educators in general and school counselors specifically play a crucial role in protecting the health and well being of children" (p. 281). Allsopp and Posen (1988) recognized that teachers may be the first adults to become aware of child sexual abuse and that they may not be trained to deal with the problem. They also point out that sexual activity between children and adults is a crime in every state. They document the fact that, in addition, persons who work with children are required by law to report all suspected cases of child sexual victimization (p. 300).

To find out what the policy and practices are in a given school, teachers should ask for information about current state laws and proposed legislation, the specific school district system procedures, the requirements for reporting suspected child sexual abuse, and the nature of support offered to teachers by school counselors.

We suggest that teachers and teacher candidates listen carefully to children. If an abuse problem is suspected, reporting it to the proper authority in the school building is the first step. We also suggest documenting observations, by writing a behavior description, recording the dates, and recording to whom and when the report was made. Remember that the well-being of a child must be considered the highest priority in a strong democratic society.

Herman (1985) identified eighteen indicators of sexual abuse that would suggest further investigation, when two or more occur at the same time. Figure 10-4 gives examples from this list.

Spiegel (1988) emphasizes the important pivotal role that counselors play during investigations of abuse. He warns that the first step is to be aware of the child abuse hysteria syndrome. While school counselors must be involved in cases and cannot simply file a form and excuse themselves, they can impress upon caseworkers their own doubts and concerns, and they can urge those individuals to exercise caution in forming conclusions.

Suicide

At first glance, you might wonder why, in a classroom organization and management book, we have included the topic of suicide. The reason is that our experiences over the last ten years have suggested that we should at least look into this topic. Teachers whom we talk with report that they confront suicide in various situations and manifestations. In our review of this topic we found that there has been an increase in suicide rates. For example, Lewis and Associates (1988) report an increase in the suicide rate since 1960 for adolescents of 5.1 per 100,000, while the general population increase was 1.6 per 100,000 during the same period. Approximately 2,200 teenagers commit suicide each year (Children's Defense Fund, 1990). Suicide rates for children ages ten to fourteen, have increased from 0.5 per 100,000 to 1.1 per 100,000 in 1982. Five- to nine-year-olds currently have a suicide rate of 0.1 per 100,000.

The authors' review of the literature also indicates a focus on suicide attempters and an effort to try to understand who they are and how to help them. Only a limited amount of literature and information on what to do to help is available; experience suggests that teachers and friends may be able to help the troubled person. Even though the need to handle suicide situations in a school context may not occur often, the problem is one with which teachers need to be familiar. Teachers who have some ideas about constructive ways to act in suicide situations will be helpful to their students. One question to ask in each teaching environment is how students who communicate that they are considering suicide may be responded to. Likewise, a school should have guidelines for dealing with the human responses to a case of successful suicide.

- Sophisticated sexual knowledge, beyond that expected for age.
- Student tells teacher about abusive behavior.
- Evidence of physical injury.
- Moodiness, excessive crying.
- Gender role confusion.
- Unnatural interest in own or other's genitals.

(*Source:* Herman, 1985, p. 174.)

FIGURE 10-4
Symptoms of potential child abuse.

A study of 26 attempters, ages nine to eighteen, were compared with 725 nonattempters on measures of school achievement, educational goals, socioeconomic status, and depression. It was found that:

> As has been found in studies using clinical samples, suicide attempters in our community-based sample had significantly lower school achievement than nonattempters. The relationship between attempted suicide and low school achievement seemed to be explained by the effects of depression. Lower-SES [Social Economic Status] youths tended to be more likely to attempt suicide than higher-SES youths. However, SES appeared to have little effect on the relationship between attempted suicide and school achievement. Results also suggest that children of mothers with low educational goals for them may be more at risk for attempted suicide than youths whose mothers have higher educational goals for their children. (Lewis et al., 1988, p. 459)

Adults who observe the deterioration of a student's mental health are in a position to take action. Often a student is demonstrating clues in the hope that a teacher will observe them and take some kind of action. However, other students do not give warning signals to anyone. Thus, a teacher must be prepared to handle the effects of an attempted or successful suicide upon the student's classmates and other teachers. Some school districts have a policy for directing the professional response to be offered when a student has committed suicide. Additionally, some districts provide opportunities for teachers to learn constructive and helpful responses to the living victims of a suicide, both in the immediate aftermath and long-term.

In some districts, classroom teachers work with counselors, administrators, and other community resources to provide a strong supportive response to the districts' students. However, some teachers are employed in school districts which are not organizationally prepared to respond to the suicide crisis. As with most situations which are not covered by federal or state law, school districts have different plans for handling problems generated by suicides. One school system has made arrangements with other school districts around the county to draw all counselors from county schools to a school where a suicide has occurred. This arrangement makes it possible for all students to talk in small groups with personnel trained to work through problems created by suicide.

In addition, parents of students who were particularly close to the victim are called to school to talk about their children's responses and learn about ways to be supportive and helpful.

When teachers are dealing with a student who is contemplating suicide, Martin and Dixon (1986) recommend, they "should immediately refer the student to the school counselor" (p. 270). After the referral, teachers should expect that the counselor will conduct an evaluation and inform the student of the counselor's right to warn others of a potential suicide. The counselor will inform the student's parents as well as teachers, the principal, and the school psychologist. Teachers should express their expectations that the school psychologist or other mental health professional of the family's choosing will take therapeutic responsibility.

Sheeley and Herllihy (1989) present a somewhat different perspective on the role of the counselor and what teachers can expect. They state:

> The balance between confidentiality and the duty to warn others is delicate. The ethical codes states that the school counselor owes a duty of confidentiality to student clients and the counselor should not disclose, or be required to disclose in individually identifiable form, any information about any student client without the client's explicit authorization, unless the disclosures would be: (a) to another mental health provider who is being consulted in connection with the treatment of the student by the counselor or (b) to a properly identifiable recipient, when it is necessary to show compelling circumstances that affect the health and safety of the student client. (p. 94)

Given that some professional counselors take this position, it is incumbent upon teachers to clarify their line of responsibility. With such serious student problems, the teacher's professional task is to identify the specific procedures and perspective under which a given school district operates. Teachers are advised to be prepared to act assertively with administrative and counseling officials to ensure that student needs are met.

Hostile-Aggressive Students

In the late 1970s and early 1980s, Brophy and Rohrkemper and classroom teachers at the Institute for Research on Teaching at Michigan State University worked together to study teacher responses to students with problem behavior. They selected teachers from two urban school districts in grades K–6 who were nominated by their principals as either outstanding or average at dealing with problem students. They found that differences between outstanding and average teachers were surprisingly small. They suggested that this might be true because teachers who worked well with one type of problem did not necessarily do well with other types. More important, they concluded that few teachers, regardless of their experience or reputation, are well prepared to deal with hostile-aggressive students.

Brophy and Rohrkemper (1989) reported that when higher-rated teachers responded to hostile-aggressive students they tended to be both power-assertive and instructive. They also had confidence in their ability to change students and determination to do so. Higher-rated teachers told students their rationales for the changes in behavior they expected. They also provided instruction in ways that students found more acceptable.

Brophy and Rohrkemper found that, in contrast, low-rated teachers were mostly coercive and not instructive in their responses. Low-rated teachers made confused attempts to control the behavior of aggressive students rather than making systematic attempts to change students in fundamental ways (1989, p. 72). These teachers had limited and vague ideas about how to respond to aggressive students. Some even tried to deny any responsibility for coping with such students. However, most indicated that they would involve the principal or other professionals, because they lacked ideas on how to handle these students.

Brophy and Rohrkemper (1989) underline the point that the lack of effectiveness of these low-rated teachers is not caused by their reliance on well-articulated but ineffective methods (such as catharsis or physical punishment). Instead, they are ineffective because they lack well-articulated ideas about how to cope with aggressive students and thus end up responding in ways that are not systematic or powerful enough to be effective (p. 71).

Arrington and Rose (1987) report that young children often use physical confrontation to resolve conflicts and speculate that this is due to the models they have experienced (i.e., the way they have been treated). When they break a rule, they are frequently spanked. Therefore, framing the classroom learning-community environment for children as one where physical aggression is not acceptable is a necessary part of stage III.

Children in our society are having trouble. The Children's Defense Fund (1990) reports that on a given day 135,000 children bring a gun to school (p. 4). Gennings-Moton (1990) reports that approximately 40,000 juveniles (over age twelve) were arrested for crimes in Michigan in 1988. The overall crime rate for children has decreased in Michigan (down 7 percent from 1987 to 1988), but the number of serious offenses has increased. She indicates that criminal behavior by children is categorized in two ways:

1. "Crimes that children commit." These are serious offenses that children commit that adults are offenders of as well (murder, robbery, rape).
2. "Status offenses." These are crimes that only children can be found guilty of (truancy, running away).

The number of crimes that children commit has increased, while the status offenses have decreased.

Finally, discipline problems may be caused by the teacher. For example, nonassertive or aggressive teacher behavior may contribute to classroom problems.

Assessment of Policy

Preparation for stage III also involves assessment of school and district policy and resources. For the purposes of this stage, what is of concern is policies on discipline, as well as the services and procedures provided by the district. The authors' work has led us to believe that, in order for teachers to get help, they must figure out who will help them and how to get the help. Policies differ at each school.

Variance in practices necessitates teacher assessment to figure out what is expected. Teachers must ask directly for information. They need to specifically assess the support staff (e.g., counselors and school psychologists) and procedures for handling problems. We recommend that teachers prepare descriptions of three problem situations and use these as the basis for interviewing building resource persons and administrative staff.

The descriptions should be context-specific: that is, they should involve context-specific situations likely to occur in that specific school. Here are three examples of problems:

1. *Attendance*   George has been absent from school on Mondays and Fridays for the first three weeks of school. He is on task in school, but is always working on makeup work. He is getting further and further behind. You called his mother this morning and she said he was sick. George told you he works Fridays through Mondays to help support the family.
2. *Homework*   Nancyann has not completed one homework assignment in three weeks.
3. *Drug use*   Howard told you that Alex is taking overdoses of pills in front of other students. Howard also said that Alex has changed a lot and that he is worried about Alex.

To create each problem vignette, identify roles, the problem, and responsible actions that the teacher would take initially to respond to the problem. Describe each situation to the counselor and the principal. Follow the description by asking questions such as: "If this were to occur, what policy and procedures would you expect me to follow? What ones would you follow?" and "What outcome would you expect relative to this situation?" Results of this sort of interviews with the principal and counselor provide teachers with clues about the individual school's actual practices as they are related to stated school and district policy.

Preparations for stage III provide a foundation for the teacher's future actions. They also provide a basis for actions that will be congruent with a learning-community culture. This is the last stage in establishing the learning community. Once progress has been made in this stage, an approximation of the learning-community environment will be visible.

IMPLEMENTATION

Some teachers hold a romantic notion that good teachers take on responsibility for the lives of their students. We hold that wise teachers know their expertise (teaching/learning) and seek other resources to help students handle serious personal problems.

Conflicts generally fall into two categories: conflicts related to learning-community life and conflicts resulting from problems that students bring to the classroom. The learning community teacher can teach students an adaptation of Gordon's no-lose process (1974), through the use of role-playing, which will help to resolve learning-community conflicts. For conflicts resulting from problem behavior brought to the classroom by students, teachers can use contracts coupled with an assertive stance that protects the group from learning disruption and supports responsible resolution of problems by students.

Teaching Conflict Resolution

The first step in implementing a plan for this stage is to teach students how to resolve problems constructively. Providing students with opportunities to role-play conflict identification and resolution before actual conflicts arise allows them to learn constructive strategies before they are needed and during a time when their emotions are under control. Thus they can focus on the impact of the process and the process itself. Starting with low-risk situations allows students to learn the process and the necessary communication skills (e.g., active listening and self-disclosure statements such as "I" statements).

One example of how to teach these communication skills to students is through the use of "Practicing Pairs" (which is also described in Chapter 9). Begin the instruction by having the whole class brainstorm topics that pairs could discuss at a later time. The topics chosen should not represent conflicts but should provide opportunities for students to communicate positions, information, and feelings. List the topics on the board so that they can be seen throughout the classroom.

Next, list the communication skills to be practiced. Provide two examples of statements that illustrate each skill and one example that is not accurate. For example, to illustrate a clarifying question the teacher might say, "You said the wax on your skis needs to be changed. Why would you change the wax?" and "I don't understand how you do that. What process do you use to change the wax?" These questions would be followed by an inappropriate example, such as, "You do *what* to your skis?"

After the teacher provides the illustrations for a given communication skill, several students are asked to give their own examples. The teacher provides positive or corrective feedback and then gives the students record-keeping forms (see Table 10-1). Pairs of students practice the skills by discussing one of the select topics recorded on the board. Students are instructed that whenever another student uses a skill, they are to tally it on the form. Likewise, whenever a student believes that his/her partner used one of the skills, they should tally that also. Once the discussion begins and each person talks at least three times (which should take about six minutes total), the pairs can compare their record sheets. If one student believes she/he asked ten clarifying questions and the partner believes it was only five, they should clarify their understandings. Each person should recall as many of the questions as possible, so that the questions can be analyzed to see whether they fit the criteria. Remember, the purpose of this practice activity is to provide individual, written, concrete experiences using specific communication skills. The record-keeping forms are to be turned in at the end of the session for teacher review.

During the practice time, the teacher listens to the students to assess their skills. After the first topics have been discussed, and students and teacher think they all have the idea of each skill, it is time to use the skills in conflict resolution.

First, the teacher should set the context for practicing conflict resolution. Students can be prepared for use of role-plays in learning conflict-resolution skills by reviewing the rationale for establishing a learning community, including expected student outcomes. Second, the teacher should point out that: (1) conflict is viewed as normal in a learning community, (2) conflict can be identified, and (3) conflict can be resolved constructively. Third, he/she should explain how the strategies to be taught for conflict identification and resolution support the expected outcomes—that is, the idea that a learning community can bring about constructive resolution.

TABLE 10-1   RECORD-KEEPING FORM FOR "PRACTICING PAIRS"

Communication Skill	Number of Times I Used the Skill	Number of times Partner Used the Skill
1. Exploratory questions		
2. Clarifying questions		
3. Self-disclosure		
4. Listening		
a. Paraphrasing		
b. Nonverbal		
5. Encouraging others		
6. Giving information		
7. Comparing		
8. Contrasting		
9. Synthesizing		

Fourth, the teacher should model the conflict-identification and conflict-resolution process. Having students role-play is one way to provide a model. Another is to a play a videotape of a conflict-resolution discussion between the teacher and another adult. Next, the teacher's personalized conflict-resolution strategy can be presented (taught). That is, the steps can be explained and illustrated. Then three students can be assigned to each group. One person is the observer, and the other two represent the different sides of a conflict. Each group of students then talks its way through one of the conflicts that are listed on the board. The observer participates by helping the others to remember to include all the steps in the problem-solving model. After two members of the group have reached some agreement about the conflict, the members switch roles and work through another role-play.

After the process has been modeled, the teacher can once again have the students brainstorm conflicts for use as practice topics, list the topics on the board, and assign the students to pairs. Each pair of students can then select two topics for discussion. Each student writes a vignette for one of the conflicts, including the context, participants, and the initial interaction that illustrates the conflict. As an alternative, the pairs of students generate descriptions of problems that might interfere with their learning community and write the vignettes.

Teachers from the primary grades through high school tell us that using role-plays to work through conflicts that typically occur between members of the learning community provides positive examples and practice. These teachers report that the role-plays provide concrete examples to refer to when a real conflict arises (e.g., how to talk to each other and potential solutions). They also report that learning a process for resolving conflicts prepares the class for handling real conflicts when they do occur.

Other teachers with whom we have worked do not use role-plays. Instead, they watch for conflicts that occur early in the year. Then they facilitate conflict resolution by working with the entire class at one time. They lead the class step by step through a problem-solving process. Once the conflict has been resolved, they go back and review what has been done, write the steps on a chart, and indicate that this model will help them to resolve their conflicts in the future.

Seeking Assistance

Though advance planning helps to prepare teachers for handling disruptions, there are two points at which teachers should seek help. Teachers should request assistance to prevent problems and to respond to crisis problems.

Preventing Problems

Before a serious problem arises, but after a pattern of potentially destructive behavior has been established, the teacher should take preventive action. He/she should seek the assistance of building or district resource personnel to help in clarifying situations and in determining whether the situations have the potential for becoming problems. Then plans can be made for the prevention of potential problem behavior.

No one understands the impact of behavior on the class as well as the teacher and the students. Thus, when the teacher asks someone from outside the learning community to help with a problem, five actions are needed, to increase the potential for a successful consultation.

First, the teacher needs to document observations of the potential problem behavior. One way to do this is to keep records on 4 x 6 index cards in the back of the schedule book or record book. Teachers who have access to a computer can create a confidential file in which to record problem behavior. When the problem behavior is observed the teacher jots down: (1) the time, (2) the date, (3) the behavior, (4) what occurred just before the behavior appeared, (5) the students' responses to the behavior, and (6) the teacher's responses to the behavior. Besides providing the necessary documentation, these notes also help the resource person to understand the history of the problem, as observed by the teacher.

Second, the teacher needs to ask the resource person to spend time in the classroom. The teacher and the resource person should work together to plan the amount of time needed for this observation. Enough time should be allowed to enable the resource person to acquire information about the duration, frequency, and effects of the potential problem behavior.

On one occasion, one of the authors was asked to observe and talk to a teacher about the behavior of a specific student. After observing the behavior several times during a two-hour period, the observer still did not understand the teacher's concern. The effects on the students and the teacher that had been reported by the teacher were not evident. When the observer told this to the teacher, the teacher said, "You haven't been here long enough; just be patient." By the middle of the afternoon, the observer was able to see an increase in the problem behavior and the effect on the other students that had been reported by the teacher. It would have been easy for the observer to decide prematurely that the problem was not real. This illustrates the danger of making outsider observations without taking enough time to acquire an understanding of the community's norms.

Third, after an outside observation, the teacher and the resource person should compare notes, so that they can clarify their ideas and develop a shared understanding from a joint perspective and on the basis of the expertise that both can bring to the situation.

Fourth, the teacher may wish to suggest to the resource person a plan for changing the situation. The plan should be congruent with the teacher's expertise and available information. In effect, the teacher is saying, "This is what I think I can do about this problem now." The resource person provides feedback, and together they develop a plan that they will carry out. The resource person, in effect, is saying, "Here is my idea about your plan and your earlier observations, and here is what I can do to provide support and to help prevent this situation from becoming a serious problem for the student."

Fifth, the teacher and the resource person should meet again, after the plan has been implemented. The purposes of this meeting are: (1) to give the teacher an opportunity to review the effects of the implementation of the plan, (2) to allow the resource person to share additional information that she/he may have gathered, (3) to determine whether the current plan is sufficient or even still needed, and (4) to determine whether additional help is needed.

Responding to Crises

Teachers also need to ask for assistance when a crisis occurs. The five problems explored at the beginning of this chapter are the sort for which teachers usually need additional help. The primary role of the teacher is to facilitate student understandings as related to the functions of schooling. Resource personnel are educated to provide support for teachers and students and to respond to problems but not to substitute for the teacher. They most frequently work with individuals or with small groups of students and are not responsible for learning outcomes for groups of twenty-two to forty students.

Teachers need to carry out their primary role of instruction and to ask resource people to provide the support that students and teachers need to solve crisis problems. We do agree with Brophy and Rohrkemper (1980) that teachers need to stay involved in supporting students who are exhibiting destructive behavior, while the resource people are trying to eliminate the behavior. Thus, a partnership between a resource person and a classroom teacher lets each take responsibility for his/her primary job; this gives the student the best of both worlds. Working together, the two professionals and the student are able to develop contracts and other strategies that will help the student to become a constructive and contributing member of the classroom learning community.

Dealing with Other Classroom Problems

Not all classroom problems are of a crisis nature. Some disruptions to learning occur because of factors that are under the control and responsibility of the teacher. Such things as inappropriate tasks, poor instruction, and a room that is too hot or too cold contribute to learning disruptions but can be remedied by action of the teacher and learners. One method for preventing disruptive behavior caused by such factors is to monitor the class and respond early to clues that students may be becoming disengaged from the learning process. These clues range from students' reactions to stuffy air, to their finishing a task within a couple of minutes of its assignment, to their simply not being engaged, even with the benefit of clear directions and individual help. Teacher responsiveness to such indicators help to make the classroom a learning environment for all children.

Responses to early cues of off-task behavior may include asking students to explain their thinking up to the point at which they got stuck or helping them to link new information to their prior knowledge. Such responses help to maintain the learning environment through instructional responses rather than through authoritarian dictates (e.g., "Get back to work!").

Thoughtful responses also contribute to learning rather than distracting learners. On occasion, a student will have an off day. If off days occur frequently, resource help may be needed for that student. However, if a student simply has an infrequent out-of-sorts day, the teacher can ask him/her to take time out, to allow for regaining self-control.

One elementary teacher taught her students to identify the times when they were having trouble being responsible members of the community. On these occasions, a student would ask to go to a time-out place in the classroom, and then would make the decision about when to reenter the group. If a student stayed in the time-out place for more than fifteen minutes, the teacher would check on the student and inquire whether there was something she could do to help. Sometimes the teacher and student would make an appointment to talk at noon, after school, or before school the next day.

When learning is disrupted in a classroom, it is the teacher's responsibility to restore the environment to one in which learning can continue. The first step is to quietly talk to the disruptive student to indicate that a particular behavior is unacceptable. If the behavior recurs, the teacher can, again quietly, ask the student what is happening/wrong/going on. Note that, when a teacher is working to restore a learning environment, there is no reason to take actions that are disrespectful and degrading to the student or the teacher. The point is to decrease the disruption so that learning can once again occur. Teachers who cause a scene in response to disruptive behavior contribute to increasing the negative emotional level and the amount of time during which the class is disrupted. Students sometimes take disrespectful and other out-of-control teacher behaviors as models for ways to assure their rights and responsibilities—which is another reason to avoid these inappropriate behaviors.

Assertive and firm statements and/or commands, when necessary, help to communicate that the teacher means business. Students who continue to bully teachers and students after all other appropriate responses have been tried must be warned about what action the teacher intends to take next. The teacher must communicate what action will be taken if the student decides to further disrupt the classroom, and must also let the student know the reasons for the action (e.g., protection of rights for learners and teacher responsibility).

Sending students out of the classroom signals either that a long-range plan is being carried out (one that was worked out among the student, counselor, and teacher) or that a crisis problem exists and that help for the teacher and student is needed. Remember Good and Brophy's (1986) principles for effective punishment. Watch to see whether sending a student from the room does in fact suppress the disruptive behavior for some period. Some students see being sent out of class as a desirable goal, and thus taking this action will actually reinforce the disruptive behavior.

Educators have two distinctly different points of view on sending students to the office of the principal, the assistant principal, the deputy principal, a counselor, or a security officer. One perspective is that teachers need to teach and others should discipline students. The second is that teaching includes the responsibility for creating a classroom culture that engages all students in learning. This is not to say that teachers don't need support in handling the crisis problems identified earlier. The authors' position is that simply eliminating students who do not initially share the teacher's excitement and interest in the subject matter or in learning is not professional. Engaging all children, so that all children will have equal access to knowledge, is the job of the professional teacher. Schools that permit streams of students to be sent out of classrooms are functioning as custodial institutions, not as learning institutions. Teachers who habitually lose control of their classrooms should either learn how to engage today's learners or seek an alternative career.

Finally, when one or more students try to push a teacher or another student around verbally or physically, it is frightening. If a teacher finds such confrontive student behavior intimidating, she/he should get professional help with either self-concept, assertive behavior, or self-defense strategies. Personal improvements such as these may help the teacher feel more secure. For some teachers, however, the problem is not confrontive behavior, but rather working with students who are not like the teacher.

Based on observations of student and teacher behavior in an urban junior high and a suburban junior high classroom, Lasley (1981) concluded that "teachers are instrumental in both causing and preventing discipline problems" (p. 149). He suggests that teachers contribute to problems when they ignore students' cultural backgrounds and learning needs and that acknowledging the presence and importance of such factors can reduce or eliminate certain kinds of problems. For example, Lasley reports that students in both urban and suburban classrooms displayed coping behaviors. These behaviors in the suburban school were more often tacit and subtle, and thus were acceptable to teachers with largely middle-class value systems. Urban students' coping behavior includes verbal jousting and posturing, which are antithetical to the middle-class value system. In both the urban and the suburban settings, students saw their coping behaviors as acceptable. Teachers in the two settings, who held similar middle-class value systems, saw one set of coping behaviors as acceptable and the other as unacceptable.

In this case, working with other teachers who are successful with a wide range of students and who have different values, backgrounds, and/or skin color may help to reduce the feelings of intimidation. If these or other strategies do not help, again the teacher should choose another profession.

REFLECTING

At this stage in the establishment of the classroom learning community, two types of reflection need to occur. First comes reflection on conflict identification and resolution, which involves assessing the ability of the teacher and students to identify and resolve conflicts. The second type of reflection at this time should cover the entire process of establishing the classroom as a learning community.

Conflict Resolution

Reflecting on the relationships between instruction and the ways in which conflict is handled involves identifying the practices that are taking place. Two sets of observations need to be made. The first set should answer the questions "When problems arise, who initiates their resolution?" and "What do students do that shows their support (or lack thereof) for each other, even in conflict situations?"

If, every time a problem occurs, the teacher has to assume responsibility to get it resolved, then students have not acquired a sense of their responsibility as members of the learning community. This conclusion leads the teachers to plan additional conflict identification and resolution activities. At this point, using naturally occurring situations contributes to helping students see their roles. The teacher can introduce the problem. She/he next reminds students about the steps they practiced and then facilitates group discussion, from agreement that there is a problem to the implementation of the resolution. The teacher can then ask the student to facilitate the process for a second problem to be discussed. The teacher then asks the students to identify their roles in problem(s) solving, helping them to see that they can manage the process without the teacher.

Another question to consider during reflection is "What type of behavior(s) do I use during conflict situations?" Frequently, teachers and teacher candidates with whom we work have trouble integrating

TABLE 10-2   NONASSERTIVE, ASSERTIVE, AND AGGRESSIVE BEHAVIORS

Nonassertive Behavior	Assertive Behavior	Aggressive Behavior
Am I violating my rights?	Am I standing up for my rights and not violating the rights of others?	Am I standing up for my rights dishonestly, or am I inappropriately violating the rights of others?
Am I communicating others' rights but not mine?	Am I communicating that we all have rights?	Am I communicating that my rights dominate others' rights?
Am I communicating that I am weak and you are strong?	Am I communicating that we both are competent?	Am I communicating that I am strong and you are weak?
Are my nonverbal actions distracting from statements?	Are my nonverbal and verbal actions congruent, fluent, and firm?	Are my communications condescending, parental, or sarcastic?
Am I afraid of approval?	Am I maximizing chances that both parties' needs can be met?	Am I afraid of losing control of myself or others?
Am I developing an image of weakness and manipulation through guilt?	Am I developing honest, constructive relationships?	Am I developing relationships in which others do not get their needs met?

Source: Adapted from concepts described in *Responsible Assertive Behavior,* by Patricia J. Kubowski and Arthur Lange. Champagne, Ill.: Research Press, 1976.

the ideas of learning-community teacher behavior and assertive behavior. They seem to develop a misperception that learning-community teachers are nonassertive. Asking the questions in Table 10-2 can help teachers to assess both their own and students' interactions. Helping students to make assertive rather than aggressive or nonassertive statements will contribute to the quality of the learning community and its smooth running.

One way to use Table 10-2 is to identify particular problems that need to be worked through. Then think through three ways (assertive, nonassertive, and aggressive) in which the problem can be discussed. Analyze each of the three kinds of interactions, identifying the essential elements of each that make it nonassertive, assertive, or aggressive. Comparing the nonassertive and aggressive messages with the assertive message will help to clarify the differences between messages that are appropriate for the learning community and those that are not.

Being sure one is clear about the roles of the teacher, the roles of specialists, and the administrators is a third area for reflection. It should be noted that, in reviewing the literature and in talking with educational resource personnel, the authors found that the norms for the behavior of such personnel were very different from the norms of regular classroom teachers. Therefore, teachers who reflect on their own actions in guiding the resolution of classroom problems and in assisting students to get the services they need from specialists may find themselves confused about the actions of specialists. For example, counselors and school psychologists, as part of their membership in professional organizations, make a commitment to a policy which supports the privacy of individuals. However, some do have legal forms, to be signed by clients, that allow the counselor to inform others in the case the clients indicate that they are going to hurt themselves or someone else. Where reflection raises questions, direct conversation with the involved specialists will help to clarify the confusion.

The authors believe that classroom teachers should take deliberate action to help students. Teachers should use the procedures made explicit by policy in a given school district, should ask for the policy statements, and should document all actions that they take in helping students to get the services they deserve and need. The documents that teachers create will provide a basis for reflection on teachers' professional responsibility to students who have problems.

Establishment of a Learning-Community Culture

Reflecting is an ongoing process. Toward the end of stage III in the establishment of a learning community is an appropriate time for systematically taking stock. Now is the time for making adjustments, changing misconceptions, and clarifying confusions. The teacher and students have spent enough time together to make it possible to determine the effects of implementation of the teacher's plans.

We suggest that, at this time, teachers review their plans and construct observation forms and checklists to support reflection. As examples, we have identified four items that provide ideas for topics for reflection instruments. These include leadership, development, problem solving, and cooperation.

The organization and monitoring tasks of teachers and students, here at the end of stage III, are to make sure they are moving toward the stated purposes and that the process is congruent with the intended outcomes. Thus, our heuristic for this section is monitoring.

We suggest that a way for teachers and students to monitor the progress of the community and individual members is by asking a set of questions and looking for evidence to answer the questions both in the literal sense and in the spirit of the learning community. The questions focus on monitoring activity in relation to community leadership, development, problem solving, and cooperation. We pose the following monitoring questions:

1. *Monitoring leadership*   Do we all raise questions, make suggestions, and offer criticism?

2. *Monitoring development*   Can all members accurately describe their individual progress and their sense of the collective progress of the group?

3. *Monitoring problem solving*   Are we solving problems together? What kind?

4. *Monitoring cooperation*   Do we all ask for help and respond to others' requests for help?

In addition to monitoring leadership, development, problem solving, and cooperating, the learning-community teacher can also assess specifics. For example, assessing the effectiveness of routines, pupil accountability, and overall problem-solving effectiveness provides useful information to the learning-community teacher. Checklists can help to focus data collection.

Checklists can be created based on insights or questions raised by monitoring of activities. For example. noticing that several students don't follow procedures raises questions about whether the procedures may need to be adjusted. A checklist of this purpose could be developed similar to the one in Table 10-3.

TABLE 10-3   CHECKLIST TO DETERMINE WHETHER THE LEARNING COMMUNITY HAS BEEN ESTABLISHED

Procedures	Yes	No	Needs Attention

Mark each of the procedures below in terms of its relevance to your specific learning community. Mark "Yes" if it needs no attention. Mark "No" if it does not belong in the community, and mark "Needs attention" if it is functioning improperly.

I.   Procedures to promote instructional time and engaged time.

   A. Occurring on a regular basis:

      1. Getting started (at beginning of the day, hour, session, activity)

      2. Taking and reporting attendance, lunch counts

      3. Movement for instruction

         Students

         Furniture

      4. Getting and putting away materials

      5. Getting and turning in student assignments

      6. Transitions

      7. Aides

   B. Occurring on an irregular basis:

      1. Visitors

      2. Administrative requests

II. Procedures to promote successful outcomes.

   A. Helping

   B. Feedback, written and verbal

   C. Bringing closure to lessons

   D. Evaluation

   E. Assuming responsibility

   F. Calling on students to promote equal access to speaking time

III. Procedures for maintaining a classroom learning community.

   A. Celebrating

   B. Explicit routines for solving problems

IV. Housekeeping procedures that promote student accountability, responsibility, and shared teacher and student ownership of the classroom.

CHANGING THE CLASSROOM MANAGEMENT PARADIGM

Metaphor One: Traditional Classroom Management Culture

George Wilson is an urban middle school English teacher. He teaches seventh and eighth grades. He is also the advisor for the school paper. Mr. Wilson says that he is a frustrated writer who is waiting for the day when he can retire and devote his life to writing critical essays for the little journals. In fact, he loves teaching poetry and literature to middle school students who are still in their formative years.

Mr. Wilson has a reputation as a strict disciplinarian: "I take no back talk from anyone, much less from my students," he says. He has five rules for classroom decorum on the bulletin board; the list is on the board before students come to the first day of class and stays in the same spot all year. If a student breaks a rule, he records it in his grade book and deals out punishment (ranging from extra homework to detention, to talks with the vice-principal) according to the severity of the infraction of Mr. Wilson's rules. The students say that Wilson is fair and not too hard if you pay attention to what he says is important and "if he says it is important, it will be on the test." They also observe that when called on, male students are asked to expand their ideas. Females are called on about once to every five males, and they are asked to expand their ideas.

Wilson says that he is strict because he cannot waste precious class time on distractions and disruptions when there is so much information for the student to learn and so much literature for them to read and appreciate. He is big on teaching literature because "it is dealing with the most cherished memory of our society, shared with us by the best writers of the past." Wilson sees his role as giving information, selecting the best examples of good literature, and introducing students to the classics. "They don't know it now," he says, "but they will thank me later for being a tough teacher with good taste." His students know the 10 most important American writers, and they can name important poets and dramatists.

The principal and visitors to Mr. Wilson's classes remark that he is an interesting lecturer and has control of the students. The role of visitors when in Wilson's class is to sit and become part of the audience for his presentation.

Metaphor Two: Classroom Learning Community Culture

John Gunnings is an urban middle school mathematics teacher. He works with three other teachers as a member of an eighth grade teaching team. Gunnings considers his classroom as a community within a larger village. He sees the school as the village and the principal as the mayor. Gunnings thinks it is all right to call his class "Gunnings' Neighborhood," even if it sounds corny. He talks a lot about his neighborhood and what makes it work. For example, he says, "there is much to do because there is much to learn, so everyone must have a role." Gunnings uses social metaphor when he is talking with the students and their parents about the class because it emphasizes the active role that every student must play if the whole neighborhood is to be a successful and satisfying place to study and learn.

Mr. Gunnings prefers to call the teaching and learning experiences "investigations." He sees teaching mathematics as a matter of inviting students to conduct investigations about numbers and other mathematical phenomena. Instead of lecturing, he most often poses problems or dilemmas for class discourse. He sees his role as engaging students in meaningful "math talk." To achieve high student participation in class discourse, Gunnings spends a lot of time early in the year developing a common vocabulary with his students. They learn to talk about "theories," to "infer from their observations," to "challenge someone's assumption," to "test an idea by finding an example," and, most of all, to "respect others and their ideas." He spends time each day "thinking with his students." A question he asks a lot is, "What is happening?" He waits for answers from students, being sure he hears from everyone every day.

Though students see him as a resource who knows a lot of stuff, he portrays himself as a learner. "Life is a journey, not a destination," he likes to say to his students. Mr. Gunnings keep his focus on how students make sense out of their experiences. "The important thing," he says, "is to try and figure out whether any real learning is going on." He asks himself everyday "are we pushing back our collective ignorance and actually gaining in the race against indifference?"

Mr. Gunnings' reactions to student responses to his or the students' questions are to ask whoever is speaking to "expand on their statement, or tell how it is linked to the current topics." His focus is to help both male and female students clearly articulate their mathematical ideas and contribute to group discussions and learning.

The principal reports that "when I walk into the room I think that it is chaotic. However, the students are engaged in learning and not communicating any confusion. After I am in the room for awhile, I realize that you cannot be in Mr. Gunnings' neighborhood without starting to feel that you must become a contributing citizen." Visitors are drawn into the "learning conversation" by students who ask them, "What is your theory about what is happening here?"

Contrasts between Traditional and Learning Community Teachers

The contrast between these two teachers is based on the differences in their underlying assumptions about teaching and learning, control, caring, gender, and classroom culture. In the first metaphor, Wilson believes teaching to be the distribution of knowledge and the shaping of the right attitudes and social behaviors. Wilson believes that learning is a matter of acquiring something that the teacher disperses to his students. He believes that he needs to control students, because if he did not they would not use their time productively. He demonstrates that he cares for the students by constantly managing their time and actions. He does not let students "get away with anything." His course work reflects his admiration of classical male authors. *Wilson's basic assumptions result in his creating a traditional protective classroom culture.*

In the second metaphor, Gunnings sees teaching as facilitating. He thinks that knowledge is something that the students put together in their heads, and thus it is essential that as the teacher he does everything possible to encourage students to actively participate in learning experiences. Participation in the discourse of the class makes what is learned a public event, not an isolated private individual affair. Bruner (1990) put this idea well when he wrote that "by virtue of participation in culture, meaning is rendered public and shared" (pp. 12–13).

Gunnings consciously teaches students to make decisions about the use of their time, their behavior, their responsibilities as learners, and accountability as members of the classroom society. He believes that he must be conscious about issues of equity. He is careful to reflect in the classroom teaching materials that he uses, the diversity of people and ideas in America. Gunnings says he cares enough about his students to let them make decisions, to make mistakes and errors, although they are held accountable and responsible for the outcomes of their actions. Gunnings' assumptions result in a reflective classroom learning community culture, as described in this text.

Argyris (1985) illustrates the contrast between reflective cultures and protective cultures. Reflective classroom cultures are led by teachers who see themselves as reflective professionals and who model life-long learning and a collaborative learning process. People working or living in reflective cultures tend to treat knowledge as constructed reality embedded in particular contexts. Students of reflective teachers perceive their teachers not as finished products, but as growing and struggling adult learners. A feature in the students' perceptions in this type of classroom culture is their acknowledgement of their teachers as members of the classroom learning community.

In contrast, Wilson's classroom is illustrative of a protective school culture where teachers such as Wilson see themselves as managers of discipline and dispensers of knowledge. They see knowledge as a complete "body," something received from the past. Since traditional protective classroom cultures are based on the belief that knowledge is a closed set of standardized information, learning is then just a matter of acquiring something that the teacher disperses to pupils. Students of protective teachers see them as the "holders of knowledge" and as the external managers of their behavior.

Changing the Classroom Culture Metaphor: The Reflective Learning Community

What difference does it make whether we challenge the traditional protective classroom metaphor or not? What difference will it make if teachers establish reflective rather than protective classroom cultures? For us the answer to these questions rests on what we believe are the purposes of schooling. Simply put, is the role of education contributing all it can to the wellness (improvement) of our society? Given the numbers of students who are not successful academically, the number of social problems in our neighborhoods, the lack of personal and social responsibility on the part of CEOs, and the continued problems of equity, the answer is no. The changes in assumptions and the resulting changes in classroom cultures are necessary if our students are to have the opportunity to learn more.

We propose that *reflective classroom cultures, classroom learning communities,* be the new management metaphor. We believe that if schools are to play their role in our democratic society, education must shift from establishing protective cultures to establishing reflective learning communities. In the next section we explore the concepts of control, caring, gender, relationships, and culture as they are related to protective and reflective classroom learning communities and to the education of teachers.

Control, Caring, Gender, Relationships, and Culture

The place we begin the reexamination of assumptions about classroom management is with assumptions related to control, caring, gender, relationships, and culture. We consider the manifestations of control, caring, gender, relationships, and culture from both protective traditional classrooms and reflective learning community classroom perspectives. McGregor (1985), Block (1993), Putnam and Burke (1992), and Schein (1985), among other scholars, provide a basis for examining assumptions related to these concepts.

Control. Control manifests itself in many different forms in both traditional and reflective school cultures. In traditional protective cultures the actions of teachers reflect McGregor's (1985) Theory X. They perceive students as people who dislike work, are distrustful, lazy, unmotivated, and unwilling to work. Teachers who hold these assumptions believe that students must be coerced or bribed into working, and appreciate being told what to do rather than thinking it out for themselves (e.g., Trice and Beyer, 1990). In sharp contrast, reflective learning community teachers' behavior reflects McGregor's Theory Y (1985). These teachers perceive their students neither liking nor disliking work, but developing feelings about it as a result of their experiences with work. Teachers who reflect Theory Y assumptions also believe that students ". . . want to grow; basically trust their surroundings and other people; and are self-actualizing, self-controlled, and self-motivated" (Trice and Beyer, 1993). We note that teachers holding Theory Y are not laissez faire nor authoritarian instructional leaders, but act as authoritative leaders.

Authoritative classroom teacher leaders see themselves as the responsible adult instructional leader. The role of students is one of responsible actions to self and the group. The authoritarian leaders see themselves as the decision maker and enforcer, and the role of learners as one of doing what they are told. Laissez faire teacher leaders see themselves as observers and learners as responsible for organization.

The concept of control explored from the "Theory Y" perspective means learning community teachers consider how to teach students to: be self-controlled; be responsible for their behavior; expect to pay consequences for decisions about one's behavior that is destructive to self or others; and, distinguish between when to comply with norms and when to challenge them. For example, learning community teachers are responsible for teaching their students how to challenge classroom and school rules and norms that marginalize or inhibit the development of independent and critical thinking, as well as situations that inhibit achievement in academics. In contrast, teachers holding "Theory X" are concerned that students obey their rules, are quiet, and do as they are told.

Caring Issues. In traditional protective classroom cultures, teachers exercise their caring actions in ways that reduce the students' ability to make decisions, and thus inhibit their capacity for developing "... ownership, responsibility (Block, 1993, p. 25), and accountability" (Block, 1993, p. 31). This kind of over-protective "caring" has long-term negative consequences for the students and the communities within which they will live and serve.

Over-protective teachers do things for their students that students can be responsible for doing themselves, or they keep students from doing things that are difficult because they want to protect them from failure and the resultant bad feelings. It is common for teachers of protective cultures to say "yes" to students when students ask or demand responses that may increase the chances of dependency later in their lives. Reflective learning school cultures promote a different kind of caring. A reflective teacher makes decisions about classroom cultural norms, procedures, rules, roles, and instructional strategies that will enable students to become autonomous and responsible members of the community.

Nell Noddings (2005) talks about the "ethic of care." Her descriptions of caring make it clear that holding high standards, providing excellent support, and clearly communicating rigorous intellectual and social-emotional demands are indicators of teachers profoundly caring for their students. Susan Katz (1999) found that caring and holding high expectations for learners were necessary in fostering positive learning outcomes. She stresses the point that teachers who demonstrate caring without holding high expectations can make a dangerous turn. In this situation teachers feel sorry for students, do not challenge them intellectually and end up demonstrating a paternalistic mode of operation.

A reflective learning community teacher is sensitive to the times when her/his caring actions change from being constructive to over-protective. Reflective learning community teachers consider their "caring actions" in light of how they will help students develop independent and interdependent behavior. Students of these teachers will learn "ownership, responsibility, and accountability" (Block 1989–1990).

Gender Issues. Thomas (1990) defines gender issues as "... a social construction (that) ... concerns the differing qualities culturally attributed to women and men" (p. 1). Many authorities (Thomas 1990; Oakley 1972; Acker 1981) agree that gender is a hotly debated issue in education. The concept of gender equity is reflected in the metaphors of protective and reflective school cultures. The traditional protective school culture is characterized by a bias protecting the basic rights of the male and/or subtle gross violation of "social justice" as a major purpose of education (Putnam & Burke, 1992). For example, Mahony (1985), Wolpe (1977), and Lees (1978) all found evidence that in co-ed schools, teachers described boys' sexual harassment of girls as "trivial" or "normal" behavior characteristic of boys that age.

The violation of female rights in traditional protective cultures also manifests itself by the marginalization and alienation of women. Aronowitz and Giroux (1985) point out how "Women, though in different degrees, experience dual forms of domination in both the home and workplace" and how "... the dynamics of these forms are interconnected, reproduced, and mediated in schools ..." (p. 101).

Teachers in reflective school cultures base their schooling outcomes of social justice on the assumption of equity. They approach their students with genuine positive regard as human beings. Their unconditional respect, for each of their students, is not dependent upon class, race, behavior, or gender societal stereotypes. To this end, reflective school cultures create an environment where the school community is equipped with the skills and sensitivity of identifying the obvious and subtle ways in which gender violates the academic, personal, social responsibility, and social justice outcomes as the major purposes of schooling. Reflective cultures empower teachers and students to change the detrimental elements of gender inequities in the culture that are mediated in the schools. This is necessary if our schools are to be effective instruments of democracy.

Relationships. The assumptions we hold about the concepts of control, caring, and gender form the parameters of the relationships we create in school. Teacher-pupil relationships have long been recognized as a factor that plays a critical role in the learning process. For example, Bush (1954) describes "Teaching ... as a problem in human relations ... as a dynamic interplay between the teacher and pupil" (p. 184–185).

Cusick (1983) described several relationship scenarios that he found in protective classroom cultures. He describes, for example, how a teacher tolerated students not paying attention during the presentation; how the elective system enables students to avoid classes of teachers who make students work hard; and how students undermine the authority of substitute teachers. Cusick (1983) also describes the examples of student-student relationships characteristic of the traditional protective school culture. He described, for example, how a discussion on racism ended in a conflict among students. He maintains that "the administrators worked so hard to avoid (general disruption) because it could have destroyed the safety and orderliness which the school has to present to the public" (Cusick, 1983, p. 17). The problem with these kinds of relationships is that they make the attainment of the purposes of schooling very difficult because when conflict is ignored, covered up, or swept under the carpet, permanent solutions are not found.

In reflective learning community cultures, relationships are built on mutual respect and expectations that individuals carry out their responsibilities and remain accountable for their actions. Open discussions about roles and responsibilities among teachers, administrators, parents, students, and teacher educators are the basis for building new relationships. Early agreement that individuals will help each other in building the constructive relationships allows opportunities for the members to risk, error, reflect, and try again without destructive consequences personally or to the community.

We believe that the main objective is to seek permanent solutions to relationship problems, no matter what it takes. We believe, like Argyris (1990), a reflective school culture cannot be built when there are present in the environment

> organizational defensive routines . . . actions or policies that prevent individuals or segments of the organization from experiencing embarrassment or threat . . . because organizational defensive routines are anti-learning, overprotective, and self-sealing (p. 25).

For example, being uncomfortable, at some times, is a normal part of seeking solutions to problems. Getting "things" on the tables so that individuals and systems can own them is a necessary step in problem solving. This is not to say that embarrassing or threatening others over "power of control" issues is appropriate. Talking through real issues that represent assumptions that interfere with developing constructive relationships is the first step in changing the basic destructive assumptions. Individuals need to own their assumptions and actions that cause relationship problems.

There are many steps that could be taken to help people acquire a reflective attitude to support relationships that ensure learning for understanding. Cusick (1983) suggests, for example, that schools should "confront the issue of racial animosity directly, try to 'deal with' it in the curriculum, and seek to ameliorate it through positive action rather than simply trying to keep its students apart" (p. 17). Senge (1990) suggests participative and reflective openness. He states:

> participative openness leads to people speaking out . . . (and) reflective openness leads to people looking inward. Reflective openness starts with the willingness to challenge our own thinking, to recognize that any certainty we ever have is, at best, a hypothesis about the world. No matter how compelling it may be, no matter how fond we are of 'our idea,' it is always subject to test and improvement. (p. 277)

The path toward the acquisition of these lifelong skills is certainly full of innumerable obstacles. It is, however, a challenge that must be accepted by students, teachers, teacher educators, and administrators who intend to build an alternative school culture, e.g., a reflective school culture.

Culture. Teacher education courses traditionally explore culture as "multicultural education" (e.g.. Blacks do one thing in a given situation, whites do other things in the same situation, and Hispanics do a third thing in the same situation). For the purposes of this book we consider culture from the perspective of schools and classrooms: cultures that as educators we create and recreate each year, and yet give little thought to over the course of time. We begin by defining the terms culture, assumptions, and beliefs.

Considerable attention is given to the concept of culture in education (Kalantis, et al., 1990; Sarason, 1971). Schein (1985) defines culture as:

a pattern of basic assumption—invented, discovered, or developed by a given group as it learns to cope with its problems of external adaptation and internal integration—that has worked well enough to be considered valid and, therefore, to be taught to new members as the correct way to perceive, think, and feel in relations to those problems (p. 9).

Ott (1989) insists that a distinction be drawn between "basic assumptions" and "beliefs." He maintains that

> Basic assumptions are beliefs, values, ethical and moral codes, and ideologies that have become so ingrained that they tend to have dropped out of consciousness. They are unquestioned perceptions of truth, reality, ways of thinking and thinking about, and feelings that develop through repeated successes in solving problems over extended periods of time. Important basic assumptions are passed on to new members, often unconsciously. Beliefs and values are consciously held cognitive and affective patterns. They provide explicit directions and justifications for patterns of organizational behavior, as well as the energy to enact them. Beliefs and values are also the birth places of basic assumptions (p. 47).

We find that some schools, over a period of time, create cultures that are unproductive in terms of promoting the attainment of the four purposes of schooling (Putnam & Burke, 1992). Cusick's (1983) work illustrates how the functions of schooling become lost. Cusick described a teacher's experience in trying to uphold academic standards in this way:

> This girl missed 55 days of class, 55 days and she hadn't handed in an assignment. I checked my book, since October 10, and so I flunked her from the class. But the parent came in and talked to the principal, so I got called in, and he said, looking right at me, 'Mr.___, is it necessary to fail that student?' and I said 'yes' and showed him what I'm showing you, and then he looked at me and said again, 'Is it really necessary to fail that student?' I said 'Yes,' but the third time he said it, I got the message. (p. 39)

Student achievement as a purpose of schooling is not considered in this interaction. The principal did everything in his/her power to please people at the expense of the four purposes of schooling. The actions are "face-saving" techniques which are the cornerstone of maintaining the traditional protective culture. In another case that warranted expulsion, Cusick (1983) pointed out:

> . . . the administrators were very careful about expulsion. . . . . The administrators really tried to avoid getting into such matters, which were of necessity time consuming, expensive, and potentially embarrassing to the school, which based its legitimacy on its ability to appeal to everyone (p. 35).

> . . . people in the central administration were concerned about that (expulsion). In fact, when the ninth grade principal went for an expulsion, he was pointedly reminded by a central administrator that he already 'had forty-five for the year' (and that) . . . 'you don't get people to vote their financial support by throwing their kids out' (p. 37).

How do students, teachers, school administrators, and the central administrators ever come to create and sustain a school culture that violates all the purposes of schooling? Argyris (1990) explained, we have been socialized to always pretend to maintain a position of authority by being defensive.

Defensiveness, further, makes it difficult for us to "detect and correct the errors . . . because fundamental rules (with which we operate are) to (1) bypass the errors and act as if they were not being done, (2) make the bypass indiscussible, and (3) make its undiscussibility indiscussible" (p. 43). This invariably leads to our refusing to take full responsibility for participating in the birth and sustenance of the culture by externalizing the blame. The result is a protective culture that has outlined its usefulness. When a school culture ceases to maximize learning, it becomes inappropriate. Such a school culture is ". . . like dinosaurs (whose) anatomy and physiology are simply inappropriate to the emerging world" (Owen, 1984, p. 209).

A new paradigm, a reflective culture, is needed because the current one is failing to help students, teachers, parents, administrators, and the central administrators solve the problems that make learning difficult. What do we, then, need to do? How do we change our paradigm about school/classroom culture?

Educational implications. In order to challenge the classroom and school management cultures, we believe that examination of educators' assumptions about the concepts of control, caring, gender, relationships, and culture must occur in relationship to Schwab's (1974) four functions of schooling. To help with this examination we consider the ideas of organizational learning and unlearning, double-loop learning, and "cultural approach."

The first metaphor that can guide us in an attempt to transform protective school and classroom cultures is organizational unlearning. "Unlearning is a process through which learners discard knowledge. Unlearning makes way for new responses and mental maps" (Hedberg, 1981, p. 18). We believe that the elements of a protective culture that we discussed in this book are learned by teachers, students, administrators, and parents. We, therefore, also believe that a reflective school culture can only be established through a conscious unlearning process. This process will create a way for new knowledge to be used to deliberately create a new culture.

The second useful metaphor is that of organizational learning. "Organizational learning (is) . . . the process within the organization by which knowledge about action-outcome relationships and the effect of the environment on these relationships is developed" (Duncan and Weiss, 1979, p. 84). Learning organizations, according to Senge (1990), are organizations "where people continually expand their capacity to create the results they truly desire, where new and expansive patterns of thinking are nurtured, where collective aspiration is set free, and where people are continually learning how to learn together" (p. 3). He further suggests that, "The learning organizations that will truly excel in the future will be the organizations that discover how to tap people's commitment and capacity to learn at all levels in an organization" (p. 3). This is possible when organizational members reorganize themselves in teams "who function together in an extraordinary way—who trusted one another, who complemented each other's strengths and compensated for each other's limitations, and who produce extraordinary results" (p. 4).

The third metaphor is double-loop learning. Argyris' concept of (1976) double-loop learning is the kind of learning that empowers the teachers, students, parents, and school administrators with the capacity "to question (their own) design and . . . purposes; . . . to reexamine their own values and assumptions in order to design and implement a quality of life not constrained by the status quo" (p. 638). He suggests that the best way to achieve this is to "help people to learn . . . how to produce disconfirmable statements; how to advocate articulately what they deeply believe in, yet simultaneously encourage inquiry, especially about whatever they are advocating" (p. 640). This is, indeed, a call for a school cultural transformation that will lead to the creation of a cultural climate that minimizes the violation of the four purposes of schooling.

The fourth metaphor is cultural approach. Alien and Kraft (1984) suggest "cultural approach" as a substitute for "cultural change." They maintain that, ". . . a weekend training is not enough. We must devise some means to install new behavior so that it becomes part of the organization . . . and in schools we must incorporate the good things planned in committee meetings into the daily norms of the classroom" (p. 38). They call their model of transforming school culture the Normative System Approach. Elements included in their model are: understanding organizational unconsciousness, planning for individual and organizational change, developing leadership, creating the structures of new culture, and identifying a renewal process.

IN CONCLUSION

Teacher candidates who are primarily interested in becoming effective teachers have a view of their future role of the teacher as carrying out their career choice. Many see teaching as an opportunity to improve on their experiences as K–12 students, in a sense to right wrongs they experienced as learners. In student teaching or internships their instruction is extremely well planned thus engaging students in learning. They practice (1) establishing communities of learning, (2) explicitly communicating expectations and (3) paying attention to each student in the beginning days of their teaching. Thus, they reduce the time, effort, and stress they might otherwise spend on the distractions of disorderliness, discipline, having to overmanage, and disinterest. They consciously work to try out and integrate the ideas, research and theories they studied in their preparation program. They also ask questions and volunteer to do paperwork.

When these people start their first year of teaching they know what paperwork is required and how to get it done without letting it pull their time from students and planning. They know how to create a plan for establishing a classroom culture, they know how to plan effectively and how to include the four functions of schooling, they know how to discipline a student when the need arises, and they are not overwhelmed during the first months as an inservice teacher. They begin to be the vision they created about the teacher they would be. They resist the socialization by the school's educators and may in fact change the culture of the school (not just the classroom) where they teach.

Other preservice teachers use their student teaching or internship as time to get by with doing as little as possible. Sometimes they invest hours in ineffective planning resulting in the creation of management problems, discipline problems, high levels of stress, and even helpless behavior ("I spent hours on my plans, I did what they said. Tell me what to do now."). They see this experience as the end and so their primary focus is on after student teaching, not what they can gain from it. They get involved in planning their wedding, finding a job, or going to conferences that they have not researched and really do not know whether or not they will contribute to their professional knowledge or skills. It really does not matter to them, they are just playing the teacher role.

When these people find themselves in their first teaching position they are quickly faced with the pressures of being socialized into the school's culture. Since their focus was on playing teacher, they quickly become one of the traditional educators.

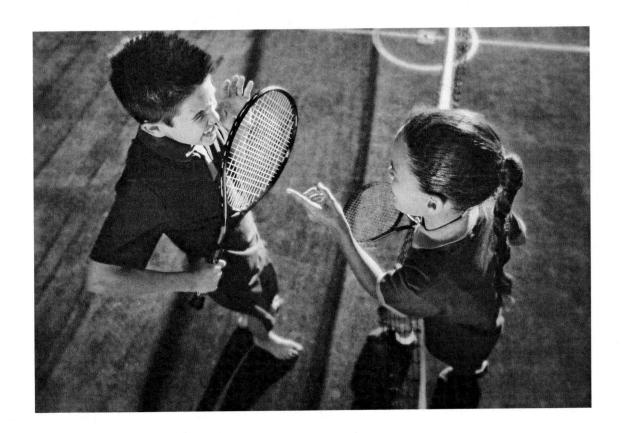

Performance Outcomes and Activities (NJPTS 2, 4, 6, 8)

Chapter 10: Stage III. Identifying and Resolving Conflicts

PERFORMANCE OUTCOMES

Teacher Candidates will:

1. Gain the knowledge and skills for professionally preparing for, carrying out, and reporting data from classroom observations that furthers their knowledge about teachers and teaching and learners and learning and schools and schooling.
2. Gain the knowledge and skills to identify Stage 3. Identifying and Resolving Conflict teacher and student behavior.
3. Gain the knowledge and skills to create an effective plan that when implemented will likely move students through Stage 3. Identifying and Resolving Conflicts with activities that are congruent with the functions of schooling for learning communities.
4. Develop communication skills necessary for the identification and resolution of conflicts with peers, students, and parents.
5. Create short-term and long-term plans to support students in the change of behavior that are re-searched based.
6. Refine interview skills, data analysis and use of data.
7. Continue practice in applying knowledge and skills necessary for carrying out child studies and action research.
8. Articulate a clear and logical rationale that could be used to explain to a learner why being treated the same as another student is not equal treatment.
9. Articulate a clear and logical rationale that could be used to explain to a learner why being treated the same as another student is not fair treatment.
10. Articulate a clear and logical explanation of how learning is maximized by treating students differently.
11. Articulate rationale as to why it is not respectful to learners, who are different and unique from each other, to have the same expectations.
12. Articulate rationale as to how it is respectful and fair to learners to hold each one to high academic, personal, social, and social justice learning standards.
13. Explain why it is unethical and disrespectful to ignore or not be aware of bullying behavior.

ESTABLISHING A BULLY-FREE CLASSROOM LEARNING COMMUNITY

The school bully causes students (the victims) and sometimes adults to feel uncomfortable and not safe in their educational environment. There is agreement that bullying occurs where there is little adult supervision (e.g., hallways, buses, playgrounds, cafeterias, lockerrooms). Bullying also occurs in highly supervised environments right under the noses of teachers who do not know what is going on, do not know what to do, or who are afraid to take action against the bully and protect the victim. It is the teachers' ethical and professional responsibility to protect all of their learners.

Beane, (1999) in *The Bully Free Classroom,* provides a series of activities that a learning community teacher can use as part of the development of the classroom learning community in Stage 2. Establishing Expectations and Stage 3. Identifying and Resolving Conflicts. Beane's top ten facts about bullying are congruent with the research and authors reviewed earlier. They are:

1. Bullying is more than just teasing.
2. Anyone can be a bully.
3. Anyone can be a victim.
4. Bullying isn't a modern problem.
5. Bullying affects everyone.
6. Bullying is a serious problem.
7. We can work together to find solutions.
8. A comprehensive plan will produce the best results.
9. Children at risk can be helped.
10. Schools are responsible for protecting students. (pp. 5–14)

It is clear that creating a bully free classroom is primarily a preventative method in classroom management. However, the knowledge and ability to respond when bullying is suspected is also a critical element of the bully free classroom. To create an authentic learning community it is essential that the teacher includes activities in Stages I, II, and III that support the establishment of a bully-free classroom culture. Equally important is the teacher's ability to respond immediately to a bully and victim as well as working with the class as a whole on the elimination of bully behavior and the increase in support, collaboration, and cooperation.

Exercise 10.1
Reviewing Your Stage I and Stage II Plans & Adding Bully-Free Classroom Activities.

A. Review your plans for Stage 2. Establishing Expectations and identify rules and norms that need to be added to your plan so that you are clearly working toward a "Bully Free Classroom." Also review your initial Stage III plans and make appropriate additions.
B. Once you have identified new rules and norms that will help to eliminate bullying from your classroom, create one activity for each that will provide instruction and practice for your students as they learn these new rules and norms.
C. Identify the activities in Stage III that will support the establishment of a "No Bullying Classroom." Add one more activity to your plans such as a role-play that you can use with your students to eliminate classroom bullying. Resources that you can use to upgrade your plans include: Beane (1999), *Bully Free Classroom: Over 100 Tips and Strategies for Teachers K–8;* Thompson (2004), *Through Ebony Eyes: What Teachers Need to Know But Are Afraid to Ask About African American Students;* Olweus (1993) *Bullying at School.*

The next set of Chapter 10 activities provide opportunities to practice identification of problems, identification of appropriate responses, and practice responding to the problems.

Exercise 10.2
Bothersome Behavior

Teacher candidates with whom we work find the problem behavior self-assessment and planning tasks that follow useful in identifying the types of behaviors that could cause them management problems in the future. In-service teachers find the following activity useful in thinking through a problem they are having with a specific student.

A.   The first task is to complete the Assessment Instrument for Identifying Student Behavior that might be a problem for you. Rank each of the items within a given category from 5–1, with 5 indicating extremely bothersome behavior, and 1 indicating that the behavior is not bothersome at all to you. The format in the box below is the scoring and analysis form for your use after filling out the Assessment Instrument.

Bothersome Behavior Scoring Form

Directions: Add the numbers for each set of behavior and list in the Total Score Column. Then find the average score for each set of behaviors. Write the Average score in the second column.

Category		Total Score	Average Score
A.	Completion of task (academic responsibility)	___	___
B.	Interaction with teacher	___	___
C.	Interactions with students (social responsibility)	___	___
D.	Self-control (personal responsibility)	___	___
E.	Self-management (personal responsibility)	___	___
F.	Dishonest behavior (social justice)	___	___
G.	Disruptive behavior (social responsibility)	___	___
H.	Bully behavior (social justice responsibility)	___	___

Circle the two categories in which you received the highest average scores.

Identifying Problem Student Behavior

Self-Assessment Instrument

A.   Completion of Tasks

___ 1. Failing to follow directions for assignments

___ 2. Failing to complete in-class assignments

___ 3. Failing to complete homework

___ 4. Refusing to participate in class activities or assignments

___ 5. Reading, writing, etc., while teacher is instructing, giving directions

___ 6. Complaining about class activities or assignments

___ 7. Asking irrelevant questions during instructional or work times

___ 8. "I don't care," appears not to care

___ 9. "So What!" Does not appear to try things

___ 10. Does not work up to or does not use abilities

___ 11. Does not want to do anything

___ 12. Daydreams or acts spaced out

___ 13. Accomplishes little

___ 14. Short attention span

___ 15. Requires individual help with most work

___ 16. No self direction, does not work independently

___ 17. Poor listener

___ 18. Does not follow rules

___ 19. Other examples of behaviors that bother me a lot in this category

B. Interaction with teacher or other adults

___ 1. Sassing or speaking rudely to teacher

___ 2. Swearing at teacher

___ 3. Arguing with teacher

___ 4. Verbally interrupting teacher while she/he is talking

___ 5. Sarcastic

___ 6. Asks a lot of unnecessary questions

___ 7. Constantly complaining

___ 8. Has to have "last word"

___ 9. Whining

___ 10. Hyperactive—does not sit still

___ 11. Tattletale

___ 12. Other examples of behavior that bother me a lot in this category

C. Interactions with other students

A. Physical

___ 1. Hitting, shoving, or tripping another student

___ 2. Throwing things at another student

___ 3. Pulling a student's hair

___ 4. Destroying another student's property

B. Emotional

___ 1. Verbally interrupting another

___ 2. Laughing at another student's mistakes or actions

___ 3. Showing disrespect for another student's opinions

___ 4. Drawing pictures to poke fun at another student

___ 5. Calling another student names

___ 6. Making fun of another student

___ 7. Swearing at another student

___ 8. Other examples of behavior that bother me in this category

D. Self-Control

___ 1. Displaying masochistic behavior to demand attention

___ 2. Throwing temper tantrums

___ 3. Always asking to go to the bathroom or get a drink of water

___ 4. Excessive complaining about feeling ill

___ 5. Crying in class

___ 6. Impatient

___ 7. Yelling in class—outburst

___ 8. Other examples of behaviors that bother me a lot in this category

E. Self-Management

___ 1. Forgetting notebooks, textbooks, or other classroom materials

___ 2. Forgetting lunch money, permission slips, or other non-academic materials

___ 3. Disorganized

___ 4. Other examples of behavior that bother me a lot in this category

F. Dishonest Behavior

___ 1. Stealing from another student

___ 2. Stealing materials from school

___ 3. Stealing from teachers

___ 4. Lying to teacher with the intent to deceive (not fantasy)

___ 5. Cheating on in-class assignments

___ 6. Cheating on homework

___ 7. Cheating on tests

___ 8. Plagiarizing

___ 9. Other examples of behavior that bother me a lot in this category

G. Disruptive Behavior

___ 1. Chewing gum in class

___ 2. Clicking pens, tapping feet, cracking knuckles, making other noises in class

___ 3. Throwing erasers, spitballs, paper airplanes, etc., in class

___ 4. Writing and passing personal notes in class

___ 5. Playing with toys, etc., in class

___ 6. Combing hair

___ 7. Putting on makeup

___ 8. Eating in class

___ 9. Whispering, making faces, or nonverbally communicating at inappropriate times

___ 10. Acts up when teacher is out of the room

___ 11. Eating in class

___ 12. Other examples of behavior that bother me a lot in this category

H. Bullying Behavior

___ 1. Boss people around

___ 2. Brag about being tough

___ 3. Make people do things they don't want to

___ 4. Pick on others because of size, shape, race, religion, gender, family, sex, culture

___ 5. Say nasty things about people to others

___ 6. Threaten people

Complete the bothersome behavior scoring form. Circle the two categories in which you received the highest average score. Then for each category: (1) Write a statement as to why the type of behaviors in the category bother you (for example, if stealing is one of the areas, you might write, "This area is very bothersome to me because I do not know how to solve this type of problem. I don't know what to do when I haven't seen someone do something and you have only their word against another student's word."). (2) Review the behaviors in each of the categories and list one thing that you could say and do for each of the behaviors.

Next, take your statements and lists and meet with a partner to discuss your and his/her findings. Discuss why each of the behaviors in your two categories bothers you. With your partner, identify two additional constructive actions that are congruent with a learning community classroom culture that you can take and what you would say for each of the behaviors. Go over the other person's categories and repeat the above process.

Exercise 10.3
Assessing and Responding to a Problem Behavior

The purpose of this activity is to provide you with an opportunity to practice assessing and planning a response to a student problem behavior.

1. Schedule one observation with a teacher and schedule an interview with the teacher after the observation. Give yourself time to do the follow-up activities to the observation and create your interview questions before you do the interview.
2. Use the following observation form for your data collection.

IDENTIFYING PROBLEM STUDENT BEHAVIOR OBSERVATION FORM
On the back of the observation form, draw an illustration of the classroom set-up.

Describe Problem Behaviors	Describe what was going on just prior to the occurrence of the problem behavior	Describe the teacher's response	Describe the student's response to the teacher
1.			
2.			
3.			
4.			
5.			

3. After the observation, on the drawing of the classroom, place the number of the problem behavior you described in the area of the room where it occurred.

4. In the chart below list the problem behaviors you described.

THINKING THROUGH POTENTIAL TEACHER ACTIONS

List Each of the Problem Behaviors You Observed	What behavior (clue) is it possible to observe that is a hint that the problem behavior will occur?	How would you respond to the "cue" behavior to prevent the problem behavior from occurring?	What could you plan to do as a part of Stage III, which would prevent the behavior from occurring the rest of the year?

5. Review your responses to the *Thinking Through Potential Teacher Actions* to respond to and prevent behavior problems.

   a. *How* are your responses congruent and/or incongruent with the philosophy for managing conflict in a learning community classroom? (indicate for each one)

   b. If there are aspects that are incongruent with the learning community, *what changes* would be necessary to bring them into congruence?

   c. What do you think would interfere with you or the teacher you observed to make these changes in practice?

   d. Put a check by any problem behavior that appears to you to be bullying behavior.

6. Preparing for the Teacher Interview

   a. First list three things you learned from your observation and reflections. Second, be prepared to show the teacher your worksheets and ask if they have any feedback to give you about your proposed responses to the problem behaviors. Third, ask the teacher what she/he thinks would be the results if she/he actually carried out your recommendations.

b. The next part of the interview will be about bullying. Prepare a list of questions to ask the teacher at the interview that will help you learn about policies and practices related to "bullying" in the schools and classrooms. Things to include in your interview (data collection) are: the law (state/national), policies, rules, and procedures related to bullying at the district, school and classroom level. Develop questions to learn about the history of bullying in the school. What are the actual practices related to bullying? What types of things are being done to prevent bullying at the district, school, and classroom level?

7. Conduct your interview with the teacher. If the teacher is unable to answer any of your questions, ask the teacher who could give you the information.

8. After the teacher's interview get the additional information about bullying by contacting the resources that the teacher recommended. Introduce yourself, explain who recommended you contact them, explain what you are studying, and request their permission to ask them your unanswered questions.

9. Analyze the responses to all of your interview questions. After you analyze and summarize your data answer the following:

a. What was the teacher's response when you asked about his/her carrying out the recommendations you created? Based on the teacher's feedback what, if any, changes would you make to your recommendations?

b. How do the policy and practices compare and contrast?

c. What are the district's, school's, and teacher's policy, norms, rules about bullying?

Exercise 10.4
Talking with the Head of District Bullying Prevention Projects or the Head of the Local Police Department Gang Prevention Task Force and Reviewing the Literature

A. *Class Activity I.* The preparation for and carrying out of this activity is done by the course members and the instructor. This is a group in-class activity.

The students in the course and the instructor identify and invite a speaker to class. The speaker should be either the District's head of the Bullying Prevention Project or the Police Department's Gang Prevention Task Force Leader. Together the instructor and members of the class identify questions to ask the expert that will help the members of the class in working to prevent bullying in early field experiences, student teaching, and when they become teachers.

Using the following role groups (Bully, victim, teacher, school principals, district administrators, parent/guardians, neighbors, the stand-byer) write a description of what the speaker should prepare to talk about.

B. *Class Activity II.* **Reading, Summarizing, Reflecting Organizing and Reporting Information**
This activity will be set up at the beginning of the semester as it requires time for course members to prepare.

The purpose of this activity is to read work by authors who care greatly about the education of all P–12 students and to summarize the material, reflect on the messages, connect the information to what you are learning about a learning community, select, organize, and report information. This activity also gives you further practice working in a cooperative learning group.

Guided Reading Cooperative Groups

Group I: Angela's Ashes, by_____ (read book, listen to audio tape or watch movie); plus Research Related to Effects of Poverty on P–12 students.

Joyce:
Need author name here

Group II: Fist Stick Knife Gun, by G. Canada

Group III: Through Ebony Eyes, by G. Thompson

Group IV: The Bully, the Bullied, and the Bystander, by B. Coloroso

Group V: Bullying at School, D. Olweus

Group VI: The Bully Free Classroom, by A. Beane

Group VII: Solving Discipline Problems, by C. H. Wolfgang (**Secondary teacher candidates**)

Group VII: The Three Faces of Discipline for the Elementary School Teacher, C. Wolfgang (**Elementary teacher candidates**)

Group VII: The Three Faces of Discipline for Early Childhood Education Teachers (**Early childhood teacher candidates**)

Guided Reading and Reporting Questions
Poverty:

Group I: Angela's Ashes, and Reports on 10 more Research Reports on the Effects of Poverty on P–12 students and through their adult years.

What are the effects of poverty on the children and adults in the story "Angela's Ashes"?

During the last 10 years, what does *the research* say are the effects of poverty?

What are the primary recommendations that come from the research, as to what can be done to minimize the effects of poverty?

Bullying:

Group II: Fist Stick Knife Gun, G. Canada

In each of your answers to the following questions, indicate two references in the book that support your generalization or inferences.

What "codes of conduct" do you observe among your students or your peers?

How do the "codes of conduct" you observe compare with those described by Canada?

What is the "big idea" that Canada is trying to make in the section titled "A Matter of Time"? How is this relevant to learning about the lives of your students?

In the section titled "The Best Way We Know How," what would you infer would be Canada's advice about the role of the teacher in an urban school?

What point would Canada make, in support of urban teachers?

If Canada were the interviewer for teaching positions in the Camden or Vineland School Districts, what questions would he ask applicants? What criteria would he use for the selection of teachers to be hired?

Group III: Through Ebony Eyes, by G. Thompson

Through Ebony Eyes: What Teachers Need to Know But are Afraid to Ask About African American Students, by Gail L. Thompson

STUDY QUESTIONS AND TASKS

Turn in your written responses to the following no later than _____.

1. Introduction Pages 1–3: Create a concept map that illustrates the connections in the content on those three pages.

2. Introduction Pages end of 3–5: In your own words, explain two reasons why Gail Thompson believes that her book needs to be read by people who are thinking of entering teaching as well as inservice teachers.

3. Chapter 1: After reading this chapter, list the studies that "blame the victims" and those that "blames schooling factors" as the reason African Americans are not achieving in school. Second, describe in your own words the argument that Thompson makes about the effects of teachers' beliefs and attitudes on African American learners.

4. Chapter 2: After reading this chapter, first explain what the tutor did to help the student in mathematics and then explain how what she did helped the student to achieve at a higher level. Second, describe specific examples of how Thompson recommends teachers help students in math, in reading, and in writing. Third, what is the common thread that runs through her recommendations to teachers? Fourth, based on what you read what would you include when you were teaching art and music?

5. Chapter 3: After reading this chapter, first, draw a map showing the relationships among the many examples presented on pages 70–98. Second, explain the connections between Thompson's seven effective classroom management strategies or practices and the stages in developing a classroom learning community culture.

6. Chapter 4: After reading this chapter, explain what the teacher did that made a difference in Thompson's life. What would it take for you to become a teacher who chooses to become a powerful and influential life-changing teacher? (e.g., what would you need to learn, what skills would you need to acquire)

7. Chapter 5: How can any teacher motivate African American student to acquire Standard English skills without silencing them or devaluing their home language or dialect? What stage of the Learning Community culture would support a teacher in this effort?

8. Chapter 6: After reading this chapter, explain how Thompson recommends teachers react if an African American student calls another African American student the N word.

9. Chapter 7: After reading this chapter, explain two ways that you can respond if a student calls you a racist.

10. Chapter 8: After reading this chapter, first, explain what "culturally relevant teaching" means. How can multicultural education be used by teachers to harm students? How can multicultural education be used by teachers to help them?

11. Chapter 9: After reading this chapter, answer the following questions suggested by Thompson:
    - "Are African American teachers more effective with African American students than non-black teachers?
    - Black or African American: Which term should we use?
    - Why do so many African Americans have a bad attitude?
    - Why can't we call them "monkey"? (to offend or not to offend)
    - Why are African American students so loud?" (p. 8)

12. How did you use the Appendices? What did you use or learn from them?

Group IV: The Bully, the Bullied, and the Bystander, by B. Coloroso

Guidelines for Reporting on Coloroso's ideas about the Bully, the Bullied, and the Bystander

Chapters 1–4. Create an activity that you and members of your group can do with the class that will communicate Coloroso's ideas of the bully, the bullied, and the bystander.

Chapter 2. On PowerPoint create a one-page document that explains the difference between teasing and taunting.

Chapters 5–6. Create an illustration (table, concept map, etc.) that shows the critical factors in identifying bullying and the critical factors in identifying if a person is a bully. Coloroso presents the information primarily in a "family situation." In your illustration show how schools can observe the actions of a bully and what schools can do to stop a bully.

Chapter 7: Create a one-page PowerPoint that explains the characteristics that you would observe if a child is being bullied, and shows what teachers can do and should not do to support a victim of bullying.

Chapter 8: Illustrate in a one-page PowerPoint, the things that teachers can do to turn a bystander into a witness.

Chapter 9: On a one-page PowerPoint describe the relationship between a learning community culture and what Coloroso says are caring schools.

Group V. Bullying at School, D. Olweus

Part I of the book includes definitions and descriptions.

What does Olweus say bullying is?

What are the characteristics of a bully?

How does he say we can identify a bully?

How does he say we can identify a victim?

He proposes that males are more prone to bullying than girls. How does this differ from Thompson's ideas about boy and girl bullies?

On page 64 is a figure outlining the parts of a successful intervention program. For each of the items in the figure give a concrete example of that element and identify the pages where you found the information.

Group VI: The Bully Free Classroom, by A. Beane

Beane has created a book that has many ideas of things that teachers can do to prevent and eliminate bullying in their classrooms. Your instructor will provide your group with a packet of the reproducible pages of this book. They are listed on page vi. The first part of your work, after reading through the book, is to take the reproducible pages and organize them into sub-packets that are related to the Stages I, II, III, IV, and V of the learning community. Add cover pages for the beginning of each stage and give the newly organized packet back to your instructor so that it can be printed for the other students in your class. Your second task is to prepare a one-page PowerPoint chart that communicates the points that you judge the most important contribution of this book. The third task is to create an activity, based on the information and activities in the book, for you to do in your course with the other members. Activity should be appropriate for college sophomores.

Classroom Management and Discipline:

Group VII: Solving Discipline Problems, by C. H. Wolfgang (**Secondary Teacher Candidates**)

Group VIII: The Three Faces of Discipline for the Elementary School Teacher, C. Wolfgang (**Elementary Teacher Candidates**)

Group IX: The Three Faces of Discipline for Early Childhood Education Teachers (**Early Childhood Teacher Candidates**)

First, after reading the book in your group, create a PowerPoint that illustrates the Teacher Power continuum and shows how each of the current discipline models fall on the continuum. Prepare this for presentation to the whole class. Second, assess yourself and find out which "Face of Discipline" you each fall into. Then each person should take a problem behavior that you've seen or read about and show how you as a teacher would respond to the problem. Prepare these as handouts. Select one example from each of the three faces and present these to the class. Use a PowerPoint presentation.

Exercise 10.5 Stage 3: Identifying and Resolving Conflicts: Assessing and Responding to a Problem.

The purpose of this activity is to provide you with an opportunity to practice assessing and planning responses to a student problem situation.

Step 1: Schedule an observation in a classroom, lunchroom, playground, hallways, or auditorium.

Step 2: Use the following form (**Data Collection**) and identify the situational context, what occurred just prior to the occurrence of the problem behavior, the problem behavior, initial teacher response, and student reaction. After you have clear notes on two or three different problem behaviors, you are ready to review and plan a response that puts into practice what you are learning about handling problem student behavior.

Step 3: Draw inferences about the reasons for why the problem behavior occurred. Write out your inferences.

Step 4: Now using the form below (**Planning Form**) create a short- and long-term responses to the original problem.

DATA COLLECTION & FIRST IMPRESSIONS

Observations		Drawing Inferences
A. Describe what is going on in the class. What happened prior to the problem behavior?		A. What inferences can you draw about the reasons for the misbehavior?
B. Describe the problem behavior, what, how long, frequency, etc.		B. What would be *your immediate* ideas for short- and long-range goals for solving this problem?
Initial Teacher Response	Student Response	1. Short-term Goal
		2. Long Term Goal
		C. What additional data would you want to collect in order to solve this problem?
D. If you were the teacher and this occurred again what would be your immediate response?		D. Is the problem one that occurs because of circumstances that would be within your responsibility and power? If yes, how; and if not, why not?

Step 5: Now that you have completed your initial responses, it is time to reflect on your specific ideas. Turn your Data Collection and First Impressions Form over and write responses to the following items.

A. How are your responses congruent and/or incongruent with the philosophy for managing conflict in the learning community culture?

B. If there are aspects that are incongruent with the learning community, what changes would be necessary to bring them into congruence?

C. What would interfere with you doing this, or making these changes in your practice?

Exercise 10.6
Identifying Building and District Discipline Policy

The purpose of this activity is to identify a process to use for identifying the policies and practices related to solving problems related to student behavior. Teachers will have students who have problem behaviors and it is critical that teachers and student teachers know the building and district discipline policies. It is the process for acquiring this information that is the important aspect to learn, so that you can use it during early field experiences, student teaching, as a new teacher, and even as an experienced teacher who changes buildings or districts.

The value that is embedded in the learning community is that the primary goal for working with a student who has problem behavior is so socialize him/her into the community. You would know you were successful when you observe the student contributing to the classroom learning community culture.

Knowing policy and practices is helpful in letting you know what the guidelines and boundaries are that administrators and parents support when implemented by teachers or administrators.

Step 1: With a partner from class, identify one type of bullying (crisis-type) and one other problem behavior that is typical of your observations in classrooms as a basis for your inquiry.

Step 2: For each one create a vignette that describes a situation where the behavior occurs.

Step 3: Write out questions you would ask a principal, teacher, or central office student affairs administrator.

Step 4: Schedule and carry out interviews with two of the above.

Step 5: With your partner analyze the responses to identify your shared understandings of how policy and practice compare and contrast. Pay special attention to differences and what you learned about how the district handles bullying.

Step 6: Based on your findings, write a recommendation to teachers concerning how to handle the two problems you investigated.

Step 7: Share your recommendations with two teachers and record the following:

a. What does the teacher infer the consequences to the pupil and teacher would be if the teacher were to follow your recommendations?

b. Why would the teacher follow or not follow your policy?

Step 8: As a matter of reflection, reanalyze your recommendations and determine if they are congruent with what you have learned about a learning community philosophy. If anything is not congruent describe what changes you could make so that the policy is congruent with the learning community culture.

Exercise 10.7
Communication Skills for Identifying and Resolving Conflict

The following task focuses on communication skills used in conflict identification and conflict resolution.

Active Listening

Step 1: The purpose of this is to provide practice in paraphrasing a speaker's verbal statements and reflecting his/her feelings. Confrontational student talk sometimes intimidates teachers, causing them to respond in a defensive mode. Defensive responses put up roadblocks rather than facilitating identification of the problem and understanding of the student's perspective.

Situation: As the teacher, you've worked really hard with a specific student on something, which is basic to the next concept you are going to teach. Because the student had trouble learning, you simplified the task by reducing the number of items she/he had to respond to at any one time. In addition, you furnished concrete materials for practice during the last two individual work sessions. Finally, the student indicates that she/he has learned what you were teaching. You decide to give the evaluation test. When you hand out the test, the student slams down his/her pencil and slumps in the seat.

A. Write an active-listening statement (e.g., "You are upset by what you saw on the test."). You say:
B. The student responds with, "This isn't a fair test! I'm not going to do it!" Write an active-listening state (e.g., "You feel that this is an unfair test."). You say: . . .
C. The student says, "Yes! And I am not going to do it. You set me up!" You active-listen again. You say:

Step 2: Write out a situation that requires active listening. Exchange descriptions with a partner then read the situation and respond with an active listening comment. Have the person who wrote the situation reply to your response so that you have an opportunity to follow-up with another active listening statement. Try to get about 4 or 5 interactions so that you push your thinking about what is being communicated to you. Do the same with the other situation.

"I" Statements

The focus of this task is on self-disclosure statements. We selected the "I" statement for use in this task because it keeps the focus on the teacher's feelings and the consequences of the student's behavior to the teacher. The purpose of the "I" statement is to communicate the speaker's perspective.

Situation: A student blurts out the answer to almost every question during a class question and answer period. You've already given him a look which says "That is enough, stop it!" You also said, "Stop answering all the time and let someone else answer." He has just done it again. You respond with an "I" statement: "When you blurt out the answer to every question (the problem behavior), I feel frustrated (the teacher's feelings), because I can't tell what the rest of the students know and who needs help with what (consequences of the problem behavior for the teacher)."

Step 1: Identify a situation which caused you to feel frustrated. Think about the student or other person involved, the behavior, your feelings, and the consequences of the behavior for you. Write an "I" statement which would have been appropriate for the situation.

Step 2: Write four "I" statements of your own to use in communicating with students about problem behavior you confront in schools.

Questioning

The focus of this part of the task is on asking questions that will help you better understand another person's ideas, problems, feelings, or all three. Questioning skills are used in problem identification.

Step 1: Working with a partner, select a topic to discuss. To begin, one person should tell what he/she knows, feels, and or wonders about the topic. The role of the listener is *to ask clarifying and exploratory questions.* Exploratory questions are an invitation to talk about something. Clarifying questions ask for additional information. During the discussion note the questions that you asked the other person.

Step 2: Next, with your partner, assess the questions that were asked. Determine whether the questions helped the listener to understand the perspective, feelings, or information communicated by the speaker. Identify the specifics of what you learned from each question.

Step 3: Reverse the roles and do steps 1 and 2 over.

Step 4: If you asked questions that did not elicit additional information figure out with your partner why you got the response you did and note those reasons.

Step 5: Turn in the list of questions and your notes.

Other Communication Skills

This part of the task gives you an opportunity to practice the five other communication skills that are used in problem solving.

Skills:

1. *Encouraging others to contribute*. For example, "Javier, what do you think about this?" "Jennifer, earlier you said how you felt about this. Now that we have talked more about it, how do you feel?"
2. *Giving information*. For example, "I saw_" "I read. . . ." "I inferred . . ." "My experience is . . ."
3. *Comparing*. For example, "This sounds like . . ." "Several characteristics of this are similar to . . . they are . . ." "I feel the same way about this situation . . . as when . . . happened." "I think almost the same way about this as I do about. . . ."
4. *Contrasting*. For example, "This appears to be different from . . . because. . . ."
5. *Synthesizing*. For example, "So far we have found three different solutions. John, Juanita, George, and Maria all indicated that. . . ."
    Step 1: Select a group of four to six people to work together in a small group.
    Step 2: Name a timer, recorder, reporter, and facilitator. The recorder's task is to tally the incidents of the use of the skills during the conversation.

Skills	Person 1	Person 2	Person 3	Person 4	Person 5	Person 6
"I" statement						
Encouraging						
Exploratory Questions						
Clarifying Questions						
Giving Information						
Comparing						
Contrasting						
Synthesizing						

Step 3: Members of the group need to identify several topics that represent a range of problems frequently confronted by teachers. Remember the focus of this conversation is to give everyone a chance to use the communications skills in a problem identification and solving situation.

Step 4: The facilitator should initiate the discussion by using one of the skills. Carry on the discussion until everyone has had a chance to use each skill. Then stop the discussion of the topic and review the use of the skills. Since the focus is on each person's talk and the form of the talk is being attended to by the group, speakers may feel uncomfortable. Different people may have trouble in using one or more of the skills. Finally, determine what the group has learned about the problems itself.

Step 5: Select a second topic and go through the process again. Provide support and help for one another when it is difficult to use a particular skill. For example, if an individual has difficulty in synthesizing, ask the person a series of specific questions about the content of the discussion to help him/her pull together the ideas.

Step 6: Turn in tally chart with discussion notes.

Exercise 10.8
Conflict Identification and Resolution

The two tasks in this activity focus on facilitating the identification of a problem or conflict and working out a plan for its resolution. Each task is to be performed by four people working together in a small group, and each has roles for a teacher, two students and an observer. Each task should be carried out four times so that everyone has a chance to play each of the roles.

In the first task, the teacher is not involved in the problem. In this task, the conflict is between two students, and the teacher's role is to provide guidance to the students by using a process designed to help them to resolve their problem.

Step 1: In your group of four people, identify who will be the observer, the students and the teacher.

Step 2: Identify several conflicts that students confront and that do not involve the teacher directly.

Step 3: Begin the first two role-plays by having the teacher introduce the conflict and the last two-role play by having the students ask the teacher for help with a conflict they have.

Step 4: Use the checklist to work through the conflic-resolving steps. The observer should record the communication skills used, the comments that interfere with a smooth problem-solving process and other notes that will help in processing the role-play.

CHECKLIST I: CONFLICT RESOLUTION WHEN THE TEACHER IS NOT INVOLVED IN CONFLICT

Step	Facilitating when the teacher is not directly involved in conflict	Monkey Wrenches (Things that happen which jam up the works.)	Record Communication skills used and comments on process
1.Assessment __Teacher observes that there is a conflict or is asked by students to help solve conflict. __Reach agreement with all people involved in the conflict that they will work on identifying the exact conflict and on resolving that conflict. __Determine whether affective or cognitive discomfort for either student is great enough to warrant pursuing problem.	__Active listening to reduce the frustration of the parties involved. __Make it clear that the teacher is not going to solve the problem and is not interested in who is right and who is wrong.	__Do participants have a history of seeing everything as a conflict. (e.g., anytime they don't get their way) __Teacher tells students what the conflict is __Teacher tells students what to do to resolve the conflict	
2. Problem Identification __Identify problem. __Formulate problem statement. __Conflicts among solutions are usually how problems are seen.	__Have the parties involved state the conflict from their perspectives. __Help parties' state own needs. __Help parties to state conflict of needs (paraphrasing being careful to state what student communicates and not teacher's ideas) __Reach agreement that the conflict of needs identified represents fairly what each party has said. __Determine that everyone feels his or her needs have been heard (disgruntled non-verbals need more active listening).	__Problem statement stays at level of conflict among solutions __Closes down and is not open to new solutions __Students do not feel their needs have been heard and feel their needs will not be dealt with. __Teacher has pre-determined results and students know it. Or __Students believe teacher has predetermined results but he/she does not.	
3. Finding Solutions __Identify alternative solutions	__Ask other to indicate what might be done to resolve problem. __Accept all responses, even illogical or irrational ones (at beginning of discussion). __Teacher or someone write down all suggestions.	__Several illogical or irrational responses usually indicate person does not: 1) trust process; 2) feels his/her needs or feelings were not heard. __If illogical or irrational responses continue, stop process and active-listen and ask exploratory questions to student. "Alice, you seem to still be upset. Maybe we have missed an important point you were trying to make. Tell me what it is you meant." __Teacher does not respond with "Don't be silly."	

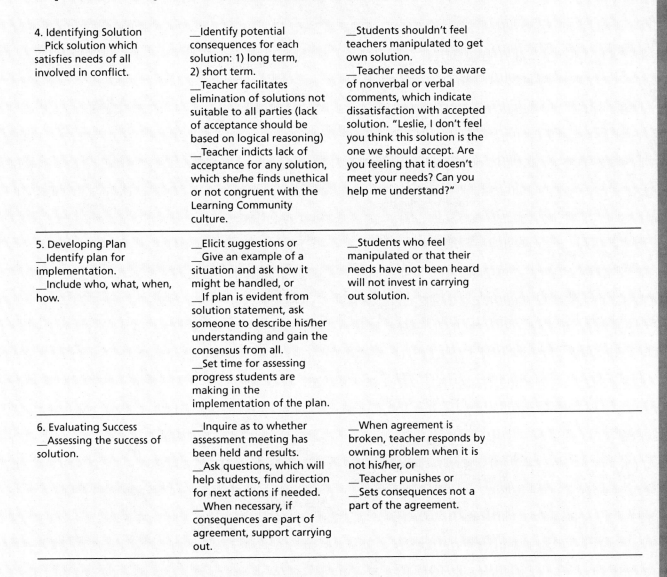

4. Identifying Solution __Pick solution which satisfies needs of all involved in conflict.	__Identify potential consequences for each solution: 1) long term, 2) short term. __Teacher facilitates elimination of solutions not suitable to all parties (lack of acceptance should be based on logical reasoning) __Teacher indicts lack of acceptance for any solution, which she/he finds unethical or not congruent with the Learning Community culture.	__Students shouldn't feel teachers manipulated to get own solution. __Teacher needs to be aware of nonverbal or verbal comments, which indicate dissatisfaction with accepted solution. "Leslie, I don't feel you think this solution is the one we should accept. Are you feeling that it doesn't meet your needs? Can you help me understand?"
5. Developing Plan __Identify plan for implementation. __Include who, what, when, how.	__Elicit suggestions or __Give an example of a situation and ask how it might be handled, or __If plan is evident from solution statement, ask someone to describe his/her understanding and gain the consensus from all. __Set time for assessing progress students are making in the implementation of the plan.	__Students who feel manipulated or that their needs have not been heard will not invest in carrying out solution.
6. Evaluating Success __Assessing the success of solution.	__Inquire as to whether assessment meeting has been held and results. __Ask questions, which will help students, find direction for next actions if needed. __When necessary, if consequences are part of agreement, support carrying out.	__When agreement is broken, teacher responds by owning problem when it is not his/her, or __Teacher punishes or __Sets consequences not a part of the agreement.

Teacher as Facilitator: When both Teacher and Students Are Involved in a Conflict

An example of a situation where both the teacher and students may be part of a conflict is when the teacher assigned a group of students to practice a presentation. She told them to use a certain spot in the classroom and later she began working with another group in an area adjoining that being used by the presentation group. When she had difficulty hearing her students, she signaled to the presentation group that they should lower their voices. At first the presentation group responded, but their voices rose again as they became involved in their work. As a learning-community teacher, the teacher avoided escalating the conflict or responding in an authoritarian manner. Instead of yelling or sending the presentation group to their seats, she walked over to them and said, "I need to hear." A student in the group said, "We need to speak loudly enough to communicate the emotions in our presentation." The teachers responded, "Any ideas on how we can work this?" One student responded, "We could go to the library or you could take your group to the other end of the room." Clearly, the teacher and these students had a history of conflict identification and resolution. Each side stated their needs. Each side was able to hear the other's needs so they moved quickly to a resolution.

Other typical conflicts include: (a) student behavior that disrupts instruction (teacher unable to accomplish expected outcomes) and learning, or (b) homework completed so late that feedback from the teacher is not timely and thus not effective (learning isn't occurring). The teacher is in conflict with the student because his/her time is wasted and the student is not benefiting.

Once again form a group of four people and follow the steps used before with Checklist I. In this part of the task the teacher facilitates the problem solving, but in this instance, she/he must communicate his/her own position, in addition to guiding the student and must participate in the resolution.

CHECKLIST II: CONFLICT RESOLUTION WHEN TEACHER IS DIRECTLY INVOLVED IN CONFLICT

Step	Facilitating when the teacher is not directly involved in conflict	Monkey Wrenches (Things that happen which jam up the works.)	Record Communication skills used and comments on process
1.Assessment __Teacher observes that there is a conflict or is asked by students to help solve conflict in which the teacher is a part. __Reach agreement with all people involved in the conflict that they will work on identifying the exact conflict and on resolving that conflict.	__Teacher begins with "I" statement. __Active listening to reduce the frustration of the parties involved. __Make it clear that the teacher is not going to solve the problem and is not interested in who is right and who is wrong. __Determine whether affective or cognitive discomfort for students or teacher is great enough to warrant pursuing problem.	__Do participants have a history of seeing everything as a conflict. (e.g., anytime they don't get their way) __Teacher tells students what to do to resolve the conflict	
2. Problem Identification __Identify problem. __Formulate problem statement. __Conflict may be of solution (usually how a problem is seen). __Conflicts among solutions are usually how problems are seen.	__Have the parties involved state the conflict from their perspectives. __Help parties' state own needs by helping them to make "I" statements. __Help parties to state conflict of needs (paraphrasing being careful to state what student communicates and not teacher's ideas). __Reach agreement that the conflict of needs identified represents fairly what each party has said. __Determine that everyone feels his or her needs have been heard (disgruntled non-verbals need more active listening). __Have students paraphrase teacher's needs.	__Problem statement stays at level of conflict among solutions rather than moving to conflict of needs. __Closes down and is not open to new solutions __Students or teacher do not feel their needs have been heard and feel their needs will not be dealt with. __Teacher has predetermined results and students know it. Or __Students believe teacher has predetermined results but he/she does not.	

3. Finding Solutions __Identify alternative solutions	__Ask others to indicate what might be done to resolve problem. __Accept all responses, even illogical or irrational ones (at beginning of discussion). __Teacher provides his/her ideas. __Teacher or someone writes down all suggestions.	__Several illogical or irrational responses usually indicate person does not: 1) trust process; 2) feels his/her needs or feelings were not heard. __If illogical or irrational responses continue, stop process and active-listen and ask exploratory questions to student. "Alice, you seem to still be upset. Maybe we have missed an important point you were trying to make. Tell me what it is you meant." __Teacher does not respond with "Don't be silly."
4. Identifying Solution __Pick solution which satisfies needs of all involved in conflict.	__Identify potential consequences for each solution: 1) long term, 2) short term. __Teacher facilitates elimination of solutions not suitable to all parties (lack of acceptance should be based on logical reasoning) __Teacher indicts lack of acceptance for any solution, which she/he finds unethical or not congruent with the Learning Community culture. __When consensus has been reached, teacher or individuals from both sides of conflict state how solution will meet their needs.	__Students shouldn't feel teachers manipulated to get own solution. __Teacher needs to be aware of nonverbal or verbal comments, which indicate dissatisfaction with accepted solution. "Leslie, I don't feel you think this solution is the one we should accept. Are you feeling that it doesn't meet your needs? Can you help me understand?"
5. Developing Plan __Identify plan for implementation. __Include who, what, when, how.	__State what, when, and how you will carry out your teacher's part of agreement. __Elicit suggestions or __ give an example of a situation and ask how it might be handled, or __If plan is evident from solution statement, ask someone to describe his/her understanding and gain the consensus from all. __Students state what, when, how they will carry out their part of the agreement. __Set time for assessing progress students are making in the implementation of the plan. __Have students write out agreement. Put in special place, post, or have participants sign.	__Student who feel manipulated or that their needs have not been heard will not invest in carrying out solution.

6. Evaluating Success
__Assessing the success of solution.

__Ask for feedback and then relate teacher feelings and observations.
__If it is obvious plan is not working, call attention to fact and schedule a meeting to create a new plan.
__Ask questions, which will help students, find direction for next actions if needed.
__When necessary, if consequences are part of agreement, support carrying out.
__Be careful to allow time and reminders to facilitate implementation of plan.

__When agreement is broken, teacher responds by owning problem when it is not his/her, or
__Teacher punishes or
__Sets consequences not a part of the agreement.

Exercise 10.9
Conflict Identification and Resolution

Creating a Plan for Teaching Students How to Identify and Resolve Conflicts

Step 1: The focus of this task is on thinking through and creating a plan for how you would teach Identification and Resolution of Conflicts to your students. Using the Planning format below create a plan for teaching a group of students the conflict resolution process. Be sure to work out role-plays that will provide concrete experience and practice.

STAGE THREE: IDENTIFYING AND RESOLVING CONFLICTS

Conflicts: Steps that are taught to Learning Community Members Describe Each Step	Introducing the Steps of Conflict Identification & Resolution Activity that will be used to teach learners specific actions of each steps	Practice and Feedback Describe the activities that learners will do in order to practice the steps. List what you will observe and give feedback about.	Evaluation Describe a conflict situation that will serve as the basis for learners to role-play. Use the conflict identification and resolution process.
Step 1. Reach Agreement			
Step 2. State the Conflict			
Step 3. Identify and Select Responses			
Step 4. Create a Solution			
Step 5a. Design a Plan that will be implemented			
Step 5b. Implement the plan with the student			
Step 6. Assess the Success of the Plan Implementation			

Step 2: Not all conflicts are resolved in an orderly non-stressful manner. There are times when the teacher must act in an assertive, responsible, authoritative manner. At these times a student's behavior has disrupted the flow of learning, the student may be on the verge of getting out of control and the teacher needs to stop what is happening and then work to socialize the student to respond in a new manner when he/she confront the same frustration in the future. Use the format below and create a plan that responds to a discipline problem that you have observed and need to think through how you would handle the immediate situation and the follow-up work with the student.

CRISIS PROBLEM BEHAVIOR REQUIRING TEACHER ACTIONS AND STUDENT DISCIPLINE

Discipline Problems Problem behavior that requires students to be disciplined. Describe Problem	New Behavior State what behavior you expect once the problem behavior is eliminated	State what strategy you will use to work with the student in order to eliminate the problem behavior	If punishment should be required what will it be? State how you will describe the punishment and how the consequences are related to the specific problem behavior

MONITORING AND EVALUATING YOUR CLASSROOM ORGANIZATION AND MANAGEMENT

At the end of the activities for this chapter, are two forms that provide guidelines for checking out our classroom organization and management performances. Using these in your planning in the future will help you remember what things to consider about management. Having a peer or cooperating teacher use them when assessing your plans and observing your teaching will provide you with feedback about your progress toward the Program's Performance outcomes.

The first form was finalized by Lanier, Putnam and Barnes (1998) and used in the MSU Multiple Perspectives Program and the Flint Teacher Education Center. Data compiled from observations of student teachers, intern teachers and inservice teachers indicates that when: (a) 20% or more of the teacher management talk falls into the restoring category, the smooth flow of instruction and learning is disrupted; (b) 0% of the teacher management talk falls in any one of the three categories, the flow of instruction and learning is disrupted; and (c) a larger % of management behaviors falls in maintaining or restoring than in creating, the teacher as well as students are disrupting the classroom. Less experienced teachers (student teachers, new teachers) and teachers who are starting the year with a new group of students are apt to have a larger percentage of teacher talk focused on management. However, more experienced teachers will establish expectations through their Stage 2 work and the rules, norms, routines, and procedures that support smooth instruction and learning are clear and functioning, thus it is not necessary for the teacher's to focus on management.

The second form is a rubric that provides a qualitative idea about how well the student teacher is progressing toward the Program's Performance Standards for management.

Exercise 10.10
Role Plays. Learning Community Teacher Practicing
(Open Reflective Disposition) Talking with Angry Parent

One of the situations that student teachers and some first-year teachers find threatening is when they are confronted by an angry parent. Parents come to school angry when they think/feel that their child is being treated unfairly, is not being listened to, is not being provided the opportunity to learn, or is being bullied. Their demeanor is dependent upon the relationships the student teacher or teacher has created prior to the occurrence of a problem. You will find less hostility when you have continuously been in contact positively with your students' parents and guardians since you learned they were assigned to your learning community and at least begun to build trust and a sense of partnership. For novice educators, beginning statements and listening is difficult. Below are a series of situations that provide you with the opportunity to practice working with an agitated parent or guardian.

Step 1: Working in pairs one person take the role of the student teacher or new teacher and the other take the role of the angry parent and work your way through situation 1.

Step 2: Reverse roles and work through situation 2.

Step 3: List the communication and problem-solving skills that were the easiest and most difficult for you to carry out. Make a concrete plan for how you will work on the communication and problem-solving skills that were the most difficult for you.

Role Play 1

A. A Message from the Principal

The principal asks to talk with you, a Learning Community teacher after school. The principal tells you that Mrs. White was in and said that unless her child starts to have a good experience at school and that there is evidence that the child is actually being taught, both Mrs. and Mr. White will remove the child from school at the end of the semester. You look at your records and note that Mrs. White was in to see you about a month ago. She was concerned at that time, but after talking with her for an hour, you thought that she went away satisfied. You agree to meet with Mrs. White before school in two days.

B. Preparing for the Conference

- What will you study and prepare for the meeting?
- What exactly do you want to communicate during the conference?
- Without knowing any more information than what the principal told you, what would you establish as the goals for the meeting?
- What questions will you ask Mrs. White that will help you understand her concerns?
- During the next day of school, what type of interactions will you have with Mrs. White's child?

C. The Conference

When Mrs. White comes to the conference she brings in a folder of papers that have been sent home since the beginning of the school year. They have been marked with *number right, letter grades,* a single number (e.g., 3), percentages or *number wrong.* The written feedback on them is general and not specific in nature (e.g., good paper, work harder, careless).

- What do you say to open the conversation?

Mrs. White is clearly upset. She does not raise her voice. However, whenever you interrupt her talk to respond to something she is saying, she glares back, communicating that she is not being listened to.

Mrs. White says that she does not think her child is being taught. She tells you that her child is doing simpler work than a year ago, that she does not see any improvements in his writing or spelling. She shows you earlier work and work from the last week to illustrate this point. She says that when she tells him to correct things he says that the teacher does not make him do that. She tells you that when she asks him what he needs so that he will do better he says I need the teacher to explain things. She says she is concerned that his teacher doesn't care about his learning or success. She takes a deep breath and indicates that she has communicated what is frustrating her.

- Based on this little information what do you say next?

Given that the parent is clearly trying to work with the school and her child to improve academic performances you and the parent create a plan of action that is congruent with the district's *Vision "no child shall be left behind."*

- Outline the action plan you might create.

D. Post Conference

After the conference, you lead the debriefing with your principal.

- What would you want to be able to tell the principal about Mrs. White after your conference?
- What new information would you want to be able to tell the principal about the student?
- What questions (that the principal would ask you) would you want to be able to answer if you had had a productive meeting?
- How would you know if you reached your goal or not?
- What is your goal for the student?
- What is your goal for the next meeting with the parent?

Role Play 2

A. Angry Parent enters Classroom

Mrs. White walks in your learning community as the students are leaving for the day. You infer from the look on her face that not everything is OK. She spots you, the teacher, and walks quickly to where you are standing . . . and shouts; "I have had it with you people! You are not teaching my child!" She flings open a folder on the table in front of you and out drops the papers that her child has taken home so far this year.

- What is the first thing you say to Mrs. White?

B. Learning Community Student Teacher Responds to Angry Parent

You then tell Mrs. White that you see she is clearly upset and that you want to get the other members of your High Performance Work Team so that you can all hear her concerns. The other teachers come and you sit down around one of the tables in the room.

- What active listening statements would you say?
- What do you say to open the conversation in a way that will end the communication of frustration and move to a problem solving mode?
- At this point what is your goal for this meeting?

C. Angry Parent Continues to be Upset

Mrs. White talks in a loud voice. If you interrupt her to respond to something she is saying, she glares back, and says, "You are not listening to me! You are just making an excuse!" Mrs. White says that she does not think her child is being taught. She tells you that her child is doing simpler work than a year ago, that she does not see improvements on his writing or spelling. She shows you earlier work and work from the last week to illustrate her points. She says that when she tells the child to correct things he says that the teacher does not make him do that. She tells you that when she asks him what he needs so that he will do better he says I need the teacher to explain things. She says she is concerned that his teachers don't care about his learning or success. She takes a deep breath and is so angry that her hands are shaking as she piles up the papers she brought with her.

- What would you say next?
- What would you say to move the conversation to the problem resolution place?

D. The Parent is Assertive that Changes Need to be Made and You are Ready to Create a Plan of Action

Mrs. White is clear that she expects changes to be made. You are anxious to work with the child and the parent to improve the child's learning and feelings about school.

- Outline the action plan that you might create to work through the problems that you identified. The action plan is congruent with the district's VISION *"that all students shall learn"* and that each child is being taught as a member of the learning community.

E. Sharing Objective Information with the Principal

As a Learning Community teacher, you are responsible for the debriefing with your principal after the conference.

- What questions would you expect to have answered as the result of a productive meeting?
- What type of documentation will you keep about the meeting?
- What follow-up will you do with the parent in a week? In two weeks?

TEACHER AND ANGRY PARENT AND CONFLICT IDENTIFICATION AND RESOLUTION

Needs Human Resource Help	Basic	Proficient	Distinguished
1. Responds aggressively or passively to parent 2. Raises own voice or withdraws and does not speak when parent is communicating frustration 3. Calls for the principal 4. Blames the student 5. Blames the parent 6. Blames the other kids, the district or the school	1. Listens to the parent 2. States the problem based on what he/she thinks is wrong 3. Says "you are angry because . . ." and the parent indicates that the teacher has reflected the parent's concern accurately	1. Active listens to the parent (reflecting the cognitive and affective messages that the parent communicates) 2. Inquires about the parents thinking in order to understand the anger and frustration that the parent is communicating 3. Finds problem and states the problem from the parents point of view 4. Working with parent and other Learning Community members creates action plan to resolve problem and concerns of all involved	1. Active listens to the parent (reflecting the cognitive and affective messages that the parent communicates) 2. Inquires about the parents thinking in order to understand the anger and frustration that the parent is communicating 3. Finds problem and states the problem from the parents point of view 4. Working with parent and other Learning Community members creates action plan to resolve problem and concerns of all involved 5. Sets up process for evaluating whether plan is working or not

At the end of this chapter is an observation form and rubric that you can use during your early field experiences and in student teaching. When you teach a small group lesson, ask a colleague to observe you so you can see where your management talk and actions are occurring. If a colleague is not available, videotape the lesson, or audio tape your talking so that you can tally your talk and actions. Having this information about yourself increases your reflection and investment in appropriate planning.

MANAGING AN EFFECTIVE LEARNING ENVIRONMENT THROUGH CREATING, MAINTAINING, AND RESTORING

Description of Situation:

Creating an Orderly Environment	Dates Observed
Efficiently distributes and collects materials	
Provides for orderly pupil movement	
Describes desired behavior and why	
Describes attention getting devices for children and teachers	
Describes purpose/rationale for the lesson (standard, performance)	
Questions students about feelings (affect)	
Questions students about present knowledge of subject (linking)	
Listens to students describe feelings (paraphrases at times)	
Listens to students describe prior experiences (synthesizes)	
Relates student feedback to present standard, task, performance	
Describes strategies for the lesson:	
a. gives concrete example of the activity	
b. describes probable time conditions	
c. describes what to do when finished	
d. describes permissions and prohibitions with rationale	
f. communicates location of rubric and example of work done at top of the standard	
Asks students to describe what they are going to do	
Clarifies student concerns	
Walks around; observing; assisting; etc., until everyone is on task	
Reinforces desired intellectual behavior and academic responsibility	
Reinforces desired social-emotional behavior (social responsibility)	
Reinforces desired personal responsibility	
Reinforces desired social justice responsibility	
Presents challenging content (not too easy or too difficult)	
Present activities that are pleasant to student (not too easy/difficult, interesting	
Observations:	

Maintaining an Orderly Environment	Dates Observed
Redirects with task involvement	
Purposefully ignores potential distraction	
Reduces frustration through task assistance	
Uses non-verbal signal interference	
Shifts instructional techniques, materials, etc., as part of lesson	
Shifts instructional techniques, content, etc., based on observations	
Provides constructive activity in face of unforeseen time problems	
Removes potential distractions	
Uses proximity-relationship control effectively	
Reinforces-rewards desired behavior	
Regroups pupils	
Spontaneous humor or affection	
Changes objectives/strategy because of on-going assessment	
Utilizes successful attention-getting devices	
Restoring an Orderly Environment	
Verbal desist techniques:	
a. calls name	
b. requests end of inappropriate behavior	
c. directs or suggests appropriate behavior	
d. give rationale for behavior change	
Limits activities space, props	
Sharpen boundaries for permissible behavior	
Conditional promise, (If you do this, then . . .)	
Punishment—gives discomfort, e.g., verbal or non-verbal censure, overtime, isolation, deprivation, physical	
Threats, warnings	
Satiation	
Comments from Observer:	

*Judith Lanier (Professor Emeritus, MSU) created the original CMR concept and observation form.

RUBRIC FOR CLASSROOM MANAGEMENT AND ORGANIZATION

Component	Below Minimal Performance Level 1	Needs Work 2	Meets Standard 3	Exemplary Practice 4
Creating an Effective Learning Environment	The Student Teacher begins talking without everyone's attention. The Student Teacher waits for attention for too long a period of time and then starts lesson.	Student Teacher performs 1 or 2 *Creating Behaviors*	Student Teacher performs a majority of the *Creating* actions. Students are compliant and asking clarifying questions when necessary without getting the group off task.	The learners respond to the Student Teacher using established routines and procedures for transitions between lessons. The Student Teacher uses minimal *Creating Behaviors* to create an effective learning environment.
Maintaining an Effective Learning Environment	The Student Teacher ignores cues that students will be off task or disruptive; May walk around room but physical position did not have the effect of keeping learners engaged	Student teacher performs 1 or 2 maintaining behaviors	The Student Teacher obviously uses *Maintaining* actions but does not disrupt the learning environment or flow of the lesson. Students are compliant.	The Student Teacher monitors learners and uses *Maintaining* actions in ways that do not distract any other learners, keeping the learners on task and progressing in the acquisition of new knowledge and skills.
Restoring an Effective Learning Environment	Student Teacher performs 1 or 2 restoring behaviors but has little or no effect on student engagement	The majority of the management and organizational behaviors performed by the Student Teacher fall into the restoring category.	Student Teacher uses restoring actions in less than 20% of his/her management talk. Restoring actions do not disrupt other learners and they stay on task.	No restoring actions are necessary during formal instruction, small group, independent work, and any type of transition.

Component	Below Minimal Performance Level 1	Needs Work 2	Meets Standard 3	Exemplary Practice 4
Observer's impression and notes support that:	In general the Student Teacher went through his/her lesson. Students were or were not engaged as they chose. Student Teacher was not in charge even in settings where students were not disruptive. Students' learning time was wasted.	The Student Teacher creates many disruptions in the flow of the lesson by over-managing students. For most of the learners instruction was a waste of time.	The Student Teacher's management and organization included less than 20% *restoring* behaviors. There is an even distribution of creating and maintaining actions. There is evidence that students are engaged in meaningful tasks and are acquiring new knowledge and skills.	The instructional part of the lesson, practice or application activities, or authentic evaluation tasks are carried out without any Student Teacher or learner disruptions to the lesson. Learners are engaged in authentic tasks that provide opportunities for them to apply knowledge and skills to real life.
Recommendation	Student Teacher should not teach again until he/she has plans for a series of lessons, with clear learner outcomes and evaluations. Mentors work on helping Student Teacher move focus from his/her performance to student learning.	Student Teacher should focus on linking the learner outcomes and the lesson activity and then write out the *Creating* behaviors that he/she will use to explain what learners will learn that is new.	Work with Student Teacher on analyzing student work for the purpose of individual assessment and use of data for creating instructional groups.	Use the Student Teacher's plans and practice as models for other student teachers that have problems with classroom management and organization.

RECOMMENDED READINGS

The following references are recommended to individuals who are interested in more detailed information about specific problem behaviors.

References and Suggested Readings
Assertiveness

Bower, S. A., and Bower, G. H. *Asserting Your Self,* Reading, Mass., Addison-Wesley.

Cummings, C. (2000). *Winning strategies for classroom management.* ASCD Publishers.

Davidson, J. (1997). *The complete idiot's guide to assertiveness.* Alpha Books, Penguin Group (USA) Inc.

Davis, M., Eshelman. (1988, 2003). E. G., McKay, M. *The Relaxation & Stress Reduction Workbook,* New Harbinger Publ., Inc., Oakland, CA.

Glenn, H. S., Nelsen, J. (2000). *Raising Self-Reliant Children in a Self Indulgent World.* Three Rivers Press. NY, NY.

Jakubowski-Spector, P. (1973). "Facilitating the Growth of Women Through Assertive Training" *The Counseling Psychologist.* 4, 75–86.

Lazarus, A. (1966). "Behavior Rehearsal vs. Non-directive therapy vs. advice in effecting behavior change: Behavioral Research and Therapy," 4, 209–12.

Caring

Katz, Susan Roberta. (1999). *"Teaching in Tensions: Latino Immigrant Youth, Their Teachers, and the Structures of Schooling."* Teachers College Record 100 No. 4, Summer, 809-840.

Noddings, Nel. (2005). *The Challenge to Care in Schools: An Alternative Approach to Education, Second Edition* (Advances in Contemporary Educational Thought Series) NY: Teachers College Press.

Poverty

Angela's Ashes (movie)

Bullying

AAUW Educational Foundation. (2001). *Hostile Hallways: Bullying, teasing, and sexual harassment in school.* Washington, D.C., May.

Baumeister, R., and Leary, M. (1995). The Need to belong: Desire for Interpersonal Attachments as a Fundamental Human Motivation. *Psychological Bulletin, 117,* pp. 497–529.

Beane, A. L. (1999). The bully free classroom: over 100 tips and strategies for teachers K–8, Free Spirit Publishing Inc., Minn., MN.

Belsey, B. Cyberbullying, Defined, *www.Cyberbulling.com*

Bullied to Death (A&E video).

Canada, G. Fist stick knife gun: A personal history of violence in American. Boston: Beacon Press, 1995.

Coloroso, B. (2004). The bully, the bullied, and the bystander: From preschool to high school—how Parents and teachers can help break the cycle of violence, Harper Resource of HarperCollins, NY, NY.

Cooper, D., and Snell, J. L. (2003). Bullying—Not Just a Kid Thing, *Educational Leadership, Creating Caring Schools, March* Vol. 60, No. 6., pp. 22–25.

Eckman, A. (2001). *Beyond Bulling: Knowing when to step in—and when not to.* Education Update, Volumn 43, Number 6, September, ASCD.

Olweus, D. (1993). *Understanding children's worlds: bullying at school.* Blackwell Publishing, Malden, MA.

Scherer, M. (2003). *Perspective/uncivil liberties.* Educational Leadership: Creating Caring Schools, March Vol. 60, No. 6, Pp. 5–6.

Shore, R. M. (1996). *Personalization: Working to curb violence in an American High Schools.* Phi Delta Kappan, January, pp. 362–363.

Walls, L. (2004). *Bullying and sexual harassment in schools.* Committee for Children, *www.cfchildren.org.*

Drug Abuse

Edwards, D. M., and Zander, T. A. (1985). Children of alcoholics: Background and strategies for the counselor. Elementary School Guidance and Counseling, 20(2), 121–128. This article reviews strategies for working with children of alcoholics and provides an extensive list of articles, books, and films, which may be useful in providing information to classroom teachers.

Horton, L. (1988). Alcohol/drug prevention: A working bibliography for educators. *Illinois Schools Journal,* 67(3), 18–27. This is a bibliography for educators who want to increase their knowledge of alcohol and other drugs and to devise prevention measures for schools and classrooms.

Layne, D. J., and Grossnickle, D. R. (1989). A teamwork approach to the prevention of chemical abuse and dependency. *NASSP Bulletin,* 73(514), 98–101. This article reviews Operation Snowball, a program that purports to engender positive attitudes in students and combats alienation and the attendant drug and alcohol abuse.

Oetting, E. R., Beauvais, F, and Edwards, R. W. (1989). "Crack": The epidemic. *The School Counselor, 37(2),* 128–136.

Powers, S., and Miller, C. E. (1988). Effects of a drug education program on third and fourth grade students. *Journal of Alcohol and Drug Education, 33(3),* 26–31. This article reviews a study and illustrates the difficulty of preventing drug use. It also shows the connections between decision making about drugs and self-esteem. (December 1988). *Elementary School Guidance and Counseling, 23(2),* pp. 139–145.

Dishonest Behavior

Miller, G. E., and Klungness, L. (1986). Treatment of nonconfrontative stealing in school-age children. *School Psychology Review, 15(1),* 24–35. Reviews studies dealing with non-confrontative stealing—that is, stealing in which there is no direct confrontation with or use of force upon the victim. We recommend this paper because it describes work relevant to aversive contingency management, positive contingency management, parent training, and self-control, as well as other prevention studies for schools and communities.

Child Abuse

Camras, L. A., Ribordy, A., Hill, J., Martino, S., Spaccarelli, S., and Stefani, R. (1988). Recognition and posing of emotional expressions by abused children and their mothers. *Developmental Psychology, 24(6),* 776–781. This paper provides information about the recognition of emotional facial expressions by abused children and their mothers.

Herman, P. (1985). Educating children about sexual abuse: The teachers' responsibility. *Childhood Education, 6(3),* 169–174.

Koblinsky, S., and Behana, N. (September 1984). Child sexual abuse: The educator's role in prevention, detection, and intervention. *Young Children, 39(6),* 3–15. An approach to this highly emotional topic. We recommend this paper for reading and discussion.

Spiegel, L. P. (1988). Child abuse hysteria and the elementary school counselor. *Elementary School Guidance and Counseling, 23(1),* 48–53.

Suicide

Lewis, S. A., Johnson, J., Cohen, P., Garcia, M., and Velez, C. N. (1988). Attempted suicide in youth: Its relationship to school achievement, educational goals, and socioeconomic status. *Journal of Abnormal Child Psychology, 16,* 459–471.

Steele, W. (1983). *Preventing teenage suicide*. Naples, Fla.: Ann Arbor Publishers. Suggestions for educating parents and students about what to do if they come in contact with people who have suicidal tendencies. Steel's videotape "Teenage Suicide: What to Do" is also available.

Wellman, M. M. (1984). The school counselor's role in the communication of suicidal ideation by adolescents. *School Counselor, 32,* 104–109.

Discipline

Cummings, C. Winning strategies for classroom management, Chapter 1. (*www.ascd.org/publications/books/100052/chapter1.html*)

Marzano, R., Marzano, J., and Pickering, D. (2003). *Classroom management that works: Research-based strategies for every teacher.* ASCD, Alexandria VA.

Wolfgang, C. H. (1996). *The three faces of discipline for the elementary school teacher: Empowering the teacher and students.* Allyn and Bacon. Boston, MA.

Wong, H., *Classroom management.*

General Information

Allsopp, A., and Prosen, S. (1988). Teacher reactions to a child sexual abuse training program. *Elementary School Guidance and Counseling, 22,* 299–305.

Bósquiz, Mario. (2005). *The Chalupa Rules: A Latino Guide to Grengolaudia.* Published by Penguin Group, NY, NY.

Brophy, J. E., and Rohrkemper, M. M. (1980). *Teachers' specific strategies/or dealing with hostile-aggressive students.* (Research Series No. 86). East Lansing: Michigan State University, Institute for Research on Teaching.

———— and ———— (1989). Teachers' strategies for coping with failure syndrome students. (IRT Research Series No. 197). East Lansing, Mich.: College of Education.

Canada, G. (1995). *FistStickKnifeGun.* Beacon, Publishers. Boston, MA.

Cohen, E. G. (1982). A multi-ability approach to the integrated classroom. *Journal of Reading Behavior, 14(4),* 439–460. (1986).

Collins, M. T., and Collins, D. R. (1975). *Survival kit for teachers (and parents).* Glenview III.: Scott Foresman.

Designing groupwork: Strategies for the heterogeneous classroom. New York: Teachers College Press.

Fagen, S., Long, N., Stevens, D. (1975). *Teaching children self-control: preventing emotional and learning problems in the elementary school.* Charles Merrill Publishing Co., Columbus, Ohio.

Gordon, T. (1974). *Teacher effectiveness training.* New York: Peter H. Wyden.

Hare, N., Hare, J. (1991). *The miseducation of the black child. The Black Think Tank,* San Francisco, California.

Lewis, R., and Lovegrove, M. (1984). Teachers' classroom control procedures: Are students' preferences being met? *Journal of Education for Teaching, 10(2),* 97–105.

Putnam, J., Singo, T. (1994). *Changing the Classroom Management Paradigm.* Michigan State University, E. Lansing, MI.

Sheets, R. H. (2002). *"You're just a kid that's there"—Chicano perception of disciplinary events.* ERIC, EJ643802.

Wong-Fillmore, L. (1991). Language and cultural issues in early education. In S. L. Kagan (Ed.), The care and education of America's young children: Obstacles and opportunities. The 90th yearbook of the National Society for the Study of Education (pp. 3–49). Chicago: University of Chicago Press.

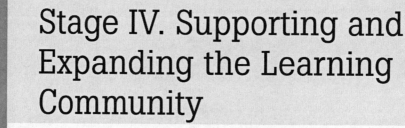

Stage IV. Supporting and Expanding the Learning Community

By the time the class has reached developmental stage IV, the learning community is a fully functioning reality. Students feel at ease with each other. They know the rules, their roles, and the norms. When problems arise, they not only know that the problems can be solved but also how it is done.

Another sign that the classroom learning community has reached stage IV is that the students have confidence in their abilities to solve problems and to be in control of their own behavior. This is the result of careful attention to the connections between the norms of the classroom and members' actions during the proceeding stages. This stage begins to emerge about the third week of the school year; it reaches maturity by about the fifth week. Throughout the rest of the year, the classroom learning community engages in productive activities, with attention given to supporting and raising the quality of community life. The class members work systematically on redefining or adding class goals for the year. These goals are used to guide decision making within the community. Both teacher and students become responsible for monitoring the progress within the classroom learning community. The teacher makes use of this formative evaluation data to organize and manage instructional activities that contribute directly to students' achievement of academic, personal, social, and equity goals of schooling.

As the community evolves to stage IV, the focus shifts from classroom governance issues to concern for student achievement consistent with the purposes of schooling. What has gone before has been, in a sense, preparation for this productive stage. Getting on with productive activity is a sign that the culture of the classroom learning community has been established.

Teachers and pupils share responsibility for supporting the quality of life in the classroom learning community. However, teachers can help all members to participate in the life of the community more fully by modeling how to make use of thoughtful plans and how to monitor themselves and others. Commonly referred to as "cooperative learning" or "multiability tasks," group work can be considered a "strategy for solving two common classroom problems: keeping students involved with their work, and managing students with a wide range of academic skills" (Cohen, 1986, p. 6). Group work does support pupil learning in all domains and is worthy of scholarly study.

This chapter, like Chapters 8 to 10, is organized according to the cycle of (1) preparation, (2) implementation, and (3) reflecting. In stage IV, the learning community becomes a public forum in which the connections between plans prepared (intentions) and actions taken (implementations) are discussed openly (reflections). The teacher's consistent use of this heuristic models for students how meaningful structures and relationships are built.

We urge teachers to discuss with students how their actions are informed by their beliefs and to tell them that all actions have consequences. If things happen in the classroom that are not productive and not valued, then the teacher knows how to examine the connections—to backtrack from consequences to actions to plans to beliefs. In this chapter, using this analysis cycle is what we mean by "reflection." We concur with Argyris (1982) that such reasoning must finally be conducted in public, in order for change (learning) to occur. The public discourse provides new data, support, and challenge for thoughts. It also includes all community members in the maintenance and improvement of the classroom culture.

We recognize that commitment to community is always particular to a specific class, school, or family. The commitment arises out of awareness that the particular group provides an array of satisfying choices, based on reliable and valid information. In a learning community, when old perceptions are found to be inaccurate, they are discarded, and replaced by new perceptions. Thus, trust in the reflective practices of the community grows. Effort does not have to be expended on pretending that some things are true when everyone knows that they are not. The energy saved can be invested in learning rather than in protecting.

PREPARATION

Planning during stage IV is an ongoing process. At this stage the community has been established. Therefore the focus of planning changes from establishing the community to: (1) ongoing monitoring of the community culture and (2) instructional planning that is focused on attaining specified functions and goals.

Monitoring

Preparing includes identifying the kinds of things that on a day-to-day basis give teachers and students cues about the state of the classroom learning community. The teacher's monitoring of what is going on includes determining that the community continues to function and that specified outcomes are being worked toward and achieved.

During the year, the teacher monitors the quality of the community. Planning specific monitoring procedures helps to provide a basis for systematically identifying needed changes. The monitoring procedures should help to answer general questions such as: "What is this about?" "What outcomes are occurring?" and "Are we using all resources?"

Specific characteristics that the teacher monitors include: (1) equity in power and status among students, (2) the mix of activities and their contributions to the classroom learning community, and (3) the contributions of the daily life of the classroom learning community to achievement of the stated purposes of schooling.

For example, learning-community teachers monitor progress related to the subject matter that is to be learned. They also monitor how the learning process (e.g., lectures and cooperative learning) contributes to those same purposes of schooling. An example is a history lesson in which the students look for "voices not represented in the text." This lesson contributes to ideas of social justice as well as other specific academic outcomes the teacher identified. Further, a related small-group research activity could also contribute to understanding: (1) the various silent positions, (2) the usefulness of cooperation in learning, and (3) the responsibility for reading critically and questioning critically (social responsibility).

Monitoring involves more than teacher assessment. Pupils also must monitor (and thus must be taught) the indicators of a successful learning community. In addition, they need to learn to monitor *their* experiences in the community. They need to ask: "How are we doing?" "Am I learning?" "What am I learning?" "Am I helping?" and "Am I getting the help that I need?" For example, in stage II, establishing expectations, pupils are taught procedures for asking for help, offering help, listening to the helper, deciding whether they can or cannot help, and saying no. During stage IV, teachers and students monitor being helpful, because helpfulness is a necessary quality in a learning community. Students'

What do you notice immediately in the pupils' behavior? Relate their behavior to:

Rules

Procedures

Roles

Norms

How do you interpret the meaning of these behaviors? Relate the students' behavior to their understanding of:

Rules

Procedures

Roles

Norms

FIGURE 11-1

Monitoring students' behavior in a learning community.

What norms seem to be operating in this classroom? That is, what do you see, and on the basis of your observations, what general guidelines appear to drive student behavior?

Observed Actions	Inferred Beliefs about norms that are operating

Compare your findings with the norms you intended to establish in your classroom learning community. Do you need to work on any particular norm? Do you need to extinguish any unintended norm?

FIGURE 11-2

Monitoring norms in a learning community.

abilities to say no, to ask for assistance, and to accept being told "I can't help you," are cues to the establishment of this norm—and these abilities can be monitored.

Following are some examples that illustrate the nature of the things that need to be monitored and the types of monitoring tasks that can be designed. Figures 11-1 and 11-2 illustrate ways of monitoring the community in general. Figure 11-3 provides a means of assessing small-group work.

Date: _____ Class: _____
Time: _____ Name: _____

Members of the group: _____

Task: _____

Product: _____

Subtasks for completing assignment: _____

Assigned roles:

Facilitator _____

Timer _____

Recorder _____

1. List the people in your group who acted as organizer:

   Give an example of how the role was carried out:

2. List the people in your group who acted as contributor:

   Give an example of how the role was carried out:

3. List the people in your group who acted as encourager:

4. List the people in your group who acted as linker:

5. If this project were assigned again, how would you like to see it done differently?

6. If this project were assigned again, what would you keep the same?

7. What are some of the problems that your group had while working on this project?

8. What are some of the problems you had with this project?

9. What study-group skill have you improved in the most?

10. Based on the criteria we have established for group work, how would you grade yourself in this project? _____ Why do you think that is the grade you earned?

FIGURE 11-3

Group work assessment form. [*Source:* The authors have used Standord's labels for roles in group development (1977, p. 111) and E. Cohen's labels for assigned groupwork (1986, p. 85).]

Figure 11-1 presents two major questions for use in monitoring the foundations of the functioning community. Asking, in effect, the questions "What is actually going on?" and "What does this mean?" provides a structure for monitoring a part of the community that could slip away if not monitored. For example, when established procedures are not followed, there is likely to be a decline in available instructional time. While this may not seem like a major problem at first, a loss of as few as three minutes a day is equivalent to over a quarter of a period (15 minutes) in a week. At a loss of five minutes a day, almost half a traditional instructional period is lost in a week.

Figure 11-2 presents a form for monitoring community norms, specifically. Determining what is actually going on and whether more needs to be invested in establishing or changing norms helps to maintain the community.

Figure 11-3 presents a form for getting feedback about individual participation in small-group work. This form may be filled out by a group working together or by individual members. A form of this nature provides monitoring information of two types: first, information about roles as they are related to effective group responsibility, and second, monitoring information about the small-group project as it was assigned.

Planning for Instruction

Teaching for understanding is integral to learning-community outcomes. Planning for instruction that promotes understanding includes: (1) reviewing subject matter, (2) clarifying expected pupil outcomes, (3) identifying the sequence of the curriculum, (4) identifying multiability tasks, (5) identifying the steps in each task, (6) identifying checkup and due dates for products, (7) identifying evaluation tasks and grading criteria, (8) preparing explicit explanations of processes and expected outcomes, and (9) identifying criteria for determining whether everyone understands (e.g., can do something or can explain).

Reviewing the subject matter is essential to teaching for understanding. Both in-service and preservice teachers use this step to refresh their thinking about the structure of the particular subject matter they are getting ready to teach. The review is focused on finding linkages between traditional lesson topics and the larger subject-matter concepts. For example, in a mathematics unit entitled "The Mouse and the Elephant" (Fitzgerald and Shroyer, 1986), four concepts are available for instruction. Rather than selecting only one (e.g., graphing), the teacher reviews the materials to see how the concepts are connected to each other. The focus of the lessons should be on understanding the concepts and their relationships to each other. The review of subject matter as a part of the planning process provides the teacher with the opportunity to clarify the subject-matter connections before planning specific lessons.

The learning-community teacher identifies the functions of schooling and specific goals for classes during the vision-building process (see Chapter 7). In stage IV, the functions and goals provide guidance in selection of content and specification of expected unit outcomes. After the content has been reviewed, review of the functions and goals results in clarification of the outcomes expected from the next sequence of instruction.

Once the outcomes have been specified, the teacher can identify where the instruction will begin and how the unit will be introduced. What follows is a probable sequence of curriculum that can be used as planned or adjusted on the basis of feedback from students during instruction.

The information about outcomes and sequence is used as the basis for identifying specific instructional methods. For example, learning-community functions of schooling require use of small-group cooperative learning and multiability tasks along with individual work, lectures, discussions, simulations, and question-answer lessons. Planning multiability and/or cooperative learning tasks along with other methods provides a concrete representation of instruction so that the teacher can review the planned experiences and determine the potential impact.

Once a general plan has been completed, more specific plans are made. For example, the steps in each lesson for both the teacher and students are listed. This provides an opportunity for the teacher to catch any points that would cause confusion for students. It also provides an opportunity to list all materials and equipment necessary for a given lesson.

Identifying dates for checking up on individual and group progress and for turning in specific products is part of the planning for the specifics of a unit. At the same time, criteria for evaluation and evaluation tasks are identified.

Next, the sequence of instruction is reviewed, and explicit explanations for processes and content are written or talked out. This process provides teachers with information about points at which they might unintentionally confuse students by skipping a step in a process, not making criteria clear, or being unclear during direct instruction.

Finally, preparation includes the specification of criteria for determining when everyone understands. Deciding what all learning-community students must learn provides a basis for deciding when the community will move on to a new unit and new material.

The process described above for preparing for instruction is used repeatedly by learning-community teachers. Variations on the process are developed individually, as teachers come to see what is essential to planning instruction so that all functions of schooling will be attended to on a regular basis. Careful, thoughtful planning provides a basis upon which teachers can make productive decisions during instruction. Teachers and students together thus promote progress toward specified outcomes rather than putting roadblocks in one another's paths.

IMPLEMENTATION

The activities in this section are examples of lessons and plans that actual teachers have worked out to use with their classes. It is always dangerous to offer specific suggestions about things to do, because the suggestions may be unintentionally misinterpreted as meaning "This is the way to do it." Remember that these examples are only examples. We selected them because we know the teachers and their pupils, and we also saw most of the lessons or units as they were taught. In the contexts in which they were used, these lessons contributed to the pupils' achievement and to the learning-community culture.

Primary Grades

The primary-grade examples have been selected to illustrate that first-graders and kindergarten children can be taught to work cooperatively in small groups. We first learned this lesson from Jannie Tibbets about twenty years ago. As we worked together in her kindergarten classroom, she mused one day, "These children operate in any organizational system we can figure out how to model and explain." The examples here were created by two other teachers who also knew how to teach primary-age children to work cooperatively.

Liset Holmes identified the learning-community goals for her first grade as to foster acceptance, communication, responsibility, decision making, all pupils learning subject matter, and constructive confrontational and problem-solving skills. She organized her class for carrying out whole-group instruction, small-group (four members each) work or instruction, and individual work or instruction. She made two rules: "You must work together" and "You must be willing to help." After working through the orientation, establishing expectations, and conflict-resolution stages, Holmes was able to use cooperative activities for teaching subject matter. One example of a cooperative activity was "Surrounding Patterns." The objective was for the children to create a series of patterns and then to name their creation. In essence, the children were to agree on a base design, to surround it with another agreed-to design, and finally to observe how patterns grow. (See Morton, *Math Their Way*, Worksheet 55, for this idea.)

Holmes began the "Surrounding Patterns" activity by having all the children sit in front of her on the floor. Behind her was a bulletin board on which two pieces of paper were taped. One was large-format graph paper. Nearby were colored squares and glue. Holmes said that she and three other teachers, Mr. Jones, Ms. Salar, and Ms. Chung, had met at lunchtime and created a "surround pattern." She then showed the group the second paper taped to the board on which was one large pattern. She read the titles "Rainbow" and "Straight Lines and Curves," which were printed on the side of the paper. She told the students that they would be working together in small groups, and that each group would make a pattern. She said that she and the other three teachers had had to work together to come up with one pattern that they all agreed to.

Holmes put out the four boxes of colored shapes. She said, "First I said I thought the pattern should be two pink squares, a yellow triangle, and a blue trapezoid." Holmes stuck the shapes she had suggested on the blank graph paper on the bulletin board. "Ms. Salar said she thought it should have at least one circle. Mr. Jones said the pattern should start with the circle. Ms. Chung said she agreed with Mr. Jones. I said I agreed, and Ms. Salar said she agreed. So we laid out the pattern on the piece of paper." Holmes moved the pieces around to represent the pattern.

"Now, we had to figure out the first surround pattern. So, each person laid out what she/he wanted. Mr. Jones took his turn first. When we looked at what he had put out, Ms. Chung said that it did not fit the rule. He changed it, but it still didn't fit the rule. Then Ms. Chung tried her idea. It fit the rule. I said I wanted to do her pattern next. Ms. Salar said she had another idea, and she laid out her suggestion. Her idea fit the rule also. Now we had two ideas that fit the rule, but we could use only one. Ms. Salar said we should vote. She asked, 'How many want Ms. Chung's pattern?' We all raised our hands. She then asked, 'Who wants Ms. Salar's pattern?' Ms. Chung raised her hand again. She should have voted only once. We agreed to put Ms. Chung's pattern on next. Each of us took one of the boxes of shapes and placed the shapes where they were to go." Holmes demonstrated by sticking the shapes onto the paper. "Sometimes we made a mistake and had to change where we put them. When they were all in place, Ms. Chung pasted them on. At the end of our work time, we looked at the paper. Mr. Jones said he wanted to call our design "Rainbows." I said I wanted to call it "Straight Lines and Curves." We wrote both names on it, here. We cooperated to create our design."

After the demonstration, Holmes assigned the students to their groups. She asked one member of each group to describe to her the sequence of the activity they were to perform and what they were to create. Next, Holmes asked the groups of students to go to their tables. One first-grader started immediately to create a design. Another member of the group said, "We don't have to use that one; we are supposed to cooperate." The designer looked up, walked to the teacher, and asked "Do we have to cooperate?" Another member of the group said loudly to the teacher, "You said we had to cooperate." Holmes said, "Yes, you need to cooperate."

Holmes circulated to each group in turn. She listened to the conversations, intervened when she could challenge pupils, let pupils work out problems, and helped to reduce frustration when it was going to interfere with learning to cooperate or with the idea of creating the patterns. When the patterns were done, each group read aloud the name of their pattern, and Holmes put all the patterns on the bulletin board.

In another school, after having worked through the initial stages of learning-community development, Mary Ann Leibenguth organized her kindergartners into groups for the purpose of working cooperatively on learning subject-matter outcomes. She had already expended the time and effort to help her pupils to create a classroom learning community. This meant that she was more explicit than many teachers about the pupils' roles and responsibilities. For this unit, she assigned the pupils to groups of four. She decided to change work groups only at the beginning of a new unit of study. Thus, in her class each group stayed together throughout a unit of study.

Leibenguth started each day's activity by showing an example of the product that the pupils would construct. Next she told the students the task. For example, "Today we are going to make a pattern using pieces of paper. Each of you will have an envelope with shapes in it. We will work in our same small groups. Within your group, you must agree on a pattern, and then together you must make the pattern go across the white paper strip that is on the table. No one can be the boss. You must talk about what you each want and then agree on what you will do. Everyone must help to start the pattern and everyone must help to keep it going to the end of the paper. When you have your pattern glued to the paper, take a minute to look at the pattern and decide on a name for it. When all the groups have finished, each group will show their pattern. In this group, Annennett will be the announcer." She went onto assign announcers to the other groups and to remind the groups where they were to work.

Leibenguth saw her role, during group work, as rotating among groups and intervening as necessary to help the group maintain their group skills. When a problem arose, she stood back long enough to give the group a chance to resolve it. If it appeared that they would need help, she would remind them of the rules for group work.

In her unit about patterns, Leibenguth also had the small groups use "junk" to create visual patterns that were congruent with word patterns that she gave them (e.g., "bumpy" and "smooth"). After that, they created quilts and then puzzles.

Middle Grades

Diana Reinsmoen developed a unit on map skills, into which she organized her activities for the development of the classroom learning community. Once the learning community had reached the productivity stage, the pupils worked in small groups to complete various map tasks related to social studies objectives. For example, students reported various generalizations (e.g., parts of the world have land, or water, or political borders), about which they reached consensus. The small groups also created multiple-cue riddles about various sections of the world. For example, the groups created riddles that ended with "What area is it?" Each group then gave the pieces of their riddle to the other members of the class. The rest of the class then figured out, using the clues and their map skills, what area was included in the riddle.

Lisa Saunders created a unit to follow up on a study of a section of twentieth-century world history that included the world wars, the cold war, and the need for building peaceful relationships in today's world. She used "The Other Side," a computer simulation in which two countries build a "bridge of peace." She finds that this simulation is fast-paced, challenging, and not so difficult that it is abnormally frustrating for the students in middle-school classes. She designed this unit so that her students will begin to understand two things: (1) just how much work it takes to have a peaceful relationship with others and (2) that working in group situations under pressure takes even more skill than they have needed so far in the school year. She also believes that this simulation will help them to see how important cooperation and communication are, not only in their groups but in what happens in larger arenas. She stated that by the end of the unit she wanted the pupils from two different classes to "understand how difficult it is to build and maintain a peaceful relationship, not only because of the actions of the 'other side' but because of a person's own conflicting needs and desires; to understand difficulties of using indirect means of communication; and [to] develop clear communication skills." Saunders' design for the unit is presented below.

Day One

Whole Group

Opening question: What does it take to build peace in this world? List the students' responses.

Lecture: Highlight the various peace initiatives throughout history, giving continuity to the unit and tying it to the "Other Side" game. The game involves negotiating peace with another country, "Rusnakland," which will be represented in the game by small groups from another class.

The game: Describe the "Other Side" game. Illustrate the use of computers as part of the activity equipment. Explain that there will be handouts that the students will use in groups to plot their moves, to plan actions and reactions, to monitor their economy, to publicize events happening in the game, to send messages, and to do various other activities. Explain the rules and procedures of the game (e.g., selling and purchasing bricks to build the bridge collaboratively.) Identify necessary roles. Stress that everyone will have a role to play and that every role is important for successful completion of the computer bridge building.

Group process skills: Tie the activity to group skills that have been identified and practiced in other small-group activities earlier in the year. Being able to understand how the other side is thinking, as practiced in the "Current Events" strategy, is critical to the game.

Journal: Provide directions for journal keeping and explain that students' feelings about the day's activities should be recorded, along with questions on the action of the game and its relationship to real life.

Evaluation: Explain that at the end of the unit there will be a quiz on the basic material we've covered. Groups will also write a 1- to 2-page paper discussing the experience of working in a group, the process of building a bridge of peace and how it related to them, and what they have learned about maintaining peace in the world today.

Homework: Students are to read the directions for the game in the handbooks. They should be prepared to describe the game and ask questions about it at the beginning of the next class.

Day Two

Whole Group

Review game directions: Ask pupils to tell, in sequence, the steps in the game. Included will be the identification of steps, rules, roles, and skills. The directions for the game are complicated, and so this will take most of the period. End the period by listing on the board the members of the various small groups. In tomorrow's class, the small groups will begin working together.

Day Three

Whole Group

Explain the importance of small groups to the larger group and the success of the activity.

Homework: Assign a question for reflective journal writing.

Small Groups

Each group is assigned a facilitator, a timer, and a recorder. The task is for the group to review the steps in the game and to ensure that all members of the group understand the task and the purpose.

Today each small group will meet for half the period and discuss their roles, both individually and as a group. The students will decide upon a facilitator and a recorder, since both positions are very necessary to complete the tasks of the groups. They will also examine copies of their worksheets, and each group will prepare a general statement on their objectives as a group. Then the entire class will meet, and a spokesperson from each group will describe to the class what the small group perceives as the role of that small group. I will stay out of this as much as possible, for it is very important to this simulation that the groups build a sense of trust between the members of each of the small groups as well as within the larger group. This is the first day during the simulation in which the groups will be using the group responsibility techniques of encouraging, organizing, responding, and linking. The groups will need to have all these skills finely tuned throughout the entire simulation, especially as they start having pressure put on them. This is why I will have the small groups spend an entire class period on just sorting out their own objectives and feelings about where they fit into the entire picture and then explaining them to the entire class. It is important to take this much time to have the groups become comfortable with each other. Then I'll give them the journal question for the next day.

Day Four

Small Groups

Once I've collected the journals, the groups will gather to start really planning their strategies. Should be big excitement today: they get on the computer and send the first message! The response which comes back from Rusnakland [class next door] will be recorded on the chalkboard. Each group will start working on the task assigned to it. Since there will undoubtedly be confusion at first, I may have to intervene just enough to remind facilitators of their jobs. However, I will have the roles and responsibilities posted on the chalkboard in the front of the room, and my intervention will be only to point out the procedures to the groups that I see slipping off-task, being dominated by one person, or generally not observing the norms. Near the end of the period we'll call a halt to the activity to discuss how the first day went, how people felt about their groups, and what problems occurred, and to have the class decide on what action to take.

Homework: Then I'll give them the journal question for the next day.

Days Four and Five

Small Groups

These two days will be totally devoted to small-group work. The process will remain the same, unless a major catastrophe occurs and the world is blown up or one of the countries becomes bankrupt. If that happens, or if they do get the bridge built, we will start over again.

Day Six

Whole Group

If it has not happened by now, I will try to introduce some conflict into the simulation to teach problem or conflict confrontation. The problem I introduce will depend upon the situation. However, once the problem has occurred, we will stop the activity for a time and decide how to resolve it. First I'll ask them whether indeed they see it as a problem, and if so, whether they feel it needs to be solved. Assuming that they decide it does (and I'd better make it enough of a problem that they do!), I'll have the entire class discuss the problem and suggest creative ways to solve it. If the problem is between small groups, I might lead the class to suggest that a monitor be set up to watch the process of interaction between the groups. I also want to have the class discuss differences between behaviors and judgments that cause conflict. One point I want to make very clear is the need for specific and accurate (documentable) descriptions of actions which appear to be causing the conflict. Then I will encourage the groups/class to practice active listening to both or all sides of the conflict, to decide *by consensus* what to do, and to be very specific in the solution they suggest.

Homework: As an evaluation of this task, the journal question for the evening will have to do with conflict and problem solving, how the students feel about their activities of the day, and how these activities relate to conflict in negotiations between countries.

Day Seven

Small Groups

By now the groups should be working together fairly well, and we should be getting close to building the bridge. One of the interesting aspects of this game is that the last brick in the bridge can be as difficult to purchase and place as all the others combined. If a group is not busy, I may divide them up and have them monitor the activities of the other groups or of the class as a whole. Then I can have them write an evaluation and compare it with mine in a class discussion at the end of the period. This will be interesting and valuable because the students will have a different perspective than I do. They may very well be much more harsh in their evaluation.

Homework: The journal question for the evening will relate to that difference and to the differences in the evaluation of information by different members of a negotiation team.

Day Eight

Small Groups

I will spend a few minutes on this next-to-last day of the group part of the unit discussing the activity as a whole with the entire class, and then I will have the small groups break off and work on their papers. I will bring up the differences in their journal question entries during the activity, because I'm sure the entries will change to reflect the greater cooperation and learning that will take place through the simulation. I will also discuss the changes in the groups from the beginning of the activity to the end, since this will be the longest period of time the groups will have worked together in this class. Also, the class will discuss the difference between working within the class and working with a group outside the physical setting of the classroom, whom they could not see or directly interact with during the simulation. (Although the work of the other class has not been discussed in this plan, it has been a vital part of all decisions and plans made.) If the other class has not been trained in group-working techniques, my class will also discuss the differences between working with people who have been trained and working with those who have not. Finally, the class will discuss how the simulation relates to negotiations for peace in the real world of foreign policy.

Day Nine

This is the day when the small groups meet and write their group papers. Since they have been writing group papers from the beginning of their group learning, I will not expect to need to give them much guidance.

Day Ten

Whole Group

This is the day of the quiz and wrap-up of the unit.

Evaluation. Four forms of evaluation will help me to determine whether or not the students have achieved the goals stated for this unit. First, since they will be writing in their journals every evening, I will be able to monitor their personal feelings and progress throughout the unit. Second, they will have a test on the information presented on communications, the specific events discussed, and the workings of a group in building a peaceful relationship. Third, I will have them write a paper, as a group, in which they describe the experience and evaluate what they have learned, including how they felt about working in this group (its strengths and weaknesses), how they felt about the "other side" group (especially if the other group has not had any training in group learning), what could have been handled differently by the other teacher and myself, and how working in this group related to what they learned about the group process in the "real world." Finally, we will see whether the bridge has actually been built!

I will also keep a daily journal, discussing my impressions about the exercise, mentioning what seems to work and what doesn't, and what I will do the next time to make it work better.

High School

Judy Murdoch created a cooperative strategy to help high school honors students learn and recall words and their definitions. She began by dividing the class into six groups of six students each. Each group was responsible for preparing twenty vocabulary words. The students wrote definitions and a set of statements for their twenty words. (See the examples in Figures 11-4 and 11-5.) Next, Murdoch created two 10-word/definition tests and answer sheets for each of the six sets of twenty words. (See the examples in Figures 11-6 to 11-9.) She also created question cards. (See the example in Figure 11-10.) Finally, she gave each group the full set of materials for the six vocabulary games.

The directions for the game, entitled "Vocabulary Recall Activity," are on p. 341.

1. Acerbity	11. Integument
2. Auscultation	12. Irrefragable
3. Billingsgate	13. Jeremiad
4. Dulcet	14. Lachrymose
5. Éclat	15. Obstreperous
6. Emendation	16. Opprobrium
7. Eugenic	17. Perspicacity
8. Excoriate	18. Recidivism
9. Gasconade	19. Stertorous
10. Insouciant	20. Thaumaturgist

FIGURE 11-4
Word List.

1. **acerbity** *n.* Bitterness of speech and temper. "The meeting of the United Nations Assembly was marked with such acerbity that little hope of reaching any useful settlement of the problem could be held."

2. **auscultation** *n.* Act of listening to the heart or lungs to discover abnormalities. "The science of auscultation was enhanced by the development of the stethoscope."

3. **billingsgate** *n.* Abusive language. "His attempts at pacifying the mob were met by angry hoots and billingsgate."

4. **dulcet** *adj.* Sweet-sounding. "The dulcet sounds of birds at dawn were soon drowned out by the roar of traffic passing our motel."

5. **éclat** *n.* Brilliance or glory. "To the delight of his audience, he completed his task with éclat and consummate ease."

6. **emendation** *n.* Correction of errors; improvement. "Please initial all the emendations you have made in the contract."

7. **eugenic** *adj.* Pertaining to the improvement of a race. "It is easier to apply eugenic principles to the raising of racehorses or prize cattle than to the development of human beings."

8. **excoriate** *v.* Flay; abrade. "These shoes are so ill-fitting that they will excoriate the feet and create blisters."

9. **gasconade** *n., also v.* Bluster; boastfulness. "Behind his front of gasconade and pompous talk, he tried to hide his inherent uncertainty and nervousness."

10. **insouciant** *adj.* Indifferent; without concern or care. "Your insouciant attitude at such a critical moment indicates that you do not understand the gravity of the situation."

11. **integument** *n.* Outer covering of skin. "The turtle takes advantage of its hard integument and hides within its shell when threatened."

12. **irrefragable** *adj.* Not to be disproved; indisputable. "The testimonies of the witnesses provide irrefragable proof that my client is innocent."

13. **jeremiad** *n.* Lament; complain. "His account of the event was a lengthy jeremiad, unrelieved by any light moments."

14. **lachrymose** (lak-) *adj.* Producing tears. "His voice has a lachrymose quality which is more appropriate at a funeral than at a class reunion."

15. **obstreperous** *adj.* Boisterous; noisy. "The crowd became obstreperous and shouted their disapproval of the proposals made by the speaker."

16. **opprobrium** *n.* Infamy. "He refused to defend himself against the opprobrium poured upon him by the newspapers."

17. **perspicacity** (-ku-) *n.* Clearness of expression; freedom from ambiguity. "One of the outstanding features of this book is the perspicacity of its author; his meaning is always clear."

18. **recidivism** *n.* Habitual return to crime. "Prison reformers in the United States are disturbed by the high rate of recidivism—the number of men serving second and third terms in prisons."

19. **stertorous** *adj.* Having a snoring sound. "He could not sleep because of the stertorous breathing of his roommates."

20. **thaumaturgist** (tho-) *n.* Miracle worker; magician. "I would have to be a thaumaturgist and not a mere doctor to find a remedy for this disease."

FIGURE 11-5
Definitions list.

Below, write the word from the word list which matches each definition.

1. Habitual return to crime _____

2. Infamy _____

3. Pertaining to improvement of race _____

4. Act of listening to the heart or lungs to discover abnormalities _____

5. Sweet-sounding _____

6. Outer covering or skin _____

7. Producing tears _____

8. Without concern _____

9. Freedom from ambiguity _____

10. Miracle worker _____

FIGURE 11-6

Test 1.

1. Recidivism
2. Opprobrium
3. Eugenic
4. Auscultation
5. Dulcet
6. Integument
7. Lachrymose
8. Insouciant
9. Perspicacity
10. Thaumaturgist

FIGURE 11-7

Answer sheet for Test 1.

Below, write the word from the word list which matches each definition.

1. Correction of errors, improvement _____

2. Bitterness of speech and temper _____

3. Lament; complaint _____

4. Abusive language _____

5. Brilliance or glory _____

6. Bluster; boastfulness _____

7. Having a snoring sound _____

8. Not to be disproved _____

9. Flay; abrade _____

10. Boisterous; noisy _____

FIGURE 11-8

Test 2.

1. Emendation
2. Acerbity
3. Jeremiad
4. Billingsgate
5. Éclat
6. Gasconade
7. Stertorous
8. Irrefragable
9. Excoriate
10. Obstreperous

FIGURE 11-9
Answer sheet for Test 2.

What type of principles are easier to
apply to raising horses or cattle than
to the development of human beings?

FIGURE 11-10
Question card.

Vocabulary Recall Activity

Goal: All students know all words.

1. The teacher hands a deck of twenty question cards to one member of the small group. This pupil acts as the monitor for a given game. The cards are passed to a second player who acts as monitor for a second game. No one person can act as monitor until all other members of the group have taken a turn. (See Figure 11-10.)

2. The person to the left of the member holding the question cards is first, and the game proceeds to the left.

3. The deck of questions is placed face down on the desk.

4. The first player takes a card from the deck, reads the question out loud, and tries to answer the question (no penalty for guessing).

5. The next player challenges, if he/she wants to. The first player then hands the question card to the challenger. If the player passes, other members of the group can challenge in turn.

6. When all have had an opportunity to challenge or pass, the group monitor checks the answer. The pupil who has answered correctly keeps the card. If no one was correct, the card is shuffled back into the deck.

REFLECTING

The reflecting function in stage IV is one of continually asking "How are we doing in relationship to having all pupils achieve all intended outcomes?" Questions that help teachers to focus on improving the quality of outcomes toward which pupils are working include: "How can we improve?" and "What can I do differently?" As indicated earlier, teachers as well as pupils have a responsibility for monitoring the outcomes and working toward improving the quality of community life and achievement.

These questions provide a guide to focus the reflection process. Of primary concern is the achievement of each student. Focusing part of the reflection on the individual progress of students provides an opportunity to identify students who may need additional challenges or extra support. Review of records (anecdotal, task-completion, and achievement) provides one set of data for reflection.

Patterns of achievement, work, and interpersonal communication skills or problems are available from records. Such patterns provide the basis for planning the next series of lessons.

Finally, using monitoring data, the learning-community teacher reflects on the health, quality, and progress of the community. As patterns of life in the community emerge, the teacher provides leadership to improve the quality of relationships and community life in general.

A group of seventh- and eighth-graders with whom we work at Otto Middle School in Lansing, Michigan, wrote the following "rap," based on their initial experiences with classroom learning communities and cooperative groupwork. The rap is a product of a cooperative group task.

The Cooperative Learning Rap
by New Ideas

We're learning together
Is how we feel.
Cooperative Learning
Is the Deal.
We all have a part
To say and do.
That includes me,
And that includes you.
Orientation is how we start.
Everyone here must learn their part.
Establishing norms
To know what to do
Helps get the job
done and have fun too!
I talk to you,
You talk to me,
We listen to all,
And then we succeed.
We all get smarter
And have a role.
We learn a lot—
And reach our goal.
I'm the recorder,
I'll do the time,
I'll get materials,
And I'll do the rhyme.
We all work together.
That was the plan.
We recognize talent.
Here's how we stand.
Now we've told you,
And we're all through.
Join our next class,
And we'll be there too.

Performance Outcomes and Activities (NJPTS 1, 2, 4, 5, 6, 8)

Chapter 11
Expanding and Sustaining the Learning Community Culture

PERFORMANCE OUTCOMES

Teacher Candidates will:

24. Gain the knowledge and skills for professionally preparing for, carrying out, and reporting data from classroom observations that furthers their knowledge about teachers and teaching and learners and learning and schools and schooling.
25. Gain the knowledge and skills to identify Stage 4-Maintaining and Expanding the Learning Community teacher and student behavior.
26. Gain the knowledge and skills to create an effective plan that when implemented will likely increase students' achievement with activities that are supported as effective teaching strategies by the National Associations and are congruent with the functions of schooling for learning communities.
27. Refine interview skills, data analysis and use of data.
28. Continue practice in carrying out child studies.

EFFECTIVE PLANNING FOR SUCCESSFUL LEARNING COMMUNITY TEACHERS

The focus of this part of your study is on effective subject matter planning and teaching. It is never too early to begin to gain and practice the application of your knowledge of (1) the subjects that matter, (2) the structures of the subject matter areas, (3) the interrelatedness of school subject matters, (4) how students learn, (5) how to plan effectively for all learners, and (6) how to select and use best teaching practices. This knowledge and skills are all necessary if you are to be an effective learning community teacher. Knowing and articulating the links among the knowledge and skills you expect students to learn from a series of instructional occasions are keys to successful student achievement. Daily *formative assessments and periodic summative evaluations* provide the data necessary for (1) the adjustment of teaching plans, (2) use of flexible grouping, (3) conferences with other educators and families, and (4) continuous progress on the part of students.

Effective teaching and learning (student achievement) are outcomes of thoughtful teacher study and planning. It is our expectation that *teacher candidates,* illustrate in writing (1) the complex connections among their knowledge of subject matters structures and linkages, (2) learner assessment data, (3) relevant child development information, (4) best teaching practices, (5) the culture, ethnicity and interests of the learners, and (6) the resources available in schools, districts, neighborhoods and communities.

Learning to plan effectively takes time and energy and is at times frustrating. At times, it is tempting to decide to "fly by the seat of your pants" and simply skip the planning stage. When you do this, you are wasting the learners' time, you are not providing them "the opportunity to learn" and you contribute to low achievement. On the other hand teacher candidates exploring a teaching career are generally not able to quickly plan multi-levels of a lesson tied to specific standards for a specific set of student needs.

The more knowledge a teacher candidate has about the core curriculum for a state, the quicker the process of planning goes as she/he can access appropriate subject matter information. Another area that teacher candidates can practice is the development of rubrics, so that during student teaching and their first year of teaching it contributes to clear communication to learners of the quality of performances that are expected. Arter and

McTighe (2001), in *Scoring Rubrics in the Classroom: Using Performance Criteria for Assessing and Improving Student Performance,* offer clear explanations of rubrics and performance criteria. The process they suggest for creating rubrics provides a clear process for beginners. We recommend that you make use of this or a similar process to develop the habit and experience needed for creating rubrics. As you become more knowledgeable about standards, performance criteria, and exceptional performances, it will not take you as long to create rubrics. You will also find that detailed rubrics are used for multiple assignments and that your collection of concrete examples, of outstanding performances will grow assisting you in illustrating for learners what is expected.

Perlman (2003) is an advocate of performance tasks and rubrics that are clearly aligned with the standards that the school or state is holding you and your students accountable. She says that a good assessment task also requires the use of critical thinking skills, is fair, and is a worthwhile use of your valuable instructional time.

Thus, it is important to learn the process for effective planning so that prior to student teaching teacher-candidates acquire the knowledge and skills necessary for teaching "each and every student" for a short time period. It is difficult to maintain for an entire year, the high quality of work required for all students to be successful in achieving academic, social, personal, and social justice responsibilities. Candidates who demonstrate for a short period, the ability to do the sophisticated thinking, instruction, management, record keeping and relationship development, have a high probability of being able to learn to work at that level for an entire year. Some new teachers may take up to three years before they are able to consistently work at this level and be able to establish a classroom learning community. Others may have the ability to quickly apply additional knowledge and skills and thus be able to consistently perform at the high level and create a classroom learning community by the end of their first year of teaching.

One of the new elements of planning that has occurred since we wrote the first edition of this textbook is the use of standards (what a student should know and be able to do, in terms of broad concepts), benchmarks, and performance outcomes. In November of 1994, the Association for Supervision and Curriculum Development reported in Update (volume 36, number 9) that the variety of work being done on national standards "are influencing curriculum deliberations at the district level . . ." (p. 6). In professional education course work, you will learn about the NJ Core Curriculum standards and the standards that each subject matter's professional organization has now identified. In your field experiences, you will have access to district standards, benchmarks, or performance outcomes. Kendall and Marzano (1994) define benchmarks; "are statements of the particular knowledge and skills expected at various developmental levels—for example 8th graders demonstrate an understanding of primes, factors, multiples, ratios, and proportions." (p. 7). They report 1,541 benchmarks embedded within 157 standards. They note that it would be not be feasible to require students to demonstrate competence in all of these. They recommend about 600 benchmarks be covered in K–12 school years. Benchmarks can be stated as lists of "declarative, procedural, and contextual knowledge; . . . An alternative is to state benchmarks as performance tasks" (p. 7). Kendall and Marzano believe that this allows for combining of benchmarks, and thus give teachers a creative and powerful way to organize content. "If performance tasks are codified and used as a means to define curriculum, however, this approach may restrict the manner in which students can demonstrate their knowledge and skills in a given domain" (p. 7).

You will work with the standards from your major subject matter area in this course as you work through the two sets of work related to planning.

The following two sets of work are the first steps in getting you started on becoming an effective instructional planner and on your way to becoming an outstanding new teacher.

Exercise 11.1
Preparing for Instruction in a Learning Community

I. Introduction:
A. Instructor and three volunteers prepare and lead a whole group activity that introduces "Concept map" to the members of the course. Examples of activities to prepare for concept mapping are located in Novak and Gowin, 1999, Table 2.3, pages 32 and 33.

B. Instructor leads initial concept mapping activities with whole group. Examples of concept mapping practice activities are located in Novak and Gowin, 1999, Table 2.3, pg. 33–34.

II. The Process for Creating a Curriculum Concept Map for Instruction
Now that you have the basic idea of a concept map, it is time to expand your understanding to include the use of concept mapping in the instructional planning process.

A. Assessment
Deciding what you will include in any instructional concept map starts in two places. First are the designated standards for the subject matters you are teaching. Second, is your students' assessment data that was provided or you collected and analyzed.

   You collected the following assessment data last semester. Study and organize these data and present them in an informative manner, as these data provide the foundation for your instructional planning.

   A.   School, classroom and district (data from previous assignment)
   B.   Neighborhood and Community (data from previous assignment)
   C.   NJ Core Curriculum in Mathematics for Elementary or Secondary Learners or other content standards for a particular subject matter area
   D.   Written Mathematics Curriculum Guide from District
   E.   Information about learners in the school, different grade levels
   F.   Testing information (mathematics or other content areas) from school (university professor provides)
   G.   Review your content area performance standards, the NJ Standards, the national standards*
         (see Table 1 at the end of this chapter)

B. Selection of Core Curriculum Standards to be taught over 10 weeks
A concept map is an instrument for explicitly describing your understanding of subject matter concepts and the relationships among them. A concept map is a tool that shows teacher candidates', teachers', and students' understandings. Thus, concept maps help you in communications of one's understandings and as an assessment tool as it is very useful for evaluating candidates' and students' understandings. Similarly, they are useful for self-assessment as the map shows what you currently think and provides an opportunity for you to evaluate the wholeness and complexity of what you are able to communicate. Concept maps also are useful for reflection and discussion of key ideas with in-class whole or small groups and study groups. They also support whole group work, when the teacher provides the leadership for a collectively constructed map. Learners though discussion and reflection, give input into the class map by supplying the key ideas and connections.

   Concept maps that you create as a part of your instructional planning provide you with a "map" of what is to be studied that you can share with your students. They function as a self-assessment to see if you need to further research the content to be taught. Knowing the relationships (structure and functions) within a given subject matter is important to a teacher if she/he is to be able to correctly instruct, assess students missing knowledge or skills, and evaluate student performance of Core Curriculum standards.

Following are steps you can use to create a concept map for your instructional planning.

1. Based on test data select an area of instruction (Instructor will provide topic; or choices)
2. Create a Concept Map that includes relevant Knowledge, Skills, Concepts, and/or Principles that shows relationships among knowledge, skills, and concepts to be taught over a ten-week period.
3. Draw lines between items to show the nature of the relationships.
4. Select one area of concept map or one set of related concepts and illustrate the prerequisite knowledge, skills and concepts to the outcomes and illustrate the outcomes that will follow once learner has acquired first outcomes.

C. Writing Performance Outcomes for Learners and Summative Tests (*See Table at end of assignments.)

1. Review your concept map and test data from the classroom that you used in your selection of content for your curriculum concept map.
2. Review the NJCC standards in that area appropriate for the low, middle and top math achievers in that class.
3. Given a ten-week period write performance outcomes and related assessment tests for a minimum of three groups of learners.
4. Write a summative exam that checks knowledge, skills, and applications of concepts and skills to real world performances that are directly related to the written performance outcomes.
5. Write a rubric for grading the students work on the exam.

D. Creating a Calendar

1. Based on your mathematics or other performance outcomes create a calendar for each of three groups for a ten-week period.
2. Mark the dates in your calendar when you will give formative assessments.
3. Mark on the calendar any holidays or other district information that will interfere with your instructional/learning progress.

E. Create Instructional Lessons, Practice Work and Application Work for three Groups

1. Beginning with group "1" using the calendar, performance outcomes, assessments, and evaluation tools
   a. Write an introduction to the line of study that will occur. Focus on the content of what will be learned and indicate the performance outcomes that you are expecting students to demonstrate at the end. Write out questions you will ask students to determine whether they understand your expectations.
   b. Write out the instructional talk for the first lesson.
   c. Write out the practice exercise you will work on with the students and write the directions to the exercise.
   d. Write out 2 more practice activities.
   e. Write out the application exercise you will assign to students and write out the directions you will give.
   f. Write out the formative assessment tasks and write a rubric to use in grading.
   g. Create a diagram for the set up you will use for instruction, small group, and individual work.
   h. For the next set of content follow steps 1–7 until you have the instruction, practice activities formative assessments for the all of the content to be taught in the 10-week period.
2. Group "2" follow steps in Group "1."
3. Group "3" follow steps in Group "1."

RUBRIC FOR INSTRUCTIONAL DESIGN

CONCEPT MAP

A. Concepts and Terminology

2.5–3	1.5–2	1	0
Candidate's map shows an understanding of the topic's concepts and principles and uses appropriate terminology and notations; uses facts, skills, concepts and principals that are appropriate for all learners in group	Candidate makes some mistakes in content terminology or shows a few misunderstandings of the content concepts and principles; range of knowledge presented does not include all learners	Candidate makes many mistakes in terminology and show a lack of understanding of the many concepts and principles in the content area; unable to tell what learner needs are included in map	Candidate's map shows no understanding of the topic's concepts and principles

B. Knowledge of the Relationships among Concepts and Principles

2.5–3.0	1.5–2.0	1	0
Identifies all the important concepts, principles and shows an understanding of the relationships among them	Identifies important concepts but makes some incorrect connections	Makes many incorrect connections	Fails to use any appropriate concepts or appropriate connections

C. Ability to Communicate Through Concept Maps

2.5–3.0	1.5–2.0	1	0
Constructs an appropriate and complete concept map and includes examples; places concepts in an appropriate hierarchy and places linking words on all connections; produces a concept map that is easy to interpret	Places almost all concepts in an appropriate hierarchy and assigns linking words to most connections; produces a concept map that is easy for others to read	Places only a few concepts in an appropriate hierarchy or uses only a few linking words; produces a concept map that is difficult to interpret	Produces a final product that is not a concept map

RUBRIC/SCORING GUIDE FOR INSTRUCTIONAL PLANS

	Evidence
I. Assessment Data about each child who will be taught this unit:	
3 Points: Prerequisite knowledge noted and related data on each child in instructional groups provided, data about strengths of each child noted, special needs noted. After the first units of the year, specific knowledge and skill data is provided.	
2 Points: Prerequisite knowledge is noted; student data is based on "negative" what they can't do; special needs noted in general statements.	
1 Point: Assessment data is specific about a few of the students not all; generalized statements about interests and strengths included.	
0 Points: No prerequisite knowledge is noted and assessment data is provided in generalized statements.	

	Evidence
II. **Learning Objectives for Unit Stated in terms identifying skills, knowledge and/or performances expected. Objectives linked to Flint Standards & Bench Marks included in Curriculum map and reflect concept map.**	
3 Points: Learning Objectives all stated in terms of outcomes; Objectives cover the subject matter in the unit; After first unit objectives are written for specific children and their individual learning plans (links to assessment data are available).	
2 Points: Learning Objectives all stated in terms of outcomes; Objectives do not cover the subject matter included in the unit; After the first unit's objectives are linked to groups of learners.	
1 Point: Learning Objectives all but one are stated in terms of outcomes; No linkages to specific learners are provided.	
0 Points: Learning Objectives include more than one statement of activities.	
III. **Evaluation Tools and/or Performances**	
3 Points: Procedures for regular "formative assessments" are described; Evaluation tools/tasks and related scoring guides are provided. Clear discriminations between "instructional or practice activities and the tasks that will be evaluated." Description of how evaluation data will be collected is included; After the first units "pre-assessment and post-tasks are included" data from prior work does not inform teachers about the current knowledge & skills in a given area; Record keeping system is used that includes information useable for decision making, Learning Community meetings and conferences with families.	
2 Points: Procedures for regular "formative assessments" are described; Evaluation tools/tasks and related scoring guides are provided; Clear discriminations between "instructional or practice activities and the tasks that will be evaluated"; Description of how evaluation data will be collected is included; Record keeping system is used that includes information useable for decision making, Learning Community meetings and conferences.	
1 Point: Evaluation tools/tasks and related scoring guides are provided. Clear discriminations between "instructional or practice activities and the tasks that will be evaluated."	
0 Points: Evaluation tools/tasks and related scoring guides are provided.	
IV. Instructional Activities	
3 Points: Activities included represent what is needed for 80% of the students to acquire knowledge and skills; Activities provided support learning of more than one of the unit's objectives; Instructional tasks are aligned with the objectives; Activities include links to students' out-of-school lives (neighborhood & community).	
2 Points: Activities included represent what is needed for 80% of the students to acquire knowledge and skills; Activities provided support learning of more than one of the unit's objectives; Instructional tasks are aligned with the objectives.	
1 Point: Activities linked to learning activities.	
0 Points: Activities linked to topics but do not provide opportunities to practice what will be evaluated.	

Exercise 11.2
Planning on Your Own

Part I: Creating a Concept Map

1. Review the New Jersey Core Curriculum Standards—The source for District Student Outcome Standards and Performances.
2. Review the District's Standards and Performances (provided for review by the school to which you are assigned).
3. Meet with your cooperating teacher and review the content that she/he will cover during the rest of this semester. They can communicate this to you by showing you the NJ standards they will be working on or by telling you the chapters in the texts that they are using.
4. Create a concept map that illustrates the subject matter to be taught and the linkages among the concepts. (If the cooperating teacher gave you text chapters, review these and select NJ standards that fit the content communicated to you.)
5. Ask your cooperating teacher to point out and give you a list of names of a group of students with whom you can teach ___ lessons (that is focused on the standards for which the teacher is responsible) during the rest of the semester.
6. Ask your cooperating teacher to review your concept map with you. Remember that a teacher will be thinking about more subject matter than we are asking you to consider. Make notes of the cooperating teacher's feedback and turn in at the end of this experience.
7. Based on the content of your concept map create your first units (start with social studies and science; see rubric for unit plans). *Ask* for feedback on your unit plans from your instructors and cooperating teachers. Review their feedback, the rubric for units and edit your unit plans until the performance standards and lesson learning objectives are written as outcomes of what students should know and be able to do.

Scoring Guide for a Concept Map (See Rubric Above)

I. Ultimately, Concept Maps will include all subject matter that will be taught during a marking period or semester. They will also illustrate connections among the subject matters. This scoring guide is for the beginning or first planning experiences.

II. Concept Maps for the rest of the program will increase in complexity. The first one will include only reading and math (or other subject area) for early childhood and elementary teacher candidates and reading and one content area for middle school and high school teacher candidates. The Rubric below provides guides for developing your first concept map.

Scoring Guide for Concept Maps

I. Concepts and Terminology

3 Points: Show an understanding of the skills, concepts, and principles that will be taught during a ten-week marking period. Shows accurate connections and uses appropriate terminology and notations.

2 Points: Makes some mistakes in terminology or shows a few misunderstanding of skills, concepts, or principles. Connections between and among concepts have a few mistakes.

1 Point: Makes many mistakes in terminology and shows a lack of understanding of many concepts or principles. Subject matter does not extend for a marking period.

0 Points: Shows no understanding of the subject matter's concepts or principles.

II. Knowledge of the Relationships among Skills, Concepts, or Principles

3 Points: Identifies all the important skills, concepts, principles and shows an understanding of the relationships among them.

2 Points: Identifies important concepts and principles but make some incorrect connections.

1 Point: Makes many incorrect connections.

0 Points: Fails to use any appropriate concepts or appropriate connections.

III. Ability to Communicate through Concept Maps

3 Points: Constructs an appropriate and complete concept map. Places concepts in appropriate relationship to each other and places linking words on all connections. Produces a concept map that is easy to interpret.

2 Points: Places almost all concepts in an appropriate hierarchy and assigns linking words to most connections. Produces a concept map that is easy to interpret.

Part II: Organizing Plans for a Marking Period

I. Using the content in your concept map . . . Write 2 performance outcomes (in two content areas) that you expect learners to accomplish during the marking period. (Given the grouping below that is a minimum of 12 performance outcomes you will write.) Also, write one performance outcome for all students in the area of personal, social or social justice performances.
   A. Group of 5 students is performing above grade level.
   B. Group of 8 students is performing at grade level.
   C. Group of 5 students is performing 2.5 grade levels below grade level.

II. Write three assessment tasks that you can have students do so that you will have data about each student as it relates to his/her knowledge about the content you think will be taught.

III. Create a calendar that includes a ten-week marking period. On the calendar sketch out how you would schedule the instructional lessons, formative and summative tests, field trips, co-operative learning activities, class presentations etc., for the two content areas for your three groups. Don't forget that you will create some instructional lessons, etc., that include all three of your groups of students. Don't forget that you would have more performance outcomes for ten-week period of time.

IV. Preparing Lesson Plans for a Limited Amount of Instruction.
  A. Assessment data from assessment tasks.
   • List names of students and describe their performance on the assessment tasks.
   • Create 3 groups using the assessment data you collected.
  B. Based on your assessment data you collected, rewrite, add, and/or delete the performance outcomes you wrote. The new ones should be suitable for the three groups of students and the assessment data you collected.
  C. Describe each Learning Activity:
   • Using references in the Resource Center (examples below) create one instructional lesson for each of your groups. (e.g., *Mosaic of Thought: Teaching Comprehension in a Reader's Workshop,* by Keene, E.O. and Zimmermann, S. *Best Practice: New Standards for Teaching and Learning America's Schools: Reading, Writing, Mathematics, Science, Social Studies, and the Arts,* 2nd Edition, by Zemelman, S., Daniels, H., Hyde, A.)
   • List materials, texts, page numbers and visual aids to be used.
   • Describe how you can tie the lesson activity or content to personal, social, or social justice outcomes.
   • Develop a list of questions to stimulate substantive student discourse and thinking about the content.
  D. Instructional Considerations to Think About and Add Responses to Your Plans:
   • How will you stimulate substantive discourse about the content; i.e., what thought questions might you ask? Are they related to the student's out-of-school experiences? (List on cards that you can use during direct instruction or as you move from group/individual to group/individual.)
   • What will you say specifically, to help student link this work with work done at an earlier time?
   • How will you motivate students to become engaged with the task? How will you explain the purpose and what is expected so that students can explain to anyone who asks what they are learning?
   • What examples or metaphors will you use to tie the lesson to students' out-of-school lives and experiences?
   • What out-of-school use of this knowledge will you suggest to students?
   • How will you bring closure to the lesson and tie this lesson to what comes next?
  E. What management concerns might arise because of the nature of the tasks or the procedures or groups you are using and how will you avoid them?
  F. What norms, student accountability, routines, reminders or other supports will you use to reinforce students' self-regulating behavior?
  G. Accommodations made for each and every student:
   • How have you modified the objectives, the procedures, the groups or other pedagogical considerations to ensure that each child will be engaged and make progress during this lesson?
   • Are the plans you made in the unit to provide needed assistance for those students who need such support working?
   • List what you will do to accommodate special needs students.
  H. Lesson Evaluation:
   • What do you need to see or hear students doing in order to decide that each student has achieved their performance outcomes; i.e., do you have an evaluation rubric? What data did you collect on which students while you were teaching? Who else do you need to observe to get the same data on them?
   • Are you systematically keeping track of each student's progress in achieving the objectives?
   • What went really well? What makes you think that it went well? What did you observe? What would you do differently?
  I. Student evaluation:
   • Use rubrics you developed.
   • Record data using a record keeping system you created.
   • Is there any work that you need to keep for the child's log/portfolio for study or parent teacher conferences?

Getting Ready to Teach your Lessons to Your Students

In order to carry out your plans, you will need to gather additional information and/or prepare some materials. You will probably not include the following in your written plans, but you should make sure that you are adequately prepared to help students achieve the lesson's performance outcomes.

The following reminders should be reviewed and carried out if needed:

- Have you researched the topic so that it is clear that you have the needed subject matter knowledge?

- Do the questions you developed reflect the nature of knowledge and skills needed by students to pass the NJ State Exam?

- What questions do you have about the content and students' developmental readiness to do anticipated tasks? Have you worked these through with your mentor or another teacher?

- Have you identified available resources to teach the content in ways that actively engage students? (e.g., using the investigation units will help you in the area of mathematics)

- Have you developed a list of questions to stimulate substantive student discourse about the content?

- What do you need to include in the visual aids, student guides or work sheets you select or prepare so that they contribute to learning and are just not busy work?

- Have you organized students into heterogeneous groups, identified student roles and responsibilities for group work, and developed other "creating" management strategies?

- What other things are important within the context in which you are teaching?

Exercise 11.3
Performance Portfolio

A Performance Portfolio is a purposeful collection of a student's work that tells the story of the student's efforts, new learning, emerging insights, progress, or achievement in specified areas of performance.

A. Review your concept map, performance outcomes, performance activities and the other aspects of your plans. Identify and list the artifacts that students who were taught your plans would include in a Performance Portfolio.

(Potential artifacts include: (1) Accounts of all activities illustrating increases, no change, or falling behind in the acquisition of knowledge and skills. (2) Self-reflection writings in journals, personal notes, reflective paragraphs, etc., which illustrate the student's personal growth and his/her progress toward the curriculum performance outcomes. (3) Video or Audio Records that provide an oral account of activities, revisions, and reflection and which illustrate the student's personal growth and his/her progress toward the curriculum performance outcomes. Videos of presentations or reports with feedback and evaluations. (4) PowerPoint and other formal written reports, articles, or presentations. (5) Observation Records and Notes that provide feedback from the teacher, peers, parents and others (e.g., letter from community members contacted during a community study) which depict the student's work, growth, and progress. (6) Data, which summarizes the numerical information that characterizes the student's progress in achievement toward academic, personal, social, and social justice responsibilities. (7) Table of Contents and Explanation of specific progress toward specific performance outcomes, goals, and or objectives.)

B. Using your concept map and plans as the basis for a performance portfolio create a table of contents explaining what would be included in the portfolio had you had the opportunity to teach your entire set of plans.

C. Using your Signature Assignments update your electronic portfolio.

RUBRIC FOR PERFORMANCE PORTFOLIO FOR TLC 1 & TLC 2 & P–12 PORTFOLIOS

	Reflections	Achievement	Artifacts
4	Self-evaluations and reflections focus upon all of the course and chapter outcomes. Showing the connections between text objectives and course performance outcomes. Specific details and/or breadth are connected directly to specific changes in academic, personal, social, and social justice responsibilities. Professional growth is organized into themes that reflect connections.	Personal goals are evident for two semesters. Clear ties between personal goals, course performance outcomes, and text objectives evident. Personal Goals challenge beyond performance outcomes for two courses. Clear statement about progress toward achieving personal, social, academic, & social justice responsibilities. Clear evidence of high motivation to tackle issues or challenges to continuously improve.	Artifacts illustrate student's top quality performances in the use of computers and a variety of media. Artifacts demonstrate personal and professional insights as they specifically relate to the course and text objectives and performance outcomes. Action research project includes report that is ready for submission to a journal for publication.
3	Self-evaluations and reflections focus on many of the course and book objectives. Personal reflections dwell upon the performance criteria and standards.	Personal goals are ever-expanding and connect across the two semesters. There is evidence of an increasing means for solving problems.	A variety of artifact formats, which illustrate significant personal and professional growth, are included. Action research report of high quality.
2	Self-evaluation and reflections focus upon many aspects of work but lack specific details and/or breadth. No central theme concerning professional growth.	Personal goals are set but restrict growth across the two semesters. Problem solving is dependent on others.	Artifacts represent a variety of course and text performances. They do not clearly convey personal or professional growth but rather appear as assignments.
1	Global statements, which focus only on a few aspects of work, objectives, and performance outcomes. Detachment from self-evaluations is evident.	Personal goals are global and focus on only a few aspects of the work, objectives and performance outcomes for TLC 1 and TLC 2.	A preference for traditional artifacts representing routine work and thinking is evident. Little risk taking to make substantive changes in thinking or performances.

Exercise 11.4
Service Learning as a Part of Integrated Instructional Planning

The purpose of this project is to provide teacher candidates with the opportunity to develop the knowledge and skills effective educators need to carry out their roles in P–12 schools. One of the roles for which teachers provide leadership is building partnerships with parents and the community. Read the article by Joyce L. Epstein in the May 1995 issue of Phi Delta Kappan, pages 701–711, entitled "School/Family/Community Partnerships, Caring for the Children We Share."

This exercise provides you with opportunities that you will help you create a classroom, school, family and community partnership as a teacher. These experiences are necessary for you to begin the development of a comfort level for interacting with family and community members so that in the future you will include them as a major part of the Learning Communities that you establish as teachers.

This exercise requires that you work directly with a teacher or principal, and a parent or community member (not working for the district) plus others as necessary for the planning and implementation process. It also requires you to link the service learning activity to school subject matter. Service Learning activities are not isolated projects for kids to do. For example, cleaning up a yard of a school neighbor without tying it to subject matter being studied about the environmental is not meeting the criteria for a service learning project. We also suggest that all of the teacher candidates in a given school work together on this project. Since all activities have multiple levels and subject matter connections, it is possible for everyone to have different instructional plans, but they can work together to carry out a superb school-wide, grade level, or building-wing activity.

This assignment will be done after you complete the whole group task of creating a long-range instructional plan. Once you begin to create your individual instructional plans, it is time for you link this assignment with specific concepts you include in your plans. Thus, this project is part of your instructional planning, just as it will be when you are a teacher. It is not being assigned as an isolated task because we do not want you to see Service Learning as "extra" or outside the curriculum for teachers and learners.

Part I: Assessing What You Need to Know Before Creating a Plan

1. What is the purpose? What would you say are the goals in your instructional plans that this project will introduce, set the direction for, illustrate or reinforce?
2. How do you go about creating a design for this adult and student activity? What are the steps involved in carrying out the activity?
3. How will you work with the Principal, Assistant Principal, Cooperating Teachers, family and community members? Would special service people in your building be a part of your planning or people with whom you would communicate on a regular basis, or just once or twice?
4. At what times would you talk with the school staff about your ideas? Do you need to present your final plan at a meeting of the entire staff?

Part II: Data Gathering and a Calendar

5. What information do you need in order to make decisions about what will support students achieving your stated goals and purposes?
6. From whom do you need to get information?
7. What questions will you ask?
8. How do you keep the plan open until you have all of the information?
9. What time-lines are you using for data gathering, analysis and decision-making?

Part III: Writing a Plan

10. By when will a design be drafted and ready to share?

11. Who will be a part of the verbal planning (individual and group discussions)? When will you meet? (Be sure to keep track of the neighborhood, community, family members who work with you, the nature of their contributions, and their interests.)

12. Outline for the Activity Plan:
    A. Assessment—State the purposes and goals, link to performance outcomes in your instructional plans, summarize the data you collected, and tie your plan to the Learning Community's values.
    B. State expected outcomes for learners. Indicate how you will collect data to determine if they achieved the expected outcomes or not.
    C. Describe the activities that are a part of your plan.
    D. Indicate who is responsible for what aspect of implementing your plan. Also indicate how things will be covered should someone not show up as planned, or not bring the materials promised.
    E. Write a budget and indicate who will provide the funds and from what resources.

13. Share your plan with appropriate groups and individuals. Collect all the feedback that they provide and make the changes necessary to have a group plan that is supported by the variety of people who were included in the planning.

Part IV: Implement your Plan

14. Once the design is completed, how will you arrange to carry it out? Carry it out.

15. How will you collect data that is useful for evaluation? Carry out evaluation.

Part V: Evaluation and Reporting

16. Final report made to planning group, teachers, school, and members of your college course. This is a product that you should include in your Portfolio.

17. Report includes
    A. Description of how you worked together with school, family and community members to create design
    B. Service Learning Plan that you implemented
    C. Evaluation of your implementation (write up of evaluation data, and observational data)
    D. Recommendations for changes should others want to do this activity.
    E. Share with others in your college course and school staff with whom you worked. On a 4 × 6 index card: Summarize your final report using one side of a 4 × 6 index card. Print copies to share with other members of your group.

Exercise 11.5
Interconnected Lesson Set
Contributed by TLC I and TLC II Instructors at
Rowan University, College of Education
Teaching in Learning Communities II

SECTION I: LESSON DESIGN AND PLANNING

This part of the assignment is designed to complement and extend the lesson that you wrote as part of your Teaching Literacy course. Specifically, you will create two additional lessons, which could be taught before or after the literacy lesson.

- The two lessons you design must follow the College of Education's lesson plan format.
- A draft of your lessons will be reviewed by your TLC II peers and TLC II instructor.
- You will submit all three lesson plans and corresponding materials.

SECTION II: ANALYZE & REFLECT

This part of the assignment is designed to help you reflect on the experience of teaching the lesson you developed for your Teaching Literacy course using feedback from your partner. If possible, you should also receive feedback from your cooperating teacher.

After teaching your lesson and discussing the experience with your partner and your cooperating teacher (if possible), reflect on the following questions:

1. What aspects of your lesson and teaching experience were successful? Why do you think so?
2. Did you modify any aspects of your lesson while you were teaching? How? Why?
3. How would you modify this lesson if you were to teach it again? Why?

4. How did your actual teaching experience compare with your expectations?
5. What did you learn about the process of teaching and learning from this experience?
6. What did you learn about the students from this experience?
7. What did you learn about the process of self-reflection and peer-reflection from this experience?

** Write a clear, well-organized essay that summarizes your thoughts. **

** Submit the feedback forms from your partner and cooperating teacher with your essay. **

LESSON PLAN FORMAT

Overview

- Title
- Teacher(s)
- Subject(s)
- Topic/Unit of Study
- Grade/Level
- Time Frame
- Rationale/Background information
- Materials and Equipment
- References/Sources

Standard/Objectives

- State and/or National Standards
- Student Outcomes (in measurable terms)

Learning Experience

- Introduction
- Sequence of Activities
- Closure/Culminating Experience
- Adaptations/Modifications

Lesson Analysis

- Student Evaluation compared to Assessment Data (Achievement)
- List the observations you made about the students' involvement, reactions, and engagement
- Self-Reflection
- Based on the data you collected list the changes you will make in this type of lesson in the future

Interconnected Lesson Set Rubric
Rowan University–College of Education
Teaching in Learning Communities II: Spring 2006

Component	Exceeds Expectations	Meets Expectations	Does Not Meet Expectations
Section I: Lesson Design & Planning	• All required components are comprehensively outlined for at least two lesson plans. • Lesson content and procedures reflect a thorough understanding of the selected students' academic / behavioral / social strengths and needs. • Lesson content and procedures are exceptionally creative and demonstrate an understanding of best practices for culturally responsive instruction in a learning community environment.	• All required components are outlined for at least two lesson plans. • Lesson content and procedures are appropriate for the selected group of students. • Lesson content and procedures demonstrate an understanding of best practices for culturally responsive instruction in a learning community environment.	• Two lesson plans do not include all the required components. • Lesson content and procedures are not entirely appropriate for the selected group of students. • Lesson content and procedures do not evidence the use of best practices for culturally responsive instruction in a learning community environment.
Section II: Analyze & Reflect	• Essay is thorough, concise, and demonstrates an advanced level of reflection about each lesson component, the students, and the teaching experience. • All ideas are supported with insightful examples/evidence.	• Essay is complete and demonstrates an acceptable level of reflection about each lesson component, the students, and the teaching experience. • Most ideas are supported with relevant examples/evidence.	• Essay does not demonstrate adequate reflection about each lesson component, the students, and/or the teaching experience. • Ideas are not adequately supported with relevant examples/evidence.
Professional Writing	• Assignment contains no significant grammatical, syntactical, or lexical errors. • Writing is clear, concise, and organized such that it would be considered exemplary within a professional setting.	• Assignment contains a few grammatical, syntactical, or lexical errors. • Writing is clear and organized such that it would be considered acceptable within a professional setting.	• Assignment contains numerous grammatical, syntactical, and/or lexical errors. • Writing is unclear and/or disorganized such that it would be considered unacceptable within a professional setting.

Scoring Guide for Beginning Planning

A. Assessment Data about each child who will be taught this unit:

3 Points: Prerequisite knowledge noted and related data on each child in instructional groups provided, data about strengths of each child noted, special needs noted. Assessment tasks given and evaluated, recorded, specific feedback to students evident and all included in materials turned in to course instructor. Teacher candidate clearly observed and collected data during their field placements and in school homework time.

2 Points: Prerequisite knowledge is noted; student data is based on "negative" what they can't do; special needs noted in general statements; assessment tasks given, evaluated and recorded.

1 Point: Assessment data is specific about a few of the students, not all; generalized statements about interests and strengths included; No clear evidence of assessment tasks related to performance outcomes.

0 Points: No prerequisite knowledge is noted and assessment data is provided in generalized statements;

B. Learning Objectives (Performance Outcomes) lessons stated in terms identifying skills, knowledge and/or performances expected. Objectives linked to NJ Core Curriculum, District performance outcomes and reflected in concept map.

3 Points: Learning Objectives (performance outcomes) all stated in terms of measurable outcomes (what, quality, how demonstrated); Performance outcomes related to specific learner data. They cover the subject matter in the lessons, and are related to marking period map. Social, personal, and social justice outcomes accurately stated (based on developmental levels and observation data).

2 Points: Learning Objectives all stated in terms of outcomes that lack all parts; Objectives do not cover the subject matter included in the lessons; Outcomes related to whole group or subgroup data.

1 Point: Learning Objectives all but one are stated in terms of outcomes; No linkages to specific learners are provided.

0 Points: Of the Learning Objectives included more than one is a statement of an activity.

C. Evaluation tools and or Performances

3 Points: Procedures for regular "formative assessments" are described; Evaluation tools/tasks and related scoring guides are provided. Clear discriminations between "instructional or practice activities and the tasks that will be evaluated." Description of how evaluation data will be collected is included. The pre-assessment and post-instructional tasks (evaluation) are included. There is written evidence that shows how data from prior work informed the candidate about the current knowledge and skills in a given area. Record keeping system is used that includes information useable for decision-making, Learning Community meetings and conferences with individuals and families.

2 Points: Procedures for regular "formative assessments" are described; Evaluation tools/tasks and related scoring guides are provided; Clear discriminations between "instructional or practice activities and the tasks that will be evaluated"; Description of how evaluation data will be collected is included; Record keeping system is used that includes information useable for decision making, Learning Community meetings and conferences;

1 Point: Evaluation tools/tasks and related scoring guides are provided. Clear discriminations between "instructional or practice activities and the tasks that will be evaluated";

0 Points: Evaluation tools/tasks and related scoring guides are provided;

D.   Instructional Activities

3 Points: Activities included represent what is needed for 80% of the students to acquire knowledge and skills; Activities provided support learning of more than one of the unit's objectives; Instructional tasks are aligned with the objectives; Activities include links to students' out-of-school lives (neighborhood and community);

2 Points: Activities included represent what is needed for 80% of the students to acquire knowledge and skills; Activities provided support learning of more than one of the unit's objectives; Instructional tasks are aligned with the objectives;

1 Point: Activities linked to learning activities;

0 Points: Activities linked to topics but do not provide opportunities to practice what will be evaluated.

Exercise 11.6
Five Questions to Ask about the District's Standards

The purpose of this task is to provide the opportunity for teacher candidates to begin to learn about the structure of standards, benchmarks, performance outcomes and how they are being used in the setting where you do your field experiences. In addition this task gives you a process for learning about standards in the district and school where you student teach and accept your first teaching position.

John Kendall and Robert Marzano of McRel (1994) advised that schools or districts should answer five basic questions prior to their setting their own standards. The five questions are provided below. Interview a classroom teacher and ask him/her these questions. What do you learn? Invite a director of curriculum to your class and have him/her respond to these questions.

1. How many standards and benchmarks will be articulated? (How many are there for the grade level of the teachers you interviewed? For the district?)
2. In what format will benchmarks be articulated?
3. Will students need to achieve all selected benchmarks to demonstrate competence in a standard?
4. Will student performance be reported using course grades or standards?
5. Will all students be required to meet all standards?

Ending Notes

You have not completed the process for effective planning and instruction. As you gain more experiences, knowledge, and skills, you will find that you create a personal format for your maps and long-range plans. Teacher candidates report that using this planning process helped them to focus on students and their learning. In addition, because they had processed the linkages as a part of their concept mapping, they found that they were able to help students visualize linkages and tie new information to their prior learning.

References and Recommended Readings for Further Information

Allen, R. (2003). The democratic aims of service learning, Educational Leadership: Creating Caring Schools, March Vol. 60, No 6, Pages 51–55.

Arter, J. McTighe, J. (2001). Scoring Rubrics in the classroom: Using performance criteria for assessing and improving student performance, Thousand Oaks, Cal., Corwin Press, Inc.

Callison, D. (2000). *Rubrics.* ERIC, EJ620187.

Cohen, E. G. (1986). *Designing groupwork.* New York: Teachers College Press. Chapter 8: Treating Expectations for Competence.

Danielson, C., Marquez, E. (1998). *A collection of performance tasks and rubrics high school mathematics.* Eye on Education, Inc., Larchmont, NY.

Duffy, G., Roehler, L., Sivan, E., Rackliffe, G., Books, Meloth, M., Varus, L., Wesselman, Putnam, J., Bassiri, D. (1986). *The effects of explaining the mental processing associated with using reading strategies on the awareness and achievement of low group third graders.* Institute for Research on Teaching, MSU, E. Lansing, MI.

Englert, C. S., and Mariage, T. V. (1996). *A sociocultural perspective: Teaching ways-of-thinking and ways-of-talking in a literacy community.* Learning Disabilities Research and Practice. Vol. 11, No. 3. pp. 157–167. Lawrence Erlbaum Associates, Inc.

Englert, C. S., Tarrant, K. L., and Mariage, T. V. (1992). *Defining and redefining instructional practice in special education: Perspectives on good teaching.* Teacher Education and Special Education. Volume 15, No. 2, pp. 62–86.

Goodland, J. I., Soder, R., and Sirotnik, K. A. (1990). *The moral dimensions of teaching.* San Francisco: Jossey-Bass.

Hale, J. E. (2001). *Learning while black: creating educational excellence for African American children,* Baltimore, Md., Johns Hopkins University Press.

Joshua, D. (2002). *Inside picture books: Where are children of color?* Educational Horizons, Spring, pp. 125–132.

Inzunza, V. (2004). Alumna Teaches Teachers Big lessons about community as classroom, in New Educator: Opportunities for all children: The college of education and urban schooling. Fall Vol. 10, No. 1.

Keene, E., Zimmermann, S. (1997). *Mosaic of Thought: Teaching comprehension in a reader's workshop.* Heinemann, Portsmouth, NH.

Kendall, J., Marzano, R. (1994). *The systematic identification and articulation of content standards and benchmarks.* January, McRel. As adapted in Update, ASCD, November 1994, Vol. 36, No. 99, Alexandria, VA.

Lanzing, J. (1997). *The concept mapping homepage, Saint Nicolas concept map. www.users.edte.utwente.nl/lanzing/cm_home.htm*

Liberman, A. (1988). *Building a professional culture in schools.* New York: Teachers College Press.

Marzano, R. J. (2000). Transforming classroom grading, McRell Institute, Alexandria, VA., ASCD.

Marzano, R. J. Pickering, D., Pollack, Jane. (2001). *Classroom instruction that works: Research-based strategies for increasing student achievement.*

Morrell, E. (2004). Linking literacy and popular culture: Finding connections for lifelong learning, Christopher-Gordon Publishers.

Napier, R. W. and Gershenfeld, M. K. (1983). *Making groups work: a guide for group leaders.* Boston: Houghton Mifflin.

Novak, J. D. (1991). *Clarify with concept maps: A tool for students and teacher alike.* The Science Teacher, 58 (7), 45–49.

Novak, J. D. (1993). *How do we learn our lesson?: Taking students through the process.* The Science Teacher, 60 (3), 50–55.

O'Flynn, S., Kennedy, H., MacGrath, M. (2003). *Get their attention! How to gain the respect of students and thrive as a teacher.* David Fulton Publishers, Great Britian.

Perlman, C. (2003). *Performance Assessment: Designing Appropriate Performance Tasks and Scoring Rubrics.* ERIC, ED480070.

Prawat, R. (1993). *Learning Community, Commitment, and School Reform.* Michigan State University, E. Lansing, MI.

Putnam, J. (1985). *Perceived Benefits and Limitation of Teacher Educator Demonstration Lessons.* Journal of Teacher Education, Nov–Dec., pp. 37–38.

Raths, L. E., Wasserman, S., Jones, A., and Rothstein, A. M. (1986). *Teaching thinking: Theory, strategies, and activities for the classroom.* New York: Teachers College Press.

Rowan, B. (2004). Teachers matter: Evidence from value-added assessments, Research Points: Essential Information for Education Policy, Summer Vol. 2, I–2.

Thompson, G. (2000). Stories from the field: What prospective and beginning secondary teacher learned from working with struggling third and fourth grade readers. Education Horizons, Fall, pp. 19–25.

Thompson, G. (2002). African American students in schools: research and effective instructional practices, educational Horizons, Spring, pp. 105–108.

Vansledright., B., Putnam, J., Shank, Pricco, P., Barger, F., *Building the Classroom Learning Community Culture.* (1993). Michigan State University, E. Lansing, MI.

Warren, S. R. (2002). *Stories from the classrooms: How expectations and efficacy of diverse teachers affect the academic performance of children in poor urban schools.* Educational Horizons, Spring, pp. 109–116.

Willis, S. (2002). Service learning puts academics into action, Education Update, June, Vol. 44, No. 4, (*www.ascd.orgaffiliates/articles/eu200206_willis.html*)

Table 1: National Standards by Mid-Continent Research for Education and Learning (McRel).

Zemelman, S., Daniels, H., Hyde, A. (1998). *Best Practice: New standards for teaching and learning in America's schools.* Heinemann. Portsmouth, NH.

GUIDELINES FOR THINKING ABOUT PLANS FOR TEACHING AND LEARNING

Guiding Questions	Your Ideas
A. Purpose and Rationale	**A. Concept Map**
1. What do I want students to begin to learn or begin to think about (concepts, processes, attitudes, semantic, syntactic, structure of disciplines, social responsibilities, and personal responsibilities)?	
2. Why is this content important?	
3. Why is it important for student to learn at this time?	
4. Are the tasks that I want students to do authentic?	
5. What will the student make of the learning experience(s) and take away from it/them?	
6. How did I decide to teach this?	

B. Relevancy of Context	A. Connections on a Concept Map & Connections with prior learning and future learning
7. How does this content relate to other content? (prior, among that included in this plan, and future)	
8. How did I decide to teach this?	
9. What do I know about this content?	

C. Assessments	C. Using Assessment Data
10. How does this content relate to what students already know?	
11. Why is it important for students to learn this at this time?	
12. How did I decide to teach this?	
13. What do I know about this content?	
14. What questions do students have about this content?	
15. What else do I need to learn about this content? Where will I find it?	
16. What might be possible areas of difficulty for students to learn this?	
17. How will I monitor what the students learn?	
18. What do I have to do to accommodate the behaviors of special needs students?	
19. What do I need to do to connect students with special learning needs to this content?	

D. Tasks	D. Instruction, Practice and Applications
20. How could students best learn this content?	
21. How can it be represented so that my students understand it?	
22. What is my role as teacher in this interaction or learning experience?	
23. What is my students' role in this learning experience?	
24. How can I create, arouse, or encourage my students' curiosity about learning this content?	
25. What materials and resources will I use?	

26. How will I begin?	
27. How will I sustain students' interest and engagement?	
28. What activities will I use for instruction?	
29. What activities will I use for practice?	
30. What activities will I use for applications?	
31. How will I bring closure?	
32. How will this be documented (writing folders, journals, charts, graphs, projects, publications, etc.)?	
33. How does the community of learners in this classroom keep track of what they have learned?	
34. What learning community goals, norms, dispositions, or attitudes are fostered by this content, tasks, and interactions? How will I foster these?	
E. Environment	**E. Environment for Learning**
35. How can I create my students' curiosity about learning this content?	
36. How can I organize the environment?	
37. What materials and resources will I use?	
38. How will I involve the neighborhood or community?	
F. Evaluation	**F. Formative and Summative Evaluation**
39. How will I know what students have learned?	
40. How will the students know what they learned?	
41. How will this be documented?	
42. How does the community of learners in this classroom keep track of what they are learning?	
43. How will learning progress be communicated to others?	
40. What is included in the rubrics I will use during these learning experiences?	
41. What performance tasks (applications) will the student carry out?	

Stage V. Disbanding: Transition and Closure

The final stage of group development includes the transition from supporting and expanding the classroom learning community to disbanding it at the end of the semester or school year. In this fifth stage, the teacher and students assess their progress, reflect on their learning-community experience, and prepare to move on to their next experiences. Teachers have a special professional responsibility to assess students' progress against the functions of schooling. They also reflect on their professional experiences and prepare for the next cycle of students and the creation of new learning communities.

While all classroom groups come to an end chronologically, only classes that have developed into effective classroom groups actually progress through transition and closure. For students and teachers involved in learning communities, ending the school year is not merely a change in a class or the beginning of summer; it is an ending of genuine, worthwhile, and successful relationships. A group of people who grew from an aggregate of individuals into a classroom learning community will be disbanding. Transition and closure begin when students and teachers realize that the special relationships in their learning community are coming to an end. Thus, a teacher begins to implement the final stage by being sensitive to feelings that students may be expressing, although the students themselves are not necessarily aware of the basis for their feelings. Disbanding can be a shock. Students will avoid the subject if teachers do not structure year-end activities. Being prepared to facilitate the passage of the group through this final stage is a responsibility of the learning-community teacher. The progression of feelings that one works through in this stage may be similar to the feelings involved in other losses (e.g., denial, anger, bargaining, resolution, and getting on with whatever comes next).

PREPARATION

Preparation for transition and closure includes planning for the following activities:

1. Dealing with feelings about ending the group and progress made during the year
2. Remembering what occurred during the previous four stages through reflection
3. Linking what you learn from assessments and reflections to your value of self and value for others. Creating a positive attitude toward your future plans

Assessment

The first set of activities includes designing three types of assessment tasks. First, students are to assess their own progress toward developing personal and social responsibility, social justice values and actions, and academic outcomes over the course of the learning-community semester/year. Second, the teacher is to assess the progress individual students have made toward the functions of schooling, the process used to create a learning community, and the quality of the expanded learning community. Third, appropriate timing for starting the transition activities, from productivity to closure, needs to be determined.

Learning-community teachers urge students to ask themselves, "What is different now about me and others in the group?" This question directs the students' attention to the contrasts between what they are now capable of doing and what they could do when the class started. At the "beginnings" stage of the learning community, assessment involved setting goals and defining what students could and could not do, what they knew and did not know. By stage V, assessment increases students' awareness of their learnings. Such awareness can contribute to building their self-confidence as learners, problem solvers, and members of the community.

The four functions of schooling, considered as instructional goals for the learning community, provide the basis for thinking about achievements made by the group and individuals. The progress made in each area includes achievements to be celebrated by the community. Many of the activities that facilitated preceding stages provide a basis for closure activities. Students' products provide a basis for statements such as, "Remember when I couldn't . . . when I learned . . . and how I figured out. . . ."

Students are urged to make comparisons between many points of time, providing a basis for the review. Changes in physical growth, interests, skills, and knowledge are included in this category. Student papers written about similar topics early and later in the year will show changes in perceptions which can be analyzed. Likewise, samples of handwriting, artwork, video "bits" from oral presentations, and clips showing group work at the beginning of the year compared to recent group work can all be analyzed for growth in process. These activities provide community members with links to past times that illustrate group and individual changes. Many students need to be reminded of how far they have come in order to get a realistic handle on their progress. Students live so thoroughly in the here and now that it is difficult for them to take a broad perspective, especially on a subject as close as themselves.

Three types of tasks also need to be designed that will enable the learning-community teacher to determine: individual students' progress during the school year; the progress of the group as a functional social unit based on learning-community principles; and the teacher's own professional development of skills and understanding, in both pedagogy and subject-matter competence.

Achievement in education is always a matter of unlearning old misunderstandings and replacing them with newer, more functional understandings. This is true of the group and of the individual. The cultural bindings that the students bring to class at the beginning of the school year are loosened during the course of development of a learning community. The results can free us from the unconscious sources of our errors and misunderstandings. The inspirations for reflection are the products of assessment: written records, recordings (video and audio), art objects, homework, posters, and other items that qualify as memorabilia.

Remembering and Reflecting

During reflection, many questions can be asked to facilitate remembering. For example, "What was celebrated by the group and by the teacher this year?" "What goals did the group set?" "What goals did individuals set?" "What did we do to begin the year?" "How did we capture the beginning of the year?" "What were the milestones?" The answers to these and similar questions provide the content of reflection and the basis for planning for the future.

We have observed that many teachers carry out special stage I activities that are designed to reappear as closure activities. For example, if teachers use a time capsule at the beginning of the year, opening it at the end of the year will facilitate the process of remembering, letting go of dependence upon the group, and getting ready to move on to the next experience. Special occasions, particular crisis situations that were successfully or not so successfully worked through, celebrations, individual achievements, group accomplishments, and problems confronted can all serve as substance for activities for the closure stage.

Teachers use these situations to provide a means for reviewing experiences, planning celebrations, and creating a monument to recognize that the group existed. For example, photographs taken during the course of the year can help all members of the community to reflect on their experiences. One teacher, at the end of the year, showed her first-graders pictures of themselves that had been taken during the year. She met with each child in an individual conference and asked him/her, "Tell me what happened when this picture was taken." When students had difficulty in identifying positive points, she asked questions that led the students to talk about themselves as learners.

Comparing and contrasting provides a basis for stage V activities for primary-grade students. For example, if teachers have filed away documents and samples of student work—such as audiotapes, photographs, stories written at different times during the year, artwork, videotapes of presentations or plays, drawings of products created by the students, and books written by the students earlier in the year—they have a rich resource for facilitating group reflection in this stage. Early products can be compared with later work to provide the group and individual students with a sense of how much they have learned— "How far we've come!" Individual students often say such things as, "Remember when I couldn't do these problems, and now I can. . . ."

Comparing and contrasting products throughout the year's experience is just as interesting to middle-grade students. Middle graders are more self-conscious about their identities and appreciate the chance to create a product that will reflect their experience.

Comparing and contrasting projects can also be carried out in high school, but at more sophisticated levels. Secondary students with whom we work enjoy personal and small-group awards. "Remember the time when . . ." and "We'll always remember [a particular person] for [a particular contribution] . . ." are sentiments that we have known students to express in the form of certificates or raps at the end of the school year.

Such activities are based on things the group did to "capture" the starting of the year. These activities provide learning-community members with an opportunity to see what they and their world were like when the year began; this tends to facilitate the process of closure and transition. Having students open time capsules, look at photos taken the first day of the year, read letters written to themselves on the first day of school, and tell others their predictions about what the year would be like are helpful ways of inviting them to focus attention on accomplishments.

Closing activities can provide opportunities to communicate what members of the community think about one another. Transition and closure activities can be based on community members' ideas about what they "will miss," "will always remember," "wish they had known sooner," and "appreciate" about others. The expressions can be made verbally, on audiotape or videotape, in "mystery letters" or drawings, or in whatever creative ways community members think up. These activities provide students with a legitimate basis for expressing how they value others and for hearing how they are valued by others in their learning community.

Memorial Activities

Activities designed to provide the group with a basis for memorializing their learning community include making a class will; planting a tree or flowers; leaving a plaque; and writing a poem, framing it, and leaving it hanging on the classroom wall. A group painting, for example, can be framed and given to the principal to hang in the hall or on the classroom wall. A class could plant a tree in the schoolyard or flower bulbs in city gardens, or it could paint a new game on a blacktop or pavement play area. These are only a few ideas of things that can be done to memorialize a classroom learning community. Brainstorming with the class can produce many new ideas for class memorials.

Such activities provide members of the community with a long-term identity. A woman whom we know still drives by the school where she attended fourth grade to see the tree that her class planted at the end of the year. Teachers who use this type of activity tell about former students coming back to their rooms to look for the "memorial" that their group left. They tell current students about their experiences and how they felt at that time.

Linking and Getting Ready to Move On

Finally, learning-community teachers can help students to move on to their next experiences (next semester's class, summer activities, the next school year). For example, the teacher can ask students to describe what they are going to be doing next, which will help to focus individual students' attention on what is coming next. Remembering the past is another way of getting ready to move on to new experiences. The teacher helps students to share their futures by asking them to describe their accomplishments. Such activities foster individual's positive beliefs about their personal progress, challenges they met, problems they worked through, successes they achieved, and other things that help them to be able to say "I believe I am valuable because I. . . ." As students and the teacher express their ideas about themselves in relationship to the class experiences, their sense of self-worth increases. People in a learning community can make public statements about themselves without fear of being labeled "braggart" because they are talking about part of their common history.

IMPLEMENTATION

Choosing the appropriate time to begin the assessment, reflection, and moving-on activities requires sensitivity. Once the activities begin, students and teachers are acting on their awareness that the community will be disbanded. The question to be answered at this time is, "When shall we start transition and closure activities in order to provide the best experience for community members?"

One way to facilitate movement through this stage is to communicate plans for transition and closure directly to the students. A plan should be integrated with the end-of-year/semester academic learning activities. Communicating plans provides an organized perspective, giving students something to look forward to and providing support for those who feel that things are falling apart, at the end of the year.

When students become concerned about ending the experience, they will provide clues. Sometimes they suggest new projects that would require enormous amounts of work. Sometimes they begin to bicker among themselves about matters that appear to the teacher to be inconsequential—behavior that they may not have exhibited since early in the year. Sometimes students become lethargic or withdraw from interaction. Some students may appear to be angry but may not be aware that their angry feelings are related to the prospect of ending relationships that are part of the classroom learning community. By observing students' changes in behavior and their attitudes about each other or schoolwork, teachers can become sensitive to students' concern about losing the community at the end of the semester or the year.

Providing a frame through which students can view the situation they are experiencing helps the class to move through this stage. The learning-community teacher talks to students about what is happening to them, and to their teacher, as the semester or year comes to a close. Providing a frame for this period of time means that the teacher expresses personal feelings about the impact of the ending of the learning community. The teacher empathizes with how the students may be feeling as they become aware that their classroom community will soon be disbanded. Also, the teacher links new student skills and understandings to feelings of loss that students have but may not have expressed openly as yet.

A teacher's talk with students about closure should be direct and should focus on the students' feelings about both their accomplishments and the disbanding of the learning community. Active listening and paraphrasing of students' comments about their feelings helps them to become aware of what is happening to them and to their learning-community group. The teacher, as an adult, needs to acknowledge the students' feelings as real; this helps students to understand the reasons for their unsettling reactions at the close of the year. By framing, the teacher assumes leadership and helps students to go through the year-end transition and, finally, to bring closure to their experience.

Framing the transition/closure experience for the classroom learning community leads to implementation of specific activities. The learning-community teacher plans activities to move the group toward closure, to continue to provide quality learning experiences, and to minimize unproductive behavior. The students by now are active community participants, and increasing their knowledge and understanding about what they are experiencing is a genuine and valuable part of their membership in the class. Various activities provide students with support for their feelings and teach them that they are not unusual because they have feelings as a part of the disbanding of the culture. Activities provide a "place" where students can celebrate, grieve, and find the support which will move them toward getting on with the next part of their lives. The activities also help individual members of the classroom learning community become aware of and share how they belong to the group, how they are valued, what they value in others, and how they are continuing to achieve during this stage. The reflections and opportunities to share provide the students with ways to talk about themselves and their experiences. Thus, in these activities learners formulate talk about their progress and experiences that they carry forward to their next experiences.

Reflection on the year's experiences leads students to feel OK about moving on. The context of the reflection is the matching of changes, growth, and accomplishments with goals set at the beginning of the year and with other things that were not predicted or planned. Teacher and students can see together what has happened and can process the information publicly. New goals can be set, based on reflection; new directions can be charted, based on new interests; and ideas for new explorations can be identified, based on past successes. Such expressions of accomplishment provide students with a basis for getting on with their life experiences."

REFLECTING

Teacher Preparation for Next Year

Assessing the end of the year and the experience of a given class or set of courses is the teacher's first step in planning for the establishment of future classroom learning communities. A teacher's preparation for establishing the next classroom learning community begins during reflection on this year's experiences. Using information about the students' achievements and the process and quality of the year's learning community provides resources for thinking about things that the teacher may wish to change next year.

Performance Outcomes and Activities (NJPTS 1, 2, 4, 5, 6)

Chapter 12
Stage 5 Disbanding: Transition and Closure

PERFORMANCE OUTCOMES

Teacher Candidates will:

29. Gain the knowledge and skills for professionally preparing for, carrying out, and reporting data from classroom observations that furthers their knowledge about teachers and teaching and learners and learning and schools and schooling.
30. Gain the knowledge and skills to identify Stage 5-Disbanding and Closure teacher and student behaviors.
31. Gain the knowledge and skills to create an effective plan that when implemented will likely move students through Stage 5 with activities that are congruent with the functions of schooling for learning communities.
32. Refine interview skills, data analysis and use of data.
33. Accurately complete a self-evaluation of a plan for establishing a classroom learning community.

Exercise 12.1
Creating Transition and Closure Activities

Design one *closure activity* that you would do with your students once you are able to create a classroom learning community culture.

Step 1: Describe the activity.
Step 2: List what the students will experience while participating in your activity.
Step 3: Describe how what the students experience is tied to the functions of a learning community culture.

Exercise 12.2
Linking the Different Parts of your Planning to Create A Plan for Establishing a Classroom Learning Community

It is time to pull together all of the various parts of the plan for establishing a classroom learning community that you have created over two semesters and make one systematic formal plan. This task requires that you review and edit your plans as you answer the following questions. Now at the end of the semester your final edition of your plans should also include both plans for creating your learning community culture as well as subject matter plans with activities that are congruent with a learning community classroom.

Analysis of Plan	Page(s) & Paragraph
I. Establishing a Learning Community Culture Goals	
A. Goals/objectives for establishing a learning community culture	
B. Goals/objectives for maintaining the established learning community culture	
C. Goals/objectives for expanding your established learning community culture	
D. Goals/objectives for disbanding an established learning community group	
II. Year-long Function of Schooling Goals	
A. Academic Goals/objectives	
B. Social justice Goals/objectives	
C. Personal responsibility Goals/objectives	
D. Social responsibility Goals/objectives	
III. Subject Matter Standards and Benchmarks	
A. Group 1	
B. Group 2	
C. Group 3	
IV. Justification for Goals, Standards and Benchmarks	
A. How are your Goals, standards, benchmarks related to the long-term functions-of-schooling outcomes?	
B. How is the subject matter related to the assessment data?	
V. Formative Evaluation	
A. What data will be collected?	
B. When and how will data be collected?	
C. How will data be analyzed?	
D. What use will be made of the data?	
E. Why is the data worth the effort?	
VI. Summative Evaluation	
A. What data will be collected?	
B. What performance tasks will be used?	
C. How will data be collected?	
D. How will data be analyzed?	
E. How will data be recorded?	
F. What use will be made of the data?	
G. Why is the data worth the effort?	

Analysis of Plan	Page(s) & Paragraph
VII. Analysis of instructional activities; subject matter; and calendar	
A. When you analyze your instructional plans, exactly what contributions do they make to the academic, person, social, and social justice outcomes?	
B. Is the sequence of content accurate?	
C. Is the subject matter accurate?	
D. Are the strategies for each group appropriate for learning the content?	
E. Are the strategies appropriate for engaging students in each group?	
VIII. Plans to Accommodate Special Needs	
A. What special needs are you accommodating?	
B. What attention are you giving to the environment to meet these needs?	
C. What attention are you giving to the learners?	
D. What attention are you giving the curriculum?	
E. What teacher needs have you made accommodations for?	
IX. Instruction—All of Lessons	
A. Label, in your plans, each activity as (1) presentation (modeling, demonstration, information giving; (2) guided practice (interactive phase in which students practice while the teacher guides their understandings; (3) application (activity in which students apply new knowledge/skill to a real-life context); or (4) independent practice (students practice independently and then receive feedback); (Use colored highlight, too)	
B. What examples of work and rubrics will you use related to the work	
X: Instruction—Single Lesson	
A. What type of student motives does a given activity support?	
B. What do you plan to say to make it clear to students what standard/benchmark they are working toward?	
C. What linkages did you make to prior knowledge?	
D. What linkages did you make to the next lesson?	
XI. Evaluation of Instruction	
A. How will you evaluate your instruction?	
B. How will you evaluate if you made appropriate changes during instruction?	
XII. Other	

Exercise 12.3
Assessing Learning-Community Development

The following checklist provides a structure for determining your degree of satisfaction with different aspects of the learning community. Use the scale below to rate your satisfaction with each item.

SCALE
5 Very frequent
4 Frequent
3 Infrequent
2 Usually happens only once
1 Doesn't happen

Think about your classroom during the first few days of school (or a group you have been teaching). Use the above scale to indicate the frequency with which the following events were observed in the class during this early stage.

_____ 1. Students watch the teacher for verbal and nonverbal clues to her/his expectations for student behavior.
_____ 2. Each student can call everyone else by name.
_____ 3. The teacher provides get-acquainted activities.
_____ 4. Cooperative students are made fun of by other students.
_____ 5. A few students seem to be always responding in class.
_____ 6. During school, students share feelings about being in a new group.
_____ 7. The teacher communicates expectations for academic work, behavior, and grading systems.
_____ 8. Some students put down, ridicule, or tease other students.
_____ 9. The teacher randomly selects students for small-group work.
_____ 10. The teacher explicitly teaches small-group work roles.
_____ 11. The teacher explicitly and systematically teaches norms.

After the first few days of school, students have gotten to know something about each other and have begun to feel more free. During the next few days, you might have observed the following events. Indicate how frequently you feel these events happened.

_____ 1. Discussion groups are often chaotic and ineffectual.
_____ 2. Students stray off discussion topics and report personal stories.
_____ 3. Students get into arguments during discussions which end with two or three students yelling at each other.
_____ 4. Students struggle with issues of power.
_____ 5. The teacher takes responsibility for setting goals, calling on people, and drawing conclusions.
_____ 6. Students take responsibility for setting goals, calling on people to contribute, and drawing conclusions.
_____ 7. Problems are solved by the teacher.
_____ 8. Problems are solved by the students.
_____ 9. Activities are planned which teach students how to become contributing.
_____ 10. Students practice paraphrasing each other during discussions.
_____ 11. Competition is the usual mode of achieving goals.
_____ 12. Cooperation is the usual mode of achieving goals.
_____ 13. When problems arise, they are usually ignored.
_____ 14. When problems arise, they are usually faced and solutions are found.

Sometimes classrooms go through periods of conflict. Indicate the frequency with which these events were observed in the classroom.

____ 1. Students rebel against the teacher's leadership.
____ 2. Students complain about the behaviors of other students or the teacher.
____ 3. Students openly disagree with each others' ideas or opinions.
____ 4. Students and teacher actively listen to each other.
____ 5. The teacher imposes stricter limits to settle conflicts.
____ 6. The students use role-plays and reverse role situations to explore their conflicts and look for solutions.
____ 7. The teacher feels that students who verbally argue with the teacher must be trying to show that they have more power than the teacher.
____ 8. Bickering among members of the class increases as students get to know each other better.
____ 9. Conflict increases with an increase in class participation.
____ 10. Students are testing the teacher.
____ 11. Teacher assigns roles to provide for equity in power and status among students.

During the time of year that teachers feel their pupils are learning the most, the following events may occur. Think about the period of time when you feel that your class was most productive. Indicate how frequently you feel these events happened in your class.

____ 1. Conflicts arise.
____ 2. Students work together to accomplish a variety of learning tasks.
____ 3. Students solve interpersonal problems.
____ 4. Students deal with disagreement in constructive ways.
____ 5. Students are generally task-oriented.
____ 6. Interpersonal needs of group members are met.
____ 7. Students can articulate functions of schooling and specifics related to your courses/class.
____ 8. All pupils are successful in all functions of schooling.

The final part of the school year has events specific to that period of time. Think about how the school year ended. Indicate how frequently you observed the following events.

____ 1. Students have conflict with each other.
____ 2. Students say "I didn't learn anything in this class," or make other negative comments.
____ 3. Teacher says the class is breaking up and gives realistic suggestions about how people can contact each other.
____ 4. The students and teacher discuss the events of the year.
____ 5. Group projects are done which can be left behind as gifts from the class.
____ 6. The teacher helps students to identify how they get involved in other groups.
____ 7. Regular lessons are scheduled and maintained until the end of the year.

Based on your assessment of the community, think about whether the class got stuck in one stage. What stage was the class in at the end of the year? Was there anything that should have been done to promote a longer stage IV? What? Why or why not? What changes will you make another time? Based on analysis of the data above, write three lists: (1) things that you should be sure to do again next year, in order to ensure the same effects as this year, (2) things that you should do to eliminate or prevent particular effects, and (3) things that you should do in order to create effects that were not present this year.

1. Things to do again:

2. Things to eliminate:

3. New things to do:

OVERVIEW

The Holmes Group is a consortium of research universities, with headquarters at Michigan State University committed to the reform of teacher education and the restructuring of schools, especially the schools that are called "professional development schools." The Holmes Group recently published a report entitled *Tomorrow's Schools: Principles for the Design of Professional Development Schools* (1990, East Lansing, MI: College of Education). Of the principles this report lists as critical for the creation of professional development schools, two specifically relate to our vision of teachers' professional practice and the kind of classrooms and schools in which teachers can fully exercise their capacities: first, the recommendation that "schools be organized as communities of learning," and second,

the conviction that teachers need to operate as partners in an environment which "will promote reflection and research on practice" (p. 7). Clearly, the scholars who were responsible for assembling *Tomorrow's Schools* believe that the future of learning community is directly linked to the quality of the professional environment in which teachers work. Without a reflective culture in which shared understandings can be tested among teachers, the chances that learning-community classrooms will succeed are small.

In the final chapter of this book, the authors argue for linking reflection with practice, for thinking about our thinking, and for talking about our discourse within communities of learning. The social foundations of both thought and language are emphasized.

The Future of Learning Community

Even a superficial review of the literature shows the reviewer that the implementation of classroom learning community cultures expanded over the last ten years. In fact, the movement progressed to the stage where *the concept* of classroom learning community can be lost in implementation and in labels. For example, we found many articles and books whose titles included "classroom learning community" but were written about other types of school communities. Analysis of the books and articles indicated that in many cases the classroom culture described was not congruent with the philosophy, principles, values, and indicators of the "learning community" culture. This reminded us that teachers, administrators and teacher educators need to be clear about the nature of the classroom cultures they are creating. The learning community classroom culture has its primary focus on **learning** in all four areas of *academics, personal, social and social justice outcomes*. The culture of the classroom learning community is also based on identified group and leader dispositions, knowledge and skills.

Teacher candidates who have the knowledge of how a classroom learning community differs from other types of classroom cultures are able to establish the learning community culture as a goal. They are then able to monitor their progress toward the goal as they develop the knowledge, skills, and dispositions necessary for providing leadership for the establishment of a classroom learning community culture.

In order to create classroom learning communities, teachers need to be part of professional learning communities. A great deal of the dysfunctionality in today's schools is tied to teachers' isolation. Teachers are cut off from the feedback of professional criticism, and their isolation dramatically reduces their chances for engaging in self-corrective testing of their beliefs and practices.

Study after study has shown that teachers feel isolated by the social context in which they work (Rosenholtz, 1989). Schools are not currently organized in ways that would support collaboration and reflection. Without helpful feedback from fellow professionals, teachers feel uncertain about their instructional practices, and they may even interpret requests for help from fellow teachers as signs of professional inadequacy. Under these circumstances, it is little wonder that teachers in traditional school contexts tend to keep to themselves.

Improving professional workplaces for teachers would require opening up the possibilities for communication between teachers and students in a whole school. Talking to one another about what they are thinking is characteristic of the members of a learning community; it is an essential norm for interaction within the group. When teachers talk about their thoughts and feelings, they invariably talk also about their talking. When we think about our thinking, we call it "metacognition." When we talk about our talking, we call it "metacommunication." **Metacommunication** means talking about the kind and quality of our communication with one another—about the kind of communication that is culturally valued by the group. We test statements made within the group as a means to think about our thinking. Thus, metacommunication and metacognition are linked in a learning community.

One reason we need to reflect on our thought and practice is that human beings have a strong propensity to create what Bateson (1972) called "double binds" for themselves. That is to say, even as we create systems for communicating our ideas and concerns within a community, we seem to maintain procedures for self-deception. This tendency results in our deceiving ourselves by hiding the truth or part of the truth about what we do from ourselves. R. D. Laing (1969) described the process of developing a divided self as a product of family rules: First, rules are created to govern conduct; then, rules are created about the rules; and finally, the rule of camouflage—the rule that says there are no rules—is created. Similarly, teachers have rules or beliefs which drive their practice in classrooms. The more hidden these beliefs are from the awareness of teachers, the harder it is to change instructional practice. Uncovering hidden rules or beliefs is a central task of reflection in a learning community.

As teachers, what we think we know and what we presume can sabotage our intentions of being helpful to our students if we do not reflect on and test our assumptions with others. We need to examine what we know about ourselves and the world for error, bias, and ignorance. Only through uncovering our mistakes, irrational beliefs, and prejudices do we have a chance to learn new things. Our perspective on reflection assumes that learning, whether among teachers or among students, is not a process of acquiring a collection of unrelated facts but basically a process of unlearning error. We do not necessarily become wiser by adding bits and pieces of wisdom incrementally. We gain wisdom by increasing our awareness of ourselves and the world we live in and disregarding the false conceptions. From the time of Socrates (470?–399 B.C.) critical thinking has been directed at self-knowledge—at knowing what we think and how we think.

Information-processing psychological research (e.g., Gardner, 1983; D. N. Perkins, 1981; Segal, Chipman, and Glaser, 1985) has been done on how we solve problems, adapt to our environment, and invent new ideas. The picture of thinking that emerges from these researchers makes it clear that thinking skills are complex mental processes which are affected powerfully by context.

For example, in a traditional school with a punitive principal, teachers invariably become secretive and think of themselves as less powerful. So too, do students think themselves to be incompetent when constantly criticized. Just as people who have experienced long periods of pain and sickness can feel less inclined to risk new experiences, so what we think possible is often formed by our social context (Bruner, 1990).

Considerable research literature on how people internalize social norms is available (e.g., Aronfreed, 1968; Bandura, 1986; Zenchenko, 1985). Such research emphasizes learning as a socialization process. Taking such research seriously leads us to define teaching as arranging social environments to achieve school goals. This understanding of teaching supports the central notion behind classroom learning communities: namely, that students must participate directly in discourse about the nature of the world, about their understandings of the world, and about themselves in relation to the world. In a learning community, discourse is the talk that shapes understanding.

Such a picture of what goes on in learning-community classrooms represents a significant modification of the traditional view of education in classrooms which focus on individual achievement, individual functioning, and individual blame or virtue for levels of achievement. Talk about "internalization," as Rogoff (1990) shows, can be interpreted as placing barriers between what is external and the process of its appropriation. If students are active participants in a classroom learning-community activity, they are engaged to such a degree that there is little contrast between internal and external aspects of their communication. Their talk happens in a great social rush. As Rogoff says, "Humans are social creatures, living in a social sea" (1990, p. 195). From a social interaction perspective, knowledge is awareness. The Russian psychologist, L. S. Vygotsky (1896–1934) argued for this position, namely that learning is not a mechanical transferring of external experience to internal meanings.

Traditional teachers tend to view knowledge as a collection of some kind of "stuff" which can be transferred, bartered, weighed, and stored, like any other commodity. In contrast to this traditional world view is the perspective that is emerging from cognitive and developmental psychology and contemporary philosophy (e.g., Gardner, 1983; Goodman, 1984). Current views hold that knowledge is more likely to be dynamic. These views are sometimes called "contextual relativism" (Perry, 1982). Goodman describes knowledge as:

> developing concepts and patterns, as establishing habits, and as revising or replacing the concepts and altering or breaking habits in the face of new problems, needs, or insights. Reconception, reorganization, invention, are seen to be . . . important in all kinds of knowing. (1984, p. 19)

The insights into our mental processes being provided by information-processing psychology require a new epistemology—one in which we treat what we know as conventional, temporary, and in constant need of checking. In the discourse of a learning community, testing what we know becomes automatic. What we are suggesting here is not simply being more logical. Logic alone is not a sufficient basis upon which to test our assumptions. Logic is useful in closed systems, like computer programs or other defined systems. However, most of the time we are dealing with open systems; they are considered "open" because we rarely know what is going to happen next. Understood from this perspective, reflective thinking and problem solving will not provide us with "right answers" to "ready-made questions." Rather, they will promote reorganization of our conception of reality. We learn by monitoring our thinking—namely, by metacognition.

The process and procedures we seek are self-correcting social adaptations, analogous to the marvelous capacity of living organisms to adapt to change. As long as changes are within a range of biochemical tolerance, organisms from simple cells to complex creatures like human beings are capable of adjusting to environmental stimuli in creative ways. Consider human body temperature as an example: a delicate balance of the body's processes requires an average normal temperature of 98.6°F. If the temperature in our surrounding environment swings from hot to cold, the body responds by adjusting to the change in temperature through chemical reactions. Too drastic a change cannot be tolerated, but the body is amazingly resilient. Maintaining the internal balance is the function of a system of checks (tests) which constantly monitor events and make adjustments. Fortunately, the vast majority of the body's monitoring is automated; we do not have to think about our body temperature, except under extreme pressures, such as disease, prolonged heat waves, or a breakdown of the home furnace in winter.

The mind seems to be organized in the same way, that is, systemically. As people learn new skills and information, what we learn is organized into clusters (Hunt, 1982) and stored in memory. The storage is neither random nor absolute. Similar material seems to be batched together, and we forget stimuli that are not repeated frequently or used regularly. Fortunately, the mind uses automatic procedures which provide efficiency of operation. Occasionally, our mental habits thwart us and we become aware of them. For example, most people who drive an automobile have had this type of experience.

The array of skills and information needed to drive a car safely is staggering. However, with practice we acquire the requisite skills, and they quickly become routine; that is, we can use them, but they are no longer in our awareness. Often the routines extend to patterns connected with the destinations to which we drive. We know the route to work so well and have traveled it so often that it becomes a habit. The route over the crosstown freeway to the exit ramp at the university can be driven almost automatically. Under normal driving conditions, the routine tempts us to review the day's schedule or engage in problem solving or daydreaming about the next vacation. If the weather turns nasty, however, and there is ice on the freeway, our attention becomes riveted on the task of negotiating the slippery surface with caution. The monitoring system serves us well, except when we want to break our habit.

Going to the airport, for example. We pack our bag, gather our papers, check that we've got our airline ticket, and get into the car to drive to the airport, to catch a flight to a national meeting. Fifteen minutes later we find ourselves driving onto campus! Instead of passing the exit ramp and driving on to the airport, automatic pilot took over and drove us to work. Changing what we think or do takes concentration.

Another popular analogy for how our mind works is to describe the brain as a computer and the mind as the programming that runs the computer. This analogy must be used with caution, because the comparison is instructive only; actually, the differences in size and capacity of the human brain compared with even the most complicated computer favor the brain by a wide margin. The computer is a very simple machine, driven by a digital system (controlled by a switch: on/off, yes/no). Programs are written which organize information, store it, and give access to it through switches that recognize "on" and "off" by using two digits: 0 and 1. (A string might look like: 001101110110001.)

A current advance in computer program design is what is called a "memory cache." This is how it works. A program is written to keep track of other programs that are used in operating a computer. That is, given a large memory by computer standards (not by human standards), a computer can perform many functions, each one requiring a program or subprogram to run it. A memory cache monitors the actual functions an operator uses most frequently, and keeps the most used programs in resident memory for instant use. This procedure increases computer efficiency and permits a greater number of user options with a smaller total memory; thus, the memory cache makes it possible to use a less expensive computer architecture to achieve results similar to those of more sophisticated machines.

Some estimates of program use calculate that a typical user will operate 5 percent of the total computer functions about 95 percent of the time. The computer can keep those 5 percent of functions ready for immediate use and be 95 percent efficient. The key to the system is the memory cache's monitoring of the actual pattern of each operator's use of computer program functions. The monitoring provides *feedback* to the computer, and that makes the system self-correcting.

The point of this analogy is not that the brain is simply a machine like a computer, but rather that *all self-correcting systems depend upon feedback*. Monitoring of human mental functions provides feedback and is a necessary process in testing for error, bias, and mistakes in our thoughts and feelings. Feedback is a central process used in analyzing our beliefs and goals.

We can distinguish between two types of thinking: one directed *by* goals and another directed *at* goals. The first type of thinking is goal-driven and as a result may be thought of as linear. That is, goal-driven thinking proceeds by steps from A to B to C, and so on, until it achieves the aim or target of the process. The type of thinking which focuses on the steps needed to reach a goal is like an arrow shot at a bull's eye on a target.

The second type of thinking focuses on the goal itself. It asks whether the goal is desirable. This type of thinking characterizes reflective thinking and is cyclical rather than linear in organization.

The distinction between linear thinking and goal-driven thinking can be illustrated by the development of systems theory. In the early stages of planning theory, actions to be undertaken were plotted along a line in a sequence. The simplest diagram looked like this:

Input ⟶ Process ⟶ Output

Systems theory grew out of cybernetics (Bateson, 1972) and depended upon the addition of the feedback loop; the diagram looked like this:

This second type of thinking is like systems processing because it asks whether a goal is worthwhile; it is circular, reflective, and self-corrective. The feedback loop completes a circuit which makes evaluation possible. In addition to asking how a goal may be achieved, feedback questions the value of the outcome and provides options for modification of the "how" as directed toward redefined goals. Systems feedback provides a learning-community teacher with a model for thinking about what happens within the class.

When we shift from a linear model to a circular model, a massive change occurs in how we think about thinking. Once reliable feedback has been added to a classroom, like the loop in the above diagram, a circuit is closed and each position within the circle becomes a trigger or switch for the next position. The idea of a circuit itself is suggestive of how learning-community teachers monitor their teaching. Consider a circuit—say, a thermostat. The thermostat is a device which measures the air temperature in a room and throws a switch when the temperature falls below a set degree. The switch is connected to the heater, which heats the air and, at another temperature, throws the switch to turn itself off. That action allows the air temperature to drop, and so on. The circle of causation becomes complete. It becomes difficult to tell which factor is in control. One naturally says: "But, of course, the whole system depends on the thermostat, it controls the process." This is a common sense response; but does it work? In a certain sense the critical factor is the air temperature, in another sense it is the heater, and so forth. The point is, the process is circular, once the loop is closed.

The idea of circular causation has been discussed in detail by Bateson in *Mind and Nature* (1980). He describes the work of Norbert Wiener, who (with Rosenblueth and Bigelow) proposed the self-corrective circuit as a model for how organisms adapt. Adaptation is a process of habituation achieved by circularity. Habits can be so automatic that they disappear from view; we literally cannot see them operating. For example, Bateson (1980, p. 120) explains that at first glance, a switch or relay might be confused with any other object in a room, like "wall" or "table." However, the function of the switch makes it disappear as an object, *from the point of view of the circuit.* Consider: in the "on" position, the switch is like the rest of the circuit, conducting the electricity; it is no different from the wire in the circuit itself; it's just another part of the circuit. In the "off" position, the gap created in the circuit makes the switch vanish. It does not exist. The switch is an artifact of *time* in the sense that *when* it is on, it disappears with the rest of the conductors of electrical current; and *when* it is off, it disappears from the view of the circuit. Therefore, the switch is "related to the notion 'change' rather than to the notion 'object'" (Bateson, 1980, p. 121).

The case can be made that all our sense organs act like switches; that is, they are of the same logical type. They are activated by difference. The senses must perceive change in order to be "on." Bateson concludes with this comment on the circularity of causation:

> *The truth of the matter is that every circuit of causation in the whole of biology, in our physiology, in our thinking, our neural processes, in our homeostasis, and in the ecological and cultural systems of which we are parts—every such circuit conceals or proposes those paradoxes and confusions that accompany errors and distortions in logical typing. (1979, p. 121)*

In other words, a systems perspective demands that we take very seriously the context in which we work. The ecology of a school is a system made up of subsystems. The classroom learning community is one subsystem in the larger ecosystem of the school. Teachers are members of several communities within the school, all at the same time, and this reality demands that they communicate across communities. Without feedback and professional communication, teachers seal off one class from another. Every teacher remains isolated from the others. Linear thinking about teaching practice (i.e., step-by-step thinking) can lead to programmed error. Programmed error is so basic that it is outside our awareness most of the time. This is how self-sealing errors can dominate a culture. Without self-correcting circular feedback, the participants in a system remain isolated, unable to integrate the whole.

It is true that humans live in a world of parts and that we perceive our world but partially. However, our guess about the whole requires some form of feedback, verification, and confirmation. The meanings we ascribe to events change according to the context in which the events occur, and that includes the perceptual frame in which we experience things. This reality supports the necessity for humans to share with each other their different perceptions, if we are to learn about the context of community. The communication of different perceptions of events helps to define the context, and that makes it possible to talk about what we value. Metacognition (thinking about our thinking) benefits from metacommunication (talking about our talking).

A basic assumption of this book has been that change or improvement in the quality of student learning happens when the quality of life experienced by students in classrooms improves. Thus, classroom culture is considered the appropriate level at which to analyze teaching practice, but the communication of reflection happens at both the classroom level and the schoolwide level among the subculture of fellow teachers. The level of analysis at which reflection on practice occurs, therefore, need not be confused with evaluation of an individual teacher's worth. Only individual teachers can assess their own worth or value to themselves. The same applies to students. Teachers can evaluate students' individual performances but not their ultimate personal worth.

Each individual, like each classroom learning community, is unique and ultimately incomparable. Analysis of what a student is doing right or wrong can only apply to this student, in this particular class, with these particular students, at this particular time (developmental stage), in this particular subject. Rarely will such analysis also apply to other students. To look at a classroom as a learning community is to look from the perspective that the classroom is an operating ecosystem, or a functional subculture—not a collection of isolation individual students.

What we have been discussing is the mistake of confusing the whole with the parts, or the isolated with the joined. We make another mistake when we seek to make inferences from isolated events. Two or more events must be compared in order to discover a pattern of meaning. We must distinguish between a collection of unique, isolated entities (students and teachers) and a pattern of behavior (culture), and recognize that they are of different logical types. Problem-solving schema have to be adapted to the level of analysis intended. If we try to analyze student performance against national norms, we will tend to make significant interpretive errors. Yet teachers, and particularly parents, seem eager to do just that: "How is my student, or my child, doing against the national norm?" This error of analysis is particularly destructive when it is applied to the planning of instructional activities. A more appropriate level of analysis would certainly be to ask how a student is doing against his/her own record last week, or last month.

John Dewey's book *How We Think* (1933) was written to help teachers to develop reflective thinking. He emphasized that humans' thinking and sharing of understanding distinguishes us from other species of animals. His description of the steps from a prereflective to a postreflective state is not just a linear heuristic. Dewey knew that the steps were not sequential and could happen in any order. His steps include:

> *In between [pre and post reflection], as states of thinking, are (1) suggestions, in which the mind leaps forward to a possible solution; (2) an intellectualization of the difficulty or perplexity that has been felt (directly experienced) into a problem to be solved, a question for which the answer must be sought; (3) the use of one suggestion after another as a leading idea, or hypothesis, to initiate and guide observation and other operations in collection of factual material; (4) the mental elaboration of the idea or supposition as an idea or supposition* (reasoning, *in the sense in which reasoning is a part, not the whole inference); and (5)* testing *the hypothesis by overt or imaginative action. (1939, p. 855)*

Dewey says that these different functions or states of thought do not follow one another in a set order. Any thought can affect another one and change the nature of the subsequent mental action. Dewey understood that the mind's functions mirror the interactions which take place in community, and that each function affects other functions, with the result that the group (the whole) is larger than the individual functions (the parts). This is particularly relevant when thought is turned to social action or social reconstruction, as opposed to the study of physical phenomena in controlled laboratory situations.

In testing ideas in professional practice, teachers take overt actions which change the social environment. Therefore, in social actions there must be a practical commitment to living by the consequences of one's actions. That is to say, there is always a moral seriousness about experimental behavior in a learning community. The thoughtful person, as Dewey wrote, "makes a problem out of the consequences of conduct, looking into the causes from which they probably resulted" (p. 856).

The usefulness of Dewey's scheme in terms of teachers' reflection on practice deserves wider application. Reflection is recursive, looking back on patterns of behavior, seeking a match or mismatch between intention and effect. This action is metacognitive because it monitors the elements which link intention to effect, as a means for making self-correcting adjustments of teaching practice.

The problems of practice that teachers experience involve tacit theories or beliefs about the nature of learning, the functions of schooling, and images of self-worth. Argyris and his associates explore tacit theories through a scheme called "action science" (Argyris, 1982; Schon, 1983; Argyris, Putnam, and Smith, 1985). The essence of action science is an elaboration upon the traditional advice, "Think before you act." In action science, one is advised, "Think before, during, and after you act." The tacit information upon which teachers base actions should be examined systematically, in order to change practices. Teachers always find it necessary to act, often quickly and without apparent premeditation. Reflecting on completed action creates the possibility that future actions will more closely match the teacher's intended goals. The process, as Schon puts it, is one of "reflective conversation with the situation" (quoted by Argyris, Putnam, and Smith, 1985, p. 52).

As we have seen, simply reflecting on professional practice may not be sufficient to restructure social action, because the definition of the problematic situation may be false. We cannot reflect on actions, if those actions are not perceived as being problematic because the beliefs driving them are false or biased. By trial and error, we can keep on inventing new actions, but to the degree that the problem is caused by a false idea about the reality situation, each new action will bring disappointment and/or failure. The cycle of repeated trials and disappointment is the self-sealing process of what Argyris (1982) calls "single loop learning."

Action science sees reflection as focused on both the action taken and the situation out of which the action arose. Action science guides teachers to examine *both their instructional activities and the context of the activities*. The activities and their context cannot be separated without falsifying both to some degree. Problem solving through public reflection includes defining the problem in the match or mismatch between beliefs and actions and their subsequent consequences. When teachers publicly test their actions against their intentions, what happens is what Argyris (1982) calls "double loop learning." He argues that correction of "error requires conditions of the good dialectic, which begins with the development of a map that provides a different perspective on the problem" (p. 106). These conditions are the variables of metacommunication in a learning community. The learning cycle of a classroom learning community is not a collection of isolated events but a continuous process of public discourse. As we have seen, learning does not mean arriving at a state that is free of error. Rather, learning is an open-ended process of error detection. The learning cycle continues to shape our beliefs, ideas, and theories.

Even if time were the only variable of the learning cycle, the discovery of what we believe and how we try to implement these beliefs would be different after each cycle. In the same sense that, as the Greek philosopher Heraclitus (ca 540–ca 480 B.C.) wrote, "We cannot step twice into the same river," by the time we reflect on our actions, we are not the same people we were when we started our actions. More than time, however, is involved when we seek to change what we do by changing what we think about. Engaging in public discourse, in a learning community in which differences are valued as precious sources of alternative explanation, changes us and our ideas about the self and the world. In this sense, we create and are created by the interdependent classroom learning community. This model of reflection (problem solving) does not require all members of a learning community be like-minded believers in the same ideology. Far from it! It calls for all the members to engage in public discussion about what is happening, so that the range of thinking in the group will be examined and matched with the apparent links between thought and action and results.

In a classroom learning community, students and teachers are respected for their contributions to the whole group, while maintaining individual personal judgment. Personal judgment involves not only the ability to think one's own thoughts but also the ability to perceive the mind at work in the words of others. Every utterance has a "mind of its own"—what we might call our "personal idiom." Development of critical skills requires the public expression of one's personal idiom. This can only happen when teachers and students trust each other. Trust comes from risking oneself openly with others, and developing trust takes time. The learning-community teacher is responsible for developing a learning environment in which such risk taking can take place. Unless students know that they can be themselves in the classroom, they do not risk exposing who they think they are; they remain protective. The learning-community teacher invites students to risk learning not only who they are, but who they may become.

The goal of a classroom learning community is the positive utilization of human resources by developing human potential to the highest levels of freedom and personal satisfaction. The function of a democratic society is to create the conditions necessary for the pursuit of happiness and harmony among people. In this sense, the school is a moral learning community (Goodlad, Soder, and Sinotnik, 1990). Paulo Freire (1974) taught that education is the practice of freedom. The authors believe that the classroom learning community comes close to creating the necessary conditions for learning about our democratic heritage and joining in the exercise of freedom.

Both Carolyn Barnes and Mark Hicks, who were introduced in Chapter 1, struggled for a time with their ideas about classroom learning communities and about their visions of professional teaching.

Carolyn Barnes has come to love her fifth-grade class. She is now in her third year at Woodville School. Her class is organized as a learning community, and she is pleased to be able to focus on the real learning needs of her students, rather than being preoccupied with classroom management problems. She believes that her class is a democratic society in which she and the students are devoted to learning about themselves and the world around them. She sees herself as playing two roles—instructional leader and participant—in the community of scholarship they are building together. Barnes believes that what is learned must be socially constructed and that what is constructed affects what it is possible to learn. She finds herself reflecting frequently on the balance between initiating actions and responding to student initiatives within the class.

One of Barnes's students, Steve, is a good example of the payoff for her approach to teaching. Steve had a low opinion of himself and of schooling in general before he started in Carolyn's fifth-grade class. He did not seem to care about anything. His favorite response to most everything was, "Who cares?" However, in Carolyn's learning community, students learn to trust their ability to think through problems in many areas of the curriculum. Steve first became excited when he discovered that he could solve simple algebraic problems. Later on, he found that he could apply his problem-solving skills in the social arena. The leadership Steve developed within his study team in dealing with mathematical problems helped him when he was faced with social problems within the team. Success in one area spread to other areas.

How did Carolyn Barnes get Steve to change so radically from a bored and indifferent nonparticipant to an enthusiastic learner? "It was not what I did, so much," Carolyn says, "as what Steve has done for himself." Steve, however, thinks differently. He says, "Ms. Barnes's class is like a continuous debate. It's nothing like any class I've known." Steve is referring to the continuing discussions that characterize Barnes's class. No matter what the subject, students are involved in defining concerns, focusing on issues, gathering information, suggesting hypotheses, and defending their theories. Instead of focusing on facts and rote learning, students in Barnes's class strive to make sense of what they experience and to communicate that sense to others. In mathematics, for example, Barnes may suggest a type of problem, but she then asks the mathematics groups to develop real-life examples and to figure out how they can be solved. In the discussion afterward, the group members defend multiple theses about the mathematical idea. They challenge each others' assumptions and go after each others' solutions with enthusiasm. This environment suits Steve's temperament.

Steve's mother has told Carolyn Barnes that she sometimes does not recognize her son. "He was a scattered child, without an idea in his head and without much interest in anything," Steve's mother said. "Now he is alive with ideas that interest him!" Barnes knows that high-order thinking calls forth a high degree of commitment from learners and that creative activities are intrinsically interesting to students. Under the right circumstances, students become involved with what they are doing. They have a stake in it, and it is important to them. The students in her class do not wait for her to play leader and tell them what to do. Instead, they say to her, "This is what we want to do because. . . ."

Teaching has become fun for Carolyn Barnes during the years that she has been having her students work in cooperative learning groups in her fifth-grade class. She feels excited each day when she comes to school. Often she wonders what new and interesting ideas her students will come up with that day.

Carolyn Barnes also feels like she is no longer working alone. Her professional life has expanded to include most of the other teachers at Woodville School. The principal supports the teachers' efforts at sharing their successes and failures. Most of the teachers' meetings are organized by the teachers themselves and deal with their own concerns—and most of the concerns discussed are professional concerns about teaching and about students' achievement. Barnes heads the committee that arranged for the computers in each classroom to be networked with the computers throughout the school, including those in the library. Her next goal on that committee is to link the school computers with the district central offices and with the university.

In her own classroom, each day provides new and varied satisfactions and challenges. As students learn to listen to each other, they begin to realize the power they have to affect each other and the community atmosphere. When a student is depressed, the rest of the class is able to cheer him/her up. Even when Barnes herself feels down, she does not stay that way for long. Her class raises her spirits. Carolyn believes that the learning community nurtures its members across all dimensions, so that nothing human is foreign to her class.

Mark Hicks now teaches social studies in the Walden Middle School in his midwestern home state. He found out about this job when he visited his parents during summer vacation, several years after he started teaching. Walden is a professional development school associated with a nearby midwestern research university and located in an urban setting in a medium-size city. Hicks is a team leader in a multiple-staffed learning community that consists of sixty students. His team includes two interns from the university; an aide who is a specialist in reading in the content area, and who is provided by the school district; a university professor who teaches language arts; and a graduate student who works as a researcher and documenter. The students are organized into study groups, and the whole group is organized into a cooperative learning community. The students leave their groups when it is time for them to take their mathematics, science, art, and physical education classes in different rooms and different groups. However, for half the day the students are all together in one area of the school. Hicks is the instructional leader for social studies (including civics, history, geography, and economics), and the professor is the instructional leader for the language arts (literature, writing, speech, and drama). Mark also teaches one history class in the afternoon, for another learning-community group.

The whole group is also considered the home room for all sixty students. Insofar as possible, Hicks and his teaching colleagues organize their instructional themes around interdisciplinary issues. The students keep journals in which they write their thoughts and feelings about what they are studying and what is happening in the class. Their entries give Hicks insights into their fears and other emotions, as well as their cognitive development. Hicks is particularly interested in what the students understand and can use conceptually to build new ideas about the world they live in. The students are challenged to connect what they are studying in school with the outside world. For example, during a national election campaign one fall, the students organized into research groups and followed particular candidates, read their speeches, watched them on television, checked on their positions, and compared their voting records. The study groups prepared presentations for the whole group and made predictions about the election outcome. After the elections, the students studied the results and compared them with their predictions. Where they missed the mark, the groups tried to find reasons for the difference between the outcomes and their predictions. This project combined many areas of knowledge and gave the students a feeling that what they were doing was relevant to the world around them.

Hicks is the collaborating teacher for the intern teachers who work with the team. They look to him for direction and support. He feels comfortable in the role of collaborator with those who are learning the profession of teaching. One reason for his positive feelings is Hicks's belief that what he is doing with the interns, university researchers, and his fellow teachers is expanding the borders of knowledge about teaching and teacher education. He now talks about himself as a "teacher educator" as well as a "teacher." Hicks says that he not only teaches conceptual understanding of history and the other social sciences, but he also teaches himself. That is, he believes that he himself is "on the line" each day. What he believes about learning, about the nature of society, and about good teaching is tested openly in every class. In reflecting on his teaching and the teaching of his interns, he explores the many levels of knowledge and of sensitivity to his students, his colleagues, and his own personal image. In these review sessions, Hicks often finds himself getting excited about the future and its possibilities, his role as an educator, and how he thinks schools need to function to meet the needs of a new century. He believes that what he is doing is helping to create a future for students who might otherwise never have had much of an opportunity to compete for jobs, much less excel in what they choose to do with their lives.

Performance Standards and Activities (NJPTS 1, 2, 4, 5, 6)

Chapter 13
The Future of Learning Communities

PERFORMANCE STANDARDS

1. Apply knowledge about learning-communities to identify outcomes for LC leaders and for educators participating in PLCs.
2. Accurately collect, summarize and report findings from interviews and speakers.

Exercise 13.1
Identifying What Educators Gain from Leading Classroom Learning Communities and Participation in Professional Learning Communities

Step 1: Design a list of questions that will provide you with the information you need in order to understand the benefits that educators gain from (1) leading the establishment and expansion of a classroom learning community and (2) participating in a professional learning community.

Step 2: Attend a presentation by teachers who are learning community leaders and/or participate in Professional Learning Communities. At the presentation listen for information that you can quote that answers your questions. At the appropriate time ask questions that you have not had answered. Listen to the responses to other people's questions and record data that answer questions you identified.

Step 3: Analyze the information you collected and write a position paper explaining the benefits and tensions that the learning community leader and participant in PLCs experiences.

RECOMMENDED READINGS

Barth, R. S. (1990). *Improving schools from within*. San Francisco: Jossey-Bass.

Bateson, G. (1980). *Mind and nature: a necessary unity*. London: Fontana Paperbacks.

Lortie, D. (1975). *Schoolteacher*. Chicago: University of Chicago Press.

Porter, A. (October 1987). Teacher collaboration: new partnerships to attack old problems. *Phi Delta Kappan*, 69(2), 147–152.

Rosenholtz, S. J. (1989). *Teachers' workplace: the social organization of schools*. New York: Longman.

BIBLIOGRAPY

AAUW Educational Foundation. (2001). *Hostile Hallways: Bullying, teasing, and sexual harassment in school.* Washington, D.C., May.

Abernathy. S., Manera. E., and Wright, R. (1985). What stresses student teachers most? *The Clearing House, 58,* 361–362.

Acker, S. (1981). *No woman's land: British sociology of Education 1960–79. Sociological Review, 29 (2), 77–104.*

Adams, F. (1982). Making production, making democracy: A case study of teaching in the workplace. Chapel Hill. N.C.: Twin Streams Educational Center.

Adams, R. S., and Biddle. B. J. (1970). *Realities of teaching: Exploration with videotape.* New York: Holt, Rinehart & Winston.

Aiello, B. (ed.) (1975). *Making it work: Practical ideas for integrating children into regular classrooms.* Reston, Va.: Council for Exceptional Children.

Allen. J. D. (1986). Classroom management: Students' perspectives, goals, and strategies. *American Educational Research Journal, 23*(3), 437–459.

Allen, R. (2003). *The Democratic Aims of Service of Learning.* Educational Leadership, Creating Caring Schools. March. Vol. 60, No. 6, pp. 60–63.

Allen, R. G., and Kraft, C. (1984). *Transformations that last: A cultural approach.* In Adam, J. D. (ed.). Transforming work: A Collection of Organizational Transformation Readings. Virginia, Miles River Press.

Allsopp, A., and Posen, S. (1988). Teacher reactions to a child sexual abuse training program. *Elementary School Guidance and Counseling, 22,* 299–305.

Alschuler, A. S. (1980). *School discipline a socially literate solution.* New York: McGraw-Hill.

American Psychologist. *Journal of the American Psychological Association, 31*(9), 638–654.

American School Counselors Association (ASCA) Position Statement: The School Counselor and Child Abuse/Neglect Prevention. (1988). *Elementary School Guidance and Counseling. 22*(4), 261–263.

Ames, R. (1982). Teachers' attributions for their own teaching, in J. M. Levine and M. C. Wang (eds.), *Teacher and student perceptions.* Hillsdale, N.J.: Laurence Erlbaum, 105–124.

Anderson, L. (1983). Responsibility in the classroom: A synthesis of research on teaching self-control. *Educational Leadership, 40*(2), 62–66.

——— (1984). The environment of instruction: The function of seatwork in a commercially developed curriculum, in G. Duffy, L. Roehler, and J. Mason (eds.), *Comprehension instruction: Perspectives and suggestions.* New York: Longman, Inc., pp. 93–103.

Anderson, L., and Evertson, C. M. (1978). *Classroom organization at the beginning of school: Two case studies.* (R & D Report no. 6003.) Austin: The University of Texas, The Research and Development Center for Teacher Education.

———, ———, and Brophy, J. E. (1979). An experimental study of effective teaching in first-grade reading groups. *Elementary School Journal, 79,* 193–223.

Anderson, L. W. (1976). An empirical investigation of individual differences in time to learn. *Journal of Educational Psychology, 68,* 226–233.

———, and Pigford, A. (1987–1988). Teaching within-classroom groups: Examining the role of the teacher. *Journal of Classroom Interaction, 23*(2), 8–13.

Apple, & J. A. Beane (Eds.), *Democratic Schools,* (pp. 1–25). Alexandria, VA.

Apple, M. W. (1981). *Ideology and curriculum.* London: Routledge & Kegan Paul.

——— (ed.). (1982a). *Cultural and economic reproduction in education: Essays on class, ideology, and the state.* London: Routledge & Kegan Paul.

——— (1982b). *Education and power.* London: Routledge & Kegan Paul.

Apple, M. W. (1993). Official Knowledge: Democratic Education in a Conservative Age. New York: Routledge.

Apps, J. W. (1985). *Improving practice in continuing education: Modern approaches for understanding the field and determining priorities.* San Francisco, Calif.: Jossey-Bass.

Argyris, (1985). Strategy, change, and defensive routines. Boston: Ballinger.

Argyris, (1986). *Theories of action that inhibit individual learning.*

Argyris, (1990). *Overcoming organizational defenses. Facilitating organizational learning.* Boston: Allyn and Bacon.

Argyris, C. (1976). *Increasing leadership effectiveness.* New York: Wiley-Interscience.

——— (1982). *Reasoning, learning, and action: Individual and organizational.* San Francisco, Calif.: Jossey-Bass.

———, Putnam, R., and Smith, D. M. (1985). *Action science: Concepts, methods, and skills for research and intervention.* San Francisco, Calif.: Jossey-Bass.

——— and Schon, D. A. (1974). *Theory in practice: Increasing professional effectiveness.* San Francisco, Calif.: Jossey-Bass.

Arlin, M. (1979). Teacher transitions can disrupt time flow in classrooms. *American Educational Research Journal, 16,* 42–56.

Armstrong, R. (1972). Towards the study of community action. *Adult Education (U.K.), 45*(1), 21–25.

——— and Davies, C. T. (1977). Community action, pressure groups and education. *Adult Education (U.K.), 50*(3), 149–154.

Arnn, J. W., Jr., and Manigeri, J. N. (1984). Teacher support teams: An examination of dynamics. *Action in Teacher Education, VI*(3), 31–34.

Arnold, D., Atwood, R., and Rogers, V. (1974). Question and response levels and lapse time intervals. *Journal of Experimental Education, 43,* 11–15.

Arnold, R., and Burke, B. (1983). *A popular education handbook: An educational experience taken from Central America and adapted to the Canadian context.* Toronto, Canada: CUSO-Development Education and Department of Adult Education, Ontario Institute for Studies in Adult Education.

Aronfreed, J. (1968). *Conduct and conscience: The socialization of internalized control over behavior.* New York: Academic Press.

Aronowitz, S., and Giroux, H. A. (1985). *Education under siege: The conservative, liberal, and radical debate over schooling.* South Hadley, Mass.: Bergin & Garvey.

Aronowitz, S., and Giroux, H. (1991). *Politics, culture, and social criticism.* Minneapolis, MN.

Aronowitz, S., and Giroux H. (1993). Education Still Under Siege. Second Edition. Critical Studies in Education Series. Connecticut: Bergin & Garvey, Greenwood Publishing Group.

Aronson, E. (1978). *The jigsaw classroom.* Beverly Hills, Calif.: Sage.

Arrington, P., and Rose, S. (1987). Prologues to what is possible: Introductions as metadiscourse. *College Composition and Communication, 38*(3): 306–318.

Arter, J., and McTighe, J. (2001). Scoring rubrics in the classroom: Using performance criteria for assessing and improving student performance. Thousand Oaks, Calif., Corwin, Press, Inc. ASCD.

Ashlock, R. B. (1976). *Error patterns in computation: A semi-programmed approach,* 2d ed., Columbus, Ohio: Merrill.

Association for Supervision and Curriculum Development. (1981). *Effective classroom management for the elementary school* (videotape). Alexandria, Va.: Association for Supervision and Curriculum Development.

Atheide, D. L. (1976). *Creating reality: How TV news distorts events.* Beverly Hills. Calif.: Sage.

——— (1985). *Media power.* Beverly Hills. Calif.: Sage.

Ausubel, D. (1963). *The psychology of meaningful verbal learning: An introduction to school learning.* New York: Grune and Stratton.

Axelrod, S. (1983). *Behavior modification for the classroom teacher* (2d ed.). New York: McGraw-Hill.

——— and Apsche, J. (eds.). (1983). *The effects of punishment on human behavior.* New York: Academic Press.

Axline, V. M. (1969). *Play therapy.* New York: Ballantine Books.

Azrin, N. H., Hake, D. G., Holz, W. C., and Hutchinson, R. R. (1965a). Elicitation of aggression by a physical blow. *Journal of Experimental Analysis of Behavior, 8,* 55–57.

———, ———, ———, and ——— (1965b). Motivational aspects of escape from punishment. *Journal of Experimental Analysis of Behavior, 8,* 31–44.

———, Hutchinson, R. R., and Sallery, R. D. (1964). Pain-aggression toward inanimate objects. *Journal of Experimental Analysis of Behavior, 7,* 223–228.

Babad, E. Y. (1985). Some correlates of teachers' expectancy bias. *American Educational Research Journal, 22*(2), 175–183.

Baker, J. A. (1992). *Paradigms. The business of discovering the future.* Harper Business. A division of Harper Collins Publishers.

Baker, K. (1985). Research evidence of a school discipline problem. *Phi Delta Kappan, 66*(7), 482–487.

Bales, R. R. (1950). *Interaction process analysis—A method for the study of small groups.* Cambridge, Mass.: Addison-Wesley.

Bandura, A. (1965). Behavior modification through modeling procedures, in L. Krasner and L. P. Ulman (eds.), *Research in behavior modification.* New York: Holt, Rinehart & Winston.

——— (1969). *Principles of behavior modification.* New York: Holt, Rinehart & Winston.

——— (1977). *Social learning theory.* Englewood Cliffs, N.J.: Prentice-Hall, Inc.

——— (1986). *Social foundations of thought and action: A social cognitive theory.* Englewood Cliffs, N.J.: Prentice-Hall, Inc.

———, Roxx, D., and Ross, S. A. (1961). Transmission of aggression through imitation of aggressive models. *Journal of Abnormal and Social Psychology. 62,* 575–582.

——— and Waiters, R. H. (1963). *Social learning and personality development.* New York: Holt, Rinehart & Winston.

Bangert, R. L., Kulik, J. A., and Kulik, C. C. (1983). Individualized systems of instruction in secondary schools. *Review of Educational Research, 53*(2), 143–158.

Banks, C. A. M. & Banks, J. A. (1997). Reforming Schools in a Democratic Pluralistic Society. *Educational Policy. 11*(2), 183–93.

Banks, J. A. *Multiethnic education: Theory and practice* (2d ed.). Boston. Mass.: Allyn and Bacon, Inc.

Barber, B. (1984). *Strong democracy: Participatory politics for a new age.* Berkeley: University of California Press.

Barker, G. P., and Graham. S. (1987). Developmental study of praise and blame as attributional cues. *Journal of Educational Psychology, 79*(1), 62–66.

Barndt, D., Cristall, F., and Marino. D. (1983). *Getting there: Images of women's journeys to equality.* Toronto: Between the Lines.

Barrett, T. C. (1985). *Youth in crisis: Seeking solutions to self-destructive behavior.* Longmont, Colo.: Sopris West, Inc.

Bartles, B. H. (1995). *Promoting Mathematics Connections with Concept Mapping.* Mathematics Teaching in the Middle School. Vol. 1, No. 7. November–December pp. 542–549.

Bartles, B. H. (1995). "Promoting Mathematics Connections with Concept Mapping," Mathematics Teaching in the Middle Schools, Mathematics Teaching in the Middle School, Vol. I. No. 7, November–December.

Bateson, G. (1972). *Steps to an ecology of mind.* New York: Ballantine Books.

——— (1980). *Mind and nature: A necessary unity.* London: Fontana Paperbacks.

Battistich, V., Solomon, D., Kim, D., Watson, M., and Schaps, E. (1995), *Schools as Communities, Poverty Levels of Student Populations, and Student Attitudes, Motives, and Performance: A multilevel Analysis.* American Educational Research Journal, 32, pp. 627–658.

Baumeister, R., and Leary, M. (1995). The Need to Belong: Desire for Interpersonal Attachments as a Fundamental Human Motivation. *Psychological Bulletin, 117,* pp. 497–529.

Beach, D. M. (1977). *Reaching teenagers: Learning centers for the secondary classroom.* Calif.: Goodyear Publishing.

Beane, A. L. (1999). *The bully free classroom: over 100 tips and strategies for teachers K–8,* Free Spirit Publishing Inc., Minn., MN.

Beane, J. A., & Apple, M. W. (1995). The case for democratic schools. In M. W. Belsey, B., Cyberbullying, Defined. www.cyberbulling.com.

Beidler, P. G. (ed.). (1986). *Distinguished teachers on effective teaching.* (New Directions for Teaching and Learning. no. 28.) San Francisco, Calif: Jossey-Bass.

Belenky, M. F., Clinchy, B. M., Goldberger. N. R., and Tarule, J. M. (1986). *Women's ways of knowing: The development of self, voice, and mind.* New York: Basic Books.

Bell, L. C., and Stefanich, G. P. (1984). Building effective discipline using the cascade model. *The Clearing House, 58,* 134–137.

Bellah, R. N. (1985). *Habits of the heart: Individualism and commitment in American life.* Berkeley: University of California Press.

Belsey, B., Cyberbullying, Defined, *www.Cyberbulling.com*

Bender, W. N. (1987). Learning characteristics suggestive of teaching strategies in secondary mainstream classes. *The High School Journal, 70*(4), 217–223.

Benne, K. D., Bradford, L. P., Gibb, J. R., and Lippitt, R. O. (1975). *The laboratory method of changing and learning: Theory and application.* Palo Alto, Calif.: Science and Behavior books.

Bennis. W. (1983). The artform of leadership, in S. Srivastva and associates (eds.). *The executive mind: New insights on managerial thought and action.* San Francisco, Calif.: Jossey-Bass.

Bennis, W. G., Schien, E. H., Berlew, D. E., and Steele, F. I. (eds) (1964). 1973 Interpersonal Dynamics: Essays and Readings on Human Interactions. The Dorsey Press. Homewood, Illinois.

Bennis, W. G., Thomas, R. J. (2002). Geeks and Geezers: How era, values, and defining moments shape leaders. Accenture LLP Harvard Business School Publ.: Boston, Mass.

Bereiter, C., and Engelmann. S. (1966). *Teaching disadvantaged children in the preschool.* Englewood Cliffs, N.J.: Prentice-Hall, Inc.

Berg, F. (1986). *Listening for the hard of hearing students.* San Diego, Calif.: College Hill Press.

Bergem. T. (1986). Teachers' thinking and behavior. An empirical study of the role of social sensitivity and moral reasoning in the teaching performance of student teachers. *Scandinavian Journal of Educational Research, 30*(4), 193–203.

Berliner, D. C., and Tikunoff, W. J. (1976). The California beginning teacher evaluation study: Overview of ethnographic study. *Journal of Teacher Education, 27,* 24–30.

Berman, L. M. (1986). Perception, paradox, and passion: Curriculum for community. *Theory into Practice, 25*(1), 41–45.

Berne, E. (1964). *Games people play: The psychology of human relations.* New York: Grove Press.

Bernstein, B. (1977). *Class, codes, and control,* Vol. 3: *Towards a theory of educational transmission* (2d ed.). London: Routledge & Kegan Paul.

Berstein, P. (1980). *Workplace democratization: Its internal dynamics.* New Brunswick, N.J.: Transaction Books.

Berte, N. R. (ed.). (1975). *Individual education by learning contracts.* (New Directions for Higher Education, no. 10.) San Francisco, Calif.: Jossey-Bass.

Birch, J. W. (1974). *Mainstreaming: Educable mentally retarded children in regular classes.* Reston, Va.: Council for Exceptional Children.

Blase, J. J. (1986). A qualitative analysis of sources of teacher stress: Consequences for performance. *American Educational Research Journal, 23*(1), 13–40.

Blitz, B. (1973). *The open classroom making it work.* Boston, Mass.: Allyn and Bacon, Inc.

Bloch, A. (April, 1977). The battered teacher. *Today's Education,* 58–62.

Block, P. (1993). Stewardship: Choosing service over self-interest. Berrett-Koehler Publishers; San Fransico, California.

Bloom, B. S. (ed.). (1956). *Taxonomy of educational objectives: Handbook I: Cognitive domain.* New York: Longman.

———— (1977). Affective outcomes of school learning. *Phi Delta Kappan, 59,* 193–198.

———— (1987). A response to Slavin's mastery learning reconsidered. *Review of Educational Research, 57*(4), 507–508.

Bongiovanni, A. F. (1979). An analysis of research on punishment and its relation to the use of corporal punishment in the schools, in I. A. Hyman and J. Wise (eds.), *Corporal punishment in American education*. Philadelphia, Pa.: Temple University Press, 126–144.

Borg, W. R. (1980). Time and school learning, in C. Denham and A. Lieberman (eds.), *Time to learn*. Washington, D.C.: National Institute of Education.

Borko, H., and Cadwell, J. (April, 1980). *Individual differences in teachers' decision strategies: An investigation of classroom organization and management decisions.* Paper presented at the annual meeting of the American Educational Research Association, Boston, Mass.

———— and Livingston, C. (1989). Cognition and improvisation: Differences in mathematics instruction by expert and novice teachers. *American Educational Research Journal, 26*(4), 473–498.

Boser, J. A., and others. (1988). Elementary school guidance program evaluation: A reflection of student-counselor ratio. *School Counselor, 36*(2) 125–135.

Boshier, R. (1986). *Toward a learning society.* Vancouver, Canada: Learning Press.

Botkin, J. W., Elmandjra, M., and Malitza, M. (1979). *No limits to learning: Bridging the human gap.* Oxford, England: Pergamon Press.

Boud, D., Keogh, R., and Walker, D. (1985). *Reflection: Turning experience into learning.* London: Routledge & Kegan Paul.

Boulding, E. (1977). Learning to image the future. In W. G. Bennis, K. D. Benne, R. Chin, and K. E. Corey (eds.), *The planning of change* (4th ed). New York: Holt, Rinehart & Winston.

Bourdieu, P., and Passerson, J. (1977). *Reproduction in education, society, and culture.* Beverly Hills, Calif.: Sage.

Bower, S. A., and Bower, G. H. *Asserting your self,* Reading, Mass., Addison-Wesley.

Bowles, S. B., and Gintis, H. (1976). *Schooling in a capitalist society: Educational reform and the contradictions of economic life.* New York: Basic Books.

———— and ———— (1986). *Democracy and capitalism.* New York: Basic Books.

Bowman, R. (1983). Effective classroom management: A primer for practicing professionals. *The Clearing House, 57,* 116–118.

Boynton, P., Di Geronimo, J., and Gustafson, G. (1985). A basic survival guide for new teachers. *The Clearing House, 59,* 101–103.

Bradley, D. F. (1988). Alcohol and drug education in the elementary school. *Elementary School Guidance and Counseling, 23*(2), 99–105.

Bransford, J. D., and Stein, B. S. (1984). *The ideal problem solver.* New York: W. H. Freeman & Co.

Bronfenbrenner, U. (1970). *Two worlds of childhood.* New York: Russell Sage Foundation.

Brookfield, S. D. (1987). *Developing critical thinkers: Challenging adults to explore alternative ways of thinking and acting.* San Francisco, Calif.: Jossey-Bass.

Brooks, D. M., and Hawke, G. (1987–1988). Effective and ineffective session opening teacher activity and task structures. *Journal of Classroom Interaction, 23*(1), 1–4.

————, Silvern, S. B., and Wooten, M. (1978). The ecology of teacher-pupil verbal interaction. *Journal of Classroom Interaction, 14,* 39–45.

Brophy, J. E. (1979). Teacher behavior and its effects. *Journal of Educational Psychology, 71,* 733–750.

—— (1981). Teacher praise: A functional analysis. *Review of Educational Research, 51*(1), 5–32.

—— (1983). Classroom organization and management. *The Elementary School Journal, 83*(4), 265–286.

—— (1983). Improving instruction: Effective classroom management. *School Administrator, 40*(7), 33–36.

—— (1985). Classroom management as instruction: Socializing self guidance in students. *Theory into Practice, 24*(4), 233–240.

—— (April 1987a). *Educating teachers about managing classrooms and students.* Paper presented at the annual meeting of the American Educational Research Association.

—— (1987b). Socializing students' motivation to learn, in M. L. Maehr and D. A. Kleiber (eds.), *Advances in motivation and achievement* (vol. 5), Greenwich, Conn.: JAI Press, pp. 18–210.

—— and Evertson, C. M. (1976). *Learning from teaching a developmental perspective.* Boston, Mass.: Allyn and Bacon, Inc.

—— and —— (1978). Context variables in teaching. *Educational psychologist, 12,* 310–316.

—— and Putnam, J. G. (1979). Classroom management in the elementary school, in D. L. Duke (ed.), *Classroom management: The seventy-eighth yearbook of the National Society for the study of education.* Chicago: The University of Chicago Press.

—— and —— (1980). *Teachers' specific strategies for dealing with hostile-aggressive students.* (Research Series, no. 86) East Lansing: Michigan State University, Institute for Research on Teaching.

—— and —— (1982). *Motivational factors in teachers' handling of problem students.* (Research Series. no. 115) East Lansing: Michigan State University, Institute for Research on Teaching.

—— and —— (1987). *Teachers' strategies for coping with hostile-aggressive students.* (Research Series, no. 185) East Lansing: Michigan State University, Institute for Research on Teaching.

—— and Rohrkemper, M. M. (1989). *Teachers' strategies for coping with failure syndrome students.* (IRT Research Series, No. 197) East Lansing: Michigan State University, College of Education.

Brown, A. L. (1978). Metacognitive development and reading, in R. J. Spira, B. C. Burke, and W. F. Brewer (eds.), *Theoretical issues in reading comprehension.* Hillsdale, N.J.: Laurence Erlbaum.

Brown, D. (1971). *Changing student behavior: A new approach to discipline.* Dubuque, Iowa: Brown.

Brown, J. S., Collins, A., and Duguid, P. (1988). *Cognitive apprenticeship, situated cognition, and social interaction.* (Report no. 6886.) Cambridge, Mass.: BBN Systems and Technologies Corporation.

Bruner, J. S. (1990). Culture and human development: A new look. Human Development, 33, 344–355.

Bruner, J. S., et al. (1966). *Studies in cognitive growth.* New York: John Wiley and Sons.

Bruner, J. S. (1983). *In search of mind: Essays in autobiography.* New York: Harper Colophon Books.

—— (1990). *Acts of meaning.* Cambridge, Mass.: Harvard University Press.

——, Brubaker, N. L., Brooks-Alleman, J., and Duffy, G. G. (1984). *Making seatwork work.* (Research Series 142.) East Lansing: Michigan State University, Institute for Research on Teaching.

——, Evertson, D., and Emmer, E. (1980). Dimensions in classroom management derived from recent research. *Journal of Curriculum Studies, 12,* 343–356.

—— and Prawat. R. (1983). A synthesis of research on teaching self-control. *Educational Leadership, 40,* 62–66.

Buchmann, M. (1986). Role over person: Morality and authenticity in teaching. *Teachers College Record, 87*(4), 529–543.

Bullied to Death (A&E video).

Burke, J. B. (1982a). *Disruptive versus nondisruptive students: Response to projective media.* Paper presented at the American Educational Research Association, April 1982, New York.

———— (1982b). Communicating with students. In D. Orlosky, (ed.) *Introduction to education.* Columbus, Ohio: Charles Merrill.

———— (1984). Interpersonal communication. In Cooper, J. (ed.) *Developing skills for supervision.* New York: Longman, Inc.

Bush, R. N. (1954). *The teacher-pupil relationship.* New York: Prentice Hall.

Cain, H. D. (1980). *Flint's emergency treatment and management* (6th ed.). Philadelphia, Pa.: Saunders.

Camras, L. A., Ribordy, A., Hill, J., Martino, S., Spaccarelli, S., and Stefani, R. (1988). Recognition and posing of emotional expressions by abused children and their mothers. *Developmental Psychology, 24*(6), 776–781.

Canada, G. (1995). Fist stick knife gun: A personal history of violence in America. Boston: Beacon Press.

Canfield, J., and Wells, H. C. (1976). *100 ways to enhance self-concept in the classroom: A handbook for teachers and parents.* Englewood Cliffs, N.J.: Prentice-Hall, Inc.

Cangelosi, J. S. (1980). *Project G.R.E.A.T. needs assessment report.* Tallahassee: Florida Department of Education.

———— (1982). *Measurement and evaluation: An inductive approach for teachers.* Dubuque, Iowa: Brown.

———— (1986). *Cooperation in the classroom: Students and teachers together.* Washington: National Education Association.

———— (1988). *Classroom management strategies: Gaining and maintaining students' cooperation.* New York: Longman, Inc.

Canter, L. (March, 1981). *Assertive discipline.* Paper presented at the annual conference of the Association of Supervision and Curriculum Development, Anaheim, Calif.

———— and Canter, M. (1976a). *Assertive discipline.* Los Angeles, Calif.: Canter and Associates.

———— and ———— (1976b). *Assertive discipline: A take-charge approach for today's educator.* Los Angeles, Calif.: Canter and Associates.

Carducci, D. J., and Carducci, J. B. (1984). *The caring classroom.* Palo Alto, Calif.: Bull Publishing.

Carter, K. (1985). *Teacher comprehension of classroom processes: An emerging direction in classroom management research.* Paper presented at the annual meeting of the American Educational Research Association. Chicago, Ill.

———— (1986). *Classroom management as cognitive problem solving: Toward teacher comprehension in teacher education.* Paper presented at the annual meeting of the American Educational Research Association. San Francisco, Calif.

Carter, T. P., and Chatfield, M. L. (1986). Effective bilingual schools: Implications for policy and practice. *American Journal of Education, 95*(1), 200–232.

Charles, C. M. (1983). *Elementary classroom management.* White Plains, N.Y.: Longman, Inc.

———— (1985). *Building classroom discipline: From models to practice* (2d ed.). White Plains, N. Y.: Longman, Inc.

Cherryholmes, C. (November 1985). Theory and practice: On the role of empirically based theory for critical practice. *American Journal of Education, 94,* 39–70.

———— (1990). *Reading research.* Unpublished paper.

Children's Defense Fund. (1990). *Children 1990: A report card, briefing book, and action primer.* Washington, D.C.

Ciardi, J. (1962). *You read to me, I'll read to you.* New York: J. B. Lippincott Company.

Clarizio, H. F. (1976). *Toward positive classroom discipline* (2d ed.). New York: John Wiley and Sons, Inc.

———— (1980). *Toward positive classroom discipline* (3d ed.). New York: John Wiley and Sons, Inc.

Clark, D. H., and Kadis, A. (1971). *Humanistic teaching.* Columbus, Ohio: Charles E. Merrill Publishing.

Clark, L. H., and Starr, I. S. (1981). *Secondary and middle school teaching methods* (4th ed.). New York: Macmillan.

Clements, B. S., and Evertson, C. M. (1982). *Orchestrating small group instruction in elementary school classrooms* (Report No. 6053). Austin, Tex.: The Research and Development Center for Teacher Education.

Cohen, D. K. (1988). *Teaching practices: Plus ça change. . . .* (Issue Paper 88-3). East Lansing: Michigan State University, National Center for Research on Teacher Education, 1–71.

Cohen, E. G. (1976). Problems and prospects of teaming. Research and development memorandum no. 143. Stanford, Calif.: Stanford Center for Research and Development.

———— (1982). A multi-ability approach to the integrated classroom. *Journal of Reading Behavior, 14*(4) 439–460.

———— (1986). *Designing groupwork: Strategies for the heterogeneous classroom.* New York: Teachers College Press.

Cohen, M. (1987). Improving school effectiveness: Lessons from research, in V. Richardson-Koehler (ed.), *Educators' Handbook: A research perspective.* New York: Longman, Inc., pp. 474–490.

Cohen, M. W. (1986). Research on motivation: New content for the teacher preparation curriculum. *Journal of Teacher Education, 37*(3), 23–28.

Collins, M. L. (February 1977). The effects of training for enthusiasm displayed by preservice elementary teachers. (ERIC Ed. 129773.) *Resources in Education, 12*(1), 57.

Collins, M. T., and Collins, D. R. (1975). *Survival kit for teachers (and parents).* Glenville, Ill.: Scott Foresman.

Coleman, J. S. (1966). *Equality of educational opportunity: Summary report.* Washington: U.S. Department of Health, Education and Welfare.

Coloroso, B. (2004). The bully, the bullied, and the bystander: From preschool to high school—how parents and teachers can help break the cycle of violence. Harper Resource of HarperCollins, NY, NY.

Como, L., and Snow, R. E. (1986). Adapting teaching to individual differences among learners, in M. C. Wittrock (ed.), *Handbook of research on teaching* (3d ed.). New York: Macmillan, 605–629.

Cooper, D., and Snell, J. L., (2003). Bullying—Not Just a Kid Thing, *Educational Leadership, Creating Caring Schools, March* Vol. 60, No. 6., pp. 22–25.

Cooper, H. M., Burger, J. M., and Seymour, G. E. (1979). Classroom context and student ability as influences on teacher perceptions of classroom control. *American Educational Research Journal, 16*(2), 189–196.

Copeland, W. D. (1980). Teaching-learning behaviors and the demands of the classroom environment. *The Elementary School Journal, 80*(4), 165–177.

———— (1987). Classroom management and student teachers' cognitive abilities: A relationship. *American Educational Research Journal, 24*(2), 219–236.

Corsini, R. J., and Howard, D. D. (eds.) (1964). *Critical incidents in teaching.* Englewood Cliffs, N.J.: Prentice-Hall, Inc.

Craig, R. T., and Tracy, K. (1983). *Conversational coherence: Form, structure, and strategy.* Beverly Hills, Calif.: Sage Publications.

Cremin, L. (1977). *Traditions of American education.* New York: Basic Books.

Cruickshank, D., and associates. (1980). *Teaching is tough.* Englewood Cliffs, N.J.: Prentice-Hall, Inc.

Cummings, C. (1980). *Teaching makes a difference.* Snohomish, Wash.: Snohomish Publishing Company.

Cunningham, A. R. (1983). The deportment chart: A student management tool that could help a classroom teacher. *The Clearing House, 56,* 421–422.

Curwin, R., and Medler, A. (1980). *The discipline book: A complete guide to school and classroom management.* Reston, Va.: Reston Publishing Co.

Cusick, P. (1983). The educational system and its nature and logic.

Cusick, P. (1983). *Egalitarian ideal and the American high school.* New York: Longmans.

Dalton, J. & Watson, M. (1997). *Among Friends: Classrooms where caring and learning prevail.* Oakland, CA: Developmental Studies Center.

Davis, M., Eshelman, E. G. , McKay, M. (1988, 2003). *The relaxation & stress reduction workbook.* New Harbinger Publ, Inc., Oakland, CA.

Deci, E. L. (1975). *Intrinsic motivation.* New York: Plenum Press.

———— (1978). Appreciation of research on the effects of rewards, in M. Lepper and D. Greene (eds.). *The hidden costs of reward: New perceptions on the psychology of human motivation.* New York: John Wiley & Sons.

———— and Ryan, R. (1985). *Intrinsic motivation and self-determination in human behavior.* New York: Plenum Press.

Deer, C. E., Maxwell, T. W., and Relich, J. D. (1986). Student perceptions of school climate over time: Two secondary schools. *Australian Journal of Education, 30*(2), 188–199.

Deiro, J. (1996). *Teaching with heart: Making healthy connections with students.* Corwin Press, Inc. Thousand Oaks, California.

Deiro, J. (2003). *Do your students know you care? Caring is not just a way of acting; it's a way of thinking.* Educational Leadership, Creating Caring Schools. Volume 60, Number 6, March, pp. 60–63.

Denham, C., and Lieberman, A. (eds.). (1980). *Time to learn.* Washington: U.S. Department of Education and the National Institute of Education.

Dewey, J. (1933). *How we think* (rev. ed.). Boston, Mass.: D. C. Heath.

———— (1939). *Intelligence in the modern world.* Ratner, J. (ed.). New York: The Modern Library.

———— (1944). *Democracy and education.* New York: The Free Press. (Originally published in 1916.)

———— (1963). *Experience and education.* New York: Macmillan Publishing Company.

Dinkmaaer, D., and Dreikurs, R. (1963). *Encouraging children to learn: The encouragement process.* Englewood Cliffs, N.J.: Prentice-Hall, Inc.

Dobson, J. (1970). *Dare to discipline.* Wheaton, Ill.: Tyndale House Publishing.

———— (1974). *Hide or seek.* Old Tappan, N.J.: Fleming H. Revell Company.

Dodson, P. K., and Evans, E. D. (1985). A developmental study of school theft. *Adolescence, 20*(79), 509–523.

Dowaliby, F., and Schumer, H. (1973). Teacher-centered versus student-centered mode of college classroom instruction as related to manifest anxiety. *Journal of Educational Psychology, 64,* 125–132.

Doyle, W. (1980). *Classroom management.* West Lafayette, Ind.: Kappa Delta Phi, P.O. Box A.

—— (1983). *Managing classroom activities in junior high English classes: An interim report.* (R & D Report 6131.) Austin: The University of Texas at Austin, Research and Development Center for Teacher Education.

—— (1984). How order is achieved in classrooms: An interim report. *Journal of Curriculum Studies, 16*(3), 259–277.

—— (1985). Recent research on classroom management: Implications for teacher preparation. *Journal of Teacher Education,* 31–35.

—— (1986). Classroom organization and management, in M. C. Wittrock (ed.), *Handbook of research on teaching* (3d ed., pp. 392–431). New York: Macmillan.

Dreikurs, R. (1968). *Psychology in the classroom* (2d ed.). New York: Harper & Row.

—— and Cassell, P. (1972). *Discipline without tears.* New York: Hawthorn Books.

—— and Grey, L. (1968). *Logical consequences.* New York: Meredith Press.

——, ——, and Pepper, F. (1982). *Maintaining sanity in the classroom: Classroom management techniques* (2d ed.). New York: Harper & Row.

Duffy, G. G., Roehler, L. R., and Putnam, J. (1987). Putting the teacher in control: Basal reading textbooks and instructional decision making. *The Elementary School Journal, 87*(3), 358–366.

Duke, D. (ed.). (1979). *Classroom Management. The 78th Yearbook of the National Society of Education, Part II.* Chicago: University of Chicago Press.

—— (ed.). (1982). *Helping teachers manage classrooms.* Alexandria, Va.: Association for Supervision and Curriculum Development.

——, and Jones, V. F. (1984). Two decades of discipline: Assessing the development of an educational specialization. *Journal of Research and Development in Education, 17,* 25–35.

Dunkin, M., and Biddle, G. (1974). *The study of teaching.* New York: Holt, Rinehart and Winston.

Duncan, R., and Weiss, A. (1979). *Organizational learning: Implication for organization design.* In Straw, B. M. Research in Organizational Behavior. An Annual Series of Analytical Essays and Critical Reviews. Connecticut: JA Press, Inc.

Dunn, L. M. (1967). Special education for the mildly retarded: Is much of it justifiable? *Exceptional Children, 34,* 5–22.

Eckman, A. (2001). Beyond Bullying: Knowing When to Step In—and When Not to, *Educational Update,* ASCD, Vol. 43, No. 6, September.

Edwards, D. M., and Zander, T. A. (1985). Children of alcoholics: Backgrounds and strategies for the counselor. *Elementary School Guidance and Counseling, 20*(2), 121–128.

Emmer, E. T., and Evertson, C. M. (1981). Synthesis of research on classroom management. *Educational Leadership, 38,* 342–347.

——, ——, and Anderson, L. M. (1980). Effective classroom management at the beginning of the school year. *The Elementary School Journal, 80,* 219–231.

——, ——, Sanford, J., Clements, B., and Worsham, M. (1984). *Classroom management for elementary teachers.* Englewood Cliffs, N.J.: Prentice-Hall, Inc.

——, ——, ——, —— and —— (1984). *Classroom management for secondary teachers.* Englewood Cliffs, N.J.: Prentice-Hall, Inc.

Engelmann, S. (1969). *Preventing failure in the primary grades.* New York: Simon and Schuster.

Epstein J. L., Salinas, K. C. (2004). Schools as Learning Communities, Partnering with Families and Communities, *Educational Leadership,* Vol. 61, Number 8, pp. 12–18.

Epstein, Joyce L. (1995). School/Family/Community Partnerships, Caring for the Children we Share. *Phi Delta Kappan,* May p. 701–711.

Erickson, F., and Mohatt, G. (1982). Cultural organization of participation structures in two classrooms of Indian students, in G. Spindler (ed.), *Doing the ethnography of schooling.* New York: Holt, Rinehart & Winston, 132–175.

Ernst, K. (1973). *Games students play, and what to do about them.* Melbrae, Calif.: Celestial Arts.

Everhart, R. B. (1987). Understanding student disruption and classroom control. *Harvard Educational Review, 57*(1), 77–83.

Evertson, C. M. (1982). Differences in instructional activities in higher- and lower-achieving junior high English and math classes. *The Elementary School Journal, 82,* 329–350.

——, Sanford, J. P., and Emmer, E. T. (1981). Effects of class heterogeneity in junior high school. *American Educational Research Journal, 18,* 219–232.

—— and Veldman, D. J. (1981). Changes over time in process measures of classroom behavior. *Journal of Educational Psychology, 73*(2), 156–163.

—— and Emmer, E. T. (1982a). Preventive classroom management, in Daniel L. Duke (ed.), *Helping teachers manage classrooms.* Alexandria, Va.: Association for Supervision and Curriculum Development, 27–40.

—— and —— (1982b). Effective management at the beginning of the school year in junior high classes. *Journal of Educational Psychology, 74,* 485–498.

——, ——, Clements, B. S., and Sanford, J. P., and Worsham, M. E. (1984). *Classroom management for elementary teachers.* Englewood Cliffs, N.J.: Prentice-Hall, Inc.

——, ——, Sanford, J. P., and Clements, B. S. (1983). Improving classroom management: An experiment in elementary classrooms. *The Elementary School Journal, 84*(2), 1983.

Faber, A., and Mazlish, E. (1987). How to talk so students will listen and listen so students will talk. *American Educator, 11*(2), 37–42.

Fallows, J. (1989). *More like us: Making America great again.* Boston, Mass.: Houghton Mifflin.

Fisher, C. W., Berliner, D. C., Filby, N. N., Marliave, R., Cahen, L. S., and Dishaw, M. M. (1980). Teaching behaviors, academic learning time, and student achievement: An overview, in C. Denham and A. Lieberman (eds.), *Time to learn.* Washington: National Institute of Education, 63–87.

Fisher, K. (1993). Leading self-directed work teams. New York: McGraw-Hill, Inc.

Fitzgerald, W., and Shroyer, J. (1986). *Mouse and elephant: Measuring growth.* Middle grades mathematics project. Cambridge, Mass.: Addison-Wesley.

——, Lappen, G., Winter, M., and Phillips, R. (1986). *Similarities and equivalent fractions: Middle grades mathematics project.* Cambridge-Mass.: Addison-Wesley.

Flavell, J. J. (1963). *The developmental psychology of Jean Piaget.* Princeton, N.J.: Van Nostrand.

———— (1979). Metacognition and cognitive monitoring: A new area of cognitive-developmental inquiry. *American Psychologist, 34,* 906–911.

Floden, R. E. (1985). The role of rhetoric in changing teachers' beliefs. *Teaching and Teacher Education, 1*(1), 19–32.

Florio-Ruane, S. (1983). *The written literacy forum: An analysis of teacher/researcher collaboration.* IRT Research Series, East Lansing: Michigan State University.

Flygar, T. J. (1987). Teachers as researchers: Learning through teaching. *Phi Delta Kappan, 68*(8), 630–631.

Frailberg, S. (1959). *Magic years.* New York: International University Press.

Franklin, J. (2004). A Safer Place for Learning, *Education Update,* ASCD March, Vol. 46, No. 2.

Fraser, B. J., and Walberg, H. J. (1984). Cooperative learning environments. *Contemporary Education Review, 3*(1), 252–260.

Freed, A. M. (1971). *TA for kids (and grown-ups too).* Sacramento, Calif.: Jalmar Press.

———— (1973). *TA for teens (and other important people).* Sacramento, Calif.: Jalmar Press.

Freire, P. (1974). *Education for critical consciousness.* New York: Continuum Publishing Co.

Freud, A. (1968). *Normality and pathology in childhood: Assessments of development.* New York: International University Press.

———— (1971). *The ego and the mechanisms of defense.* New York: International University Press.

Frieberg, H. J. (1999). Consistency management and cooperative discipline: From tourists to citizens to the classroom. In H. J. Freiberg (Ed.) Beyond Behaviorism: Changing the classroom management paradigm (pp. 75–79). Boston: Allyn and Bacon.

Frieze, I. H. (1980). Beliefs about success and failure in the classroom, in J. H. McMillan (ed.), *The social psychology of school learning.* New York: Academic Press.

Fuchs, E. (1969). *Teachers talk.* Garden City, N.Y. : Anchor Press.

Gallup, A. M. (1984). The 16th Annual Gallup Poll of the public's attitudes toward the public schools. *Phi Delta Kappan, 66,* 23–28.

———— (1986). The 18th Annual Gallup Poll of the public's attitudes toward the public schools. *Phi Delta Kappan, 68,* 43–59.

Galluzzo, G. R., and Minix, N. A. (April, 1988). *Student teacher thinking: A comparative study of elementary and secondary student teachers.* Paper presented at the annual meeting of the American Educational Research Association, New Orleans, La.

Gamoran, A. (1987). Organization, instruction, and the effects of ability grouping: Comment on Slavin's "best-evidence synthesis." *Review of Educational Research, 57*(3), 341–345.

Gangey, W. J. (1981). *Motivating classroom discipline.* New York: Macmillan Publishing Co.

Garbarino, J., and deLara, E., Words Can Hurt Forever, *Educational Leadership, Creating Caring Schools,* March Vol. 60, No. 6., pp. 18–21.

Gardner, H. (1972). *The quest for mind.* New York: Vintage Books.

———— (1983). *Frames of mind: The theory of multiple intelligences.* New York: Basic Books.

Gaudiani, C., and Burnett, D. (1985–1986). Academic alliances: A new approach to school/college collaboration. *American Association for Higher Education, 1*(31).

Gazda, G., Asbury, F. R., Balzer, F. J., Childers, W. C., and Walters, R. P. (1977). *Human relations development: A manual for educators* (2d ed.). Boston, Mass.: Allyn and Bacon, Inc.

Gettinger, M. (1984). Achievement as a function of time spent in learning and time needed for learning. *American Educational Research Journal, 21*(3), 617–628.

——— (1985). Time allocated and time spent relative to time needed for learning as determinants of achievement. *Journal of Educational Psychology, 77*(1), 3–11.

Ginott, H. G. (1965). *Parent and child.* New York: Avon Books.

——— (1972). *Teacher and child.* New York: Avon Books.

Giroux, H. A. (1988). *Teachers as intellectuals. Toward a critical pedagogy of learning.* Massachusetts: Bergin and Garvey Publishers, Inc.

Glachan, M., and Light, P. (1982). Peer interaction and learning: Can two wrongs make a right? in G. Butterworth and P. Light (eds.), *Social Cognition.* Chicago: University of Chicago Press, 238–262.

Glass, R. M., and Meckler, R. S. (1974). Preparing elementary teachers to instruct mildly handicapped children in regular classrooms: A summer workshop, in G. J. Warfield (ed.), *Mainstream currents.* Reston, Va.: Council for Exceptional Children.

Glasser, W. (1969b). *Schools without failure.* New York: Harper & Row.

——— (1975). *Reality therapy: A new approach to psychiatry.* New York: Harper & Row.

——— (December, 1976). Presentation to the School Council of Ohio Study Group, Delaware, Ohio.

——— (1977). Ten steps to good discipline. *Today's Education, 66*(4), 61–63.

——— (1978). Disorders in our schools: Causes and remedies. *Phi Delta Kappan, 59,* 331–333.

——— (1986). *Control theory in the classroom.* New York: Harper & Row.

——— *Glasser's approach to discipline.* Los Angeles, Calif.: Pamphlet published by Educator Training Center. No date.

———, Bassin, A., Bratter, E., and Rachin, R. (1976). *The reality therapy reader: A survey of the work of William Glasser.* New York: Harper & Row.

Glickman, C. (1985). *Supervising instruction: A developmental approach.* Boston, Mass.: Allyn and Bacon, Inc.

——— and Wolfgang, C. (1979). Dealing with student misbehavior: An eclectic review. *Journal of Teacher Education, 30,* 7–13.

Gnagey, W. J. (1981). *Motivating classroom discipline.* New York: Macmillan Publishing Co.

Gold, S. R., and Cundiff, G. (1980). Decreasing the frequency of daydreaming. *Journal of Clinical Psychology, 36,* 116–121, 1987.

Good, T. L. (1979). Teacher effectiveness in the elementary school: What we know about it now. *Journal of Teacher Education, 30,* 32–64.

——— and Brophy, J. E. (1977). *A realistic approach.* New York: Holt, Rinehart and Winston.

——— and Brophy, J. E. (1978). *Looking in classrooms* (2d ed.). New York: Harper & Row.

——— and ——— (1986). *Educational psychology,* 3d ed. New York: Harper & Row.

———— and ———— (1987). *Looking in classrooms,* 4th ed. New York: Harper & Row.

Goodlad, J. I. (1984). *A place called school: Prospects for the future.* New York: McGraw-Hill.

————, Soder, R., and Sirotnik, K. A. (1990). *The moral dimension of teaching.* San Francisco, Calif.: Jossey-Bass.

Goodman, N. (1983). *Fact, fiction, and forecast.* Cambridge, Mass.: Harvard University Press.

———— (1984). *Of mind and other matters.* Cambridge, Mass.: Harvard University Press.

Goodwin, D. L., and Coates, T. J. (1976). *Helping students help themselves: How you can put behavior analysis into action in your classroom.* Englewood Cliffs, N.J.: Prentice-Hall, Inc.

Gordon, D. T. (1999). Rising to the discipline challenge. Harvard Educational Letter Research on-line. Sept/Oct

Gordon, D. T. (1999). Turning frustration to fullfillment: New teachers need more help with discipline. Harvard Educational Letter Research on-line. Sept/Oct

Gordon, T. (1974). *Teacher effectiveness training.* New York: Peter H. Wyden.

Grant, C. A., and Sleeter, C. E. (1986). Race, class, and gender in education research: An argument for integrative analysis. *Review of Educational Research, 56*(2), 195–211.

Gray, J. (1967). *The teacher's survival guide: How to teach teenagers and live to tell about it!* Belmont, Calif.: Fearon Teacher Aids Publishers.

Gray, W. H., and Gray, M. (November 1985). Synthesis of research on mentoring beginning teachers. *Educational Leadership, 43*(3), 37–43.

Green, J. L. (1983). Research on teaching as a linguistic process: The state of the art, in E. W. Gordon (ed.), *Review of Research in Education,* vol. 10. Washington: American Education Research Association, 151–252.

Green, K. (1985). The paired comparison method in educational research. *Educational and Psychological Measurement, 45*(3), 567–575.

Green, L., and Foster, D. (1986). Classroom intrinsic motivation: Effects of scholastic level, teacher orientation, and gender. *Journal of Educational Research, 80*(1), 34–38.

Greene, M. (1978). *Landscapes of learning.* New York: Teachers College Press.

———— (1986a). Philosophy and teaching, in M. C. Wittrock (ed.), *Handbook of Research on Teaching,* 3d ed. New York: Macmillan, pp. 479–501.

———— (1986b). Perspectives and imperatives: Reflection and passion in teaching. *Journal of Curriculum and Supervision, 2*(1), 68–81.

Greene, T. F. (1985). The formation of conscience in an age of technology. *American Educational Research Journal, 94*(1), 1–32.

Greenwood, C. R. (1991). Longitudinal analysis of time engagement and academic achievement in at-risk and non-risk students. Exceptional Children, 57, 521–535.

Greenwood, C. R., Horton, B. T., and Utley, C. A., (1999). *Academic engagement: current perspectives on research and practice.* "Journal of Education for Students Placed at Risk," 4(1), 65–82 Copyright © 1999, Lawrence Erlbaum Associates, Inc.

Greenwood, G. E., Good, T. L., and Siegel, B. L. (1971). *Problem situations in teaching.* New York: Harper & Row.

Griffin, G. (1978). Guidelines for the evaluation of staff development programs. *Teachers College Record, 80*(1), 126–139.

Gump, P. V. (1982). School settings and their keeping, in D. L. Duke (ed.), *Helping teachers manage classrooms.* Alexandria, Va.: Association for Supervision Curriculum Development.

———— (April, 1985). *An environmental perspective on classroom order.* Paper presented at the annual meeting of the American Education Research Association, Chicago, 111.

Gunnings-Moton, S. (1990). *Hostile aggressive students.* Michigan State University, E. Lansing, Mich., unpublished paper.

Guzzetti, B. (1987). Humanism in the classroom. *The Journal of Classroom Interaction, 22*(2), 23–27.

Haberman, M. (2004). Can star teachers create learning communities? *Educational Leadership,* Vol. 61, No. 8, May 2004, p. 52–56.

Haberman, Martin. (1999). Victory at Buffalo Creek: What makes a school serving Hispanic Children in poverty successful? Instructional Leader, 17 (2).

Hall, E. T. (1977). *Beyond culture.* New York: Doubleday & Co., Anchor Books, 1977.

Haller, E. J. (1985). Pupil race and elementary school ability grouping: Are teachers biased against black children? *American Educational Research Journal, 22*(4), 465–483.

Hallinan, M. T., and Teixeira, R. A. (1987). Students' interracial friendships: Individual characteristics, structural effects, and racial differences. *American Journal of Education, 95*(4), 563–583.

Hamachek, D. E. (1982). *Encounters with others: Interpersonal relationships and you.* New York: Holt, Rinehart and Winston.

Hanes, R. C., and Mitchell, K. F. (1985). Teacher career development in Charlotte-Mecklenburg. *Educational Leadership, 43*(3), 11–3.

Harmin, M. (1977). *What I've learned about values education.* Bloomington, Ind.: Phi Delta Kappa Educational Foundation.

———— and Saville, S. (1977). *A peaceable classroom: Activities to calm and free student energies.* New York: H. Winston Press.

Harris, B. M., Bessent, W., and McIntyre, K. E. (1969). *In-service education: A guide to better practice.* Englewood Cliffs, N.J.: Prentice-Hall, Inc.

Harris, T. A. (1969). *I'm OK—you're OK: A practical guide to transactional analysis.* New York: Harper & Row.

Hassett, J. D., and Weisberg, A. (1972). *Open education: Alternatives within our tradition.* Englewood Cliffs., N.J.: Prentice-Hall, Inc.

Hawkins, D. (1974). *The informed vision: Essays in learning and human nature.* New York: Agathon Press.

Hawley, R. C. (1975). *Value exploration through role playing.* New York: Hart Publishing.

Heath, S. B., and McLaughlin, M. W. (Editors, 1993). *Identity and inner-city youth, beyond ethnicity and gender.* Teachers College, Columbia University, NY, NY.

Hedberg, H. (1981). *How organizations learn and unlearn.* In Nylstrom, P. C. and Starbuck, W. H. (eds.). Handbook of Organizational Design. Adapting Organizations to Their Environments. New York: Oxford University Press.

Heil, G., Bennis, W. and Stephens, D. C. (2000). *Douglas McGregor, Revisited: Managing the Human Side of the Enterprise.* John Wiley and Sons, NY, NY.

Herman, P. (1985). Educating children about sexual abuse: The teachers' responsibility. *Childhood Education, 6*(3), 169–174.

Hessman, T. (1977). *Creating learning environments—The behavioral approach to education.* Boston, Mass.: Allyn and Bacon, Inc.

Hewett, F. M., and Forness, S. R. (1977). *Education of exceptional learners* (2d ed.). Boston, Mass.: Allyn and Bacon, Inc.

Holt, J. (1972). *Freedom and beyond.* New York: E. P. Dutton.

Homme, L. (1970). *How to use contingency contracting in the classroom.* Champaign, Ill.: Research Press.

Horton, L. (1988). Alcohol/drug prevention: A working bibliography for educators. *Illinois Schools Journal, 67*(3), 18–27.

Houston, J. P. (1986). Classroom answer copying: Roles of acquaintanceship and free versus assigned seating. *Journal of Educational Psychology, 78*(3), 230–232.

Huffman, J., Hipp, K. A. (2000). *Creating Communities of Learners: The interaction of shared leadership, shared vision, and supportive conditions.* Paper presented at Annual AERA meeting, New Orleans, LA, April.

Hunt, D. E. (1971). *Matching models in education.* Ontario, Canada: The Ontario Institute for Studies in Education.

Hunt, M. (1982). *The university within.* New York: Simon and Schuster.

Hunter, M. (1967). *Reinforcement.* Los Angeles, Calif.: Theory into Practice Publications.

Hurmence, B. (Editor, 1984). *My folks don't want me to talk about slavery: Twenty-one oral histories of former North Carolina slaves.* John F. Blair, Publisher, Winston-Salem, North Carolina.

Hyman, I. A. (1978). A social science review of evidence cited in litigation on corporal punishment in the schools. *Journal of Child Psychology, 30,* 195–199.

———— and Wise, J. H. (eds.). (1979). *Corporal punishment in American education.* Philadelphia, Pa.: Temple University Press.

Illich, I. (1973). *Deschooling society.* New York: Harper & Row.

Issacs, S. (1972). *Social development of young children.* New York: Schocken Books.

Jakubowski-Spector, P. (1973). "Facilitating the Growth of Women Through Assertive Training." *The Counseling Psychologist.* 4, 75–86.

James, M., and Jongeward, D. (1971). *Born to win: Transactional analysis with gestalt experiments.* Boston, Mass.: Addison-Wesley.

Johnson, D., Marvyama, G., Johnson, R., Nelson, D., and Skon, L. (1981). Effects of cooperative, competitive, and individualistic goal structures on achievement: A meta-analysis. *Psychological Bulletin, 89,* 47–62.

Johnson, D. R. (1982). *Every minute counts: Making your math class work.* Palo Alto, Calif.: Seymour.

———— (1986). Making minutes count even more: A sequel to every minute counts. Palo Alto, Calif.: Seymour.

Johnson, D. W. (1980). Group processes: Influences of student-student interactions on school outcomes, in J. McMillan (ed.), *The social psychology of school learning.* New York: Academic Press, 123–168.

—— and Johnson, R. T. (1974). Instructional goal structure: Cooperative, competitive, or individualistic. *Review of Educational Research, 44*(2), 213–235.

—— and —— (1978). Cooperative, competitive, and individualistic learning. *Journal of Research and Development in Education, 12*(1), 3–15.

—— and —— (1983). The socialization and achievement crisis: Are cooperative learning experiences the solution? in L. Bickman (ed.), *Applied social psychology annual.* Beverly Hills, Calif.: Sage, 307–318.

—— and —— (1985). Classroom conflict: Controversy versus debate in learning groups. *American Educational Research Journal, 22*(2), 237–256.

—— and —— (1987). *Learning together and alone: Cooperative, competitive, and individualistic learning* (2d ed.), Englewood Cliffs, N.J.: Prentice-Hall, Inc.

Johnson, J. (1977). *Use of groups in schools: A practical manual for everyone who works in elementary and secondary schools.* New York: University Press of America.

Johnson, R. T., and Johnson, D. W. (1980). The social integration of handicapped students into the mainstream, in M. Raynolds (ed.), *Social environment of the schools.* Reston, Va.: Council for Exceptional Children, pp. 9–38.

—— and —— (1981). Building friendships between handicapped and nonhandicapped students: Effects of cooperative and individualistic instruction. *American Educational Research Journal, 18*(4), 415–423.

——, ——, and Stanne, M. B. (1986). Comparison of computer-assisted cooperative, competitive, and individualistic learning. *American Educational Research Journal, 23*(3), 382–392.

Jones, V. F. (1979). The gentle art of classroom discipline. *National Elementary Principal, 58,* 26–32.

—— (1980). *Adolescents with behavior problems: Strategies for teaching counseling, and parent involvement.* Boston, Mass.: Allyn and Bacon, Inc.

—— and Jones, L. S. (1981). *Responsible classroom discipline: Creating positive learning environments* (1st ed.). Boston, Mass.: Allyn and Bacon, Inc.

—— and —— (1986). *Comprehensive classroom management: Creating positive learning environments* (2d ed.). Boston: Allyn and Bacon, Inc.

Joyce, B. R., and Harootunian, B. (1967). *The structure of teaching.* Chicago, Ill.: Science Research Associates.

——, Hersh, R. H., and McKibbin, M. (1983). *The structure of school improvement.* New York: Longman, Inc.

—— and Showers, B. (1982). The coaching of teaching. *Educational Leadership, 40*(1), 4–16.

—— and Weil, M. (1980). *Models of teaching,* 2d ed. Englewood Cliffs, N.J.: Prentice-Hall, Inc.

—— and —— (1986). *Models of teaching,* 3d ed. Englewood Cliffs, N.J.: Prentice-Hall, Inc.

Kagan, S., and Madsen, M. (1972). Experimental analysis of cooperating and competition of Anglo-American and Mexican-American children. *Developmental Psychology, 6,* 49–59.

Karlin, M. S., and Berger, R. (1972). *Discipline and the disruptive child: A practical guide for elementary teachers.* West Nyack, N.Y.: Parker.

Karniol, R. (1987). Not all failures are alike: Self attribution and perception of teachers' attributions for failing tests in liked versus disliked subjects. *British Journal of Educational Psychology, 57*(1), 21–25.

Kendall, J., and Marzano, R. (1994). *The systematic identification and articulation of content standards and benchmarks.* January. McRel. As adapted in Update, ASCD, November 1994, Vol. 36, No. 99. Alexandria VA.

Kerr, M. M., and Nelson, C. M. (1983). *Strategies for managing behavior problems in the classroom.* Columbus, Ohio: Merrill.

Khemsara, R. (2004). Educators attempt to fight bullying in schools. April 12, 12:16, University of Houston. Quality Education.

King, N. (1975). *Giving form to feeling.* New York: Drama Book Specialists.

Klinger, E. (1978). Modes of normal conscious flow, in K. S. Pope and J. L. Singer (eds.), *The stream of consciousness.* New York: Plenum Press.

Koblinsky, S., and Behana, N. (1984). Child sexual abuse: The educator's role in prevention, detection, and intervention. *Young Children, 39*(6), 3–15.

Koestler, A. (1969). *The act of creation.* New York: Macmillan.

Kohlberg, L. (1975). The cognitive-developmental approach to moral education. *Phi Delta Kappan, 56,* 10.

Kohn, A. (1986). *No contest: The case against competition.* Boston, Mass.: Houghton Mifflin.

Kohut, S., and Range, D. G. (1979). *Classroom discipline: Case studies and viewpoints.* Washington: National Education Association.

Kounin, J. (1970). *Discipline and group management in classrooms.* New York: Holt, Rinehart and Winston.

Kounin, J. S., and Gump, P. (1974). Signal systems of lesson settings and the task related behavior of preschool children. *Journal of Educational Psychology, 66,* 554–562.

———— and Sherman, L. W. (1979). School environments as behavior settings. *Theory into practice, 18,* 145–151.

Krampen, G. (1987). Differential effects of teacher comments. *Journal of Educational Psychology, 79*(2), 137–146.

Krathwohl, D. R., Bloom, B. S., and Masia, B. B. (1964). *Taxonomy of educational objectives: Handbook II: Affective domain.* New York: Longman, Inc.

Krumboltz, J. D., and Krumboltz, H. B. (1972). *Changing children's behavior.* Englewood Cliffs, N.J.: Prentice-Hall, Inc.

Kubowski, P. J., and Lange, A. (1976). *Responsible assertive behavior.* Champagne, Ill.: Research Press.

Kyriacou, C. (1987). Teacher stress and burnout: An international review. *Educational Research, 29*(2), 146–152.

Laing, R. D. (1969). *The politics of the family.* Toronto: Canadian Broadcasting Corporation.

Lambiotte, J. G., Dansereau, D. F., Rocklin, T. R., Fletcher, B., Hythecker, V. I., Larson, C. O., and O'Donnell, A. M. (1987). Cooperative learning and test taking: Transfer of skills. *Contemporary Educational Psychology, 12*(1), 52–61.

Langer, S. (1967). *Mind: An essay on human feeling,* vol. I. Baltimore, Md.: The Johns Hopkins Press.

Lanier, J. (1970). *Creating, maintaining and restoring.* Unpublished paper. East Lansing: Michigan State University, College of Education.

———— and Little, J. (1986). Research on teacher education, in M. C. Wittrock, (ed.), *Handbook of research on teaching.* New York: Macmillan, pp. 527–570.

Lanier, P. (1981). Mathematics classroom inquiry: The need, the method, and the promise. *(IRT Research Series, No. 101.)* East Lansing: Michigan State University.

Larson, C. O., Dansereau, D. F., O'Donnell, A. M., Hythecker, V. I., Lambiotte, J. G., and Rocklin, T. R. (1985). Effects of metacognitive and elaborative activity on cooperative learning and transfer. *Contemporary Educational Psychology, 10,* 342–348.

Lasley, T. J. (1981). Research perspectives on classroom management. *Journal of Teacher Education, 32*(2), 14–17.

—— (1985). Fostering nonaggression in the classroom: An anthropological perspective. *Theory into Practice, 24,* 247–255.

—— (1987). Classroom management: A developmental view. *The Educational Forum, 51*(3), 285–298.

Latham, G. I. (1984). *Time-on-task and other variables affecting the quality of education of handicapped students.* Logan: Utah State University.

Layne, D. J., and Grossnickle, D. R. (1989). A teamwork approach to the prevention of chemical abuse and dependency. *NASSP Bulletin, 73*(514), 98–101.

Lazarus, A. (1966). *Behavior Rehearsal vs. Non-directive therapy vs. advice in effecting behavior change.* Behavioral Research and Therapy, 4, 209–12.

Leinhardt, G. (April, 1983). *Routines in expert math teachers' thoughts and actions.* Paper presented at the annual meeting of the American Educational Research Association, Montreal, Canada.

—— and Bickel, W. (1987). Instruction's the thing wherein to catch the mind that falls behind. *Educational psychologist, 22*(2), 177–207.

——, Weidman, C., and Hammond, K. M. (1987). Introduction and integration of classroom routines by expert teachers. *Curriculum Inquiry, 17*(2), 135–176.

Lemlech, J. K. (1977). *Handbook for successful urban teaching.* New York: Harper & Row.

—— (1979). *Classroom management.* New York: Harper & Row.

—— (1984). *Curriculum and instructional methods for the elementary school.* New York: Macmillan.

—— (1988). *Classroom management: Methods and techniques for elementary and secondary teachers* (2d ed.). New York: Longman, Inc.

Lessinger, L. (1970). *Every kid a winner: Accountability in education.* New York: Simon and Schuster.

Lewin, K., Lippitt, R., and White, R. (1939). Patterns of aggressive behavior in experimentally created social climates. *Journal of Social Psychology, 10,* 271–299.

Lewis, R., and Lovegrove, M. (1984). Teachers' classroom control procedures: Are students' preferences being met? *Journal of Education for Teaching, 10*(2), 97–105.

Lewis, S. A., Johnson, J., Cohen, P., Garcia, M., and Velez, C. N. (1988). Attempted suicide in youth: Its relationship to school achievement, educational goals and socioeconomic status. *Journal of Abnormal Child Psychology, 16,* 459–471.

Lipson, J., (Ed.) (2001). Hostile hallways: bullying, teasing, and sexual harassment in school, AAUW Education Foundation, Washington D.C., Researched by Harris Interactive, NY, NY.

Loo, C. M. (1977). *The differential effects of spatial density on low and high scorers on behavior problems indices.* A paper presented at the annual meeting of the Western Psychological Association, Seattle, Wash.

Lucker, G. W., Rosenfield, D., Sikes, J., and Aronson, E. (1976). Performance in the interdependent classroom: A field study. *American Educational Research Journal, 13*(2), 115–123.

Lyerly, K. Z. (1982). *Daydreaming and its implications to reading instruction among gifted children.* Unpublished master's thesis. Jacksonville: The University of North Florida.

Madison Project. *Independent exploration material.* Syracuse, N.Y.: Syracuse University, Webster College.

Madsen, C. H., and Madsen, C. K. (1981). *Teaching/Discipline a positive approach for educational development* (3d ed.). Boston, Mass.: Allyn and Bacon, Inc.

Maeroff, G. I. (1983). *Team building for school change. Equipping teacher for new roles.* New York. Teachers College Press.

Mager, R. E. (1968). *Developing attitude toward learning.* Palo Alto, Calif.: Fearon Publishers.

Maher, F. A., and Rathbone, C. H. (February, 1986). Teacher education and feminist theory: Some implications for practice. *American Journal of Education, 94*(2), 214–235.

Maifair, L. L. (October, 1986). Helping kids resist drugs. *Instructor, XCVI* (3), 72–74.

Manning, B. H. (1988). Application of cognitive behavior modification in first and third graders, self-management of classroom behaviors. *American Educational Research Journal, 25*(2), 193–212.

Markman, E. M. (1979). Realizing that you don't understand: Elementary school children's awareness of inconsistencies. *Child Development, 50,* 643–655.

Marsh, H. W. (1986). Verbal and math self-concepts: An internal/external frame of reference model. *American Educational Research Journal, 23*(1), 129–149.

Martin, G., and Pear, J. (1983). *Behavior modification: What it is and how to do it* (2d ed.). Englewood Cliffs, N.J.: Prentice-Hall, Inc.

Martin, N. K., and Dixon, P. N. (1986). Adolescent suicide: Myths, recognition, and evaluation. *The School Counselor, 33*(4), 265–271.

Marzano, R. J., and Marzano J. S. (2003). The Key to Classroom Management, *Educational Leadership, Building Classroom Relationships,* September, Vol. 61, No. 1, pp. 6–13.

Maslow, A. H. (1962). *Toward a psychology of being.* New York: D. Van Nostrand.

———— (1968). *Toward a psychology of being* (2d ed.). New York: D. Van Nostrand.

———— (1970). *Motivation and personality.* New York: Harper & Row.

May, W. T. (April 1988). *Unveiling professional inequities through drawing.* Paper presented at the annual meeting of the American Educational Research Association, New Orleans, La.

McClelland, D. C. (1973). Testing for competence rather than for "intelligence." *American Psychologist, 28,* 1–14.

McClure, J. S. (2003). Civilized assertiveness for women: Communication with backbone . . . not bite. Albion Street Press, Denver, CO.

McDaniel, T. R. (1986). A primer on classroom discipline: Principles old and new. *Phi Delta Kappan, 68,* 63–67.

McGarity, J. R., and Butts, D. P. (1984). The relationships among teacher classroom management behavior, student engagement, and student achievement of middle and high school science students of varying aptitude. *Journal of Research in Science Teaching, 21,* 55–61.

McGregor D. (1985). *The human side of enterprise.* McGraw/Hill.

McKibbin, M., Weil, M., and Joyce, B. (1977). *Demonstration of alternatives.* Washington: Association of Teacher Educators.

McLemore, W. P. (1981). The ABC's of classroom discipline. *The Clearing House, 52,* 205–206.

McLuhan, M., and Fiore, Q. (1967). *The medium is the message.* New York: Bantam Books.

McMurrain, T. (1975). *Intervention in human crisis.* Atlanta, Ga.: Humanics Press.

McNeal, L. (1987). Talking about differences, teaching to sameness. *Journal of Curriculum Studies, 19*(2), 105–122.

Medley, D. M. (1977). *Teacher competence and teacher effectiveness: A review of process-product research.* (ERIC Document No. 143–629). Washington: American Association of Colleges of Teacher Education.

Mendler, A. N., and Curwin, R. L. (1983). *Taking charge in the classroom: A practical guide to effective discipline.* Reston, Va.: Reston Publishing.

Miller, G. E., and Klungness, L. (1986). Treatment of nonconfrontative stealing in school-age children. *School Psychology Review, 15*(1), 24–35.

Millman, H. L., Schaefer, C. E., and Cohen, J. J. (1980). *Therapies for school behavior problems.* San Francisco, Calif.: Jossey-Bass Publishers.

Minsky, E. (1986). *Review of the learning partners program.* (ERIC Document No. ED277712.) Washington: American Association of Colleges of Teacher Education.

Morales, C. A. (1978). Discipline: Applicable techniques for student teachers. *Education, 101,* 122–124.

Morton, L. (1983). *Math their way.* Menlo Park, Calif.: Addison-Wesley. (Worksheet 55).

Mosston, M., and Ashworth, S. (1985). Toward a unified theory of teaching. *Educational Leadership, 42*(8), 31–34.

Moustakas, C. (1972). *The authentic teacher.* Cambridge, Mass.: Howard A. Doyle Publishing.

Muriel, F., and Jongeward, D. (1975). *The people book: Transactional analysis for students.* Menlo Park, Calif.: Addison-Wesley.

Nash, R. (1976). Pupils' expectations of their teachers, in M. Stubbs and S. Delamont (eds.). *Explorations in classroom observation.* New York: John Wiley & Sons, 83–100.

National Commission on Excellence in Education. (1983). *A nation at risk: The imperative of educational reform.* Washington: U.S. Government Printing Office.

National Education Association (1972). *Report of the task force on corporal punishment.* Washington: author.

——— (1982). *Status of the American public school teacher 1980–81.* Washington: author.

——— (1894). *Report of the committee often on secondary school studies.* Washington: author.

Neill, A. S. (1962). *Summerhill: A radical approach to child rearing.* New York: Hart Publishing.

Nelson, J. W. (1987). A new dimension to accountability? Educational negligence claims against teachers. *Australian Journal of Education, 31*(3), 219–235.

Newcomb, M. D., and Bentler, P. M. (1989). Substance use and abuse among children and teenagers. *American Psychologist, 44*(2), 242–248.

Newmark, G. (1976). *The school belongs to you and me.* New York: Hart Publishing.

Norlander-Case, K. A., Reagan, T., G., and Case, C. W. (1999). *The professional teacher: The preparation and nurturance of the reflective practitioner.* Jossey-Bass Inc., San Francisco, California.

Novak, Joseph D., Gowin, D. Bob. (1999). Learning How to Learn, Cambridge University Press.

Nucci, L. P. (1984). Evaluating teachers as social agents: Students' ratings of domain appropriate and domain inappropriate teacher responses to transgressions. *American Educational Research Journal, 21*(2), 367–378.

Oakes, J. (1999). *Limiting students' success and life chances: The impact of tracking.* In A. C. Ornstein and L. S. Behar-Horenstein (eds.), Contemporary Issues in Curriculum (2nd ed). Needham Heights, Mass., Allyn and Bacon.

O'Brien, R., and Cohen, S. (eds.). (1984). *The encyclopedia of drug abuse.* New York: Facts on File.

O'Donnell, A. M., Dansereau, D. F., Rocklin, T. R., Hythecker, V. I., Lambiotte, J. G., Larson, C. O., and Young, M. D. (1985). Effects of elaboration frequency on cooperative learning. *Journal of Educational Psychology, 77*(55), 572–580.

———, ———, Hall, R. H., and Rocklin, T. R. (1987). Cognitive, social/affective, and metacognitive outcomes of scripted cooperative learning. *Journal of Educational Psychology, 79*(4), 431–437.

———, Rocklin, T. R., Dansereau, D. F., Hythecker, V. I., and Young, M. D. (1987). Amount and accuracy of information recalled by cooperative dyads: The effects of summary type and alternation of roles. *Contemporary Educational Psychology, 12,*(4), 386–394.

Oetting, E. R., and Beauvais, F. (1988). Adolescent drug use and the counselor. *School Counselor, 36*(1), 11–17.

———, ———, and Edwards, R. W. (1989). "Crack": The epidemic. *The School Counselor, 37,* 128–136.

Ogbu, J. U. (1988). Class stratification, racial stratification, and schooling, in L. Weis (ed.), *Class, race, and gender in American education.* New York: State University of New York Press, (pp. 163–179).

Oja, S. N., and Ham, M. C. (1984). A cognitive-developmental approach to collaborative action research with teachers. *Teachers College Record, 86*(1), 171–192.

Olweus, D. (1993). *Understanding children's worlds: bullying at school.* Blackwell Publishing, Malden, MA.

Olweus, D. (2003). A Profile of Bullying at School, *Educational Leadership, Creating Caring Schools,* March Vol. 60, No. 6., pp. 12–17.

Onions, C. T. (ed. with the assistance of G. Friedrichsen and R. Burchfield) (1966). *The Oxford dictionary of English etymology.* Oxford, England: The Clarendon Press.

Ornstein, A., and Levine, D. (1983). Sex differences in ability and achievement. *Journal of Research and Development in Education, 16*(2) 66–72.

——— and ——— (1985). *An introduction to the foundations of education* (3d ed). Boston: Houghton Mifflin.

Osborn, D. K., & Osborn, J. D. (1981). *Discipline and classroom management.* Athens, Ga.: Education Associates.

Owens, L. (1987). Cooperation, in M. J. Dunk (ed.), *The International Encyclopedia of Teaching and Teacher Education.* Oxford, England: Pergamon Press, 345–349.

Paley, V. G. (1986). On listening to what children say. *Harvard Educational Review, 56,* 122–131.

Pames, S. (1976). *Guide to creative action.* New York: Scribner.

Parker, W. C. (1987). Teacher thinking: The pervasive approach. *Journal of Teacher Education, 38*(3), 50–56.

——— and Gehrke, N. J. (1986). Learning activities and teacher decisionmaking: Some grounded hypotheses. *American Educational Research Journal, 23,* 227–242.

Parsons, T. W., and Tikunoff, W. (1974). *Achieving classroom communication through self-analysis.* El Segundo, Calif.: Prismatica International.

Penman, R. (1987). Discourse in courts: Cooperation, coercion, and coherence. *Discourse Processes, 10*(3), 201–218.

Perkins, D. N. (1981). *The mind's best work*. Cambridge, Mass.: Harvard University Press.

Perkins, H. (1969). *Human development and Learning*. Belmont, Calif.: Wadsworth.

Perlman, C. (2003). *Performance Assessment: Designing appropriate performance tasks and scoring rubrics*. ERIC, ED 480070.

Perry, W. G. (1970). *Forms of intellectual and ethical development in the college years: A schema*. New York: Holt, Rinehart, & Winston.

———— (1978). Sharing in the costs of growth, in C. A. Parker (ed.), *Encouraging development in college students*. Minneapolis: University of Minnesota Press, 37–70.

———— (1981). Cognitive and ethical growth: the making of meaning, in A. W. Chickering (ed.), *The Modern American College*. San Francisco: Jossey-Bass, 76–116.

Peterson, P. L., and Swing, S. R. (1982). Beyond time on task: Students' reports of their thought processes during classroom instruction, in T. Good and W. Doyle (eds.), *Focus on Teaching*. Chicago: University of Chicago Press, pp. 228–238.

———— and Janicki, T. C. (1979). Individual characteristics and children's learning in large-group and small-group approaches. *Journal of Educational Psychology, 71*(5), 677–687.

Petreshene, S. (September, 1986). Management made easy. *Instructor, XCVI*(2), 70–74.

———— (October, 1986). What can you do in 10 minutes? Transition activities that make kids think! *Instructor, XCVI*(3), 68–70.

Piaget, J. (1965). *Moral judgment of the child,* (Marjorie Gabain, trans.). New York: The Free Press.

———— (1971). *The construction of reality in the child*. New York: Ballantine Books.

Pittman, S. I. (1985). A cognitive ethnography and quantification of a first-grade teacher's selection routines for classroom management. *The Elementary School Journal, 85*(4), 541–557.

Podeschi, R. (1987). Purpose, pluralism, and public teachers education. *Journal of Thought, 22*(2), 8–13.

Popp, J. A. (1987). If you see John Dewey, tell him we did it. *Educational Theory, 37*(2), 145–152.

Popper, K. (1957). *The poverty of historicism*. London: Routledge & Kegan Paul. (Ark Edition, 1986.)

———— (1966). *The open society and its enemies,* vol. I *Plato* (5th ed.). London: Routledge & Kegan Paul.

———— (1974). *Unended quest: An intellectual autobiography*. LaSalle, Ill.: The Open Court Press.

Pottebaum, S. M., Keith, T. Z., and Ehly, S. W. (1986). Is there a causal relation between self-concept and academic achievement? *Journal of Educational Research, 79*(3), 140–143.

Potter, E. F. (1974). *Correlates of oral participation in classrooms*. Unpublished doctoral dissertation. Chicago, Ill.: University of Chicago.

Powers, S., and Miller, C. E. (1988). Effects of a drug education program on third and fourth grade pupils. *Journal of Alcohol and Drug Education, 33*(3), 26–31.

Pratt, D. (1980). *Curriculum design and development*. New York: Harcourt Brace Jovanovich.

Presbie, R. J., and Brown, P. L. (1985). *Behavior management* (2d ed.). Washington: National Education Association.

Presno, V., and Presno, C. (1980). *The value realms: Activities for helping students develop values*. New York: Teachers College Press.

Pulaski, M. A. S. (1980). *Understanding Piaget: An introduction to children's cognitive development* (2d ed.). New York: Harper & Row.

Putnam, J. G. (1976). *Helper-helpful and harmer-harmful.* Teacher Corps, East Lansing: Michigan State University.

Putnam, J., Lillard, R., Singo, T. (1998). The Role of the University in a Professional Development School.

Putnam, J., Straham, B., & Singo, T. (1996). Leadership for Educational Reform in Professional Development Schools: Initial Findings—The High School.

Putnam, J., Wright, A., & Singo, T. (1997). The Study of the Principal and His Role in the Professional Development Middle School.

———— (1984a). *One exceptional teachers' systematic decision-making model* (Research Series 136, January). East Lansing: Michigan State University, Institute for Research on Teaching.

———— (1984b). *Developing an elementary school learning-community classroom.* (Research Series 145, November). East Lansing: Michigan State University, Institute for Research on Teaching.

———— (1987a). Applications of classroom management research findings. *Journal of Education for Teaching, 11*(2), 146–164.

———— (1987b). *Basic knowledge and skills for developing an effective classroom management and organization system.* Unpublished manuscript. East Lansing: Michigan State University, College of Education.

———— (1987c). Multiple Perspectives Program Resource Manual. Unpublished raw data.

———— (1987d). *Outline for management and organization plan.* Unpublished manuscript. East Lansing: Michigan State University.

———— (1987e). *Preservice teachers' perceptions about classroom management and organization.* Unpublished manuscript. East Lansing: Michigan State University, College of Education.

———— (1988). TE 811A: *Classroom management and organization.* Unpublished course packet. East Lansing: Michigan State University.

———— and Johns, B. (April 1986). *Classroom management and organization: Preservice teacher outcomes.* Paper presented at the annual meeting of the American Educational Research Association, San Francisco, Calif.

Ramsey, R. D. (1981). *Educator's discipline handbook.* New York: Parker Publishing Company.

Raths, L. E., Harmin, M., and Simon, S. B. (1966). *Values and teaching: Working with values in the classroom.* Columbus, Ohio: Charles E. Merrill Publishing.

Reardon, F. J., and Reynolds, R. N. (1979). A survey of attitudes toward corporal punishment in Pennsylvania schools, in I. A. Hyman and J. H. Wise (eds.), *Corporal punishment in American education.* Philadelphia, Pa.: Temple University Press.

Reder, L. M. (1980). The role of elaboration in the comprehension and retention of prose: A critical review. *Review of Educational Research, 50,* 5–53.

Redl, F., and Wineman, D. (1972). *When we deal with children: Selected writings.* New York: The Free Press.

Reeve, R. A., Palincsar, A. S., and Brown, A. L. (1987). Everyday and academic thinking: Implications for learning and problem solving. *Journal of Curriculum Studies, 19*(2), 123–133.

Rich, J. M. (1984). Discipline, rules, and punishment. *Contemporary Education, 55,* 110–112.

Robert, S. C. (ed.). (1970). *Robert's rules of order* (rev. ed.). Glenview, Ill.: Scott Foresman.

Roetter, P. (1987). The positive approach in the classroom. *The High School Journal, 70*(4), 196–202.

Rogers, C. R. (1951). *Client-centered therapy: Its current practices, implications, and theory.* Boston, Mass.: Houghton Mifflin.

——— (1961). *On becoming a person: A therapist's view of psychotherapy.* Boston, Mass.: Houghton Mifflin.

——— (1962). The interpersonal relationship: the core of guidance. *Harvard Educational Review, 32.4,* 416–429.

——— (1969). *Freedom to learn.* Columbus, Ohio: Merrill.

Rogoff, B. (1990). *Apprenticeship in thinking.* New York: Oxford University Press.

Rogus, J. F. (1985). Promoting self-discipline: A comprehensive approach. *Theory into Practice, 24,* 271–276.

——— (1988). Teacher reader programming: Theoretical underpinnings. *Journal of Teacher Education, 39*(1), 46–51.

Rohrkemper, M. (1984). *Individual differences in students' perceptions of routine classroom events.* (Research Series No. 144.) East Lansing: Michigan State University, Institute for Research on Teaching.

——— (1985). Individual differences in students' perceptions of routine classroom events. *Journal of Educational Psychology. 77*(1), 29–44.

——— (1986). The functions of inner speech in elementary school students' problem-solving behavior. *American Educational Research Journal, 23*(2), 303–313.

Rorschach, E., and Whitney, R. (1986). Relearning to teach: Peer observation as a means of professional development. *American Educator, 10*(4), 38–44.

Rose, T. L. (1984). Current uses of corporal punishment in American public schools. *Journal of Educational Psychology, 76,* 27–441.

Rosenholtz. S. J. (1989). *Teachers' workplace.* New York: Longman, Inc.

——— and Cohen, E. G. (1983). Back to basics and the desegregated school. *The Elementary School Journal, 83*(5), 515–527.

Rosenshine, B. (1983). Teaching functions in instructional programs. *Elementary School Journal, 83*(4), 335–351.

——— (1987). Explicit teaching and teacher training. *Journal of Teacher Education, 38*(3), 34–36.

——— and Furst, N. (1973). The use of observation to study teaching, in R. Travers (ed.), *Second handbook of research in teaching.* Chicago: Rand McNally.

——— and Stevens, R. (1986). Teaching functions, in M. C. Wittrock (ed.), *Handbook of research on teaching* (3d ed.). New York: Macmillan.

Rosenthal, R., and Jacobson, L. (1968). *Pygmalion in the classroom: Teacher expectations and pupils' intellectual development.* New York: Holt, Rinehart and Winston.

Ross, S. M., and DiVesta, F. J. (1976). Oral summary as a review strategy for enhancing recall of textual material. *Journal of Educational Psychology, 68,* 689–695.

Rowan, G. (2004). Teachers Matter: Evidence from Value Added Assessments, *Research Points,* Summer, Vol. 2, Issue 2, pp. 1–4.

Rubin, L. J., and Balow. B. (1971). Learning and behavior disorders: A longitudinal study. *Exceptional Children, 38,* 293–299.

Rust, J. O., and Kinnard. K. Q. (1983). Personality characteristics of the users of corporal punishment in the schools. *Journal of School Psychology, 21,* 91–105.

Safran, S. P., and Safran, J. S. (1985). Classroom context and teachers' perceptions of problem behaviors. *Journal of Educational Psychology, 77*(1), 20–28.

Salter, A. (1949). *Conditioned reflex therapy.* New York: Farrar, Straus & Giroux.

Sanders, D. P., and McCutcheon, G. (1986). The development of practical theories of teaching. *Journal of Curriculum and Supervision, 2*(1), 50–67.

Sandven, J. (1979). Social sensitivity as a factor in the teaching process. A theoretical discussion and an experimental contribution. *Scandinavian Journal of Educational Research, 23*(3), 131–150.

Sanford, J. P., Emmer, E. T., and Clements, B. S. (1983). Improving classroom management. *Educational Leadership, 40,* 56–61.

Santrock, J. W. (1984). *Adolescence: An introduction* (2d ed.). Dubuque, Iowa: Brown.

Sarason, S. G. (1971). *The culture of the school and the problem of change.* Boston: Allyn and Bacon, Inc.

Schallert, D. (1982). The significance of knowledge: A synthesis of research related to schema theory, in W. Otto and S. Whits (eds.), *Reading Expository Material.* New York: Academic Press, 160–192.

Schaps, E. (2003). *Creating a school community.* Educational Leadership, ASCD. March, Volume 60, Number 6, pp. 31–33.

Schaps, E., Battistich, V., and Solomon, D. (1997). School as a caring community: A Key to Character Education. In A. Molnar (Ed.), *The construction of children's character, part II: 96th yearbook of the National Society for the Study of Education.* Chicago: University Press.

Schein, E. H. (1985). *Organizational Culture and Leadership.* Jossey-Bass. San Fransico, California.

Scherer, M. (Ed.) (1999). The Constructivist Classroom. *Educational Leadership.* 57 (3).

Scherer, M. (Ed.) (2004). Schools as learning communities. *Educational Leadership,* 6(8).

Scherer, M. (2003). Perspectives/Uncivil Liberties, *Educational Leadership, Creating Caring Schools,* March Vol. 60, No. 6, pp. 5.

Schmuck, P., and Schmuck, R. A. (1977). Formal and informal aspects of classroom life: Can they be harmonized for academic learning? *The History and Social Science Teacher, 12,* 75–80.

Schmuck, R. A. (1980). The school organization, in McMillan J. (ed.), *The Social Psychology of School Learning.* New York: Academic Press, 169–213.

——— (1985). Introduction, in Slavin, R., Sharon. S., Kagan, S., Lazarawitz, R. H., Webb, C., and Schanch, R. A. (eds.), *Learning to cooperate, cooperating to learn.* New York: Plain Press.

——— and Runkel., P. (1985). *The handbook of organizational development in schools,* (3d ed.). Palo Alto, Calif.: Mayfield.

Schon, D. (1983). *The reflective practitioner: how professionals think in action.* New York: Basic Books.

Schrag, P. (October 4, 1986). What the test scores really mean. *The Nation,* pp. 297, 311–313.

Schunk, D. H. (1987). Peer models and children's behavior change. *Review of Educational Research, 57*(2), 149–174.

Schwab, J. J. (1974). The concept of the structure of a discipline, in E. W. Eisner and E. Vallance (eds.), *Conflicting Conceptions of Curriculum.* Berkeley, Calif.: McCutchan.

——— (May/June 1975). Learning community. *The Center Magazine,* 30–44.

———— (1976). Education and the state: Learning community, in *The Great Ideas Today.* Chicago, Ill.: Encyclopeadia Britannica, Inc.

Seeman, H. (1984). A major source of discipline problems. *Educational Horizons, 62,* 128–131.

Segal, J. W., Chipman, S., and Glaser, R. (1985). Thinking and learning skills, vol. 1 in *Relating instruction to basic research.* Hillsdale, N.J.: Laurence Erlbaum.

Senge, P. (1994). *The fifth discipline.* Currency Doubleday. NY, NY.

Senge, P., McCabe, N. H., Lucas, T., Kleiner, A., etc. *Schools that learn: Fieldbook for educators, parents, and everyone who cares about education.* Currency Doubleday. NY, NY.

Shalaway, L. (1980). *How teachers deal with problem behavior.* (Educators Report, vol. 8, no. 1.) East Lansing: Michigan State University, College of Education.

Shannon, J. (1986). In the classroom stoned. *Phi Delta Kappan, 68,* 60–62.

Sharan, S. (1980). Cooperative learning in small groups: Recent methods and effects on achievement, attitudes, and ethnic relations. *Review of Educational Research, 50*(2), 241–271.

———— (December, 1987). Cooperative learning: New horizons, old threats. *The International Association for the Study of Cooperation in Education Newsletter,* p. 3.

————, Kussell, P., Hertz-Lazarowitz, R., Bejarano, Y., Raviv, S., and Sharan, Y. (1984). *Cooperative learning in the classroom: Research in desegregated schools.* Hillsdale, N.J.: Laurence Erlbaum.

———— and Sharan, Y. (1976). *Small-group teaching.* Englewood Cliffs, N.J.: Educational Technology Publications.

Shaughnessy, J. (1998). *Initial guidelines on becoming a learning community.* OERI Event No. 36, November 16. Northwest Regional Educational Laboratory, Portland, Oregon.

Sheeley, V. L., and Herllihy, B. (1989). Counseling suicidal teens: A duty to warn and protect. *The School Counselor, 37,* 89–97.

Sheperd, C. R. (1964). *Small groups.* San Francisco: Chandler.

Shore, R. M. (1996). *Personalization: Working to curb violence in an American High Schools.* Phi Delta Kappan, January, pp. 362–363.

Shroyer, J., and Fitzgerald, W. (1986). *Mouse and elephant: Measuring growth.* Reading, Mass.: Addison-Wesley Publishing Co.

Shulman, L. (2004). *This wisdom of practice: Essays on teaching, learning, and learning to teach.* San Fransico, California: Jossey-Bass.

Shulman, L. S. (1987). Knowledge and teaching: Foundations of the new reform. *Harvard Educational Review, 57*(1), 1–22.

Shultz, J., and Florio, S. (1979). Stop and freeze: The negotiations of social and physical space in a kindergarten/first grade classroom. *Anthropology and Education Quarterly, 10*(3), 166–181.

Sieber, R. T. (1979). Classmates as workmates: Informal peer activity in the elementary school. *Anthropology and Education Quarterly, 10*(4), 207–235.

Silberman, M., and Wheelan, S. (1980). *How to discipline without feeling guilty: Assertive relationships with children.* New York: Hawthorn Books.

Silbert, J., Carnine, D., and Stein, M. (1981). *Direct instruction mathematics.* Columbus, Ohio: Charles E. Merrill.

Silverstein, J. M. (1979). *Individual and environmental correlates of pupil problematic and nonproblematic classroom behavior.* Unpublished doctoral dissertation. New York: New York University.

Simmons, R. (2002). Odd girl out: The hidden culture of aggression in girls. Orlando: Harcourt Brace.

Simon, S. B., Hawley, R. C., and Britton, D. D. (1973). *Composition for personal growth: Values clarification through writing.* New York: Hart Publishing.

———, How, L. W., and Kirschenbaum, H. (1972). *Values clarification: A handbook of practical strategies for teachers and students.* New York: Hart Publishing.

Skinner, B. F. (1953). *Science and human behavior.* New York: Macmillan.

——— (1954). The science of learning and the art of teaching. *Harvard Educational Review, 24,* 86–97.

——— (1971). *Beyond freedom and dignity.* New York: Alfred A. Knopf, Inc.

——— (1982). *Skinner for the classroom: Selected papers.* Champaign, Ill.: Research Press.

Skon, L., Johnson, D. W., and Johnson, R. T. (1981). Cooperative peer interaction versus individual competition and individualistic efforts: Effects on the acquisition of cognitive reasoning strategies. *Journal of Educational Psychology, 73*(1), 83–92.

Slavin, R. E. (1973). *Using student team learning.* (The Johns Hopkins Team Learning Project.) Baltimore, Md.: Johns Hopkins University, Center for Social Organization of Schools.

——— (1980). Cooperative learning. *Review of Educational Research, 50*(2), 315–342.

——— (1983). *Cooperative learning.* New York: Longman, Inc.

——— (1985). An introduction to cooperative learning research, in R. Slavin, S. Sharan, S. Kagan, R. H. Lararowitz, C. Webb, and R. Schmuck (eds.). *Learning to cooperate, cooperating to learn,* New York: Plenum Press, pp. 5–15.

——— (1987a). Cooperative learning: When behavioral and humanistic approaches to classroom motivation meet. *The Elementary School Journal, 88*(1), 29–37.

——— (1987b). A theory of school and classroom organization. *Educational psychologist, 22*(2), 89–108.

——— (1987c). Ability grouping and its alternatives: Must we track? *American Educator, 11*(2), 32–48.

——— (1987d). Ability grouping and student achievement in elementary schools: A best-evidence synthesis. *Review of Educational Research, 57*(3), 293–336.

——— (1987e). Grouping for instruction in the elementary school. *Educational Psychologist, 22*(2), 109–128.

——— (1987f). Small group methods, in Dunkin, M. J. (ed.), *The international encyclopedia of teaching and teacher education.* New York: Pergamon Press, 237–243.

——— (1988). A message from IASCE president-elect. *The International Association for the Study of Cooperation in Education Newsletter, 9*(2), 2–3.

——— and Madden, N. A. (1979). School practices that improve race relations. *American Educational Research Journal, 16*(2), 169–180.

———, Sharon, S., Kagan, S., Lazarowitz, R. H., Webb, C., and Schmuck, R. A., (eds.). (1985). *Learning to cooperate, cooperating to learn.* New York: Plenum Press.

Smith, M. J. (1975). *When I say no, I feel guilty: How to cope—using the skills of systematic assertive therapy.* New York: Dial Press.

Snider, M., and Borel, K. (2004). Stalked by a Cyberbully, *Maclean's Magazine,* May.

Spiegel, L. P. (1988). Child abuse hysteria and the elementary school counselor. *Elementary School Guidance and Counseling, 23*(1), 48–53.

Spitz, R. (1957). *No and yes.* New York: International University Press.

Sprinthall, N. A., and Thies-Sprinthall, L. (autumn 1980). Educating for teacher growth: A cognitive developmental perspective. *Theory into Practice, 19*(4), 278–286.

Stallings, J. A. (1976). How instructional processes relate to child outcomes in a national study of follow-through. *Journal of Teacher Education, 37,* 43–47.

Stanford, G. (1977). *Developing effective classroom groups: A practical guide for teachers.* New York: A & W Visual Library.

————— and Roark, A. E. (1974). *Human interaction in education.* Boston, Mass.: Allyn and Bacon, Inc.

Stanford, J., and Evertson, C. (1981). Classroom management in a low SES junior high: Three case studies. *Journal of Teacher Education, 32,* 34–38.

Stanlaw, J., and Peshkin, A. (1988). Black visibility in a multi-ethnic high school, in Lois Weis (ed.), *Class, race, and gender in American education.* New York: State University of New York Press, pp. 209–229.

Stiggins, R. J., and Bridgeford, N. J. (1985). Performance assessment for teacher development. *Educational Evaluation and Policy Analysis, 7*(1), 85–97.

————— and Duke, D. (1988). *The case for commitment to teacher growth.* New York: State University of New York Press.

Stradley, W. E., and Aspinall, R. D. (1975). *Discipline in the junior high/middle school: A handbook for teachers, counselors, and administrators.* New York: The Center for Applied Research in Education, Inc.

Strike, K., and Soltis, J. (1986). Who broke the fish tank? And other ethical dilemmas. *Instructor, 95,* 36–39.

Strom, R. D. (1969). *Psychology for the classroom.* Englewood Cliffs, N.J.: Prentice-Hall, Inc.

Stroot, S., Keil, V., Stedman, P., Lohr, L., Faust, R., Schincariol-Randall, L., Sullivan, A., Czerniak, G., Kuchcinski, J., Orel, N., and Richter, M. (1998). *Peer assistance and review guidebook.* Columbus, OH: Ohio Department of Education.

Sulzer-Azaroff, B., and Mayer, G. R. (1977). *Applying behavior analysis procedures with children and youth.* New York: Holt, Rinehart and Winston.

Sweeney, R. E. (1977). *Environmental concerns of the world.* New York: Harcourt Brace Jovanovich.

Swick, K. J. (1985). *Disruptive student behavior in the classroom* (2d ed.). Washington: National Education Association.

————— (1985). *Parents and teachers as discipline shapers.* Washington: National Education Association.

Swing, S. R., and Peterson, P. L. (1982). The relationship of student ability and small-group interaction to student achievement. *American Educational Research Journal, 19*(2), 259–274.

Talmage, H., and Pascarella, E. T. (1984). The influence of cooperative learning strategies on teacher practices, student perceptions of the learning environment, and academic achievement. *American Educational Research Journal, 21*(1), 163–179.

Tennyson, R. D., and Park, O. (1980). The teaching of concepts: A review of instructional design research literature. *Review of Educational Research, 50*(1), 55–70.

Thelen, H. A. (1954). *Dynamics of groups at work.* Chicago, Ill.: University of Chicago Press.

———— (1981). *The classroom society: the construction of educational experience.* New York: Wiley.

Thomas, K. (1990). *Gender and subject in higher education.* Suffolk: St. Edmunsbury Press, Ltd.

Thomas, K. F. (1985). Early reading as a social internationalism process. *Language arts, 474.*

Thompson, C. (1988). *Report of the taskforce for reform of teacher education at Michigan State University.* Unpublished raw data.

Thompson, G. (2004). *Through Ebony Eyes: What teachers need to know but are afraid to ask about African American students.* Jossey-Bass: San Francisco, CA.

Thornton, S. J. (1984). *Curriculum consonance in U.S. history classrooms.* Paper presented to College and University Assembly Annual Meeting of National Council for Social Studies, Washington, D.C.

Tiene, D., and Buck, S. (1987). Student teachers and classroom authority. *The Journal of Educational Research, 80*(5), 261–265.

Tikunoff, W., Berliner, D., and Rist, R. (1975). *An ethnographic study of the forty classrooms of the beginning teacher evaluation study.* (Technical Report 57-10-5.) San Francisco, Calif.: Far West Regional Laboratory.

Tillman, M. (1982). *Trouble-shooting classroom problems.* Glenview, Ill.: Scott Foresman.

Tobbin, K. (1986). Effects of teacher wait time on discourse in mathematics and language arts classes. *American Educational Research Journal, 23,* 191–200.

———— (1987). The role of wait time in higher cognitive level learning. *Review of Educational Research, 57*(1), 69–95.

Tomorrow's schools; Principles for the design of professional development schools. (1990). East Lansing, Mich.: The Holmes Group.

Trice, H. M. and Beyer, J. M. (1993). *The culture of work organizations.* New Jersey: Prentice Hall.

Ulrich, R. E., and Azrin, N. H. (1962). Reflexive fighting in response to aversive stimulation. *Journal of Experimental Analysis of Behavior, 5,* 511–520.

Van Dyke, H. T. (1984). Corporal punishment in our schools. *The Clearing House, 57,* 296–300.

Van Horn, K. L. (April 1982). *The Utah pupil/teacher self-concept program: Teacher strategies that invite improvement of pupil and teacher self-concept.* Paper presented at the annual meeting of the American Educational Research Association, New York.

van Oudenhoven, J. P., van Berkum, G., and Swen-Koopmans, T. (1987). Effect of cooperation and shared feedback on spelling achievement. *Journal of Educational Psychology, 79*(1), 92–94.

Veldman, D. J., and Sanford, J. P. (1984). The influence of class ability level on student achievement and classroom behavior. *American Educational Research Journal, 21*(3), 629–644.

Wagner, L. A. (1985). Ambiguities and possibilities in California's mentor teacher program. *Educational Leadership, 43*(3), 23–29.

Waiters, P. A. (1971). Drugs and adolescents: Use and abuse, in Blaine, G. B. and McArthur, C. C., (eds.) *Emotional problems of the student.* New York: Appleton-Century-Crofts, 148–162.

Walker, J. E., and Shea, T. M. (1976). *Behavior modification: A practical approach for educators.* Saint Louis, Mo.: C. V. Mosby.

——— and ——— (1984). *Behavior management: A practical approach for educators* (3d ed.). Saint Louis, Mo.: Times Mirror/Mosby.

Walkins, Chris. (2005). Classrooms as learning communities: a review of research. London Review of Education. March, Vol 3, No. 1, pp. 47–64(18) Carfax Publishing.

Wallen, N. E. (1966). *Relationship between teacher characteristics and student behavior.* (Part 3, Cooperative Research Project No. SAEOE 10-181.) Salt Lake City: University of Utah.

Waller, W. (1961). *The sociology of teaching.* New York: Russell and Russell.

Walls, L. (2004). *Bullying and sexual harassment in schools.* Committee for Children, *www.cfchildren.org.*

Ward, B. A., and Tikunoff, W. J. (1976). The effective teacher education program: Application of selected research results and methodology to teaching. *Journal of Teacher Education, 27,* 48–53.

Warner, D. (1985). Using cognitive discrimination training to develop classroom knowledge. *Journal of Teacher Education, 36*(3), 55–60.

Warring, D., Johnson, D. W., Maruyama, G., and Johnson, R. (1985). Impact of different types of cooperative learning on cross-ethnic and cross-sex relationships. *Journal of Educational Psychology, 77*(1), 53–59.

Watson, J. B. (1914). *Behavior: An introduction to comparative psychology.* New York: Holt, Rinehart and Winston.

Webb, N. M. (1982). Student interaction and learning in small groups. *Review of Educational Research, 52*(3), 421–445.

———, Ender, P., and Lewis, S. Problem-solving strategies and group processes in small groups learning computer programming. *American Educational Research Journal, 23*(2), 243–261.

Webster, N. (1979). *Webster's deluxe unabridged dictionary* (2d ed.). New York: Simon and Schuster.

Weinstein, C. S. (1979). The physical environment of the school: A review of the research. *Review of Educational Research, 49*(4), 557–610.

Weissbourd, R., *Moral Teachers, Moral Students.* Educational Leadership, Creating Caring Schools, March Vol. 60, No. 6, pp. 6–11.

Wellman, M. M. (1984). The school counselor's role in the communication of suicidal ideation by adolescents. *The School Counselor, 32*(2), 104–109.

Welsh, R. S. (1985). Spanking: A grand old American tradition? *Children Today, 14,* 25–29.

Wheeler, C. (July 1988). Personal correspondence.

Wilcox, K. (1982). Differential socialization in the classroom: Implications for equal opportunity, in G. Spindler (ed.), *Doing the ethnography of schooling.* New York: Holt, Rinehart, & Winston, 456–488.

Wilcox, R. T. (1983). Discipline made gentle. *The Clearing House, 57,* 30–35.

Wilde, J., and Sommers, P. (1978). Teaching disruptive adolescents: A game worth winning. *Phi Delta Kappan, 59,* 342–343.

Wilford, A. W., and Stripling, K. E. (1984). *Urban elementary school teacher perceptions regarding the effectiveness of specified classroom management strategies.* Paper presented at the annual meeting of the American Educational Research Association, New Orleans, La.

Williams, R. (1983). *Keywords: A vocabulary of culture and society.* London: Fontana Paperbacks.

Williams, R. L. M. (1985). Children's stealing: A review of the theft-control procedures for parents and teachers. *Remedial and Special Education, 6*(2), 17–23.

Wittrock, M. C. (1986). Students' thought processes, in M. C. Wittrock (ed.), *Handbook of Research on Teaching* (3d ed.). New York: Macmillan, 297–314.

Wolf, M. M., Hanley, E. L., King, L. A., Lachowicz, J., and Giles, D. K. (1970). The timer game: A variable interval contingency for the management of out-of-seat behavior. *Exceptional Children, 37,* 113–117.

Wolfgang, C. F. (1977). *Helping aggressive and passive preschoolers through play.* Columbus, Ohio: Charles E. Merrill Publishing.

——— (1978). It's O.K. I'm bionic! *Phi Delta Kappan, 59*(10), 26–32.

Wolfgang, C. H., and Glickman, C. D. (1986). *Solving discipline problems: Strategies for classroom teachers* (2d ed.). Boston, Mass.: Allyn & Bacon.

Wolpe, J., and Lazarus, A. A. (1966). *Behavior therapy techniques: A guide to the treatment of neuroses.* Oxford, England: Pergamon.

Wong, H. and Wong R. T. The first days of school. Harry Wong Publishing, Inc.

Wood, F. H. (1982). The influence of public opinion and social custom on the use of corporal punishment in the schools, in F. H. Wood and K. C. Lakin (eds.), *Punishment and aversive stimulation in special education: Legal, theoretical and practical issues in their use with emotionally disturbed children and youth.* Reston, Va.: Council for Exceptional Children, 127 pp.

Woods, J. (2002). *Hostile Hallways.* Educational Leadership, Vol. 59, No. 4, December/January 2001–2002.

Woolridge, P., and Richman, C. L. (1985). Teachers' choice of punishment as a function of a student's gender, age, race, and IQ level. *Journal of School Psychology, 23,* 19–29.

Workman, E. A. (1982). *Teaching behavioral self-control to students.* Austin, Tex.: Pro-Ed.

Yager, S., Johnson, D. W., and Johnson, R. T. (1985). Oral discussion, group-to-individual transfer, and achievement in cooperative learning groups. *Journal of Educational Psychology, 77*(1), 60–66.

Yinger, R. J. (1987). Learning the language of practice. *Curriculum Inquiry, 17*(3), 295–318.

Zenchenko, V. P. (1985). Vygotsky's ideas about units for analysis of mind, in J. V. Wertsch (ed.), *Culture, communication and cognition: Vygotskian perspectives.* Cambridge, Mass.: Harvard University Press, 94–118.

Zuker, E. (1983). *Mastering assertiveness skills: Power and positive influence at work.* New York: American Management Association.

Zumwalt, K. K. (January 1978). The problems of discipline and violence in American education. Special issue. *Phi Delta Kappan.*

——— (ed.). (1986). *Improving teaching: 1986 ASCD yearbook.* Alexandria, Va.: Association for Supervision and Curriculum Development.

INDEX

Contributed by Rowan Teacher Candidate 2005
Melissa Dickson

is for **learning** and the knowledge we share.

is for **equity** - our community is fair.

is for **achievement**, we honor every day.

is for the **roles**, the many we portray.

is for the **norms**, we establish from the start.

is for **interaction**- we can all take part.

is for **negotiating** the rules for our team.

is for our **goals**- we share common dreams.

is for **caring**- we value one another.

 is for **offering** our help to each other.

 is for **motivation**- it comes from inside.

 is for our **morals**- truth, respect, and pride.

 is for **understanding** we grow in unity.

 is for **nurturing** our learning community.

 is for **individuality** of our classmates.

 is for **teamwork**- we all cooperate.

 is for **year-round** in which we celebrate!